TOTAL LEARNING

TOTAL LEARNING

Developmental Curriculum for the Young Child

Third Edition

Joanne Hendrick
University of Oklahoma

Merrill, an imprint of
Macmillan Publishing Company
New York

Collier Macmillan Canada, Inc.
Toronto

Maxwell Macmillan International Publishing Group
New York   Oxford   Singapore   Sydney

Cover photo: Joanne Hendrick

This book was set in Goudy Old Style

Administrative Editor: David Faherty
Production Coordinator: Linda Bayma
Art Coordinator: James H. Hubbard
Cover Designer: Cathy Watterson
Photo Editor: Terry Tietz

Photo on p. 178 by John Hutzimarkos. All other
photographs were taken by the author with the
assistance of the children, staff, and parents of the
Institute of Child Development, the Oaks Parent-
Child Workshop of Santa Barbara; Ridgeview
Elementary School of Oklahoma City; City College
Children's Center of Santa Barbara.

First edition copyrighted 1980 by C. V. Mosby
Company.

Macmillan Publishing Company
866 Third Avenue, New York, New York 10022

Collier Macmillan Canada, Inc.
1200 Eglinton Avenue East
Suite 200
Don Mills, Ontario M3C 3N1

Library of Congress Catalog Card Number:
89−62574
International Standard Book Number:
0−675−21188−3
Printed in the United States of America
3 4 5 6 7 8 9−93 92 91 90

Preface

Total Learning is an unconventional book about curriculum because it focuses on the developmental needs of the child rather than on specific subject areas. Thus the book is divided according to the emotional, social, creative, physical, and cognitive selves rather than according to social studies, science, or art. To be sure, these topics *are* included, but they are incorporated into discussions about the self they predominantly benefit. However, in an attempt to provide the best of both worlds, an index based on subject matter is included on the front endpaper of the book to facilitate finding discussions of specific topics when these are needed.

EMPHASIS

The primary emphasis of *Total Learning* is on teaching students to design curriculum that fosters competence in children in all areas of the self. The book advocates the use of curriculum that is developmentally based, nourished by play, and intended to encourage children to become independent, creative people. Emphasis is placed throughout on the importance of fostering emotional health and building satisfying social relationships.

MAJOR CHANGES AND ADDITIONS

Although many old friends such as the stress on the value of multiethnic and nonsexist curriculum remain, *Total Learning* has been carefully revised, and several hundred new reference citations are included in the text.

The most wide-reaching change is the inclusion of a particularly interesting and/or significant research study in each chapter. The intention is to introduce undergraduate students to the value of relevant investigations and stimulate graduate students to further endeavor.

Some of the studies, such as the material from the Lazar Consortium and Smilansky's pioneer research on play, were selected because they are well known. Others, such as Birch's study of the influence of peer model food choices and Lubeck's investigations of sandbox society were included because they were particularly appropriate or just plain unusual and interesting.

The studies are described in concise and simple, yet accurate, terms. Each study includes a paragraph or two on the implications for teaching that may be drawn from the results of the research.

Another change in this edition is the addition of Self-Check Questions for Review at the end of each chapter. These questions feature both content-related questions and integrative ones that require users to apply their higher-order thinking skills.

In addition to these overall improvements, new material has been added on writing informal objectives, knowing about Haemophilus influenzae, type B, coping with the threat of AIDS, confronting bias, and developing true literacy versus teaching reading per se. The information on developing cognitive competence now emphasizes teaching reasoning skills rather than discussing content and process learning—a change in terminology my own students find easier to grasp. Of course, a number of new and revised charts and examples of planning have been added. These include material on toy selection, developmental steps toward literacy, and examples of developmentally appropriate group times.

ACKNOWLEDGMENTS

Writing a book of this kind is a major undertaking that requires not only the work of the author but other people's support and contributions as well. In particular, I want to thank the staff of the Children's Center at Santa Barbara City College, Donna Coffman, Clevonease Johnson, Marilyn Statucki, and Zoe Iverson. Since my transfer to the University of Oklahoma, Head Teachers Cené Marquis, Jane Vaughn, and Ruth Ann Ball have also contributed mightily to my enlightenment. Over the years these people have shared so many ideas and suggestions, and our philosophies are now so entwined that it would be impossible to say any longer who was responsible for what. The same thing can be said of the students; if students like this book, it is because of what former students have taught me they needed and wanted—and many of their ideas and requests are incorporated here.

Several instructors reviewed the second edition of *Total Learning* and offered countless valuable suggestions for improving it. They were Beth Anderson, Moorehead State; Jean Billman, Winona State University; Eleanor L. Cook, Central Connecticut State; and Kathryn S. Turner, University of Montevallo. I thank them all for the hours they devoted to their evaluations.

The staff at Merrill Publishing Company have been of great assistance. I am especially grateful to David Faherty, administrative editor; Linda Bayma, production coordinator; and Terry Tietz, photo editor for their understanding and encouragement as well as their professional expertise during the book's production.

The quality of the illustrations was much enhanced by my friends at Color Chrome Photographic Laboratories, who continue to make my work look much better than I have any right to expect. To them goes a special thank you!

Contents

14

15

16

1 The Purpose of Curriculum

Have you ever

- Wondered what young children really should learn in preschool?
- Been questioned about your philosophy of teaching and felt unable to give a clear answer?
- Wanted to know how to plan curriculum more effectively?

If you have, the material in this chapter will help you.

As parents, and . . . teachers, we have the greatest gift to give children—a positive self-concept. We can do this by treating them as though they were already what they could only hope to become. Let them, through our eyes, see themselves as competent, worthy and in control of their destiny. Give them direction to their longings and leave them with the conviction that their fate can be molded by their hopes and deeds; that their lives need not be shaped by accident; that their happiness does not depend upon happenstance. Introduce them to themselves. Allow them to learn who they are and what they can be. If this is accomplished, they will no longer be strangers to themselves. They will feel at home in the world.

DAVID L. GALLAHUE (1982)

This book concerns itself with answering the questions: (1) what is the purpose of early education? and (2) what should curriculum for young children include?

WHAT IS THE PURPOSE OF EARLY EDUCATION?

The answers to these questions can be deceptively simple. The purpose of early education is to foster competence in young children, though not only competence in intellectual areas. Competence should be thought of as relating to all aspects of the self (Connolly & Bruner, 1974): learning to live comfortably with others, learning to master and safely express one's feelings, and learning to love life and welcome new experience. The purpose of education then is to foster competence in dealing with life.

WHAT SHOULD CURRICULUM FOR YOUNG CHILDREN INCLUDE?

Curriculum, which is the design of experience and activities developed by teachers to help children increase their competence, should include everything that happens to children during

their time at the preschool, nursery school, or children's center. The task of the teacher is to develop curriculum that enables such total learning to take place.

But how can teachers go about this? How is it possible to promote creativity, emotional health, physical prowess, social expertise, and cognitive skills in a few brief hours each day? Moreover, how is it possible to weave these into a consistent whole? At first glance it may appear an overwhelming task. However, if we break the task into smaller parts, we will see that it is possible to develop curriculum that does accomplish these goals and brings satisfaction and fulfillment to children and teachers.

The most common way of breaking curriculum into parts is according to subject matter (Hildebrand, 1986; Leeper, Witherspoon, & Day, 1984; Seefeldt & Barbour, 1986). This approach may feel natural and sensible to us because we have been brought up in an educational tradition in which curriculum is divided according to that system. As children we moved from art class to science class to history class, seeing little relationship between subjects and often ignoring our feelings.

But life is not like that. In life many kinds of learnings happen together and affect each other. Feelings often strongly influence learning ability, and the need for social involvement takes priority over the acquisition of information. In real life all aspects of the person must be treated together and educated together. Only when this is recognized and provided for in the curriculum can true learning and competence develop. For this reason, I prefer to discuss curriculum in terms of these aspects, or selves, and to design curriculum that provides the various learning experiences that are most suitable for the development of competence for each of these selves. This life-oriented approach places the emphasis where it belongs—on the child, not on impersonal subject matter.

In this book the selves are identified as the physical, emotional, social, creative, and cognitive selves. The physical self is discussed first because a healthy body provides the foundation that enables the other selves to develop and flourish. Curriculum for the physical self not only covers recommendations for the development of physical abilities, but also includes discussions regarding nutrition, cooking, caring for the body, and understanding the cycle of life and death.

The emotional self is emphasized because emotional stability contributes so much to children's sense of well-being and self-confidence. Emotionally healthy children do not need to pour their energies into defending themselves from worries and insecurities; instead, they are free to channel their energy into developing their total being, thereby enriching the growth of all five selves. Curriculum for the emotional self involves the planning of experiences that inspire trust, autonomy, and initiative and that teach children to remain in contact with their feelings. Such curriculum uses dramatic play to clarify these emotions and help children understand that other people have feelings, too.

The social self is vital to consider because children must live with other people all their lives. The earlier children can gain skills that help them get along easily and happily with others, the more likely they are to enjoy life and

to feel successful. Learning for the social self usually depends on interpersonal encounters between the child and other people, both grownups and children. Curriculum to aid such learning promotes the ability to control antisocial impulses. It helps children get along in a group, enjoy playing with other youngsters, and learn to lend them a helping hand from time to time. If this curriculum is well presented, it encourages children to treasure their own ethnic and sexual identities and those of other people as well.

The creative self is another vital aspect because creativity greatly contributes to children's sense of self-worth and individuality and increases the probability of unique contributions that they may ultimately make to society. Curriculum for the creative self contains materials that encourage self-expression and pretend play and strategies that enhance the growth of original thought.

Finally, the curriculum for the cognitive self must be as carefully planned as the rest because the ability to reason and to put the results of this reasoning into words enhances children's potential for later academic success. Therefore, the cognitive self, though discussed last, has an important place in preschool curriculum. Such curriculum includes experiences and activities that enhance verbal fluency and that also elicit the use of particular mental abilities.

But while thinking of the individual selves, the reader is also asked to remember that a sound curriculum not only provides opportunities to enhance the individual selves. In some ways, children are like bicycles: they are greater than the sum of their parts. It is the way the selves of the child operate together that produces the personality, just as gears and wheels operate together to become the bike. Therefore, well-designed curriculum should be planned to foster this kind of wholeness by providing opportunities for integrating learning. Teachers should intend that every subject they include, whether it be cooking, carpentry, or caring for an animal, educates all the selves, even though it may emphasize only one in particular.

WHAT IS COMPETENCE?

This chapter began with the statement that the purpose of education is to foster competence in dealing with life. But what *is* competence, and why is it of such value? Competence can be defined as the wonderful feeling of assurance exemplified by the statements: "I can do it," "I am able," "I know how," and "I am an effective person." These reveal a security and belief in oneself that are the fundamental cornerstones of self-esteem. The fortunate possessors of such confidence are willing to risk and to explore for the sake of learning because they believe themselves to be worthwhile, competent people.

According to Robert White (1968), the desire for competence is one of the basic motivators of human behavior. In addition to needing to satisfy hunger, thirst, and other basic physiological needs, human beings have an inherent drive for mastery and competence. It is this drive, White maintains, that urges the infant on in his relentless practice of rolling over or sitting up,

Hard to believe that 4-year-old Anthony could be this competent, but he performed this feat a number of times. (He is also the son of the basketball coach!)

and it is the same drive that motivates many adults to pursue evening education classes after a long day's work.

Competence may also be considered in terms of its opposite: helplessness. Nelson (1987) reviewed a number of studies that demonstrate that feelings of helplessness result when children find that their personal efforts have little impact on how things turn out. In other words, when children experience consistent failure, some of them conclude that nothing they do makes any difference, and as children grow older, they are more likely to draw the conclusion that they are ineffective in coping with circumstances (Rholes, Blackwell, Jordan, & Walters, 1980). People often express this helplessness by acting anxious and depressed and becoming unable to take action (Garber & Seligman, 1980). They just stop trying.

On the other hand, when individuals feel competent, they see themselves, at least to some degree, as in control of their own destinies, and as a result, they feel good about themselves. Bronson (1974) claims that the person who sees himself as competent expects that "under most conditions he is likely to encounter, he will be able to cope with whatever demands he meets, and to derive joy from the encounter" (p. 243). What a marvelous educational goal this is for teachers—to help children attain competence so they may experience joy. And what a powerful antidote this could be for children of the poor, whose helplessness is often a hallmark of the family's attitude toward life.

HOW IS COMPETENCE ACQUIRED?

Granted that competence is a fundamental goal desirable for education, the question remains, what do teachers need to know and do to foster competence in young children?

What Do Teachers Need to Know to Foster Competence?

First, teachers need to understand the general capabilities and interests common to each age of childhood so that they can plan curriculum that is neither so difficult it is discouraging nor so easy it is uninteresting. They also require knowledge of each child, since every youngster, although like other children of his age in some ways, is unique in others.

There are studies and checklists available that identify general developmental levels and characteristics for particular ages. One such list is included in Appendix A. To appreciate the uniqueness of individual children, however, teachers have to rely on themselves and on their developing sensitivity and expertise, as much as on these more objective measures. For example, a teacher needs to know not only how a child behaves at school, but also how he is at home. Many factors there affect his life: How much television does he watch, and what kinds of programs does he see? Is his family undergoing hard times? Has there been a recent crisis of any kind? Is he an only child, a twin, a sixth of seven? How does his family feel about him? What do they expect of him in the way of behavior? What do they anticipate this experience at school will be like? What is his neighborhood like? With whom does he play? All these bits and pieces garnered by the teacher contribute to her understanding of the child and to her ability to interpret his behavior accurately. Actually, it is all these individual circumstances and variations that make teaching fascinating.

Teachers need to know how young children learn. The question of how to enable each child to learn as fully and completely as possible, without pushing him too hard or letting him drift into boredom, remains the continuing challenge of education. Because of an increasing pressure to push formal academic learning on young children before they are ready for it (Hills, 1987; National Commission on Excellence in Education, 1983), teachers must be knowledgeable about what constitutes developmentally appropriate curriculum. Fortunately, the National Association for the Education of Young Children has issued a publication entitled *Developmentally*

Appropriate Practice in Early Childhood Programs Serving Children From Birth Through Age 8 that spells out in considerable detail what is and is not appropriate teaching practice for children of that age (Bredekamp, 1987).

Once teachers have a reasonable knowledge of what young children are like, they need to understand how to teach them effectively, since the more easily children learn, the more competent they will feel. Although recent evidence indicates this is a complex question and that the answer varies from child to child, there are some basic principles about how all young children learn that are generally regarded as true.

One such principle is that children pass through a series of stages as they grow. Children learn to sit up before they learn to stand and to use their fingers before learning to hold a spoon. Such stage-related development has been substantiated by such widely diverse researchers as Brittain (1979), Erikson (1963), Gesell and colleagues (1940), Kohlberg (1985), and Piaget (1983).

Another related principle is that children learn things a step at a time. This step-by-step learning is often termed *hierarchical learning* because the child moves up a hierarchy rung by rung as skill is acquired. Teachers therefore should plan to teach skills gradually, first teaching simple skills and then more advanced ones as the children gain competence. An important implication of this principle for teaching is that the curriculum must offer a variety of levels of challenge concurrently, since different children in the same group are at different steps on the learning ladder during the same period.

Still another basic principle of learning is that children and adults learn best through actual experience and participation. John Dewey's concept of learning by doing is as true today as it was 40 years ago. The truth of this can be seen by reflecting on the process of learning to teach. One can read about teaching forever, but all the reading and discussion in the world cannot substitute for the learning that results from actually encountering the liveliness and variabil-

ity of young children in the classroom. It is learning by doing, not learning by talking about it, that makes the difference.

For young children who cannot read and for whom language is still new and tenuously grasped, the value of experience-based learning is even more crucial (Hunt, 1986; Piaget & Inhelder, 1969). Discussion and verbal learning that are isolated from actual experience have little educative power for such young learners. Instead, learning must be accomplished through all the sensory channels. Children must live through, explore, and try things out to attach meaning to them. As Bruner says, competence in the form of objective intelligence comes from knowing how, not knowing that (Connolly & Bruner, 1974).

The final principle to remember is that preschool children learn by using play to translate experience into understanding (Piaget, 1962; Piaget & Inhelder, 1969). As Frank (1968) remarked, "Through play, children learn what no one can teach them." For young children, play *is* the lifeblood of learning, so it is vital that teachers provide extensive opportunities for children to learn through play every time they come to school.

Teachers must realize that parents are the most important influence in the development of the child. Teachers sometimes fail to see that they have a limited role in the child's educational experience. The truth is that parents exert a much more profound influence than teachers do, particularly during the early stages of development (Anthony & Pollock, 1985; Feldman & Nash, 1986; Patterson, 1986). This is true not only because of the greater amounts of time children and parents are likely to spend together, but also because of the strong emotional bonds that exist between them. Teachers therefore need to keep their perspective about their relative importance and to realize the benefits of including parents in the life of the school. As an aid to teachers, suggestions concerning this home-school cooperation are made throughout this book, and Chapter 19 is entirely devoted to this subject.

Learning through all the sensory channels is important.

What Do Teachers Need to Do?

First, teachers have to work hard. Occasional newcomers to the field of early childhood education have the impression that young children are easier to teach or less challenging to control than older children are. Of course, this is not true. Teaching 2-, 3-, and 4-year-olds requires very special energies. The hours are long, and the demands on teachers' patience, attention, and good judgment are endless. Since research indicates it is during these very early years of childhood that much of the child's basic intellectual ability is formed (Bloom, 1964), the work of early childhood teachers carries a very special

responsibility—and the next day it is there to do all over again.

Teachers need to pay attention to research and apply the results of research findings when it is appropriate to do so. This book includes a summary of a research study in almost every chapter. Some of these studies were included because they are well known, while others were selected because they provide a variety of different and occasionally ingenious ways of finding out answers to questions about children. Well known or not, they all contain valuable implications for teaching.

I hope that these summaries will convince the reader that research can be fascinating, and that

RESEARCH STUDY
Early Education Can Make a Difference

Research Question   The Consortium for Longitudinal Studies asked the basic question, Can quality preschool education produce long-term, lasting benefits for children who attend such programs?

Research Method   This follow-up study gathered data about how young children turned out who had attended high-quality experimental preschool programs in the early 1960s. These 11 programs were distributed over the entire United States and included center-based, home-based, and combined center- and home-based programs. Most of the children came from low-income Black families. The total number of children included in the follow-up study was 2,008.

All the studies offered the advantage of experimental groups (children who had attended the programs) and reasonably similar control groups (children who had not attended the programs). This circumstance was crucial to the success of the follow-up study because researchers could compare what happened to the children who had attended preschool with what happened to the children who had not attended preschool.

The investigators checked school records, scores on intelligence tests, and interviewed the parents and young people who ranged from 9 to 19 years of age at the time of the follow-up study.

Results   The results of the follow-up study clearly indicated that the preschool programs *did* provide the following long-term benefits for the children who attended them:

1. The children were more competent in school. Although results varied from program to program, children in the preschool programs were only half as likely as children in the control groups to be assigned to special education classes, and fewer of them were required to repeat a grade in school. (Only 13.8% of the preschool children were assigned to special education classes as compared to

---

teachers need to pay attention to it because it can produce results that are directly relevant to what happens every day in early childhood classrooms. My frustration is that the studies could not be presented in their entirety. Perhaps these overviews will stimulate readers to pursue the original publication or, better yet, resolve to carry out research themselves in the future. The field of early childhood offers endless opportunities for such activity.

Teachers should take pride in knowing that preschool education can make a difference. In the past, the value of preschool education was often ignored or denigrated, and even today teachers must still fight the stereotype of being "just baby-sitters."

Unfortunately, there are still many people who are unaware of the growing body of evidence that quality preschool child care programs can produce substantial, long-term benefits for children who participate in such environments. For this reason, it is important for all of us to know about the landmark study described in this chapter. We must be well informed so we can stand up for the value of what we do and be able to cite the research findings that prove its worth.

28.8% of the control children. Only 25% of the preschool children had to repeat a grade as compared to 36.6% of the control children.)

2. Children who had attended preschool programs scored significantly better on intelligence tests during their early years in school; however, those differences disappeared after 3 to 4 years, so the final conclusion was that the effect of early education on intelligence test scores was not permanent.

3. Early education had an effect on the family—mothers of the preschool group were more satisfied with their children's performance in school and had higher occupational aspirations for their children than did mothers of children in the control group.

Implications   These findings are important because the effect on the children themselves is significant. How much better it is for children's self-esteem to remain in regular school classes than to be made to repeat a grade or suffer the potential humiliation of placement in a special education classroom.

The financial savings to society must also be taken into account. Providing special education and having students repeat grades costs a lot of money, and any time this can be avoided legislators and school administrators sit up and take notice. Therefore, educators can use these research results in their fight for additional quality preschool programs.

Finally, the Consortium study was the first longitudinal study to provide solid, well-researched evidence that early education actually does produce tangible, positive, long-term results. Thanks to it and to numerous additional studies since that time (Berrueta-Clement, Schweinhart, Barnett, Epstein, & Weikart, 1984; Hunt, 1986), legislators and administrators now look more favorably towards providing preschool programs for young children because the research has made them aware that providing quality early education has lasting benefits for society.

Note. From "Lasting Effects of Early Education: A Report from the Consortium for Longitudinal Studies" by I. Lazar, R. Darlington, H. Murray, J. Royce, and A. Snipper, 1982, *Monographs of the Society for Research in Child Development, 47*(2–3, Serial No. 195).

Teachers need to develop a clear philosophy of teaching. This involves identifying those educational values they consider to be most worthwhile and determining the methods of instruction that will implement these values most effectively.

The curriculum advocated throughout this book is founded on a philosophy that encourages children to make decisions for themselves whenever possible and appropriate, to learn through actual involvement, and to participate in experiences that provide balanced opportunities for all aspects of the child to grow and develop.

For this reason, this book advocates presenting curriculum in an "open" school, where during many portions of the day, children are expected to take responsibility for self-selecting how they will use their time.

Three Educational Philosophies. Franklin and Biber (1977) discuss three psychological perspectives and illustrate how these are reflected in current preschool education. They identify these perspectives as the *behavioristic learning theory approach,* the *Piagetian cognitive-developmental approach,* and the *developmental-interaction ap-*

proach. In actuality, no preschool is likely to be purely behavioristic or purely Piagetian, but rather it tends to follow one approach more than the others, while remaining somewhat eclectic.

Franklin and Biber (1977) characterize the behavioristic learning approach as being based on behavioristic psychology, which has as its basic tenets that "(a) observable behavior or performance constitutes the primary datum for the scientific investigation of learning processes and for approaches to behavior change and (b) the basic principles of learning are the laws of classical and operant conditioning" (p. 3). This is commonly referred to as a *behavior modification* approach. Although behaviorists recommend procedures that seem to many teachers to be rather cut-and-dried or calculated, behavior modification does encourage the development of clear-cut analyses of behavior and teaching goals.

Behaviorists also recommend that teachers wishing to change a child's behavior begin with a careful observation of his current behavior, determine which rewards are preferred by that child, develop a description of what behavior would be more desirable, and finally develop and implement a reinforcement plan or schedule that will use the preferred rewards to select and reinforce the more desirable behavior. Two programs that have attempted to put this educational theory into deliberate, consistent practice are the ones by Bereiter and Englemann (1966) and the Portage Project (Shearer, 1987).

There's no denying that teachers, either consciously or unconsciously, make use of the principles of positive reinforcement every time they smile in approval at what a child has done, just as they use negative reinforcement when they reprimand him. Moreover, understanding learning theory may prevent naive teachers from unwittingly causing unwanted behavior to continue because they fail to perceive and put a stop to the rewards a behavior holds for a child who persists in behaving a particular way.

However, there are limitations to this approach that must be noted. According to Frank-

lin and Biber, these include (1) whether specifically trained behaviors generalize to other behaviors, (2) how long the reinforced behavior is likely to continue once the reward is removed, and (3) how tangible rewards (such as candy) can be exchanged for more intangible ones later. In addition, I raise the question of how such a reward system can be translated into internal rather than external gratifications, so that the child ultimately becomes inner- rather than other-controlled. Franklin and Biber also comment that programs presently based on behavior modification techniques seemingly value the more traditional, academic forms of education. These programs often emphasize the use of learning drills and rote memory as educational techniques; the program of Bereiter and Englemann (1966) is a particularly clear-cut example of this.

The second perspective discussed by Franklin and Biber is the cognitive-developmental perspective based on the theories and research of Jean Piaget and his colleagues at Geneva. This approach sees the child as the source of action and as an interactor with the environment, rather than as being manipulated from the outside. The child is viewed as gradually developing underlying cognitive structures that help him make sense of his world and that govern "his modes of transaction with the social and physical environment in which he lives" (Franklin & Biber, 1977, p. 10). The authors continue, "Since learning is an active process, and knowledge is constructed rather than 'acquired,' the child must be provided with an environment which furthers his own natural tendency to act on and with objects, to explore, manipulate, and experiment" (p. 11).

Piagetians, who are proponents of the cognitive-developmental perspective, maintain that direct exploration and handling of objects are vital elements in early education. They also stress the stage theory of development, which maintains that individuals pass through different stages in such areas as cognition and moral development as they mature, and they have documented examples showing that children actually do think differently than adults (see Chapter 17). An example of how this theoretical base has been translated into practice is contained in the book by Hohmann, Banet, and Weikart, *Young Children in Action* (1979).

According to Franklin and Biber, considerable closeness of viewpoint exists between Piagetian-based educators and those who subscribe to the third perspective: the developmental-interaction perspective. The primary difference between the two is that Piaget focused mainly on only one area—cognition. (This focus is of great value to early childhood teachers. Piaget developed his theory at a time when intellectual-cognitive learning was assuming increasing importance and his work provided a humane, child-oriented means of approaching such learning.)

Although the developmental-interaction approach[1] often makes use of Piagetian theory, it moves beyond this to encompass a larger, more eclectic approach. It is this point of view that the philosophy of *Total Learning* and its companion book *The Whole Child* (Hendrick, 1988) most nearly matches.

This philosophy is based on the concept that children pass through a number of predictable, orderly stages in their growth. It uses Erikson as the model for emotional development, Piaget in relation to cognitive growth, and Gesell and other more recent authors for stages of physical development.

The developmental-interaction approach views interaction as taking place not only between the child and the environment, but also between the various aspects or selves within the child. The way the child sees himself and feels about himself influences his ability to learn, just as his potential sense of mastery over cognitive materials increases his positive sense of self-worth (Weber, 1984; Zimiles, 1987).

---

[1]An excellent description of this model in its purer original form is provided by Zimiles (1987) and Weber (1984) in their discussions of the Bank Street Model.

For this reason it is important to enhance the child's sense that he is a competent, autonomous person in all aspects of his being. The child who sees himself as socially adept, emotionally self-possessed, physically skilled, and intellectually able feels secure and masterful—ready to cope with changes in his environment as they occur—ready to relish life and welcome new experiences.

Although it is necessary to discuss these different aspects of the child's self individually as this book progresses, the overall intention is to blend the needs and education of all of them together in the total curriculum and to deal with the child as a whole being. With such a philosophy, learning through play and by means of actual experience is as essential to the curriculum as is the planning that provides for many choices within a carefully arranged overall structure. Throughout this book, emphasis is placed on process learning. This learning helps children acquire skills that enable them to cope with many situations rather than to merely learn facts or content (though the teaching of facts and content is included).

Although environments that favor such process learning are often spoken of as being "open," this should not be interpreted as meaning haphazard. Indeed, the sensitivity needed for planning for self-selection and open choice that truly meets the needs of children requires more thought on the teacher's part than does the teacher-dominated approach in which children are conveniently marshalled from one activity to another according to the clock and the teacher's wish.

What *open* actually means according to the philosophy of this book is that a variety of carefully selected learning opportunities based on the children's needs and interests are offered. These are geared to the appropriate developmental level and are intended to develop all five selves. Some of these, particularly in the area of cognitive activities, may involve active participation by child and teacher; some are more child centered. The environment is open in the sense that children are encouraged to involve themselves in these experiences as their needs and desires dictate, provided that they do not injure themselves or others or damage property. But this is not just a case of child plus activity. The social milieu provided by other children and adults contributes much to the richness and value of this learning experience. It is the people, both grown-ups and children, who provide the opportunities for the questions, interchanges, and compromises, which are the essence of successful open education.

Finally, the teacher must present learning within a climate of caring. Although climate is composed of many elements, it is primarily a product of the teachers' attitudes toward the children and their work and the children's response to these feelings. We must ask ourselves therefore what kind

Children flourish when they know the teacher cares about them.

of teacher attitude is most likely to promote learning in the classroom. Is it warmth or positive regard or even love? Surely all these qualities are of value in teaching. Who would not prefer a warm teacher to a cold one or an approving teacher to one who rejects children unless they conform to her demands?

The difficulty with advocating warmth and acceptance does not lie in whether or not they are desirable. The difficulty lies in asking teachers to feel this way at times when they cannot do it sincerely—times, for example, when a child has deliberately twisted the rat's paw to see it wince or bitten another child hard enough to draw blood. In such circumstances can one feel warm or accepting? And if not, what is left? Is it possible to advocate *any* attitude that is genuine and can be evoked in such highly charged situations that promotes positive growth for teacher and child?

It *is* possible, and that attitude is best described by the word *caring.* Perhaps it is really this quality that Sullivan (1940) has in mind when he comments: "Love exists when the satisfaction or security of another person becomes as significant to one as is one's own" (p. 20). I prefer to substitute the word *caring* for *love* because in our society the word *love* has so many different connotations. Thus we can say that caring exists when the satisfaction or security of another person becomes as significant to one as is one's own. This attitude fits even difficult circumstances, since it is possible for the teacher to continue to care, and to care intensely, about a youngster even while being appalled at what he has done. In tense confrontations, it is deeply reassuring to children to sense this true concern. It assures them that no matter what they have done, they are important to the teacher and she will not abandon them. Moreover, this reaction has the additional virtue of being absolutely genuine, thereby making unnecessary such false declarations of approval as, "I like *you* but not what you do."

One final aspect of the Sullivan definition requires comment. The reader may recall the definition states that caring exists when the well-being of another becomes as important to one as one's own. Good teachers give much of themselves to the children and families whom they serve, but this should never be accomplished at the expense of caring for themselves. That is why it is so important to remember the second part of the definition, which makes it plain that it is necessary and acceptable to care for oneself as well as for other people. Caring should never be offered in a spirit of self-sacrifice, lest it become martyrdom.

SUMMARY

Since the purpose of education is to foster competence in all aspects of life, curriculum should provide opportunities for total learning. This is best accomplished by considering the five aspects of the child's personality (the physical, emotional, social, creative, and cognitive selves) when planning curriculum.

To make this a reality, teachers need to know what children are like. They must be knowledgeable about developmental sequences and about individual differences to keep the curriculum both age- and child-appropriate. They need to remember that children learn things a step at a time, that they learn best through experience, and that they use play to interiorize knowledge. Teachers also need to value the family as the most important educational influence in the life of the child.

Teachers need to work hard; they need to pay attention to research findings and their implications for the classroom; they need to know that what they do can make a positive, long-term difference in the lives of the children they teach; they need to develop a clear philosophy of teaching; and they need to present learning in a climate of caring, where the well-being of the children is as important to them as is their own. This climate of caring is fundamental to the growth of competence.

SELF-CHECK QUESTIONS FOR REVIEW

Content-Related Questions

1. According to the author, what is the basic purpose of education?
2. Should curriculum focus mainly on cognitive, intellectual learning?
3. Name the five selves and mention some areas of curriculum that belong to the separate selves.
4. Why is a feeling of competence so valuable?
5. Name three important principles about how all young children learn. Why do teachers need to know what these principles are and how to apply them?
6. Are teachers or parents more important influences in children's lives?
7. Name two important pieces of research information produced by the Consortium for Longitudinal Studies. Why are these findings so important?
8. Give a brief description of the strengths and weaknesses of the behavioristic philosophy of education.
9. How does a pure Piagetian philosophy of education differ from that of the developmental-interaction approach?
10. Describe some cornerstones of the developmental-interaction approach that underlie teaching young children.
11. What is the second part of Sullivan's definition of love or caring, and why is it as important as the first part?

Integrative Questions

1. Select one activity, such as playing with blocks, and give examples of how creativity, emotional health, physical prowess, social expertise, and cognitive skills can be enhanced while the children are participating in that activity.
2. Compare teacher behaviors that might contribute to a child's feelings of helplessness with behaviors that would increase a child's sense of competence.
3. Taking into account the factors discussed in Chapter 1, discuss your own personal requirements you feel a child-care situation should meet before you could accept a staff position.

QUESTIONS AND ACTIVITIES

1. Nobody is competent at everything. Think of an area in which you do not regard yourself as skilled, such as playing tennis, using a power tool, or separating eggs. How do you respond when asked to participate in such an activity? And how do you feel when forced to participate?
2. Watch closely the next time you teach. See if you can spot any circumstances in which a child feels incompetent. How did you cope with this circumstance? Was there some way you could have helped him cope more satisfactorily?
3. Considering the opposite of what should be done often stimulates thought. For this reason, suppose you wanted to make children feel as helpless as possible. What could you do to make them feel this? Give several everyday examples.
4. What would you say is the effect of helplessness on self-esteem?
5. Put the difference between knowing *how* and knowing *that* into words. Use an example to illustrate what you mean.
6. *Problem:* A mother has just entered her child in your preschool. She asks if he will be learning to write his name, the alphabet, and other skills that he needs to learn before entering elementary school. How would you explain the learning program at your school so that the mother understands what kinds of learning will take place?
7. Do you agree that caring is the most valuable attitude for a teacher to express? What other attitudes are important to project?
8. Is there any difference between the "openness" in a preschool setting as described in the text and allowing children to do anything they please when they please? Where should the teacher draw the line?

REFERENCES FOR FURTHER READING

Overviews

Bredekamp, S. (Ed.). (1987). *Developmentally appropriate practice in early childhood programs serving children from birth through age 8: Expanded edition*. Washington, D.C.: National Association for the Education of Young Children. This resource carefully spells out both good and undesirable teaching practices. It is valuable particularly because its basic principles of good practice can be applied to many differing educational approaches.

Griffin, E. F. (1982). *Island of childhood: Education in the special world of nursery school*. New York: Teachers College Press. Griffin conveys a sense of the atmosphere that should surround children and teachers during these early years. Highly recommended.

Hymes, J. L. (1981). *Teaching the child under six* (3rd ed.). Columbus, Ohio: Merrill Publishing Co. This warm, highly readable paperback discusses the current state of the art in nursery school curriculum and includes excellent, down-to-earth discussions of what young children are like and what kinds of programs serve them most adequately.

Read, K., Gardner, P., & Mahler, B. C. (1987). *Early childhood programs: Human relationships and learning* (8th ed.). New York: Holt, Rinehart & Winston. This book remains the best description of the underlying attitude and approach I hope teachers can achieve when working with young children.

Competence

Fowler, W. (Ed.). (1986). Early experience and the development of competence. In W. Damon (Ed.), *New directions for child development*. San Francisco: Jossey-Bass, Publishers. This paperback from the *New Directions* series considers competence from a variety of viewpoints. A useful place to begin.

Murphy, L. B., & Moriarty, A. E. (1976). *Vulnerability, coping, and growth from infancy to adolescence*. New Haven, Conn.: Yale University Press. The authors emphasize the variety of coping strategies used by children to attain mastery of themselves and their environments. Interesting reading.

White, R. W. (1968). Motivation reconsidered: The concept of competence. In M. Almy (Ed.), *Early childhood play: Selected readings related to cognition and motivation*. New York: Simon & Schuster. In this classic discussion, the author reviews various theories about the nature of motivation and then proposes that certain behaviors are motivated by the need to achieve competence rather than by hunger or thirst.

Descriptions of Various Programs and Philosophies

Morrison, G. (1988). *Early childhood education today* (4th ed.). Columbus Ohio: Merrill Publishing Co. Morrison offers a useful overview of the kinds of early childhood settings available in the United States.

Roopnarine, J. L., & Johnson, J. E. (Eds.). (1987). *Approaches to early childhood education*. Columbus, Ohio: Merrill Publishing Co. Another survey of programs that stresses the research procedures and findings associated with their implementation.

Caring

Buscaglia, L. (1984). *Loving each other: The challenge of human relationships*. New York: Holt, Rinehart & Winston. The author offers some sensible advice about what loving really means.

Warren, R. M. (1977). *Caring: Supporting children's growth*. Washington, D.C.: National Association for the Education of Young Children. This pamphlet, which is filled with wise observations on fostering the emotional health of children, illustrates many aspects of caring related to preschool education.

For the Advanced Student

Bellack, A. S., Hersen, M., & Kazdin, Q. E. (Eds.). (1982). *International handbook of behavior modification and therapy*. New York: Plenum Publishing. This is a very long book that offers a tremendous variety of articles related to the subject of behavior modification. For serious students of this approach, it is an outstanding reference.

Berrueta-Clement, J. T., Schweinhart, L. J., Barnett, W. S., & Weikart, D. P. (1984). *Changed lives: The effect of the Perry Preschool Program on youths through age 19*. Ypsilanti, Mich.: High/Scope Educational Research Foundation. This book summarizes not only the Perry research, but also various other longitudinal studies reporting the effect of early childhood programs on later development.

Biber, B. (1984). *Early education and psychological development*. New Haven: Yale University Press. Biber outlines the basic principles of the developmental-interaction approach—the educational philosophy on which *Total Learning* is based—and illustrates them with specific examples drawn from her work at Bank Street College.

Harter, S. (1985). Competence as a dimension of self-evaluation: Toward a comprehensive model of self-worth. In R. L. Leahy (Ed.), *The development of the self*. New York: Academic Press. This chapter explores the relationship between competence and feelings of self-esteem.

Piaget, J. (1983). Piaget's theory. In P. H. Mussen (Ed.), *Handbook of child psychology* (4th ed.). W. Kessen (Ed.), *Vol. I: History, theory, and methods*. New York: John Wiley & Sons. This work, by the master himself, is a classic explanation of Piagetian theory.

Schweinhart, L. J., Weikart, D. P., & Larner, M. B. (1986). Consequences of three preschool curriculum models through age 15. *Early Childhood Research Quarterly, 1*(1), 14–46. This long-term follow-up study indicates that children who participated in the High/Scope program or in a classical nursery school program experienced far less delinquency in adolescence than did children in the highly regulated DISTAR program. This article generated a good deal of commentary by others. For a number of responses to it see *Early Childhood Research Quarterly*, (1986), *1*(3), 287–311.

White, B. L., & Watts, J. C. (1973). *Experience and environment: Major influences on the development of the young child* (Vol. 1). Englewood Cliffs, N. J.: Prentice-Hall. The chapter titled "The Development of Competence" is of particular interest because of the lists of competencies it includes and White's comments on how these can be generated in children from 1 to 6 years of age.

2 Play

The Integrative Force in Learning

Have you ever

- Fumbled for words when a parent says, "Well, I'm glad they're having fun, but when do you really teach them something?"
- Known that play was an important mode of learning but doubted whether it contributed much to mental development?
- Wondered what you could do to encourage the children to get more out of their play experiences?

If you have, the material in this chapter will help you.

As with love, play can be a many-splendored thing with many faces and ages. Play must be alive and come from inside, and, as with love, it can never be a spectator sport. It is active and self-initiated. Watching a football game may be fun, but it is not play. We cannot program play, just as we cannot program love. We cannot impose upon children what we think they need to play, or what we think they should feel about play.

Play is the doing. "I'd rather do it myself, Mother," is packed with meaning. We cannot hand the child an idea or word and expect it automatically to become a part of the child. Children may accept our offering, but they are the only ones capable of the incorporation of the idea into their growing selves. For the young child, play is the single most effective means to accomplish integration and growth.

SUE SPAYTH RILEY (1984)

Chapter 1 advocates not only the planning of curriculum for each of the child's selves, but also the consideration of the child as a whole, because the whole is more than the sum of the individual parts. We never want to lose sight of the child as being this complete human being. So, as we plan our teaching, we must ask ourselves, what method do we use to bring about this sense of wholeness for children? What glue can we supply that will stick the parts of that small person together to form a complete, fully functioning person?

To answer this perplexing question, we have only to go to the children and observe what they use to accomplish this integration. The answer is that children use play to achieve this goal. Play provides children with unparalleled opportunities for integrating their personalities, because when children play, all the selves are used simultaneously. Thus, a child taking the father's role in house play may be developing the physical self by practicing eye-hand coordination as she pours pretend juice, practicing social skills as she ingratiates herself with the group, developing emotional insight when the recalcitrant baby protests, "No! No! Baby not go to bed," and using her cognitive creative abilities as she substitutes a necktie for a leash while walking the

family dog. I can think of no other experience in the child's life that provides the same opportunity for all the selves to interact and grow simultaneously as does the opportunity for play.

Play further acts as an integrative force by providing opportunities for children to clarify who they are and who they are not. Playing the role of a police officer, mother, baby, or bus driver is one way of doing this, of course, but the ordinary social interactions that occur during play also help children form concepts of their total self. During play they may define themselves, or may be defined by others, as someone who is liked, or disliked, or good at climbing, or a crybaby, or myriad other things. Such labels tend to push a child into a particular mold or framework that can be desirable or undesirable.

Play also acts as an integrative force by helping children discriminate not only between who they are and who they are not, but also to discriminate between what is real and what is not. Two- and three-year-olds, in particular, may require the teacher's help in remembering that dramatic play is "just pretend" and that they are acting "as if" something were true (Curry & Arnaud, 1982). For example, I recently helped a child work out some of his fear of dogs by allowing him to hit a stuffed dog at nursery school while stuttering out all the terrible things he would like to do to it because it had bitten him. Suddenly he stopped and said uncertainly, "But if I bite him, he won't bite back, will he?" He needed me to ask him, "Is the puppy real?" before he could continue with his play. That moment of uncertainty demonstrated how thin the line can be between reality and fantasy in young children's play and how important the teacher is in providing reassurance when it is necessary.

As children mature, they learn to handle the real/not real continuum themselves and need less frequent direction from the teacher. Garvey (1983) explains that they do this by developing ways of signaling between themselves when they begin to play and make the transition from reality to pretend. For example, they may begin an interchange with "Pretend that . . ." or "I'll be the mommy and you be the daddy, okay?" This kind of gambit is an accepted social signal among preschoolers that they are entering a period where literalness is suspended and imaginative play substituted in its place.

BUT WHAT IS PLAY?

There are as many differing theories and definitions of play as there are people who write about it, and the arguments continue (Vandenberg, 1986). Schwartzman (1978) is quite accurate when she says, "Today we are still flying theoretical 'kites' in the study of play—only now there are more of them. This is as it should be because play requires a multiperspective approach . . . and resists any attempts to define it rigidly" (p. 325).

Definitions of Play

Definitions range from Montessori's, "Play is a child's work," to Dewey's, "Play is what we enjoy while we are doing it. Work is what we enjoy when we have accomplished it." Views on the purpose of play also vary, ranging from Freud's

contention that play provides opportunities to clarify and master emotions to Piaget's proposal that play enables children to substitute symbols in place of reality (Elkind, 1981a).

A current definition that has particular merit for preschool teachers is offered by Johnson and Ershler (1982): "Play may be defined as behavior that is intrinsically motivated, freely chosen, process-oriented, and pleasurable" (p. 137). This definition is useful because it provides us with a set of standards against which we can measure the play activity in our classrooms. It is only necessary for us to translate these standards into a series of questions to use them in this way. For example:

- *Play is intrinsically motivated.*
  (interpretation) Will children choose to become involved in the curriculum I have planned because the activities are inherently satisfying or because they will be rewarded by the teacher?
- *Play is freely chosen.*
  (interpretation) Does this play allow children to choose freely what they wish to do for at least a portion of the time they are at school?
- *Play is process-oriented.*
  (interpretation) Will children find satisfaction while doing the activity and not just in the end result?
- *Play is pleasurable.*
  (interpretation) Will the children have fun while they are participating in the activity?

We need to ask ourselves these questions continually because all too often teachers lose sight of them when planning to include play in the curriculum. For example, teachers may set up a block corner to carry out a particular theme such as farm animals or transportation, thereby stifling the children's opportunities for freely choosing how they wish to play with blocks that day.

Sutton-Smith (1987) speaks of such guided play as the "domestication of early childhood play." He suggests that some teachers tend to see "educational play" as being the only really good, worthwhile kind and the more spontaneous, vigorous, child-instigated play as less desirable and hence not worthy of encouragement.

Although there can be a place for controlled play experiences in the curriculum, we must always remember that guided play does not meet the criteria of being child generated or freely chosen since teachers tend to push children into following the theme and the teacher's idea. There must also be many opportunities for children to play freely and spontaneously as their *own* ideas and internal states dictate. It is only when such open opportunities abound that children can fully develop their ideas and passions. It is this kind of open play that provides the best opportunities for integration of all the selves.

Stages of Play

Researchers do agree that play passes through a series of developmental stages, although once again they differ in their categorization of these.

One tried and true categorization still in use today, which investigates the social aspects of play, was developed by Parten in 1932. She viewed play as advancing from *solitary play* (playing alone, with little reference to what other children nearby are doing—characteristic of very young children), to *parallel play* (playing beside, but not with, a companion child with toys that are similar—often seen in the play of 2- and 3-year-olds), to *associative play* (playing together, but not subordinating their individual interests to a common goal—often witnessed in the play of 3½- to 4½-year-old children), and finally to *cooperative play* (playing together for a common purpose—often apparent in the play of 4- and 5-year-olds who organize themselves into a group). These stages are not mutually exclusive, however. Kenneth Rubin (1977a) demonstrates that solitary play can be quite sophisticated and that the same child may use various forms and combinations of these stages at different times of the day and in various circumstances throughout his early childhood. Therefore, teachers should not view solitary and parallel play as necessarily being evidence of immaturity.

Another well-known way of categorizing stages of development in play was developed by

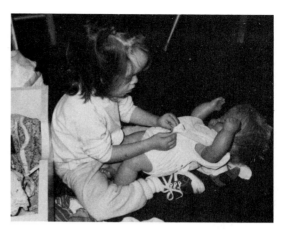

This kind of solitary play is typical of "old" twos.

Smilansky (1968) following Piagetian theory. This categorization has also been widely used by researchers (Henniger, 1985; Rubin, Watson, & Jambor, 1978). Smilansky divides play according to *functional play* (the child makes simple use of movements to provide exercise—characteristic of infants and young toddlers), *constructive play* (wherein the child works toward a goal of some sort, such as completing a puzzle or picture—characteristic of children up to about 3½ years), and *sociodramatic play* (the child assumes roles and uses language for pretending). By age 7 the child reaches the stage of *games with rules*, which is described as the highest form of cognitive play.

Table 2–1 summarizes these two systems of categorizing play activity. Note that Parten's system focuses on social interaction whereas the Smilansky/Piaget model concentrates on intellectual growth.

Smilansky used one of the Piagetian stages, *sociodramatic play*, in the research study described in this chapter. It is included here not only because the results are valuable, but also because her work pioneered an entire new generation of research studies on play.

The value of understanding and identifying these stages is that it allows teachers to plan play

TABLE 2–1
Definitions of play categories

Social play

Solitary play

The child plays alone with toys different from those used by other children; although the child may be within speaking distance, there is no attempt at verbal communication with the peer group. The child is centered on his or her own activity.

Parallel play

The child plays independently but among other children. The child plays with toys that are similar to those the other children are using. In short, the child plays beside rather than with other children.

Group play

Associative play. The child plays with other children. The children are borrowing, following each other with play things. All engage in similar if not identical activity. There is no division of labor and no organization of activity.

Cooperative play. The child plays in a group that is organized for making some material product, striving to attain some competitive goal, dramatizing situations of adult or group life, or playing formal games. There is a division of labor, a sense of belonging, and an organization in which the efforts of one child are supplemented by those of another.

Cognitive play

Functional play

Simple muscular activities and repetitive muscular movement with or without objects are used in functional play. The child repeats actions or initiates actions.

activities that are appropriate for the ages of the children they are teaching. It is as inappropriate to expect a 2-year-old to understand how to play duck-duck-goose as it is to expect a 4-year-old to be satisfied with a rattle and set of nesting blocks. Knowledge of developmental levels prevents boredom or frustration in young children.

PRINCIPLES FOR ENCOURAGING PLAY

Play flourishes best in an atmosphere of acceptance and approval. Children sense when teachers are not fully convinced of the worth of play and just permit it to occur, rather than accepting

Cognitive play

Constructive play

The child learns use of play materials, manipulation of objects to construct something or create something. There is an attempt to create something (e.g., drawing a person, building a playdough house, measuring with water beakers).

Dramatic play

The child takes on a role; he or she pretends to be someone else, initiating another person in actions and speech with the aid of real or imagined objects.

Games with rules

The child accepts prearranged rules and adjusts to them, controlling actions and reactions within given limits.

Miscellaneous categories

Unoccupied behavior

The child is not playing in the usual sense but watches activities of momentary interest, plays with his or her own body, gets on and off chairs, follows the teacher, or merely glances around the room.

Onlooker behavior

The child watches the others play and talks to, questions, and offers suggestions to the children playing but does not enter into the activity.

Reading

The child is being read to by the teacher.

Rough and tumble

Children in a group of two or more run and chase each other or engage in mock fighting.

Note. From "Social and Cognitive Aspects of Play in Young Handicapped Children" by G. Mindes, 1982, *Topics in Early Childhood Special Education*, *2*(3), p. 41. The author wishes to thank Kenneth Rubin of the University of Waterloo, Waterloo, Ontario, for permission to use his working draft of this play observation scale.

it in a wholehearted way. On the other hand, teachers who fully understand that play is a productive avenue for learning and who thus make a commitment to it subtly convey this message to children. In this climate, play and all its attendant goods thrive and children lead rich, engrossed, and happy lives at school.

In addition to commitment, there are some more obvious and generally applicable principles that teachers who wish to encourage play can incorporate into their teaching repertoire. One such principle is that *planning enough time for play to be generated is essential.* It takes time for children to develop their play ideas fully—to

RESEARCH STUDY
Teachers Can Help Children Learn to Play More Effectively

Research Question In a previous study, Smilansky observed significant differences in the play activity of middle-class European Jewish children and lower-class Jewish children who came from Middle Eastern countries. She became interested in what could be done to improve the quality of play for the less-developed second group.

Therefore, she formulated the question, What methods of adult intervention are most effective in developing the ability for sociodramatic play in children from culturally deprived backgrounds? (The term *culturally deprived* is no longer used because everyone comes from a culture. The children Smilansky designates by this term were Jewish children from low-income families who emigrated to Israel from various Middle Eastern countries.)

Research Method Three groups of "disadvantaged orientals" (Groups A, B, and C) totalling 420 children of kindergarten and preschool age, and two control groups were included. Control Group D was composed of children matched to the experimental group (n = 362) and Control Group E was composed of European children (n = 427). Teachers in Group A were trained to enrich the children's informational background by taking them on field trips, talking over experiences, and so forth. Teachers in Group B concentrated on teaching the children how to play by using active intervention and suggestions, and teachers in Group C combined enriching experiences with techniques for improving the quality of the children's play. In the control groups the children played as they usually did. All the teachers used the same themes: visiting the health clinic, going to the grocery store, and a theme based on a storybook.

move all the way in their play from packing their suitcases to trundling them through the school, visiting their friends, pretending to have a snack, and finally returning. Another is that *equipment must be stored in readily accessible areas.* Teachers should feel free to move with the children's play and produce materials on request, rather than saying, "It's in the shed—we'll get it tomorrow."

Plentiful materials also encourage children to play freely because having enough equipment to go around promotes comfortable, harmonious play. This does not mean it is necessary to have 20 little red cars so that everyone can have one, but it does mean it is wise to try to have at least two of whatever items that are very popular.

Equipment should also be age appropriate. Table 2–2 offers many suggestions for the kinds of age-appropriate materials and equipment children love to use in their play.

Wherever play takes place, teachers should be aware of it and seek to continue and extend it. We sometimes think of play as occurring only in the housekeeping area or in the block corner, and it is true that these are highly popular places for such activity to take place. However, play can occur anywhere: in the sandbox as children imagine they are digging to the bottom of the earth, on the climbing gym as it becomes an eagle's nest, at the manipulative table as they play zoo with small models and cubical counting

Each child in the experimental and control groups was classified at the beginning of the experiment according to the level of his sociodramatic play skills based on a series of observations. Following 9 weeks of the experiment, the level of the children's play was observed for a second time.

Results   The sociodramatic play of Group A, who had only experiences and discussions, did not improve significantly. Nor did the play of Control Groups D or E change significantly.

On the other hand, the level of sociodramatic play of Group B (who were exposed to direct instruction in developing play skills) and Group C (who were exposed to direct instruction combined with experiences) improved to a significant extent. Group C improved the most.

Implications   This study is important for two reasons. First, it demonstrates that children from so-called "deprived backgrounds" can learn to enrich their styles of play. It also supports the idea that play combined with experience and teacher interaction is an effective way of changing children's play behavior.

There is a second, even more important result of Smilansky's work, however, and it is the reason why a study done in 1968 is included in this book. It is important because it marks one of the first times a fairly rigorous research study focused on play! Until then many investigators assumed that the activity of play was too difficult to evaluate, so almost no research was conducted on that subject. Inspired by Smilansky's work, however, studies have proliferated, and we now possess a respectable, though sometimes tantalizing, body of research on this vital topic.

Note. From *The Effects of Sociodramatic Play on Disadvantaged Preschool Children* by S. Smilansky, 1968, New York: John Wiley & Sons.

blocks. Play can also be a wagon transformed into an ambulance, a young parent nursing a doll, or two children laughing together as they do stunts on the crawl-through blocks.

Encouraging play is like pulling taffy. Just as the accomplished taffy puller can stretch and bend the candy as far apart as his arms will reach, so the accomplished teacher can do the same thing with play—drawing it forth, stretching it out, extending it, so that children can obtain the maximum benefit from the experience.

To do this successfully, the teacher should anticipate what the children might go on to next in their play. Offering a mild suggestion as the play begins to wane or falter can save and continue it by adding an additional episode. ("Well, here you are, sitting at the cash register! Has anyone phoned in an order? Oh, here comes Ryan. Are you the man picking up the hamburgers?") Teachers can find inspiration for this by assuming the children's perspective and asking themselves what they would enjoy doing next if they were that age.

A note of caution: be prepared to accept rejection of your idea by the children without feeling offended. Remember, it is *their* play and you are the supporter, not the creator, of it. It is all too easy for insensitive teachers to force ideas on children in play, thereby dulling the spontaneity and creativity of the children.

These 3-year-olds are at the stage defined as associative play.

It is also important for teachers to allow some space between themselves and the children so that the youngsters do not feel suffocated by too much close attention. Yet, at the same time, it is necessary to remain alert and willing to set limits when these are needed. Two- and three-year-olds may require intervention for the sake of their own safety. Four-year-olds are more likely to benefit from restraints for the sake of others' safety, as when they are involved in such activities as monster play.

In summary, when children are involved in play, the ideal attitude for teachers to assume is that of attentive approval. Teachers with this attitude remain aware of what is happening, are willing to contribute ideas and materials when this seems desirable, are able to clarify and interpret the children's actions to each other should this be necessary, and are appreciative of the value of this activity as the play unfolds.

ADDITIONAL BENEFITS OF PLAY

If the integrative function of play were its only value to children, this would be reason enough to include it as a basic element in planning curriculum. But, when analyzed, play provides many additional benefits. When children play, they are more completely themselves than at any other time. Play leaves children free to express ideas and to play things out safely with no penalties attached. While playing, they make choices and decisions for themselves, they assume command, they are masterful and in control of what is happening, and they are able to seize endless opportunities to try out, to experiment, and to explore. Moreover, they can subtly regulate their play, so that it offers challenges that are neither too difficult nor too easy. Knowledge of these benefits is important to teachers, since they need to be able to explain to

Still another benefit of play is the opportunity it provides for learning to get along together.

parents and administrators why play is a vital ingredient when planning learning situations for young children.

Encourage the Development of the Physical Self Through Play

The joy, freedom, and vigor that are so characteristic of children as they use their bodies in physical play is certain evidence of how deeply satisfying this is to them. Knowing what one's body can do and feeling physically confident enhances the basic feelings of security and self-esteem in a special way.

What can teachers do to help the physical self develop through play? It is important to maintain a reasonable balance between allowing children to experiment with taking risks and practicing common sense control. A sound rule to follow is to intervene in *any* play that is genuinely dangerous to the child or to others around her while encouraging as much movement and

TABLE 2–2
What are some good toys and play materials for young children?

All ages are approximate. Most suggestions for younger children are also appropriate for older children.

	Sensory materials	Active play equipment	Construction materials
2-year-olds and young 3's	Water and sand toys: cups, shovels Modeling dough Sound-matching games Bells, wood block, triangle, drum Texture matching games, feel box	Low climber Canvas swing Low slide Wagon, cart, or wheelbarrow Large rubber balls Low 3-wheeled, steerable vehicle with pedals	Unit blocks and accessories: animals, people, simple wood cars and trucks Interlocking construction set with large pieces Wood train and track set Hammer (13 oz. steel shanked), soft wood, roofing nails, nailing block
Older 3's and 4-year-olds	Water toys: measuring cups, egg beaters Sand toys: muffin tins, vehicles Xylophone, maracas, tambourine Potter's clay	Large 3-wheeled riding vehicle Roller skates Climbing structure Rope or tire swing Plastic bats and balls Various sized rubber balls Balance board Planks, boxes, old tires Bowling pins, ring toss, bean bags and target	More unit blocks, shapes, and accessories Table blocks Realistic model vehicles Construction set with smaller pieces Woodworking bench, saw, sandpaper, nails
5- and 6-year-olds	Water toys: food coloring, pumps, funnels Sand toys: containers, utensils Harmonica, kazoo, guitar, recorder Tools for working with clay	Bicycle Outdoor games: bocce, tetherball, shuffleboard, jumprope, Frisbee	More unit blocks, shapes, and accessories Props for roads, towns Hollow blocks Brace and bits, screwdrivers, screws, metric measure, accessories

Note. From *Choosing Good Toys for Young Children* by S. Feeney and M. Magarick, 1983, Washington, D.C.: National Association for The Education of Young Children. Copyright 1983 by National Association for the Education of Young Children.

Manipulative toys	Dolls and dramatic play	Books and recordings	Art materials
Wooden puzzles with 4–20 large pieces Pegboards Big beads or spools to string Sewing cards Stacking toys Picture lotto, picture dominoes	Washable dolls with a few clothes Doll bed Child-sized table and chairs Dishes, pots, and pans Dress-up clothes: hats, shoes, shirts Hand puppets Shopping cart	Clear picture books, stories, and poems about things children know Records or tapes of classical music, folk music, or children's songs	Wide-tip watercolor markers Large sheets of paper, easel Finger or tempera paint, ½" brushes Blunt-nose scissors White glue
Puzzles, pegboard, small beads to string Parquetry blocks Small objects to sort Marbles Magnifying glass Simple card or board games Flannel board with pictures, letters Sturdy letters and numbers	Dolls and accessories Doll carriage Child-sized stove or sink More dress-up clothes Play food, cardboard cartons Airport, doll house, or other settings with accessories Finger or stick puppets	Simple science books More detailed picture and story books Sturdy record or tape player Recordings of wider variety of music Book and recording sets	Easel, narrower brushes Thick crayons, chalk Paste, tape with dispenser Collage materials
More complex puzzles Dominoes More difficult board and card games Yarn, big needles, mesh fabric, weaving materials Magnets, balances Attribute blocks	Cash register, play money, accessories, or props for other dramatic play settings: gas station, construction, office Typewriter	Books on cultures Stories with chapters Favorite stories children can read Children's recipe books	Watercolors, smaller paper, stapler, hole puncher Chalkboard Oil crayons, paint crayons, charcoal Simple camera, film

SUREFIRE PRETEND PLAY ACTIVITIES

Here are a few suggestions for settings that will spark dramatic play among the children.

- *Playing house.* A trusty standby that holds endless appeal for children. Try an apartment set up with two houses side by side made from hollow blocks; this often facilitates social interaction between groups of children and quells arguments as well.
- *Marketing.* Offer paper bags, empty cans and boxes, imitation fruits and vegetables, play money, and something to use as shopping carts (for example, doll buggies and wagons). Children enjoy both the buyer and seller roles. Works well as an enrichment to house play.
- *Running a fast food restaurant.* Although some of us may deplore certain aspects of this industry, there is no denying that children are very familiar with placing orders, with take-out features, and with the virtues of "with pickles or without." Ride 'em trucks or possibly trikes, as well as cash registers, trays, sacks, containers, and hats, add joy to the play.
- *Camping.* Bedspread tents hung on **A**-frames and whatever camping equipment is available such as canteens, firewood, or sleeping bags make this play lots of fun. Flashlights also add delight.
- *Hospital play.* Children are deeply interested in participating in this activity. Inclusion of a stethoscope, some kind of shot needle (turkey basters or large eyedroppers can be used to represent these), and masking tape and gauze for bandages add interest. When one of our students assembled a transfusion unit from a plastic bottle and tubing, the children played with it repeatedly.
- *Business office play.* Old typewriters past the possibility of repair, calculators, stamps with stamp pads, used envelopes, paper clips, and surplus paper bring appeal and realism to this play.
- *Baby washing.* Baby washing combines the delights of water play with family life. Because boys often can be enticed into this activity, it is particularly valuable as a way of providing experience in a nurturing role. Towels, bar soap, cornstarch powder, and diaper wipes add reality.
- *Birthday party play.* Boxes (either with or without something inside) and recycled party wrappings, cards, pretend birthday cakes (boxes with candles stuck in them), paper plates and cups, and possibly hats provide a surprising amount of rather ritualized, yet satisfying, play on this theme. Children enjoy wrapping up the "presents" as much as unwrapping them—perhaps because adults often restrict such activity so that gifts will "look nice."
- *Taking a trip play.* Children find great pleasure in packing suitcases and lugging them around. Play may include plane tickets, maps, magazines, peanuts for snack, and special hats for the pilots and flight attendants to wear. Discussions about destinations, possible weather anticipated there, and so forth can encourage children to do a little thinking and planning ahead.

---

freedom as possible. More protection is necessary for 2-year-olds than for 4-year-olds because the former are less experienced and consequently have poorer judgment. Although 4-year-olds are thirsty for risks and infatuated with challenges, they can be asked to evaluate dangers for themselves, rather than being constantly controlled by the teacher.

Adding variety to the possibilities for outdoor play will also support it in a positive way. When the same trikes, swings, and climbers are present day after day, no wonder children succumb to boredom and wild behavior. However, a bedspread tent over the climber or lengths of hose and a ladder combined with the tricycles can suggest new play potential that will sustain their interest and cultivate new ideas, as well as encourage continued physical effort.

Finally, play emphasizing physical activity between children can be influenced by the

It only takes a few props to stimulate camping play.

choice of equipment furnished to them. Large, portable items they can haul together, such as boards and hollow blocks, encourage cooperative, physical play. These "open-ended" materials allow children to work together to construct all kinds of play situations, which constitutes an added bonus for the creative self. (For further discussion of curriculum for the physical self please refer to Chapters 7, 8, and 9.)

Enhance the Emotional Self Through Play

We hear repeatedly that play can be the great reliever of feelings, and there is no denying the truth of this statement. Play *does* permit unacceptable impulses to be expressed in acceptable ways. It can also reduce stress, as Elkind (1983) explains:

> Play is, first and foremost, an individual's way of dealing with the stress of life. By transforming reality play makes unmanageable situations manageable at the same time that it provides socially acceptable outlets for stress. Children, no less than adults, are under stress, particularly today. Accordingly, children need to play for the same reason adults do—to enable them to go on with the difficult task of adapting to an ever more complex and bewildering society. (p. 232)

But play does something else for the feeling aspect of the child. It promotes the positive feeling of healthy delight. What fun it is to become absorbed in building an oven in which to bake the sandbox cookies or to feel satisfied when at last the blocks balance or the car runs through the tunnel all the way. What joy it is to play with another child and feel she has become your friend.

Of course, other feelings also arise in play: anger, when someone else becomes dominant; pain, when one is left out; fear, when an activity becomes too scary. The virtue is that play allows children to experience this wide range of emotion under relatively safe circumstances and to learn to deal with these feelings bit by bit. How valuable it is to learn that sadness and anger can be coped with and that they do not last forever.

How can teachers help? First, teachers can allow the expression of feelings while drawing the line when necessary between feeling like doing something and actually doing it (see Chapter 10). It is just as acceptable to feel angry while playing as it is to feel silly or happy or excited. As a matter of fact, a child most probably will experience all these emotions when playing with other children. It is far better to realize this and to encourage children to express these safely through words than to insist they conceal or suppress such feelings, thus causing children to act them out by hurting someone else.

Second, teachers can help the child's emotional self grow during play by providing play experiences that draw out a problem when a child seems blocked from dealing with it by herself. Perhaps, for unknown reasons, a child has become afraid of the dark. The teacher might provide some large boxes and flashlights in a darkened corner of the playroom so that the youngster can control the situation and play through her fear. Of course, if the fear appears to be increasing or extreme, the teacher would take some additional steps besides providing opportunities for such play. Depending on the severity of the behavior, these steps might include talking with the child, reading some stories during group time about how other

SUPPORTING MULTICULTURAL LEARNING THROUGH PLAY

Play presents delightful possibilities for including multicultural materials and instilling positive attitudes about ethnic and cultural differences into the lives of children. For instance, the multicultural addition one week might be Hawaiian clothes in the dress up area. These should be introduced casually to the children: "Aren't these pretty? You're welcome to put them on. Leilani's family is sharing these for the fun of it this week. Did you know that she was born in Hawaii?" or a hammock from Guatemala could be hung outside, and as the children enjoy swinging in it, the teacher could explain that it comes from another country, Guatemala, where it is so hot that people sleep this way to stay cool. He might say, "See, the air comes right through when you swing. Isn't that a practical idea? And it's fun, too."

Another aspect of multicultural play is the occasional problem encountered by teachers who have groups of children from different cultures in the same room. Of course, it is understandable that children who speak the same language find it convenient to play together. (I'm thinking here of some Head Start situations in which I have worked, where the Spanish-speaking boys played together, apart from their English-speaking companions.) Sometimes teachers appear to make no effort to encourage the children to intermingle as they play. In fact, they sometimes seem completely unaware of the split in the group. However, children can and *should* be encouraged to overcome language barriers while playing, as well as while participating in more structured situations. A child does not have to speak fluent English to enjoy building a block tower with another youngster, and the noises little boys make while pushing toy cars around the sandbox appear to stem from some universal reservoir of language.

Teachers should search for multicultural learning possibilities and encourage play among all the children whenever possible. Children are basically friendly, and teachers who provide tactful encouragement add one more building block to the bridge of interracial friendliness among people. (For a more detailed discussion please refer to Chapter 12.)

children coped with similar concerns, or having a parent conference.

Usually, however, providing appropriate play opportunities will clarify feelings and provide relief—particularly when teachers realize how helpful such experiences can be. Teachers should also remain aware of their limitations in such circumstances. They are not professional psychologists. When a child's play appears to be anxiety ridden or highly ritualized and repetitious, they should recognize these signals as calls for help that go beyond their training. At this point, referring the family for psychological consultation is usually the wisest step.

Help the Social Self Develop Through Play

Although children gain many benefits from playing by themselves (solitary play) or side by side (parallel play), it is when they play together in associative or cooperative play that the social self benefits most because these kinds of play provide the richest opportunities for social learning. Preschool teachers typically spend a large part of each day helping children develop this aspect of themselves. During such play, children learn about getting along together, entering a group, handling exclusion and dominance, sharing power, space, and ideas with other people, making compromises, driving bargains, and cooperating to gain satisfaction.

Children also learn about the social world that lies beyond childhood as they assume the role of a mother or a teacher or Godzilla (!) during play. Moreover, some researchers (Rubin & Howe, 1986) maintain that such role taking has the additional benefit of allowing children to put themselves in another's place, which probably encourages children to understand other people's feelings and to develop their ability to feel empathy for them. Social play therefore presents an unsurpassable means by which the social self can develop.

What can teachers do to help? The most important contribution teachers can make to social play is to pay attention to what is happening so they can facilitate this in a beneficial way. Perhaps one child is hovering on the edge of the play and needs a suggestion on how to enter the group; perhaps an argument is brewing over who will drive the truck and who will ride; perhaps someone is crying angrily because she thinks her friend tripped her on purpose. To deal with these situations, the teacher must act as arbitrator, negotiator, and clarifier. At the same time, he models strategies that the children will eventually learn to use for themselves as the teacher gradually encourages them to take over the roles he has demonstrated.

When seeking to facilitate social play, teachers have to walk a fine line between being at the center of attention and withdrawing too far from what is going on. The teachers' behavior must vary with the needs of the group. Some children, as Smilansky (1968) and Butler, Gotts, and Quisenberry (1978) point out, are so inexperienced that they need help even to begin play. For such youngsters it may be necessary for the teacher to participate very directly by suggesting possibilities for play ("My goodness! It looks like there are some babies here that need to be fed. What shall we make them for dinner? Shredded Wheat? Oh, that would be delicious. What can you use for bowls?") For other inexperienced children, supplying equipment as the need arises is the answer. For older 4-year-olds it may be sufficient to extend their play by asking questions, such as "Now you've got the carriages loaded up, are you fellows going on a trip, or what?" Through it all, the teacher should remember the goal of promoting play *among* the children, rather than between the children and himself. He should also be ready to intervene quickly when it is necessary, but to remain an attentive observer when it is not.

Some kinds of activities and equipment appear to promote social interaction among children, whereas others do not. For example, K. H. Rubin (1977a,b) reports that children usually engage in solitary or parallel play while using play dough, clay, and sand and water. This finding is supported by a current study at my institute.[1] On the other hand, some equipment invites or even requires participation by more than one child to be maximally satisfying. Parachutes, rocking boats, balls, long jump ropes (for slightly older children), wagon and trike combinations, and horizontally hung tire swings are all examples of equipment that encourage play by more than one child at a time. Teachers who wish to foster cooperative social interaction among children and who wish to help them develop their social selves as fully as possible should search for and acquire such equipment.

Foster the Creative and Cognitive Selves Through Play

Recent reviews of research concerned with finding a possible link between divergent thinking (the ability to produce more than one answer to a problem) and play report that children who have been involved in free play before being asked to participate in situations requiring divergent thinking produce more various and creative answers to those problems than do children who were exposed to structured experiences before the problem was posed to them (Görlitz & Wohlwill, 1988; Saltz & Brodie, 1982). For example, Pepler (1982) set up an experiment using 3- and 4-year-olds in which the children either played with pieces that could fit into formboards (a convergent, only-one-correct-way activity) or played with these pieces without the board (a more-than-one-correct-way activity). The control groups just watched the experimenter engage in convergent or divergent activ-

---

[1] The institute refers to the Institute of Child Development at the University of Oklahoma, Norman, Oklahoma.

Some equipment invites socialization.

ities. The results indicated that the children who had played freely with the block pieces gave more unique responses when presented afterward with a divergent thinking task than did the children in the other three groups who had not been involved in free play.

What can teachers do to help? The most important thing to do is to remain open-minded about possibilities and recognize the value of creative ideas as they appear in such free play. Such positive support by teachers reinforces and encourages this kind of behavior in children.

Welcome the unconventional use of equipment whenever possible. Just the other day, as I waited in line at the bank, I watched a number of youngsters playing with one of those velvet-covered ropes, which banks use to designate where people should stand. Although adults saw only this function to the rope, the children saw a number of other possibilities. These included brushing their hands back and forth along it (a blissful sensory experience judging from one little girl's face), playing follow-the-leader and winding back and forth between its poles, hitting it with a little stick and making it swing, and running under it in a game of tag. The children's behavior clearly illustrated the playful, creative powers children bring to almost any situation.

Teachers should generally accept unconventional uses of equipment by young children, since this is of great value to the children's creative selves. Thus children should be permitted to ride tricycles backward, balance along the handle of a broom left on the sidewalk, or go down the slide toboggan-style on a bit of carpet.

Unfortunately, the same inexperience that enables children to perceive unusual possibilities in the equipment may also make it difficult for them to assess potential dangers, so teachers must remain alert to such potentially dangerous situations if they arise. The child who attempts to convert a tier of dresser drawers into a set of stairs may be in for a painful surprise.

Encourage imaginative substitutions. Although there are times when children's activity can genuinely cause harm or destroy property and teachers must intervene, there are many more times when the unconventional, original use of equipment would not be damaging or dangerous, and teachers need not discourage the children's idea. For example, there is really no reason why unit blocks cannot be used on a table instead of the floor or a hat cannot double as a shopping bag.

Sometimes this original, unconventional approach is expressed by the imaginative substitution of something for something else. Piaget (1983) terms this activity *symbolic play* and maintains that this representation of reality on a symbolic level is an important step in mental development. Pretend play almost always makes use of this kind of creative imagination at some point. For instance, the guinea pig may represent a lion, the doll carriage may become a hospital

Here Zac has transformed our sawhorses into horses of quite another kind!

cart, or an oatmeal carton can suggest a toadstool. By age 4, children often do not need the object at all, and we see pretend coffee being poured into a nonexistent cup or an imaginary rocket taking off with all the appropriate sound effects.

Such creative, symbolic play can be particularly encouraged if the children's center makes a point of offering unstructured equipment, since the less structured (less reality bound) the equipment is, the more imagination the children are free to put into it (Pepler & Ross, 1981). This is because whenever something looks like something in particular, it generally will be used as the thing it resembles, thus restricting the children's imaginations. If a series of boxes in the play yard is painted to look like a series of quaint houses, the children are likely to play house in them, but not as likely to think of turning them over and converting them into a boat or train, as they would if the boxes were plain and accompanied by some boards, blocks, and old tires.

One February, for example, our staff decided that the housekeeping corner was not really attracting children anymore despite its enchanting array of beds, artificial fruit, lifelike replicas of stoves and iceboxes, and charming little dishes. So we took it all away. In its place we set out boards and large, hollow blocks and sawhorses and then neatly laid out a few dolls, blankets, and dishes on one of the boards. We said nothing and just waited. It was really interesting to see the children expand on the possibilities. The creative play began at a very primitive level, with the "furniture" consisting of a bed of blankets arranged on a couple of blocks and a kind of picnic set up on the floor. Over the weeks the children played more and more intensely and for longer periods of time as they developed and extended their ideas and perceived additional possibilities. Their play varied on different days and included the construction of an elaborate, two-room house, a two-deck camper, and an operating room. As their enthusiasm mounted, they added unit blocks, cubical counting blocks, pictures from our file, and rug scraps. This became one of the most satisfying experiences for the children at our school.

Rasmussen (1979) sums it up well by saying:

Perhaps the most incalculable error that adults make in respect to children's play is assuming that expensive, fixed structures are somehow better than inexpensive or discarded raw materials. Such notions could be dispelled if adults would open their eyes to children at play and see for themselves the genius of imaginative creative minds at work, transforming the simplest material into the stuff of excitement and joy. (p. 39)

Ask questions that encourage children to think for themselves. Free play time is the time par excellence to foster the development of thinking by asking children questions. The right question at the right time can stimulate creative solutions by children and also allows them to realize that the teacher values their ideas. Some examples of questions that can encourage young children to think creatively include "We don't have a truck. What could you use instead?" or "Is there some way I could help you? Something I could get for you?" or "I've been wondering, how will you figure that out?"

SUMMARY

As Lawrence Frank (1968) remarks, "Play is how children learn what no one can teach them." To this I would add that the activity of play is what children use to integrate their experiences and themselves into a meaningful whole.

There are many definitions of and purposes ascribed to play, and all reflect some degree of truth. One definition is especially useful for preschool teachers to use: "Play may be defined as behavior that is intrinsically motivated, freely chosen, process-oriented, and pleasurable" (Johnson & Ershler, 1982, p. 137). Teachers can profit by using the elements of this definition as standards against which to measure the freedom and richness of play in their schools.

Investigators agree that play develops through a series of stages as children mature. Two examples of these stage theories are presented in the text because an understanding of them helps teachers plan age-appropriate play experiences for the children.

Some general ways teachers can encourage rich, full play include creating an atmosphere of acceptance and approval, providing enough time for play to develop fully, storing equipment in accessible places, providing enough of it, and extending and prolonging play.

Teachers can foster the development of the physical self through play by helping children keep a reasonable balance between taking risks and being safe, by adding variety to outdoor activities, and by providing equipment that encourages them to use their bodies in different ways. Play that promotes the development of the emotional self can be encouraged by providing ample opportunities for play and by permitting the expression and ownership of the full range of feelings by children. Teachers can enhance the social self by paying close attention to play and by teaching social skills to children as the need

arises. While doing this, teachers must avoid becoming the center of attention yet they must be ready to stimulate and extend play if it begins to falter.

Play offers excellent opportunities for children to develop their creative and intellectual faculties. This is particularly true when teachers remain open-minded about unusual, but harmless, uses of equipment, establish a climate of acceptance and admiration for the children's ideas, provide plenty of unstructured equipment, ask helpful questions, and avoid distracting the children by interrupting too often.

SELF-CHECK QUESTIONS FOR REVIEW

Content-Related Questions

1. Name three ways play acts as an integrative force for children's personalities.
2. List the four standards recommended by the author that should be applied when evaluating whether a teacher's idea about a play activity is truly play from the child's point of view.
3. One of the principles for encouraging play is that the teacher needs to accept its value in a whole-hearted way. Name four or five additional principles listed in the text.
4. Pretend you are giving a talk to a group of parents and that you wish to explain to them why play is important in the lives of young children. (You'll probably give this particular talk many times during your teaching career!) Give some reasons why play benefits the physical, emotional, social, creative, and cognitive selves of the child.
5. What are some practical things teachers can do to foster play for each of the child's five selves? (These are the physical, social, emotional, creative, and cognitive selves.)

Integrative Questions

1. It is Easter time and the children have been to visit a family that raises rabbits. Upon return, the teacher passes out rabbit-ear hats and encourages the children to hop around like rabbits. What do you think Sutton-Smith would say about that activity?
2. If you agree with the definition of play provided in this book, then how would you define work?

3. Take a closer look at the picture that shows some 4-year-olds playing camping. Now suppose they have been playing this for quite some time, and that the play is beginning to falter. What might you do to continue and extend it?
4. Compare the suggestions about what teachers can do to help foster emotional growth in play with suggestions for fostering physical growth through play. How do the suggestions differ?

QUESTIONS AND ACTIVITIES

1. You are planning your first parent meeting of the year, and you want to base it on play and its value as a mode of learning. Think of two or three different ways you might present this topic so that it would be genuinely interesting to the parents.
2. *Problem:* You have a group of young Mexican-American boys in your room who spend most of their time playing "Bullee, Bullee" (a game where one boy acts the part of the bull by holding finger horns at the side of his head, and the other boys play matador). What would you do about this kind of play? Does it encourage cruelty to animals? Is it too aggressive? What about the other children who do not join in?
3. *Problem:* There always seem to be some pieces of play equipment that are rarely used by the children because they are stored in inaccessible places. Think about the storage where you are teaching. How could some of the less used, but potentially play-full, materials be stored so that they would be more readily available to teachers and children?
4. Take time to observe some children playing at the water table. Record what they do, and then identify what they are learning from the activity while enjoying themselves. Compare your notes with others who have also observed the activity.

REFERENCES FOR FURTHER READING

Overviews

Bergen, D. (Ed.). (1988). *Play as a medium for learning and development: A handbook of theory and practice.* Portsmouth, N.H.: Heinemann. For a good overview of the values of play written in readable form by well-known specialists in the field, this book is hard to beat. Highly recommended.

Johnson, J. E., Christie, J. B., & Yawkey, T. D. (1987). *Play and early childhood development.* Glenview, Ill.: Scott, Foresman and Co. The authors present a comprehensive analysis of factors affecting play. The material is well grounded in research yet remains readable. Highly recommended.

McKee, J. S. (Ed.). (1986). *Play: Working partner of growth.* Wheaton, Md.: Association for Childhood Education International. McKee presents a collection of short articles intended mainly for the practicing teacher. Particularly noteworthy is a list of play materials for various ages and an extensive bibliography.

Rogers, C. S., & Sawyers, J. K. (1986). *Play in the lives of children.* Washington, D.C.: National Association for the Education of Young Children. The authors provide a good introduction to the topic of play, including explanations of why it is so valuable, stages of its development, and practical suggestions about ways to encourage it. Highly recommended.

Westland, C., & Knight, J. (1982). *Playing, living, learning: A worldwide perspective on children's opportunities to play.* State College, Pa.: Venture Publishing. This unusual book with a strong international approach reviews the many ways in which people make play available to children. These range from adventure playgrounds and mobile play units to "new games" and suggestions for family play.

Practical Advice on Generating Play

Adcock, D., & Segal, M. (1983). *Making friends: Ways of encouraging social development in young children.* Englewood Cliffs, N.J.: Prentice-Hall. Adcock and Segal offer many practical suggestions for promoting social play between children.

Cherry, C. (1976). *Creative play for the developing child: Early lifehood education through play.* Belmont, Calif.: Fearon Publishers. This book deals with play in the broadest sense of the word and includes discussions of such topics as gross and fine motor activities, science experiences, and dramatic play.

Frost, J. L., & Sunderlin, S. (Eds.). (1985). *When children play: Proceedings of the International Conference on Play and Play Environments.* Wheaton, Md.: Association for Childhood Education International. This wide-ranging collection of articles is crammed with useful information that is research-based but practically oriented.

Hendrick, J. B. (1988). *The whole child: Developmental education for the early years* (4th ed.). Columbus, Ohio: Merrill Publishing Co. The chapter entitled "Fostering Creativity in Play" presents many practical suggestions on how to encourage play and how to emphasize its creative aspects.

For the Advanced Student

Bretherton, I. (Ed.). (1984). *Symbolic play: The development of social understanding.* New York: Academic Press.

Various chapters recount advanced research studies concerned with the effect of play on children as they interact with other people.

Fein, G., & Rivkin, M. (Eds.). (1986). *The young child at play: Reviews of research* (Vol. 4). Washington, D.C.: National Association for the Education of Young Children. This review offers study after study documenting the value and impact of play on children's development.

Görlitz, D., & Wohlwill, J. F. (Eds). (1987). *Curiosity, imagination, and play.* Hillsdale, N.J.: Lawrence Erlbaum Associates, Publishers. The editors present a mix of European and American authors who are interested in carrying out research about play and its relationship to developing curiosity and imagination. A difficult but valuable reference.

Gottfried, A. W., & Brown, C. C. (Eds.). (1986). *Play interactions: The contribution of play materials and parental involvement to children's development.* Lexington, Mass.: D. C. Heath and Co. This book provides a good example of how research on play has proliferated in the past decade. Title is self-explanatory.

Guerney, L. F. (1984). Play therapy in counseling settings. In T. D. Yawkey and A. D. Pellegrini (Eds.), *Child's play: Developmental and applied.* Hillsdale, N.J.: Lawrence Erlbaum Associates, Publishers. Guerney presents a concise overview of the way play is used by varying schools of psychotherapy.

Hartley, R. E., Frank, L. K., & Goldenson, R. M. (1952). *Understanding children's play.* New York: Columbia University Press. This old but invaluable book discusses the virtues of specific play materials and what each contributes to the healthy development of young children.

Monighan-Nourot, P., Scales, B., Van Hoorn, J. V., & Almy, M. (1987). *Looking at children's play: A bridge between theory and practice.* New York: Teachers College Press. This book is written for experienced, thoughtful teachers as it discusses the concept of play and issues related to that subject. It demonstrates how three teachers moved from developing questions related to play to carrying out research to answer those questions.

Opie, I., & Opie, P. (1969). *Children's games in street and playgrounds.* Oxford, England: Clarendon Press. The Opies, who are famous for their studies of children's games, nursery rhymes, and fairy tales, have produced a classic and fascinating reference that deals chiefly with the play of somewhat older youngsters.

Rubin, K. H., Fein, G. G., & Vandenberg, B. (1983). Play. In P. H. Mussen (Ed.), *Handbook of child psychology.* E. M. Hetherington (Ed.), *Volume IV: Socialization, personality, and social development.* New York: John Wiley & Sons. This is an invaluable, comprehensive starting point for serious students of play.

Schaefer, C. E., & O'Conner, K. J. (1983). *Handbook of play therapy.* New York: John Wiley & Sons. A treasury of information on play therapy is contained here. It presents a number of differing approaches to therapy and also devotes special chapters to the use of therapy in specific situations.

Yawkey, T. C., & Pellegrini, A. D. (1984). *Child's play: Developmental and applied.* Hillsdale, N.J.: Lawrence Erlbaum Associates. This book covers many different aspects of play ranging from play while hospitalized to the self-building potential of pretend play.

3 Planning for Total Learning

Creating Supportive Curriculum Plans and Schedules

Have you ever

- Been puzzled about how to begin making a curriculum plan?
- Needed an example of a basic schedule for a full- or half-day program?
- Wondered how to manage a rainy day successfully?

If you have, the material in this chapter will help you.

At no other level of education does a teacher have so much free-dom and so few constraints concerning content, method and ex-pected outcomes. Inherent in this freedom is both challenge and responsibility for careful, imaginative, resourceful planning for the education of young children.

ORALIE McAFEE (1981)

Discussing how to plan a curriculum for total learning before discussing the basic elements that compose it is somewhat like explaining how to plan a nourishing meal before teaching anything about good nutrition, cooking, or even shopping for food. I believe, though, that it is helpful to see the intended whole before going on to discuss the individual elements. For this reason, this chapter concentrates on planning curriculum (*what* will happen) and developing schedules (*when* it will happen). Chapter 4 discusses constructing environments for children (*where* it will happen).

THE BASIC INGREDIENTS OF PLANNING: WHAT SHOULD BE INCLUDED IN THE CURRICULUM

Know What You Want the Children to Learn

Chapter 1 stated that the basic purpose of education is to enhance children's feelings of being competent and cared for. Since future chapters will describe in detail how to achieve such feelings of security and self-worth for each of the five selves, we will content ourselves here with reviewing a basic list that is intended only as a summary of the most valuable skills children should begin to acquire as they move through a well-planned day at preschool. Teachers need to be aware of these skills in order to include them when planning curriculum.

In addition to those activities that provide for the health and safety of the children and help them understand and value life, there are those activities specifically for the *physical self* that should be included in the preschool curriculum. These include activities that provide practice in the following:

- Participating in movement and locomotion activities
- Practicing static and dynamic balance
- Developing body and space awareness
- Practicing rebound and airborne activities
- Fostering rhythm and temporal awareness
- Engaging in throwing and catching activities
- Using daily motor skills
- Participating in relaxation and tension-releasing activities

A curriculum that favors the development of *emotional health* in children should include opportunities for learning to do the following:

- Separating comfortably from their families
- Achieving the basic attitudes of trust, autonomy, and initiative
- Remaining in contact with their feelings while maintaining emotional control
- Using dramatic play and other self-expressive materials to come to terms with emotional problems
- Facing reality
- Beginning to understand other people and feel empathy for them

Learnings for children's *social selves* should encompass the following:

- Learning to control unsocial impulses
- Acquiring socially acceptable strategies for getting what they want
- Learning to function successfully as a member of a group
- Finding satisfaction in helping each other
- Finding pleasure in accomplishing meaningful work
- Understanding their place in the world, and feeling good about their gender roles and ethnic heritages.

Opportunities for children to develop their *creative selves* should include the following:

- Using a wide range of self-expressive activities
- Participating in imaginative dramatic play
- Engaging in creative thinking and problem solving

Finally, the children's *cognitive selves* should be enhanced by the following:

- Fostering *verbal ability* through:
- Putting their ideas into words throughout the day and enjoying communicating with other people
- Participating in carefully planned group times

- Developing *cognitive* skills by:
- Analyzing choices and making decisions
- Discovering answers for themselves

- Using the specific mental abilities of:
- Matching
- Perceiving common relations
- Grouping
- Temporal ordering
- Graduated ordering (seriation)
- Determining simple cause-and-effect relationships

Know How to Teach These Skills

There are two questions teachers should ask themselves when thinking about how to teach any particular skill to a young child: (1) What activity can I include that provides the best opportunities for learning this skill? and (2) How can I help the child experience success in that activity?

I recall a teacher who had a 4-year-old in his group named Angie who went out of her way to tease Jeanne, a Down syndrome child. So he asked himself, "How can I stop the teasing and turn Angie's attitude into a more positive one?" and, even more important, "How can I help her understand a little about Jeanne's difficulties?" Although he was puzzled at first about how to accomplish these goals, he finally decided to encourage Angie to hold Jeanne's coat every day. He explained to Angie privately that although Jeanne looked as big as the other children, she was actually younger *inside* and so needed help just as Angie's little sister did. She did learn to help Jeanne with some quiet coaching from him

(and some louder coaching back to him from Angie. "Not that way, dummy," she once said to him in exasperation. "It works best if you hold it this way for her. Here, you'd better let me do it."). Eventually this led to Jeanne putting her coat on by herself, much to Angie's satisfaction. Thus, the activity resulted in a growth in competence for both children. Although these were different kinds of competence, each was well suited to the different ages and abilities of the children.

DRAW UP THE PLAN: DECIDE HOW TO INCORPORATE THE *WHAT* AND *HOW* INTO AN OVERALL PLAN

Developing a curriculum plan is accomplished most easily by dividing the process into a series of steps.

The First Step: Choose a Topic Drawn From the Children's Interests

From my observations, it appears that the most frequent way inexperienced teachers begin planning a day or week is to choose a topic or theme first and then list a large number of possible activities related to that topic. This is a sensible way to begin *as long as the topic is drawn from some concern already expressed by the children or from something that happened the previous week.* This helps ensure that the children will be interested in the subject. Perhaps a house is being torn down nearby, so construction equipment would be of interest, or a mother rat is due to have babies, or one of the children wants to bring her garter snake to school.

Any of these would make a good topic, but for the sake of discussion, let us suppose the teacher chooses the mother rat. Knowing that the rat is about to produce a litter and that children are always intrigued by baby animals, the teacher could begin listing many ideas related to pregnancy and baby animals. At this stage it is best for the teacher not to criticize ideas or eliminate possibilities because this tends to inhibit the flow of other ideas that might be developed into good activities. Some of these possibilities might include the following:

- Observing how the mother rat cares for her babies, then comparing this with the way other mothers care for their babies
- Having kittens or puppies visit
- Visiting a farm to see baby animals such as chicks and calves
- Hatching eggs in an incubator
- Using various books about baby animals and their mothers at group time
- Showing pictures of elephant mothers and their babies, then using stuffed toy elephants in the dramatic play area
- Having a mother bring her baby to school and nurse him
- Talking about how animals give birth
- Measuring the mother rat to see how her abdomen is expanding
- Providing special nesting materials and discussing what she and other animals do to prepare for their babies
- Using the series of pictures of baby animals and their mothers from the picture file
- Keeping track of how quickly the baby rats grow by measuring them and taking pictures to turn their progress into a temporal ordering activity at the flannel board
- Asking if anyone has a baby goat or lamb they can bring to school
- Going to the zoo to see the recently born lion cubs
- Getting out the relationship cards that link mother animals with their babies
- Showing pictures at group time of different ways animals carry their young after they are born
- Spotlighting baby play in the dramatic play area

Beginning with an idea like this invariably produces a feeling of enthusiasm in teachers, and when teachers feel interested and enthusiastic, they convey this to the children.

The Second Step: Face the Reality of What Is Possible and What Is Not

In the second step of curriculum design, teachers must consider various realities as they evaluate each of the possibilities they have brainstormed.

Reality One. How appropriate is the idea for the children in the group? Older 4-year-olds would greatly enjoy a trip to the children's zoo (providing it is kept simple and no attempt is made to visit the entire zoo in one afternoon). The 2-year-olds might benefit more from a simpler experience, such as having some baby ducks

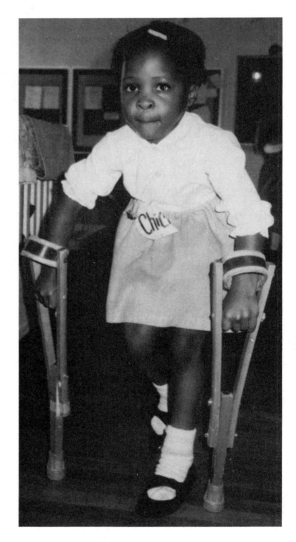

Opportunities to try out experiences help children gain social understandings.

visit, watching them eat, comparing them with an adult duck, and watching them paddle about in the wading pool.

Reality Two. How feasible is the idea? For example, does the teacher know where to locate some fertile eggs? If the topic right now is baby animals, will the children still be interested after 3 weeks when the eggs are ready to hatch? Will someone be available on weekends to turn the eggs so that the chick embryos develop properly?

Reality Three. Are activities reasonably consistent with each other? Is the topic focused enough, or do activities cover too wide an area? Are there some wonderful but extraneous ideas that could best be used another week? For example, perhaps the ideas about human babies would relate better as a follow-up, rather than in combination with the topic of animal babies this week.

Reality Four. Can this topic be used to provide curriculum that develops all five of the children's selves? This is unlikely, since topics usually meet some of the needs for the selves, but additional activities must be added so that the curriculum becomes sufficiently comprehensive. For example, the topic of baby animals offers many possibilities for the development of the cognitive self, such as practicing common relations by linking pictures of mother animals with their babies and discussing whether the visiting kittens are all the same or not (a matching activity) and how they are similar to, and different from, puppies (grouping). The children could be encouraged to develop their creative problem-solving ideas by thinking of ways to protect the baby rats while their cage is cleaned or ways to corral the little goat when she visits. They could also learn some facts about procreation and develop wholesome attitudes about that, thereby adding to their understanding of the cycle of life.

On the other hand, self-expressive activities related to baby animals are difficult to find. Occasionally teachers will have children glue cotton balls on pictures to make baby rabbits, but this is more an exercise in following directions and conformity than in being truly self-expressive. However, it might be fun to offer "baby" colors at the easel, such as pink, gray, and white (the colors of the baby rats) or to encourage older children to make up stories about the adventures or feelings of the baby animals that are visiting.

Reality Five. Can the topic be presented so that it is not too stimulating or overwhelming for the children? Student teachers in particular are sometimes so excited (and worried) about their curriculum that they plan too much in one day or even in one week. The result of too much variety can be cranky, fatigued, confused children who are in no condition to learn well. Therefore, it is necessary to caution beginning teachers to practice moderation in their planning, while at the same time hoping that, as they become more experienced, they will retain their sense of enthusiasm every time they plan a week's curriculum.

Reality Six. Does the curriculum take the needs of individual children into consideration? For example, the teacher could ask the shy child to bring the puppies to school. Or the unpopular youngster who tends to bully the weaker children can contribute positively to the group by inviting them to visit his family's dove cage to see the newly hatched chicks. Is there some way a particularly intelligent little girl can pursue an interest related to the topic in more depth? Perhaps the teacher could suggest a family trip to see the dinosaur egg at a nearby museum.

Reality Seven. Does the list include anything that can be used to promote a multiethnic or nonsexist approach? Teaching about the role of both parents in conception, for example, would answer the nonsexist aspect (see Chapter 9 for more detail). Discussing pictures during group time of African children playing with their baby goat, for instance, would satisfy the multiethnic requirement.

RESEARCH STUDY
Pinpointing Areas of Weakness in Curriculum Planning

Research Question   Can the Early Childhood Environment Rating Scale (Harms & Clifford, 1980) be used to identify strong and weak areas of quality for a child-care center or group of centers, and, hence, identify areas where the staff of the centers would benefit from training to remedy the weaknesses?

Research Method   The investigators observed 21 child-care centers from rural and urban settings, profit and nonprofit programs. They used the Early Childhood Environment Rating Scale to rate areas of the center environments, including personal care routines, furnishings and display, language-reasoning experiences, gross-motor activities, creative activities, social development, and adult needs. Then they analyzed the data to look for patterns of strength and weakness in the centers that were observed.

Research Results   Two of the areas that received the lowest ratings in the study were social development and adult needs. The items most frequently lacking under social development were soft, cozy places, opportunities for the children to have privacy or work alone, and free play time where teachers paid attention to the potential educational value of that activity. Multicultural materials, another facet of social learnings, were also in short supply.

In the adult needs category the investigators reported that "provisions for separate adult meeting areas and facilities for adults' personal needs were frequently lacking. . . . In addition, professional libraries and staff development opportunities were typically less than ideal in size and accessibility" (p. 12).

They also found that the two subscales that differentiated most clearly between the centers rated highest and lowest were the scales having to do with furnishings and display, and creative activities. Furnishings in the higher-quality centers included sand/water tables, woodworking benches, easels and art, cozy areas, interest centers, and displays of children's art at their eye level. Poorer-quality centers lacked these amenities.

After Analysis, Relist the Remaining Topics. As the realities of planning are considered, some ideas are removed from the list, some are simply deferred, and some are added as inspirations strike the teacher. At this point the process moves to Step Three.

The Third Step: Block in Activities Throughout the Week

In this step of curriculum design, teachers must block in the thematic activities over a week's time. The simplest way to do this is to prepare a chart, such as the Quick Check one shown in Table 3–1 to ensure that something particular has been planned for each of the children's selves each day. Such a chart does not need to be elaborate. It is merely a shorthand way of making certain that the program is comprehensive and balanced.

Although experienced teachers clearly see the purposes for each activity they plan, beginning teachers often do not have this clear perception

On the creative scale, higher-quality centers offered sand/water play, dramatic play that went beyond housekeeping equipment, and teacher behavior that enhanced and extended the children's play. "Supervision in lower-quality centers focused only on safety, neatness, or proper use of materials and was frequently minimal in quantity" (p. 13).

The authors concluded that it is possible to use rating scales to measure the quality of environments. The study highlighted those areas where teachers appeared to either need more training or be reminded of what they once knew and had ceased to put into practice.

Implications for Teaching These findings single out potential soft spots in planning and curriculum that apparently creep up on centers unless steps are taken to guard against them. Teachers should heed these warnings and prevent these soft spots from appearing in their own programs and spoiling their quality. They should ask themselves as they plan, "Are we being careful to include quiet places where children can do individual work? Are we paying attention to what the children are doing and facilitating play as well as we can? Are we consistently including multicultural materials and activities?"

"Are we paying attention to our own needs as teachers? Is there a place, or can a place be developed, where we can talk and use resources to stimulate our teaching?

"Are we making certain we include a wide range of creative activities, and are these presented in a way that extends and supports the children's use of them? Have we included sand and water play, carpentry, and an art area on a consistent basis? Are our rooms arranged in a number of interest areas? Are we sharing the results of the children's creativity where they can also see and enjoy them?"

Being able to answer "yes" to these as well as other questions will help assure that we are maintaining quality environments for young children.

Note. From "Pinpointing Staff Training Needs in Child Care Centers" by N. Benham, T. Miller, and S. Kontos, 1988, *Young Children, 43*(4), pp. 9–16.

---

and so it is essential that they use a second chart, such as the one shown in Table 3–2, as well as the Quick Check Chart. This second chart should pinpoint the purpose for offering the activity to the children by providing an explanation or reason for its inclusion in the curriculum. If the teacher cannot supply a worthwhile reason for including an activity, she should consider selecting another activity for the children that will be more beneficial.

A chart combining weekly planned activities and their respective purposes is shown in Table 3–3. I strongly recommend that beginning teachers write out the purpose for each activity as is done in this chart for at least a number of weeks. This is valuable to do for two reasons. First, pinpointing the major reason for including the activity clarifies the teacher's purpose and helps her emphasize that aspect when presenting it. Second, doing this makes it easier to explain to parents why various activities that look like "just fun" are included in the curriculum.

TABLE 3–1
Quick check curriculum chart

Part of self being developed	Monday	Tuesday	Wednesday	Thursday	Friday	
Physical self						Planned activity
Emotional self—understanding feelings						Planned activity
Social self Social skill						Planned activity
Multicultural and non-sexist emphasis						Planned activity
Creative self						Planned activity
Cognitive self Cognitive skill						Planned activity
Language development						Planned activity
Special activities for children with special needs						Planned activity

Theme: Date:

Age of children:

The Fourth Step: Fit Activities into the Daily Schedule

In the fourth step of curriculum design, teachers must fit the activities into the daily schedule. Such schedules can be a blessing if they are used to help children and teachers know what comes next and to contribute to the feeling of security such knowledge produces. Or they can be a burden if they are allowed to dominate the day in a rigid, minute-by-minute fashion that ignores children's needs and prevents teachers from exercising good judgment. A well-designed schedule not only provides for orderly planning, but it also allows for flexibility so that time periods can be extended or contracted depending on whether the children are deeply occupied or particularly restless.

The Fifth Step: Evaluate What Happened and Decide How to Improve the Activity Next Time

There is nothing more satisfying than finishing a day with children and knowing that it was a good one—that the children learned what was intended and that everyone has grown a little toward decency and happiness. When that happens, it can be a temptation to leave well enough alone and simply bask in the pleasure of work well done.

TABLE 3-2
Examples of possible activities and purposes or reasons for including them

Name of self	Activity	Purpose or reason for inclusion
Physical self	Dropping beans in bottles with tweezers	Fine muscle—eye-hand coordination
	Introduce Irish mail (an arm-pumped, foot-steered, wheeled vehicle)	Large muscle—develops arm movements in opposition to each other
Emotional self	Playing hospital	Express feelings (fears) and bring them under control
	Kicking slide with heels	Sublimate angry feelings—express them indirectly
	Play in housekeeping corner	Play being the baby—regress to younger age
	Learn to use brace and bit	Develop new skill—enhance self-esteem by gaining competence
Social self	A group of children will pump up large inner tube together	Generate cooperative endeavor to reach mutually desired goal—both sexes
	Push younger child on swing	Experience satisfaction in helping another person
	Sponge off lunch table	Experience pleasure in work and in benefitting the group
Multicultural and nonsexist emphasis	Learn La Raspa (a Mexican dance)	Enjoy and respect another's culture
	Group time: talk over pictures of children from different cultures bathing in different ways	Teach children that people may do things differently but they have needs in common
	Carpentry for both sexes	Prevent "instrumental incompetence" from developing in girls
Creative self	Collage	Use self-expressive material to experience pattern and design
	Hospital play	Imaginative play that expresses child's "personal" idea of what the hospital is like
	Think of ways to protect baby guppies from their cannibal mother	Foster development of creative problem solving
Cognitive self	Lotto	Matching skills: pairing identical pictures
	Button box	Grouping skills: sorting according to categories determined by child
	Cooking banana nut bread	Temporal ordering: set ingredients out in order in which they will be used
	Cooking banana nut bread	Cause and effect: put some bread in oven, leave some out temporarily, and compare
Language development	Encourage conversation between children at snack time	Foster receptive and expressive language by increasing pleasure in communication
	Talk about plants during gardening	Foster receptive language by increasing comprehension of new vocabulary
Plans for children who have special needs	Have Angela help care for baby rats	Angela shut door on mother rat's tail last week. She feels badly about that mistake. Helping will make her feel better.

TABLE 3–3
Weekly curriculum analysis chart—morning*

Part of self being developed	Monday	Tuesday
Physical self	Creative dance Emphasize rhythm, tension release, creative self-expression	Obstacle course Emphasize balancing, bouncing (airborne), and body-perception skills
Emotional self—mental health	Read *Curious George Goes to the Hospital* Use discussion to broaden understanding and overcome fear	Hospital play Play out concerns and fears about hospital using hospital kit
Social self	Making dough Older children "read" the illustrated recipe to younger ones, thereby helping them	Share twins' baby book Enhances twin's self-esteem Bonds home with school
Multicultural and non-sexist emphasis	Dance: practice La Raspa Pleasure in another's culture	Black mother brings twins' baby book to share with group Emphasize that babies from various cultures have a lot in common
Creative self	Making dough; dancing Using dough is creative; making it is not	Hospital play; easel painting Foster creative, dramatic play, and self-expression
Cognitive self	Dough: recipe illustrated for children to read by themselves Temporal ordering; use of symbols; common relations (tools with materials)	Compare pictures of twins Matching: Are they identical?
Language development	Group time: read *Curious George Goes to the Hospital* Provide information on what a hospital is like and facts for later, realistic play	Use book about babies at group time Encourage children to discuss "when they were little!"

*Focus of interest for mixed group of 3- and 4-year-olds is the hospital (selected because one youngster was undergoing a hernia operation). Refer to same subject in Chapter 16.

This chart includes only special activities. Standard activities such as sand, tricycles, books, and so forth are assumed to be present.

Wednesday	Thursday	Friday	
Beanbag game: throw in tires	Carpentry Health examination	Health examination	Nature of activity
Projectile management	Carpentry: fine muscle skills Health screening	Health screening	Specific purpose
Group time: Pass around a stethoscope and tongue depressor; discuss their use	Water play in bathroom	Block play with rubber people as accessories	Nature of activity
Prepare children for brief health examinations on Thursday and Friday	Tension relief: important because of doctor's visit	Perhaps play family or hospital with them	Specific purpose
Make group card for child in hospital	Doctor's visit: help doctor set out instruments		Nature of activity
Pleasure in doing something for someone else Maintain social bonds with absent child	Career education Opportunity for meaningful work		Specific purpose
Field trip: Cinco de Mayo celebration See dance group dance La Raspa, return to center and dance	Female doctor conducts examination	Male doctor conducts examination	Nature of activity
Generate positive feelings toward Mexican-American culture	Teach principle that both men and women can be doctors		Specific purpose
Large collaged get-well card and dough	Repeat hospital play Carpentry	Fingerpainting	Nature of activity
Collage: design and arrangement Dough: free, self-expression	Opportunities for self-expression	Relaxation, tension release Free, nondemanding experience	Specific purpose
Health discussion	Lotto game: seasons	Set out Montessori cylinders	Nature of activity
Cause and effect: "What makes us keep well?"	Grouping skills based on seasonal changes of weather	Practice seriated ordering	Specific purpose
Emphasize "what if" questions at snack	Turn pages of *Curious George Goes to the Hospital*	Have children dictate stories	Nature of activity
Foster development of alternative answers	Have children tell the story; practice recall and temporal ordering	Subject: "What happened when the doctor examined me"; use language to describe experience to express feeling	Specific purpose

TABLE 3–4
Activity analysis sheet

Theme: The five senses   Age: 2-year-olds   Time: Tuesday morning

Name of self	Activity	Purpose	Evaluation
Physical: small muscle	Making orange juice	Develop eye/hand coordination: squeezing and pressing; tasting sweet and sour.	Children were extremely interested in this activity. They loved squeezing the oranges and tasting them. *Next time* I will offer this activity at beginning of self-select (individual choosing) time, instead of in the middle (we had to wait for the cook to be free to help). That way, more of the children could have participated.
Physical: large muscle	Obstacle course	Foster coordination of bodies in crawling, balancing, climbing, and spatial awareness. Talk about feeling body as it moves.	Children really enjoyed crawling through the tunnel and climbing up the stairs. I emphasized feeling how hands hold on, feet sting after jumping down. They modified the activity to satisfy their love of throwing beanbags into the tires. They rearranged the large hollow blocks and balance beam in a row and threw the beanbags into the tires. *Next time* I will have the beanbag throwing separate from the obstacle course so the activities won't interfere with each other. If both require close supervision, I'll move one outside for later play.
Social	Washing dishes in the water table	Encourage children to play side by side; encourage conversation and meaningful work. Have warm soapy water and cold rinse water—ask children to sense the difference.	The children enjoyed washing dishes (including the orange juice ones) and playing with the bubbles. Some brought more dishes from the dramatic play area. Children tried to feel the bubbles. *Next time* I would offer this activity right next to dramatic play to facilitate play in both places. Use only warm water—children disliked the contrast, even though it did fit the theme.

Nonsexist	Wood train and blocks	Encourage both girls and boys to use blocks and train.	Children were engrossed with the trains—both boys and girls enjoyed building the track and using the little people and animals I added. *Next time* I might have more blocks out and try harder to interest girls. It helps immensely to have a teacher in that area.
Emotional	Hiding in large box included in obstacle course	Work on fear of dark; controlling strength of experience by self-regulation. Talk about seeing better in light than in dark.	Children played cooperatively, shutting each other inside the box. It was too scary and/or stimulating for several of them. There was considerable screaming and excitement. *Next time* I'd do this as a separate activity; perhaps with flashlights. It was too much to supervise, so I finally pushed the box over to the wall and closed the flaps so the children couldn't get in. We talked about feeling scared in large group afterwards. Tried shutting our eyes to make it dark.
Creative	"Finger painting" with feet	Provide semi-creative experience. Concentrate on sensation via feet as compared to sensation via hands.	Painting was very slippery. Children had to sit on chairs, not walk on paper. Required lots of supervision because of safety and cleanup and putting on shoes and socks. *Next time* I would talk about it first—prepare children for "sitting" rule. Offer only if plenty of help is available.
Cognitive	"Smell" cannisters used in Let's Find Out. Asked children to match identical smells and to label smells they knew.	Practice concept of matching using a different sensory mode. Attach names to smells.	Most children were cautiously interested. *Next time* It's important to keep correct lids on cannisters so smells don't get mixed up. Color coding tops and bottoms would make this easier to do.

Note. Based on work by Jill Staab, student teacher, University of Oklahoma. Reprinted by permission.

On the other hand, everyone has days when just the opposite occurs and nothing seems to have gone right. The temptation then is to wallow in misery and see everything in shades of gloom.

Actually, neither of these responses is desirable. What *is* preferable to either of them is taking a more clear sighted view of how the children responded to each activity and then asking oneself what can be done next time to make the activity more effective.

Table 3–4 provides an example of how one student teacher evaluated some of the activities she included on a particular day she taught.

DEVISE THE DAILY SCHEDULE

Meeting the Needs of the Children

The schedule should provide for alternating periods of quieter and more active experiences. A sound schedule provides a daily pattern of activities that reduces the possibility of excitement escalating to the point of wild exhaustion. This is accomplished by interspersing quieter times, such as group or snack, with more vigorous experiences, such as outdoor play or dance.

In addition to this overall alternation, it is also important to plan for a variety of quieter and more vigorous activities within the larger time block, since individual children have different activity level requirements. Sometimes, for example, a child needs to be allowed to leave the group early, just as another youngster may relish the chance to withdraw to a shelter of blocks when the rest are rolling giddily down the hill outside. All schools should provide cozy book corners and rocking chairs to which children can retire when they wish to find peace and quiet.

The schedule should provide for indoor and outdoor play. While thinking about the value of alternative quiet and active learning situations, it also makes sense to consider whether the schedule will require all the children to be inside or outdoors at once or whether they will be free to move in and out as they desire.

If the staff is large enough and weather permits, allowing children to go in and out at will provides the best mix of large and small muscle activities. Schools in warm climates often operate on this kind of plan year around, but schools situated in more wintry areas usually prefer to go through the routine of snowsuits, boots, and mittens only once a morning and afternoon. What these colder climate schools sometimes forget, however, is that it might be possible to operate on a more open plan during early fall and late spring. If the staff is limited in number, part of the indoor and outdoor areas can be blocked off so that supervision remains adequate. The increased freedom and reduction of tension that results can make the effort of modifying the schedule well worth the trouble.

Sometimes, however, all-indoor or all-outdoor scheduling is necessary. Staff who must operate according to this plan should take special pains in planning the schedule to see to it that large-muscle activities are planned for inside and small-muscle activities are included outside to maintain a satisfactory balance in the curriculum.

The schedule should provide for a reasonable pace throughout the day. I began this section by mentioning the beneficial effects of adjusting the tempo of particular days to the needs of the children as these become apparent, but it is necessary also to allow enough time overall, every day, in the schedule to permit children to become truly engrossed in what they are doing. Plans that cause children to be constantly shifted back and forth from one thing to another reduce their chances for concentration and deep involvement, to say nothing of the general feeling of harassment they promote throughout the school.

Elizabeth Jones (1977) puts this eloquently, when she says:

Michael said of school when he was in fifth grade or so and we were talking about the possibility of his taking things to school to do when he finished his work. *"No point in starting anything. You never get to finish."* As a parent aide I saw the same lesson being carefully taught

A well-planned schedule allows time for children to experience quietness—a real chance to be themselves.

to Suzy's kindergarten: *Don't get interested. You'll just get interrupted.* The schedule was set up in short blocks of time apparently based on a theoretical 5 year old's attention span. Every time children got out an activity, it was time to put it away—at least so it seemed to me (and, I hope to them, because I hope they haven't learned at age 5 not to care). (p. 43)

In addition, it is necessary to allow a realistic amount of time for transitions if harassment is to be avoided. Little children do not "hurry" well. It takes time for them to shift gears from one activity to the next, and the wise teacher allows for this when planning. Particularly at the beginning of the year or in complicated change situations, a transition may require as long as 15 minutes.

A reasonable pace also means that staff has time to create those intimate moments of relationship with each youngster that lie at the heart of the preschool learning experience—a truly vital ingredient in early education.

Finally, the schedule should provide for a balance between individual self-selected learning experiences and participation in the more structured small-group times described in Chapter 15. Another way of saying this is that the day should provide for a combination of open and more structured activities. Openness is desirable so that children learn to make responsible choices, develop their autonomy and independence, and have many opportunities to participate in activities that suit their individual interests and needs, whereas the more structured opportunities are needed to help them learn to function as members of a somewhat more formal group and to ensure comprehensive coverage of some areas of the curriculum, such as particular mental abilities.

Meeting the Needs of the Adults

Adults, as well as children, have needs, and it is important that the schedule take these into consideration as well (Benham, Miller, & Kontos, 1988). For example, beware of the schedule that assumes that the same staff member will be at the same place at the same time each day. Adults need variety just as children do. Chang-

A SPECIAL PROBLEM IN SCHEDULING: WHAT TO DO WHEN THE WEATHER IS TERRIBLE

It is one of those difficult days that happen in every child-care facility. The weather has not been good all week, but until now the children have been able to go outside at least for a little while. Not today—it is only Thursday with the weatherman predicting more of the same on Friday. (One thing teachers cannot count on is having fewer children in school on a day with bad weather. Under such circumstances parents are more faithful than mail carriers and neither rain nor sleet nor snow seems to stay them from their appointed rounds of car pools.)

Long-Term Remedies

Make out an emergency daily schedule well in advance so that you are not caught in a frenzy of last minute planning.

Develop a list of volunteers and substitutes who have said they would be willing to rise to the occasion and help out on days that are especially taxing. When these people arrive, be certain you have simple but worthwhile activities for them to do with the children, such as reading to them or cooking with them. It is important for these people to feel successful enough so that they want to return. Try to give them advance warning, if possible, and be prepared for some excuses and refusals.

Consider having some kind of shelter constructed in the play yard: an outdoor covered area is both a summer and winter blessing, as is a wall that blocks out prevailing winds.

Short-Term Remedies

Stay as positive as possible. Help the children savor the day—after all, it *is* special. Get out special weather poems, stories, and pictures. Encourage them to watch the thermometer or rain gauge. Serve hot soup for snack (keep some dehydrated packets on hand for this purpose.) Put a pan of ice outside and see how many days it takes to melt.

Find some extra space and use it for "spill-over" activities, such as water play in a large bathroom, tricycles in the hall, carpentry on a covered porch— or block off part of an indoor room for trikes. Be willing to make some exceptions for rambunctious behavior. Look around, sometimes available space will surprise you.

Large-muscle activities are essential. Dancing and marching offer controlled opportunities for active, large-muscle play. Remember to combine it with relaxation experiences.

Offer absorbing favorites. Water play, cornmeal in tubs, or wheat to pour will occupy children for hours, and the cornmeal and wheat activities require little supervision. Cover some table or A-frames with old bedspreads or sheets and ask the children to furnish these houses with what they need.

Divide and conquer. If you teach in a self-contained classroom, suggest trading some children for part of the day with another teacher; the change can provide relief for both groups. Or if the weather permits travel, send part of the group on an excursion to the library or market.

Control the noise level. Noise tends to escalate particularly on such days. Be sensitive to this. Lower your own voice, turn the phonograph off, and insist that everyone use indoor voices.

Finally, treat yourself to something special when you go home. Congratulate yourself for a job well done and reward yourself with a luxurious bath, a good book, or a favorite TV program. After all, you deserve it.

---

ing areas frequently and encouraging staff to decide among themselves in which area they will be teaching during the coming week help ensure cooperation and enthusiastic participation.

Particularly in full-day centers, teachers also need respite from being constantly with the children. They need this not only to go to the restroom or take a coffee break or to talk to a colleague; they also need time to prepare materials and hold staff meetings. Unless such opportunities are deliberately included in the schedule, such times are often nibbled away, morale

Rainy days present fine opportunities for discussing the weather and what to do about it.

and energy decline, and both teachers and children suffer from the results.

Finally, as noted in Chapter 19, the schedule must provide time for teachers to greet and chat with parents at the beginning and end of the day. These friendly, comfortable contacts are indispensable in creating the bonds between home and school.

Reviewing the Schedule from Time to Time

Children change during the year, and a schedule that suits them in the fall more than likely requires modification in the spring. For example, it is probable that the time allocated to large group should be lengthened as the children's abilities to concentrate and get along together increase, and it is likely that transition times can be shortened because the children have learned to move easily through such routines.

It is also useful to examine the schedule from time to time for trouble spots where things are not going smoothly and consider whether an adjustment might alleviate the difficulty. Perhaps congestion and scuffling in the toilet room might be reduced by sending the 3-year-olds through first and feeding them a little sooner than the 4-year-olds are fed, or restlessness at group time might be alleviated by offering it earlier in the morning when the children are less tired. Remember, it is always possible to experiment with a variation for a week or two and then go back to the previous pattern if the change fails to solve the difficulty.

Special Comments on Half- and Full-Day Schedules

Half-day schedules, in particular, require attention to the comments about pacing the day well. If long enough blocks of time are to be included, the pattern that usually works best is two large time periods divided in the middle by snack and group time.

Short days also mean that most of the preparation must be done before the children arrive or after they go home, and, to be realistic, staff time for this purpose should be scheduled and paid for.

I am including an interesting example of an unusual 3½-hour schedule as an illustration of what can be done to meet special needs (see Figures 3–1 and 3–2). In this particular situation, two Head Start classes cooperate to use one large room and yard. Although the room is legally large enough to serve both groups at once, in actuality the staff found this situation produced bedlam, so they worked out an alternative plan. It must be admitted that such a solution would not be feasible in all climates. Los Niños is fortunate to be located in a part of the country that makes much outdoor activity practicable.

A Schedule for a Full-Day Center. Full-day centers are blessed with many scheduling advantages; among these are the leisurely pace the longer day affords combined with plenty of time for involving children in activities and for forming close relationships with them.

7:30–9:00
  Children arrive, play indoors until it warms up; time of going outside varies, also, in accordance with children's energy needs.
9:00–9:15
  Transition: wash hands, toileting, move to snack tables.
9:15–9:45
  Breakfast or substantial snack—everyone sits down together, transition, including brief large muscle activity.
9:45–10:15
  Planned experience group time (most intellectually challenging group time of day presented at this point).
10:15–11:45
  Activity time, indoors and out, field trips, and so on.

FIGURE 3–1
Staggered schedule serving two groups of morning children using the same room

	Group I		**Group II**
9:00	Children arrive	11:30	Children arrive
9:00-9:10	Snack	11:30-12:10	Table activities and indoor play
9:10-10:00	Table activities and indoor play	12:10-12:30	Small group time
10:00-10:15	Small group time	12:30	Lunch
10:15-10:25	Rest with a story	1:00-1:10	Rest time with a story
10:25-10:55	Large group time (music and physical movement)	1:10-1:40	Large group time (music and physical movement)
10:55	Clean up for lunch	1:40-2:00	Free choice time and clean up
11:00-11:30	Lunch	2:00	Children leave for home
11:30	Children leave for home		

I am indebted to Los Niños Head Start, Santa Barbara, for allowing me to include this schedule as an example.

FIGURE 3–2
Rainy day schedule serving two groups of morning children using the same room

	Group I		**Group II**
9:00	Children arrive		
9:00-9:10	Hearty snack		
9:10-9:55	Indoor activities		
9:55-10:00	Clean up and transition	10:00	Children arrive
10:00-10:15	Small group work	10:00-10:15	Outside time
10:15-11:30	Outside time (including field trips)	10:15-10:30	Hearty snack (indoors)
		10:30-11:10	Indoor activities
		11:10-11:15	Cleanup and transition
		11:15-11:30	Small group time
11:30-12:00	Transition, wash hands, lunch, brush teeth	11:30-12:30	Outdoor time (including field trips)
12:00-12:10	Transition, quiet story time as group gathers		
12:10-12:30	Large group time		
12:30	Leave on bus to go home.	12:30-1:00	Transition, wash hands, lunch, brush teeth
		1:00-1:10	Transition and quiet story time as group gathers
		1:10-1:30	Large group time
		1:30	Leave on bus for home

I am indebted to Los Niños Head Start, Santa Barbara, for allowing me to include this schedule as an example.

11:45–12:00

Transition: cleanup, toileting, wash hands, gather for lunch.

12:00–12:30

Lunch.

12:30–12:45 or 1:00

Wash hands, brush teeth, gradually settle down for nap.

1:00–2:30

Nap: children are expected to at least rest quietly for ½ to ¾ of an hour; most will sleep a bit longer than that; children get up gradually as they waken.

3:00

Last child up by this time.

2:30–3:15

Snack set out: children may come to table and eat as they are ready.

2:30–4:30

Activity time, indoors and out, includes opportunities for field trips, purposeful play, and so forth.

4:30–5:15

Story time for those who desire it, quiet play, get cleaned up with hands washed, hair smoothed, ready to go home with families.

The major problem in scheduling that full-day centers must take into account is the problem of monotony and lack of variety in curriculum that results from teacher fatigue and burnout. This is likely to be particularly true in the afternoon portion of such programs when all too often children are simply turned loose on the playground for hours at a time.

Rather than allowing this to happen, the staff should face the problem of teacher burnout squarely and attempt to solve it in two ways. First, make certain that the schedule provides respite for teachers from continual contact with children. The second effective scheduling strategy is to combine full-time and half-time staff so that some half-time people arrive in the afternoon armed with new ideas and equipped with the energy to see these through. (Young teachers in training and volunteers are both good sources for such afternoon help, but if these resources are drawn on, supervising teachers must play fair and make certain they provide them with sufficient guidance and support.)

Translated into an actual schedule, the plan might appear as shown in Table 3–5. Note that this plan uses the material included for Tuesday in Table 3–3.

TABLE 3–5
Activity schedule for fifteen 4-year-olds* in a full-day center

Date: Tuesday, September 12, 1989
Topic or theme for week: Babies and hospitals (chosen because of new baby in one family and because another child is due for a hernia repair the next week)

Time	Staff†	Activity	Purpose and notes
7:30-9:00	Two staff	*Welcome children*	Ease transition to school; conduct health check
		Collecting baby pictures	Use pictures for bulletin board and group discussion—continues interest from yesterday.
		Table top activities, including books about babies	
		Outdoor play for a while if warm enough	Weather is nice, better take advantage of it.
9:00-9:15	Two staff	*Transition*	Eveyone to toilet if necessary and wash hands; get one adult seated with children as quickly as possible; make sure cook has breakfast ready as children sit down.
9:15-9:45	Two staff	*Breakfast* (or snack) Fruit, cereal, and milk with buttered toast.	Special event: serve fruit in baby food jars, baby cereal, and milk to fit baby theme.
9:45-10:15	Two staff with divided group, or one adult sets up while other conducts group	*Planned experience time* Book: *Curious George Goes to the Hospital*	Generate questions about hospital; may read half of book, rest later if too long; during hospital discussion point out that doctors and nurses can be of either sex.
		Song: "Rock A Bye Baby"	Use B sound at beginning of each word for fun and for auditory training.

---

*Group is composed of seven Anglos, four Mexican-Americans (all English speaking), and four Black children (including a pair of twins).
†Identity of staff changes as their shifts are completed.

TABLE 3–5 (continued)

Time	Staff	Activity	Purpose and notes
9:45-10:15 —cont'd		Discussion: What was it like when you were a baby?	Use baby pictures to discuss "now and then" (temporal ordering).
		Poem: "Five Little Monkeys"	Use flannel board—may lead to doctor discussion; also talk about bouncing on mattress, which the children will do later outside.
		Transition—dismissal	Dismiss according to who is wearing sneakers, jeans, etc.; provides practice in mental abilities of grouping or matching.
10:15-11:45	Two staff	Highlights of self-select activity time	
		Hospital and baby play	Set up outside if weather permits.
		Blocks	Accessories: ambulance and biracial wooden medical figures.
		Make salad	Salad made with children if cook has time.
		Dough	Made by children without teacher help; illustrated recipe encourages left-to-right "reading" and provides practice in temporal ordering.
		Outside: swings, trikes, dampened sand, and obstacle course	Balance on low wall, jump off onto mattress, bounce, throw ball into tire, run up ramp, repeat (while they are jumping, remind children of "Five Little Monkeys"); practice in dynamic balance, locomotion, rhythm, rebound, throwing and catching activities.
11:45-12:00	Two staff	Transition	Toilet, wash hands (teachers, too), calm down, move transition along by singing and discussing what is for lunch.
12:00-12:30	Two staff	Lunch	
		Tortillas with beans, green salad, yogurt with fresh fruits for dessert, milk	See if cook has time for children to help make salad during self-select; meal is multicultural emphasis for day—use one of the Mexican-American family's recipes for beans.

TABLE 3–5 *(continued)*

Time	Staff	Activity	Purpose and notes
12:30-12:45 or 1:00	Two staff	*Transition to nap*	Toilet, wash hands, brush teeth; emphasize quiet.
1:00-2:30	One staff during nap Two staff as children wake up (in nap room)	*Nap*	Children get up gradually as they wake up. Second staff preparation time.
2:30-3:00	One staff	*Transition*	Last child up by this time; toilet, wash hands.
2:30-3:15	Two staff	*Snack* Cut up oranges and raisins; water if desired	Children come to eat as they get up and move on to play; second staff member sets up afternoon.
2:30-4:30	Two staff (after supervising nap and snack)	*Self-select activity time* Water play outdoors; then get out baby buggies, plus usual outdoor activities	Wading pool with hoses (requires supervision with both staff); fun, coolness, social play, and facts about volume and what the power of water can do.
4:30-5:15	Two staff and visitor	*Indoor activity time* Story time, quiet play; children cleaned up to go home Special visit from mother of Black twins who brings their baby book to share with the group.	Offer drinks of water to thirsty children. As crowd diminishes, one staff sets up for morning activities. Builds self-esteem of twins who are shy and tend just to play together; provides practice in concept of matching (do the twins look the same as babies and now?) and cross-cultural learning.

SUMMARY

Careful scheduling lies at the heart of all well-run early childhood programs. To accomplish this task successfully, teachers need to include activities that foster the development of all five selves of the child.

Drawing up an effective curriculum involves going through a series of steps. These include selecting a theme related to the children's interests and brainstorming a large number of possible activities related to that theme, analyzing these ideas according to a number of realities that must be considered when planning, blocking out the activities over a week's time, making certain there is a worthwhile purpose or reason for including each one, fitting the activities into the daily schedule and evaluating the day when it is over. Examples of different kinds of schedules complete the chapter.

SELF-CHECK QUESTIONS FOR REVIEW

Content-Related Questions

1. Think of the five selves and list some skills for each of them that should be included in a curriculum plan.

2. Why is it most satisfactory to select a topic for a curriculum theme drawn from the children's interests?

3. A number of reality tests proposed in the chapter should be applied to curriculum ideas to make certain the activities are practical and appropriate. List and discuss as many of these as you can.

4. Why is it valuable for teachers to pinpoint the purpose or reason why they are offering a particular activity for the children to do?

5. When planning the schedule, what are some of the children's needs the teacher should take into account? And what are some of the adult's needs that must also be considered?

6. Discuss some practical ideas teachers can use to make a spell of bad weather more tolerable in their classrooms.

7. The research study reported in this chapter singles out several kinds of equipment and activity areas that were lacking in the poorer-quality child-care centers. Which ones were usually missing?

Integrative Questions

1. Assume that you are teaching a group of 2-year-olds and that you intend to use birds as a theme because one of the children wants to bring her pet canary to school. Read through the following list of activities and evaluate them in terms of the seven realities discussed in the text. Which ideas would you select? Which ones would you discard? Explain your reasons for each decision. *

   • Use a stuffed bird or dead bird for close observation.
   • Put a bird feeder outside the window for the children to check on every few days.
   • Raise a baby wild bird who has fallen from its nest.
   • Provide tubs of feathers and other objects to contrast how they feel on the children's feet or hands.
   • Offer a snack (popcorn and water in flat bowls) so that children can eat and drink as birds without using their hands.
   • Visit the bird room in the museum.
   • Have children make a birdhouse.

---

*Bird ideas kindness of Cené Marquis, Head Teacher, Institute of Child Development, University of Oklahoma.

   • Emphasize the American Indian culture since birds have always held a place of importance in that culture.

2. Identify and compare the differences in supervision that existed between the good- and poor-quality centers revealed by the Benham, Miller, and Kontos study.

3. You are making a decision about which of two jobs to accept. One is in a full-day center, and the other is in a half-day center. Based on the discussion of scheduling in this chapter, assess the advantages and disadvantages of each kind of schedule, explain which one you would choose, and why you personally prefer it.

QUESTIONS AND ACTIVITIES

1. Is there anything wrong with turning children loose on the playground in the afternoon? After all, don't they need this free time to generate creative play ideas?

2. This book has talked a good deal about the benefits of using a focus of interest as a center for developing curriculum, but is there another side to it? What might be the disadvantages of centering on a particular topic?

3. Are there some consistent trouble spots (times of day when teachers seem to consistently discipline or control the children) in teaching situations you have observed or in which you have worked? Share some of these with the class and consider possible rearrangements of the schedule that might alleviate these situations.

4. Assume that the Quick Check Chart (Table 3–1) is a useful planning tool for you to employ. If you wanted to use it for planning a group time or for just one morning, explain how the headings might be modified to make this possible.

5. *Problem:* It is 4:30 in the afternoon at your day-care center. The children have been through snack time, they have done the special activity for the afternoon, they have played outside until they are exhausted, and now they are fighting and bickering among themselves, and there is still an hour to go. What activity would you recommend scheduling that would enable the children to remain in at least partial control of themselves during this time rather than spending it in a state of tantrums, attacks, and just galloping around?

REFERENCES FOR FURTHER READING

Overviews

Brown, J. F. (Ed.). (1982). *Curriculum planning for young children*. Washington, D.C.: National Association for the Education of Young Children. This book is a compilation of articles from *Young Children* which offers many practical ideas for building curriculum in a variety of areas. Very worthwhile.

Planning with Individual Children in Mind

Bredekamp, S. (Ed.). (1987). *Developmentally appropriate practice in early childhood programs serving children from birth through age 8* (expanded edition). Washington, D.C.: National Association for the Education of Young Children. Although this has been cited previously, it is such a valuable reference it merits citing again because of its emphasis on planning curriculum that is developmentally appropriate for children.

Cassidy, D. J., Myers, B. K., & Benion, P.E. (1987). Early childhood planning: A developmental perspective. *Childhood Education*, 64(1), 2–8. The authors pose useful questions to ask when developing curriculum and demonstrate how to suit curriculum to children in the same group who have varying developmental needs.

Developing Curriculum Based on a Topic or Theme

Eliason, D. F., & Jenkins, L. T. (1986). *A practical guide to early childhood curriculum* (3rd ed.). Columbus, Ohio: Merrill Publishing Co. Eliason and Jenkins provide a large number of ideas related to specific themes and accompany each one with a purpose.

Flemming, B. M., Hamilton, D. S., & Hicks, J. D. (1977). *Resources for creative teaching in early childhood education*. San Diego: Harcourt Brace Jovanovich. This book is a rich resource of all kinds of activities to use in curriculum, categorized according to such topics as family celebrations, seasons, and animals. Highly recommended.

Developing an Overall Plan for the Day

Dodge, D. T., Goldhammer, M., & Colker, L. J. *The creative curriculum for early childhood*. Washington, D.C.: Creative Associates International. This book offers good discussions on scheduling and routines. It also discusses specific areas of curriculum such as blocks, table toys, sand, and water.

Hildebrand, V. (1984). *Management of child development centers*. New York: Macmillan Publishing Co. The chapter entitled "Improving Children's Programs: The Manager's Role" offers considerable practical advice about overall planning and scheduling.

Discussions of Scheduling

Maxim, G. (1989). *The very young* (3rd ed.). Columbus, Ohio: Merrill Publishing Co. Maxim provides interesting examples showing how schedules can reflect the educational values of the school.

Seefeldt, C., & Barbour, N. (1986). *Early childhood education: An introduction*. Columbus, Ohio: Merrill Publishing Co. In Chapter 5, the authors offer a variety of schedules as well as a clear discussion of how to go about planning curriculum to meet the needs of children.

For the Advanced Student

National Association for the Education of Young Children. (1984). *Accreditation criteria & procedures of the National Academy of Early Childhood Programs*. Washington, D.C.: The Association. This document sets forth the criteria used by the Academy for accrediting half- and full-day child-care centers. Highly recommended.

Relevant Journals

Child Care Information Exchange. 17916 NE 103rd St., Redmond, Washington 98052. Six issues a year, $25.00. The timely, practical articles in CCIE fill a gap in the literature on how to work in and operate child-care centers. Topics range from dealing with staff burnout to informing parents about tax exemptions. A valuable publication.

4 Designing the Supportive Environment

Have you ever

- Hated the room in which you teach?
- Needed to save money when buying equipment?
- Wished there were more interesting things for the children to do when they played outside?

If you have, the material in this chapter will help you.

*Your classroom should be a room richly hung, full of challenge
and excitement, full of experience, full of warmth and feeling
that can sustain from time to time the inevitable failures and
frustrations of growing up. A place of now. A place that recognizes the best way to learn is to live.*

JOHN COE (1987)

Now that we have the elements of a good curriculum in mind and understand how to plan and schedule it, there is one more thing to consider: what to do about arranging the physical setting and materials so they facilitate and support the curriculum. This means that as teachers plan this physical environment, they must review once again the basic educational purposes that they consider important to make certain that this plan embodies their philosophy.

SOME YARDSTICK QUESTIONS TO APPLY

For example, if teachers believe that the purpose of education is to increase competence for each of the child's selves, they might apply the following yardstick question to evaluate the environment: *Will this arrangement help children be competent and successful?* Accomplishing the goal implied by this question might involve something as simple as placing a row of tires as a barrier between the tricycle activity and the sandbox area so that riders need not be continually reprimanded for intruding on the diggers' space, thereby preserving their self-esteem by avoiding criticism of their behavior. It also might involve using small, transparent pitchers at snack time to make it easier for children to pour skillfully without spilling. Or it might involve enlarging the block corner so that children are less likely to antagonize each other by stumbling over each other's constructions.

If teachers believe that children learn best when all their senses are involved, they will continually incorporate these kinds of opportunities into the physical environment. They will

tie visual experiences to concrete ones whenever possible. Perhaps they will start by opening a book to an exquisite drawing of a growing plant and placing it beside plants that the children have started for themselves or ones that they can touch and handle. Perhaps they also will encourage the children to listen to the silkworms chewing on their leaves and to feel their soft, dry bodies, as well as to look at them. A good yardstick question to ask here might be, *What will the children be able to do with what is set out here?* When the answer is "Just look," this is a clue that something should be modified.

If teachers believe that curriculum topics should stem from the interests of the children, they will listen to these concerns carefully and create not only a curriculum that is based on these interests, but also a physical environment that reflects them. An example of a good question to ask here is, *Where did this idea come from?* Did it come from the children, or is it simply a piece of "embalmed" curriculum I find convenient to get out once again? Although physical settings often benefit from the use of resources accumulated from past years, they also derive great benefit from the addition of new resources. Adding these fresh items sustains both the teachers' and children's interest in the subject and helps ensure that teaching materials will be relevant to the interests of the current group of youngsters.

Finally, if the teacher is convinced that children learn to appreciate beauty by experiencing it, he will ask himself these questions as he regards the entire environment:

- *What does the room look like today? Is it colorful but not garish?*

- *Is it orderly and clean but not bare or stark?*
- *Is it interesting without being overwhelming?*
- *Is it beautiful?*

DOES ROOM ARRANGEMENT REALLY MATTER?

In addition to considering the empowering and aesthetic values related to arranging indoor and outdoor environments, there is another practical reason teachers should consider this subject with care. The way the environment is arranged definitely affects children's and adults' behavior. A number of studies in recent years (Campbell & Dill, 1985; Phyfe-Perkins & Shoemaker, 1986; Smith & Connolly, 1980; Wohlwill & Van Vliet, 1985) confirm that this is true. This area of study is often spoken of as the *ecology* of child-care centers because ecology has to do with the relationship between living things and their environments. The research study by Teets which is included here provides an example of how these studies are carried out.

SUGGESTIONS FOR ARRANGING THE ENVIRONMENT

Starting from Scratch

Occasionally teachers have an opportunity to design a children's center right from the start. Even though such opportunities are relatively rare, such a design is included here (Figure 4–1) because so much interest has been displayed in this particular center by visitors.

This center is a good example of a building planned to meet many needs during the day. Each of the indoor play areas can be, and frequently is, divided into smaller spaces by flexible dividers, and a third "special activities" room is used for children's large-muscle activities, as well as for college classes and parent meetings. The large storage units placed in the center of the indoor play rooms make frequently used equipment readily accessible. Note also the numerous storage closets. Outdoors the fixed

play apparatuses, such as swings and climbing complexes, have been deliberately situated in the far corners of the yard to encourage the children to make use of the entire space. The building accommodates 55 children as well as numerous student teachers and staff members.

Planning the Basic Indoor Arrangement

Suppose that the building is already there and that you, the teacher, are stepping into the room for the first time, and it is completely empty. (Sometimes when teachers have been teaching in the same room for a while, they find it worthwhile to put everything out in the hall and simply experience the empty space while thinking about it and the children who will occupy it.) Now take note of such unchangeable items as the location of doors, windows, built-in cabinets, water facilities, and light plugs, and examine how these "givens" affect the way things must ultimately be arranged in the room. (For example, the most convenient place for the cooking table is near both the sink and a power supply.)

Next, think about the traffic patterns. Can furniture be arranged to provide unimpeded pathways to the "go-home" door, bathrooms, and outdoor play areas? Can it be used as buffers and dividers to prevent undesirable patterns from developing so that block and book corners and the dramatic play area are protected from unnecessary intrusions?

Then go out in the hall and look at the available furniture with a fresh perspective. Try to see the playhouse stove or the book cabinet in terms of its potential as an area demarcator or as an empty space on which a child's picture could be displayed or as a countertop for holding an interesting exhibit. Sometimes it is helpful to play the game, "If I couldn't . . .": "If I couldn't use this cabinet as a bookcase, what else could I use it for?" Doing this can allow you to discover new possibilities in even the most mundane furnishings.

Noise levels must be considered, too. It is wisest to separate noisy areas as far from each

FIGURE 4-1

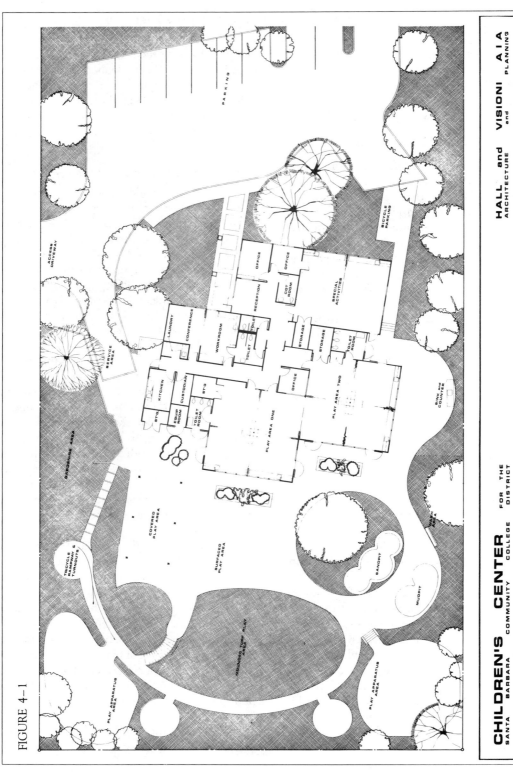

CHILDREN'S CENTER FOR THE
SANTA BARBARA COMMUNITY COLLEGE DISTRICT

HALL and VISIONI AIA
ARCHITECTURE and PLANNING

64

other as possible. For example, if carpentry cannot be done outside, consider placing it at one end of the room, which will keep it out of the traffic pattern and will prevent (at least partially) the sound of hammering from rocketing through the school. Consider also whether it might be possible to use part of the hall for this purpose, since a teacher must devote her undivided attention to it anyway.

Quiet areas must be created to balance the more noisy, high-activity ones. Consider how tiring it is even for an adult to be in the constant company of other people. Although we think of children as generally seeking the company of other children, it is equally exhausting for them to endure the continual stimulation and adjustments from constant contact with other people. Children need quieter, somewhat secluded places to which they can withdraw when they have had enough contact. Such arrangements may vary from a comfortable sofa with books nearby to an unused fireplace where children snuggle down into a mass of pillows (Benham, Miller, & Kontos, 1988).

Finally, think about the various activities you want to include and where these would be most sensibly placed, taking into consideration the unchangeable "givens," the desirable and undesirable traffic patterns, the need for noise and stimulation control, and the available equipment. Remember also to place activity areas with an eye to the accessibility of storage, the level of illumination needed, and the desirability of distributing activities throughout the room. Plan also for open spaces into which activities and children can spread as needed.

Typical Indoor Activities. Particular activity areas commonly included indoors are the unit block area, a reading and story corner, one or more places for dramatic play (this usually includes a housekeeping area but should be able to accommodate many other pretend play situations from time to time), space for creative self-expressive activities and for tabletop activities, and a let's-find-out exploration area that varies with the current focus of interest. Many areas in the children's center serve more than

Sometimes children create their own quiet places!

RESEARCH STUDY
Changing the Environment Can Change Behavior

Research Question   Can reducing problems in the child-care environment improve children's behavior?

Research Method   The investigators used the Environmental Inventory developed by Prescott, Jones, and Kritchevsky (1972) to rate the initial environmental quality of three classrooms, one of 2-year-olds, one of 3-year-olds, and one of 4-year-olds (N = 39). Ratings covered the areas of organization, complexity, number of places available per child, and special problems. All of the rooms scored in the low- to poor-quality range.

Then the children's behavior was observed and scored for 2 weeks according to the amount of child/child interactions, teacher/child interactions, use of materials in appropriate areas, and level of involvement with materials. Twenty behavior samples were gathered for each child.

Next, the rooms were arranged so they qualified for high scores on the Environmental Inventory, and the children's behavior was observed and scored under those conditions for another 2 weeks.

Finally, the rooms were returned to their original condition, and the children's behavior once again recorded.

Examples of the changes made during the second, high-quality phase included moving tricycles outside that had been stored near the door where children were tempted to ride them in the room, and separating interest areas so that, for example, music and science activities were not located in the same place. Rugs and soft cushions were added to a library area to increase its usage.

Results   The investigators reported that during the time the rooms were arranged to meet high-quality standards, the children talked more together and did less standing around than during the times when the rooms were poorly arranged. The

---

one purpose during the day: the carpeted block area, for instance, readily converts to a comfortable group time spot, and most full-day centers must use all available floor space for cots and mats at nap time.

Planning Environments for Aesthetic Appeal

Now that the functional aspects of the arrangement have been considered, it is time to consider the asthetic aspects of the environment. A room should be beautiful and appealing, as well as practical. Purchasing well-designed basic equipment certainly is important in accomplishing

this,[1] as is using harmonious colors and including a variety of textures.

Teachers often put a good deal of emphasis on bulletin boards as well. These can tell children something valuable about how the school views their abilities if consistent use is made of what they have painted or otherwise created. Material on such boards should be placed low enough that short people (that is, children) can see it easily.

---

[1]Moyer (1986) is an invaluable resource for selecting such equipment. See the references at the end of the chapter for a fuller description of this pamphlet.

children used materials in appropriate areas more of the time, the amount of constructive play increased, and random and deviant conduct decreased. All of these results met a satisfactory level of statistical significance. When the rooms were restored to their original condition, the children returned to their earlier, less-desirable behaviors.

Therefore, Teets concluded that the study demonstrates that good-quality environments *can* produce positive changes in children's behavior.

Implications Previous studies of child care environments, such as that by Smith and Connolly (1980), had centered on the effects of overcrowding, but had not demonstrated that such effects can be corrected by changing the environment. Teets' study goes beyond that work and offers evidence (and hope!) to teachers that they can change what is happening in their classrooms by paying careful attention to the effect room arrangement has on children's behavior.

When children seem rowdy or at loose ends or consistently get in trouble, the wise teacher should stand off and review the way the room is arranged. Are the children running back and forth because they're "naughty," or are they running because the room is arranged like a long, narrow tunnel? Are they stomping on each other's blocks because they're destructive or because there's insufficient space for them all to build as they wish? Are they standing around doing nothing because they're withdrawn or because there isn't enough for them to do?

Although not all undesirable behavior can be attributed to poor design of the environment, some of it certainly can be. Teachers can make their own lives and the lives of the children they teach so much easier if they will take care when planning how to arrange their rooms.

Note. From "Modification of Play Behaviors of Preschool Children Through Manipulation of Environmental Variables" by S. T. Teets, 1985, in J. L. Frost and S. Sunderlin (Eds.), *When children play: Proceedings of the International Conference on Play and Play Environments,* Wheaton, Md.: Association for Childhood Education International.

Often adults unthinkingly place items of interest at their own height, and the children do not benefit from such displays if they must crane their necks to see them. It is a sound principle to get right down to the children's height when planning wall arrangements and take a look at them from the children's position—the results can sometimes be surprising.

In their delightful books on teaching-learning environments, Jones (1977) and Jones and Prescott (1978) speak of the hardness-softness dimensions in the school environment. Softness should surely be a part of the aesthetics of the center. Cozy furniture, carpeting, sand, rocking chairs, and laps all fall into this category, as do play dough, animals, and strap swings. These might all be thought of as simply "soft to touch," but the authors define their common quality in a different way. They describe a "soft" environment as one that is sensorily responsive. For example, a playground with grass, sand, and tires to bounce on is more sensorily responsive than is an asphalt one with metal play equipment. If we wish to make this sensorial responsiveness part of the room itself, as well as part of the curriculum, we must strive for an overall effect that is homey and comfortable—"soft" in every sense of the word.

PLANNING FOR MULTIETHNIC AND NONSEXIST AREAS IN THE CURRICULUM

The value of consistently incorporating multiethnic and nonsexist materials and activities into curriculum plans *cannot* be overemphasized. Although Chapter 12 devotes many pages to this topic, I do not want the reader to wait until then to begin thinking about this important subject. Basically, multicultural curriculum should stress two things: first, that all people have many things in common—they get sleepy, they feel hungry, and sometimes they are sad or happy; second, that everyone has different, unique, and valuable contributions to make to the life of the group.

Even though teachers want to be casual and matter-of-fact about teaching these values, they also should be persistent in planning for their inclusion as part of the environment. For example, the fact that all kinds of people have some needs in common could be taught by borrowing a tatami mat and quilts from a Japanese friend and ecouraging the children to play "going to bed" using the Japanese bed and also using a western-style sleeping bag. Meanwhile the teacher could point out that everyone gets tired and sleepy and that they meet this need in different, but equally practical and comfortable, ways.

When planning for nonsexist activities, beware of subconsciously thinking of some activities and areas as being "for the boys" and others as being "for the girls." Think instead of what *all* the children might do if you added the rubber pigs and wooden cows to the block corner after a visit to a family's cow barn. *Expect* that both boys and girls will be drawn into play there, and encourage use of the block area by children of both sexes.

It also contributes to the feeling of homeyness and comfort when the ethnic and cultural backgrounds of children are matter-of-factly represented in the physical environment of the school. Although it is not as significant an influence in the generation of positive feelings and attitudes as the activities discussed in the book, the inclusion of multiethnic pictures, books, and artifacts does contribute to the children's overall feelings of being valued for their own cultural richness.

Once you have decided where everything should go and what aesthetic components should be included, then it is time to move it all into place and observe how the staff and children live within this environment together. Ask yourself if the plan is achieving the desired purposes. If not, why not? Never hesitate to rearrange things once again to achieve the educational goals you deem most desirable.

It is refreshing to rearrange rooms from time to time for the sake of variety, as well as for more functional reasons, by changing materials from one place to another or moving indoor equipment outside or vice versa. It also can be exhilarating to empty the room and encourage the children to do the arranging for a change. One school that experimented with this reported that the children scarcely used the tables at all in their own arrangements, and yet some preschools are positively littered with tables. A side benefit reported by this staff was that, as they paid particularly close attention to what the children were telling them and as they encouraged the children to carry out their own ideas, the amount of conflict between children was reduced and they began to solve more of their social difficulties for themselves (Pfluger & Zola, 1972).

Planning the Outdoor Environment

The outdoor play area is just as valuable and important to plan and arrange wisely as is the indoor area. Too often teachers who take pains over their interior rooms think of outdoor play as primarily having large-muscle values, but a well-

The children loved using this hammock from Guatemala.

arranged play yard includes opportunities for the development of all the child's selves. Therefore, in addition to swings, sandboxes, slides, and wheeled toys, outdoor areas should contain gardens, animals, and places for water and mud play. Opportunities for pretend play can be especially rich outdoors if a plentiful supply of sturdy boxes, boards, and ladders is available. Science activities, particularly those in natural science and physics, fit in well outside if equipment such as water, pulleys, ropes, and living materials is included in the environment; and many art activities such as fingerpainting are better suited to the more easily cleaned and less restrictive outdoor area.

Schools in colder climates lack the freedom of having some of these activities take place outside in winter months, but they do possess the advantage of vastly changing weather conditions, which can provide an appetizing variety of activities—if teacher and children dress warmly enough! A well-planned environment in the north contains dry outdoor playing areas that are larger than usual and surfaced with asphalt, cement, or tanbark so that the children do not become wet and chilled. Particular attention should be given to wind protection so that the children can spend considerable time outdoors almost every day.

Many of the principles mentioned in regard to indoor planning apply equally to outdoor planning. It is important to provide clear pathways that invite children to move to different areas. Planning to prevent congestion by dispersing interesting areas throughout the yard is also valuable, and placing activities near their storage units makes effective use of equipment more probable. Shaded areas and a diversity of surfacing materials where possible are important to consider, too.

In addition, the analysis of kinds of outdoor equipment done by Kritchevsky, Prescott, and Walling (1969) and Jones and Prescott (1978) has particular merit, since there tend to be many more "simple" units used there than inside. According to all these researchers, a *simple unit*

Schools in colder climates have the advantage of vastly changing weather conditions that provide an appetizing variety of activities.

has "one obvious use and does not have sub-parts or a juxtaposition of materials which enable a child to manipulate or improvise. (Examples: swings, jungle gym, rocking horse, tricycle.)." This kind of equipment is limited in play value because of the number of children it can interest at one time and the length of time it is likely to keep even one child occupied. A *complex unit* is defined as one "with sub-parts or juxtaposition of two essentially different play materials which enable the child to manipulate or improvise. (Examples: sand table with digging equipment; play house with supplies.) Also included in this category are single play materials and objects which encourage substantial improvisation and/or have a considerable element of unpredictability. (Examples: all art activities such as dough or paints; a table with books to look at; an area with animals such as a dog, guinea pigs, or ducks.)." A *super unit* is a complex unit that has "one or more additional play materials, i.e., three or more play materials, juxtaposed. (Examples:

sand box with play materials and water; dough table with tools; tunnel, movable climbing boards and box, and large crates)" (Kritchevsky, Prescott, & Walling, 1969, pp. 10, 11). These units can involve more children at the same time and sustain each child's interest longer. Jones (1977) reported in another publication that "a super unit is about eight times as effective in holding a child's attention as a simple unit; a complex unit about four times as effective" (p. 12).

Certainly teachers who wish to promote positive social action, creative problem solving, and richer play as part of their outdoor curriculum will do well to assess the outdoor play equipment and convert it to complex and super units wherever possible. One of the easiest and most productive ways of doing this is to acquire the supply of boards, saw horses, crawl-through blocks, mattresses, and large hollow blocks recommended in Chapter 8. If these are moved to various areas at different times and are used in conjunction with other, less-movable equipment, they add instant complexity and play possibilities to areas as diverse as the sandbox and jungle gym. Adding dramatic play props, such as dolls, housekeeping paraphernalia, or fire hats and hoses is another easy way to change a simple unit to a complex or super one.

When arranging and developing the outdoor activity areas to increase their potential for richer play, teachers should ask themselves, "How can I arrange this area so that the children will be encouraged to play together?" and "What is there in reserve that might be added to deepen and extend the play as it progresses?" (Chapter 2 offers additional suggestions about how to do this effectively.)

MAINTAINING THE TOTAL ENVIRONMENT IN GOOD ORDER

There is another aspect of the development of the physical environment to consider: the overall impression that the physical environment conveys is of great significance. Mundane as it may seem, orderliness and cleanliness play vital roles in that impression.

Of course, some items, such as the plastic cover used at the clay table, are better left uncleaned. Maintaining good order should not become a fetish in a children's center, but cleanliness is appreciated by experienced visitors who have all too often come across schools with sticky chairs, smudged blocks, and grubby puzzles. Days at a center move at a quick and ever-changing pace, which makes it difficult, though not impossible, to keep things looking fresh and well maintained. Table 4–1 contains many suggestions for keeping maintenance simple and for saving money, too.

TABLE 4–1
Money-saving tips on maintaining and preserving equipment

Preservation and maintenance	Additional comments
Furniture	
Buy varnished or lacquered shelves, cabinets, and so on, rather than painted ones. They require less frequent refurbishing.	Buy furniture with casters whenever possible to aid movement. Avoid "built-ins" when you can; they reduce flexibility.
Look for easily cleaned plastic surfaces on tabletops and chairs. Chairs, in particular, soil easily, so purchase ones that will hold up under frequent washing and do not require repainting; ones with plastic backs and seats are good choices.	Scratched and marred surfaces can be recovered with plastic similar to Formica, but which can be cut with scissors and glued with a special adhesive.
Check all furniture regularly to make certain that nuts and bolts are tight.	Buy good quality, substantial items or have them made; it saves money in the long run.
Wax all wood and plastic furniture with paste wax before using initially and after washing. This cuts work and saves surfaces. (Children like to help polish the result.)	Haunt thrift shops and rummage sales for low dressers, shelves, old tables, and so forth. Tables are easy to shorten—all it takes is a saw, muscles, and careful measurement. It makes money go further.
Floors	
Use linoleum as the basic surface (carpeting is impossible to keep clean in eating or art areas), but provide carpeted spaces where possible. (Keep carpets away from outdoor entries.)	Carpeting adds warmth, comfort, noise control, and "softness" to the room; tightly woven ones are best for easy vacuuming. Small area rugs that can be shaken out and moved easily are nice if they don't wrinkle too much; use nonskid mats underneath.
An old-fashioned carpet sweeper is very handy for quick rug cleanup.	
String mops are more effective than sponge mops to use after water play.	
A drain in the bathroom floor facilitates frequent cleaning and disinfecting; it makes indoor water play more welcome.	
Files (picture, poetry, flannel boards, songs)	
Mount them on stiff cardboard or mat board. (Rubber cement is most satisfactory adhesive.) Spray with clear, flat, acrylic spray. File under topic headings for easy identification.	These files are invaluable educational resources and cost relatively little.

TABLE 4–1 *(continued)*

Preservation and maintenance	Additional comments
Books	
Purchase durable, "library grade" bindings to start with or cover with clear contact paper.	It adds variety to put some books away for use another day.
Repair books promptly with mending tape.	Keeping books sorted according to some simple classification system makes finding that "special" book easier.
Teach children to handle books with loving care.	
Unit blocks	
Wax with paste wax before use.	Stack on shelves according to kind; never dump in bins.
It is occasionally necessary to wash really dirty blocks. Do *not* soak. Dry immediately to avoid roughening and raising grain.	Use on flat, "tight" carpeting: it deadens noise, is warmer for children to sit on, and protects corners of the blocks.
	Can use homemade, soft wood blocks as money stretchers. They don't wear well but will do in a pinch—so will sealed and stapled milk cartons if money is really tight. Be sure you provide a lot of them.
Tabletop activity materials	
Mend broken corners of storage boxes immediately.	Storage in see-through plastic boxes is ideal.
Have a special, centrally located little pot or box, and drop stray bits and pieces into it for weekly sorting; include nuts and bolts, Tinker Toys, puzzle knobs, and so forth.	Presenting some items, such as colored bears, pegs, and cubical counting blocks, in a shallow basket makes them readily visible and appealing.
Label puzzle pieces with individual symbols on back for rapid sorting and reassembly.	When cardboard boxes are used for storage, draw a picture on the side or top so children can "read" what's inside.
Teach children to keep small, many-pieced items on the table; don't permit these to scatter. Using carpet squares, one per child, helps keep an activity focused in one place.	
Count pieces of some items before setting out, mark quantities on box, and recount before putting away (for example, doctor's kit and simple games).	
Protect teacher-made activities with acrylic spray or clear contact paper.	
Inspect all items regularly for cleanliness, and wash when necessary.	
Tools (cooking, woodworking, gardening)	
Keep tools out of the weather and keep them oiled and painted when necessary.	Purchase sturdy equipment that really works.
Teach children to use them for their intended purpose; don't discourage experimentation but don't permit destructive abuse.	Store tools of all kinds with care; don't just dump in a box.

TABLE 4-1 (*continued*)

Preservation and maintenance	Additional comments
Self-expressive materials	
Present messy activities away from carpeted areas.	Stack large sheets of paper on a series of narrow shelves rather than on one deep one for easy access; paper is heavy to lift.
Store cleanup materials used together in the same place; for example, keep sponges, detergent, and scrub brushes assembled in the fingerpainting bucket.	Store construction paper in closed cabinets to reduce fading.
	Sort donated materials as they arrive.
Wash glue and paint brushes thoroughly, every time; store on end, wood tips down.	Buy art materials in quantity whenever possible (test quality first: tempera paint varies a good deal, as does paper).
	Consider forming a purchasing co-op with other schools; bargain for discounts.
Wheel toys	
Always store under cover.	In the long run it pays to buy the expensive preschool-grade quality of this equipment; check warranties.
When possible, buy toys that do not require painting.	
Check nuts and bolts frequently; oil occasionally.	
Outdoor equipment (swings and slides)	
Avoid buying painted equipment; if you have it, sand, prime, and paint it regularly.	Inspect rigorously for safety.
Repair instantly, for safety's sake and to discourage further abuse.	Purchase removable, fiber swing seats with extra hooks.
Wooden jungle gyms placed on grass or dirt rot quickly.	If affordable, rubber matting under such equipment is wonderful.
Hollow blocks, boards, sawhorses, boxes, and so on	
These should be lacquered with a product such as Deft every year.	Some brands of large plastic blocks are reported to bow in or out or to be too slippery to be satisfactory for climbing on and for stacking.
Use only on grass or carpet to prevent splintering (indoor-outdoor carpeting or artificial turf can be used for this purpose when the entire play area is paved).	Store molded plastic items in a warm place and wooden equipment in a dry place.
Animal cages	
Bottoms should be made of mesh to be self-cleaning. No animal should have to live in squalor.	Outdoor cages require shade, wind protection, and ventilation.
	Protect from vandals by keeping cages carefully mended and using quality padlocks.

MATERIALS

Recommendations for the actual presentation of various materials to children are included throughout this book, so here in closing we will content ourselves with the remarks by Harms (1972) on the importance of how materials are maintained and displayed:

> Everything present in the environment, even the spatial arrangement, communicates to the child how to live in that setting. Materials that are in good condition and placed on open shelves tell a child that the materials are valued, that they are meant to be considered, and that a child may take them off the shelf by himself. When they are taken off the shelf, they leave a big empty space so it is easy to put them back where they belong. What kind of message does a child get from open shelves crowded with an odd assortment of materials, few with all the pieces put together? What kind of message does he get from a closed cupboard? (p. 59)

When materials are plentiful, whether they be collage supplies or blocks, this tells children they need not pinch and scramble for their share, thus allowing them to be more generous. When materials are changed regularly, this tells them that school is a varied and challenging place. When they are complete and well cared for, this teaches them to take care also. When they are in good taste or, better yet, beautiful, this helps form children's taste for things of beauty and quality. When materials are multiethnic and nonsexist, this reminds them repeatedly of the fundamental equality and worth of every human being.

SUMMARY

Everything related to the careful arrangement of the physical setting contributes in substantial ways to the overall effect, the *ambiance,* of the school. But, like the child herself, ambiance is more than the sum of its parts. Ambiance is composed of many things; it includes the intangible glow the staff radiates in the morning; the feeling that there is time for everyone; the splash of color on the walls; the rocking chair in the corner; and the blooming plant on the windowsill. These all contribute to the sense of caring, personal concern, and beauty that careful planning and sound room arrangement convey.

SELF-CHECK QUESTIONS FOR REVIEW

Content-Related Questions

1. The author recommends two "yardstick questions" to use when evaluating the environment. What are those questions? Why are they worthwhile ones to ask?
2. List some points that should be considered when arranging equipment in a classroom, and give practical examples of how equipment could be arranged to take these factors into consideration. For example, suggest a variety of purposes a bookcase might fullfill in addition to holding books.
3. What are some ways a teacher could add touches of beauty to her room?
4. Suppose you have a child from Nicaragua in your room. Suggest some items you might include that would help him feel culturally at home.
5. Think of the room where you are teaching and of the equipment included there. Using the suggestions in Table 4–1, suggest some practical ways to preserve and maintain that equipment.
6. Give some practical examples drawn from the research study that illustrate how rearranging a room can affect the children's behavior.

Integrative Questions

1. Select a piece of outdoor play equipment and explain how it could be used as a simple, complex, or super play unit.
2. The text emphasizes that the environment should reflect the teacher's underlying philosophy. Give four examples of the way *you* would set up an early childhood room so that it would reflect *your* philosophy.

QUESTIONS AND ACTIVITIES

1. You are now the teacher and you have six Vietnamese children as part of your preschool

group. In terms of creating the physical environment, what multiethnic touches would you add from their culture to help them feel at home?

2. Halloween is coming soon, and you want to give your room a festive air in honor of that season. What would you do to make this a truly *participatory* environment for the children?

3. Draw a floor plan of your ideal preschool room, suitable for 15 children. Show how you would arrange the major elements to foster positive social interaction between the children.

4. What is the best storage idea you have observed in a child-care center? Share it with the class.

5. Estimate what you think the costs of the following items of equipment are likely to be and then look up the actual costs in an equipment catalog: (a) a large set of hollow blocks, (b) an aluminum tricycle, (c) a set of rubber wild animals for the block corner, (d) a dozen building boards approximately 10 inches × 60 inches each, and (e) a starter set of hardwood blocks.

REFERENCES FOR FURTHER READING

Discussions about Planning the Overall Environment

Baird, J. C., & Lutkus, A. D. (Eds.). (1982). *Mind child architecture*. Hanover, N. H.: University Press of New England. Books that specialize in the topic of appropriate environmental designs for young children are rare indeed. This one is the result of a conference involving psychologists and architects. Interesting reading.

Frost, J. L., & Sunderlin, S. (Eds.). (1985). *When children play: Proceedings of the International Conference on Play and Play Environments*. Wheaton, Md.: Association for Childhood Education International. This publication is a particularly rich resource for those interested in the design of outdoor play spaces. Highly recommended.

Greenman, J. (1988). *Caring spaces, learning places: Children's environments that work*. Redmond, Wash.: The Exchange Press. Greenman offers an original and refreshing book that should not be missed by anyone interested in the care of young children. Highly recommended.

Johnson, J. E., Christie, J. C., & Yawkey, T. D. (1987). *Play and early childhood development*. Glenview, Ill.: Scott, Foresman and Co. Chapter 10, "Physical Environment and Play," presents a valuable discussion of space arrangements that is extensively documented by research.

Jones, E. (1977). *Dimensions of teaching-learning environments; handbook for teachers*. (Available from Pacific Oaks College, 714 W. California Blvd., Pasadena, California 91105). This publication presents a useful way of looking at the overall environments of the school, both indoors and out.

Noyes, D. (1987). Indoor pollutants: Environmental hazards to young children. *Young Children, 42*(6), 65–75. Noyes reminds us of how important it is to police our indoor environments for dangerous substances and also provides lists of valuable resources for pursuing the subject further. Highly recommended.

Prescott, E. (1984). The physical setting in day care. In J. T. Greenman & R. W. Fuqua (Eds.), *Making day care better: Training, evaluation, and the process of change*. New York: Teachers College Press. Prescott presents a sound philosophical overview of essentials that must be considered when planning an environment for children.

Weinstein, C., & David, T. (1987). *Space for children: The built environment and children's development*. New York: Plenum Press. This is an extraordinarily useful book that covers topics ranging from the physical environment in child-care centers to playgrounds for able and disabled children. Children's participation in planning is also discussed. Highly recommended.

Evaluation of Preschool Settings

Harms, T., & Clifford, R. M. (1980). *Early childhood environment rating scale*. New York: Teachers College Press. Ever wonder how the environment you teach in might measure up in terms of how effectively it is meeting the needs of children and adults? The Harms/Clifford Scales are simple to use and cover seven areas, ranging from personal care routines of children and creative activities to how well the needs of the adults are met.

National Association for the Education of Young Children. (1984). *Accreditation criteria and procedures of the National Academy of Early Childhood Programs*. Washington, D.C.: The Association. This is another very useful set of criteria for measuring many aspects of quality programs, including the physical environment.

Equipment

Moyer, J. (Ed.). (1986). *Selecting educational equipment and materials*. Wheaton, Md.: Association for Childhood Education International. No teacher should be without this gem of a reference which includes equipment lists that set priorities for purchases according to essential first-year ones, second- and third-year additions, and luxury items. Information extends from infant centers through upper elementary school. An indispensable resource.

Money Stretchers

Miller, J. B., & Miller, K. M. (1979). Informed purchasing can stretch short dollars. *Young Children, 34*(6), 15–20. A rare and valuable article for nonbusiness-oriented teachers on how to specify standards, ask for bids, and find sources for equipment.

Moore, N. R. (Ed.). (1983). *Free and inexpensive learning materials* (21st ed.). Nashville: George Peabody College for Teachers. (Distributed by Incentive Publications, Incorporated.) The title is self-descriptive.

For the Advanced Student

Lindberg, L. (no date). *Facility design for early childhood programs: An NAEYC resource guide.* Washington, D.C.: National Association for the Education of Young Children. This guide is useful because it gathers together in one place a list of resources on a subject where information can be difficult to locate.

Phyfe-Perkins, E., & Shoemaker, J. (1986). Indoor play environments: Research and design implication. In G. Fein & M. Rivkin (Eds.), *The young child at play: Reviews of research* (Vol. 4). Washington, D.C.: National Association for the Education of Young Children. The authors first present an extensive review of relevant research and then base their implications for design on that review.

Smith, P. K., & Connolly, K. J. (1980). *The ecology of preschool behavior.* Cambridge, England: Cambridge University Press. This is an account of a research project that sought to determine the actual relationship between such things as the number of children in the group, the physical environment, and staff ratio. Interesting reading for an advanced student.

5

Planning with Individual Children in Mind

Using Educational Objectives in the Preschool

Have you ever

- Heard someone mention behavioral objectives and wondered what they were?
- Felt like you knew in a general way what was important for little children to learn but had trouble translating general goals into specific curriculum?
- Wanted to make a plan to help a particular child behave better?

If you have, the material in this chapter will help you.

Once upon a time the animals had a school. The curriculum consisted of running, climbing, flying, and swimming, and all the animals took part in all the subjects.

The Duck was good in swimming, better, in fact, than his instructor, and he made passing grades in flying, but he was practically hopeless in running. Because he was low in this subject, he was made to stay after school and drop his swimming class in order to practice running. He kept this up until he was only average in swimming. But average is acceptable, so nobody worried about that except the Duck.

The Eagle was considered a problem pupil and was disciplined severely. He beat all the others to the top of the tree in climbing class, but he used his own way of getting there.

The Rabbit started out at the top of the class in running, but he had a nervous breakdown and had to drop out of school on account of so much makeup work in swimming.

The Squirrel led the climbing class, but his flying teacher made him start his flying lessons from the ground instead of the top of the tree down, and he developed charley horses from overexertion at the takeoff and began getting C's in climbing and D's in running.

The practical Prairie Dogs apprenticed their offspring to a Badger when the school authorities refused to add digging to the curriculum.

At the end of the year, the abnormal Eel that could swim well, run, climb, and fly a little was made valedictorian.

ANONYMOUS

N ow that we have looked at the overall schedule and environment in terms of the entire group of children, it is time to think about individual children and their needs. Many preschool teachers store an informal list of such needs and the ways they intend to meet these in their heads. Some examples might include:

- Next time I'll turn over the rocking boat, creating an arch of stairs, to give Cecile [who is 2 years old] practice in alternating her feet as she climbs up them.
- I think I'll serve soba [Japanese noodles] for snack to help Fumie feel more at home with us.

These teachers believe that such mental notes are sufficient and that they allow them to be flexible and adjust quickly to children's needs as they change from week to week.

For some teachers, however, such casual lists of what they intend to do about a problem do not suffice. They make a good case for the value of pinpointing what individual children need to learn. They maintain that, once these needs are clearly stated, it is much easier to make individualized curriculum plans that will help particular children acquire specific skills and become more competent. For example, a teacher who prefers this more definite approach might add the following objective to a little boy's record: "When Miles builds in the block area, he will do it with another child twice a week." Then she might include a few notes or a plan for helping Miles play with others in this area.

1. Suggest that another child carry some blocks over to help him build.
2. Get out the large boards that require two children to lift them together.
3. Add the small cars to block play—these seem to encourage interaction between the children.

When children's learning needs are stated in this specific way, they are called *educational* or *behavioral objectives*.

PROS AND CONS OF USING BEHAVIORAL OBJECTIVES

In the late 1960s and 1970s the pros and cons of using such objectives were hotly debated by educators. Some believed that using them stifled and narrowed educational programs. They cited cases in which writing objectives required much of the teacher's time and then they were never looked at again. They disapproved of objectives because they believed that they encouraged a cut-and-dried approach to teaching based mainly on the principles of behavior modification. Others argued that some of the more valuable kinds of social and emotional learning could not be specific in behavioral terms. Another criticism was that often such objectives were written to specify behavior that had the sole virtue of being readily observed but that was of little importance otherwise (Combs, 1972; Ebel, 1970; Eisner, 1969).

There is no denying that objectives can be miswritten or misused (Eisner, 1985). However, when objectives are properly employed, they can help teachers think seriously about which goals have the greatest value. They also enable teachers to clearly define how they will be able to tell when the child has reached these goals. The clearsightedness that results is a welcome antidote to the high-minded pronouncements that abound in education and that give the reader a pleasant glow but do not actually mean much when given careful attention.

Consider the following excerpt from a center brochure: "Our little school, nestled amid the rustic pines and hills of _____ has as its goal the development of the whole child—we want him to be mentally healthy, physically able, authentically creative, and socially sensitive." There is nothing wrong with this statement as a long-range, general foundation for an educational program. But many teachers never bother to ask themselves seriously what practical steps they will take to translate such lofty goals into the daily reality of the children's lives. Behavioral objectives can help teachers bridge this gap between broad purposes and actuality.

DEFINITION OF BEHAVIORAL OBJECTIVES

Behavioral objectives are not as appalling as they may sound. An objective is simply a clear statement that identifies a behavior the teacher deems important. It usually consists of one or two sentences describing how the child will behave when he has reached the desired goal. The outstanding characteristic of behavioral objectives is that *they must be based on behavior that the teacher can actually see.*

Objectives can and should cover many areas of learning rather than just the cognitive domain. Thus, a teacher who believes that originality of ideas is important might write this objective: "When presented with a problem that requires a solution, Claire will think of and try out a variety of ways to solve it until she has found an effective solution. For example, when unable to get into a swing that is too high, she will think of and try out several ways to reach the seat until she achieves success." Another teacher who believes that physical development is valuable might compose this objective: "Given one or two trials, Jackie will be able to catch a large ball thrown to him from a distance of 5 feet."

The worst pitfall for beginning teachers is a tendency to select insignificant behaviors to document (Tyler, 1973). This is probably because certain behaviors, such as finger snapping or color naming, are easy to observe and count. Fortunately, it is equally possible to write behavioral objectives for the affective or cognitive domain that identify richer, more significant behaviors (Lee & Merrill, 1972), as illustrated by many examples used throughout this chapter.

Moreover, it is not necessary to write objectives in a stiffly classical form in order for them to be explicit and useful. Although that approach is included in this book because it is still required by many school systems, this chapter also illustrates how to write objectives that say the same thing in a less stilted, more palatable-to-teachers manner.

STEPS IN WRITING BEHAVIORAL OBJECTIVES

There are four steps to writing an objective. The first step is to identify the desired, broad goal. The next step is to translate this goal into several behaviors that reflect the accomplishment of the goal and to write specific objectives for the most significant of these behaviors. The third step is to add the conditions and performance levels of the objectives, that is, where, when, and how often the child must exhibit the behavior for the teacher to decide he has attained the objective. The final step, which may or may not be included because it is not really a part of the objective, is a list of possible activities that the teacher could use to help the youngster reach the objective.

Step One: Select the Broad Goal

Selecting a broad goal is the most logical starting point because this requires teachers to think carefully about what they really want children to learn. If they consider the area of mental health important, then they must identify a series of broad goals that contribute to mental health. Identifying these goals also helps ensure that they cover every area of curriculum it is valuable to include.

One approach that helps ensure thorough coverage is to use outlines of educational goals. These outlines are often called *taxonomies* (several are listed in the references at the end of this chapter). It is not necessary to use taxonomies devised by other people, however; the staffs of many centers feel they are quite capable of developing their own outlines of goals. Working together to write such outlines has the advantage of tailoring the goals to the specific philosophy of the school and to the particular needs of the children's families as well.

Some examples of broad goals that might be selected by full- or half-day children's centers include the following:

Physical Development

1. The child will be able to demonstrate or acquire physical skills appropriate to his age.
2. He will develop a sense of himself as being physically competent both in relation to his personal aspirations and in comparison with his peers.

Emotional Stability and Mental Health

1. The child will remain in touch with the full range of feelings, including positive and negative ones, within himself and will be encouraged to recognize and acknowledge their presence and express them in appropriate ways.
2. As he matures, the child will begin to achieve empathy and insight into the feelings and concerns of other children and members of the staff.
3. The child will build a sense of self-esteem basic to mental health by acquiring those skills and competencies he sees as valuable.
4. The child will develop a sense of identity by learning who he is in relation to the space around him, in relation to other members of his family and their cultural background, and in relation to the children and staff in the school.

Creative Self-Expression

1. The child will express his own ideas and feelings through the use of self-expressive materials and play.
2. He will learn to produce alternative solutions to problems when this is necessary.

Social Competence

1. The child will gain the ability to care about the rights and needs of other people. (This is related also to the mental health goal of having empathy for the feelings and needs of others.)
2. He will develop the ability to tolerate separation from his parents.
3. He will develop the ability to share staff attention with other children part of the time.
4. He will develop the ability to feel pleasure in working for the good of the group.
5. He will develop the ability to play with other children by accepting leadership from others on occasion and also by contributing his own ideas when desirable.

Language and Cognitive Development

1. The child will be able to express himself verbally by increasing his vocabulary and by gradually extending the length and complexity of his syntax.
2. He will increase his communication skills by learning to listen to other people and grasp what they mean.
3. The child will develop his intellectual ability by performing a variety of tasks that provide practice in particular mental abilities relevant to later success in school. These abilities include:
   a. The ability to group and classify items
   b. The ability to arrange items in logical order and tell what comes next (using both spatial and temporal sequences)
   c. The ability to formulate common associations
   d. The ability to identify objects that are identical and match these together
   e. The ability also to identify items that are different and label them as such
   f. The ability to grasp elementary principles of cause and effect
   g. The ability to transfer learning to facilitate the solving of problems

Step Two: Compose an Objective That Describes the Desired Behavior

After identifying the broad goals, the next step is formulating the objectives. This involves deciding what behaviors can be used to indicate that the child has reached the goal. For example, in the first goal from the area of social competence

("The child will gain the ability to care about the rights and needs of other people"), it is necessary to think of several more specific situations that would require the child to consider the rights and needs of other people. One such occasion might be lunchtime when everyone is entitled to a fair share of food. Other possibilities include respecting the privacy of other children's cubbies, being quiet at nap time so that all may sleep, not breaking other children's toys, or refraining from constantly demanding to be the center of attention. Suppose that sharing food at lunchtime has been picked as one of the situations to use when assessing whether the goal of caring about the rights of others is being attained.

Write the Objective. After considerable trial and error, an objective to fit lunchtime is developed: "When given a bowl of a favorite food, Terry will show he cares about the rights of others by serving himself a portion and leaving enough for the other children, too." There are two special points to note about this objective. The first is that the teacher used *action* verbs to describe the way Terry will behave when he has accomplished the goal; that is, instead of the objective being written as, "Terry will *think* of others and *be aware* that everyone is hungry at lunchtime," it is written as, "Terry will *show* he cares . . . by serving himself . . . and leaving enough food. . . ." Good verbs to use when writing objectives include *identify, name, describe, show, tell about, construct, arrange in order, show what comes next,* and *demonstrate.* These are far superior to verbs like *think, be aware, understand,* or *appreciate* because such action verbs describe behavior that can actually be seen; they make it unnecessary to guess at what is happening.

The second point to note about this objective is that it does not explain how the child will learn to take some and leave some. Since teachers are likely to be teachers before they become objective writers, they often fall into the trap of trying to explain how the goal will be reached. Such teachers might formulate the

Sometimes it requires direct intervention by the teacher to help children learn to "take some and leave some."

following objective: "The child will learn to share food at lunchtime by having to wait until last when he grabs out of turn." Aside from whether this describes a sound teaching technique, it explains how the teacher intends to reach the goal of teaching social concern. This is incorrect. *An objective should state only the desired outcome, not the means by which it is to be attained.* It specifies only how the child will behave once he has reached the objective.

Here is an objective written by a hard-pressed preschool aide with a particular little boy in mind: "At snack time Henry will wait until the basket of fruit is passed to him. He is not to grab or yell, 'Give me!' If he can usually wait until the basket has been passed to two other children before him, the goal is accomplished." Note how specific her goal is. Note also that the objective does not describe how to teach him "not to grab or yell, 'Give me!' " Note particularly the last sentence of this objective because it is an example of the final items that must be included to make an objective complete.

Step Three: State the Conditions and Performance Level of the Objective

Once the desired behavior is identified, two more items must be added to make the objective complete: the conditions and levels of performance the child is expected to reach to accomplish the objective. In Henry's case the condition is that he can "wait until the basket has been passed to two other children before him," and the level, or frequency, of performance is "usually."

This portion of the objective, which stipulates when and how frequently a child must display the behavior, can be one of the most significant parts of writing objectives, since such statements of expectations force teachers to examine underlying values, as well as standards of performance. Consider an objective that states, "The child will provide evidence that she likes to eat by eating everything on her plate at each meal." Another example, written for a group of 3-year-olds, might be, "The children will sit quietly during story time. They will never interrupt the reader or talk to their neighbor while the story is being read." But are "eating everything on her plate" and "sitting quietly during story time" truly desirable educational goals? Are there more desirable ones that could be selected in place of these? What are the most fundamental values that should be stressed and turned into goals?

Consider the level of expectation in the examples above. No one can be expected to be 100% perfect. It is unreasonable to demand that a youngster always clear her plate or that a group of 3-year-olds always sit quietly during story hour. Unless these objectives are modified, they imply an expectation of perfection. For the behavioral objective to be successful (and to enhance the self-esteem of the children), it is necessary to take the children's developmental level into account and to set a reasonable standard of performance for them.

Step Four: Create a List of Activities to Help the Child Reach the Objective

After teachers have formulated an objective for a youngster, they often go on to develop a plan for reaching it. When such a plan of action is desired, it should be included as a separate fourth step. Remember, it is not technically a part of the objective per se.

For the objective we have been discussing ("When given a bowl of a favorite food, Terry will show he cares about the rights of others by serving himself a portion and leaving enough for the other children"), a plan might include the following:

1. I will check the kitchen and make sure the amount of food supplied will be plentiful.
2. I will delegate Terry as the one to return to the kitchen for seconds to show him there is plenty.
3. When food is passed, I will remind him to take some and leave some, showing him what I mean if this is necessary.
4. I will make sure he has a second helping when he wants one.

5. I will praise Terry when he does help himself and remembers to leave enough for the other children.

CREATING INFORMAL OBJECTIVES

Writing objectives in the manner described above often seems so unnatural to teachers that they become hostile to the whole idea of writing them. As mentioned previously, this is unfortunate because objectives can serve a useful function by clarifying exactly what the teacher wants the child to learn. One solution to this problem is to write informal objectives instead. It often works well to begin objectives with the words "I want" followed by what you want the child to learn.

For example, a formal objective might be phrased, "While playing in the sandbox Lotus will add her own ideas to our play activities two times each day." When this same objective is translated into an informal objective, it might be phrased, "I want Lotus to be more confident and tell us her ideas a couple of times a day when the children play together in the sandbox."

The joy of this more informal approach is that it lends itself to a final step that feels natural, too. It is the addition of an objective for the teacher that clarifies her plan (objective) for her own behavior; that is, what she intends to do to turn the plan into reality. In this case it could be, "I'll watch for a problem-solving situation—Lotus is so smart—and ask her what she'd do about it. Maybe the children will need to carry water, or something like that, and they'll need a way to transport it. I think if I asked her directly she wouldn't be too shy to tell me what she thinks."

Note that the less formal way of writing the objective still focuses on what the child will actually be doing when she has reached the objective, it says how frequently the behavior is expected to take place, and it tells the circumstances in which the behavior will occur. The informal objective also keeps the plan of action separated from the child objective by including it in the teacher's objective instead.

Following are a few more examples illustrating the two forms of objective writing.

Formal Objective: Maggie will participate in an interpersonal activity with at least two other people this week.

Informal Objective: I want Maggie to play with a couple of other children sometime during the week.

Teacher Objective: I'll invite Maggie, Mike, and Lisa to tell me what we need to play "going camping." I'll see if I can generate some togetherness that way.

Formal Objective: Jonelle will try out the medium slide this month.

Informal Objective: I want Jonelle to overcome her fear of the medium slide and be willing to use it when we go outdoors, hopefully by the end of this month.

Teacher Objective: I must think of some way to help Jonelle understand that going down slides is fun and that she doesn't need to be scared. I guess I'll start with sliding the dolls down the little slide. I'll also offer to slide down with Jonelle on my lap. I have to remember to take it easy and not push her too hard.

Formal Objective: Brad will ask for a toy when he wants it at least once today.

Informal Objective: I want Brad to learn to ask instead of grabbing everything he wants at least once a day.

Teacher Objective: I will stay with Brad when he plays in the block area. When the chance comes up and I can see that he wants a block another child has, I'll coach him how to get it instead of just grabbing it and point out how much more friendly the other child acts when he behaves that way.

CARRYING THE OBJECTIVES THROUGH: A FINAL COMMENT

It is all very good to make out a list of goals and objectives for the group as a whole or for individual children, but these will have little effect on the actual program unless they are reviewed from time to time to make certain that the curriculum is focusing on these goals and objectives. If the review indicates that the

Sometimes teachers who have the kindest of intentions push too hard.

objectives and activities do not match what is actually happening in the school, then they should be rewritten in terms of the actual program or the program should be modified to reflect the desired goals.

SUMMARY

The use of behavioral goals and objectives in curriculum planning can be a helpful strategy. If properly developed, they can help teachers examine their value systems, select goals they feel are significant, and translate lofty ideas into practical behavioral expectations for the children in their groups.

A well-written objective confines itself to specifying behavior that can be readily observed and to stating the frequency and conditions under which the behavior is expected to take place. Although many school districts prefer teachers to use more formal objectives, they may also be written according to a less formal style and phrased in terms of what the teacher wants the child to accomplish. When these are accompanied by objectives for the teacher, the resulting changes in behavior can be very rewarding.

However, it is not sufficient only to write objectives. Checks must be made during the year to find out whether the objectives are being implemented in the actual curriculum, and evaluations of children's behavior should be carried out to determine whether the teaching has been effective.

SELF-CHECK QUESTIONS FOR REVIEW

Content-Related Questions

1. List some pros and cons about writing behavioral objectives.
2. Explain the difference between a goal and an objective, and give an example of a goal. Then show how you might change that goal into an objective.
3. There are two special points to remember when writing an objective. One is that it is important to use action verbs. List some action verbs. Also list some that should be avoided because they are not verbs that describe behavior that can be seen.
4. What is the second important point to remember when writing an objective?
5. In this text, what do the terms *conditions* and *performance level* mean?
6. Write a formal objective. Then demonstrate how it could be turned into an informal objective. Next, write an objective for the teacher to accompany the informal objective.

Integrative Questions

1. Read over the parable at the beginning of the chapter. What is the meaning or moral of this tale?
2. Write a goal and objective for some aspect of social behavior. Compare them and explain what they have in common. Also explain how they differ from each other.

QUESTIONS AND ACTIVITIES

1. What educational values do you think would be most likely to be overlooked when writing a set of behavioral objectives for a young child?
2. What might be some important educational values that are so intangible that you feel it might not be feasible to write objectives that could cover them?
3. Identify and explain the differences between the broad goals listed in the first part of the chapter and the behavioral objectives discussed later.
4. Select one of the broad goals and practice identifying specific activities that would represent the goal in action; then write objectives based on the satisfactory performance of these activities.
5. One of the most effective ways to learn to write good objectives is to use negative practice; therefore, write the very worst objective you can think of. Be sure to make it an objective that is difficult to observe and that represents a value you feel would be inconsequential. Share these morsels with the class.
6. Which of the two forms of writing objectives do you prefer? Explain why this is the case. What might be the advantage of using the unpreferred form?

REFERENCES FOR FURTHER READING

Taxonomies

Beaty, J. J. (1988). *Skills for preschool teachers* (3rd ed.). Columbus, Ohio: Merrill Publishing Co. This text lists specific objectives for teachers for many areas of curriculum.

Beaty, J. J. (1989). *Observing development of the young child* (2nd ed.). Columbus, Ohio: Merrill Publishing Co. Beaty begins each chapter with a list of skills children should acquire. These skills could be readily translated into objectives. She then suggests many activities that might be provided for practice in skill acquisition.

Hoepfner, R., Stern, C., & Nummedal, S. G. (1971). *CSE-ERIC preschool/kindergarten test evaluations.* Los Angeles: School Evaluation Project, Center for the Study of Evaluation and the Early Childhood Research Center, University of California at Los Angeles. This applicable and useful taxonomy was developed following consultation with teachers, supervisors, and early childhood specialists. The goals identified by these sources were then translated into operational definitions. The outline covers the affective, intellectual, psychomotor, and subject achievement domains. Worth pursuing at the library.

The Case Against Behavioral Objectives

Combs, A. W. (1972). *Educational accountability: Beyond behavioral objectives.* Washington, D.C.: Association for Supervision and Curriculum Development. For a strong statement of the case against behavioristic psychology and behavioral objectives, the student should read this excellent pamphlet.

Writing Effective Objectives

Hatoff, S. H., Byram, C. A., & Hyson, M. C. (1981). *Teacher's practical guide for educating young children: A growing program.* Boston, Mass. Allyn & Bacon. The chapter in this book entitled "Directions for Growth: Goals, Objectives, and Plans" explains how to suit objectives to individual children.

Mager, R. F. (1984). *Preparing instructional objectives* (2nd ed.) Belmont, Calif.: Pitman Learning. Dr. Mager's short book explains in a clear and amusing way how to write instructional objectives.

Popovich, D. (1981). *Effective educational and behavioral programming for severely and profoundly handicapped students; A manual for teachers and aides.* Baltimore, Md.: Paul H. Brookes Publishing Co. Chapter 1 presents a crystal-clear discussion of how to write behavioral objectives.

Seefeldt, C., & Barbour, N. (1990). *Early childhood education: An introduction* (2nd ed.). Columbus, Ohio: Merrill Publishing Co. In their chapter on planning, Seefeldt and Barbour include numerous examples of goals translated into objectives. This book is helpful for students who need more practice in distinguishing between goals.

For the Advanced Student

Bloom, B. S., Engelhart, M.D., Furst, E. J., Hill, W. H., & Krathwohl, D. R. (1956). *Taxonomy of educational objectives; Handbook I. The cognitive domain.* New York: David McKay Co.

Krathwohl, D. R., Bloom, B. S., & Masia, B. B. (1964). *Taxonomy of educational objectives: Handbook II. The affective domain.* New York: David McKay Co. The Bloom and Krathwohl taxonomies are listed here because they are frequently referred to in the literature on behavioral objectives. However, these particular taxonomies do not specify overt behavior outcomes, and it may be difficult to translate the sophisticated skills listed in them into behavior that is characteristic of preschool children.

Tyler, R. W. (1950). *Basic principles of curriculum and instruction.* Chicago, Ill.: University of Chicago Press. Tyler's work is a famous exemplar of the behavioral objectives movement.

6

Practical Methods of Recording and Evaluating Behavior

Have you ever

- Had a parent ask you how her child was getting along and been unable to say anything concrete or specific in reply?
- Read an advertisement for a new preschool test and wondered how to tell if it was any good or not?
- Been asked to prove that the children in your group were really learning?

If you have, the material in this chapter will help you.

Observe, interview, interact, take notes and write goals for learning. Use your own collected information as the true picture of the child's performance. Measure specific behaviors when necessary to diagnose entering ability or when transitions to more complex material require it. And above all, reduce both your and the child's anxiety level by keeping the extent of "testing" to an absolute minimum. Finally, guard against what Goodlad calls "CMD" (chronic measurement disease): preoccupation with pulling up plants to look at them before the roots take hold. Remember, learning will develop its roots if the conditions provided for learning and the kinds of learning supported are as important as what is being taught.

JOHN R. CRYAN (1986)[1]

The subject of evaluation and measurement of the abilities of children as young as 2, 3, and 4 years of age is usually passed over in texts on early childhood education. Perhaps this is because evaluation has been regarded as beyond the ken of beginning teachers, or perhaps it is because evaluation procedures have not been used extensively by children's centers in the past.

However, current educational practice makes it imperative that all preschool teachers have at least an understanding of basic principles of evaluation and how to keep adequate developmental records. For one thing, more states are now requiring children to take screening tests before admission to kindergarten (NAEYC, 1988), so early childhood teachers need to know what these entail in order to discuss the subject with parents.

It is also vital for teachers to make certain that whatever evaluation measures are used with their children are closely related to what is being taught in the school. The disastrous results from the early days of Head Start when tests that were not related to the curriculum were used to measure the program's effectiveness remind us just how significant such matters can be. Head Start was almost scuttled as a result of those early, incorrectly selected tests (Cicerelli, Evans, & Schiller, 1969; Smith & Bissell, 1970). Finally, there is a growing trend toward requiring schools, even schools for very young children, to be accountable. More and more frequently schools are expected to furnish proof that what they are doing with children makes a difference to the children's learning and behavior.

For all these reasons, as well as for other educational ones considered later in this chapter, it behooves teachers to understand methods for measuring and evaluating the behavior of young children.

PURPOSES AND ADVANTAGES OF USING EVALUATION PROCEDURES

Basic Purposes

Evaluation serves two basic purposes. First, it can be used to describe the current behavior of a child and what she knows, and if the evaluation is repeated, it can show ways the child has changed over a period of time. Second, when data on a number of children are combined, the results give a picture of the current status of the group, as well as identify changes that have occurred since the previous evaluation.

---

[1]Cryan, J. (1986). Evaluation: Plague or promise? *Childhood Education, 62* (5), 350. Reprinted by permission of the Association for Childhood Education International, 11141 Georgia Ave., Suite 200, Wheaton, Md. Copyright 1986 by the Association.

The reader should not picture this process as requiring the services of a psychologist who comes in and administers a series of commercially developed tests. Although such formal measures have a definite place in sophisticated research programs or when working with children who appear to have special problems, useful information can also be obtained by means of simpler, less costly procedures that teachers can employ themselves as part of their ordinary routine. The drawback to developing such procedures is that it takes time and effort, but if the advantages of assessing children are fully understood, teachers may be better motivated to include this process in their busy schedules.

Educational Advantages

Regardless of what method teachers decide on for recording behavior, its use will result in their gaining increased knowledge and awareness of every child in their group. Simply considering the same questions for each child also helps ensure that no one has been overlooked.

Evaluation can increase the quality and specificity of the curriculum. Once the degree of the children's skills is known and their strengths and weaknesses are identified, the planning of a curriculum becomes easier and more focused. For example, the majority of the children in a Head Start group might be evaluated in September as "usually showing interest in field trips." However, the majority also might be placed in the "hardly ever" category on "able to tell a connected story." A curriculum that uses the group's strength (shows interest in field trips) to help remedy the weakness (inability to tell a connected story) could then be planned. Perhaps one such activity would be a field trip in which the teacher takes the children to visit a car wash and afterward asks them to tell what happened when the car went through the wash and she forgot to roll up the windows.

Moreover, evaluation permits specific inabilities of particular children to be noted, and plans can then be developed to work on these difficulties. For instance, a staff member at our center noted in her running observation record that one of her lively little boys had a difficult time sitting through lunch. Rather than criticizing and constantly restraining him, she resolved to ask him to be the kitchen messenger. This individualized, prescriptive activity helped him contribute to the well-being of the group, made him feel genuinely important, and gave him an opportunity to move around. This did help him eventually to become less restless and better able to settle down to his meals.

Evaluation can improve teacher morale. It is surprising how easy it is to forget in May what a child was like in September. Many center teachers have been left at the end of the year with only the hazy impression that the children have learned a good deal and a few more specific memories, such as Leroy no longer bites or Elizabeth no longer screams when her mother leaves. It was not until I participated in a research project that measured certain abilities in the fall and again in the spring that I realized how much tangible records of progress can raise teacher morale by substituting concrete evidence of progress for a handful of memories.

Evaluation aids the compilation of reports to parents. Parents are always concerned about the welfare of their young children at school and like to know how they are getting along. In addition to the daily chats that are such a valuable part of binding home and school together, occasional conferences are also helpful. There is an obvious advantage to being able to produce carefully kept records at such times. Parents really appreciate having the information, and they are also reassured when shown evidence that the teacher has cared enough to make this special effort to know about their child.

Evaluation is an invaluable resource to draw on when compiling reports to boards and funding agencies. The trend that requires preschools and children's centers to be accountable to qualify for continued public support means it is important that teachers in such schools use sound, relevant evaluation procedures to measure change and growth. The following methods may serve not only the attractive purpose of directly benefiting children in the group, but also may be used to furnish evidence that progress has taken place and that further financial support of the facility is justified.

THE PROS AND CONS OF USING SCREENING TESTS

There is a growing trend toward using screening tests to determine the time of admission to kindergarten and/or first grade (Wolf & Kessler, 1987). This trend requires discussion here because preschool teachers are often questioned by parents about this subject and because more and more frequently teachers are being asked to accept 5-year-olds into their 4-year-old groups who have scored as not being ready for kindergarten.

The value of providing extra time for children to develop has long been recognized by early childhood teachers and researchers (Gesell Institute, 1987; Wood, Powell, & Knight, 1984). This is thought to be particularly true for boys born during the second half of the year before kindergarten entry. Just about every teacher can cite examples of children who made satisfying growth during that extra year—growth that enabled them to function more effectively when they entered formal schooling a year later.

The intention of screening tests is to assist administrators in identifying those children who are "developmentally immature" and in finding children with special handicaps who need special services. There is another side to the issue, however, which warrants discussion. This is the argument that simply allowing extra time for a child to mature is not enough (Meisels, 1987). There is more to healthy development than maturation. Children, particularly those who are immature, require stimulation and the opportunity to learn. When children are "held out," there is no accurate way to tell if they might have

caught up and benefited from their year in kindergarten since they have not had the opportunity of attending. Proponents of this side of the argument maintain that it is *the school* that should change, not the child (Gold, 1987). *The school* should adjust its curriculum and teach what these youngsters need to learn rather than penalizing them by holding them out of school for a year.

This argument is not settled yet and since there is merit on both sides, it remains up to the reader to decide which faction to agree with. But whichever side is selected, there are two important points to remember. One is that if a screening test does single out a particular child as needing help, the screening test must be regarded as just the first step in the diagnostic process. Screening tests are notoriously brief and inaccurate (Meisels, 1985). Therefore, follow-up, diagnostic testing is essential before any final decisions are made. The other point to remember is that the kinds of problems reported in the Joiner research study found in this chapter are still with us today (Michigan Department of Education, 1984). It is very important to choose screening tests with great care if they are to be of any value at all.

BASIC PRINCIPLES OF EVALUATION

Before reviewing the actual methods of evaluation, the teacher needs to understand some general principles that apply to all forms of evaluation.

Observe confidentiality and professional discretion at all times. All records concerned with children and their families must be regarded as confidential. This means that they must never be left lying around for someone to pick up and read even while the teacher is working on them. The competence of individual children should never be discussed with people outside the school or with other parents who do not have a right to know about it. Above all, results of evaluations should be interpreted with caution and mercy, since it is possible that the teacher may have reached an incorrect conclusion about the child's abilities or that the test is a faulty one.

Select evaluation measures that match the educational goals of the school. Perhaps the staff has selected the development of self-esteem as one of the most important educational goals. To find out if the children are developing good self-esteem, it is vital that the teacher use either a school-developed measure or a commercial test that evaluates this specific trait. General measures of socialization, personality, or intelligence should be avoided, since they are unlikely to reveal progress in specific areas. However, if a list of behavioral objectives has already been developed to define more clearly what is meant by self-esteem, that list would be a fruitful source for developing adequate evaluation measures.

Be sure to carry out more than one evaluation. Sometimes teachers employ measures of evaluation only at the end of the year. This provides a summing up for the family and for the next teacher (who may or may not read it) but is of little value to the teacher who has done the work. It is more useful to employ evaluative measures shortly after the youngster enters the program and again later on. Early assessment helps the teacher quickly become acquainted with the child and begin to plan around the youngster's needs and interests. It also provides a pretest to be used as a comparison at the middle and end of the year. Without this measurement at the beginning, there is no way to show how much the child has learned during her time at school.

Be careful to present checklist material to each child in the same way. Sometimes it can be a temptation to change the way a checklist item is presented in accord with the personality or skills of a particular child. For instance, a teacher might unconsciously take a few steps forward to shorten the distance when throwing a ball to a younger child; or in recording balance beam walking she might allow more accomplished

children to walk on the narrow beam but use the wider side for a less able child, yet she will mark all the children as successful on the checklist. Such inconsistencies make comparison between children impossible and spoil the accuracy of the group report. Hard hearted as it may seem at first, if a specific measure of accomplishment is included, it is essential to measure all the children against the same standard. The way to adjust a checklist to include less skilled children is to provide several different task levels, ranging from easier to more difficult, for the children to attempt. In the case of the balance beam this might mean that all children are asked to try both the broad and narrower beams.

Sometimes also the teacher gradually changes her method of presenting a checklist item as she becomes more experienced using it and figures out a "better" way to do it. Doing this must also be avoided. Every item must be presented in the same manner from the first test to the last if comparisons are to be drawn between subjects or even if comparisons are to be made between early and later performances of the same child. To draw valid conclusions, the teacher must compare the same behaviors, not different ones.

Beware of the getting-better-and-better syndrome. Although it is a happy fact that many children will make progress, it is also true that some children will not, at least not in all areas. To avoid tester bias, which may view every child as getting better and better all the time, the teacher must discipline herself to observe behavior objectively so that she sees it as it *is* rather than as she wishes it to be. The development of explicit descriptions of behavior as checklist items will help the teacher be objective in her judgment. It is also helpful to have another teacher participate in the evaluation when possible.

A different kind of tester bias that must also be guarded against is the tendency of some teachers to check the same level of accomplishment for most items on a child's checklist. This is sometimes termed the *halo effect.* Again, the teacher must discipline herself to consider each item on the list on its own merits to resist the influence of the halo effect as much as possible.

METHODS OF EVALUATION IN THE PRESCHOOL

It is easy to become carried away when talking about evaluation and to advocate methods that, though excellent in many respects, are simply not practical for daily use. If the method of record keeping requires too much time and effort, it is almost certain to be dropped by the wayside as the year progresses and the teacher puts it off in favor of preparing for the parent potluck or Valentine's Day. Occasionally schools

Taking time to really listen to children can help teachers find out a lot about what they are thinking.

have access to extra help (parent cooperatives and laboratory schools are particularly fortunate in this regard) and are able to employ a more elaborate system of recording behavior, but this is not the case in most working situations. For this reason, elaborate case studies, long written observations, and even the suggestion that the teacher carry a little notebook in his pocket in which to jot down bright sayings and astonishing incidents are not advocated here as practical methods of evaluating children at the center. There is a valuable place for such activities in teacher training and for occasional studies of children who have special needs (Cryan, 1988), but I do not believe it is realistic to suggest that such lengthy methods be used as primary ways of gathering information on the majority of the children.

However, there are at least four briefer kinds of evaluation that have proved useful and feasible: the parent interview, the use of commercial tests, the maintenance of brief anecdotal records, and checklists.

Use of Parent Interview as a Source of Information

The parent interview remains one of the outstanding means of collecting information about the child. Some information may be obtained in written form, but some is best gathered by means of personal interviews. Effective methods of talking with parents are discussed in Chapter 19, but the interview deserves special mention here because it is such a good way to find out about a child's skills. Children's behavior is sometimes quite different at school and at home. For instance, a child who is silent as a sphinx at school may be quite talkative at home. This is important for the teacher to know when evaluating her language development, as well as when making recommendations for a prescriptive curriculum.

Use of Commercial Tests

The advantages of using published tests for preschoolers should not be overlooked. If the teacher selects a test that has been normed on many other children of varying ethnic groups and cultural backgrounds, it is possible to compare the performance of her group or of individual children in her group with the larger, national sample. Standardized tests, if sold by a reputable company, are likely (but not necessarily) to have been developed by experts.

Well-developed tests will always include information on what kinds of children and how many of them were included in the original standardization of the test. In order for the test to be fair, it is of great importance that this original sample include an adequate mix of youngsters from various economic levels and ethnic groups in our society.

High-quality tests also make a point of reporting *validity* and *reliability*. The *content validity* of a test has to do with whether the test measures what it says it does. For example, if the test claims that it measures self-esteem, is that what it really measures? Another kind of validity, known as *predictive validity*, has to do with how well the test predicts future outcomes (e.g., how well the test might predict future performance of the child in school).

Reliability is the degree to which test scores can be counted on to be consistent when the test is repeated. For example, if the same child took the test again within a few days, would his score be about the same?

When carefully administered and correctly interpreted, well-constructed tests can be valuable diagnostic aids. However, the drawbacks to using commercial tests must also be considered. An inspection of test information compiled by Hoepfner, Stern, & Nummedal (1971) and reconfirmed by Johnson (1979) reveals the following weaknesses: the majority of such tests require one-to-one administration, which can be time consuming and inconvenient to arrange, even for a class of 15 children; many tests have professional restrictions requiring that they be administered by a psychologist, a service rarely available to centers or preschools; and tests that measure exactly what the early childhood

teacher wishes to measure can be difficult to find. The research report concerning screening tests that is included in this chapter paints a picture of the problems of test selection and administration that are still prevalent today (Michigan Department of Education, 1984).

Finally, there is the disadvantage that many tests appear to favor the white, middle-class child and are inappropriate to use with children who come from poor families, who are bilingual, or who come from backgrounds that differ from that of middle-class, white society (Reynolds, 1984).

For these reasons, it is evident that selection of commercial preschool tests remains a difficult problem for teachers not specifically trained in measurement and evaluation. Teachers who wish to make use of such instruments will find the references listed at the end of this chapter to be helpful starting points (Goodwin & Driscoll, 1980; Johnson, 1979). They can then write to the publisher of a desired test and request data on its population sample, reliability, and validity. These reports should be shown to someone who is knowledgeable about test construction and administration. School psychologists, for instance, are usually glad to help with this kind of evaluation and can determine whether the reliability and validity are high enough to make the test of real value.

Use of Observations as Records

In addition to information gathered from parents or from commercially developed tests, teachers draw on observations they have made to learn about the child. The observations should be recorded either as brief anecdotal records or, even more briefly, on checklists.

Maintaining Anecdotal Records. Basically, anecdotal records are the notes made by teachers about individual children recording behaviors that they think are particularly important to remember. Probably the simplest method of maintaining these records is to use large index cards, one for each child. These should have the

RESEARCH STUDY
Can Screening Tests Be Dangerous?

Research Questions   Because school districts in New York state were using various methods of screening young children in order to identify those with special handicaps, Joiner wanted to know, "How much variety is there in the tests being used to identify the children?" "How adequate are the major screening tests?" and "Are the tests being used for the purpose the developer intended them to be used?"

Research Method   The investigator surveyed the 736 school districts in the state and gathered information about whether the children were being screened for disabilities and, if they were, what tests were being used for this purpose. Then he analyzed the information and checked all the standardized tests for quality in Buros (1965) and Hoepfner, Stern, and Nummedal (1971). He also interviewed users of the tests to see what they thought about them.

Results   Out of 736 districts, only 177 conformed to federal law (PL 94–142) and screened children for disabilities. (Note that this study was carried out in 1977 when the law had not been in effect very long.)

Within the 177 districts that were involved in screening, 151 different tests were used. The majority of these were unpublished, locally developed measures that completely lacked any evidence of validity or reliability.

Districts that used standardized tests were not doing much better in terms of quality. Thirty different tests were in use, and when these were checked with Buros and Hoepfner, Stern, and Nummedal for ratings, evaluations ranged from predominantly poor to only fair in quality of test. Moreover, almost half the time the tests were misused; that is, they did not screen adequately for the disabilities the administrators intended them to identify.

---

child's name, birth date, and date of entering school at the top. The observer's name or initials should be included also.

Notes about what the child does or says that is important or revealing are added on these cards as often as possible. Some teachers like to add to each of these cards once a week so that they can be aware of every child and of how he is progressing. Others prefer to do half the children one week and the other half the next.

In addition to noting behavior that seems particularly significant, it is also useful to draw some conclusions about what the behavior probably means. Such conclusions need to be somewhat tentative, since it is always possible for observers to draw incorrect conclusions about

the reasons for behavior. Nevertheless, drawing conclusions may help teachers see what the child is ready to learn next so that they can develop appropriate, timely objectives for the youngster. These objectives, which may change from week to week as the child gains skills, make the formulation of simple, practical plans much easier.

In the example that follows note how the teacher describes the behavior in one section and then enters his interpretation (conclusions) separately in the summary. This is done to keep the behavioral record as factual and unbiased as possible. The learning objective for the next week is written very simply in the "I want" form discussed in Chapter 5. Many teachers find this

Implications Few would disagree with the premise that it is worthwhile to identify children who have special developmental difficulties and arrange to provide them with the help they need as early in their lives as possible.

However, we must always remember that important decisions about children's lives are often based on the results of tests, so it is extremely important to understand the limitations and problems inherent in their use. This is particularly true of brief, poorly constructed screening instruments. At best, such testing should be regarded as the first, very tentative step toward identifying children who need or do not need special help. At worst, it should be disregarded altogether.

Although teacher-made tests and checklists are worthwhile to use as measures of change in individual classrooms, they should not be used as screening tests to hold children out of school or to diagnose difficulties because they have not been standardized against a larger population. Short of using elaborate statistical methods, there is no way to measure their predictive validity or reliability.

Even when standardized tests are used, great care must be taken in their selection because their quality is often inadequate. Only well-trained psychologists are qualified to evaluate the reliability, validity, and other technical matters related to test quality—and even they usually defer to the expert publications cited above.

Finally, if any kind of statewide statistics or funding plans are to be developed based on the results of screening tests, it is essential for every district to use the same procedures and measures so that the data compiled from those tests are truly comparable.

Note. From *A Technical Analysis of the Variation in Screening Instruments and Programs in New York State* by L. M. Joiner, 1977, New York: City University of New York, New York Center for Advanced Study in Education. ED 154 586.

---

kind of phrasing easier to use than the more formal objective, "Dean will play with Charlie at least two times in the block corner during the coming week," which was described in the previous chapter.

Dean W.[2]; Birth date: August 2, 1984; Entry to School: September 1989; Observer: H.B.J.

Week One: September 5

Dean is new to Center. Tall for age, slender, a little pale. First day stayed by door with mother, looked uncertain—stoic. Mother took off work to spend morning with D. She took him home after lunch, which he was unable to eat. Hid head when urged to say goodbye. During week, hardly knew he was there. Quiet, watchful, and attracted to book corner. Liked *Billy Goats Gruff* story a lot.

Summary: D. seems anxious, not sure he likes Center. Has made little contact with other children.

Objective: I want him to feel more at home and join in some of the activities this coming week.

Plan: Build bond with him myself. Talk with him about books he likes; suggest he bring one of his favorites to school for me to read to children. Don't push him too hard to join in.

Week Two: September 11

D. refused to bring book. However, at group time he brought me *Billy Goats Gruff* from our

---

[2]The names of the children have been changed to protect their privacy.

shelf and was delighted when I read it and told the children he had chosen it for the group. Spends most of time alone; used easel as vantage point for watching other activities. Able to eat more at lunch, especially bread and milk. Played a long time in blocks at end of day when Charlie (a vigorous block builder) had gone home.

Summary: D. is still a loner but is becoming interested in what is going on. Eating better so he's probably less anxious. Likes blocks.

Objective: I hope he will move into activities more and relax.

Plan: Make sure there's as much bread and milk as he wants until he's comfortable enough to eat the rest of the meal. Work on security bond. Read him special story. He likes trucks; add them to block corner. Invite him to go with small group to story hour at library.

Week Three: September 18

Turned down library—not surprising. Blocks are D's passion. Used trucks and blocks, built bridge. Said trucks were billy goats and they would fool the ogre. Later in week built elaborate structure; it was near 5:00 and he couldn't finish so left it for the next day. He arrived *smiling* and set to work; Charlie joined him. Boys worked together until every block in school was used. Dean was even noisy as they knocked it down afterward.

Summary: Seems D. is mastering anxiety by playing out the Billy Goat Gruff theme. Wonderful he's making friends with Charlie; relationship would be a good balance for each.

Objective: I hope D. will play with Charlie at least some of the time next week.

Plan: Suggest boys feel free to use cardboard blocks and boards with unit blocks if they need more scope. Show them pictures of other children building with all sorts of blocks in *The Complete Block Book* [Provenzo & Brett, 1983] to encourage them. Seat them together at lunch table.

Week Four: September 25

Had a setback with Dean. At mention of the practice fire drill he began to look anxious. Since everyone else wanted to hear the alarm, I turned it on. D. covered ears, scrunched down

to bury head in carpet. I told him it was only practice, but he still looked worried. Retreated to book corner. Next morning cried as he came in door. I tried to reassure him. When drill came, I took his hand and he huddled against me. That afternoon told his mother he didn't want to come anymore. I explained what had happened. She said she would explain at home, too.

Summary: The noise and fire talk frightened him—reawakened his anxiety. I think maybe I would have been smarter to have had fire drill right after hearing the alarm so that he wouldn't worry about it over the night.

Objective: I want D. to play through his fears about fire so he wants to come to the Center again.

Plan: Not sure, but must be careful not to make things worse. Start gently with fireman book. Be steady and not act overly concerned. Stress we can keep ourselves safe by knowing what to do when we hear the alarm.

Week Five: October 2

D. wouldn't let me read the fire book to him, but *did* look at it behind the bookcase by himself. What really worked was Charlie, Heaven bless him! He asked for the fire trucks to use in the block area. Dean hovered on the sidelines. Charlie said, "Hey, Deano—I'm squirtin' you with the hose," and he made fire siren sounds. Instead of retreating, D. said, "No you ain't—I'm squirtin' *you*," and he grabbed up another truck and shoved it at Charlie. They laughed hysterically at this, rolling on the floor (I could see Dean's relief on his face). Played in blocks with fire trucks, staked out fire area. Wouldn't let anyone else come in to get burned up. Play lasted intermittently rest of the week.

Summary: Never underestimate the power of play. I'm relieved for him. He is mastering his anxiety once again and building a friendship, too.

Objective: I want Dean to continue to play through his fear of fire and his anxiety during the coming week—and to play with Charlie.

Plan: Get out fire hats and some hose. See if children will use them with the trikes when they go outside to play.

Construction and Use of Checklists and Rating Scales

For potential comprehensiveness of coverage in the preschool, nothing beats the checklist rating scale. Checklists may be developed on almost any conceivable aspect of child development or behavior. Since they are criterion referenced, which means that they are designed to match specific objectives, checklists are congruent with what is going on in the teacher's own classroom. They offer an excellent means of assessing whether educational objectives have been accomplished, and they can be filled out at the teacher's leisure and need not be completed in one sitting.

Possible Ways to Use and Develop a Checklist. A checklist is merely a convenient way to take an inventory of behavior. It may be a list of anything that the teacher deems important and wishes to check the child on. Thus, it might be a list of all the activities available in the center's program, with spaces beside each activity to check whether the child participates in it. Or it could be a list of various ways children cope with anxiety or a list of all the children in school, with places to fill in the child's close companions and those whom he particularly avoids.

A checklist may also be used to assess whether an educational goal is being reached. When writing this kind of checklist, the teacher should list the educational goal first and then include several kinds of behaviors preferably defined in behavioral objective terms that are likely to be present when the goal is accomplished, as discussed in Chapter 5.

Thus, when the staff of our children's center chose the general goal of fostering emotional health in the children, the following behaviors were selected as representing coping behaviors related to emotional health: able to express liking for other children and adults, able to express anger in a way that does not damage people or equipment, able to confront an adult directly when the adult has caused the child to feel angry, able to maintain sustained friendships with other children.

Next, the process of making the checklist was refined by including measures of how often the behavior occurred. For our purposes we selected the following categories of frequency: *no opportunity to observe, hardly ever, about half the time,* and *usually* as being quantitative measures we could all understand. The addition of these measures of frequency changed our modest checklist into a more useful measure—a rating scale.

Since we knew how desirable it is to assess the child's abilities shortly after she begins school, as well as at midyear and year's end, we found it helpful to allow space for the three evaluation periods on one sheet of paper. This made comparison simpler and also reduced the bulkiness of the file for each youngster.

Finally, additional items were added to cover other aspects of emotional and social behavior that the staff felt were important. Bear in mind that there is nothing holy about this particular list; other staffs would select other items suited to their own goals and children.

The final form of our chart looked like the one shown in Figure 6–1.

Suggestions About Compiling Checklists. Although it is often helpful to go through the checklists of other schools to garner ideas, each school should really develop its own set, because each school has its own list of educational goals, and the checklists should be designed to fit these goals. It is astonishingly easy to be trapped into evaluating children on skills that have not been emphasized in the curriculum. Results of such mismatched evaluations can only be disappointing.

The teacher should be as explicit and clear as possible when describing the behaviors that will be evaluated. For example, suppose that the following formal educational objective has been selected by the school: "Following an initial period of adjustment, the child will demonstrate emotional independence by tolerating separation from meaningful family members during her day

FIGURE 6–1
Social-emotional competence scale [4-year-olds]

Child's name: _____ Birth date: _____

Last   First   Middle

	Pretest				**Midtest**				**Posttest**			
	Not able to observe	Hardly ever	About half the time	Usually	Not able to observe	Hardly ever	About half the time	Usually	Not able to observe	Hardly ever	About half the time	Usually

Self-confidence

Able to hold her own when challenged (confident, not unduly intimidated)

Likes to try new things

Takes criticism and reprimands in stride

Able to adjust to change in routines or people in the center

TOTAL

Autonomy and dependence

Enters into center activity within 10 minutes after mother's departure

Spends more time with own age group than with adults

Relates to more than one adult at school

Appears independent—when given the opportunity, able to make decisions for herself

TOTAL

98

Social competence

Able to share teacher with others				
Willing to bargain to attain goals				
Able to share when she has enough for herself				
Able to show or express concern for other people				
TOTAL				

Coping techniques

Able to express liking for other children and adults				
Able to express anger in a way that does not damage people or equipment				
Able to confront adult directly when adult has caused child to feel angry				
Able to maintain sustained friendships with other children				
TOTAL				
GRAND TOTAL				

Date: _____   Date: _____   Date: _____
Recorder: _____   Recorder: _____   Recorder: _____

From Santa Barbara City College Children's Center, 1975.

at nursery school." Which of the following checklist items should be selected as the most explicit one to use as a measure that the child is achieving independence?

1. The child rarely demonstrates her anxiety.
2. The child can wave goodbye to her mother without undue stress.
3. The child enters into a nursery school activity within 10 minutes after her mother's departure.
4. The child exhibits a favorable attitude toward her teachers.

Numbers 1 and 4 are not clearly related to the stated goal. Number 2 is probably a good item to use, although the phrase "without undue stress" may vary in interpretation from teacher to teacher. Number 3 is the clearest statement of the four and should be included on the list.

When composing such lists, the teacher also must keep them within reason in terms of developmental levels. It can be frustrating and discouraging to both child and teacher if the teacher expects behavior that lies beyond the child's developmental ability to achieve. For this reason, it cannot be recommended too strongly that developmental charts, such as the one included in Appendix A, be consulted when checklists are being constructed. Several resources are listed at the end of this chapter. Where such material is not available, the lists should be based on recommendations of experienced early childhood teachers.

One final admonition about the construction of checklists must be added. If the list is to be used in the manner suggested at the end of this chapter to summarize data for fiscal reports, it is necessary to phrase the behavior items so they are all positive behaviors that the teacher desires to have increase during the school year. An item should be phrased "able to share teacher with others" rather than "clings to teacher, fights other children off from her." If a positive goal form is not followed and a mixture of positive and negative descriptions is used, some of the behaviors will be marked as increasing and others as decreasing during the year. The result would be that the losses and gains cancel each other

out, and no improvement could be revealed by the final scores.

USING THE INFORMATION THAT HAS BEEN COLLECTED

Developing a Prescriptive Curriculum

For the individual child's well-being, the most important use of checklists, observations, and interviews is the use of the material to identify strengths and difficulties so that learning activities may be prescribed that will help the youngster develop as well as she is able to.

For example, when the teacher looked over one such checklist, she was alerted to the fact that Jeannie had several "hardly ever" ratings on a portion of her Social-Emotional Competence Scale. A further perusal of the anecdotal records contributed to the picture of a 4-year-old girl who was new to school and who, though appearing to like the other children, stuck close to the teacher and was unable to share whatever she played with. The parent interview added the information that Jeannie was an only child who lived in a neighborhood where there were no other children. When these pieces of information were put together, Jeannie emerged as being a socially inexperienced 4-year-old rather than the "spoiled little girl" she might have seemed at face value. The information not only increased the teacher's understanding but also her liking for the child. It helped her plan a curriculum that was built on Jeannie's liking of other people and that sought to develop her confidence and trust. This enabled Jeannie to gradually let go of teachers and equipment more easily and make friends with the other youngsters.

Making Reports to the Family

Preparation for a parent conference is much easier when records have been kept in a systematic manner. The material is already at the teacher's fingertips and needs only to be reviewed before the family's arrival. Such records may be referred to in a general, summarizing way or in terms of more specific behaviors as the occasion warrants. Many teachers find these reports invaluable to use as points of reference when reviewing the year's progress with the parents.

Preparing Reports for Official Boards and Funding Agencies

With increasing frequency, teachers and directors of day-care centers are being required to present annual summaries of the children's progress to justify continuation of funding. Many staff members are uncertain about how to present such information effectively, even though they have faithfully kept track of the children's growth during the year. A useful method of summarizing such data is found in Appendix B.

SUMMARY

Evaluation is a valuable process that early childhood teachers can use for describing children and measuring changes in their behavior. However, great care must be taken when selecting such measures. Teachers must be careful not to place too much confidence in the results of preliminary screening devices. They should also restrict conclusions based upon their own teacher-made tests.

Practical methods of recording and evaluating behavior include the use of parent interviews, commercially developed tests, anecdotal records, and checklists.

Evaluation that is systematically carried out increases knowledge of the individual child, facilitates the planning of an individualized curriculum, and makes reporting to parents a simple matter. It also provides useful data on which to base reports to advisory boards and funding agencies.

SELF-CHECK QUESTIONS FOR REVIEW

Content-Related Questions

1. What are the advantages of including evaluation procedures in an early childhood program?

2. The text lists some basic principles of evaluation. Tell what these are and explain why each is important.

3. Parent interviews are one useful source of information about children. What are three additional sources teachers can use to obtain useful information about children?

4. Commercial tests can be helpful to use, but they also have potential drawbacks. Discuss the pros and cons of using such tests.

5. What are the potential benefits of using screening tests for young children? Why do some people argue against their use? What do these people say should happen instead of starting children in school a year later?

6. Discuss the "dangers" of using locally developed tests.

Integrative Questions

1. Joiner's research reveals some particular difficulties encountered by schools using screening tests. What are some of the implications that could be drawn from the results of that research?

2. Joiner's report points out the dangers of using nonstandardized tests, yet the chapter spends considerable time explaining how to construct such tests. Does the discussion about making such tests contradict what Joiner has to say?

3. Compare checklists and rating scales. How are they alike and how do they differ?

4. The people who argue against the value of holding "developmentally immature" children out of school for a year maintain that it is the school that should change rather than the child who should wait. Which solution do you think is the more practical way to deal with the maturity variability of young children? Should they be held out of school for a year? Or should the expectations of the school be changed?

QUESTIONS AND ACTIVITIES

1. Testing and keeping checklists are a lot of work and also time consuming. Are these activities really worth the time and trouble? What other equally satisfactory methods of identifying skills or lags in development might be employed in place of these?

2. *Problem:* Your school is funded by a state that

requires you to administer a variety of pretests and posttests to the children to determine the effectiveness of the program. This year you are horrified to discover that the posttest results indicate that the children have made little improvement in language development when compared with the national norm included with the test information. You are in charge of the program. What would you do about this result?

3. In your opinion, what should become of evaluative records once the child has left the preschool? Should they be forwarded to his next school, for example? Should they be destroyed? Should they be saved for a number of years? Think carefully about the pros and cons of taking any of these actions.

4. Assess the needs of some youngsters in your school as they have been revealed by your evaluation materials. On the basis of these findings, suggest activities that you feel could be used to develop the youngsters' weaker areas by drawing on their strengths as identified by the evaluation procedures.

5. If you were the teacher and had written the following notes in Patty's anecdotal record, how would you summarize her behavior? Then what objective might you pick for the following week, and what plans would you suggest to implement that objective?

When our new child, Willie, hit Patty and grabbed the book she was holding, she said, "You stupid! You spastic!—give it back!" Later on I heard her call someone else a "Dummy" because they wouldn't play with her. Last week she called a teacher a "nerd" because he wouldn't let her go outside.

6. You have been appointed to work with another staff member to develop a checklist to evaluate what the children have learned in the Let's Find Out corner. She has a friend who works in another school that also offers a discovery area, so she suggests that you just use their checklist for the evaluation because it would save so much work. Would you agree to do this? Explain why or why not.

7. You are now a parent and you have a child getting ready to enter kindergarten. You have heard that the district is considering using a prekindergarten screening test for the first time. Would you

encourage or discourage the adoption of this policy? Explain the basis for your preference.

REFERENCES FOR FURTHER READING

References of General Interest

Ames, L. B., & Chase, J. A. (1980). *Don't push your preschooler* (rev. ed.). New York: Harper & Row. Ames and Chase make a good case for allowing children to grow naturally and at their own pace.

Leshan, E. J. (1971). *The conspiracy against childhood.* New York: Atheneum Publishers. This is a popular presentation of the case against forcing development in children. The chapter entitled "Any Dope Can Have a High IQ" is particularly appropriate to read in connection with the topic of evaluation.

Resources for Evaluating Commercial Tests

Goodwin, W. L., & Driscoll, L. A. (1980). *Handbook for measurement and evaluation in early childhood education.* San Francisco: Jossey-Bass Publishers. For anyone with more than a passing interest in various measures of evaluation, this book is indispensable. It covers testing and observation and reviews methods of assessing programs. Highly recommended.

Hoepfner, R., Stern, C., & Nummedal, S. G. (1971). *CSE-ECRC preschool/kindergarten test evaluations.* Los Angeles: School Evaluation Project, Center for the Study of Evaluation and the Early Childhood Research Center, University of California at Los Angeles. This publication, though dated, remains an excellent compendium of tests appropriate for use in preschool and kindergarten.

Lichtenstein, R., & Ireton, H. (1984). *Preschool screening: Identifying young children with developmental and educational problems.* New York: Grune & Stratton. Because this book reviews screening instruments useful for separating children who require special help or those too immature for admission to kindergarten, it covers an important aspect of evaluating children.

Child Study Techniques

Almy, M., & Genishi, C. (1979). *Ways of studying children: An observation manual for early childhood teachers* (2nd ed.). New York: Teachers College Press. This book is particularly valuable because of its attention to ways of studying young children who come from differing ethnic and cultural backgrounds and children who have handicaps.

Boehm, A. E., & Weinberg, R. A. (1987). *The classroom observer: Developing observation skills in early childhood settings* (2nd ed.). New York: Teachers College Press. This book offers practical advice on how to structure observations, checklists, and so forth so they are clearly stated and very usable.

Murphy, L. B. (1956). *Personality in young children: Methods for the study of personality in young children* (Vol. 1). New York: Basic Books. Volume 1 contains an interesting description of various open situations that can be used for evaluating young children. These include the use of miniature life toys, sensory toys, dough and cold cream, painting, the Rorschach test, and play situations. The discussion is based on responses of particular children. The interpretations are first rate, and the book supports the philosophy that it is not always necessary to resort to intelligence tests to learn a great deal about children.

Developmental Checklist Information

Beaty, J. J. (1990). *Observing development of the young child* (2nd ed.). Columbus, Ohio: Merrill Publishing Co. Beaty offers many examples of appropriate checklist items.

Bentzen, W. R. (1985). *Seeing young children: A guide to observing and recording behavior.* Albany, N. Y.: Delmar Publishers. This is a how-to book distinguished by the inclusion of lists of developmental characteristics.

Discussions About the Pros and Cons of Testing

Cryan, J. R. (1988). Evaluation: Plague or promise? In J. S. McKee & K. M. Paciorek (Eds.). *Early childhood education, 88/89.* Guilford, Conn.: Dushkin Publishing Group. Cryan presents a thoughtful analysis of the purposes evaluation can serve. He also includes descriptions of formal and informal methods of conducting it.

Meisels, S. J. (1987). Uses and abuses of developmental screening and school readiness testing. *Young Children, 42*(2), 4–6, 68–73. The author discusses various problems related to the misuse of developmental and readiness tests and criticizes the Gesell School Readiness Screening Test in particular. Note that the same issue of *Young Children* also includes a reply from the Gesell Institute, and a reply from Meisels to that reply. Interesting reading.

For the Advanced Student

Clemens, P. S. (1983). *The psychologist's test file.* Novato, Calif.: Academic Therapy Publications. This is an interesting reference for readers who would like to see some samples of test questions representing many different kinds of tests.

Eisner, E. (1985). *The art of educational evaluation: A personal view.* London: The Falmer Press. In a series of essays, this leading theorist considers various aspects of evaluation.

Frankenburg, W. K., Emde, R. N., & Sullivan, J. W. (Eds.). (1985). *Early identification of children at risk: An international perspective.* New York: Plenum Press. This book presents chapters by experts wherein many technical aspects of screening and follow-up procedures are discussed.

Meisels, S. J. (1985). *Developmental screening in early childhood: A guide* (rev. ed.). Washington, D.C.: National Association for the Education of Young Children. Following a discussion of screening tests and their presentation, the author lists several he considers to be adequate for that purpose.

Mitchell, J. (Ed.). (1985). *The 9th mental measurements yearbook.* Lincoln, Neb.: University of Nebraska Press. Formerly edited by Oscar Boros, this is the classic reference in the field of test evaluation. It contains descriptions and tough-minded assessments of tests in print that are written by authorities in the field.

National Association for the Education of Young Children. (1988). NAEYC position statement on standardized testing of young children 3 through 8 years of age. *Young Children, 43*(3), 42–47. Early childhood professionals who are considering using standardized tests should follow the seven specific guidelines advocated in this position paper when selecting such measures. A significant publication.

Smith, M. S., & Bissell, J. S. (1970). Report analysis: The impact of Head Start. *Harvard Educational Review, 14,* 51–104. The authors assess the Westinghouse Head Start report (Cicercelli, Evans, & Schiller, 1969) and criticize the study on the basis that tests and methods of evaluation employed did not fit the goals of the Head Start program.

Wolf, J. M., & Kessler, A. L. (1987). *ERS Monograph: Entrance to kindergarten: What is the best age?* Arlington, Va.: Educational Research Service. This is a balanced review of research related to the subject. An in-depth discussion of alternative ways of coping with the differential readiness of children is also included.

7 Keeping Children Safe and Well Fed

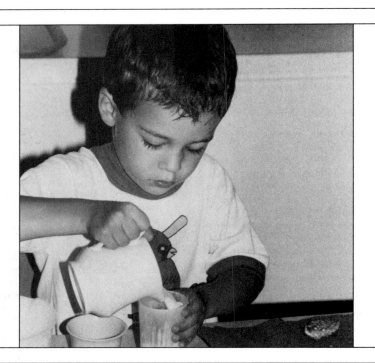

Have you ever

- Worried how to tell whether something was safe for the children to do?
- Wondered if there was any way to stem the tide of colds that were sweeping over your center?
- Wanted to include cooking for the twos but thought they were too young to do it?

If you have, the material in this chapter will help you.

Sittin' in a High Chair[1]

Sittin' in a high chair, big chair, my chair,
Sittin' in a high chair, bang my spoon!
Sittin' in a high chair, big chair, my chair,
Sittin' in a high chair, feed me soon!!

Bring on the plate, bring on the cup,
Never going to fill this baby up!
Bring on bananas, bring on the bread,
Mama's gotta get this baby fed!

Sittin' in a high chair, big chair, my chair,
Sittin' in a high chair, bang my spoon!
Sittin' in a high chair, big chair, my chair,
Sittin' in a high chair, feed me soon!

Bring on the carrots, bring on the peas,
Mama come serve this baby please!
Bring on the pancakes stacked in a pile,
Papa's going to make this baby smile!

Sittin' in a high chair, big chair, my chair,
Sittin' in a high chair, bang my spoon!
Sittin' in a high chair, big chair, my chair,
Sittin' in a high chair, feed me soon!

Bring on the napkins, bring on the sponge,
Clean me up cuz I'm all done!

HAP PALMER and MARTHA CHENEY (1984)

I love this song because of its lustiness. If we can convey this same sense of gusto and delight to children, we will transmit a worthwhile value about the pleasures their bodies can provide.

There are really two ways of helping children feel good about their bodies. The first consists of all the things we do to foster good health and sound physical development while we care for children during the day. The second comprises the curriculum we plan that encourages children to understand, cherish, and care for their bodies.

Both approaches, however, should have the same basic goals: keeping children safe and healthy, feeding them well, teaching them to understand and value life, and providing plenty of pleasurable opportunities for the growth of physical expertise.

KEEPING CHILDREN SAFE

Good teachers must be unceasingly aware of what children are doing and must occasionally move quickly to forestall an accident. The problem for beginning teachers is to know when to intervene and when not to. It is very easy for them to be so overprotective that the children absorb their apprehension and, interpreting this as a vote of no confidence, lose confidence in

[1]To be sung to the tune, "Short'nin' Bread." From "Babysong" by Hap Palmer and Martha Cheney, 1984, Topanga, Calif.: Hap-Pal Music. Reprinted by permission.

themselves. This is surely undesirable. On the other hand, there is no doubt that children must be stopped quickly from running in front of a moving swing or stepping backward off the playhouse roof. The question is, how can you as a teacher tell when an activity should be stopped and when it should be allowed to continue?

Use common sense and learn to worry about the right things. If whatever the child is doing is likely to seriously hurt himself or someone else, then it is time to stop him; but if the danger is relatively slight and he is likely to learn something valuable from the experience (such as it is a good idea to keep your fingers out of the way when using a hammer), then let him continue. Anytime you are truly dubious about the safety of a particular activity, it is wiser to stop it temporarily and ask the master teacher to help you and the child evaluate the situation. Certainly it is better to be safe than sorry (Comer, 1987).

Look over the play yard with a critical eye for safety before the children arrive. Tricycle handle bars unprotected by rubber end guards can deliver nasty cuts to the forehead of a child who tips over on them; wooden swing seats can loosen teeth; and rickety climbing equipment can come to pieces and really harm youngsters. Glass bottles (no matter how small and sturdy) at the water table may cut, as may rusty cans and metal toys in the sandbox. Splintery boards literally leave painful reminders behind. Constant vigilance is needed to make certain that all decaying equipment is either removed or repaired immediately (Frost & Wortham, 1988; Lovell & Harms, 1985).

Enlist parents in the campaign to keep children safe. Two examples of possible safety programs that parents should attend include fire safety in the home and the use of safety car seats for young children.

Fire departments are usually delighted to send speakers and pamphlets on fire safety. All families should discuss and practice ways of leaving their homes in emergencies, and all children should be taught to "stop, drop, and roll," rather than run should their clothing catch fire. If a

parent program presents this material in a calm, matter-of-fact way, it can be done without arousing too much anxiety, and, more important, it may save lives or the terrible pain and disfigurement resulting from burns.

Fortunately, in the past few years many states have passed legislation encouraging the use of safety car seats. As an early childhood teacher who sees families deliver children by car every day, you are in an excellent position to remind and encourage parents to obey this law. The teacher should become acquainted with the resources in the community that make these seats available free to families who could not otherwise afford them. An evening program could emphasize this information and make it available to all (Scott, 1985).

Teach children to think about safety for themselves; this is probably the best way to keep them safe. Help them anticipate consequences and

Gates must be closely supervised at all times.

evaluate *beforehand* what the result will be of what they want to do. This is hard to accomplish without moralizing. A frightened teacher finds it easy to blame a child for an accident by saying something like, "See I told you not to run with your socks on. I told you the floor is slippery—I was right, wasn't I? See, you hurt yourself, didn't you?" How much better it would have been if the teacher had said before the accident, "Our rule is, 'we only dance in bare feet.' Now why do we have that rule?" The teacher also should demonstrate how slippery the floor is when wearing socks. Or, when out of doors, she might say, "That looks pretty high to me. Try jumping from lower down first and see what that feels like—then we'll decide together whether it's safe to jump from higher up in the tree."

KEEPING CHILDREN HEALTHY

Teaching Children to Follow Simple Rules of Hygiene

Perhaps because health and cleanliness do go together and "cleanliness is next to godliness," teachers tend to get preachy when they talk about health. At least at the preschool level, good health practices are generally better taught by example, than taught in such units as "Our Friends, the Teeth" or "Four Basic Foods for Health."

Very young children are largely unaware of their bodies as such and completely ignorant of how to care for them, so teachers can help them learn about good health care by setting a good example and by making sure the children follow certain basic rules of hygiene.

One of the most important of these is washing hands after toileting and before handling food (American Academy of Pediatrics, 1986). The importance of washing hands and learning to keep them away from eyes, noses, and mouths cannot be emphasized strongly enough for both children and adults. Doing this not only sharply reduces the number of colds in children's centers, but also has been shown to reduce the

number of hepatitis A infections (Kendrick, Kaufmann, & Messenger, 1988). Yet teachers frequently supervise hand washing by the children and fail to take advantage of this opportunity to wash their own or they allow children to cook food without scrubbing up first.

Adjusting the amount of clothing to changes in temperature is another health rule well worth observing. Although doctors swear that becoming chilled is not related to catching a cold, experience has taught me that it is tempting fate to allow hot, sweaty children to get up from a nap and run outside into a cold wind. Unless temperature changes are called to the children's attention, it is unlikely that they will notice them and take their sweaters off or put them on as needed. Teachers must remind them to do this.

Conducting a health check as children arrive is a mandatory part of the regulations of many states and should be carried out whether mandated or not. Parents are often hurried in the morning and fail to take a close look at their youngsters in the rush of getting off to the center. Moreover, a sick child presents a terrible dilemma for parents who may be torn between needing to go to work and needing to stay home to care for an ailing child. This is a dilemma for teachers, too. However, we must remember that the welfare of the group must be taken into account, as well as the needs of a particular family. Children who are contagious cannot be allowed to stay in the group even if they seem to feel up to doing so. (Refer to Appendix C for a chart of communicable diseases and methods of control.)

Some schools attempt to resolve this problem by maintaining lists of women who will care for children in such emergencies, but most schools just encourage parents to make plans in advance to handle such emergencies. A new and promising solution for sick child care is the development of daily outpatient hospital care for children who are too sick to come to school and whose parents must go to work. Many families feel that the charges for this service, which are generally a few dollars more an hour than the usual provider care, are well worth the cost (NAEYC, 1987). When these resources fail or when the child becomes ill during the day, he should be isolated from the other children and kept comfortable and quiet until he can be taken home.

Keeping immunization records up to date also prevents the spread of various contagious diseases in the center as well as protects the community at large. Children's centers and nursery schools are typically the first institutions entered by young children; therefore, they can act as the first line of health checks for immunizations provided that they enforce their licensing requirements for admission.

Teachers often take immunizations for granted, yet research indicates that levels of immunization against polio, measles, rubella, diphtheria, whooping cough, and tetanus declined between 1980 to 1985 (Education Week, 1988a). For example, the proportion of 2-year-olds receiving the rubella vaccine dropped from 83.2% to 77.3% during that period (Education Week, 1988a). Mumps has also shown an alarming increase, with the number of children so afflicted jumping from 7,800 cases in 1986 to more than 12,000 in 1987 (Education Week, 1988b).

In recent years another disease nicknamed HIB (Haemophilus influenzae, type B) has come to the attention of pediatricians because of its potential seriousness for children of preschool age. HIB attacks 1 out of every 200 children in the United States before age 5 and is responsible for over half of all the cases of meningitis in children. It also produces joint infections that result in arthritis-like conditions and is thought to be responsible for the majority of ear infections as well. Fortunately, there is a new, safe vaccine for this disease, and although most states do not presently require it, many pediatricians recommend its administration. This protection is particularly desirable for children in day care and kindergarten since they come into close contact with so many other children every day (Oklahoma City-County Health Department, 1988).

Teachers should be aware of this potentially serious disease and encourage parents to discuss the possibility of having their children vaccinated against it.

The fifth important health rule to follow is to take special care of children who have been sick. When a child returns to school following a bout of flu or an earache or something as serious as chickenpox or measles, he must be watched carefully for signs of complications, be kept warm, and not be allowed to become overtired. Even though his doctor has said that he can come back, this does not mean that he is in tip-top shape.

FEEDING CHILDREN WELL

Children, like the army, march on their stomachs. Yet some schools still rely on the old juice and cracker routine to see youngsters through the morning. Often today this is not even real fruit juice but some dye-laden, sugar-saturated synthetic. The only advantages of this policy are that it is quick and cheap, neither of which is in the best interests of children. Instead of settling for such trash, think of food as being one of the most important parts of the curriculum and plan for it accordingly.

Problems of Malnutrition

Perhaps the reader feels that the significance of good food is being emphasized unnecessarily since it is true that in many parts of the world children suffer from malnutrition to a much greater extent than they do in the United States. However, it is also true that hunger is far from unknown in our own land (Birch, 1980). This is the case particularly among families of the poor (Dobbing, 1987), but malnutrition also exists in special forms among more well-to-do families who allow their children to feast on the junk foods so persistently touted on television (Brewster & Jacobson, 1978). Such inadequate diets result in decaying teeth, lowered resistance to infection, a reduced ability to pay attention, and (in more severe cases) general lethargy and slower-than-normal physical development (Barrett, 1987; Grantham-McGreagor, 1987).

Two Specific Health Problems. In the United States there are two aspects of malnutrition among children of all economic levels that deserve special discussion: dental decay and iron deficiency.

It has been estimated that 99% of all American children are affected by dental decay at one time or another (Williams, S.R., 1986). Although decay is related to a number of factors, including a child's inherent ability to resist infection, it is well substantiated that a diet high in refined sugar is directly associated with increased tooth decay. The most destructive sweetener is sucrose (common table sugar), the same sugar that occurs in brown sugar and molasses (Pipes, 1985). Sweet food that is sticky, such as candy, should be particularly avoided, since it stays on the teeth for a long time.

It is also important to realize that it is the *frequency* of eating sugar, rather than the total amount consumed, that makes the difference (Gustafson, 1954). Indeed, I have heard a children's dentist say desperately that he did not care how much sugar children ate if only they would eat it just once a day. But if a child eats jam or sweetened cereal for breakfast and then is fed a snack of graham crackers (think of how sticky they are) and then has pudding for lunch, sugar has been added at convenient 2-hour intervals to nourish the bacteria that secrete the acids and enzymes that make teeth vulnerable to decay. This is the reason it is worthwhile to plan snacks of popcorn, homemade peanut butter (most commercial peanut butter contains sugar), or carrot sticks with cottage cheese dip. Desserts of fresh fruit should also be featured. Reducing the sugar intake by these means controls bacteria by starving them. Day-care centers also should require toothbrushing after lunch so that teeth are cleaned at least once a day. The brushes should be stored out of reach and exposed to light and air so that they dry as quickly as possible.

Grating cheese is something almost all children enjoy doing.

Iron deficiency anemia, according to Pipes (1985), is the most prevalent nutritional deficiency in the United States today, especially among infants, adolescent boys, and women during the childbearing years. It is also common among preschool children. H. G. Birch and Gussow (1970), for instance, reported that one early Head Start study found that between 20% and 40% of the children suffered from insufficient iron and that deficiencies as high as 80% were identified among some of the children living in the deep South.

Insufficient iron produces pale, apathetic children who catch cold easily. Teachers should watch for children who match this description, since there are probably such youngsters in their rooms. When this condition is suspected, it should be drawn to the parents' attention so that they can discuss it with their physician. Meanwhile, the school can do its part in preventing anemia by planning meals that include organ meats (especially liver), meats, egg yolks, whole wheat, seafood, green leafy vegetables, nuts, dried fruit, and legumes.

Planning Nutritious Food

One of the best things about children's centers is that most of them still retain the privilege of planning their own meals and snacks. This is

TABLE 7–1
Nutrition needs for preschool children based on the basic four food groups

Basic daily needs	Ages 1–3	Ages 4–6	
Meat group			
Meat, poultry, fish, organ meats, or meat substitutes	Two servings (1 ounce each)	Two servings (1½ ounces each)	Substitutes for the protein of 1 ounce meat: 1 egg, 1 ounce cheese, ¼ cup cottage cheese, ¼ cup peanuts, ⅓ cup other nuts, ½ cup cooked dry peas or beans, 2 tablespoons peanut butter.
Milk group			
Milk (whole, skim, dry, evaporated, buttermilk) and other dairy products	Two cups	Two cups	Substitutes for the calcium of 1 cup milk: 1 cup yogurt, 1⅓ cups cottage cheese, 1½ cups ice cream, 1¼ ounces (⅓ cup grated) natural cheese, 1¾ ounces processed cheese.
Vegetable-fruit group			
For vitamin A: deep yellow-orange or very dark green vegetables	Four servings or more (3 tablespoons each)	Four servings or more (3 tablespoons each)	Eat one vitamin C source daily, one high vitamin A source at least every other day. Other fruits and vegetables fill out this food group.
For vitamin C: citrus fruit, melon, strawberries, broccoli, tomatoes, raw cabbage			
Basic cereal group			
Whole grain or enriched bread, cereal, rice, pasta	Three servings	Four servings	Very active children, teens, adults and athletes need more for energy. A serving is 1 slice bread, 1 roll, ½ cup cooked cereal products, 1 ounce dry cereal

Note. From "Feeding the Special Needs Child" by E. H. Croup, *Children in Contemporary Society,* 12(1), 7–9.

U.S. DIETARY GOALS

1. To avoid overweight, consume only as much energy (calories) as is expended; if overweight, decrease energy intake and increase energy expenditure.
2. Increase the consumption of complex carbohydrates and "naturally occurring" sugars from about 28 percent of energy intake to about 48 percent of energy intake.
3. Reduce the consumption of refined and processed sugars by about 45 percent to account for about 10 percent of total energy intake.
4. Reduce overall fat consumption from approximately 40 percent to about 30 percent of energy intake.
5. Reduce saturated fat consumption to account for about 10 percent of total energy intake; and balance that with poly-unsaturated and mono-unsaturated fats, which should account for about 10 percent of energy intake each.
6. Reduce cholesterol consumption to about 300 mg. a day.
7. Limit the intake of sodium by reducing the intake of salt to about 5 grams a day.

The Goals Suggest the Following Changes in Food Selection and Preparation

1. Increase consumption of fruits and vegetables and whole grains.
2. Decrease consumption of refined and other processed sugars and foods high in such sugars.

3. Decrease consumption of foods high in total fat, and partially replace saturated fats, whether obtained from animal or vegetable sources, with poly-unsaturated fats.
4. Decrease consumption of animal fat, and choose meats, poultry and fish which will reduce saturated fat intake.
5. Except for young children, substitute low-fat and non-fat milk for whole milk, and low-fat dairy products for high fat dairy products.
6. Decrease consumption of butterfat, eggs and other high cholesterol sources. Some consideration should be given to easing the cholesterol goal for pre-menopausal women, young children and the elderly in order to obtain the nutritional benefits of eggs in the diet.
7. Decrease consumption of salt and foods high in salt content.

Persons with physical and/or mental ailments who have reason to believe that they should not follow guidelines for the general population should consult with a health professional having expertise in nutrition, regarding their individual case.

Note. From *Creative Food Experiences for Children* (p. 208) by M. T. Goodwin and G. Pollen, 1980, Washington, D.C.: Center for Science in the Public Interest.

ideal because it allows the director and staff to combine what they know about the food preferences of young children (plain familiar food, small portions, and finger foods are preferred) with knowledge of good nutrition. Appendix D provides examples of a set of menus that appeal to young children and satisfy nutritional requirements as well.

In addition to including information on the basic food groups outlined in Table 7–1, recent reports on nutrition inform teachers that they must also be aware of the amounts of salt and fat that are added to children's food. Including large amounts of these in their diet forms food preferences in early life that lead to increased probability of heart and artery disease and high blood pressure in later life.

Based on recommendations from the U.S. Senate Select Committee on Nutrition and Human Needs and the Surgeon General's Office, the Center for Science in the Public Interest has summarized the recommendations for good food selection and preparation listed in the box on page 111.

For meals to have maximum appeal, they should reflect the cultural backgrounds of the children, as well as be nutritious. There is nothing that fills a newcomer's heart with such despair as the sight of bowls and bowls of food he does not recognize and fears to eat. With a little imagination and sensitivity on the teacher's part, the misery of this experience can be avoided.

Young Black children, for example, may find mustard, turnip, and collard greens especially appealing and may like black-eyed peas and hominy grits. Mexican-Americans, on the other hand, may find tortillas, pan dulce, salsa, and chili more to their taste. Japanese youngsters may prefer food flavored with soy sauce and may particularly enjoy fish, rice crackers, and soba (whole wheat noodles). Although these dishes are likely to be special favorites of children from these backgrounds, it is probable that *all* the children will come to enjoy them if they are gradually included in the menus. Since the majority of the group may be unfamiliar with these foods, the best approach may be to serve only one unfamiliar item at a time. Remember that to some of the children who come from differing backgrounds, most of the food at the center may be unfamiliar at least at first.

An example of one approach to dealing with a child's unfamiliarity and/or having to confront foods he might dislike is detailed in the research report included in this chapter. Note in the report that there was no pressure on the teacher's part to encourage the children to enjoy or even taste the unpreferred food. Instead, the children were merely exposed to the example set by the other children.

One final word on nutrition. Children and adults need to drink plenty of fluids. Little children do not always realize they are thirsty, and so they often translate their discomfort into crabbiness. Although teachers may have to discourage children from filling up on milk and

skipping the rest of their lunch, they should make certain that plenty of liquids are offered during the day. It is especially wise to be aware of this on hot afternoons and to offer every child a *cup* of water—a few swallows from a drinking fountain are insufficient.

Keeping Costs Down

As in all aspects of preschool management, costs must be taken into consideration when preparing menus. Table 7–2 presents a thoughtful plan that can keep down costs and still provide solid nutrition. Many schools, either privately or publicly supported, can also obtain additional funds for feeding children if they serve low-income families. More information on this subject may be obtained from the U.S. Department of Agriculture. School systems can usually supply the nearest address of this government agency.

INCLUDING COOKING IN THE CURRICULUM

Feeding children well in terms of snacks and lunches is important, but this is only half the nutrition story. The other half relates more directly to the children, since it centers on involving them in understanding about good food through cooking activities.

The value of providing such experiences frequently in the preschool is extraordinary because cooking offers so many different kinds of learning for all the child's selves. For the cognitive self there is learning how to measure and weigh, learning temporal sequence (first break the egg, then beat it, then mix it with the margarine), and learning the different flavors, textures, and consistencies which teachers love to bring to the attention of children. Much cause-and-effect learning also is related to cooking, such as "Is it the water or the heat that made the egg hard?" Many plain facts are presented, too, such as the fact that eggs come from chickens.

RESEARCH STUDY
Can Children's Food Preferences Be Changed?

Research Question Birch asked the following questions: "Can the attitude of peers affect a child's attitude toward a particular food?" and "If it can, is this a temporary change or does the change in attitude persist?"

Research Method The sample consisted of 39 middle-class 3- and 4-year-olds. Each child was asked to rank nine vegetables from most to least preferred. (Vegetables such as corn, peas, raw mushrooms, and carrots were included.) Then a child who ranked corn, for example, as least liked and peas as most liked was seated for 4 days at lunchtime with three or four children who ranked corn as most liked. Each day the teacher offered a choice of corn or peas to the children. The first day the corn hater chose first. The next three days the corn lovers chose first, and the child who disliked corn chose his vegetables after seeing the other children's selection.

Results Twelve of the 17 children who had originally disliked a particular vegetable showed an increased preference for it following exposure to children who preferred it. This result was statistically significant at .05.

More of the younger children changed their food preferences than older children did. There was no difference in behavior between boys and girls. Later on, when children were again asked to rank the same nine foods, the change in preference rankings continued for at least several weeks.

Therefore, it is reasonable to conclude that the attitude of peers *can* affect a child's attitude toward certain foods, and that these changes in attitudes are not short-lived but have at least some lasting effect on a child's food preferences.

Implications Birch says it well when she concludes, "If children were routinely exposed to children with differing food preferences, the set of foods they prefer could be enlarged" (p. 495).

I would add that if this positive condition is true, a negative one may also be true. If a child hears a number of his peers being consistently negative about a particular food, he might also shift his opinion to an unfavorable one. For this reason, it is wise to encourage positive comments at snack and lunchtime and to discourage negative comments about food such as "This looks like dog poo-poo" while casually but quietly permitting children to refuse foods they dislike.

Note. From "Effect of Peer Models' Food Choices and Eating Behavior on Preschooler's Food Preferences" by L. L. Birch, 1980, *Child Development, 51,* pp. 489–496.

TABLE 7–2
Money stretchers to make food dollars go further

Food groups	Usually less expensive, more food value for the money	Usually more expensive, less food value for the money
Milk products	Concentrated, fluid, and dry nonfat milk, evaporated, buttermilk	Fluid whole milk, chocolate drink, condensed milk, sweet or sour cream
	Mild cheddar, Swiss, cottage cheese	Sharp cheddar, Roquefort or blue, grated or sliced cheese, cream cheese, yogurt
	Ice milk, imitation ice milk, imitation ice cream	Ice cream, sherbert
Meats and meat substitutes		
Meat	Good and standard grades	Prime and choice grades
	Less tender cuts	Tender cuts
	Home-cooked meats	Canned meats, sliced luncheon meats
	Pork or beef liver, heart, kidney, tongue	Calf liver
Poultry	Stewing chickens, whole broiler-fryers, large turkeys	Poultry parts, specialty products, canned poultry, small turkeys
Fish	Rock cod, butterfish, and fresh fish in season, frozen fillets, steaks, and sticks	Salmon, crab, lobster, prawns, shrimp, oysters
Eggs	Grade A	Grade AA
Beans, peas, and lentils	Dried beans, peas, lentils	Canned baked beans, soups
Nuts	Peanut butter, walnuts, other nuts in shell	Pecans, cashews, shelled nuts, prepared nuts

Note. Revised by M. J. Ferree and C. C. Groppe. From *Balanced Food Values and Cents* (pp. 6–7) by F. Cook, C. Groppe, and M. Ferree, 1975, Berkeley, Calif.: University of California, Division of Agriculture Sciences, Leaflet 2220.

Information about health and nutrition can be incorporated casually, but persistently, into cooking activities. This helps children understand the value good food has for keeping their bodies in good condition and helps them learn to take care of their physical selves.

Other, even more basic values than those listed above are inherent in the preparation of

TABLE 7–2
(continued)

Food groups	Usually less expensive, more food value for the money	Usually more expensive, less food value for the money
Vegetables, fruits	Local vegetables and fruits in season	Out-of-season vegetables and fruits, unusual vegetables and fruits, those in short supply
Vitamin A rich	Carrots, collards, sweet potatoes, green leafy vegetables, spinach, pumpkin, winter squash, broccoli, and in season cantaloupe, apricots, persimmons	Tomatoes, brussels sprouts, asparagus, peaches, watermelon, papaya, bananas, tangerines
Vitamin C rich	Oranges, grapefruit, and their juice, cabbage, greens, green pepper, cantaloupe, strawberries, tomatoes, broccoli in season	Tangerines, apples, ,bananas, peaches, pears
Other	Medium-sized potatoes, nonbaking types	Baking potatoes, new potatoes, canned or frozen potatoes, potato chips
	Romaine, leaf lettuce	Iceberg lettuce, frozen specialty packs of vegetables
Breads, cereals	Whole wheat and enriched flour	Stone-ground, unenriched, and cake flour
	Whole grain and enriched breads	French, Vienna, other specialty breads, hard rolls
	Homemade rolls and coffee cake	Ready-made rolls and coffee cakes, frozen or partially baked products
	Whole grain or restored uncooked cereals	Ready-to-eat cereals, puffed, sugar-coated
	Graham crackers, whole grain wafers	Zwieback, specialty crackers, and wafers
	Enriched uncooked macaroni, spaghetti, noodles	Unenriched, canned, or frozen macaroni, spaghetti, noodles
	Brown rice, converted rice	Quick-cooking, seasoned, or canned rice

food, and these are closely bound up with the psychological value of nourishment. Young children equate food with love. This arises from their early feeding experiences in which love was embodied by the mother relieving the child's hunger with milk. What better ways then to continue to express caring and love to children than by feeding them well and allowing them to

Scrambled eggs are interesting to prepare because changes in texture happen with gratifying quickness.

cook for themselves and for other people. Cooking permits children not only to satisfy their own needs, but also to experience the satisfaction of nourishing others—an excellent opportunity for encouraging the development of the social self.

Moreover, because of the intense gratifications involved, cooking is one of the most ideal ways to incorporate multicultural values into the lives of young children. How better to learn that Jewish or Black or Italian or Mexican people are attractive than by preparing and eating something delicious that is typical of their culture.

Basics for Choosing a Recipe

Pick a recipe that is not too delicate. Part of the cooking experience for children inevitably in-cludes tasting everything, and this does take its toll in proportions. For this reason, it is often best to begin the cooking year with some items whose proportions do not matter much. For example, scrambled eggs with cheese, fruit salad, green salad, spaghetti, and vegetable soup all turn out well no matter what gets sampled along the way. (Incidentally, a good base for vegetable soup is tomato juice; this provides body, color, and flavor, without requiring that meat be added.)

Pick a recipe that has a lot of things for the children to do. Many recipes for little children seem to concentrate only on stirring, which usually means that everyone waits impatiently while each child takes two whacks with the spoon. To counteract this, look the recipe over and note whether there is enough variety to it. For example, compare the following two recipes and ask yourself these questions: How many different things will the children be able to do in each? What is the learning potential of each recipe? What is my opinion of the nutritional benefits to be obtained from each? Which would I choose as providing the most desirable curriculum opportunities for the children?

Nutritious-Delicious Cookies[2]

Measure and stir together the dry ingredients:

1⅓ c. flour (unbleached)	1 tsp baking soda
½ tsp. salt	½ tsp. cinnamon
½ tsp. nutmeg (or less)	¼ tsp. cloves (or less)

Put the following in bowl and beat, combining first margarine and honey, then adding egg, and last the zucchini:

½ c. margarine (softened)	⅔ c. honey
1 c. grated zucchini	1 egg beaten

Combine blended ingredients with dry ingredients. Then add the following:

½ c. rolled oats	1 c. dates, finely chopped
1 c. walnuts, chopped	½ c. coconut (optional)

Drop by heaping spoonfuls onto an oiled cookie sheet. Bake at 325° for 15 minutes until cookies are golden brown. Makes 36 cookies.

Instant Pudding[3]

Pour 2 cups of cold milk into bowl. Add mix. Beat slowly with rotary blender until well blended. Pour into bowls and serve. (Ingredients include sugar, dextrose [corn sugar], modified tapioca starch, sodium phosphates [for proper set], salt, hydrogenated soybean oil with BHA [a preservative], di- and monoglycerides [emulsifier—for uniform dispersion of oil], artificial and natural flavors, nonfat dry milk, artificial color.)

Whenever possible, choose recipes that avoid refined flour and sugars because these have a deleterious effect on teeth. The use of whole grains, fresh fruits, and vegetables provides wonderful opportunities to talk with children about eating those foods that both taste good and are good for them. Two examples of good cookbooks that stress nutrition are Ellen Ewald's *Recipes for a Small Planet* (1975), and Goodwin and Pollen's *Creative Food Experiences for Children* (1980). But nourishing recipes can be found anywhere. One of my student teachers modified a standard recipe and came up with the following:

Basic Muffins[4]

Measure and combine the dry ingredients:

2 c. whole wheat flour
3 tsp. baking powder
½ tsp. salt

Mash 4 ripe bananas—several children can do this in several small bowls. Put the following together in a bowl, combining first margarine and honey, then adding milk and beaten eggs:

½ c. margarine (soft and warm)	¾ c. milk
½ c. honey	2 eggs, beaten

Stir in banana (mashed). Combine wet and dry ingredients and pour into oiled muffin tins. Bake at 400° for 20 to 30 minutes. Yield: 18 large muffins.

Age-Appropriate Cooking Activities

Recipes must also be appropriate for the developmental levels of the child, and even children as young as 2½ enjoy cooking. Table 7–3 offers some examples of activities that are appropriate for children of various ages.

In addition to being durable, nutritious, and age appropriate and providing opportunities for participation, the recipe should be multiethnic if possible. Many adult cookbooks contain recipes from a variety of cultures. There are also two books from UNICEF written especially for children. They are beautifully illustrated, tell a bit about the customs of the featured countries, and also rate each recipe according to difficulty. Here is a sample one from Nigeria that tastes better than it sounds.

---

[2]From *Zucchini Cookbook* by V. Lemley and J. Lemley, 1976, Cave Junction, Ore.: Wilderness House.

[3]From *Instant Pudding and Pie Filling, Vanilla* by General Foods, 1977, White Plains, N.Y.

[4]From Andrea Davis, class of 1978, Santa Barbara City College.

TABLE 7–3
Cooking activities for young children of differing ages*

Ages of children	Suggested cooking activities	Comments
2- to 3-year-olds	Washing and scrubbing vegetables Peeling hard-boiled eggs Tearing lettuce for salad Fruit milkshakes (mash fruit, shake in plastic bottle) Mixing cottage cheese dips Fondue (grating cheese, etc.) Squeezing orange juice (press-down-type electric juicer) Potato salad (begin with boiled potatoes) Bananas rolled in honey and wheat germ Arranging pizza ingredients Deviled eggs Kneading bread Nachos	Utensils that work well with twos include wooden spoons, dull knives (for spreading things and for cutting soft substances, such as bananas), vegetable brushes, graters (particularly four-sided plastic ones), and sieves. Twos are interested in contrasting substances, such as cornmeal compared with unbleached flour and molasses with milk. Be prepared for a great deal of tasting and touching. Although fairly conservative about trying new foods at the table, they are often willing to taste bits of less familiar items while cooking them. Although these rules are important for all ages to remember, twos must be taught the simple rules of hygiene—you must wash your hands before cooking, and you must not touch your nose and then touch food the group is going to eat.

TABLE 7–3 *(continued)*

Ages of children	Suggested cooking activities	Comments
3- to 4-year-olds	Vegetable soup Scrambled eggs French toast (with whole wheat bread) Fruit salad Frozen juice bars (allow them to squeeze oranges first) Applesauce Filled celery stalks Meatballs Tacos Tabouli Asian dishes that require chopping and cutting Hamburgers Greens with bacon	Threes are able to use utensils, such as measuring cups and spoons, sharper knives, graters, peelers, juice squeezers, manually operated rotary egg beaters, and rolling pins. They like to mash, mix, measure, and talk about the order in which things go together. They can use recipes that require more heat, although they will need close watching. They are able to wait a bit longer for results. They enjoy doing things that help the entire group, such as making part of the snack for everyone to enjoy later.
4- to 5-year-olds	Bread Quiche Ice cream Anything grown in their garden Butter Beef jerky Fruit leather Read-for-yourself recipes Recipes from other cultures†	Fours, particularly if this is their second year in school, are accomplished cooks and can do just about everything except deep fat frying. They are able to use tongs and pancake turners, assemble equipment, such as ice cream freezers and food grinders, use a barbecue grill, and even separate eggs. If recipes are illustrated with cups, spoonfuls, and labels, they will enjoy following these with only minimal help from the teacher.

I want to thank Donna Coffman, former Director of The Santa Barbara City College Children's Center, for some of the suggestions included in this table.

*Teachers who are uneasy about using heat while cooking with young children may want to refer to *Cold Cooking for Kids: Recipes and Nutrition for Preschoolers* by P. McClenahan and I. Jaqua, 1976, Belmont, Calif.: Fearon Pitman Publishers.

†Recipes from the UNICEF book, *Many Friends Cooking* by T. T. Cooper and M. Ratner, 1983, New York: Philomel Books, are particularly appropriate to use with the fours because it contains information on the eating customs of the countries from which the recipes come.

Watching can also be learning, but it's best when children don't have to wait too long.

Groundnut Soup[5]

1 large tomato	1 C shelled, unsalted,
1 large potato	roasted peanuts (or use
1 medium onion	½ C crunchy peanut
2 C water	butter—peanuts are
1 beef bouillon cube	better)
1 tsp salt	½ C milk
	2 T rice

[5]Adaptation of "Groundnut Soup," (page 15) from *Many Hands Cooking: An International Cookbook for Girls and Boys* by Terry Touff Cooper and Marilyn Ratner (Thomas Y. Crowell). Text copyright © 1974 by Terry Touff Cooper and Marilyn Ratner. Reprinted by permission of Harper & Row, Publishers, Inc.

(1) Peel potato and onion, and (2) dice potato, tomato, and onion into very small pieces. (3) Place the bouillon cube, water, and salt in a saucepan with the chopped vegetables. Cook for 30 minutes. (4) Chop peanuts with the chopper or cut in very small pieces with a knife (a chopper works best, because the nuts roll around when cut with a knife). Combine nuts with milk, or mix the peanut butter with milk. Add this mixture and the rice to the vegetable mixture and mix well. Simmer for 30 minutes. Serves 6 liberally. (NOTE: We only cook the whole thing for 30 minutes, but the advantage of doing the vegetables first and cooking longer is that it gives more children a chance to participate.)

Recipes that come from teachers' families are always cherished by the children. At Thanksgiving our head teacher shares a recipe and tradition from her Louisiana family.

Sweet Potato Pie[6]

2 c. cooked sweet potatoes	1 tsp. cinnamon
1¼ c. sugar	2 tbs. butter
3 eggs	¼ c. evaporated milk

Mix all ingredients together and pour into an 8 inch uncooked pie shell. Bake 30 minutes or until done in a 375° oven.

Sometimes a member of a child's family will join the class and reminisce about how they cooked when she was little, and this intensifies the children's interest when they make the same recipe.

Children also enjoy bringing some special foods from home to share with the group. At Thanksgiving they find it fun for each to bring a piece of fruit for a gigantic fruit platter. This helps them appreciate the bounty and plenitude of the earth and also encourages the idea, once fundamental to the holiday, of sharing with others. Since we like the idea of the school also sharing with families, our center prepares quantities of cranberry-orange relish and sends a cup home with each youngster to share at Thanksgiving dinner.

Suggestions for Making Life Easier

When cooking, overcrowding should be avoided because this means that each child gets to take only one stir. It may even be dangerous if the children start shoving for the knife or arguing over a hot pan. Overcrowding can be prevented if at least one other, very attractive activity is deliberately offered at the same time—preferably as far away from the cooking area as possible. Crowding can be reduced also if two adults make the same recipe at separate tables or if one adult repeats the recipe twice so that additional children can participate the second time. Choos-

ing a recipe that offers many things to do that do not require close supervision or that an additional staff member can supervise also alleviates crowding. Finally, the best way to reduce overcrowding is to offer cooking frequently enough that the novelty wears off, while the satisfaction remains. When children know there are plentiful opportunities to take part in an experience, they lose that desperate I-gotta-do-it-now feeling.

Avoid recipes that are too difficult, and allow plenty of time for the children to participate fully. The test of whether a recipe is too difficult is how much of the work the teacher ends up doing herself and whether most of the children remain interested throughout the process. Roll-and-cut cookies seem to me to be a prime example of an activity that requires too much teacher assistance and supervision, although some teachers seem to thrive on making these.

It is always wise to try out a recipe at home before using it with the children. This enables the teacher to anticipate problems and also provides a time line. It is a pity to hurry children through a cooking experience that has such rich learning possibilities, so it is wise to plan plenty of time on cooking days.

Remember that cleanup is half the fun, and plan enough time for children to participate in this process. Children love to do dishes and mess about with soapy sponges, and cooking gives them a fine opportunity to do this while experiencing the satisfaction of meaningful work as well. Think of cleanup as being an integral part of the cooking experience and plan so that children can usually participate in this satisfying aspect of the activity.

Integrate Information About Food Into the Curriculum

Besides actually cooking, it is desirable to include talking about food and good nutrition during the day. There are so many delightful books about food that it is impossible to mention them all, but such treasures as *Blueberries for Sal* (McClosky, 1948), *The Enormous Turnip* (Par-

---

[6]From Clevonease Johnson, head teacher, Santa Barbara City College Children's Center. (We make special exceptions to the ban on sugar when other positive values make this necessary.)

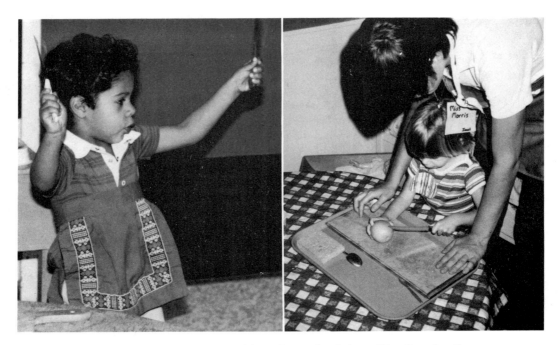

Children require careful, continuing supervision when using knives. Standing directly behind them provides good protection and control for everyone.

kinson, 1986), *Gregory the Terrible Eater* (Sharmat, 1980), *Give a Dog a Bone* (Wildsmith, 1985), *If You Give a Mouse a Cookie* (Numeroff, 1985), and *Bread and Jam for Frances* (Hoban, 1964) tie in well with cooking and eating and are great fun besides.

Parents appreciate knowing what their children are eating during the day, so posting menus in a prominent place helps assure them that the children are being well fed. At the institute, where we have a general policy of serving no dye, no sugar, low-fat and low-salt foods, we have made a point of telling parents about the policy and why we follow it. We couple this with suggestions of nourishing treats they can supply in place of the sticky birthday fare so often provided. Most parents are pleased to comply with our requests for these wholesome substitutes that can include popcorn, trail mix, fresh and dried fruits, and nuts.

SUMMARY

There are many ways of developing the physical well-being and competence of young children. This chapter stresses two of them—keeping children safe and healthy and feeding them well.

When considering physical safety, teachers must use their common sense to decide when to intervene and when not to intervene. They must also continually assess the condition of school equipment to make certain that it has not deteriorated, and they should teach children gradually to think about safety for themselves.

Basic rules of health include consistent hand washing by children and adults, conducting health checks, excluding children from school when they are contagious, maintaining up-to-date immunizations, and taking special care of children who have been ill.

Feeding children well is best approached from

two points of view—planning meals and snacks that are nutritionally sound and offering cooking as a continuing part of the curriculum. Eating well deserves a good deal of attention in children's centers because problems of malnutrition, particularly dental decay and iron deficiency anemia, are widespread among children in the United States.

When choosing recipes to cook with the children, the teacher should select ones that are not too delicate, that offer many things for children to do, that are nourishing and age appropriate, and that come from a variety of cultures.

Recipe for a Happy Day[7]

1 cup friendly words
2 heaping cups of understanding
4 heaping tsp time and patience
A pinch of warm personality
Dash of humor

Mixing:

Measure words carefully. Add heaping cups of understanding. Use generous amounts of time and patience.

Cook on front burner, but keep temperature low; do not boil.

Add generous dash of humor and personality. Season to taste with the spice of life.

Serve in individual molds.

SELF-CHECK QUESTIONS FOR REVIEW

Content-Related Questions

1. What is a good rule of thumb to follow when deciding whether or not an activity is safe for a child to continue?
2. Name some items that would be dangerous to allow in a play yard.
3. Give an example of something you might say to a child after an accident that would be moralizing. Then rephrase it in a more appropriate form.
4. Explain why it is becoming even more important

---

[7]From *Recipes for Busy Little Hands* by D. J. Croft, 1967, Palo Alto, Calif.: Author.

than it used to be to insist that children have their immunizations up-to-date before admission to school.
5. What is HIBS? And how is it best controlled?
6. List some valuable ways of keeping children healthy.
7. What are the two most important health problems related to malnutrition among children of all economic levels in the United States?
8. What are the changes recommended for food selection and preparation that could lead to better health for everyone?
9. List some expensive and less expensive kinds of food that offer adequate nutrition.
10. Explain some helpful points to consider when choosing a recipe to cook with young children.
11. Imagine you are teaching a group of 2-year-olds. Suggest some cooking activities that are appropriate for them. Now do the same thing for 3- and 4-year-olds.
12. Suggest some policies you would follow when planning a cooking experience with children that would make the experience fun and enjoyable for everyone.
13. List some wholesome substitutions for birthday cake that you could suggest parents bring to the center to celebrate their child's special day.

Integrative Questions

1. A mother is enrolling her child in your school and explains that although the youngster's immunizations are not up to date, she will take care of them as soon as possible. Would you or would you not allow that child to enter school? Explain the reasons for your decision.
2. The research study in this chapter on the influence of peers presents interesting possibilities. Could there be other situations where peer example might influence a child's preferences? Propose a possible situation where this might be the case.

QUESTIONS AND ACTIVITIES

1. Do you think women teachers are more likely to be overprotective than men teachers are? Be ready to explain why or why not you think this is true.
2. *Problem:* Elizabeth's mother arrives with her child in tow and says, "Oh, by the way, Elizabeth threw

up in the middle of the night, but she seems to be all right now—I'd appreciate it if you'd keep an eye on her today." How would you handle this situation? Should Elizabeth be allowed to stay at school? Should she be sent home? What would you say to the mother?

3. Suppose you are in charge of planning snacks for the coming week. As a consciousness raising activity, develop five different snacks that have minimal food value but that the children would like a lot. Now develop five with sound nutritional values that children would also relish.

4. What was the most serious accident that has occurred at your center or at one where you were observing in the past month or so? Benefit from this experience by analyzing what could be done to prevent its happening again.

5. *Problem:* You are now teacher in a day-care center, and there is a youngster in your group whose family are strict vegetarians—they eat no animal protein at all, including milk. You serve not only a snack and lunch, but also breakfast. Do you think that you should provide this youngster with a special diet? Should he merely make do with the fruits and vegetables the other children eat, ignoring the animal proteins they also have as part of the planned nutrition program? How do you think you should handle this situation?

6. *White Elephant Corner:* What was the most awful cooking experience you ever had with children? Give the class the fun of hearing all the reasons why it was so awful.

7. Share a recipe with the class that represents your own cultural background.

8. Maintaining adequate immunity against infectious diseases is important for everyone. This is particularly true for young women who may be contemplating pregnancy because rubella (3-day measles) can have such a disastrous effect on the fetus. How up to date are your own immunizations? Investigate the services of your county health clinic and report to the class. Which immunizations are available there at nominal cost?

REFERENCES FOR FURTHER READING

Health and Safety

Kendrick, A. S., Kaufmann, R., & Messenger, K. P. (1988). *Healthy young children: A manual for programs.* Washing-ton, D.C.: National Association for the Education of Young Children. The authors cover everything from nutrition to child abuse and infectious diseases. The writing style is simple and practical in tone.

National Association for the Education of Young Children. (1987). *Child care center disease and sick child care.* Washington, D.C.: The Association. This is a resource guide that includes addresses of specialists, reading resources, the accreditation standards of the National Academy related to health care, and a research article on the links between child care and disease.

Scott, D. K. (1985). Child safety seats—They work! *Young Children, 40*(4), 13–17. This article offers practical suggestions on the value and use of car seats.

Nutrition—General Information

Brody, J. (1981). *Jane Brody's nutrition book.* New York: W. W. Norton & Co. This book has been reviewed by the Center for Science in the Public Interest as "the best all-around nutrition text currently available."

Endres, J. B., & Rockwell, R. E. (1990). *Food, nutrition and the young child* (3rd ed.). Columbus, Ohio: Merrill Publishing Co. This is the best book on feeding young children I have ever seen. Full of practical information, it covers everything from extensive information on menu planning to nutrition education and preparing baby formula.

Williams, S. R. (1986). *Essentials of nutrition and diet therapy* (4th ed.). St. Louis: Times Mirror/Mosby. This book is a well-written, comprehensive introduction to the science of nutrition. Noteworthy for a chapter on food preferences of various ethnic groups. Highly recommended.

Teaching About Good Nutrition and Cooking With Young Children

Baxter, K. M. (1978). *Come and get it: A natural foods cookbook for children.* Ann Arbor, Mich.: Children First Press. This cheerful book offers a wide array of simple, wholesome recipes that children can make. Highly recommended.

Ferreira, N. (1982). *Learning through cooking: A cooking program for children two to ten.* Palo Alto, Calif.: R & E Associates. If you could afford just one such book for your school, I believe this would be the one to choose. All the recipes pay careful attention to nutrition and have been used with children of prekindergarten age.

Goodwin, M. T., & Pollen, G. (1980). *Creative food experiences for children* (rev. ed.). Washington, D.C.: Center for Science in the Public Interest. This is partly a cookbook and partly a book about things to do with children to help them learn about food and sound nutrition. Absolutely first rate and very inexpensive.

Whitener, C. B., & Keeling, M. H. (1984). *Nutrition education for young children: Strategies and activities.* Englewood Cliffs, N.J.: Prentice-Hall. This book offers rich resources on nutrition, feeding procedures, recipes and carryover nutrition activities. Highly recommended.

Wishik, C. S. (1982). *Kids dish it up . . . Sugar-free*. Port Angeles, Wash.: Peninsula Publishing. The recipes in this book are free of sugar, molasses, honey, and artificial sweeteners. They are accompanied with clear illustrations that older fours could learn to interpret.

Taking Cultural Food Preferences Into Account

Three of the references already listed have useful information on this subject. Endres and Rockwell devote an entire chapter to food preferences of various ethnic groups, as does Williams. Goodwin and Pollen offer many recipes from various countries. For additional recipes, I suggest the Sunset series on foreign foods published by the Lane Publishing Company. These books are relatively low in cost, reasonably authentic, and sensible in directions.

Knight, F. D. (1962). *The Ebony cookbook: A date with a dish*. Chicago: Johnson Publishing Co. Because the Sunset line does not include a book on recipes from the Black culture, I include this one from Ebony. Highly recommended.

Tharlet, E. (1987). *The little cooks: Recipes from around the world for boys and girls*. New York: UNICEF. Colorful step-by-step illustrations plus the one-world flavor and costumes of the children make this a recipe book to be used and treasured.

Money Savers

United States Department of Agriculture. (1985). *Your money's worth in foods*. Washington, D.C.: United States Government Printing Office. This publication is filled with simple, practical information on economical shopping and meal preparation. Highly recommended.

Special Problems Related to Eating

Javernick, E. (1988). Johnny's not jumping: Can we help obese children? *Young Children, 43*(2), 18–23. Javernick discusses the problem and recommends planned physical activity as the primary remedy for obesity in young children.

Kessler, J. W. (1966). *Psychopathology of childhood*. Englewood Cliffs, N.J.: Prentice-Hall. This book is written for the serious student who wants to know more about handling special behavior problems. It devotes an entire chapter to eating and toileting problems.

For the Advanced Student

Dobbing, J. (Ed.). (1987). *Early nutrition and later achievement*. London: Academic Press. The articles in this book present chilling evidence that early nutrition significantly affects the growth and development of young children. Reports are readable but quite technical.

Kane, D. N. (1985). *Environmental hazards to young children*. Phoenix: ORYX Press. Kane includes grim evidence documenting the importance of safety. The author explains the necessity of protecting children from hazards such as traffic, fire, and poisonous substances.

Journals and Organizations of Particular Interest

Center for Science in the Public Interest. 1501 16th St., N.W., Washington, D.C., 20036–1499. CSPI publishes a first-rate advocacy newsletter entitled *Nutrition Action Health Letter* and also various attractive charts and books about nutrition. The Goodwin and Pollen book, previously listed, is one of their efforts.

Child Health Alert. Box 338, Newton Highlands, Massachusetts 02161. This monthly publication covers subjects ranging from what to do about head lice to sports and their effect on the epileptic child. It provides a quick way to keep up to date on a wide variety of child health issues.

Child Health Talk. Published by the National Black Child Develoment Institute, 1463 Rhode Island Ave., N.W., Washington, D.C. 20005. The Institute newsletter features health and nutrition advice about young children.

8 Developing Physical Competence

Have you ever

- Thought that although preschool teachers paid a lot of attention to creative and social development, they did not do much to help children develop their perceptual-motor skills?
- Wondered what should be offered to enhance those skills?
- Wondered not only how to start a dance experience but also how to prevent it from turning into chaos?

If you have, the material in this chapter will help you.

What joy is in the body! The joy of work and of hard purposeful effort, the joy of singing, the joy of sport and activity, the joy of tenderness and physical touch, the joy of controlling physical things. Children have a tendency toward them all. Softly feel a baby's head, rough-house with a two-year-old, watch a three-year-old squeeze shapes from a square block of clay, and you'll see the opening melodies of the body's joy.

Inhibition and fear take away the body's joy. Children learn inhibitions and fear from us. How can we avoid it? First, we must help them to try physical things without intimidation, embarrassment, or fear. We must help them begin to sense the simple enjoyment of the functioning of their bodies. Then beyond that, we must help them find and concentrate on the particular physical things that they do especially well, the things in which they are gifted, be they sports, music, crafts, dance, or whatever their own particular gifts suggest.

LINDA EYRE and RICHARD EYRE (1984)

In addition to making sure that children's bodies are well nourished and that the children are learning to cherish and care for them, teachers also need to do all that they can to encourage sound physical development through exercise. This is because recent studies indicate that physical fitness is declining among young children in the United States. For example, 40% of 5- to 8-year-old children show at least one of the following risk factors for heart disease—elevated blood pressure, higher than desirable cholesterol ratings, or low levels of physical activity (Javernick, 1988). This situation is bound to become worse as children spend longer and longer hours squatting in front of television sets and playing with computers.

The word *exercise* may sound ominous if the reader immediately pictures children lined up in rows performing like a drill team, yet physical exercise is surely one of the activities dearest to the hearts of these youngsters, who are busy acquiring all kinds of large- and small-muscle skills during the early years of their lives.

Physical activity benefits all the selves. No other kind of activity offers such rich opportunities for the development of all the selves. Obviously the body benefits—and so does the emotional self, as the child acquires feelings of competence through the acquisition of new skills, or uses physical activity as an acceptable channel for aggressive feelings, or involves herself in creative dance to explore a wide range of emotions. The cooperative interplay between children and the satisfaction of doing things together develops the social self. The cognitive self is enhanced as children learn about body image and spatial relationships, and the creative self is provided with opportunities for original thinking that are encouraged by movement exploration activities and also nourished by the marvelous creative opportunities inherent in dance experiences.

Because of these benefits, physical activity is of great value to the young child, and it behooves teachers to think carefully about its educational potential to help children make the most of its possibilities. What is needed is the

EVALUATION CRITERIA FOR A 5-YEAR-OLD CHILD

A 5-Year-Old Child Should Be Able:

1. to balance on his preferred foot, with eyes open, with arms folded, for at least 4 seconds.
2. to catch a 16-inch rubber ball bounced chest high from distance of 15 feet, four out of five times.
3. to jump forward and to hop forward on one foot three consecutive times.
4. to identify body parts, limbs, front, back, and sides.
5. to run in a coordinated manner, with integration of arms and legs.
6. to jump over a 10-inch high barrier.

It Is Unlikely That a 5-Year-Old Will Be Able:

1. to identify his left and right body parts better than would be expected by chance (i.e. better than 50% correct responses).
2. to alternately hop from foot to foot, without undue hesitation or placing both feet on the ground simultaneously, in either a ½, ⅓, or ⅔ pattern.
3. to touch a ball swinging on a 15-inch string through a 180° arc, arm's distance away.
4. to jump or hop with accuracy into small squares.

Note. From *Perceptual-Motor Efficiency in Children: The Measurement and Improvement of Movement Attributes* by B. J. Cratty and M. M. Martin, 1969, Philadelphia: Lea & Febiger.

---

development of a comprehensive physical development program that does not regiment the children, but does provide opportunities to practice many different kinds of skills.

The best way to achieve this lies in acquiring general knowledge of the likely ages for acquisition of various skills and specific knowledge of the developmental needs of the individual children. This information should then be used to plan a comprehensive program using perceptual-motor activities, movement exploration, and creative dance. These experiences should be offered in attractive forms so that children will seek them out, rather than having to be coerced into participation.

IDENTIFYING LEVELS OF DEVELOPMENT

It only makes sense to plan physical activities that fit the developmental stages of the children. Threes, for instance, are a lot more likely to be interested in simple climbing skills and riding tricycles than they will be at catching balls or skipping rope.

For the approximate ages at which the average preschooler attains various skills, Table 8–1 provides a useful index.

Once the teacher has an idea of the general level of ability in his group and is also aware of children who have special talents or who lack motor skills that most children have acquired by their age, he has a solid foundation for knowing what level of activities he should include in his program. One word of caution is in order, however. Although the sequence in which children develop physical skills remains fairly constant, the time of acquisition varies considerably, and this must be taken into account when evaluating developmental status. Just because a child is 6 months ahead or behind the time listed in Table 8–1, the teacher should not conclude that he is either an athletic genius or a potential klutz. Gross deviations, on the other hand, should be cause for further investigation by a pediatrician.

It is also of interest to refer to the box on this page from Cratty and Martin to obtain a general feeling for the kinds of things children are able to do and not do by the time they enter kindergarten.

TABLE 8–1
Sequence of emergence of selected locomotor, manipulative, and stability abilities

Movement pattern	Selected abilities	Approximate age of onset
Locomotor abilities		
Walking		
Walking involves placing one foot in front of the other while maintaining contact with the supporting surface	Rudimentary upright unaided gait	13 months
	Walks sideways	16 months
	Walks backward	17 months
	Walks upstairs with help	20 months
	Walks upstairs alone—follow step	24 months
	Walks downstairs alone—follow step	25 months
Running		
Running involves a brief period of no contact with the supporting surface	Hurried walk (maintains contact)	18 months
	First true run (nonsupport phase)	2-3 years
	Efficient and refined run	4-5 years
	Speed of run increases	5 years
Jumping		
Jumping takes three forms: (1) jumping for distance; (2) jumping for height; and (3) jumping from a height. It involves a one- to two-foot takeoff with a landing on both feet	Steps down from low objects	18 months
	Jumps down from object with both feet	2 years
	Jumps off floor with both feet	28 months
	Jumps for distance (about 3 feet)	5 years
	Jumps for height (about 1 foot)	5 years
Hopping		
Hopping involves a one-foot take-off with a landing on the same foot	Hops up to three times on preferred foot	3 years
	Hops from four to six times on same foot	4 years
	Hops from eight to ten times on same foot	5 years
	Hops distance of 50 feet in about 11 seconds	5 years
	Hops skillfully with rhythmical alteration	6 years
Galloping		
The gallop combines a walk and a leap with the same foot leading throughout	Basic but inefficient gallop	4 years
	Gallops skillfully	6 years
Skipping		
Skipping combines a step and a hop in rhythmic alteration	One-footed skip	4 years
	Skillful skipping (about 20 percent)	5 years
	Skillful skipping for most	6 years

Note. From *Developmental Movement Experiences for Children* by D. L. Gallahue, 1982. Copyright © 1982, John Wiley & Sons, Inc. Reprinted by permission of John Wiley & Sons, Inc.

TABLE 8–1 (*continued*)

Movement pattern	Selected abilities	Approximate age of onset
Manipulative abilities		
Reach, grasp, release		
Reaching, grasping, and releasing involve making successful contact with an object, retaining it in one's grasp and releasing it at will	Primitive reaching behaviors	2-4 months
	Corralling of objects	2-4 months
	Palmar grasp	3-5 months
	Pincer grasp	8-10 months
	Controlled grasp	12-14 months
	Controlled releasing	14-18 months
Throwing		
Throwing involves imparting force to an object in the general direction of intent	Body faces target, feet stationary, ball thrown with forearm extension only	2-3 years
	Same as above but with body rotation added	3.6-5 years
	Steps forward with leg on same side as the throwing arm	5-6 years
	Mature throwing pattern	6.6 years
	Boys exhibit more mature pattern than girls	6 years and over
Catching		
Catching involves receiving force from an object with the hands, moving from large to progressively smaller balls	Chases ball; does not respond to aerial ball	2 years
	Responds to aerial ball with delayed arm movements	2-3 years
	Needs to be told how to position arms	2-3 years
	Fear reaction (turns head away)	3-4 years
	Basket catch using the body	3 years
	Catches using the hands only with a small ball	5 years
Kicking		
Kicking involves imparting force to an object with the foot	Pushes against ball. Does not actually kick it	18 months
	Kicks with leg straight and little body movement (kicks *at* the ball)	2-3 years
	Flexes lower leg on backward lift	3-4 years
	Greater backward and forward swing with definite arm opposition	4-5 years
	Mature pattern (kicks *through* the ball)	5-6 years

EQUIPMENT FOR PHYSICAL DEVELOPMENT

It was stressed in previous chapters that equipment should be durable, safe, and well maintained. (See also the discussion of outdoor equipment in Chapter 4, and note particularly the discussion of simple, complex, and super play units on pages 69–70.) We often think of *equipment* as meaning large, permanent structures, and some sorts of vigorous activity do require this kind of installation. However, many activities suggested in Table 8–2 do not require large, elaborate equipment at all.

TABLE 8–1 (*continued*)

Movement pattern	Selected abilities	Approximate age of onset
Manipulative abilities—cont'd		
Striking		
Striking involves sudden contact to objects in an overarm, side-arm, or underhand pattern	Faces object and swings in a vertical plane	2-3 years
	Swings in a horizontal plane and stands to the side of the object	4-5 years
	Rotates the trunk and hips and shifts body weight forward. Mature horizontal patterns	5 years 6-7 years
Stability abilities		
Dynamic balance		
Dynamic balance involves maintaining one's equilibrium as the center of gravity shifts	Walks 1-inch straight line	3 years
	Walks 1-inch circular line	4 years
	Stands on low balance beam	2 years
	Walks on 4-inch wide beam short distance	3 years
	Walks on same beam, alternating feet	3-4 years
	Walks on 2- or 3-inch beam	4 years
	Performs basic forward roll	3-4 years
	Performs mature forward roll	6-7 years
Static balance		
Static balance involves maintaining one's equilibrium while the center of gravity remains stationary	Pulls to a standing position	10 months
	Stands without handholds	11 months
	Stands alone	12 months
	Balances on one foot 3-5 seconds	5 years
	Supports body in basic inverted positions	6 years
Axial movements		
Axial movements are static postures that involve bending, stretching, twisting, turning and the like	Axial movement abilities begin to develop early in infancy and are progressively refined to a point where they are included in the emerging manipulative patterns of throwing, catching, kicking, striking, trapping, and other activities	2 months- 6 years

As the research study presented in this chapter substantiates, the best resource for physical play activity remains the child's ideas and her body, combined with a variety of readily obtainable accessories, such as boards, ladders, tires, barrels, boxes, and blocks. These kinds of materials have the capacity for infinite rearrange-ment necessary for the generation of creative, large-muscle play.

Some of these items, such as hollow blocks, are best purchased, though I once saw a very substantial painted set that had been made from old whiskey boxes. However, much portable equipment can be built. Some can even be

TABLE 8–2
Some suggestions for perceptual-motor and movement education activities

Physical ability	Perceptual-motor activity		Movement education activity
	Easier	More challenging	
Tension releasers—relaxation strategies See discussion in text: Helping children learn to relax			
Locomotion			
Rolling (5 months)* (mats are nice but not essential)	Roll over and over, sideways—both directions. Roll downhill (and try rolling up!)	Roll with arms overhead or do forward roll somersault (age 5), arms around knees—roll "butterball" style. Roll about, balanced on top of very large ball. Be rolled by someone else while braced in large tire	Roll to music "I roll myself over and over". Roll toward sound of drum with eyes closed—changing directions as drummer moves
Creeping and crawling (10 months)	Can use legs straight or bent. Crawl with arm and leg on same side of body parallel or in opposition (X) movement. Encourage crawling on textured surfaces for increased sensory input	Crawl while pushing a ball with head or following a line. Wriggle across floor using only arms (GI crawl)	Play at being various crawly animals—snakes, lizards, turtles, bears, cats, and so on. For control, creep slowly and then pounce—while singing "Old Grey Cat Goes Creeping"—or be spider singing "Eensy Weensy Spider". Ask children can they crawl under, over, through, and so forth—try big cardboard boxes for this
Climbing (as early as age 2; proficient at 4) (ladder climbing mastered by age 6)	Slide ladder is often only fixed ladder on playground; can also use jungle gyms, arched climbers, cargo nets, or A-frames—good to encourage hand-over-hand, foot-over-foot activity	Rope ladder or fireman's ladder. Ladders with more distance between rungs are more difficult. Steeper is harder. Ramp to top of sewer pipe, jump off. Attaching rope to top of slide and climbing up hand over hand	For children who know the story, "Jack and the Bean Stalk" provides lots of pretend climbing

Stair climbing (going up alternating feet with support, 29 months; going down alternating feet with support, 48 months)	Climbing can also include hills, ramps, and so on Ramp to low block, jump off	Short stair risers and brief flights Fun to look for stairs on excursions	Go on to higher risers, and longer flights	Try an escalator. Pretend children are on an escalator that breaks down
Walking	By age 3, walking should be automatic and skillful	Walk in different styles Tiptoe (after 30 months) Step between rungs of ladder laid on floor, or onto large hollow block stepping stones	Can you walk on only part of your foot? Vary steps—force (stomp and pussyfoot); space (baby steps and giant steps); time (quick and slow); to music Walk duck style—crouched down, holding ankles Walk in deep snow Walk on ice Walk through honey Walk on wet sidewalk Dance barefoot on different textures—carpet and smooth floor, or on grass and then through sandbox Sliding (step together, hop) is quite difficult, but fun	
Use of wheel toys	Kiddy cars (18 months +) Trikes (proficient at 3 if experience has been available)	Two types of Irish Mail (parallel pumping with hands, steering with feet; alternate pumping with hands, steering with feet) Obstacle courses that challenge steering of trikes can be fun if not overregulated	The song "Wheels on the Bus" fits well here	

Based on Arnheim, D.D., and Sinclair, W.A. (1978). *The clumsy child* (2nd ed.). St. Louis: The C.V. Mosby Co.

*Age standards for developmental skill acquisition obtained from tables in Espenschade and Eckert (1967) or Sinclair (1973). These standards usually reflect point at which 50% of children have acquired the skill. For precise definition of skill, refer to references.

TABLE 8–2 (continued)

| Physical ability | Perceptual-motor activity | | | Movement education activity |
	Easier	More challenging		
Locomotion—cont'd				
Jumping (28 months)	Jumping is easier than hopping Jump over lines or off low heights	Jump over low objects Jump off higher things onto mattress Jump rope swung in half arc slowly, or whirled in circle on ground Jump and land "on target" marked with tape or carpet square		Rabbits, grasshoppers, popcorn, and birds all jump Can act out emotions of animals, such as a scared rabbit Position in space by jumping in and out of hoops; more advanced form, one child jumps in as another jumps out; be a frog jumping on a lily pad; jump in something sticky like molasses
Hopping (age 3—hop two or three times, same foot)	Hop one or two steps on one foot, over lines, and so on	Hop several times, same foot		For alternate hopping activity, Claire Cherry suggests Indian dancing What can you do on one foot? On one arm?
Skipping		14% of fours and 22% of fives can skip; therefore, not appropriate to stress at nursery school level		
Running and leaping (children are accomplished runners by age 4)	Very desirable to have large open space for this—conveys marvelous feeling of pleasure and freedom	Can foster agility by encouraging figure-8 runs; this is quite difficult for fours		Crouch down and "explode" on signal by leaping up; run and stop in time to music or play "freeze"; leap over "puddles" on floor Can you run like a mouse? Like an elephant? Run as if the wind is pushing you Run as butterflies fly Do shadow running and leaping, moving as partner does
Balance				
Static (balance while still)	Stand on tiptoe; try balancing lying on side	Balance on hollow block Balance on one foot Stand still with eyes closed		Hold still as long as drum doesn't beat Can you balance on three parts of your body? Without touching the floor? Without using your feet? Play "statues"

Dynamic (balance while moving) (both feet on beam, walk part way, 38 months)	Use a balance board—wider is easier Walk, with one foot on, one foot off beam; walk along log, curb, edge of wall, or thin chalk line	Both feet on beam (4-inch beam or, if proficient, use narrow side of beam), or walk sideways, foot over foot on beam Visit a "clatter" bridge (may overwhelm some children) Walk on well anchored gang-plank between A-frames Skate on one roller skate Use a scooter Walk around an edge of tire or "toober" (big inner tube) Step over thin ropes laid across balance beam Walk on edges of ladder	How can you get to end of balance beam without walking on it? Imagine you're on a tightrope Dance on tiptoe—slowly for greater challenge
With object	Roll a tire Crawl, with beanbag on back Walk with beanbags, arms extended from sides	Roll a hoop Balance beanbag on back of hand Balance balloon or small ball on hand Walk on wide plank—with one weighted pole on one side or carrying bottle of sand on one side Walk carrying something spillable in bowl	Dance with hoop or paper parasol or very large fans (can be obtained from stores specializing in oriental goods) and retain balance What can you do with the fan? How far can you bend over with it?
Body and space perception	How many people can fit in the box? Guess, then try it How high can you reach? Any activity that fosters knowledge of body parts such as "Head, Shoulders, Knees, and Toes"	Play "Simon says" Use screen that just lets shoes show—guess who the shoes belong to Shut eyes—guess who you are touching by touch alone Do something with body and tell what you did in words Work on identifying more difficult body parts—eyebrows, elbows, toenails, eyelids Traffic course on bikes requiring careful steering	Any activity requiring movement in space, varied in *tempo* (pace and rhythm); *force* of motion, particularly where awareness is stressed All body-object relationships—"on," "under," "behind," and so on, that is, directionality How slow can you creep? How fast can you run? Practically any kind of finger play Move in water if a pool is available All activities where expression of emotion or physical states is encouraged—a "tired" dance, for instance

TABLE 8–2 (continued)

Physical ability	Perceptual-motor activity		Movement education activity
	Easier	More challenging	
Body and space perception—cont'd			Have child move like an animal of his choosing—ask others to guess animal
			Use "mirror" or shadow dancing
			How close can you get to your partner and not touch him?
			Ask "what can you do with your toes?" and "Anything else?"
			Have children propose ways to use the parachute
Rhythm and temporal awareness	Any activity that has a regularly recurring rhythm to it—rocking boats, swings, even tricycles, rocking chairs	Jump over rope	Rocking with partner—singing "Row, Row, Row Your Boat"
(even newborns are sensitive to different rhythms)		Jump rope swung in half arc	Marching and other moving to music activities that emphasize response to "beat"
For further discussion, see text: Movement education (p. 145) and Helping children enjoy creative dance (pp. 145; 148–149)	Any kind of bouncing equipment (see Rebound and airborne activities below)	Galloping has definite rhythm (rudiments acquired by age 4)	Shaking activities—like wet dog, like salt shaker, "Looby Lou" (rhythm band is a conforming, not creative, rhythmic activity)
	Fingerpaint to music	Can clap hands in pattern—knees, hands, head	Dance to holiday music—contrasting rhythm of "Jingle Bells" to "White Christmas," for instance
	Ride bouncy horses to music		Move according to poetic chants— "John Brown's body" has a lot of appeal
			Marching and using instruments at same time is more difficult
Rebound and airborne activities			
Jumping activities	Involves jumping skills combined with timing	Jump on "toober"	Can you bounce another way? Sitting down? Squatting?
	Equipment such as mattress, box springs, bouncing boards are appropriate	Try turning while jumping	Bouncing activities are particularly satisfying when music is added
		Jump on and off low mattress	Vary tempo to encourage variety of kinds of bounces

	Do not use trampolines; they require too much supervision and training (Many insurance companies now refuse insurance on this equipment.) Bouncing has added value as an aggression reliever		
Hanging and stretching activities	Simply hang and stretch from exercise bar	Use hand-over-hand exercise ladders Use trapeze for swinging and hanging Hang by knees from exercise bar	

Projectile management

Throwing (easier than catching—children not really proficient until 5)	Roll large balls to partner Throw soft balls, such as Nerf balls	Roll at target—large empty bleach bottles Throw at target or through hoop For advanced children, try combination of running and throwing	Pretend you're rolling something big and heavy—or as light as thistledown Scarves and streamers for waving in air
Catching (also not well developed at preschool level)	Begin with catching a rolled ball between legs; encourage child to keep eyes open Requires adult to throw ball to child for proper chance of catching; best to use large ball Bounce ball with two hands	Catch slightly smaller ball Bounce and catch ball Try a pitchback net	Catch soap bubbles (watch out for slippery floor)
Kicking (requires ability to poise on one foot)	Kick large, still ball	Kick gently rolling ball Can roll faster to increase challenge	
Striking (makes teachers nervous but children enjoy it even though it takes close supervision)	Keep balloons in air with hand Hit punching bag mounted on spindle Hit whiffle ball poised on traffic cone with plastic bat	Hit balloon with paddle Hit ball hung from string with paddle Use large plastic bat and ball; adult pitches	Dance with balloons

TABLE 8–2 (continued)

| Physical ability | Perceptual-motor activity | | Movement education activity |
	Easier	More challenging	
Management of daily motor skills (essentially tool manipulation skills that require not just eye-hand or eye-foot coordination, but also eye-finger coordination)	Use of tools that do not require extremely fine control, including such cooking utensils as potato mashers and spoons; carpentry tools, such as hammers and saws; and self-expressive items, such as paint brushes and gluing activities; also manipulative items, such as pegs, puzzles, blocks of various descriptions	Tools that require more control such as scissors, braces and bits, rotary egg beaters, tweezers, and large needles	
	Skills, such as simple buttoning	Self-care skills—fitting zipper parts together, buttoning small buttons, and occasionally, shoe tying	
	Bead stringing—large beads Puzzles—large pieces, few in number, within a frame	Bead stringing—small beads Puzzles—smaller pieces, more numerous ones, greater variety of types	
	Simple manipulation of scissors	Using scissors to cut on lines or to cut fabric	
	"Bristle" blocks, cubical counting blocks Pegs in peg hole boards	Lego blocks; Tinker Toys; Lincoln Logs	

wheedled for free from businesses such as milk companies that donate old milk crates or tire companies that give away worn tires.

When larger structures are needed, there is no other place in the preschool where one can spend so much money so quickly. There is no denying there are some beautiful, physically satisfying structures available for purchase, but fortunately there are also many ways of achieving equivalent play value without spending a fortune. Several good resource books on this subject that demonstrate how to apply ingenuity and free labor to the problem of building satisfying play equipment for children are listed at the end of this chapter.

Each community offers its own potential for free materials for such construction. Among ones frequently available are railroad ties, logs sawn into various heights, boulders for climbing, chipped sewer pipes for tunnels, and strong dead trees.

People, too, are good free resources. Park and street department people are often generous with advice and surplus materials if contacted by day-care centers. Park and recreation people, in particular, are deeply interested in and knowledgeable about large-muscle play equipment. Ask them for suggestions about planning and for community sources of free materials—they are used to making dollars stretch.

It is of utmost importance to ensure that whatever is built is safe, and that it is *twice* as strong as you think it should be. Never assume that just because the children are small, equipment need not be well braced and firmly built. In fact, young children are very hard on equipment. They use apparatus vigorously and constantly, and construction must take this into account if the equipment is to last more than a few months.

Finally, every center has its own unique potential for physical experiences. It may be a large, blank wall to bounce balls against, or a gentle slope for the children to roll down, or something as seemingly undesirable as a completely paved playground that also means a quickly drying surface in almost all weather. The point is that there are hidden assets in every situation if teachers will take a fresh look at their environment from time to time and then put these possibilities to work.

MAKING A PLAN FOR COMPREHENSIVE PHYSICAL DEVELOPMENT

Besides identifying the current level of the children's physical skills, the teachers also need some kind of comprehensive outline (taxonomy) to follow to make certain that they are not leaving out an important motor ability. I favor using the outline by Arnheim and Sinclair (1978) and Arnheim and Pestolesi (1978) as a guide because it requires relatively few categories, is reasonably comprehensive, and is easy to understand.

These categories include *locomotion,* which encompasses various ways of moving from one place to another, and *balance,* which pertains to balancing either while standing still or while moving. Awareness of one's body (where it is and what it can do) not only is important in such activities as gymnastics, but also is significant to children's sense of identity and self-esteem; thus, *body and space perception* is the third category. *Rhythmic activities* help children integrate and pace their physical movements, as well as add pleasure to what they are doing. *Rebound and airborne activities* refer to the bouncing and jumping so dear to the hearts of preschoolers, and also to the stretching and swinging movements entailed in the use of hand-over-hand exercise bars. *Projectile management* is a somewhat fancy term for throwing, catching, and otherwise moving an object through space by hitting it. *Daily motor skills* comprise what early childhood teachers usually speak of as fine muscle skills.

It will be evident from examining Table 8–2 that some kinds of activities, such as climbing activities and swinging, are best included through informal, spontaneous play and are

RESEARCH STUDY
What Kinds of Play Equipment Do Children Prefer?

Research Question   Which kind of outdoor play environment is most attractive to young children during free play?

Research Method   The subjects consisted of 138 middle-class Anglo children enrolled in kindergarten, first, or second grade in a private school.

The children had the choice of using three differing outdoor play environments. Environment A was a wood structure containing interior and exterior space for climbing and dramatic play, including tire swings, a slide, and a fireman's pole and ladder. It was basically a single structure with several activities included. Cost was about $5,000.

Environment B offered an array of 16 wood structures including balance beams, chinning bars, obstacle climbers, a suspension bridge, slide, jungle gym, and so forth. Equipment was linked together and the primary intention was to promote gross motor activity. Cost was about $5,000.

Environment C was made by parents and staff of the school according to a design furnished by the researchers. It consisted of a slide, fort, boat, car, storage, picnic table, three types of climbers, wheel vehicles, and used materials including tires, spools, barrels, railroad ties, and utility poles. It provided a wide range of experiences with opportunities for self-expression combined with action-oriented equipment (wheel vehicles and some movable items). Cost was $1,425, with some materials donated.

The children's choice and use of the three environments was recorded for one 30-minute free-play session a week for 6 weeks, and each child was recorded three times during that 30-minute period. Selection of play area was left entirely to the individual children.

Results   During these observations, Environment C (the most varied one) attracted the most children, comprising over 63% of choices. Environment A (the

usually available in most children's centers. Others, such as relaxation strategies, balancing techniques, and beginning throwing and catching skills, may be less familiar and require planned inclusion.

Teachers should supply appropriate vocabulary along with each activity, since children are unlikely to possess such language without such assistance. This helps children identify what

they are doing, extends their range of information, and may enhance, in some fashion that is not yet completely understood, their motor planning skills by tying the cognitive component to the action. This vocabulary may be as simple as this statement to a young two: "Jumpy, jump, jump!" or as elaborate as this comment to a 4-year-old: "See how your toes are gripping the edge of the tire underneath—they're inside, and

single structure) attracted the next most, with over 23%, and Environment B (the "linked" gross-motor unit) the least, with just over 13%. In terms of total numbers of choices made by the children, Environment C attracted 1,641 children, A attracted 600 children, and B attracted 345 children during the time of the study.

The younger children chose C much more frequently than they chose A or B. As grade level increased, A and B became more popular as did play involving games with rules.

Implications for Teaching The investigators concluded that, particularly for children of kindergarten age, providing a single-play structure (Environment A) or a combination that only elicits gross-motor play (Environment B) is not sufficient for meeting the free-play needs of young children.

Children prefer complex structures that offer several play options and equipment that is movable and does something. They also prefer play equipment that they can change to meet the requirements of their play, rather than having to adjust to an immovable arrangement where they must conform to the dictates of the structure. If teachers want to promote balanced outdoor play involving dramatic and imaginative play as well as simple gross motor activity, they need to provide a variety of equipment to promote such play.

It is also worthwhile to consider the cost/use ratio apparent in the three environments. For teachers of young children seeking the most play value for their dollar, clearly the design of Environment C not only provides the greatest variety of play experiences for the children but is also the most economical one to construct.

Note. From "Equipment Choices of Young Children During Free Play" by J. L. Frost and E. Strickland. In *When Children Play: Proceedings of the International Conference on Play and Play Environments,* edited by J. L. Frost and S. Sunderland, 1985, Wheaton, Md.: Association for Childhood Education International.

---

you're outside." Either statement identifies and enriches the child's experience at an appropriate level.

Note that Table 8–2 includes easier and more difficult items to demonstrate how curriculum can be developed to suit the developmental levels of younger and older children.

It is particularly important to be aware of fine muscle skills (referred to in Table 8–2 under the heading "Management of Daily Motor Skills"). These skills are so inherent to and pervasive in activities of the early school years that teachers sometimes fail to think of them as psychomotor skills and take them more or less for granted. We must realize however that such fine muscle skills are not equally easy for all youngsters to master and that *expecting young children to work at such skills for too long at a time without relief can be a real*

Sometimes it's good to just take a rest from climbing.

source of strain. Moreover, teachers should regularly take a careful look at all the children as they are handling small manipulative items, such as beads or puzzles, and be on the alert for undue clumsiness, excessive frustration, and for children who habitually hold such work too close to their eyes or who avoid such activities altogether. All these behaviors are indications that children may be having special eye-hand coordination problems. Such youngsters should be referred promptly to their pediatricians, ophthalmologists, or optometrists for further identification of the difficulty.

PRESENTATION OF ACTIVITIES

In general, the more informal the presentation of such activities is, the more ideal, since an easy-going, casual approach is the antithesis of regimentation. However, the reader should not construe informal to mean unplanned. A good

physical development program *does* require careful planning to make certain that opportunities for practice are provided for developing each of the listed skills at various levels of challenge.

Basics to Remember

No matter which skill and level of skill the teacher has selected, there are some general principles to remember that apply to all of them.

1. Remember to welcome ideas and variations suggested by the children—in the final analysis they know better than the teacher what they are ready to learn next.
2. It is necessary to offer repeated opportunities for practice when children are learning new skills—once is not enough.

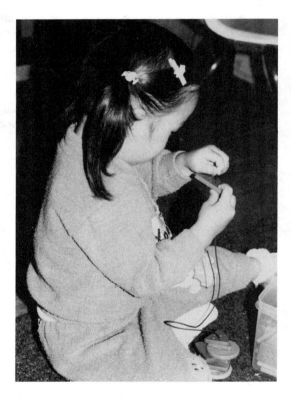

Never underestimate the degree of skill and concentration required for fine muscle work.

Swinging from a trapeze is a good example of a combined airborne and rhythmic activity.

3. Encourage movement backward and sideways, as well as forward. Keep possibilities open—do not settle for "visual, frontal, and flexed" activities.

4. Encourage children to try the same movement on each side of the body.

5. Plan activities that use more than one level in space—lying on floor, sitting, kneeling, and standing.

6. Ask children to stop and change direction while moving.

7. Include movements, such as fingerpainting or playing elephant, that require swinging arms or legs across the midline of the body. It is thought that these movements enhance shifting control centers between the hemispheres of the brain.

8. Look for ways to increase tactile input (input from sense of touch), such as dancing barefoot on a variety of surfaces.

9. Keeping safety in mind, encourage children to try activities with their eyes closed to help them be more aware of their kinesthetic sense (sensory information coming from joints and muscles).

10. Include movements that sometimes require parallel and sometimes cross-action patterns of arm and leg movements.

11. Do not emphasize teaching the concept of left and right—preschool children are too young for this to have much meaning.

12. Remember to include a variety of activities that provide quietness and relaxation, as well as more energetic ones.

13. Keep movement sessions short enough to be fun. Do not push children to the edge of exhaustion.

14. Remember to keep safety in mind—and help children think about it, too.

Including Activities in the Daily Schedule

Plan Specific Activities. One way to include activities is to refer to Table 8–2 and make certain that one or two activities are offered each day that enhance the specific skills listed there. This not only helps ensure coverage, but also breaks the sterile monotony of many outdoor play times in which the only variations may be the way hollow blocks are used or a few new toys in the sandbox. Children appreciate the changing opportunities and often work seriously and persistently until they have mastered the new skill—a sure indication that the activity has more to offer than mere novelty.

Develop Obstacle Courses. Another way to present perceptual-motor activities is to offer obstacle and action courses once or twice a week. This can put both the teacher's and children's ingenuity to work if the teacher asks, "Let's see, what could we use to jump into today?" or "What would be fun to balance on?" It is interesting to note that the children often concoct things to do that are a lot harder than what the grown-up considers reasonable.

Some general things to remember about obstacle courses are that they require a large, maneuverable area, that they should be supervised carefully (particularly if the teacher has some specific skills in mind that he hopes the children will practice), and finally that it is fun to change them while they are being used.

Honoring Developmental Tastes and Preferences

Two-year-olds love to crawl (through tires, plastic snap-together blocks, and large, open pipes), climb (sets of stairs and A-frames), and jump from low heights onto mattresses or other spongy materials. They love balancing tasks on low, wide boards, but are easily frightened of being too high up or of being shut in tunnels or boxes. Repetition of basic physical activities can be such a passion with twos that it may seem almost obsessive to the adults in charge.[1]

Three-year-olds enjoy activities similar to those enjoyed by twos, but they are much more competent, particularly in the domain of balance and coordination. They like to develop their own ideas of how to build tunnels and construct other exciting physical experiences.

Whereas 2-year-olds require careful supervision because they are inexperienced and cannot always anticipate results adequately, 4-year-olds require supervision because they enjoy taking risks and doing daring stunts. It is as though, now that they have acquired basic physical competencies, they feel impelled to test these to the utmost. They enjoy tumbling activities, balancing on more difficult beams, hanging upside down by their knees, and jumping from considerable heights. Of all the ages of children, fours are the ones for whom teachers need to offer the most challenge and variety.

---

[1] I am indebted to Paula Machado, former specialist in 2-year-olds for the Santa Barbara City College Children's Center, for these comments.

Table 8–3 is an example of a student assignment illustrating how the full range of activities may be incorporated into the daily schedule.

Helping Children Learn to Relax

Early childhood teachers have long recognized the necessity of having quiet times during the day, such as nap or midmorning rests. The ability to make good use of these times by genuinely relaxing varies a good deal from child to child. The more tense the child, the more difficulty she will have letting go—and the more she needs to do so. We often think of tension as being revealed by restlessness or a strained facial expression, but there are many other signs to look for. These are seen in children who hold their bodies in tense positions (hunched shoulders or clenched jaws), who appear immobile, or who are awkward or inhibited in movement. Other indicators of tension that are familiar include the inability to eat or a compensatory need to eat more than necessary, breathing difficulties, blushing or turning pale, cold hands or feet, the need to urinate frequently, tension headaches, and insomnia (Rathbone, 1969). When one reviews this list, the value of freeing a child from such burdens by teaching her to relax becomes apparent.

Teachers can help children learn to relax by using the simple method advocated by Jacobson (1976). Described in very general terms, this involves helping children learn to perceive how their bodies feel when they are tense and how they feel when they are relaxed and then helping them learn to relax at will. Young children can grasp this fairly readily if asked to make themselves as stiff and tight as possible or to walk like a robot, and then to make themselves as floppy as a soft rag doll or to melt like a Popsicle. Mirrors are helpful accessories because the children can observe their faces when they scrunch them up tight and then let them go soft. They can also be encouraged to look at other children and tell when they are tensing or relaxing. Emphasis should be placed on repeatedly contrasting tense and relaxed states until the children identify them easily and produce each state at will. Once they have mastered whole body relaxation, they can work on isolated areas, such as legs or arms or hands.

Stretching and yawning are excellent relaxation inducers, as are simple yoga exercises for breathing that can be used with older fours and fives. Of course, using soothing music and reducing extraneous stimulation, such as that caused by children and staff going in and out of the room during rest period, are basic to achieving success when teaching relaxation.

Movement Education

In addition to the kinds of activities that have already been discussed, an additional activity teachers often use to foster the physical development of children is termed *movement education.*

Although not as free as creative dance, there are creative aspects to it, since teachers using this approach stress creative thinking on the part of the children. Movement education also helps children become more conscious of their bodies and what their bodies can do. Thus, the teacher might ask the children to show him all the ways they can balance a beanbag or show how they might get from one corner of the room to the other without using their feet. Because this approach often uses music, it is pleasurable to children and thus can make physical development seem less like exercise and more like fun. A combination of movement exploration activities and creative dance makes a good blend— movement education helps ensure that the range of perceptual-motor activities is complete and that concepts of body image are developed, and dance (discussed in a later section of this chapter) ensures opportunities for rhythmic improvisation and self-expression.

In my opinion, teachers must be careful that this kind of direction— "Can you put your body behind something or in front of something" —doesn't become overly academic and dull. Movement education can easily be corrupted and

misinterpreted if the teacher is insensitive and allows the experience to degenerate into an instructional situation intended only to teach the meaning of adverbs.

Yoga exercises are an alternative approach to movement education that teachers might find interesting to use with young children if they have a good grasp of this philosophy. These exercises feel good and can be presented quite simply, as Rachel Carr's book (1980) demonstrates.

Helping Children Enjoy Creative Dance

By far the freest method of providing experiences that use some of these motor abilities is through creative dancing. This requires *combining some open-ended suggestions from the teacher with spontaneous activity generated by the children.* Beginning teachers (and more experienced ones, too) sometimes approach creative dance with apprehension. They usually fear two things—losing control of the group and not being able to get the children to participate. The problem may also be compounded by their feeling self-conscious about dancing.

Maintaining Control of the Group. To keep control of the group, it is necessary to draw the line between active movement and wild running around. Fortunately, there are several things to do that will help. Among them are keeping the group a reasonable size (for a beginning teacher this can mean as few as four or as many as eight children) and always having an idea about what you intend to do next. It is important to employ a variety of slower and quicker rhythms and to provide relaxation periods so that the session does not keep building and building to a disastrous climax. It will also help teachers retain control if they incorporate movements that involve sitting and lying down part of the time, as well as those that require standing and moving about. Life will generally be easier if an assistant is available to help with shoes, records, and so forth. (If dance activities are offered toward the end of the morning, often a mother can be

TABLE 8–3
One-day physical development curriculum plan

Physical ability	Perceptual-motor or movement education activity	Modifications needed	Children's response
Locomotion	Roll about balanced on top of large balls on grass outside.	Needed more *really* large balls. Balls kept blowing away so might be better inside.	D. and J. used the one very large ball and repeatedly enjoyed it. Children kicked smaller balls.
	On the way to play outside, go on walk from east door around south of building. Go up and down stairs, take long giant steps, short steps, walk fast then slow, tip-toe, stomp, and jump over the cracks on sidewalk.	First in line did well. Later ones needed to hold back for space between so children could have freedom to move.	H. and J. did everything on suggestion with enthusiasm. P. had difficulty, partly because he did not have one hand free for balance (arm was in splint).
Balance	Place rope on floor in block area for children to walk down.	Had to demonstrate rope repeatedly; children couldn't understand instructions alone. Finally removed it.	L., J., and E. had no trouble once it was demonstrated, but lost interest quickly.
	Make orange juice. Ask children to go to large container of water at another table and fill a cup and carry back to table.	Moved container so children wouldn't spill in main walkway.	E. asked if she could take two turns. Almost everyone helped. Very few spills.
Body and space perception	"Head, Shoulders, Knees, and Toes" during group.	It should have been repeated since it was new. Should be slowed down.	Quite a few children participated, which is good for first time.
	Bean bag toss with body target (conversation about body) at rug no. 1.	Teacher had to hold bags in her lap to keep everyone from throwing at once or just dropping them in. A taped line on floor might have helped.	J. stayed with it for a long time and also counted the bags. R. refused to stand back as did many others. They preferred to get close or to just drop them in.

Rhythm and temporal awareness	Fingerpaint with shaving cream to music.	Teacher in charge forgot to bring music.	H. stayed with it almost the whole time. Children washed hands a lot.
Rebound and airborne activities	Jump on mattress in block area.	Teacher had to participate to get them started. Added steps made out of blocks at one end to jump from.	E. is a strong jumper. L. jumped repeatedly once I held her doll.
Projectile management	Bean bag toss at body target.	See Body and space perception.	
Management of daily motor skills	Fingerpainting with shaving cream. Make orange juice. Use tools such as juicer, spoon to stir, knife to cut oranges, pour and measure orange juice. Manipulative materials such as puzzles, seriation cylinders, and Bristle Blocks included during rug time.	See Rhythm and temporal awareness. Substituted an electric juicer because children were unable to use customary type.	Children needed help learning to start juicer by pressing down. Did fine with spooning.
Relaxation	Fingerpainting with shaving cream to relaxing music. Jumping on mattress, relaxing on mattress.	Teacher in charge forgot music. Teacher tried to structure activity so only two were on mattress at one time, but explaining and carrying this out resulted in the children losing interest and walking away. Alternative of allowing the children to pretty much control number using mattress only got out of hand once.	Seemed relaxing to children even without music to set the pace. L. and J. really did relax.
	Rolling on large ball would be relaxing for some children.		Rolling on the ball did seem relaxing for D. and J.

Plan kindness of Cené Marquis, student teacher, The Institute of Child Development, University of Oklahoma, 1982.

prevailed on to return early and assist before picking up her car pool.)

How to Begin. Getting children to participate need not be difficult if the teacher does some planning ahead and also participates in the activities. Such enthusiasm is contagious. It often works out well to begin a dance session with some simple, sitting-on-the- floor activities, such as finger plays, dancing with the arms to music, and movement education activities. These "beginners" help overcome self-conscious-ness by not making everyone be up on their feet moving around right away. Sad to admit, even as early as preschool, some little boys have already decided that dancing is sissy. If this is the case, it is wiser to call it *movement time* or some other less prejudice-laden term than *dancing*.

Using simple props can help start the dance session also; scarves, balloons, tubes of stretchy jersey material, crepe paper streamers, tie-on skirts made of tulle sewn to ribbon waist bands, capes, and even piles of dry leaves may help distract the self-conscious child from thinking of himself. (It is better not to depend on props too much, though, because they can become dis-tracting.)

Thinking about the children instead of one-self is a good basic remedy for overcoming self-consciousness, but other activities will help, too. Taking a modern dance class where every-one is moving together is one way of working through this feeling. Another way to reduce the overall sense of anxiety is by planning everything well and having a reassuring reservoir of ideas on which to fall back. Some beginning teachers prefer to be left completely alone with the children and provided with the assurance that absolutely no one will interrupt them; others feel more comfortable if they pair with another person at the start.

Incidentally, dance experiences provide ex-cellent opportunities for identifying children with possible hearing difficulties. Watch for children who do not respond at all to changes in rhythm, who lose interest as soon as softer music

Using props such as balloons can help open children up to moving freely.

is played, or who seem to stay consistently close to the source of the sound. These behaviors may be indicators that the child is not hearing well and would benefit from a referral to a physician.

Using Music. Music contributes a great deal to the satisfaction of a dance experience. A piano equipped with accompanist is ideal but not necessary. Probably the best solution to the problem of music is to make tapes of your own to fit various moods and rhythms. It is also possible to purchase records to fit these categories, but there always seem to be some selections on each record that you do not want to use, and it can be tedious to stop and hunt for particular items while the children stand, restlessly waiting.

Be wary also of a multitude of so-called children's records that feature vocals that are arch, condescending, and insincere. When listening to these recordings, it is obvious that the people who have produced them do not know much about little children, because so often the tempo is too fast, the pitch is too high, the lyrics inane, and the activities inappropriate. Remember that children's tastes are being formed by the music you use; do not settle for second-rate tripe when there are performers like Ella Jenkins, Marcia Berman, and the Boston Pops around.

It is not necessary to use music the entire time. Percussion instruments, such as drums and tambourines, are very effective, and chants and songs are useful, also. For example, Clare Cherry (1971) has a helpful book of songs set to familiar tunes that fit various dance activities well.

Never forget that music offers fine opportunities for incorporating multiethnic materials into the center's day. Every culture has its own tradition of folk dances, drum patterns, and songs. Music can also bring the culture of the home to the school if children are invited to bring records or tapes of popular music from home to share—after all, most popular music is written to be danced to.

Folk dances have both strengths and weaknesses for the dance group at preschool. Because they follow prescribed patterns, we cannot deceive ourselves that they are creative, and they may also be too complicated if presented in their original form. It is important to remember that they can be simplified, that they do provide a way of honoring other people's culture, and that they offer opportunities for children to accomplish something together in a group. Therefore, they deserve their place in the dance experience as long as the student realizes their limitations as well as their virtues.

Expression of Ideas and Feelings. Once the children are moving freely, the time is ripe to draw suggestions from them about what the music is saying to their feet. From here it is but a short step to encouraging children to express their feelings and helping them make contact with those feelings, whose presence they may otherwise be denying to themselves. For example, the teacher might move from playing an action game based on the song "Here We Go Round the Mulberry Bush," featuring the things done at nursery school (swinging, eating snack, hammering wood), to dancing the way they would dance if they felt sad when their mother left them at school, or if they felt a little angry about being left, or if they were happy to come. During the activity, the teacher also can comment casually that children often feel all these ways—a mixture of feelings. The same approach could be applied to going to the hospital, receiving a measles shot, or the new baby arriving.

Ingredients of a Good Creative Dance Experience. To sum up, then, a good plan for dancing includes some nonthreatening warm-up activities to begin with, some multiethnic music for cultural richness, at least one idea that encourages the expression of feelings related to the children's life experiences, and plenty of encouragement for the children to dance freely to a variety of tempi and rhythms (Morningstar, 1986). A good plan also includes a reserve of ideas in the teacher's head in case something does not go as well as he had hoped and a good selection of records or tapes with which he is so familiar that he can locate the music he needs quickly.

SUMMARY

Activities that enhance their physical skills are very dear to young children, as well as vital to their growth and development. For this reason, it is well worth teachers' time and attention to plan a comprehensive program that develops each kind of basic perceptual-motor skill.

To do this successfully, teachers must know about general developmental levels and also know specific facts of physical development about each youngster. Once they have this information, they should refer to a thorough outline of perceptual-motor skills to make certain that their curriculum plans are truly comprehensive.

It is valuable to offer both portable and solidly fixed apparatus to encourage the growth of physical skills. Although all these items may be purchased, it is also possible to build many of them for reasonable sums of money.

There are several ways to incorporate the needed activities into the center's day: offering perceptual-motor activities per se, building obstacle courses, and including movement education and creative dance activities on a regular basis. Learning how to relax should also be included as an important kind of exercise.

SELF-CHECK QUESTIONS FOR REVIEW

Content-Related Questions

1. Give some examples of how physical activity benefits each of the five selves.
2. What are the approximate ages when children become proficient at letting go of something voluntarily (controlled releasing)? Catching a small ball using only their hands? Skipping skillfully?
3. Name some movable types of equipment that are inexpensive and useful to offer when developing a play space for children that stimulates large-muscle play.
4. What are some of the basics to remember that were cited in the discussion on presentation of activities?
5. Why is it important to teach children how to relax? Suggest some strategies for teaching relaxation that are helpful to use with young children.
6. How do movement education and creative dance differ from each other? What are the benefits of each of these activities?
7. List some helpful principles to remember when leading children in a creative dance experience.

Integrative Questions

1. Think of several outdoor play yards you have seen in children's centers. How does the equipment in those yards compare to that recommended by the research of Frost and Strickland?
2. Table 8-2 provides many examples of activities children can use to develop various physical abilities. Suggest an activity not included in the chart for each of the eight abilities. Explain how you could make the activity easier or more challenging, depending on the skill and age level of the children.
3. How do movement education and creative dance differ from each other? What are the benefits of each of these activities?

QUESTIONS AND ACTIVITIES

1. Suppose you wanted to make certain that all the children participated in every physical activity each day. Explain to the class what the value of doing this might be and what the drawbacks might be.
2. *Problem:* There is a little 3-year-old boy in your group who is terrified of going down your 7-foot slide. His father sees this as being "sissy" and urges his son to attempt the slide every time he brings him to school. If you were this youngster's teacher, what would you do about this situation?
3. If you could only add one piece of outdoor equipment to the preschool where you teach, what would it be? And why would you select it? How could you obtain it for the least cost?
4. Is there a piece of equipment where you observe or teach that the children rarely use or always use the same way? Suggest two things you might try with it to make it more attractive to them.
5. Play through your popular records at home, and bring two contrasting ones to share with the class that you feel would be nice to use in a dance session with children.
6. The weather has been very bad for the past 4 days—so bad that no child or teacher has ventured outdoors. Can you suggest a number of large-muscle activities that could be used indoors to provide relief? What if you put all the furniture out in the hall? Or could you use the hall?
7. *Problem:* You are just setting up a neighborhood day-care center that you expect about thirty 3- and 4-year-olds to attend. You have little money,

but lots of strong friends who own some good power tools. List the most important pieces of equipment you think your play yard needs, and explain how you plan to obtain them.

8. If you could not use a newsletter or have a parents' night, how else might you keep the parents informed about the physical development program at your school?

9. You are the head teacher at last, and so you are in charge of scheduling. How would you design a simple, clear schedule for physical activities that would cover all the skills listed in Table 8–2?

10. Share with the class the most successful things you have done with the children so far to encourage creativity in dance.

REFERENCES FOR FURTHER READING

Sequential Physical Development

Cratty, B. J. (1979). *Perceptual and motor development in infants and children.* Englewood Cliffs, N. J.: Prentice-Hall. Cratty's work does a comprehensive job on the subject of physical development.

Gassier, J. (1984). *A guide to the psycho-motor development of the child.* London: Churchill Livingstone. Gassier's work covers children from birth to age 3 and includes information on physical, social, and language development. Concise and well-illustrated.

Wickstrom, R. L. (1983). *Fundamental motor patterns* (3rd ed.). Philadelphia: Lea & Febiger. Wickstrom discusses and illustrates the development of various skills such as running and throwing, beginning with preschool children and extending to those who are physically mature.

Theories of Perceptual-Motor Development

Gearheart, B. R., & Gearheart, C. J. (1989). *Learning disabilities: Educational strategies* (5th ed.). Columbus, Ohio: Merrill Publishing. This book has several good chapters that describe the most important schools of thought on perceptual-motor development.

Activities for Physical Development and Movement Education

Curtis, S. A. (1982). *The joy of movement in early childhood.* New York: Teachers College Press. Part I analyzes the development of various motor patterns. Part II contains many suggestions for developmental activities designed to improve children's ability to move skillfully and with satisfaction. The book contains chapters on equipment and a series of observation checklists.

Kelly, N. T., & Kelly, B. J. (1985). *Physical education for pre-school and primary grades.* Springfield, Ill. Charles C Thomas. The Kellys offer many stimulating suggestions for physical activities with young children. There is a nice emphasis on inexpensive equipment that preschool teachers will appreciate.

Miller, K. (1989). *The outside play and learning book: Activities for young children.* Mount Rainier, Md.: Gryphon House. Many age-appropriate, attractive, fresh suggestions for outdoor activities are included here. Topics range from ideas for riding toy play to snow and woodworking activities.

Orlick, T. (1982). *The second coopoerative sports & games book.* New York: Pantheon Books. The games in this book are suggested for various ages, including toddlers. They are simple, fun, and noncompetitive activities that encourage children to work together. Material from differing cultures is included. Highly recommended.

Pangrazi, R. P., & Dauer, V. P. (1981). *Movement in early childhood and primary education.* Minneapolis: Burgess Publishing Co. Unlike the majority of physical education books, this one includes several chapters on divergent movement, creative play ideas, and creativity in learning. Highly recommended.

Sullivan, M. (1982). *Feeling strong, feeling free: Movement exploration for young children.* Washington, D.C.: National Association for the Education of Young Children. *Movement exploration* provides suggestions for children from ages 3 to 5 and 5 to 8. Sullivan does not hesitate to discuss how to obtain and retain control of the group. She also provides many suggestions for activities. Highly recommended.

Weikart, P. (1987). *Round the circle: Key experiences in movement for children ages 3 to 5.* Ypsilanti, Mich.: High/Scope Press. Weikart discusses eight aspects of helping children with movement experiences, ranging from using language to describe movement to moving with others to a common beat.

Weikart, P. (1988). *Movement plus rhymes, songs, and singing games: Activities for children ages 3 to 7.* Ypsilanti, Mich.: High/Scope Press. *Movement Plus. . . .* accompanies *Round the Circle* and offers many additional suggestions.

Dance

Cherry, C. (1971). *Creative movement for the developing child: A nursery school handbook for non-musicians* (rev. ed.). Belmont, Calif.: Fearon Publishers. This inexpensive paperback offers activities that are appropriate for preschool children. By using familiar melodies and simple verses, the book neatly makes the point that teachers can have a good movement activity program with no records or tapes at all.

Morningstar, M. (1986). *Growing with dance: Developing through creative dance from ages two to six.* Point Roberts,

Wash.: Windborne Publications. Morningstar offers stories and ideas according to the age and developing abilities of the children. These are intended to spark creative responses from them.

Stinson, S. (1988). *Dance for young children: Finding the magic in movement.* Reston, Va.: American Alliance for Health, Physical Education, Recreation and Dance. This book offers a helpful mixture of practical ideas, suggestions for themes, approaches with handicapped children, and sound dance theory.

Relaxation Strategies

Cherry, C. (1981). *Think of something quiet: A guide for achieving serenity in early childhood classrooms.* Belmont, Calif.: Pitman Learning. This is a truly rare book; it deals with various aspects of quietness, ranging from recommendations on presenting naps to suggestions for teaching relaxation.

Jacobson, E. (1976). *You must relax* (5th ed.). New York: McGraw-Hill Book Co. Everyone should be acquainted with this landmark book on relaxation. Simply written.

Money Stretchers

Beckwith, J. (1980). *Make your backyard more interesting than TV.* New York: McGraw-Hill Book Co. Beckwith covers everything from free materials to complex play equipment—includes material on adventure playgrounds.

Dickerson, M. (1977). *Developing the outdoor learning center.* Little Rock: Southern Association for Children Under Six. This is an intensely practical, step-by-step description of how to design and construct a play yard with mainly volunteer labor. Highly recommended.

Hewes, J. J. (1974). *Build your own playground: A source of play sculptures, designs and concepts from the work of Jay Beckwith.* Boston: Houghton Mifflin Co. Exciting equipment designs are complete with useful advice on tools and hardware. This book is a *must* when designing play equipment.

Marston, L. (1984). *Playground equipment: Do-it-yourself indestructible, practically free.* Jefferson. N.C.: McFarland & Co. Title is self-explanatory.

Playgrounds

Allen, Lady of Hurtwood. (1968). *Planning for play.* Cambridge, Mass.: MIT Press. Lady Allen, a very progressive thinker, was among the first to advocate the development of adventure playgrounds. She describes the purpose of this book as being "to explore some of the ways of keeping alive and sustaining the innate curiosity and natural gaiety of children." It does that—a classic.

Frost, J. L., & Klein, B. L. (1979). *Children's play and playgrounds.* Boston: Allyn & Bacon. This is a well-illustrated book, rich with ideas for contemporary playgrounds and how to facilitate play within them.

Frost, J. L., & Sunderlin, S. (Eds.). (1985). *When children play: Proceedings of the International Conference on Play and Play Environments.* Wheaton, Md.: Association for Childhood Education International. The authors devote an entire section of this book to designing and developing playgrounds.

For the Advanced Student

Curtis, S. R. (1987). New views on movement development and the implications for curriculum in early childhood. In C. Seefeldt (Ed.), *The early childhood curriculum: A review of current research.* New York: Teachers College Press. Curtis reviews research concerned with the integration of movement and its development as children mature.

Gärling, T., & Valsiner, J. (1985). *Children within environments: Toward a psychology of accident prevention.* New York: Plenum Publishing. An international publication, this book presents interesting new perspectives on the psychology of safety as it relates to young children.

Gesell, A., Halverson, H. M., Thompson, H., & Ilg, F. (1940). *The first five years of life: A guide to the study of the preschool child.* New York: Harper & Row, Publishers. This classic reference details step-by-step development of young children in many areas, including various physical skills.

Seefeldt, V. (Ed.). (1986). *Physical activity & well-being.* Reston, Va.: American Alliance for Health, Physical Education, Recreation and Dance. This book documents the value of physical activity to all aspects of the developing person. Particularly noteworthy for readers of *Total Learning* are the chapters entitled, "Acquisition of Motor Skills During Childhood" and "Development of Sensory-Motor Function in Young Children."

Associations Having Related Interests

American Alliance for Health, Physical Education, Recreation and Dance. 1900 Association Dr., Reston, Virginia 22091. The Alliance offers many publications and media materials related to an astonishing range of physical activities.

9 Helping Children Understand and Value Life

Have you ever

- Wondered whether little children understand anything about the cycle of life?
- Wished you knew how to avoid total chaos when an animal visits?
- Needed to know what to do when there has been death in a family and parents come to you for advice?
- Wanted to help little children avoid sexual abuse?

If you have, the material in this chapter will help you.

The nursery school is a place where the pulse of life is sensed and celebrated. Encountering the wonders of existence, the beauty and mystery of life and birth, the joy of music, and the fun of movement, pulses life-enabling energies. One of the goals of nursery school is to help a child feel life pulsing within, and animating his community and his world.

MARTHA SNYDER, ROSS SNYDER
and ROSS SNYDER, JR. (1980)

Teaching children to understand and value life may seem too abstract or advanced a subject for such little children, but when it is broken down into specific topics, it becomes clear that we have many opportunities to establish basic attitudes toward life (and death) at this early age.

For example, even very young children are interested in their own bodies and what goes on inside of them. They often ask such questions as these: If we eat watermelon seeds, will they really grow out of our ears? When Sue broke her arm, did it really fall off and did the doctor sew it on again? When I want a baby sister, why can't I buy one of those little jars at the market, take it home, and just water it real good? (The child who asked this was convinced that babies came from baby food jars.) Why doesn't the bird fly anymore? Why can't we wake him up? Why is our mouse so stiff, and why does he smell so funny?

These and innumerable questions like them provide evidence that questions about life and its cycle come up frequently and naturally in preschool classrooms. The difficulty with this subject matter is that some adults feel uncomfortable about dealing with it themselves, much less discussing it with young children. Then, too, some families feel strongly that such material should be handled only within the family, and not in the school. For these reasons, individual teachers must decide what the appropriate approach is for their particular group of children and use the material in this chapter accordingly. It is to be hoped that most teachers will be able to include information about life and death in a matter-of-fact and wholesome way as the opportunity arises.

HELPING CHILDREN LEARN TO CHERISH THEIR BODIES

One of the most meaningful areas of life education for young children is learning about their own bodies and how to cherish them. Children like to know what is inside themselves. They are interested in seeing x-rays of arms and legs, listening to heartbeats, and comparing parts of their bodies that are soft such as ears and tongues with parts that are hard such as fingers and heads. They love drinking a glass of water and then rocking in a chair to feel the splash inside, and they are fascinated with blood—what it is and what it does.

They are also interested in urination and bowel movements, since they went through toilet training not long before. Children often attach strong feelings to defecation, since toilet training remains a point of strain in some families. Indeed, some psychologists and teachers with Freudian backgrounds maintain that one of the most significant values of offering mud and play dough and fingerpainting is that these allow children opportunities to express some of their more hostile feelings about toileting in a socially acceptable (sublimated) way. For this reason, they recommend that remarks likening these substances to bowel movements should be accepted casually rather than deplored, since such

Here Katie is performing major surgery on a model from the biology department.

remarks are frequently a part of such play. On the other hand, a reasonable line must be drawn so that children do not spend their lunchtimes talking about how the gravy is made of poopoo lest it make the food seem unpalatable to the listeners.

Discussions about excretions should be frank, as should discussions about anatomical differences between boys and girls. The usual preschool practice of using the same bathroom for both sexes is a great aid in dispelling the mystery of sexual differences. Using correct vocabulary for various body parts and functions also is more desirable than using slang or street language,

though teachers certainly need to understand what a child means when he urgently whispers "kaka" or "peepee."

The most wholesome attitude to encourage is that our bodies are sources of pleasureful feelings and that they deserve good care. It feels good to stretch and yawn, it feels good to eat and be satisfied, it feels good to wake refreshed from sleep, and it feels good to go to the toilet. Bodies are not parts of us to be punished by being ignored or mistreated; they should be carefully cared for and cherished. This includes allowing our bodies to rest when they feel tired, nourishing them well, and appreciating the joys of good health, pleasures which all too often are taken for granted. Teachers must help children learn to honor their bodies and treat them well so that they remain a source of delight to them all their lives.

What to Do When Children Masturbate

Sooner or later most children discover that one source of physical pleasure comes from masturbation. They may do this almost absentmindedly while watching television or listening to stories; they may masturbate as part of lulling themselves to sleep or as a means of passing time during a sleepless nap period; they may retreat to this when feeling anxious and insecure in new surroundings.

The difficulty is that this behavior, although natural, is not socially acceptable. Besides that, many of us adults feel very uncomfortable when we discover a masturbating child. On one level we are acquainted with research about masturbation that has shown for more than a quarter of a century that the practice is commonplace among children and adults (both men and women) (Kinsey, Pomeroy, & Martin, 1948; Kinsey Pomeroy, Martin, & Gebhard, 1953). We also know that masturbation is neither perverted nor self-destructive, that penises do not drop off as a result of it, that dark circles do not show under eyes because of it, and so forth. Therefore, at least intellectually, we would like to regard masturbation as being a simple, natural part of human sexuality. But, on an emotional level, our feeling selves may respond in quite a different way, and we may feel embarrassed, disapproving, flustered, and perhaps even angry when coming across a masturbating child.

The problem is how to handle these reactions in a way that does not mortify children or make them feel guilty and yet realistically takes into account society's expectations and our own feelings. At present, the best solution seems to be to teach children as calmly as possible that masturbation is something people do only in private, just like nose picking—neither activity is socially sanctioned behavior done in front of other people. Simply take the child aside and quietly explain this without making him or her feel like a criminal.

We must also be aware that many adults (both parents and teachers) would not agree with this point of view—they condemn masturbation entirely. But it is to be hoped that these people can at least learn to refrain from issuing those dire threats that some of us were subjected to in our own childhoods—threats about what happens to little boys and girls who "do that."

Teaching Children to Protect Themselves From Sexual Abuse

We cannot leave this discussion of caring for our bodies without including information on how to teach children to protect themselves from sexual advances. From evidence that has accumulated in the past decade about the sexual abuse of children, it becomes clear that such experiences happen far more frequently than we might expect. Estimates of the number of sexual abuse cases among young children vary widely, ranging from 100,000 to 500,000 per year. Perhaps as much as 5 or 10 times that total goes unreported each year (MacFarlane et al., 1986).

Although the standard advice about never taking candy from strangers or getting into a car with someone you do not know remains sound,

research reveals that in most cases of sexual abuse the perpetrator is well known to the child and is often a relative or family friend.

In conducting education about sexual abuse, teachers must walk a delicate line between frightening children unduly and instructing them on what to do if they are approached. Children should be taught that their bodies belong to them alone and that their genitalia are private areas that no one has the right to invade in any way. If someone tries to do this and offers them presents or threatens them or their families, their best protection is to refuse and to tell their parents, teacher, or another adult immediately, regardless of how frightened they are.

Children need to understand that there is a big difference between an abusive kind of touch and the physical affection of hugs and cuddling that both children and those who love them rightfully enjoy and require to feel emotionally fulfilled. Children need to be taught to discriminate between nurturant behaviors and those of a more frightening and unusual nature.

Because of recent publicity about sexual abuse taking place in day-care centers, some adult caretakers have become hesitant about showing physical affection to children. Fortunately, it appears that most trained early childhood educators understand that expressing affection *is* not only natural, but is also a necessary part of building sound relationships between adults and the children they care for. The research report included in this chapter makes these differing points of view plain. However, it is also necessary to understand how to protect both children and adults from experiencing or being accused of committing sexual abuse.

Protecting Teachers From Accusations of Sexual Abuse

The sensational publicity about incidents of sexual abuse in child-care centers has caused both parents and teachers to worry about this possibility. Although careful study of the prevalence of such incidents reveals that such episodes are rare, occurring at the rate of 5.5 children for every 10,000 children enrolled in such centers (Stephens, 1988), everyone agrees that even one such episode is one too many.

Besides that, there is the problem of false accusations. Experts tell us we should never ignore reports by children that they have been abused because it is unusual for children to make up such stories. However, such false allegations have been known to occur (Jones & McGraw, 1987). In my own relatively small community, two such episodes have happened in the past 3 years. Of course, such misunderstandings or false accusations can be disastrous for the accused staff member and for the school, too, unless people are able to defend themselves by documenting the steps taken to protect both children and staff.

Basic precautions include making certain that parents know they are always welcome to visit at any time. They do not need to call ahead or alert the center in any way that they are coming (Winters, 1985). Parents should be educated about the difference between sexual abuse and the affectionate hugging and cuddling so necessary to the well-being of children. They should be encouraged to become well acquainted with their children's teachers so that a bond of confidence can develop between them.

Parents should be informed that staff always work in pairs, so there is always a "witness" to what is going on. Indeed, one study even recommends rotation of paired staff in order to avoid what is termed "accomplice abuse" (Stephens, 1988).

Arrange rooms and play yards so they are open to view, with no hidden corners or out-of-the-way unsupervisable spots. Stall doors in bathrooms (if they are used at all) should be either half-height or not go all the way to the floor. Finally, directors must be careful about whom they hire. They should follow up written references with telephone inquiries, and they should make background checks of criminal records in states where this is either required by regulation or at least possible to do.

The suggestions given above concerning operation of the center should always be followed as a matter of course. If all of these procedures are followed consistently, it is probable that both children and staff will be well protected and can go their happy, affectionate way without worrying that their behavior will be misconstrued.

Teaching Reverence for Life

Coupled with teaching children to understand and appreciate their own bodies should go the concept of reverence for life. The world is filled with exquisite life forms, and every time you teach children to step over a spider, or point out the fragile beauty of the rat's paw, or share the delicate wonder of a sprouting seed, you are helping them acquire this concept.

Experiences with animals should be a pleasure for both participants.

RESEARCH STUDY

Has Publicity About Child Abuse Influenced Public Opinion About Touching Children?

Research Question Does publicity about sexual abuse in day-care centers generate a negative attitude towards positive touching and physical affection in parents and teachers?

Research Method Participants were 301 middle-class adults—88 were parents; 86, early childhood educators, and 127, nonparent university students.

The investigators asked these groups to read material supporting the value of physical affection between adults and children *or* material that said "recent publicity about sexual abuse had made physical contacts between adults and children the focus of increased concern" (Hyson et al., p. 60). Next, half of the participants in each group were told they were to look at videotapes of day-care providers interacting with children, and the other half of each group were told they were to look at videotapes of parents and children interacting together. Actually, the same tape was used for both groups. The tapes presented a series of brief episodes showing adults being physically affectionate by touching children (e.g., hugging them) or being positive and friendly but not touching the children (e.g., watching a child on a climber). Viewers were asked to rate their degree of approval after viewing each episode.

Results Results indicated that publicity about child abuse can influence attitudes about the value of physical affection. The subjects who had read the comment about sexual abuse before viewing the tape disapproved more of affectionate touching and approved more of nontouching behavior. Viewers approved more of physical affection when it was done by a "parent" rather than by a "day-care provider." Men approved less of adult-child physical affection than women did, and

---

Our obligation to conserve and protect nature's wonders also should be a part of teaching reverence for life. Such mundane activities as building a compost heap, digging rabbit droppings into the garden, and returning a rotten pumpkin to the earth can all help children realize they can participate in a simple, practical effort to sustain natural life cycles.

Best of all, teaching reverence for life can be woven beautifully into cross-cultural learnings from the American Indians. These people have understood better than most how to live in harmony with nature, abusing neither animals nor earth.

In no other area of subject matter are there so many books that can be used to extend the child's feelings for the beauty of the world. Even when the text is too advanced, as is the case with the books by Holling Clancy Holling, the illustrations alone may be worth the price of the volume. There is even a magazine[1] published especially for prekindergarten children that stresses conservation and understanding nature.

---

[1]*Your Big Back Yard.* Published by the National Wildlife Federation, 1412 16th St. N.W., Washington, D.C. 20036.

early childhood teachers were more approving of physical affection than the other groups were.

Implications for Teaching People are rightfully concerned about the possibility of sexual abuse happening to young children wherever this might take place. In day-care centers, where parents may be uneasy or feel guilty about leaving their children anyway and are uncertain about what happens beyond the reach of their supervision, worry about this problem is particularly serious and has been exacerbated by recent reports that such abuse has taken place. The research points out how readily uninformed people are influenced by even the words *sexual abuse* and how quickly they tend to equate any form of physical affection with that concept.

This means that teachers must go out of their way to clarify the difference for parents between sexual abuse and physical affection. Teachers need to reiterate how important it is for young children to experience love and caring through touch as well as words, and they need to become well acquainted with every parent in order to establish bonds of trust between themselves and the families of the children they care for.

An encouraging fact is that the early childhood teachers who participated in this research remained convinced of the value of affectionate touching, despite the influence of negative publicity. Hopefully, such convictions will remain steady. Yet, if suspicions continue and incidents of abuse increase, teachers may eventually lose the confidence of their convictions and come to view the expression of physical affection with young children as something it is wiser to avoid. Hopefully, this outcome will never come to pass.

Note. From "Influences on Attitudes Toward Physical Affection Between Adults and Children," by M. C. Hyson, L. C. Whitehead, and C. M. Prudhoe, 1988, *Early Childhood Research Quarterly,* 3(1), pp. 55–75.

Teachers can make quite an occasion of its arrival each month.

Teaching about reverence for life also involves teaching about the entire life cycle of human beings. Children love the idea that they are growing bigger and stronger every day. They relish visits by babies, and they are quicker than people of many ages to appreciate the value of older adults, who can become treasured participants in the life of the school (Kornhaber, 1983). Not only do older people need children, but also children genuinely need them to enrich their understanding of the stages of human life. Most communities have organizations composed of older adults who can be approached in the search for congenial volunteers.

ANSWERING QUESTIONS ABOUT REPRODUCTION

Many adults feel uneasy about discussing sex and reproduction with children. (The development of sex roles and nonsexist curriculum is discussed in Chapter 12.) Fortunately for those of us who feel awkward about this subject, the questions nursery school–age children ask are likely to be simple and not very distressing to answer. Young

A SUREFIRE ACTIVITY—HELPING CHILDREN UNDERSTAND AND APPRECIATE THE WONDER OF ANIMALS

Having animals at school can be a delight or a pain in the neck, depending on the manner of presentation. Most children love animals and are likely to be very excited when one comes to visit. The advantage of having the visitor stay a few days or at least several hours is that as some of the newness wears off, the children have time to become more familiar with the animal. This allows them to overcome either their intense excitement or possible apprehensions. Remember, never force an animal on a reluctant child or vice versa.

When presenting an animal, choose not only one that you enjoy yourself, but also (if possible) one that is fairly slow moving and emotionally placid. Always consider safety first, and prepare for safety in advance. This is essential. Make certain that the animal can be adequately confined (we once had an octopus that escaped through an incredibly small hole in the mesh screen). A tippy, temporary cage increases the teacher's anxiety and the consequent number of warnings that she must naggingly give to the children. Make certain that cages are secure and steady and that they require adult assistance to open. Since tired animals, like tired children, are more apt to lose control, make provisions so that the animal can be withdrawn from circulation and have a rest when it needs this.

When presenting the visitor, it is very important to have firm control over the situation. *Insist* that the children sit down and be as calm as possible. It can be helpful to have carpet squares arranged in a circle to mark where they should sit (chairs can also be used for this purpose). Remind the children of what gentleness means—sometimes telling them "Remember, use soft hands and quiet voices" helps them understand this concept better than using the word *gentle* does. Remind them also to move slowly.

Crowd control will need to be considered as well. Older fours can manage suggestions and rules for themselves, but the younger children will need more direct teacher control. Offering something else of equal interest at the opposite end of the room, for example, will help. Perhaps water play with some new equipment can be offered, or having some children play outdoors while a few come in at a time may reduce pushing. Presenting the animal during large-group time is still another effective method of crowd control. When all else fails, the rule of "only three or four at a time—please come back later" can also be enforced.

Discussion before the animal arrives should include instructions about whether it can be held or should be

children often do not even realize that dogs always have puppies and cats, kittens.

They typically want to know where babies come from or why that lady is so fat. The answer to these queries is simple enough—a baby grows inside its mother in her uterus until old enough to be born and them comes out of a special place between her legs called the vagina.

What teachers usually fear is that youngsters will also want to know how the baby got in there in the first place. Actually this a very uncommon question for children under 5. In case it should come up, it is accurate to say that the father and mother start the baby growing in the mother by being very loving and close to each other—and

when they are feeling this way, the father fits his penis inside the mother's vagina and a fluid passes into her that helps start the baby growing. This kind of explanation is desirable because it incorporates both the importance of affection and biological facts.

It often confuses children to talk about planting seeds in relation to human babies. When teachers uses this analogy, youngsters naturally think of gardening and this can lead to very odd misconceptions about conception.

In discussions about reproduction, teachers should find out what the children really want to know, make answers truthful and simple, encourage children to say what they think, and

watched, how to hold the visitor if this is possible, and how to refrain from frightening it. Animals that can be handled are the most desirable kind to have at school. Rabbits, guinea pigs, rats, land turtles, slow-moving snakes, puppies (who have had their shots), and even baby goats and lambs are all good candidates. If a young animal is to be studied, taking pictures as it grows or, better yet, measuring and weighing it every few days helps children relish and understand the growth process. (Ducks, rabbits, guinea pigs, and rats grow almost as swiftly as radishes.) In some instances, it works well to have the animals live at school during this time, but in others, particularly with puppies, it is best to have them visit periodically.

Give some thought to what you want the children to gain from the animal experience. The title of this section intentionally contains the word *appreciate*. Think about how you can help children take time to really look at and appreciate the animal's wonderful qualities, to examine the delicacy of its paws, the beauty of its markings, the softness of its fur, and the whiteness of its teeth. (Children are extremely interested in teeth and whether the animal will bite.) Discuss how various features have helped it adapt to its particular environment: Why do rabbits need such large ears? Why do snails leave that trail of slime behind them? How can the snake move without any legs?

Books on natural history, such as the Golden Book series, are good sources of information on wilder forms of animal life, but often the adequate sources for more domesticated animals are the pamphlets found in pet stores or the local library. The 4-H Clubs sponsored by county extension programs also offer useful information on caring for various barnyard animals.

Whatever the source of information, you should be prepared to offer the children fascinating factual tidbits as they watch and hold the animal: Isn't it interesting that snails have 10,000 little, rough teeth on their tongues to rip up leaves? Imagine—that whole duck came out of a shell just this big! Do you know that some birds carry shells away in their beaks and drop them far from their nest to keep predators from finding their chicks?

Children love feeding animals, so it is wise to have an ample supply of food on hand. Guinea pigs and rats make very desirable pets, since their appetites are almost insatiable.

But with feeding inevitably comes the problem of keeping the animal clean. Nothing is sadder or smellier than a forgotten animal living in a cage badly in need of cleaning. Such a beast cannot help itself; it is up to us to care for it and keep it clean. If you wish to have animals as permanent tenants, you must be willing to work with the children in keeping the animals in immaculate condition.

help them understand that warmth and caring should be important elements in the experience of intercourse.

ANSWERING QUESTIONS ABOUT DEATH

No discussion of the life cycle would be complete without including information on the topic of death. Yet, for many people, this remains a subject even more taboo than sex and one that they prefer to avoid completely when teaching young children. They may believe that children should be shielded from experiencing sadness or

that death is too difficult for children to understand. Perhaps the whole subject of death is so frightening and distasteful to them that the thought of mentioning it to children seems overwhelming.

If we face reality, however, we must admit that death is all around us, just as life is: animals die, insects die, flowers die, and people die —even people children know. If, as adults, we are able to acknowledge to ourselves that death is part of life, then we may be more willing to include the subject of death when talking about the cycle of life with children. This comes up very naturally when animals die or when roses fade or pumpkins rot. Even young children can

When you've just turned 3, each day is filled with interesting experiences.

be allowed to investigate how a dead animal differs from a living one and to mourn its passing. Moreover, this experience provides sound opportunities to learn that grief is more endurable when shared and that it does not last forever.

It is helpful to understand that preschool children view death as being a temporary condition from which people may return and continue living (Koocher, 1973; Sahler, 1978), a viewpoint unhappily encouraged by animated cartoons that feature exactly this happening. When discussing death with children, the early childhood teacher has to take this kind of magical thinking into account and realize that it is not necessarily an attempt to deny the reality of death, but merely an indication that children do not grasp the irreversibility of the event. Since this idea of returning to life appears to be a developmental characteristic, about all the

teacher can do is to reiterate patiently the fact that death is permanent. Preschool children also tend to equate death with sleep—another concept unfortunately reinforced by some adults, which may induce a certain reluctance for bedtime among sensitive youngsters. For this reason, comparing death to sleep should be avoided.

Children are very interested in funerals and enjoy participating in burying pets and nursery school animals that have died. This should be permitted because it contributes to understanding the life cycle and the process of mourning. Such interest should not be regarded as morbid or macabre—it is natural. It becomes morbid only when shocked adults force it to be clandestine.

These participatory understandings can be supplemented with books that touch on the subject of dying. Teachers can use such books to introduce matter-of-fact discussions that may dispel some of the more bizarre misconceptions children harbor about death, the worst one being that death is unmentionable. There are several good books that serve this purpose, ranging from *Charlotte's Web* (White, E. B., 1952) for older children to *The Tenth Good Thing About Barney* (Viorst, 1972) for some of the youngest ones. There is also at least one record, *Spin, Spider, Spin*,[2] that has a song about a dead bird. A list of a few such books is included at the end of this chapter.

Coping With the Threat of AIDS

As discussions of AIDS (Acquired Immune Deficiency Syndrome) become prevalent on television as well as in other media, even children of preschool age are becoming aware of its existence and seriousness.

While it is important for adults to understand the basic ways that this condition is transmitted and the consequences of not taking precautions

---

[2]AR 551, Educational Activities, Freeport, NY 11520.

One day last winter a well-informed child at the institute decided her time had come, so she gave birth while our student teacher interpreted the event to an interested bystander.

Children are interested in death as well as life and, if provided with the opportunity, will ask many questions about it.

to avoid it, for young children it seems more important to concentrate on the aspects of AIDS most likely to concern or frighten them and their families. For one thing, there is the difficult moral issue of whether youngsters infected with the AIDS virus should be admitted to children's centers or nursery schools. The plight of such youngsters cannot help but touch all our hearts. They are truly innocent victims of this plague, having acquired the condition before or during birth, while being breast fed, or from transfusions. AIDS is difficult to transmit from person to person and not one case of such transmission resulting from contact at school, preschool, or child-care center has been reported (Aronson, 1987). Children in homes where an infected person is present, and who have been hugged and kissed by that person have not become infected (Skeen & Hodson, 1987).

Nevertheless, opinion remains divided over the advisability of admitting children suffering from AIDS to child-care centers because people are so frightened of the disease. Some authorities advocate such admissions, provided that reasonably careful policies of hygiene are followed. These advocates maintain that it is actually the infected children who require protection, not the other way around because they are so vulnerable to infection (Merahn, Shelov, & McCracken, 1988). Others are not so sure (Raper & Aldridge, 1988). Even well-informed people express concern that focuses on the possibility that the Human Immunodeficiency Virus (HIV) might be transmitted through biting or through contact with the blood from an infected child.

Many states are currently in the process of establishing guidelines and policies about such admissions (Tourse & Gundersen, 1988). Until these are in place, it remains the prerogative of individual centers to make the difficult decisions about such admissions. For those who do opt for admitting children with this condition, the importance of maintaining the privacy of the child and his family is stressed over and over by authorities writing on this topic, as is the necessity for following very conscientious policies related to hand washing, diaper changing, and wearing gloves when dealing with injuries involving bleeding (Aronson, 1987; Mehran, Shelov, & McCracken, 1988).

The second concern about AIDS that is directly related to the majority of young children in our care is what we should tell them about this terrible disease. It has been interesting to me, as I reviewed the literature on this subject, to note that although general information and reassurance abounds, almost nothing has been written about what young children need or do not need to know. Yet, even young children are bound to have questions about AIDS as we are flooded with information by the media, particularly television. They are also likely to pick up the tone of the messages and become frightened and/or confused by them.

The exception to this dearth of information is an article by Skeen and Hodson in the May 1987 issue of *Young Children*. Following a lengthy discussion about what adults need to know about AIDS, they turn to the subject of young children and point out how important it is to be careful when we approach this topic with them. They remind the reader that little children know very little about sexuality, blood, or death and that we do not want to confuse or frighten them about these matters. At the same time, it will be necessary to deal with their worries about AIDS if these arise.

Skeen and Hodson suggest that "children [of preschool age] . . . need a little information and a lot of reassurance" (1987, p. 69). Children should be told that the chances of their getting AIDS is very, very slight, that almost no children have it, and that they are safe. They recommend if they want to know more, that it is sufficient to say that AIDs " 'is caused by a virus, a tiny germ.' Issues of sexual transmission, the spread of the disease through the sharing of contaminated needles during drug use, and the transmission of AIDS through infected blood of mother to fetus, are issues that can be discussed when the child is older" (p. 70).

For most youngsters of preschool age, this will be enough. However, for the tragic few who must cope with a loved one's infection or death, much more extensive help will be needed than can be discussed in this chapter. Three resources for such help are listed in the footnote below.[3]

Helping Families When Death Occurs

Inevitably there will be occasions during the year when a member of one of the children's family dies. Since families frequently turn to the teacher for advice about how to handle this situation with young children, it seems wise to include a few basic principles here. Some additional books on this subject are included in the references at the end of the chapter.

The most important thing for parents to realize is that the death should neither be restricted from conversations nor concealed from youngsters. Children always know when something is wrong (Furman, 1974, 1986), and their fantasies can be much more frightening to them than reality would ever be. Truthful statements are generally the best approach.

If possible, parents should prepare children in advance for the death of a loved one. This may be done with a statement such as, "The doctors are doing everything they can to help your granny, but sometimes there's just nothing else to do, so she may die."

It is not necessary to try to conceal all grief from children—seeing others cry may help them be able to express their sadness and learn to cope

with it. As time passes, they also have the chance to realize that gradually the pain of losing someone lessens and life can continue.

Some Special Things to Caution Parents About. Parents should be informed that children (and adults) experience more than pain when someone dies. They are often angry at being abandoned. Sometimes this anger is mixed up with guilt. This may develop because children feel guilty about being angry—"I shouldn't feel mad"—or because they perceive themselves as having caused the death—"If only I hadn't stamped my foot. . ." or "If only I'd been quiet like Mommy said." When families and parents discuss these feelings with children, the youngsters are able to recognize that these are acceptable and natural and that they are in no way responsible for the person's demise.

It may take quite some time for children to grasp that the person is truly gone. For example, one of the youngsters at our center who seemed to have understood his aunt's death surprised us one day by telling us what he thought she would be sending him for his birthday.

Children also require honest reassurance about who will take care of them and how the family structure may change. They wonder, What will happen? What if the other parent dies? What about life will be the same? Occasionally, adults are shocked at what seems to them to be such a self-interested attitude. But young children *are* self-centered. Their experience is extremely limited, and the world as they know it does orbit around them. They also know very well how young and helpless they are. When life is disturbed in such a significant way, it is only natural that they require reassurance and explanations that someone will continue to take care of them.

Finally, families should know that children benefit from recalling memories of the person who has died. Adults sometimes avoid doing this with children because it may also reawaken the pain of loss, but if the life cycle is to be

---

[3]National AIDS Network (NAN), 1012 14th St., N.W., Suite 601, Washington, D.C. 20005; National Association of People With AIDS (NAPWA), 2025 Eye Street N.W., Suite 415, Washington, D.C. 20006. Both of these groups will refer you to local community-based AIDS organizations. The Public Health Service also maintains a toll-free hotline; their telephone number is 1-800-342-AIDS.

understood and human relationships valued, recalling happy times with departed family members is most worthwhile. This also provides valuable opportunities to finish working through grief and clear up any misunderstandings or concerns the child may be harboring.

SUMMARY

Teaching children to understand and value life should be a basic element of curriculum intended to stress physical well-being. It includes often taboo subjects such as death, sex, sexual abuse, and AIDS as well as learning about other aspects of children's bodies—what is inside them, how they work, and how good they feel. In addition, even very young children can begin to develop a reverence for life; the chapter includes several suggestions of ways to teach this reverence.

SELF-CHECK QUESTIONS FOR REVIEW

Content-Related Questions

1. What is the wholesome attitude we want children to have toward their bodies?
2. Should masturbation be discouraged at all times? What is the recommended way to deal with a child who masturbates?
3. Why is it valuable to cuddle and hug little children? How have reports on sexual abuse in children's centers affected the behavior of some teachers in those centers?
4. Discuss some practical ways teachers can protect themselves from accusations of sexually abusing young children.
5. What are the results of the research conducted by Hyson, Whitehead, and Prudhoe on attitudes toward expressing physical affection? Discuss the implications for teachers that can be drawn from that research.
6. What is "reverence for life"? Give some examples of how this principle can be taught to young children.
7. What kinds of questions about reproduction are young children likely to ask? Name a couple and practice answering them.

8. How does the young child's concept of death differ from that of grown-ups? Why is it important not to conceal death from children?
9. Is AIDS a disease that is easily caught by young children?

Integrative Questions

1. Suppose you had a baby goat visit the children in your class. What plans and precautions would you take to make the visit most satisfactory to the children *and the animal?*
2. Parents are rightfully concerned about their children's safety while attending child-care centers. What will you do and say to reassure families that their children will be safe in your care?
3. Compare what young children need to know about AIDS with what adults need to know.

QUESTIONS AND ACTIVITIES

1. *Problem:* One of the 3-year-olds in your group comes to school in tears because a neighbor has run over her kitten with his car. How do you think this situation should be dealt with at school? The mother also wants to know if they should stop at the pet store on the way home from school and get another kitten. What would you advise?
2. *Problem:* You suddenly realize that you are missing two or three of the 4-year-olds from your group and when you investigate, you find them hiding in the playhouse comparing differences in their sexual anatomies. How do you think this situation is best handled? What approaches do you feel should be avoided? Why?
3. *Problem:* You are devoted to cross-age grouping, and you have a grandma who volunteers regularly at the school where you teach. You also are devoted to the value of teaching reverence for life. One day you find the grandma outdoors leading the children in stamping all over a spider's nest. How are you going to cope with this situation so that (1) the volunteer is not humiliated and (2) the children do not kill any more spiders?
4. There is no denying that many people are still not at ease with such topics as life and death and sexuality. How would you advise them to go about becoming more comfortable with these subjects?
5. *Problem:* You are now teaching in a parent cooperative preschool, and the program committee has

decided that the group would like a program on what every young child and his parents should know about sex. They want you to lead the group. There are three families who are very conservative and believe all sex education should take place in the home, and there are others who believe the school should play a part in such education. What kind of program would you present? What do you believe yourself?

6. *Problem:* One of the children in your school is in an automobile accident. He is seriously hurt and after 4 days dies. How would you handle this situation with the children in your group? His twin sister is due to return to school in a few days.

REFERENCES FOR FURTHER READING

Overviews

Carson, R. (1956). *The sense of wonder.* New York: Harper & Row, Publishers. Rachel Carson was one of the first to awaken us to our responsibilities for maintaining the earth in a healthy state. In this classic, she is concerned with helping children learn to wonder about the world around them.

Eyre, L., & Eyre, R. (1980). *Teaching children joy.* New York: Ballantine Books. This book expresses a wonderfully positive point of view towards children and towards life. Highly recommended.

Education About Sex

Bernstein, A. (1978). *The flight of the stork.* New York: Delacourt Press. *The Flight of the Stork* describes Bernstein's research on what children know about reproduction at different stages of their growth. The author provides suggestions about what adult responses and information are appropriate for each stage. A truly excellent and delightful book.

Calderone, M. S., & Ramey, J. W. (1982). *Talking with you child about sex: Questions and answers for children from birth to puberty.* New York: Ballantine Books. The authors provide a world of information couched in plain, positive language.

Gordon, S., & Gordon, J. (1986). *Raising a child conservatively in a sexually permissive world* (rev. ed.). Fayetteville, N.Y.: Ed-U Press. This book features sensible, down-to-earth discussions including specific answers to questions that are likely to be posed by children of various ages.

Koblinsky, S., Atkinson, J., & Davis, S. (1980). Sex education with young children. *Young Children, 36*(1), 21–31. This useful, sensible article suggests a number of practical guidelines for teaching young children about gender differences and sexuality.

Recommended Books on Sex Education for Children[4]

Suggested age levels are designated with overlapping age ranges as follows:

N—nursery, up to age 5
K—kindergarten, ages 4–6
P—primary, ages 5–9

The Birth of Sunset's Kittens. Carla Stevens. New York: Young Scott, 1969. NKP Black and white photographs illustrate the birth of kittens. The text includes correct terminology for body parts and the birth process and subtly relates the birth of kittens to the child's own birth.

Bodies. Barbara Brenner. New York: Dutton, 1973. NK Beautiful photographs of males and females from all age groups and cultural backgrounds are used to explore the fascinating topic of bodies and what they can do. The text stresses the uniqueness of each child's body.

Did the Sun Shine Before You Were Born? Sol and Judith Gordon. Fayetteville, N.Y.: Ed-U Press, 1974. NKP With a focus on the family, the book explains male-female genital differences, intercourse, conception, and the birth process with multicultural illustrations and suggestions for parents and teachers.

Girls Are Girls and Boys Are Boys: So What's the Difference? Sol Gordon, Fayetteville, N.Y.: Ed-U Press, 1979. P The differences between boys and girls are explained in terms of body build and function, rather than play, clothing, or career preferences. Masturbation, menstruation, intercourse, birth, and breast-feeding are discussed. The illustrations are multicultural.

How Babies Are Made. Andrew C. Andry and Steven Schepp. New York: Time-Life, 1968. KP Simple, eye-catching illustrations enhance a long book that covers sexual differences, intercourse, and the birth process. Children may be confused by the sequential presentation of plant, animal, and human reproduction.

How Was I Born? Lennart Nilsson. New York: Delacorte, 1975. P A story of conception, prenatal development and childbirth is told in a sequence of beautiful photographs by the author/photographer. The text is clear and scientifically accurate and may be edited for younger children. The photos depict body differences in the sexes from early childhood to adulthood.

---

[4]From "Sex Education with Young Children," by Sally Koblinsky, Jean Atkinson, and Shari Davis. Reprinted by permission from *Young Children*, Vol. 36, No. 1 (November 1980), pp. 30–31. Copyright © 1980 by National Association for the Education of Young Children, 1834 Connecticut Ave. NW, Washington, DC 20009.

Making Babies. Sara Bonnett Stein. New York: Walker & vivid photographs of the fetus. There is a separate text for children and adults on each page, with the adult text suggesting strategies for responding to children's sexual curiosity.

Where Did I Come From? Peter Mayle. Secaucus, N.J.: Lyle Stuart, 1973. P An amusing text with cartoon-like illustrations explains body differences, sexual arousal, intercourse, conception, fetal development, and the birth process. The text may be too long for some children.

Where Do Babies Come From? Margaret Sheffield. New York: Knopf, 1972. NKP A beautifully and sensitively illustrated book that discusses intercourse and fetal development and depicts natural childbirth and genital differences in infancy, childhood, and adulthood.

Information on Sexual Abuse and Children's Centers

Koblinsky, S., & Behana, N. (1984). Child sexual abuse: The educator's role in prevention, detection, and intervention. *Young Children, 39*(6), 3–15. This article summarizes what young children should be taught about saying no to bad touches. It offers a list of resources for further information.

Nelson, M., & Clark, K. (Eds.). (1986). *The educator's guide to preventing child sexual abuse.* Santa Cruz, Calif.: Network Publications. This valuable book covers everything from issues to guidelines to bibliographies and programs. Highly recommended.

Stephens, K. (1988). The First National Study of Sexual Abuse in Child Care: Findings and recommendations. *Child Care Information Exchange, 60,* 9–12. This is a valuable research study. The findings have important implications for schools that wish to avoid any possibility that sexual abuse might take place on their premises.

Children's Picture Books About Death

Abbot, S. (1972). *Old Dog.* New York: Coward, McCann, & Geoghegen.

Bernstein, J., & Gullo, S. (1976). *When people die.* New York: E. P. Dutton.

Brown, M. W. (1938 and 1965). *The dead bird.* New York: Young Scott Books.

DePaola, T. (1973). *Nana upstairs and Nana downstairs.* New York: G. P. Putnam's Sons.

Fassler, J. (1971). *My Grandpa died today.* New York: Behavioral Publications.

Kantrowitz, M. (1973). *When Violet died.* New York: Parents Magazine Press.

Miles, M. (1971). *Annie and the old one.* Boston: Little, Brown & Co.

Stein, S. B. (1974). *About dying: An open family book for parents and children together.* New York: Walker & Co.

Tresselt, A. (1972). *The dead tree.* New York: Parents Magazine Press.

Viorst, J. (1972). *The tenth good thing about Barney.* New York: Atheneum Publishers.

Zolotow, C. (1974). *My grandson Lew.* New York: Harper & Row, Publishers.

Books About Death for Teachers and Parents

Crase, D. R. (1986). Ideas! Helping young children deal with death. *Dimensions, 14*(3), 15–18. Age-appropriate advice is included in this practical article.

Fox, S. S. (1985). *Good grief: Helping groups of children when a friend dies.* Boston: New England Association for the Education of Young Children, 35 Pilgrim Road, Boston, Massachusetts 02215. In this sound, practical book, Fox covers just about every aspect of death and young children that the teacher needs to know. Highly recommended.

Knowles, D., & Reeves, N. (1983). *But won't Granny need her socks? Dealing effectively with children's concerns about death and dying.* Dubuque: Kendall/Hunt Publishing Co. This is a first-rate primer on how the subject of death can be approached with children of various ages, as well as on helping us come to terms with our own feelings about it. Highly recommended.

Lonetto, R. (1980). *Children's conceptions of death.* New York: Springer Publishing Co. Lonetto devotes a chapter to what children 3 to 5 years of age understand about death according to various theorists. He includes many drawings of dead people done by children, revealing their thoughts, feelings, and levels of understanding about this subject.

Oakley, M. (1984). The year we had Aaron. In J. L. Thomas (Ed.), *Death and dying in the classroom: Reading for reference.* Phoenix: ORYX Press. A touching but unsentimental account of how a teacher worked with her second graders to welcome a child with a fatal illness and helped them face the fact of his approaching death.

Riley, S. S. (1989). Pilgrimage to Elmwood Cemetery. *Young Children, 44*(2), 33–36. Riley suggests taking children to visit a cemetery and describes the outcome and potential value of that experience.

Thomas, J. L. (Ed.). (1984). *Death and dying in the classroom: Readings for reference.* Phoenix: ORYX Press. A reference that is particularly helpful for the early childhood teacher because it includes several articles focusing on children of preschool age.

Information About AIDS and Preschool Children

Aronson, S. S. (1987). Health update: AIDS and child care programs. *Child Care Information Exchange, 58,* 35–39. Aronson presents basic information about AIDS and discusses problems related to admission of such children into child-care centers.

Merahn, S., Shelov, S., & McCracken, G. H. (1988). Special report: AIDS: What teachers, directors & parents want to know. *Pre-K Today, 2*(6), A1–A7. An informative, practical article. Highly recommended.

Reece, C., & Rowe, P. (Eds.). (1988). *Children Today, 17*(3). This issue devotes several article to AIDS and related problems.

For the Advanced Student

Furman, E. (1974). *A child's parent dies: Studies in childhood bereavement.* New Haven, Conn.: Yale University Press. This intensive study of bereavement contains many case histories and general discussions. It is a valuable reference that approaches the subject of loss from a psychoanalytic perspective.

Furman, E. (1984). Children's patterns in mourning the death of a loved one. In H. Wass and C. A. Corr (Eds.), *Childhood and death.* Washington, D.C.: Hemisphere Publishing Corporation. This is an extraordinarily helpful reference—not to be missed.

Koblinsky, S. A. (1983). *Sexuality education for parents of young children: A facilitator training manual.* Fayetteville, N. Y.: Ed-U Press. Although this is, as the title indicates, primarily a training manual, the resources, attention to multiethnic families, and summary of facts about sexuality make this book an outstanding reference.

Kübler-Ross, E. (1969). *On death and dying: What the dying have to teach doctors, nurses, clergy, and their own families.* New York: Macmillan Publishing Company. This is the classic work by a distinguished psychiatrist who made this subject her life's study. The publication of this book opened the subject of dying for general discussion.

MacFarlane, K., Waterman, J., Conerly, S., Damon, L., Durfee, M., & Long, S. (1986). *Sexual abuse of young children: Evaluation & treatment.* New York: The Guilford Press. This is a comprehensive reference that deals with molestation of preschool children.

Schowalter, J. E., Buschman, P., Patterson, P. R., Kutscher, A. H., Tallmer, M., & Stevenson, R. G. (1987). *Children and death: Perspectives from birth through adolescence.* New York: Praeger. This book covers many facets of death and children. The subject matter ranges from children's concepts of death to working with children who are mortally ill and helping parents cope with losing a child. Some particularly good advice is included in the chapter by William Sack entitled "A Manual for Medical Students on Chronic Illness and Death in Children."

Wass, H., & Corr, C. A. (Eds). (1984). *Helping children cope with death: Guidelines and resources* (2nd ed.). Washington, D.C.: Hemisphere Publishing Corporation. Wass and Corr's book is comprehensive enough to make it the most useful reference in the field.

Resources of Special Interest

Centering Corporation. P.O. Box 3367, Omaha, Nebraska 68103. This is a nonprofit organization that publishes many inexpensive, worthwhile pamphlets on grief and how to deal with it.

Compassionate Friends. P.O. Box 1347, Oak Brook, Illinois 60521. An organization for parents whose child has died.

Siecus Report. Published by the Sex Information and Education Council of the United States, 80 Fifth Avenue, New York, New York 10011. This newsletter is affiliated with the Department of Health Education of the School of Education, Health, Nursing, and Arts Professions of New York University. It provides an excellent way to keep up with various publications in the area of sex education. Liberal in tone.

10 Achieving Emotional Competence

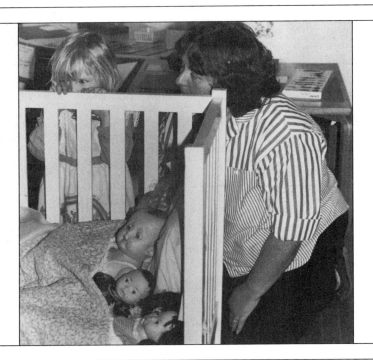

Have you ever

- Wondered how to help children express their feelings without hurting other children?
- Wanted to know some practical ways to reduce feelings of tensions and aggression in children?
- Worried over how to help a child through a family crisis?

If you have, the material in this chapter will help you.

Teachers need to recognize that emotionally tinged play often deals with the less pleasant aspects of children's daily and fantasy lives (e.g., death, destruction, evil figures such as witches, monsters, and ghosts). Such content can make many adults uncomfortable and they may terminate or prohibit such play for their own comfort, unaware of the emotional value it can have for children. Well-timed suggestions and clarifications from invested adults can provide the structure and support children need to deal with emotional issues in play, so that they do not become frightened by or flooded with emotion that may seem unmanageable without adult buffering. Voicing fears and fantasies, trying out alternative strategies in dealing with them, and discovering solutions are steps children can negotiate in play that will have emotional, as well as cognitive, payoffs.

NANCY CURRY *and* DORIS BERGEN (1987)

The difficulty with talking about curriculum for the emotional, or affective, self is that the very word *curriculum* has an academic ring that can lead us into overintellectualizing our teaching if we are not careful. We must guard vigilantly against this tendency by remembering that the most effective kind of learning and teaching about the emotional self is embedded in the everyday happenings of life rather than in self-conscious discussions of feelings in artificially contrived group times (Martorella, 1975). To deal with feelings in the most effective way, we must seize teachable moments as they occur to help children perceive and cope with their feelings so they can lead comfortable, emotionally healthy lives.

Sometimes such learning is best accomplished at school by capitalizing on opportunities as they spontaneously arise between children and other children or between children and staff. Sometimes it is best accomplished by working with parents to deepen their understanding of their children's emotional needs and how to meet them at home. But whichever approach is used, the competencies we wish children to attain are basically the same.

ONE: HELP THE CHILD LEARN TO SEPARATE FROM HER FAMILY

The first competency the child has to acquire to survive away from home is the ability to separate from her parent with a reasonable degree of ease and feel comfortable at school. Ideally, entrance to a children's center or nursery school will not be her first experience in separation, but even if it is not, the length of the absence combined with the unfamiliar environment makes some children uneasy and a few even frantic (Jervis, 1987).

To make the transition as painless as possible, separation should be accomplished gradually. This allows the youngster to make friends with her teacher and possibly one or two of the children and be involved in activities before her parent "abandons" her. Some schools make friends by having staff visit the child at home, or they send each child a personal letter welcoming her to school (children get so little mail and enjoy it so much). Schools that begin anew each fall often invite small groups of children to attend at different times of the morning for the first day or two to provide personal attention for each youngster and prevent feelings of being overwhelmed.

A parent should be encouraged to stay for the first few times until the child has settled in, but he may also need to be instructed to be matter of fact and definite when he is ready to leave, since it increases separation difficulties considerably if the adult debates and vacillates between leaving and staying. However, no matter how well acquainted the child is and how well handled the departure, teacher and parent should realize that tears or a quivering lip is a possibility. Teachers who allow themselves to feel frightened and guilty when a child is upset surely add to her anxiety, whereas teachers who take these upsets in stride convey their own sense of security to the child and thus reassure her.

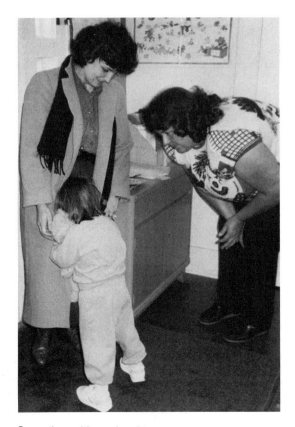

Sometimes it's so hard to say goodbye.

Unfortunately, feeling secure in the midst of a disturbing scene is more easily recommended than attained by beginning teachers. This is particularly true because such upsets so often take place while other parents are coming and going. The way to become more at ease with these situations is to resolve to see them through in as calm and confident a way as you can, comfort the child as well as you are able without pleading with her or acting apologetic, and distract her as quickly as possible from her grief. Experience over a period of time helps most of all, for everyone, but the only way to obtain that experience is to work the separation situation through with the child and her family as it arises.

Families, as well as children, benefit from the teacher's assurance, and it can comfort worried parents if they are invited to telephone later to check on whether the child is still crying. Ironically, usually the parent who is the most prone to worry is also shyest of calling about the child unless specifically invited to do so. Fathers, in particular, may be wary of appearing too concerned.

Although it is vital to realize that little children can be desolated by a parent's departure, it may also help teachers feel better if they remember that there is sometimes a touch of drama in the experience. I well recall a young friend of mine, clinging pathetically to the door, while sobbing, "Goldilocks has lost her Mama!" The moral of this tale is that it is important to discriminate between the child who is really distressed and the one who is less disturbed (even though making quite a fuss over the separation) and to respond accordingly.

For children who are deeply anxious, the basic task of teacher and parent is to establish a bond of trust between the three of them. Needless to say, the mother or father who sneaks away without letting the child know she or he is leaving is hardly establishing such a bond. Teachers should be careful to see that this does not happen.

For an anxious child, the separation should be kept short in the beginning. Sometimes it helps if the parents leave something tangible that belongs to them for the child to keep. (I know of one instance where the youngster wrapped himself in the mother's old sweater for several days.) Sometimes a surrogate comfort object, such as a favorite blanket or stuffed animal, helps bridge the gap. If the child is generally accustomed to toting such an item around, the first days of school are not the time to separate her from it (Jalongo, 1987).

Transition to school is also made easier if beginning days are kept simple and uncomplicated and if standards for behavior are not set too high. It can be difficult not to expect a new group of children to begin in the fall where the "sophisticated" former spring group left off. Teachers should bear in mind that the most vital learning tasks for the child's emotional self at the start of school are learning (1) that school is a comfortable place to be and (2) that the parent will return as promised.

Of course, even when children appear to have made the transition comfortably, they may be holding some feelings back. I am reminded of one of our institute's children whose mother asked him how he had liked school that day. "Well," he replied, "you know, I've been playing a joke on the teachers." "You have?" she asked in surprise. "Yes," he said, "they think that I'm having a good time—but really I'm not!"

TWO: FOSTER BASIC ATTITUDES OF TRUST, AUTONOMY, AND INITIATIVE IN THE CHILD

A second fundamental goal of curriculum for the emotional self is encouraging the child to be trustful, independent, and able to reach out and investigate her world. Erik Erikson (1963, 1971, 1982) has made a valuable contribution to our understanding of the significance of these attitudes in the emotional life of the child and how to encourage their development.

He hypothesizes that during their life span, individuals pass through a series of stages of emotional development wherein basic attitudes

are formed. Early childhood encompasses three of these: the stages of trust versus mistrust, autonomy versus shame and doubt, and initiative versus guilt. Although children of preschool age are likely to be working on the second and third sets of attitudes, it is important to understand the implications of the first set, also. This is because Erikson theorizes that the resolution of each stage depends in part on the successful accomplishment of the previous one.

In the stage of *trust versus mistrust,* the baby learns (or fails or learn) that other people can be depended on and also that she can depend on herself to elicit needed responses from them. This development of trust is deeply related to the quality of care that the parent provides and is often reflected in feeding practices, which, if handled in a manner that meets her needs, help assure the infant that she is valued and important. Although by the time she enters preschool, the balance between trust or mistrust will have been tipped in favor of one attitude or the other, the need to experience trust and to have it reaffirmed remains with people throughout their lives. This is also true for the other attitudes as they develop.

Therefore, it is vital that the basic climate of the center encourage the establishment of trust among everyone who is part of that community. If the teacher thinks of establishing trust in terms of letting the children know that they can depend on him, it will be fairly easy for him to implement this goal. For example, consistent policies and regularity of events in the program obviously contribute to establishing a trustful climate. Being reasonable also makes it clear to the child that she can depend on the teacher. In addition, if he is sensitive to the child's individual needs and meets them as they arise, the teacher can confirm the message of her infanthood once again that she is worthy of love and thus further strengthen trust and self-esteem.

In our society the second stage, wherein the attitudes of *autonomy versus shame and doubt* are formed, occurs during the same period in which toilet training takes place. During this time, the child is acquiring the skills of holding on and

Allowing children to do things for themselves helps foster their sense of autonomy.

letting go. This fundamental exercise in self-assertion and control is associated with her drive to become independent and to express this independence by making choices and decisions so often couched in the classic imperatives of the 2-year-old, "No!" "Mine!" and "Me do it!" Erikson maintains that children who are overregulated and deprived of the opportunity to establish independence and autonomy may become oppressed with feelings of shame and self-doubt, which result in losing self-esteem, being defiant, trying to get away with things, and, in later life, developing various forms of compulsive behavior.

The desirable way to handle this strong need for choice and self-assertion is to provide an environment at home and at the center that makes many opportunities available for the child to do for herself and to make decisions. This is the fundamental reason why self-selection is an important principle in curriculum design. At the same time, the teacher must be able to establish decisive control when necessary, since young children often show poor judgment and can be tyrannized by their own willfulness unless the teacher is willing to intervene.

Gradually, as the child develops the ability to act independently, she embarks on building the next set of basic attitudes. Around the age of 4 or 5, she becomes more interested in reaching out to the world around her, in doing things, and in being part of the group. At this stage, she wants to think things up and try them out: she is interested in the effect her actions have on other people (witness her experimentation with profanity and "bad" language); she formulates concepts of what her family feels are appropriate sex roles; she enjoys imaginative play; and she becomes an avid seeker of information about the world around her. This is the stage Erikson has so aptly named *initiative versus guilt.*

To feel emotionally satisfied, a child of this age must be allowed to explore, to act, and to do. Children's centers are generally strong in meeting the children's need to explore and create, but they often underestimate the ability of older 4- and 5-year-olds to participate in making plans and decisions for their group or to attempt challenging projects. Of course, the teacher must make allowance for the fact that 4- and 5-year-olds are better planners and starters than they are finishers. Satisfaction in completing projects is more likely to be part of the developmental stage that follows this one: the stage of *industry versus inferiority,* which is characteristic of children during their early years in primary school. But encouraging the ability to initiate plans and take action will enhance children's feelings of self-worth and creativity, as well as their ability to be self-starters—all highly desirable outcomes necessary for future development and happiness.

THREE: HELP THE CHILD REMAIN IN CONTACT WITH HER FEELINGS WHILE LEARNING TO CONTROL WHAT SHE DOES ABOUT THEM

Unfortunately, much of our culture appears dedicated to teaching children to suppress and deny feelings. As early as age 2 or 3 some children have already learned that there are certain feelings that are not acceptable for them

to "own." These vary according to family standards and may include jealousy in one family, anger toward adults in another, or fearfulness expressed by crying in a third. Whatever they are, such denial, if imposed firmly enough, causes a child to disown part of herself and believe that some part of herself is not acceptable.

The reason for such denial and suppression seems to be that people assume that feeling inevitably leads to acting or that acknowledging a feeling will make it stronger. These assumptions are coupled with the conviction that if one pretends something does not exist, it will go away. But such assumptions are psychologically unsound (Moustakas, 1959; Murphy & Moriarty, 1976). What *is* true is that repressing, denying, or ignoring feelings *increases* the probability that the child will act them out—either directly or indirectly. In other words, the child who is unable to *tell* someone how she feels is almost inevitably driven to *show* that person how she feels. Perhaps she hits someone; perhaps she messes her pants; perhaps she knocks over the block construction of an innocent bystander; perhaps she retreats to a quiet place and rocks there, endlessly, in a solitary way. None of these behaviors is an emotionally or socially productive solution, and many of them could be avoided if parents and teachers would learn to take the risk of helping children recognize their feelings and express them safely. They should use simple terms that children can understand: "Feel what you wish, feel all your true feelings, but control what you *do.*"

The problem is that, although the most effective way of dealing with feelings is by telling somebody about them, many adults do not welcome some disclosures. Furthermore, little children are often unable to put feelings into words. Reality forces me to admit that some parents will always interpret this directness as insolence, but the success of such books as Ginott's *Between Parent and Child* (1965) and Satir's *People Making* (1975), as well as the Parent Effectiveness Training of Gordon (1976), provides encouraging evidence that it is also possible for many adults to learn to listen and respond to children's feelings without being unduly threatened by the experience.

Help Children Express Their Feelings

The clearest way to show the child that you have really listened is to take time to describe her feelings before saying anything else. When attempting this, you should keep sentences describing feelings *short, uncomplicated,* and *tentative.* It is particularly important to be tentative because identifying feelings involves sensitive guesswork. Since you have to surmise the child's probable emotion, there is always the possibility of injustice and inaccuracy. To avoid hurting the child through misunderstanding her it is best to begin interpretations with such phrases as, "You seem to me . . .," or "I wonder if you're feeling . . .," or "Is your face telling me that . . .?" In short, always remember that such interpretations should be offered as caring guesses rather than as dogmatic labels. Another advantage of concentrating on the child's feelings is that this also begins the lengthy task of teaching her the difference between self-report (telling another person how one feels inside oneself) and verbal attack (hurting the other person's feelings by name calling and so forth)—a valuable distinction, albeit difficult to learn.

Also, because young children's comprehension of language is so limited, it is better teaching to go beyond using an adjective such as mad or happy or jealous to describe the emotion. These words are only beginning to acquire meaning to children. Expert teachers try to be more descriptive than that, so they may say, "You look to me like your stomach's all churned up inside," or "I think your eyes are telling me you wish you hadn't done that!" rather than telling a child she looks excited or remorseful.

Although teachers should make a point to recognize all kinds of feelings, not just unhappy ones, experience has taught me that it is the unhappy feelings that are most likely to be passed over—not so much unhappy, sad feelings as unhappy, angry ones. Yet taking time to identify the angry feelings of each child so that both youngsters hear them stated plainly should always be one of the first steps in settling a fight. Doing this takes some of the pressure to act out of an encounter. Once the teacher has stopped the actual battle, it only takes a minute extra for him to say something as simple and caring as, "Jon, you really want that rabbit badly, and, Heather, you aren't ready to give it up, and you don't want him to grab it—is that right?" Such teaching has to be done again and again, but if the teacher is persistent, this technique will gradually bear fruit. These brief descriptions of feelings let each child know the teacher or parent cares enough about her to understand and recognize her feelings without passing judgment on their worth—feelings are neither good nor bad, they simply are. But what we do about them is another matter, and so we are reminded once again of the importance of the second part of the basic mental health principle, "Feel what you wish, but *control what you do.*"

Young children frequently require clear reminding, sometimes coupled with physical restraint, that it is not all right to act out a feeling by socking somebody or biting them, no matter how angry they feel. To continue with the rabbit incident, the teacher might say, "Jon, I know you want that rabbit badly, and you, Heather, aren't ready to give it up, and you don't want Jon to grab it. I know it's hard to wait and hard to share, but I can't let you pull the rabbit's leg that way—it hurts him too much." *In other words, the pattern of intervention from the teacher should include a statement of the children's feelings, a statement of what they can or cannot do, and a simple, clear reason for the restraint.*

In addition to implementing sound mental health practices, this particular strategy has the added advantage of instilling the beginnings of internalized consciences in children. Research indicates that two of the most effective ways of building an internal conscience are combining warmth and control with simple reasons why a child must not act a particular way (Cooper-smith, 1967; Hoffman, 1970). These occasions are *not* the time to moralize and talk about how good little girls would feel or what nice little boys would do. The teacher should state the reason firmly and briefly why the child cannot do as she wishes and move on with her to something else.

Do Not Ask About Motives

One more thing about describing and discussing feelings must be emphasized: it just does not work to ask a young child *why* she did a partic-ular thing. I have occasionally heard well-intentioned students inquire, "Why did you hurt the puppy like that?" or "Why did you cry when your Mother left?" It is a rare child who can deal with this question effectively and explain in any depth why she hurt the puppy or poured paint all over her neighbor's picture. An incident in my own family illustrates this point. My oldest child, then aged 4, pushed her brother down the cellar stairs one winter day. I still remember those terrible thumping sounds as he rolled down those stairs. After assuring myself that he was all right, I turned to her and roared that fatal question, "Why, Nancy, why on earth did you push him down the stairs? Don't you know that's danger-ous? You could have killed him!" "Well," she said, looking at me sidewise, "Well . . . it's really just too complicated to explain." And that sums it up. The motivation for such acts *is* too complicated for most little children to explain.

FOUR: HELP THE CHILD LEARN TO USE PLAY AND CREATIVE MATERIALS TO RESOLVE EMOTIONAL PROBLEMS

Describing children's feelings to them is one valuable method of helping children remain in touch with their emotional selves, but its effec-tiveness depends on the sensitivity of the teacher, as well as on his being right on the spot. Fortunately, additional activities can be pro-

vided in the curriculum that also serve this purpose and do not require such close attention from the teacher. These are primarily pretend play situations and self-expressive creative activ-ities. When such activities are provided, chil-dren make use of them in a very natural way to work through troubling situations, repeating them until they have diluted their impact to manageable proportions and have attained some mastery over them (Curry & Bergen, 1987).

For example, children often play out hospital experiences, or enact scenes from home in which they assume adult roles, or retreat to infantile behavior and roles as their feelings dictate. I even recall one youngster who consistently played at being the father: beginning with a dinner table scene, he would roughly shove his "wife" aside, tip over furniture, and dump the doll children from their beds before rushing out and slamming the door. Although no such violence had actually transpired in his own home, the mother and father had recently separated, and it seemed to the teachers that the child's own feelings and his perception of the father's feelings were mingled together in his angry play.[1]

Use Pretend Play to Strengthen the Emotional Self

Children can use almost anything that comes to hand for pretend play, and to help them exercise their imaginations it is best to choose equipment that lends itself to many possible uses. Blocks, for example, can be used to represent roads, cars, baby bottles, buildings, or fences. Scarves can be made into aprons, diapers, reins for horses, veils,

---

[1]It should be noted that the teachers did not simply let this child struggle through this alone in his play. They offered some simple, understanding comments about how everyone feels like breaking things when families are separating and reassured him that he would often be able to see his father (something that was true in that particular case) and that both his mother and father still cared about him.

or elegant sashes. Of course, it also facilitates certain kinds of play if some items of a more structured nature, such as dolls and dress-up clothes, are provided. These lend themselves beautifully to playing out episodes of domestic happiness as well as contention. Then, too, special circumstances can warrant inclusion of other structured items (we added leg braces and crutches shortly after a youngster with a handicap joined our group), and equipment for general hospital play is always valuable to offer.

Use Specific Themes. It is also possible and occasionally desirable to stimulate play around a particular theme to meet a special problem. We once had a youngster at school who had been badly frightened at Halloween by some older boys who cornered her while wearing terrifying rubber masks. It is not exaggerating to say that this episode colored the child's life with terror,

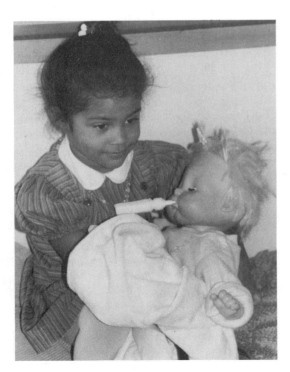

Of course, feelings aren't always unpleasant.

and she became apprehensive of many new experiences as a result. Gradually, we made simple masks available in the dramatic play area and then went on to make paper bag ones and finally introduced the rubber, pullover kind. She learned to approach these with bravado and finally mastered her fear through the medium of play. I can still see her stalking up to another child, mask in hand, saying to him solicitously, "I'm going to frighten you, Frankie—are you ready?" and then slipping on the mask and growling at him fiercely while he coped in a very adequate fashion by growling back.

Encourage Storytelling by Children. Still another way of using imagination to help children understand how they feel is by encouraging them to dictate stories. Fours and fives often relish dictating such accounts, and these are clearly influenced by their personal concerns.

This story was told by a 4-year-old in response to a picture of a little girl sitting on a beach playing:

She's sad because she's out there by herself at the beach. And it's dark out there because she's been bad. She ran away and she got lost!

This one was in response to a picture drawn by another child, also aged 4:

A kitten and a bluebird are talking about the sun. They think that the sun goes to a big barn at night. I think that's true! The bluebird gets the sun out in the morning. He punches the barn down. The end!

This story was accompanied by a kind of antiphonal chant from another youngster:

Joshua: I've got a story—a scary one—about Godzilla. Oh, he's scary—in the dark, he glows! The shark makes him do it—and sharks are really scary, but Dracula was the scariest—and a fire hose is scary—he's really scary!

Angie: (who has been listening nervously) I'm not scared of dark or ghosts!

Joshua: . . . and an alligator comes along—and King Kong. . . .

Angie: I dreamed about King Kong—and it was *dark*—but *I* wasn't scared—and I came out and I patted him and he was friendly!

Joshua: Let's see—hummmm! More scary—Aha! I got it! And the lizard came! Aha! And a crocodile!

Angie: (firmly) But I'm not scared of anything!

Joshua: (to me) Write this down! (looking disgustedly at Angie) And they all ate each other up—even the lizard! There, baby![2]

Finally, from a 3-year-old:

I saw a little snail and the snail got on him—on this little guy! And he went on him, and that guy ate the snail! That's all![3]

Sometimes the teacher can help focus the child's concern by starting the story in a particular vein. Perhaps he might begin, "Once upon a time there was a little girl who was supposed to stay at the baby-sitters, but she ran home instead. When she got there . . .," or "Once upon a time there was a child named Henry who went to the doctor and he said, 'Henry, you're going to have to have your tonsils out.' Well, that was quite a surprise to Henry. . . ."

Or children may be drawn into playing out stories and experiences by using puppets or little rubber dolls (Fuchs, 1976). These items are often particularly successful with excessively "bland" children who permit themselves only sharply restricted ways of expressing strong feelings and who may find actual dramatic play in the housekeeping corner overwhelming. My guess is that using dolls and puppets has the advantage for such youngsters of allowing them to be bigger than the puppets and somewhat apart from them—conditions that are reassuring to children who are uneasy about getting too close to strong emotions.

In addition to meeting special needs, miniature dolls and puppets are also useful to employ with children in general, particularly those older than age 3. Besides fostering their imaginations, puppets give them the sense of being in obvious command of the play, and this contributes to their feelings of mastery and strengthens their ego controls.

Use Self-Expressive Materials to Express Feelings Safely

In addition to supplying materials for imaginative play, teachers can provide for the socially acceptable expression of various emotions by offering expressive art materials such as paint and dough. These substances have additional cardinal virtues as outlets for creative ideas and aesthetic satisfactions, but they are without peer in the realm of expressing feelings. (Chapter 13 presents an extensive discussion of the creative possibilities offered by paint and dough.)

It is not realistic to expect young children to use these materials to produce actual pictures of their problems. Nevertheless, the youngster who uses her fingernails to scratch tensely through the fingerpainting paper or who limits herself to using only the center of the paper is expressing her feelings, just as the child swooping and squishing her way through a fingerpainting is expressing her happiness and lack of constriction (Hartley, Frank, & Goldenson, 1952). Some of these materials lend themselves particularly well to the sublimated expression of aggression, and some to the relief of more generalized tension.

Aggression-Relieving Activities

We may as well realize that the world is full of frustrating circumstances for young children (Murphy, 1987). Their wants are immediate, intense, and personal, and inevitably they are prevented numerous times every day from satisfying their desires. Such frustrations range from seeing that another child already has the ball they want, to having a passerby stumble over their blocks, or to finding that lunchtime has cut short their play on the swings. The intensity of frustration and amount of ensuing anger and aggression vary from child to child (Patterson, Littman, & Bricker, 1967), but all children need

---

[2] These stories are from children in the California Preschool Program, Santa Barbara City Schools.

[3] From a child in the Santa Barbara City College Children's Center.

USING MUD, SAND, AND WATER TO RELIEVE TENSION

Mud or sand, combined with water, provides an excellent example of a material that is both absorbing and relaxing for young children. Some psychologists and psychiatrists think that the smearing associated with messy materials such as mud has special emotional value to young children who have only recently passed through toilet training. They maintain that learning to conform to society's expectations by controlling their urine and bowel movement can be a difficult task for young children, and the opportunity to play with messy things seems to relieve some of the stress of this situation. Perhaps this is because the children can be allowed to do as they like (within reason) with the mud.

Whether one accepts this theory or not, there is no denying that these materials can settle down tense children to absorbed play for long periods of time. Water alone provides soothing pleasures to children, which, I believe, are unmatched by those of other materials. The opportunity to pour, swish, or generally delight in using water is one of the true joys of childhood. When combined with mud or sand, it is even more pleasurable.

Some schools are able to purchase special water tables for such play, but less expensive deep galvanized tubs work just as well. If the bathroom is large and has a drain in the floor, water play can be set up there to make access to water and mopping up simpler. The addition of containers, shakers, sieves, funnels, spoons, and pans will furnish literally hours of deeply involved play, and they may be acquired very cheaply at rummage sales or thrift stores.

In addition to the tension-relieving aspects of mud and water, there are many other virtues to these materials (D. M. Hill, 1977; James & Granovetter, 1987). For example, children can learn such facts of physics as water always runs downhill and it can change from solid to liquid to solid again in wintery weather. Pouring, mixing, and experimenting with textures of sand and mud and with the properties of wetter versus drier mud offer additional learning experiences. The use of moist sand encourages con-struction of tunnels and towers, as well as all sorts of pretend bakery products, thereby fostering the imagination. Sand also provides excellent opportunities for cognitive learning. Because these are rarely mentioned in the literature, some examples of activities are given on p. 181. *

In addition, opportunities for social cooperation abound in sand and mud play. Water play, in particular, is so absorbing and relaxing that it is often a time of pleasant harmonious interaction. (I mention this because inexperienced teachers often dread water play thinking it will make the children wild. However, if there is plenty of space and time and water to go around, this is not typically the case.)

Presenting These Materials Effectively

The most delightful kind of mud, sand, and water play involves warm days, trickling hoses, and barefoot, lightly dressed children. In these circumstances children can puddle and play to their heart's content. Cleanup is simple because it is easy to hose everything down at the end of playtime. The satisfaction evident on the children's face as they muck and squish about makes it plain that this is an activity of great value to them.

Fortunately, such play need not be limited to warm weather. It is possible to teach children that they must keep their clothes and shoes dry when it is a chilly day. Board tables can be set up on sawhorses in the sandbox to keep pant knees from soaking through, or if the activity must be carried on inside, waist-high, indoor sand tables can be used and aprons provided. Cornmeal may be used as a variation for sand if the teacher does not want the sand inside; however, one must remember that cornmeal makes floors very slippery and so must be swept up continually while it is in use. Wheat is also delightful to pour and sift, though it cannot be molded.

Several points about sand require mentioning. First, because sand is so often offered to children in only its dry state, which is relatively uninteresting and useless for play, the sandbox or table should be checked every day to make certain that at least half of the sand is moist enough for molding and modeling. Second, although children love this material so much that they will uncomplainingly make do with the same old equipment day after day, the teacher should offer a variety of play equipment to stimulate imagination and attract more children to the sandbox. *Stout* shovels are important to provide, as are sturdy spoons. Big and small cars and trucks make wonderful additions, as do cooking utensils. Sifters and sieves with various-sized holes are also useful. The inclusion of sturdy, little plastic people or animals (or both) will stimulate the playing out of pretend adventures. We have also found that an old set of wooden blocks is interesting to add occasionally. Plumber's pipes and joints and sewer tile (particularly when combined with water) add a whole new dimension. Finally, a soft hand brush stored in the sand area makes it easy for children to brush off their clothes before leaving if their clothes are very sandy. Indoors, a brush and dustpan are essential for cleaning up both floors and children.

Activities*	Learnings
Use shovel to fill pail with sand:	Sand takes the shape of the container
Pour sand from pail:	Pours like a liquid
Fill and pour from different sizes and shapes of containers:	Full/empty
	More/less
	Quantity of sand remains the same when poured into containers of different shapes (conservation)
	Volume
Shake sand in a shallow container:	Small grains of sand sift to the bottom and large grains come to the top
Look at sand with magnifying glass:	Each grain looks different in size and shape
Blow sand:	Air moves sand
Use fingers to make holes and lines in the sand:	Sand moves easily when pushed
	Hole fills when finger is moved
Sift sand:	Sand grains are different sizes
	Sand falls through space
Use balance to weigh wet and dry sand:	Wet sand is heavier than dry sand
Form sand in molds:	Sand can be pressed into different shapes
Build tunnels:	Space exists even though not seen
	Spatial relationships of under, over, inside, outside
Write and draw in sand in a shallow container, shake and change:	Tactual impression of letter and number shapes
	Designs can be erased
Dramatic play:	Language development
examples: drive cars, trucks, tractors; prepare foods; home for people and animals	Careers
	Sharing
	Representation of reality
	Construction

*From "Teachers Make Curriculum Decisions" by S. D. Taylor, 1984, *Dimensions, 12*(3), 21.

to learn to redirect their aggressive feelings into channels that harm neither themselves nor others.

Ways to Relieve Anger Harmlessly. One of the best ways of relieving such anger, as already discussed, is dealing with the feeling directly by letting the child know that you are aware of her anger and that you will help her confront it squarely.

Other, less direct methods, such as vigorous physical activity, are also helpful. Jumping hard on a mattress or throwing beanbags can be useful. Vigorous crying is an outstanding way to achieve relief. Dancing—particularly if offered with therapeutic questions such as, "What's the strongest dance you do?" or "What's the angriest thing you can think of to be? Show us what that would look like"—provides a valuable avenue of expression. Hammering is still another excellent aggression-redirecting activity, particularly if large peg-and-hammer sets are used, since these can take brutal punishment while not requiring

The sandbox offers wonderful invitations for creative play.

close supervision. Beating large drums also offers a safe aggression reliever, if the teacher can tolerate the noise (outdoors is infinitely preferable to indoors for this activity). Squirting water is still another satisfying, though milder, way of getting feelings of frustration and anger out of the system.

Regardless of what aggression reliever is provided, teachers should bear in mind that they need to be on hand to exert control if necessary. Children using these materials forcefully must still stay within the bounds of safety. It is important to be very clear with them about the rules, before they start. The hammer may be used only with the peg set, no matter how the child feels, and the water may be squirted on the fence or the tree, but not on another child or the teacher. (Note that direct methods of preventing and controlling aggression are discussed in the next chapter.)

Although such restraints are obviously necessary, it is important to remember also that the basic intention of such activity is to reduce frustration, not build it. For this reason, it is best to select materials that do not require much skill to use. This is why it is better to use a peg-and-hammer set rather than a hammer and nails for relieving aggression. Having to fiddle with a pesky nail in itself contributes to rage.

Tension-Relieving Activities

There are some general tension-relieving activities that are also of great value. Two of these are so practical that we often forget about them. They are (1) taking children who are acting restless to the toilet and (2) offering children something to eat or drink when they are out of sorts. I would not want these suggestions to be misconstrued so that every restless little boy is continually escorted to the bathroom or that food is used as a means of continually placating children, but there are occasions when these solutions are worth trying. Children are often unaware that physiological needs are making them cranky; they just know that nothing feels quite right, and sometimes this gets them into unnecessary trouble.

Other tension-relieving activities include rhythmic ones such as swinging and rocking, which are very soothing to young children. The close physical contact while rocking in the teacher's lap, in particular, provides its own special relaxing comfort. Other, more specific relaxation techniques discussed in Chapter 8 ("Developing Physical Competence") are also valuable. Finally, fingerpainting, dough, mud, and water play offer excellent opportunities for children to relax and mess about to their heart's content (Fingerpainting and dough are discussed in Chapter 13.)

Whatever is offered in the way of materials that relieve feelings, it must be remembered that such items are intended to help children over the inevitable humps and hollows of growth. As such, they are only temporary measures—first aid, not long-term cures. It is the overall environment of the school, where frustration is kept to a tolerable level by careful planning and by sound knowledge of children's needs and where overstimulation is avoided, that produces the basic facilitative climate that helps children gradually attain understanding and mastery of their feelings.

FIVE: HELP THE CHILD LEARN TO FACE REALITY

On first thought, it might seem to be ideal for children to experience childhood as a perfect, golden time devoid of frustration and anxiety, but many contemporary psychologists do not agree with this point of view. For example, in his classic work, *The Meaning of Anxiety* (1977), Rollo May maintains that properly harnessed anxiety can be a powerful incentive for creativity; and Lois Murphy (1976) cites children who cope well with anxiety as possessing the qualities of confidence, flexibility, resourcefulness, and definiteness in using the environment and managing their frustrations. It seems, then, that

experiencing at least a certain amount of frustration and anxiety so often associated with facing reality can have beneficial results for young children, particularly if parents and teachers help them learn to cope with these situations in a productive way. Part of this learning to cope involves accepting what cannot be changed.

Accepting What Cannot Be Changed

Everyone has to learn at one time or another that there are some things in life that cannot be changed. No amount of tears can affect the fact that the cut must be stitched, any more than tears can bring about a reconciliation of parents determined to separate. This does not mean that the child should not protest or mourn. Such behavior is natural, but at the same time adults can provide reassurance and comfort by taking the position, "You may not like whatever is happening, and I can understand why you feel bad, but it is something that cannot be changed. It's going to be tough, but we'll see it through together. After a while, you'll feel better again."

Fortunately, most reality facing for young children is not so emotionally disturbing. Indeed, when speaking of facing reality, I am reminded of an old cartoon that pictures two men leaning up against a bar. One man says philosophically to the other, "Well, I've finally learned what 'facing reality' means—it means doing what my wife wants!" This kind of everyday situation is what facing reality means for most children, too. It means doing what grown-ups want. Part of the art of teaching is keeping these adult demands within reasonable bounds so that children do not have to face the reality of conforming more than is truly necessary.

Learning to Accept Alternative Satisfactions

There can even be a silver lining to the dark cloud of learning to accept what cannot be changed. It is that children can learn to extend their coping abilities by creatively seeking alternative solutions (see also page 204). For example, one alternative strategy they can acquire is the ability to accept compromises to get part of what they want. The child who wants to build a tower of blocks, for instance, may be willing to substitute the oblongs in place of the cylinders for this purpose if the cylinders are all in use. Or she can be encouraged to strike bargains with another youngster—she will let him use her truck if he will share some of the blocks with her. (Four-year-olds are particularly adept at using this solution.)

One additional comment about providing alternative satisfactions is in order here. Sometimes when a serious crisis strikes a family, the teacher is tempted to "make it up" to the youngster by becoming a surrogate mother. The teacher should realize, however, that it is neither possible nor desirable for him to fill this void by behaving this way. For one thing, the relationship between teacher and child is only temporary; it draws to a close at the end of the year, and so its value is necessarily limited. Besides that, the teacher has the obligation to be involved with all the children, not with one in particular. Finally, allowing such a relationship to become established is unfair to the family, no matter how kindly the teacher's intention, because doing this robs parents of their right of parenthood.

Using Mechanisms for Protecting the Emotional Self From Too Much Reality

Neither children nor adults learn to face reality in one fell swoop or with unwavering consistency. All people develop ways of protecting themselves from time to time, and these methods of protection (or coping) serve the useful purpose of reducing stress to tolerable limits. In her book *Vulnerability, Coping and Growth* (1976), Lois Barclay Murphy summarizes a long-term study that presents a particularly interesting analysis of the coping strategies developed by young children. Some examples of coping strategies listed by her include asking for help, conforming to

routines, shifting to easier tasks, drawing on previous experience to help deal with a new one, avoiding situations, using humor, and protesting actively by crying or by using other emotional means of expression. She also discusses how preschoolers use what she terms *self-protective devices*. Among such devices are the ability to fend off excessive stimulation by controlling the impact of the environment, timing rest periods, using strategic withdrawal, using delay to appraise a new situation, and forestalling danger by knowing when to stop.

Each youngster develops her own personal repertoire of coping skills for everyday life situations. It can be fascinating, as well as enlightening, to pick a particular event (such as arriving in the morning or settling down for sleep) and then note how each youngster manages this event each day. A sensitive observer will find that there are likely to be as many different ways of making these transitions as there are children attending school. Part of the purpose of teaching is to help children extend their repertoires of adaptive coping responses, thereby increasing their ability to adjust more easily to changing life circumstances.

Using Withdrawal and Regression as Ways of Coping With Reality. Two self-protective devices warrant special comment here because they appear so commonly in early childhood and are often regarded with undue alarm by teachers: withdrawal and regression. Both of these behaviors are indicators that the child feels overwhelmed and needs to retreat for a bit. The goal of the teacher should not be to deprive the child of these strategies, but to recognize them when they occur, appreciate their value, and also perceive them as signals by the child that all may not be well in her world.

Sometimes withdrawal is quite literal: the youngster hovers behind an easel, dabbling idly with a brush, or builds herself a corral of blocks and sits inside, or even hides under a table. Such children should not be forced into participation before they are comfortable, no matter how unsocial the behavior may appear to the teacher. Indeed, the more the teacher pushes the more resistance he may incite. On the other hand, patience combined with enticing materials and a low-key approach that does not reward nonparticipation with attention will almost always draw such youngsters into activities.

Regression, the second of these two defense mechanisms, occurs when the child retreats to behavior appropriate for a younger child. Thus, we see examples of bed-wetting when the new baby arrives, or wanting to be pushed on the swing, or insisting on being helped with boots and coat when only a week before putting these on herself was a jealously guarded prerogative.

Teachers are so growth oriented that they seem especially threatened by this kind of emotional backsliding. However, if they relax and meet this dependency in an understanding way by satisfying the child's emotional hunger rather than trying to starve it to death, the child will almost always return to a more independent status as soon as she is emotionally able to do so. Children have a compelling desire to grow, and wise teachers count on this fact as their most useful ally.

SIX: HELP THE CHILD COPE WITH CRISIS SITUATIONS

Give Children Credit for Being Resilient

Crises of one sort or another happen to all children from time to time. They can be as serious as the death of a parent or as mild as moving to a new neighborhood or starting nursery school. Sometimes crises are of long duration and sometimes they are as brief as having stitches in the emergency room. What is interesting about this subject is the fact that some children crumble under such experiences while others cope more effectively and recover quickly. What is it about these survivors that causes them to come through such difficulties sunny-side-up?

Not too much is known about the factors that lie behind these effective livers. For all too long, the emphasis has been on the other kinds of children—the crumblers—and what to do to rescue them. It is the old medical model of dealing with illness rather than fostering wellness.

Certainly, the crumblers need help, but it is also true that if we knew more about why some children *don't crumble*—why they remain stable despite adversity—we could use that information to help all children as they grow and develop. This is what the long-term research study included in this chapter has attempted to ferret out. Werner and Smith wanted to know why some of the children they studied bounced back from adversity (i.e., they were resilient) while others did not.

Besides having confidence that many children possess some inner strengths that will help them cope with crises, teachers should also know how to help children make the most of these strengths when special problems arise. Although space does not permit an extensive discussion of specific crises, some basic principles that apply to most of them are detailed below. For further information, the reader is referred to materials listed in the references at the end of this chapter.

Prepare Children in Advance for Crises Whenever Possible

Some crises, such as accidents, occur so suddenly that advance preparation is not possible, and child and parent must simply see them through with whatever fortitude they can muster. Other potential emergencies can be prepared for, at least to a degree, by using a technique called *crisis proofing* (Kliman, 1978).

Crisis proofing seeks to arm the child against crises by providing her with a mild, diluted form of the experience before a more serious crisis occurs. One example of such advance crisis proofing is the use of pet funerals discussed in Chapter 9. The opportunity to experience death in moderately saddening, but not devastating,

RESEARCH STUDY

The Kauai Longitudinal Study: Why Do Some Children Survive Hardships Better Than Others?

Research Question The investigators wanted to find out why some children exposed to biological insult, unstable families, and chronic poverty grew up to be emotionally healthy, effectively functioning individuals while others did not. What were the sources of the survivors' strengths?

Research Method The sample of 698 children included all youngsters born on the island of Kauai in 1955. These children were followed from before birth to the age of 18 using various methods of gathering information about them. These methods included home visits, maternal interviews, physical examinations, reviews of agency records, and psychological tests. Even at age 18 the investigators were able to locate a surprising 88% of the original group for study.

As part of the study, they compared the children (N = 129) who developed serious coping problems resulting from chronic poverty and a series of stressful life events with children (N = 72) of similar background who coped well. Then they analyzed what there was about the two groups that made them different.

Research Results Two categories of discriminating factors emerged from the study. One set involved the environment, and the other involved the personality of the children as they responded to the environment. Among the characteristics of the successfully coping children were the qualities of being good natured, responsive to people, possessing age-appropriate sensorimotor and perceptual skills, and the ability to focus attention and control impulses.

Support from the environment for successful copers included such factors as having four or fewer siblings spaced more than 2 years apart, much attention

---

circumstances can help prepare a child for a more serious experience later such as the death of a family member or friend.

Other crisis-proofing activities might involve having an ambulance visit the school so that the children can see what is inside, visiting a kindergarten before actually attending, or touring the children's ward before having surgery (Gnepp, 1982). Such experiences are included in the curriculum to provide opportunities for the children to gain advance understanding and knowledge, thereby reducing their fear of the unknown and partially preparing them for similar, but more powerful, situations.

Reading topical books to children is an additional way to provide advance preparation for a crisis. (These can also be read after one has occurred.) This technique is called *bibliotherapy,* and it can be an excellent way to free children to ask questions and become involved in discussion (Jalongo, 1983). Two good reference resources for these books are included at the end of the chapter.

Before presenting such a book, it is important to read it through carefully. Make certain that it is appropriate for the particular group and situation. Anticipate questions that may arise from the children and consider how you might

during the first year of life, positive parent-child relationships in early childhood, availability of family and neighbors for emotional support, structure and rules in the household, and an overall sense of coherence.

Implications for Teaching   Werner and Smith concluded that what is important in helping children cope effectively is maintaining a good balance between the power of the person and the power of the environment. There are two significant ways to help children at risk. One way is to decrease the child's exposure to risk and stress, and the other is to increase the child's competencies and sources of support as means of protection against stress. Teachers are in an excellent position to offer support by increasing the child's competencies and sense of worth as well as helping him gain skills in relating to other people.

Teachers should appreciate the value of the extended family in contributing to the healthy development of children. It can be of great benefit in children's centers if the children's extended families are matter-of-factly included in the life of the center.

Finally, it is most important to be optimistic about the inner strengths many children possess as well as what their families have to offer them in the way of emotional support. These strengths can be present despite poverty, possible mental illness of parents, low educational status of mothers, and various short-term crises. Teachers should not automatically assume that children from such backgrounds will perform poorly. This study shows that a great many such children are astonishingly resilient and will turn out all right. Therefore, we need to have confidence in children's ability to bounce back as we do everything we can to help them regain their equilibrium when crises occur.

Note. From *Vulnerable But Invincible: A Longitudinal Study of Resilient Children and Youth* by E. E. Werner and R. S. Smith, 1982, New York: McGraw-Hill Book Co.

best handle these. Prepare some discussion questions of your own that would encourage the children to talk about the material. Perhaps you might want to supplement the book with some pictures from the picture file or with poetry. Plan to repeat the story or theme on additional days, just as you would any other theme. Children need time to understand new information; they need time to consider what was said and to ask questions that may occur to them later.

The purpose of crisis proofing and bibliotherapy is to help children gain strength and understanding without causing them to be excessively anxious. For this reason, it is important to point out the positive, as well as the negative, aspects of a situation. For example, when discussing hospitalization, although you should not gloss over the possibility of pain with false reassurances, you should explain that hospitals help children feel better and get well.

Encourage Parents to Explain the Crisis to Children

As mentioned in the discussion about death, it is important to include children as part of the family when crises arise. Children will sense tension and problems in the family anyway, and

Using a flashlight lets Ken control how dark it is—thereby helping him master his fear of darkness.

the uncertainty they experience of not knowing the reason for the strain is likely to be worse than the certainty of knowing what the trouble is (May, 1977). However, little children should not be expected to bear the burden of feeling responsible for either causing or helping cure the problem. We do not want them to feel blamed for the situation or that they must do something to correct it. Still, they do benefit from simple explanations about what the emergency is and what is being done to relieve it. If there is some not-too-burdensome way that they can be helpful, this will also provide comfort to children by enabling them to feel somewhat in control.

Children Also Benefit From Sharing Feelings

Parents should be informed that it is not necessary or desirable to shield children from all expressions of dismay, grief, or feeling upset *as long as reassurance is provided along with the expression of feeling.* Children learn about handling strong emotions partly by seeing how others cope with them. For example, a mother might say to her son, "I do feel bad about Aunt Mary. I love her, and when she's hurt it makes me cry . . . and then I feel a little better. We'll have to think of some way to help her." Sharing concerns, revealing a moderate amount of feeling, and showing children how to cope with that feeling is recommended. Exposing children to floods of emotion is not.

Provide Children With Chances to Ask Questions

Sometimes questions about crises arise at home, and sometimes at school. Whenever they come up, the adults in charge should make every attempt to answer them simply and truthfully:

"Yes, when they take the stitches out, it will hurt a little—it will feel like a sharp little twitch or pinch, but then it will be over and your cut will have grown together again."

Rather than plunging into a lengthy explanation, it often works best to ask questions in reply to a question to find out what the child really wants to know. Does Jeremy really want to know all the details of the divorce, or is he actually most worried about whether he will see his father again?

Play Is the Great Healer

Earlier in this chapter, and in Chapter 2 as well, considerable time was devoted to discussing how to use play to promote emotional health. When children are undergoing a crisis, provision for working through their feelings via play can bring them great relief.

Curriculum that is particularly worthwhile to use with children in times of emotional stress includes tension-relieving activities and sublimated ways of expressing aggression. Pretend play involving relevant themes can often be sparked by the inclusion of items suggesting that theme in play. The inclusion of a grandmother doll, for instance, led one of our children to contrive a wheelchair from a market basket and to spend considerable time pushing the grandma up and down the halls of the pretend rest home.

Sometimes when families are troubled, play can also alert the teacher to the fact that the youngster needs special help. Curry and Arnaud (1982) list a number of signals to watch for; these include the use of themes that are not appropriate for the child's age, single-minded repetition of one theme or role, very unusual play themes, and excessive preoccupation with one object.

The manner in which children play may also reveal to the teacher that they are having particular difficulties. Perhaps they seem particularly flushed or intense about the play, or perhaps they seem to actually become what they are playing and are unable to divest themselves of an assumed role. For instance, at one school in

which I taught, there was a little girl who almost literally became a rabbit. Unless she had on her ears and tail and had her stuffed rabbit with her, she seemed frozen and unable to participate in the life of the school. What had begun as an amusing quirk ultimately became an obsession, which required the help of a psychologist to correct.

Keep the Environment as Stable and Reasonable as Possible

Children's centers can make a wonderful contribution to the child's well-being in the area of stability. The steadiness of routine and calm affection of the teacher can provide a haven for children who are living in stressful situations at home. Simply knowing what is going to happen next and what is expected in the way of behavior at school is comforting. When this is combined with the use of play to clarify feelings, children can return home strengthened and reassured.

While keeping the environment as stable as possible, it also may be necessary to reduce expectations of good behavior for children experiencing crises who may be feeling miserable; they may cry more easily or fly off the handle more readily; they are more likely to tire sooner; they may be unable to settle down at nap; and anxiety may reduce their appetites, making them feel even more fatigued.

When children display these behaviors, they require extra comforting combined with toleration. Yet, at the same time they cannot be allowed to become tyrants—a difficult balance to maintain. The best approach to balancing routines and expectations with children's special needs is to use common sense, mercy, and patience. As their lives return to normal, expectations can be readjusted accordingly.

Other Children May Be Aware of the Crisis

In numerous situations families confide in teachers about intimate problems, and *teachers need to keep such information completely confidential.* However, a crisis often becomes known to other children in the group, as when someone's house has burned down, a car pool mother has fallen ill, or a child has had an accident. The children may feel quite distressed or anxious at the news, and they often wonder if such a thing could happen to them or their families.

Be aware that these youngsters need much of the same kind of help as that recommended for the individual children to enable them to come to terms with their anxieties. This includes crisis proofing, chances to discuss their concerns, and opportunities to deepen their understanding through play.

In addition, remember that such crises can provide very desirable opportunities to help children do something thoughtful for the child with the trouble. If the teacher asks them how they could help, children often have quite delightful ideas: "We could draw him a get-well picture." "We could give her hugs." "We could be nice and let her choose first at snack time." "We could let him feed the fish this week." These are suggestions I have heard from 3-year-olds. They are nice, practical ideas for expressing concern and offering comfort. Moreover, they benefit the children in the group by allowing them to do something kind for someone else.

SEVEN: HELP THE CHILD BEGIN TO BUILD EMPATHY FOR OTHER PEOPLE

Throughout this chapter we have been concentrating almost exclusively on how children feel and how to help them gain understanding of their feelings, as well as competence in dealing with them. The chapter would not be complete, however, without discussing a different kind of goal, even though it is one that can be only partially achieved by such young children. This is the goal of instilling empathy in children—the ability to put oneself in another's place and feel as that person is feeling. This ability is related partly to the emotional self and partly to the social self.

As Piaget (Piaget & Inhelder, 1969) has indicated, this is a difficult task because young children are essentially centered on themselves and have great difficulty grasping how others feel. Instead, they imagine that everyone feels as they themselves do. Therefore, teachers must be patient and approach this learning step by step, keeping it on a simple level, and allowing time for both learning and maturation to take place.

Bearing these limitations in mind, there are three fairly practical ways of beginning to foster empathy in young children. These are using self-report, role playing in pretend situations, and "remember when" experiences. (These strategies can also be used to deepen insight and empathy in adults. Self-report is an extremely valuable skill to use with other adults, as well as with children, and role playing and gaining insight by referring to one's own experience are excellent ways of increasing understanding of other's feelings.)

Using Self-Report

Self-report, which in this case really should be called "other" report, can be used in two ways to foster empathy when teaching young children. The first way of using it is to encourage other children to tell the child how they feel. Thus, you can ask a child being pushed off the bench by another youngster, "Do you like what he's doing? Well, tell him how you feel about it," or "Do you want him to do that? Well then, tell him you don't."

The second way to use self-report is to make a point of honestly reporting your own feelings to the children. This is valuable as long as you are not too forceful or use the report of a "bad" feeling as a threat to induce better behavior. An example of an undesirable threat is, "Boys and girls, you'd better watch out—I'm getting angry!" On the other hand, an appropriate self-report statement might be, "I'm worried you children won't remember to wait with me when we get to the curb," or "I feel irritated today because we have so much to do to get the presents ready to go home." It is even all right, when stopping a fight, to say, "Just a minute—I haven't decided what to do about this yet; I need some time to make up my mind." This is more satisfactory than making an impulsive decision that you regret later but cannot change without losing face. Honest self-reporting not only helps the children understand the teacher better, but also sets a model for them to copy.

There are some reasonable limits to the use of self-reports by teachers. One is that care must be taken so that they are not used as a means of justifying the expression of rage or abandonment to grief, since such flood tides of feeling from grown-ups frighten children too much. When properly used, self-reports allow teachers to present themselves as human beings who experience a range of feelings, just as children do. The books of Haim Ginott (1965, 1972) and Virginia Axline (1964, 1969) contain many wonderful examples of sincere communication between children and adults and can be read with benefit by every parent and teacher.

Using Role Playing

The cultivation of insight through imaginative role playing, which happens so often in dramatic play, is a second valuable way to begin building empathy for other people within the child. Although it is true that the child who is feeling brave while being the firefighter or petulant while being the baby is playing out her own feelings and ideas of that role, it is also true that she is obtaining a little insight into how other people act and respond in particular instances. This helps lay a framework on which to build later understanding (Selman, 1971).

Using "Remember When"

Finally, it is possible to build understanding of how another child feels by using the "remember when" approach. For instance, the teacher might ask, "Remember when your mother left you here for the first time? Remember how you cried? Well, that's how Janie feels right now. [Wait a bit for this to sink in.] What do you think we could do to help her?" or "Remember how mad you got when Scotty took that red car from you? Well, that's how Jim is feeling." Note there is no moralizing attached to these questions; they are asked to remind the child of how they felt and to help them understand that someone else feels that way, too.

This remembering approach is a much stronger teaching method to use with young children than is the following approach: "What if you were him—how would you like it if he took your truck?" Phrasing the question in this way (which we call "pulling a switch" at our school) is too difficult for a little child to grasp because it requires him to (1) imagine himself as Jim and (2) imagine Jim as being him—a difficult task indeed for a child who, as Piaget informs us, has not yet decentered. No wonder that the usual response to such a query is one of baffled indecision.

SUMMARY

The emphasis of curriculum for the emotional self should be on helping children become as resilient as possible by using everyday life situations as the medium for teaching. Such situations should be used to build the following competencies in young children: learning to separate from their families with a reasonable degree of ease; attaining basic attitudes of trust, autonomy, and initiative; remaining in contact with all their feelings while learning to control what they do about them; using play and self-expressive materials to clarify feelings and resolve emotional problems; facing reality; learning to cope with crises; and beginning to build empathy and understand that other people have feelings, too.

SELF-CHECK QUESTIONS FOR REVIEW

Content-Related Questions

1. It is August, and you are getting ready to welcome a new group of children on their very first day of school. List some procedures you would follow to help them adjust as easily as possible to their new surroundings.

2. Which stage of emotional development comes first—the stage of initiative versus guilt, or autonomy versus shame and doubt? What is the name of the first stage babies go through? Describe some characteristics of each stage.

3. How can play and other creative materials be used to help children resolve emotional problems?

4. Why is it helpful to offer mud, sand, and water to children who are emotionally upset?

5. Give some alternatives you could suggest to a child who wants something another child won't let her have.

6. Name some ways children protect themselves from having to cope with too much reality.

7. The Kauai Longitudinal Study identified several factors that made the difference between children who coped well with crises and those who had more difficulty. Name some factors that were related to the environment and some others that involved the personality of the children.

8. What is "self-report," and why is it a useful strategy to use with young children?

9. Why is it more effective to use "remember when" instead of saying to a child, "What if you were him? How would you like it if he took your truck?"

Integrative Questions

1. This chapter includes discussions about presenting mud, sand, and water play to children. Why are these activities included in the chapter on building emotional health? How would you explain the emotional value of such material to parents?

2. Why should teachers be optimistic about the inner strengths many children possess? Should teachers assume that all children will be able to cope with their problems successfully and, therefore, will not need help from time to time?

3. Describe a situation where someone you know was upset or lost her temper. Then put that person's feelings into words by describing what she felt or would like to do.

4. There are some general principles that are helpful to follow when dealing with almost any crisis. Think of a particular crisis situation you have come across, and explain how you would apply the principles in that situation.

QUESTIONS AND ACTIVITIES

1. Can you remember being allowed (or forbidden) to play with mud, sand, and water when you were a young child? How did you feel about this experience then? How do you feel about it now?

2. Does it seem to you that nowadays children are more restricted or less restricted in the amount of free playtime they have at their disposal?

3. Do you think that parents are sometimes right in setting limits on what they allow their children to say to them to express their feelings? If limits should be set, at what point should they occur?

4. *Problem:* You have had a 3-year-old girl in your school every weekday for 5 weeks, and every time she comes she cries bitterly for at least half an hour after her mother departs. Both you and the mother are quite concerned. Do you think this child should stay in school? If not, what other solution would you propose? Explain the reason for your particular position.

5. With a tape recorder, record yourself talking with various children. Listen to the results carefully, and identify some of your replies that were insensitive to what the children were feeling. Explain what you plan to say next time to respond more effectively to their real feelings.

6. Set up some role-playing situations in class in which students play children who are acting out their feelings. These might include a coming-to-school situation, a sandbox situation, and a snack time interlude. Observe the "children's" feelings closely and then suggest various things you might say to the children that would describe what they are feeling. Try to go beyond just labeling the feelings as glad, mad, and so forth.

7. Take an hour or so and do nothing but sit near the block or housekeeping corner and keep track of all the different strategies children employ when needing to enter a new group of children. Note also how the other children cope with the newcomers.

8. Is there a child in your preschool class who has recently come through some kind of crisis? Suggest some activities that you could plan in the curriculum to help her work through and understand her feelings about this crisis.

9. Review the personal characteristics of the children in the Kauai study who were resilient. How much of their attractive behaviors do you think were due to born temperament and how much was the result of the way other people treated them?

REFERENCES FOR FURTHER READING

Overviews

Curry, N. (Ed.). (1986). *The feeling child: Affective development reconsidered.* New York: The Haworth Press. These articles will help the reader understand the significance and role that emotions play in the lives of developing children.

Developmental Stages and Emotional Needs of Children

Curry, N., & Bergen, D. (1987). The relationship of play to emotional, social, and gender/sex role development. In D. Bergen (Ed.), *Play as a medium for learning and development; A handbook of theory and practice.* Portsmouth, N.H.: Heinemann. This chapter provides a comprehensive review of how the emotional self develops.

Erikson, E. H. (1963). *Childhood and society* (2nd ed.). New York: W. W. Norton & Co.

Erikson, E. H. (1971). A healthy personality for every child. In R. H. Anderson & H. G. Shane (Eds.), *As the twig is bent: Readings in early childhood education.* Boston: Houghton Mifflin Co. This publication contains original source material explaining Erikson's concepts of the eight stages of human development and the emotional attitudes of paramount importance at various stages of development.

Griffin, E. F. (1982). *Island of childhood: Education in the special world of nursery school.* New York: Teachers College Press. The chapter "Between Teacher and Child" contains many actual examples of how a teacher may respond in a positive way to common situations that arise during the nursery school day.

Riley, S. S. (1984). *How to generate values in young children.* Washington, D.C.: National Association for the Education of Young Children. Here is a sound book that is simply and clearly written. It contains many thoughtful suggestions on helping children stay emotionally healthy.

Resilient Children

Anthony, E. J., & Cohler, B. J. (Eds.). (1987). *The invulnerable child.* New York: The Guilford Press. A refreshing change in emphasis is provided by these authors because they recount several studies where the wholesome emotional process of coping and adapting successfully have been studied.

Communicating With Children (and Other People)

All of the books listed below provide sound advice on this subject.

Ginott, H. (1972). *Teacher and child.* New York: Macmillan Publishing Co.

Gordon, T. (1976). *P.E.T. in action.* New York: Peter H. Wyden Publisher.

Moustakas, C. E. (1966). *The authentic teacher: Sensitivity and awareness in the classroom.* East Dennis, Mass.: Howard A. Doyle.

Satir, V. (1975). *People making.* Palo Alto, Calif.: Science & Behavior Books.

Listening and Talking With Children

Axline, V. M. (1964). *Dibs: In search of self.* Boston: Houghton Mifflin Co. This highly readable account, based on a case study of an appealing little boy named Dibs, illustrates what goes on in child-centered therapy and gives many examples of how to respond to children by accepting and reflecting their feelings. Available in paperback.

Brazelton, T. B. (1984). *To listen to a child: Understanding the normal problems of growing up.* Reading, Mass.: Addison Wesley Publishing Co. Although this book deals mainly with toddlers and babies, it is so full of good sense about routines and common problems that it should be read by everyone who cares for young children.

Samalin, N., & Jablow, M. M. (1987). *Loving your child is not enough.* New York: Viking Press. The chapter on acknowledging feelings provides many examples of how to reflect and describe feelings to children. Helpful reading.

Schaefer, C. E. (1984). *How to talk to children about really important things.* New York: Harper & Row, Publishers. This book would be an excellent addition to the parent's library. Paperback.

Szasz, S. (1980). *The unspoken language of children.* New York: W. W. Norton & Co. This is an absolutely remarkable book of photographs and comments about what children's expressions and postures can tell the observant teacher about their inner states.

Resources for Bibliotherapy

Jalongo, M. R. (1983). Using crises-oriented books with young children. *Young Children, 38*(50), 29–36. The author provides a useful list of books dealing with various crises.

Pardeck, J. A., & Pardeck, J. T. (1986). *Books for early childhood: A developmental perspective.* New York: Greenwood Press. These books are subdivided according to anger and emotions, family relationships, and so forth. Each is classified according to age, and the story is summarized.

Helping Children With Common Emotional Difficulties

Balaban, N. (1985). *Starting school: From separation to independence.* New York: Teachers College Press. Every teacher of young children should read this practical, insightful book. Includes a valuable bibliography.

Furman, E. (Ed.). (1986). *What nursery school teachers ask us about: Psychoanalytic consultations in preschools.* Madison, Conn.: International Universities Press. There is a lot of practical advice on such matters as discipline, regressive behavior, death, and helping the abused child in this short book.

Humphrey, J. H. (Ed.). (1984). *Stress in childhood.* New York: AMS Press. Humphrey discusses the causes of stress and then reviews numerous ways to bring it under control.

Schaefer, C. E., & Millman, H. L. (1981). *How to help children with common problems.* New York: Van Nostrand Reinhold Co. This book focuses mainly on older children and covers everything from tantrums to nightmares to running away.

Use of Specific Materials to Foster Emotional Competence

Cherry, C. (1976). *Creative play for the developing child: Early lifehood education through play.* Belmont, Calif.: Fearon Publishers. Cherry provides an excellent discussion of how children use play to express feelings and come to terms with them.

Hendrick, J. (1988). *The whole child: Developmental education for the early years* (4th ed.). Columbus, Ohio: Merrill Publishing Co. The chapter entitled "Tender Topics: Helping Children Master Emotional Crises" deals with general and specific recommendations related to various kinds of crises.

Hill, D. M. (1977). *Mud, sand, and water.* Washington, D.C.: National Association for the Education of Young Children. Hill's booklet emphasizes the virtues of using these materials for play and learning.

James, J. C., & Granovetter, R. F. (1987). *Waterworks: A new book of water play activities for children age 1 to 6.* Lewisville, N.C.: Kaplan Press. Title is self-explanatory.

For the Advanced Student

Blatchford, P., Battle, S., & Mays, J. (1982). *The first transition: Home to pre-school: A report on the "Transition From Home to Pre-school" project.* Windsor, Berkshire, England: NFER-Nelson Publishing Co. This research study recounts what did happen during separation at nursery school rather than suggesting what should happen. The case studies are particularly interesting.

Bowlby, J. (1969). *Attachment and loss.* Vol. I: *Attachment.* New York: Basic Books.

Bowlby, J. (1973). *Attachment and loss.* Vol. 2: *Separation.* New York: Basic Books. These are important references by a man who pioneered studies of separation and young children.

Dougherty, D. M., Saxe, L. M., Cross, T., & Silverman, N. (1987). *Children's mental health: Problems and services: A report by the Office of Technology Assessment.* Durham, N.C.: Duke University Press. This report presents basic information on what constitutes emotional health and the current status of delivery services for children in the United States. The presentation is succinct and clear.

Powell, G. J. (1983). *The psychosocial development of minority group children.* New York: Brunner/Mazel. This excellent book devotes over 200 pages to the emotional development and mental health of children from a wide variety of ethnic groups.

Schaefer, C. E., & O'Conner, K. J. (1983). *Handbook of play therapy.* New York: John Wiley & Sons. A treasury of information on play therapy is contained in this book. I like it because it presents a number of differing approaches.

Werner, E. E. (1984). Resilient children. *Young Children,* 40(1), 69–72. Werner cites many research studies identifying factors that influenced children who developed soundly despite many crises in their lives.

Journals of Continuing Interest

American Journal of Orthopsychiatry. American Orthopsychiatric Association, 49 Sheridan Ave., Albany, New York 12210. The journal describes itself as being dedicated to providing information "relating to mental health and human development from a multidisciplinary and interprofessional perspective."

Journal of Children in Contemporary Society. Haworth Press, 28 E. 22 St., New York, New York 10010. This journal concentrates on a specific topic for each quarterly issue.

Pediatric Mental Health. P.O. Box 1880, Santa Monica, California 90406. A bimonthly newsletter, this publication covers research and practice on such topics as supporting parenting, play, and preparation for hospitalization.

11 Getting Along Together

Achieving Competence in Interpersonal Relations

Have you ever

- Worried about what to do next when children continue to disobey?
- Wished that you knew how to teach children to get what they want without just grabbing it?
- Wanted to know how to help children get along well together in a group?
- Tried to think of ways children could be genuinely helpful at the center?

If you have, the material in this chapter will help you.

Young children have to have adults who accept the authority that is theirs by virtue of their greater experience, knowledge and wisdom.

This proposition is based on the assumption that neither as parents nor as educators are we caught between the extremes of authoritarianism or permissiveness. Authoritarianism may be defined as the exercise of power without warmth, encouragement or explanation. Permissiveness may be seen as the abdication of power but offers children warmth, encouragement and support as they seem to need it. I am suggesting that young children have to have, instead of these extremes, adults who are authoritative: i.e., adults who exercise their very considerable power over the lives of young children with warmth, support, encouragement and adequate explanations. The concept of authoritativeness also includes treating children with respect: i.e., treating their opinions, feelings, wishes and ideas as valid even when we disagree with them. To respect people we agree with is no great problem: respecting those whose ideas, wishes and feelings are different from ours may be a mark of wisdom in parents and genuine professionalism in teachers.

LILIAN G. KATZ (1977)

One of the most frequent requests families make when they bring their youngsters to a children's center is that they learn to get along with other children. Teachers would surely agree with parents that this is a very important competence to acquire.

When children are socially competent, they are basically "fit to live with." They also possess healthy feelings of self-worth, which stem from a number of sources: knowing they are able to control their aggressive impulses much of the time is one of them. Socially competent children also know and employ a number of methods of obtaining what they want from other children. They are able to form friendships, and they understand what constitutes acceptable behavior at the lunch table or during large group. They find satisfaction in helping other people from time to time, and they relish the ego-enhancing experience of occasionally performing what they think of as being grown-up work.

Of course, most youngsters do not arrive at school possessing all these skills. It is up to us, the teachers, to help them acquire these. How to do this is the subject of this chapter. (For a developmental chart that traces the growth of social and self-help skills from birth to age 6, please refer to Appendix A.)

HELP CHILDREN LEARN TO RESTRAIN UNSOCIAL IMPULSES

The ability to control unsocial or asocial impulses is absolutely basic to getting along with others. When the recommendation is phrased in this way, however, it may sound simpler than it really is. In actuality, we must never forget or underestimate the fact that children's wants are *immediate, intense,* and *personal.* This means that when a young child wants something, he wants it right now, he wants it very much, and he wants it because *he* wants it. Yet, we continually expect him to wait, to defer gratification, and even to be pleasant while doing this. When comparing what children prefer to what adults prefer, I am always surprised at just how often youngsters are agreeable about going along with our expectations.

The most effective way to keep our demands and expectations within reason so that the child is not driven to desperation over the conflict between his wants and our expectations is to be quite clear in our own minds about what behavior must be stopped and what can be overlooked. The rule of thumb to apply here is that we must not allow the child to seriously hurt himself or someone else or damage anyone else's property. The word *seriously* is used to make it clear that we should not err on the side of being overly protective. Children learn best through experiences—unpleasant as well as pleasant ones—and if the consequences are not too dangerous, it may be desirable to let children simply experience the consequences of their actions. For example, a child who shoves another youngster down in the play yard may learn more from getting shoved back than from our preventing this relatively harmless encounter. On the other hand, if it looks as though he is going to push someone off the top of the slide or poke another child in the face with a stick, immediate action must be taken to forestall this.

Besides the general rule-of-thumb standard, it is also necessary to have a set of well-defined rules that are agreed on and enforced by all the staff. All teachers new to the center should become acquainted with these rules and enforce them, also. Unfortunately, beginning teachers do not always realize the importance of consistency, and since they dread having to confront children, they allow them to get away with behavior that the rest of the staff does not permit. The reason consistency matters so much has been explained by behavior modification research and borne out by practical experience with children. One of the principles of learning theory (behavior modification) is that reinforc-

ing behavior intermittently is a very powerful way of causing it to continue. When children are sometimes stopped from doing something they want to do but sometimes allowed to do it (a positive reward), this intermittent gratification greatly increases the probability that the children will repeat that behavior at every opportunity—the very thing teachers hope to avoid.

Short-Term Methods of Controlling Behavior

Since beginning teachers are often most concerned about handling situations that require immediate control, it seems best to outline six steps for controlling impulsive behavior first and

Boys don't have a monopoly on aggressive feelings!

then discuss ways of working toward the longer-term goal of building inner controls.

These steps include (1) redirecting the child to more positive behavior and reminding him of the rule and the consequence for violating it, (2) removing him, (3) discussing feelings and rules, (4) waiting for him to decide when he is ready to return, (5) helping him return and be more successful in an acceptable way, and (6) when all else fails, taking firmer action.

Please pay special attention to the third and fourth steps. Step three, taking time to describe the child's feelings to him, is vital because this says to the child, "I understand what you're feeling, even though I have to stop what you're doing. I care enough about you to take time to show you I understand." This also means, as explained in the previous chapter, that he does not need to continue showing you how he feels by acting out the angry feeling, which helps him control the behavior. In addition, telling him a simple rule helps the child see the sense and reasonableness of the restriction.

Step four, having the child decide when to return, is equally important because this puts the responsibility for his behavior on *his* shoulders, not on yours. If you want children to become *self*-controlled, allowing them to make these decisions for themselves has great significance.

Table 11–1 offers a sampling of possible things teachers might say to carry out this short-term method of controlling behavior. Bear in mind that steps two through six should be used only when other methods, such as distraction and redirection, have failed. (Note that, for practice, two examples of distraction and redirection have been included; can you identify them?)

Longer-Term Methods of Building Inner Controls

As the sandbox example in Table 11–1 demonstrates, it is not always easy for little children to control their immediate, intense, and personal

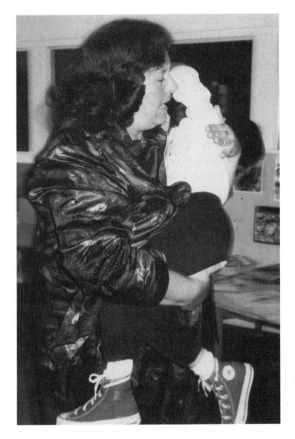

Physical control is sometimes necessary.

impulses, and adults must be ready to take swift, effective action. Helping children establish inner controls goes far beyond this immediate action, however. There are several additional things teachers and parents can do to make life easier and more pleasant for everyone, and, at the same time, build self-control within the children.

Analyze the reasons for repeated misbehavior and correct or prevent such conditions when you can. Some "discipline" situations have a way of recurring. For example, teachers may find themselves constantly telling two or three of the children not to run into the wall with their trikes

TABLE 11–1
Dealing with behavior problems on an emergency basis

General principles	Examples of what to say
Step one	
Remind the child, and redirect him if he will accept such redirection. For example, you might warn a youngster that if he continues to throw sand, he will lose the privilege of staying in the sandbox; then suggest a couple of interesting things he could do with the sand instead of throwing it. It is important to make the child understand that his behavior is up to him. It is *his* choice, but if he chooses to continue, see to it that you carry out your warning.	What could we get out that would be fun? How about some water? Or could you put the sand in the dump truck? Remember, Zac, keep the sand down—when you throw it behind you that way, it hits the other children. Why not turn around and dig the other way? Make sure you put the sand beside you here—if you throw it, it might get in someone's eyes. Do you need something to put the sand in? Let's look around and find something so you don't have to throw it. Our rule is "you have to keep the sand down so it's safe." If you throw it, you might get some in Beth's eyes. Then she'll feel bad and you'll lose the privilege of playing here for a while. Mae, I'm going to warn you once about keeping the sand down so it's safe—if you do that again, you'll have to come sit with me for a while until you decide you can control yourself.
Step two	
Warn only once. If he persists in doing what he has been told not to do, act calmly and promptly. Remove him and insist that he stay with you, telling him he has lost the privilege of playing in the sand. This is much more valuable than just letting him run off. Having him stay beside you interrupts what he wants to do—a mildly unpleasant consequence of his act, which also prevents his substituting another, more pleasant activity. At the institute, we prefer this method to putting the youngster off by himself because it allows the teacher to stay bonded to the child. This feeling of closeness seems to lend the child additional ego strength. He is also less likely to feel punished by being ostracized and feeling abandoned.	Well, you decided you would throw it again, so you've lost the privilege of using the sand. Come and sit with me and we'll talk about it. That's really against our safety rules—up you come! [Pick up the child.] Sit over here with me until you can control yourself. Jennifer, you've been warned about that, but you chose to keep right on doing it. You've lost the privilege of staying here for now—come sit with me awhile. I told you boys, we just can't have that kind of behavior with sand. It hurts too much when it gets in people's eyes. You'll have to come over here with me until you calm down.

TABLE 11–1 (*continued*)

General principles	Examples of what to say
Step three	
Take time to describe his feelings in an understanding way, but state the rule and the reason for it clearly and firmly. Don't moralize or rub it in too much. Don't talk too much.	I guess you wanted to see whether I really meant what I said when I warned you. I can see you were very mad at Janie and you wanted to get even, but I can't let you hurt her. You must keep the sand down.
	It looks to me like you were so busy with that hole you just couldn't remember to think about where you were tossing the sand.
	I can understand why you feel that way—it's okay to be mad at Janie or me, but it isn't okay to hurt somebody. Throwing sand can hurt if it gets in people's eyes. We have to keep the sand down in the sandbox.
Step four	
Allow the child to decide when he is ready to return to the activity. Many teachers say something like, "Now you sit here until lunch is ready," thus shifting the responsibility for the child's behavior to their own shoulders instead of putting the child in command of himself. It is better to say, "Now, tell me when you can control yourself, and I will let you go back." Some children can actually say they are ready, but others need help from the teacher, who can ask them when they look ready if they are ready to go back.	When you can remember to keep the sand down, tell me and then you may go back and play. It's up to you.
	[To a child who is too shy or young to put the intention into words] Are you ready to go back now? [Perhaps he just nods or looks ready.] Good, your eyes tell me you are. What would you like to do for fun there?
	When you decide you can use sand the safe way, nod your head and we'll think of something that it's all right to do with it.

or to stop tapping the table with their cups or not to poke their neighbor at group time.

When such situations happen again and again, change the situation rather than nag the child. A board on sawhorses in front of the wall or passing the cups just before milk is poured, for instance, will eliminate some of the difficulties. Rescheduling group time for when children are less tired or shortening it makes it easier for the children to be in better control of themselves. Why make it harder than necessary for children to obey?

Take individual needs into account. Children misbehave for a variety of reasons: fatigue, illness, social inexperience, and immaturity are among them. Some of these causes can be mitigated with the teacher's help. For example,

TABLE 11–1 (*continued*)

General principles	Examples of what to say
Step five* Return with the child and help him be successful so that he has the experience of substituting acceptable for unacceptable behavior. It will probably be necessary to take a few minutes to get him interested. Be sure to congratulate him when he has settled down.	Well, let's see what you've decided to do that's fun and safe. I'll help you get another bucket so that you don't need to take Lashonda's. Would you like to use these little red cars? Maybe they need a tunnel to run through. That's the way to do it—now everyone's safe. Show me what's the safe way. That's right. Good for you! Now you're doing the right thing. I'm proud of you!
Step six Occasionally, the teacher will come across a more glib customer who says hastily when removed from the sandbox, "I'll be good, I'll be good!" but then goes right back to throwing sand when he returns. At this point, it is necessary to take firmer action. Have him sit beside you until he can think of something acceptable to do, but don't permit him to go back to the sandbox. After he has calmed down, have him select a different place to play. Go with him or alert another teacher to be sure that he becomes involved in an acceptable activity. The same may be done if two or more children are involved. However, it may be wiser to separate them. In this case, take them to different activities and provide an explanation to the attending teacher. Comment favorably on his regained self-control as soon as you possibly can.	What you did [be explicit] shows me that you haven't decided to do the right thing, so you'll have to come back and sit with me until you can think of somewhere else to play. You've lost the privilege of playing in the sandbox. [To the other teacher] Jane and Maggie have lost the privilege of playing in the sandbox. They have decided they'd like to push each other on the swing awhile. Could you get them started on that?

*I cannot help but think that if the teacher had done and said some of these things earlier, she might have avoided steps two through four.

careful scheduling of activities can reduce the effects of fatigue, and inexperience can be modified by seizing on social learning experiences as they arise and by gradually teaching children how to handle these without resorting to fighting. Other causes of misbehavior must be remedied by the processes of time, growth, instruction, and patience.

Realize that children misbehave sometimes because of problems or crises at home. I have already spoken of the effect family crises may have on behavior in Chapter 10, but even when not dealing with crises, puzzled parents may resort to using ineffective child-management techniques. Sometimes, too, they feel at their wit's end and simply do not know what to do. Teachers can offer real help in these situations, particularly if they are sympathetic rather than seeming antagonistic by implying that the parents are to blame for all the child's problems. Chapter 19 provides many suggestions for offering guidance to parents when this is needed.

Warn ahead. Many noncompliance situations (and much misbehavior can simply be thought of as noncompliance with teacher expectations) can be avoided by giving children advance notice of what will be happening next. Doing this gives children time to adjust to the new idea. Perhaps the teacher might say, "Pretty soon it's going to be time for snack. I wonder what it will be today?" or "In a few minutes I'll be back to help you finish the puzzle because it's going to be group time," or "It's almost time to go in. Would you like to leave the snowman up and work on it some more after nap?"

Tell children what they should do; that is, provide positive instructions instead of negative or neutral ones. This is another tactful way of encouraging desirable behavior. The teacher who says, "Put the sand in the truck" or "Keep the sand down" rather than "Don't throw the sand" helps children behave well because she has provided positive guidance before they get in trouble.

Be alert to potential difficulties and step in before disaster strikes. This advice to intervene promptly must be balanced against the value of letting children learn from direct experience. However, when teachers know that they ultimately will have to intervene, it is far better to do it when everyone is still relatively calm and no one has experienced gratification from aggressive action. Children learn much better under such circumstances than after everything has blown sky high.

This advice also means that teachers must pay consistent attention to what is going on around them. Particularly for beginners it can be a real temptation to focus on only one amiable child and avoid watching a wider area, but good teachers learn to do both things at once. They retain a kind of peripheral awareness of the entire yard or room, no matter what other adult is present, and also pay attention to individual children at the same time. It is an art—but a very necessary one to learn.

Make a point of recognizing good behavior and commending it from time to time. This does not have to be fulsome praise. Such simple statements as "Thank you" or "That's exactly the right thing to do!" or "I appreciate your help" are satisfying without being gushy or overdone.

Convey a feeling of warmth along with a sense of firmness. Admittedly, this can be tricky advice to give novice teachers, because some misinterpret it and attempt to buy good behavior from the children by being too friendly or "chummy" with them. The role of teachers is different from this: they must set a tone of warmth and caring concern while also maintaining a posture of firm reasonableness that is quite different from being the children's buddy.

Children (and adults) flourish in this climate of sincere approval and warmth. When they sense the teacher likes them, they try harder to retain this approval by behaving in accordance with her wishes. On the other hand, if they feel continually criticized and attacked, they gradually abandon hope and give up the effort of behaving well.

They will also feel more secure and trustful if they know that the teacher cares enough about them to prevent them from doing anything seriously out of line. This is why there is often a feeling of comfort between child and teacher after they have worked through a "scene." Although an inexperienced teacher often fears that the child will avoid or hate her following an encounter, usually an increased sense of closeness and confidence between teacher and child is the result—but it certainly takes courage on the teacher's part to see the first two or three such storms all the way through. Perhaps it is not only the child who feels more secure following such an encounter.

Be reasonable. By this I do not mean reasonable in the sense of not expecting too much, although that is certainly important, too. *Reasonable* here means that a simple reason for conforming to the rules should always be included along with the prohibition. Supplying a simple, clear-cut reason not only makes it plain that the rule is not just a whim of the teacher, but also puts into practice some well-supported research findings that firm control combined with warmth and accompanied by a reason are the most effective agents in building inner controls and establishing the beginnings of conscience in young children (Hoffman, 1970).

Be a good example yourself. It is true that children *do* learn from models and that they may express more direct aggression when they have witnessed a model behaving aggressively (Bandura, 1973, 1977). Therefore, to reduce aggressive behavior, it is important to remain in control of yourself so that you do not model such behavior for the children to copy. Unfortunately, it is all too easy to pull two struggling children apart and angrily dole out instant punishment to both of the culprits as a way of relieving your own aggressive feelings—and then regret the severity of that punishment a few moments later. How much more desirable it is to stop what the children are doing immediately,

and say, before doing anything more, "Wait just a minute. I need to calm down myself and think this over—then we'll talk about it." Doing this stops the action, gives everyone a minute to draw breath, and allows you to proceed in a less aggressive, better-considered way.

Profit by your experience. Of course, not all discipline situations work out perfectly, and adults often feel badly about this. Although mishandling a situation cannot be condoned, it is also valuable to realize that one poorly handled encounter will not result in permanent damage to child or teacher.

The important thing to do when this has happened is not to sink into the depths of self-abasing despair but to think the situation over carefully, learn from it and *decide what you will do differently next time.* Doing this helps prevent the useless repetition of ineffective responses to misbehavior, and planning ahead confers an invaluable sense of assurance on the teacher. In an interesting way, children are similar to animals—both sense immediately who is afraid of them and who is not, and they

Remember, children learn by example. Modeling good behavior helps them to do the right thing.

respond accordingly. Confident teachers who know what their next step will be if matters go awry often find that such steps become unnecessary.

TEACH CHILDREN SOCIALLY ACCEPTABLE WAYS OF GETTING WHAT THEY WANT

Of course, we need to go far beyond simply stopping children from doing harm if we want them to learn to get along well in groups. Although it may sound as if we are teaching selfishness, one of the most valuable things to do is to teach them alternative ways of getting what they want, bearing in mind that children also have to learn to balance what they want with what reality makes it likely they can get.

When children resort to force, it is often because they know of no other way to get what they want. This is why it is so worthwhile to teach children the alternative strategies that are discussed in the following sections. Children who possess a number of these advanced social ploys are less likely to resort to physical attack. Moreover, possession of these skills increases their feelings of being competent and masterful.

If teachers keep on the lookout for potential snatch-and-grab situations, they can use them as a basis for practical social teaching provided they are aware of the range of alternative solutions that can be proposed to children. These include teaching children to ask to use something when the other child is done ("Ask him, 'Can I have that when you're through?' ") or to trade one thing for another ("Maybe if you gave him your hat, he'd let you use the cane") or to work out some kind of compromise in which each child obtains some satisfaction ("I know she's holding both crayons. Perhaps she'd let you use the orange while she's using red, and then you could swap"). Other alternatives include suggesting that the child use something else as a substitute or encouraging him to do something else while waiting ("The elephant puzzle's in use right now.

How about doing the giraffe while you're waiting?"). Sometimes a genuinely cooperative arrangement can be worked out in which the play is enriched by the newcomer's contribution ("Janice, if they let you play, would you help them carry the blocks? Well, why don't you tell them that?").

When children are old enough (around age 3½ to 4), it is even possible to ask them to tell you what they could do instead. This helps them think up their own alternatives. For example, the teacher might ask, "It sure didn't work to tip over her trike, did it? Now she's mad and won't let you play. The next time you want Tricia to let you ride, what could you do instead?"

At the preschool level, any of these alternatives generally work better than insisting that the children take turns regulated by the teacher or expecting that a youngster will gladly surrender something he is using just because someone else has asked for it. After all, why should he? Moreover, these alternatives are more desirable because they do not depend so much on adult enforcement, nor do they place an unreasonable expectation of generosity on either of the children involved.

Of course, these approaches do not always work—and when a youngster just begins to try them out, teachers need to remain with the child and lend their support to make them as effective as possible. It is also helpful to preface the suggestions with such phrases as *"Maybe it would work* if you tried trading him this truck for that little car," or *"Perhaps* he'd let you play if you'd sit on that side of the swing to balance it." This leaves the way open, if the other child simply refuses, to say, "Well, I guess she needs that herself right now. We'll just have to find something else for you to do instead. Maybe she'll come and tell you when she's through —would you do that, Susan?" (Incidentally, one thing that is almost certain *not* to work as a social approach for 4-year-olds is to coach them to ask, "Can I play?" There is such strong in-group feelings among fours that the answer to this plaintive inquiry will more than likely be a resounding "No!")

What to do when both want to ride and no one wants to pull? With a little guidance from the teacher, 4-year-olds can usually solve such problems for themselves.

Finally, it is important to show approval when you see children accepting and using these alternatives. ("I'm sure glad to see you ask Jim for that instead of biting him the way you used to—and he likes you better, too!" or "Well, that trade worked out pretty well, didn't it? Both you children got something you wanted.") This makes the children more aware of what they are doing, and the positive reinforcement makes repetition of that behavior more probable.

Help children respond generously. Children are more likely to feel generous about welcoming newcomers into their play or sharing equipment with them if they know that their own rights are protected. This is the reason many children's centers observe the rule, "You can keep something until you're done with it, but if you've stopped using it, then someone else can have a turn." This policy helps reduce the need to cling jealously and vigilantly to things lest they be arbitrarily taken away by the teacher. It also

means that when children are finished and have had enough, they give the item up willingly instead of grudgingly. In other words, they are sharing because they *want* to, not because they *have* to. There is a world of difference in what children learn in those two circumstances.

Children should also be taught how to stand up for their own rights because this, too, is an aspect of being socially competent, and, paradoxically, children who know they can protect themselves are likely to be less defensive and protective of their possessions. For example, the teacher might encourage a child to defend himself by asking an indecisively whimpering 3-year-old, "Do you want her to take your buggy? Well, then, tell her you don't," or say to another child, "Hang on! You don't have to let him have that, you know. Tell him the rule!"

Generous behavior will be encouraged if the teacher occasionally points out to a youngster who has shared something that the other child is now feeling gratified and friendly. ("Gee, you really made her feel good," or "Look how he's smiling at you. I think he's feeling friendly because you let him use that box.") Perhaps a quick hug can be used to show pleasure in his altruistic behavior.

Finally, simply having enough equipment and materials to go around makes a difference that cannot be overlooked. As frustration increases, constructiveness in play decreases (Barker, Denbo, & Lewin, 1976), and nothing is more frustrating or breeds more closehandedness than having only enough blocks to build one tower or enough dough for tantalizing little fistfuls. It is not always necessary to have a large budget to provide plentiful amounts of materials and equipment. Many can be made or scrounged at reasonable cost if teachers and parents are willing to make the effort (Moore, 1983).

INCREASE THE CHILD'S ABILITY TO MAKE FRIENDS

What Makes a Good Friend?

One of the reasons it is valuable to teach children to get along easily with other children is that they are more likely to have friends when they are able to do this, and even for children of preschool age, having friends contributes to happiness (Wolf, 1986).

Although some may have the impression that friendships between preschool children are largely temporary and haphazard, preschool teachers know this to be untrue and current studies of actual behavior bear this out as well (Axtmann & Bluhm, 1986). It is obvious that in most preschool groups there are children who prefer each other's company, as well as those who are more likely to be shunned or shut out of play.

When asked about why someone is a good friend, preschoolers usually give quite simple answers which boil down to "Because I like him!" (Rubin, K. H., 1982). Hayes (1978) pursued this question in more depth and found

that children gave additional reasons for friendship, including liking to play with the child, nearness (propinquity), and possession of interesting toys to play with. Hayes found that youngsters disliked children who were aggressive, who behaved in unusual ways, or who broke the rules. Some additional qualities that make a young child more likely to be selected as a friend include being physically attractive and acting friendly and outgoing (Hartup, 1983).

Increasing the Child's Likeability

To help children make friends, teachers must realize that they can help with some factors but that other ones are part of the child's temperament. Some children, by temperament, are quiet and less outgoing than others are and so appear to be less friendly. Some children seem to feel most comfortable with one or two good friends, whereas others manage well with a number of different playmates.

While taking temperament into account, there are some things teachers can do that may increase a child's likeability. They can help children learn to control their tempers or become more skillful at using alternative methods to get what they want. Increasing children's feeling of competence in any area helps them feel more confident, and this confidence helps them be more open and less defensive with other children. Hence, they act more friendly.

Sometimes even physical attractiveness can be increased if the teacher is very tactful about this. Some years ago, we had a 4-year-old youngster in the group who was very pretty and intelligent. Unfortunately, she smelled of urine. It got to the point where the children were telling her at snack time, "Sit somewhere else — you smell like peepee!" This was a delicate matter to bring to the mother's attention, to say the least. Yet, we could not go on allowing the child's feelings to be hurt. The teacher approached the problem by asking the mother if the little girl had ever had any previous urinary problems because we noticed that her panties were often just a little wet when she went to the bathroom. The mother agreed and said she had been concerned and had been meaning to take her daughter to the doctor. This conversation motivated her to take action, and it turned out that the child did have a physical problem, which they were able to correct.

Fortunately, not all friendship problems are this ticklish to handle. There are additional, simple things teachers can do to help children form friendships. One is pairing children for special experiences. Asking a pair to help set up a cooking experience may lead to their cooking together afterward, for instance. Others include restructuring a car pool or suggesting that a mother invite a child regularly to play after school. Sometimes finding a common interest helps generate a bond.

Occasionally, providing a clear explanation of how the child is offending other children becomes necessary. ("You know, when you walk into the block corner and kick over their things, they feel really mad at you. That's why they won't let you play. Maybe if you got that truck, you could deliver some blocks when they need them. When you help people, they like you better.")

Helping Children Cope with Rejection

Although all children experience occasional rejection and exclusion by others, sometimes more extreme cases occur. This seems to happen more frequently with fours than with threes. The child continually hangs around a particular child, and the harder he presses the issue, the more vehement the rejection becomes. After trying some of the alternatives listed above, the teacher may just have to help the child accept the fact that a particular child does not want to be friends with him. There is no way to force such relationships. If he chooses to continue his wistful pursuit, that is his own decision, but the teacher can point out that there are other children available to play with if he wishes to do that instead.

INCREASE THE CHILD'S ABILITY TO FUNCTION SUCCESSFULLY AS PART OF A GROUP

Use Play Situations to Help Children Develop Group Social Skills

Children learn a lot about getting along with people by playing with them. They learn what others will tolerate and what they will not, how to maintain a balance of satisfaction so that everyone has enough fun that they want to stay and play, when to give in, and when to assert themselves. Maintaining this delicate balance between compromise and getting one's own way is an essential social skill that seems to come more easily to some children than it does to others as the research report by Trawick-Smith reveals.

Playing with other children varies in accordance with children's age, temperament, and amount of social experience. Two- and three-year-olds play more frequently by themselves or alongside each other, whereas older threes and fours play more frequently together, often instructing each other quite specifically in the roles they should assume ("You be the mommy, and I'll be your little girl"), stipulating conditions ("I'll play, but you don't give me no shots!"), and using their imagination to set the stage ("This stuff over here is the tree, and we're the lions who live there"). Twos and threes tend to focus more on playing with objects and play materials, investigating their properties, sometimes investing them with imaginary play themes and sometimes not, whereas older threes and fours participate in more interactive dramatic play (Adcock & Segal, 1983).

Once play has begun, teachers should bear in mind the value of prolonging and extending the interaction so children benefit from maximum social experience. It does take a delicate hand to know when to intervene and when not to. My impression is that some inexperienced teachers tend to participate too fully by acting childlike or make themselves the center of attention or

RESEARCH STUDY
The Social Value of Compromise

Research Question Trawick-Smith asked, "Why are some children more successful in leading play activities than other children are? What is it about the way they behave that causes other children to accept their ideas so readily?"

Research Method He studied the behavior of 32 preschool children while they engaged in natural free play at nursery school. While the children were playing together, he counted the number of episodes of leading and following behavior he observed.

Leadership behavior was defined as how frequently a child's directives, suggestions, or contributions to the play theme were actually accepted by the other children. Following behavior was defined as being the opposite of leadership behavior (i.e., how often a child accepted directives, suggestions, or contributions to the play proposed by the other child).

Research Results Analysis of the results revealed something surprising. It was not the strongly outspoken, somewhat aggressive children who were the most effective leaders. Rather, the children who had the greatest number of their suggestions accepted by others turned out to be the ones who also accepted the most suggestions *from* other children. The high leadership children had many novel ideas to contribute, but they were also willing to concede some control of the play to the other youngsters.

On the other hand, unskilled leaders whose suggestions were not as frequently accepted fell into three categories. One group included the children who attempted to force their ideas on other children, whom the investigator classified as

---

become the source of too many of the ideas, all of which rob the children of the initiative.

On the other hand, some teachers lean too far in the other direction and do not encourage the children enough, with the result that the play falls apart too quickly or lacks richness. These people should acquaint themselves with the research by Smilansky (1968) and Feitelson and Ross (1973), which reports that intervention is particularly necessary with children from families of the poor who may lag behind in the development of their sociodramatic play skills and who need special modeling and encouragement in how to play to develop these skills more fully. Of

course, limited richness of play may not be restricted to those children who are living in poverty. As more and more youngsters of all economic classes spend longer hours in front of television sets, their play may also require added support from teachers.

Such intervention may take the form of suggestions ("Perhaps you boys need a bag if you're going to go to the market. Let's see, I wonder what you could use?"), supportive comments ("You children are really busy in there," or "My goodness, little kitten you *do* look snuggly—your mother is sure taking good care of you!"), or even direct participation and model-

"bullies." The second group, which he named "boot lickers," were so eager to be included in the play they were overly compliant and did as they were told, while the third group, termed "isolates," usually played alone.

Implications for Teaching This research highlights a particular social skill that it is worthwhile for children to learn during their early years. This is the willingness to listen to suggestions from other children and incorporate them along with their own ideas as they play together—in short, to practice the art of compromise. In this sort of amiable situation, the value of everyone's ideas is recognized, and everyone gets at least a little bit of what he wants.

Additional conclusions drawn by the investigator include recommendations that bullies be taught to adopt more following behaviors, to ask for things rather than just demand them, to bargain, to accept compromises, and to understand the "futility of using force."

He suggests that boot lickers be encouraged to speak up for their own ideas and learn to exercise their right of choice, and that isolated children be encouraged to play, at least occasionally, with other children.

In essence, a major goal to keep in mind when teaching children social skills is teaching them to maintain a balance between insisting on their own ideas and using the ideas put forth by others, a balance between compliance and self-assertion, and a balance between solitary and social play. It is the ability to maintain that balance that provides the key to playing successfully with other children.

Note. From " 'Let's Say You're the Baby, OK?' Play Leadership and Following Behavior of Young Children" by J. Trawick-Smith, 1988, *Young Children, 43*(5), pp. 51–59.

---

ing ("Yum, yum, yum! Thanks for that delicious mashed potato cake! Should I feed some to the baby until you're not so busy?").

In general, if teachers remember that the purpose of intervening is not to dominate but to sustain and continue the play, as well as to foster positive social interaction among the children, they will not go far wrong.

Table 11–2 provides many suggestions for ways teachers can foster positive social interaction among children. Two areas of curriculum have been singled out to illustrate their potential for doing this. Actually, all areas of curriculum have equivalent potentials for positive and negative social learning. Consider what these might be when setting up each area—whether it be the block corner, the water play table, or the sandbox. Good planning facilitates desirable social learning.

Use Mealtimes to Foster Social Competencies

Sometimes we lose sight of the fact that eating together is one of the most profoundly social activities available to human beings. In many cultures around the world, the act of breaking bread together is a sign of peace and also lies at

TABLE 11–2
Ways to increase positive social interaction among children

Approaches likely to induce positive social action	Approaches likely to induce negative social action
Dramatic play centering on the home	

Dramatic play centering on the home

Be prepared to suggest on-going ideas from time to time when play appears likely to lag or fall apart. ("Hmmm—do I smell vegetable soup?")

Provide both male and female items in order to welcome both sexes and provide opportunities to try out other-sex roles. These might include shaving equipment, tools, wedding dresses, or boots.

Stimulate variety in the play by varying the equipment. Offer market supplies, hospital things, or the large blocks and boards.

Vary the location. Move equipment to a new area—perhaps outside or into a large bathroom for water play.

Include items that attract children particularly, such as water, several large empty boxes, or guinea pigs.

Foster cultural respect by offering multiethnic equipment, such as wooden bowls from Africa, a bedspread made of Guatemalan material, or dolls of various ethnic backgrounds, and speak casually, but respectfully, of such things as our "Mexican chair," our "Zambian bowl," and so forth.

Offer more than one piece of the same large equipment, such as two baby buggies or two suitcases.

Split the housekeeping equipment into two households, and encourage the children to improvise additional needed items.

Set up an office or a market in conjunction with the housekeeping area.

To encourage role playing, offer items large enough for the children to get into themselves, such as a regular high chair and a child-sized bed.

Increase the reality-information base of the play by having a baby visit, going to a real market, or actually visiting places where parents work to see what their mothers and fathers do there.

Offer a simple cooking experience, such as making peanut butter sandwiches in the housekeeping corner.

Encourage more than one age to play together. This is fairly easy to do in housekeeping because of the variety of family roles that are available.

Encourage the children to solve problems together. How could they turn the house into a camper? What could they use for bananas?

Make the play area too small and congested so that the children get in each other's way much of the time.

Allow clothing or other equipment to accumulate on the floor so that the children stumble over it, mistreat it, or can't find what they need.

Offer only female-type items, with the result that the boys feel subtly excluded. This makes attacks by the boys more likely.

Don't set up the homemaking area before the children arrive. Leave it as it was the day before.

Provide no physical barriers, so that children who are passing through intrude either intentionally or unintentionally.

Keep equipment skimpy so that children have to wait too long for a chance to use it.

Allow equipment to become broken or dirty. This tells the children that this play area and what happens there aren't really important and that you don't care about them.

TABLE 11-2 *(continued)*

Approaches likely to induce positive social action	Approaches likely to induce negative social action
Pay attention to the children's requests and ideas. This helps them feel valued and important and encourages children to listen to each other, also.	
When necessary, help new arrivals enter the group successfully by suggesting how they could help, what they could be, or what they might say to the children who are already playing there.	
Put all the regular equipment away and encourage the children to develop their own house, using blocks, boards, and accessories.	

Outdoor large-muscle play

Whenever possible, select equipment that invites or requires more than one child's cooperative use for best success, such as double rocking boats, a hammock, large parachute activities, jump ropes, wagons, and horizontally hung tire swings.	Provide no focus for the play—let the children mostly just run around.
Offer several of one kind of thing, not only to reduce bickering, but also to induce social play. Several bouncy horses together facilitate social congeniality, for example.	Keep the children indoors so long that they are pent-up and desperate for physical activity when they do get out.
Provide plentiful equipment for dramatic play. In particular, a good assortment of blocks, ladders, sawhorses, and boards encourages the children to build things together. Smaller equipment, such as ropes, hats, and horses, also encourage this kind of social play.	Sit idly by.
	Offer the same kind of large muscle activities every day. This lack of variety breeds boredom and fighting.
Think of the sandbox as providing an interesting social play center (particularly for younger children), and provide things to do together, such as a fleet of little cars or a good supply of pans and sturdy spoons and shovels.	Store equipment in inaccessible places so that it's difficult to get out and hence will not be frequently used.
Stay alert and aware of what is going on to provide input and control in time when it is needed.	Suggest competitive activities—who can run fastest, get there first, and so forth. This breeds ill feeling and hurt feelings.
Occasionally encourage more physically proficient children to teach less skilled children how to do something.	Encourage games with many rules. This baffles the younger children, increases frustration and reduces spontaneity and creativity.
Encourage children to help each other—push each other on the swing, for example.	Permit the older, more powerful children to monopolize the equipment.
Read and apply what Kritchevsky, Prescott, and Walling (1969) have to say about developing play spaces so that complex and super play units are offered rather than simple ones.	
Offer outdoor sand, mud, and water play whenever possible. This encourages peaceful social interaction for lengthy periods of time.	
Offer large-group projects that involve doing something together, such as painting a large refrigerator box to make something to play in, or gardening. This isn't exactly play, but it's so much fun it feels like play to the children.	

Buying equipment that fosters social interaction encourages children to cooperate.

the heart of many celebrations. These lofty practices may seem far removed from a group of 3-year-olds spooning up fruit and yogurt. Yet, it is valuable for people working with children to keep the more profound social value in mind even while mopping up milk and showing children how to scrape their plates because it will help the adults remember that the fundamental goal of eating together is to have a congenial experience in which everyone is both physically satisfied and socially replenished.

Moreover, if well presented, mealtimes offer the best opportunity of the day to foster the feeling of home and family so important to young children and all too often missing from large day-care situations. This feeling of "familiness" can be generated not only by the overall climate of warmth and human interchange, but also by attention to such details as serving food that is culturally familiar (note that *familiar* comes from the same root as *family*) and by encouraging families to participate in meals at the center by occasionally having lunch with their youngsters or sending birthday goodies or sharing their surplus garden produce with the school — though there is a limit to the amount of zucchini even a center can willingly consume.

Create a climate of intimacy and calm. In addition to linking home and school, three other practices will help achieve a climate of easy comfort right from the start of the meal. The group at the table needs to be kept as small as possible: five children and an adult is ideal, though not always possible. Younger children require an even higher adult/child ratio because they need so much more help. What should be avoided at all costs is putting all fifteen or sixteen children around one table with no adult present, since pandemonium results. The children have to wait too long for food to be passed to them, and there is almost no way to generate conversation in such bedlam.

Second, the food should be right there, ready to be passed as soon as all the children are seated. The only drawback to this is that it may cool a little more than desired but having a meal ready is infinitely preferable to nagging at children to sit still and stop tapping their cups or poking their neighbor.

Finally, *it is very desirable for adults to be present and sitting down* as the children come to the table. It is not the function of these adults to get up and run after sponges, go to the kitchen for refills, and so forth. The sponges should already be available on the service trays, and children should be allowed the social opportunity of going for refills. The adults are present to help generate a peaceful, welcoming, happy atmosphere in which each child has the chance to talk with the teachers and with his friends, and also has the opportunity to help others by passing food, mopping up, and so forth.

Keep mealtime policies consistent with the basic educational philosophy of the school. Nowhere in curriculum is the fundamental educational philosophy of the teacher revealed more plainly than in the way the food situation is handled.

Who makes the final decision on what to eat? Does the teacher decide by arbitrarily doling the food out on each plate and making the child eat everything? Or does the child decide by serving himself and being allowed to go easy on food he does not like or is suspicious of?

Who passes the food around the table? Does the teacher move from child to child, or are individual children allowed to serve themselves

and pass it on to their neighbors, learning social consideration by taking some and leaving some?

Who generates conversation? Is it always teacher centered, or does it become talk *between* children as a result of her encouraging that focus? Remember that conversation is thought to be one of the earliest (if not the earliest) forms of turn taking that children learn (Bruner, 1978; Sacks, Schegloff, & Jefferson, 1978). Learning to allow space and time for others to reply is an intensely valuable social skill.

Use Group Time to Foster Social Competencies

Too often teachers think of group time as being primarily a time to read a book or two to the children, and books do have a valuable place in that activity, as discussed in Chapter 15. But, in addition to the opportunities for language and cognitive growth inherent in group time, teachers should also use it to foster positive social interaction and learning.

This time of day offers excellent opportunities for children to become interested in other youngsters and what they have been doing. Perhaps someone has brought his pet mouse from home, or perhaps three or four of the children have just returned from seeing a poodle get its hair clipped at the groomer's. Such experiences are of genuine interest to children. However, teachers get in trouble with having children share their experiences at group time when they assume it is necessary to go entirely around the circle and have each child tell something each day. This takes too long, and instead of generating interest, this practice generates seething boredom, because the children are pushed beyond their limits of self-control for holding still. Yet, if groups are kept small, and experiences are shared naturally by different children on different days, group time can be interesting and can also provide another opportunity to value things from home at school.

Occasionally discussing social problems also fosters social learning at group time, particularly with 4-year-olds (Shure & Spivack, 1978). For example, on the day before a new tricycle will be made available, the group might discuss how to work things out so that everyone will have a chance to use it, or they might discuss how to keep children from picking the tomatoes in the garden before they are ripe enough to eat. It is important that this kind of discussion not center on the past misdeeds of some small sinner in particular, but focus instead on making a group decision that will bring about socially positive behavior.

The teacher who leads such a discussion should know that, as in many other aspects of child development, children's ideas of right and wrong (and hence their ideas of what constitutes justice) pass through a series of developmental stages (Kohlberg, 1978; Piaget, 1983; Turiel, 1980). She should not be surprised if the rules they suggest are quite severe, definite ones, because children of this age believe what is right is right and what is wrong is wrong. Their idea of justice is one of reciprocity, the eye-for-an-eye and tooth-for-a-tooth variety, so the teacher may need to help the children temper their suggestions with mercy. However, if such group discussions are not overdone, they can help children think about the effect individual actions have on the group as a whole and what should be done about it.

ENCOURAGE THE CHILDREN TO FIND SATISFACTION IN HELPING EACH OTHER AND THE GROUP

Young children are largely self-centered in the sense that they see the world in terms of their own needs and point of view, but they are also capable of offering comfort and help to other people if properly encouraged and if the example has been set for them in the past (Goffin, 1987; Moore, 1982). This was brought vividly to my attention one day when I shut my hand in the door of my car. It hurt so much that I just collapsed on the seat of the car, tears oozing down my cheeks. At that point my 3-year-old climbed over, snuggled up close, and began to pat my back sympathetically, murmuring something over and over in my ear as I had done for her so many times before. When my senses cleared, I realized to my amusement that what she was crooning as she patted me was, "Pretty soon, pretty soon, you'll be all right—you're just tired and hungry! Tired and hungry!"

If not overdone, older children also benefit by helping younger ones at school. This should not be construed as meaning that a four should surrender his doll to a three just because he's older, but it does mean that the four might hold the bunny's feet so it won't kick while the three is petting it, or that he might show the younger child where the napkins are kept or pull a towel out of the holder for him when it is too high to reach. This willingness to help others need not be limited to assisting younger children. The child who volunteers to open a door for a teacher

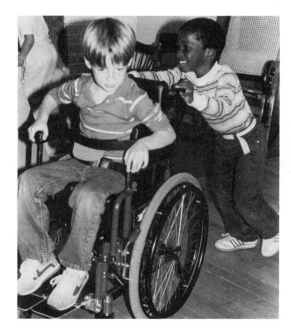

Doing something for someone else makes everyone feel good.

whose hands are full or who helps his friend push a wagon up the hill is also demonstrating his ability to care for and help other people.

Children also feel very positively about caring for animals, and it is nice to give them this opportunity. Baby animals, in particular, elicit a kindly feeling in younger children, who are also likely to be concerned and critical about the quality of care the mother animal is providing.

Then, too, children are quick to worry and feel concern when they see another child crying or when someone is hurt. If the teacher welcomes this concern and involves the child in providing comfort and fixing the small injury, this not only helps reassure him, but also lets him experience the benefit of helping another child feel better.

Meaningful Work Offers Opportunities for Helping

There are numerous places around a day-care center where children can find real pleasure in working, as long as the teacher avoids turning the work into an onerous chore. Some examples include almost any kind of cleaning up that involves water, such as scrubbing easels, doing dishes, hosing off sidewalks or sandy toys, scrubbing chairs, or washing doll clothes. Working by fixing things, such as repairing pages from torn books, breaking up dried potter's clay with a hammer so it can be moistened and reconstituted, sawing off the handles of paint brushes that are too long, tightening tricycle seats, decorating the picture file box with collage, and putting up the swing seats in the morning, are other possibilities. Still another kind of work that contributes to the well-being of the group might be fetching second helpings from the kitchen, taking old material down from bulletin boards, spreading out the plastic door mats on snowy days, helping set up cots, feeding the fish, or reassembling a puzzle that the teacher finds too difficult. When more than one child has to cooperate to accomplish a task, the value is even greater. Perhaps two are needed to fold the larger

blankets, or several children can work together to wash the teacher's car or carry the housekeeping equipment outside.

These kinds of opportunities should be available every day and will be most enjoyed by the children if the teacher allows them to choose how they want to help, keeps the jobs short, is not too critical of the results, and remembers to say "Thank you" afterward. It is particularly valuable to help them enjoy their feeling of accomplishing something genuinely worthwhile, which means that the job cannot be "make-work." Children love the sense of competence that comes from hard work well completed. It is one of the finest avenues for building self-esteem. As one youngster put it the other day, "I did it because I was so *big!* One of these days, teacher, I'll be *so* big you won't even *know* me!"

SUMMARY

If we want children to learn to balance their own needs and desires with concern for those of other people, we must have a clear grasp of the most basic social skills that are worthwhile to teach them so they will become happy, social people.

Among the most important of these competencies is the ability to control unsocial impulses and to use alternative ways of obtaining what they want rather than just snatching and grabbing. Learning to accept other children's ideas and incorporate them in the play is a particularly valuable social skill for children to acquire. Three group situations that occur during the center day offer fruitful possibilities for developing these social skills. These are sociodramatic play situations, eating together at mealtimes, and small-group sharing and learning times.

As the children gain experience and become more mature, they should also be encouraged to find satisfaction in helping each other and in doing things to help the group as a whole. Meaningful work can be used to provide this kind of satisfaction.

SELF-CHECK QUESTIONS FOR REVIEW

Content-Related Questions

1. According to Katz, what is the difference between adults who are authoritarian and those who are authoritative?
2. What is the rule of thumb to apply about when to stop behavior?
3. Why is it important to be consistent in enforcing center rules?
4. List and discuss the six recommended steps when dealing with behavior problems. Illustrate each step with an example.
5. There are also many longer-term methods of building inner controls. What are some of those recommended methods? Again, illustrate each with a practical example.
6. What are some alternative methods children can learn to use in order to get what they want?
7. What are some things teachers can do that may help a child be better liked by the other children?
8. According to the research report discussed in this chapter, what social skill separates the effective leaders from the other children?
9. Discuss some ways teachers can foster social competencies in the children during play, group times, or at meals.
10. Suppose you wished to *discourage* positive social interactions during dramatic play or outdoor time. Suggest some ways you could make this happen.
11. What are some ways children can be encouraged to help other people while they are at the center?

Integrative Questions

1. Mandy has just snatched some train track from Jan and is holding onto it fiercely while Jan is trying to tug it back. Both girls are crying loudly as they struggle. Describe how you would go through the six learning steps about discipline with Mandy, giving actual examples of what you would do or say. Then describe how you would use the situation to teach Jan what she needs to do next time.
2. Using the form on positive and negative social actions (Table 11–2), choose an indoor activity and show how you could arrange and manage it to foster either positive or negative behavior by the children.
3. Does the research carried out by Trawick-Smith have implications for adult as well as for child

leaders? If so, what are those implications? Can you provide examples from your own experience of adults who fit the various categories of ineffective leaders that he describes in the study?

QUESTIONS AND ACTIVITIES

1. *Problem:* It is springtime, and you and the children have planted a vegetable garden. The children are really interested in this, and someone has been unable to resist pulling up the radishes to see if they are ready to eat. Since they are no more than little, pale pink roots and far from ready, you find them shriveled on the sidewalk where they have been tossed aside. Although you hope to have only a general discussion about this at group time, when the matter is brought up, one of the children says immediately, "Teacher, teacher—I know who did it—Richard did it!" Thinking back over this particular situation, how would you handle it next time? And what do you plan to do about it right now?
2. Picking up the small blocks is often regarded as a real chore by both teachers and children. Suggest some things to do that would make this task more palatable.
3. What do you think of the idea of making a chart, listing on it all the jobs that must be done in school, and putting up children's names beside the items each day so they will know who is supposed to do what?
4. Describe some situations you have recently seen at your center in which it was *not* necessary to intervene in an argument between two children.
5. This book talks quite a lot about fostering alternatives to physically aggressive action. Pick out some of the more aggressive situations you have witnessed, and propose two or three alternative solutions that the children might have been encouraged to use.
6. Choose an area or activity in your own teaching situation, and list various ways positive social action could be increased.
7. Are there times when you now realize that you helped a child do something when another youngster might have helped him instead?

REFERENCES FOR FURTHER READING

Overviews

Hendrick, J. (1988). *The whole child: Developmental education for the early years* (4th ed.) Columbus, Ohio: Merrill Publishing Co. This book, which focuses on methods of instructing young children, contains several chapters on self-discipline, aggression, and social competence.

Maccoby, E. E. (1980). *Social development: Psychological growth and the parent-child relationship.* New York: Harcourt Brace Jovanovich. Maccoby combines research with experience, and the result is a clearly written, sensible, helpful book. Highly recommended.

Building Self-Control

Carlsson-Paige, N., & Levin, D. E. (1987). *The war play dilemma: Balancing needs and values in the early childhood classroom.* New York: Teachers College Press. The difficult question of what to do or not do about allowing war play and guns in children's centers is discussed here. The authors favor the controlled use of this kind of play.

Isaacs, S. (1986). *Who's in control? A parent's guide to discipline.* New York: Putnam Publishing Group. This plain-spoken book offers excellent help to teachers and parents. Highly recommended.

Marion, M. (1987). *Guidance of young children* (2nd ed.). Columbus, Ohio: Merrill Publishing Co. Marion's book is filled with a sound combination of research, theory, and practical advice.

Miller, C. S. (1984). Building self-control: Discipline for young children. *Young Children, 40*(1), 15–19. This practical article outlines basic principles. Highly recommended.

Mitchell, G. (1982). *A very practical guide to discipline with young children.* Marshfield, Mass.: Telshare Publishing. Mitchell's book is a favorite of my students—it is down to earth, dealing with general approaches and then more particular problems.

Helping Children Form Friendships

Adcock, D., & Segal, M. (1983). *Making friends: Ways of encouraging social development in young children.* Englewood Cliffs, N.J.: Prentice-Hall. Although focusing on friendship, the authors also offer many sagacious comments about helping children with different social styles get along comfortably together. Highly recommended.

Goffin, S. G. (1987). Cooperative behaviors: They need our support. *Young Children. 42*(2), 75–81. Goffin stresses the value of cooperative play between children and offers practical ideas on how to foster such positive interactions.

Rubin, A. (1980). *Children's friendships.* Cambridge, Mass.: Harvard University Press. I love this book because Rubin understands children so well. He discusses friendship at various ages and includes sensible comments on how to facilitate the growth of these relationships.

Wolf, D. P. (Ed.) (1986). *Connecting: Friendship in the lives of young children and their teachers.* Redmond, Wash.: Exchange Press. In a series of easy-to-read articles this book offers an overview of the value of friendship to young children along with comments on ways to enhance its flowering.

Importance of Nonviolence

Cryan, J. R. (1987). *The banning of corporal punishment in child care, school and other educative settings in the United States.* Wheaton, Md.: The Association for Childhood Education International. For those who need ammunition in the fight against corporal punishment, this position paper is persuasive. Highly recommended.

McGinnis, K., & Oehlberg, B. (1988). *Starting out right: Nurturing young children as peacemakers.* Oak Park, Ill.: Meyer, Stone, and Co. A thoughtful presentation of ways to encourage peaceful solutions of difficulties is presented here. The opposite point of view about permitting war play is included.

Understanding the Value of Work

Wenning, J., & Wortis, S. (1984). *Made by human hands: A curriculum for teaching young children about work and working people.* Cambridge, Mass.: The Multicultural Project for Communication and Education. While mainly dwelling on understanding work done by others, *Made by Human Hands* does include a brief discussion of jobs children can do. Teaching units and bibliographies are included.

For the Advanced Student

Eisenberg, N. (Ed.). (1982). *The development of prosocial behavior.* New York: Academic Press. Eisenberg's book considers the development of prosocial behavior in depth as reported by prominent researchers in this field.

Hetherington, E. M. (Ed.). (1983). *Volume IV: Socialization, personality and social development.* In P. H. Mussen (Ed.), *Handbook of child psychology* (4th ed.). New York: John Wiley & Sons. One volume of a thoroughly updated version of Carmichael's *Manual of Child Psychology,* Volume IV covers a number of subjects related to this chapter. An indispensable reference for the serious student.

Honig, A. S. (1985). Compliance, control, and discipline. *Young Children, 40*(2), 50–58 and 40(3), 49–51. Honig reviews research that emphasizes the significance of attachment and reasoning with children as important factors in obtaining compliance. Also included are suggestions that foster a positive approach to discipline.

Parke, R. D., & Slaby, R. G. (1983). The development of aggression. In P. H. Mussen (Ed.), *Handbook of child psychology* (4th ed.), E. M. Hetherington (Ed.), *Vol. IV: Socialization, personality, and social development.* New York: John Wiley & Sons. This article offers a definitive review of research related to aggression.

Wolfgang, C. H., & Glickman, D. C. (1986). *Solving discipline problems: Strategies for classroom teachers* (2nd ed.). Boston: Allyn & Bacon. Seven theoretical approaches to discipline are outlined by the authors before they go on to discuss special problems such as helpless- ness, verbal aggression, and so forth. Written primarily for the teacher of older children.

Additional Resources of Further Interest

The National Center for the Study of Corporal Punishment and Alternatives in the Schools, 253 Ritter South, Temple University, Philadelphia, Pennsylvania 19122. The Center is a valuable source of references, research, and workshops about the evil results of corporal punishment.

12 Who Am I?
Who Are You?

Developing Social Competence and the Sense of Self

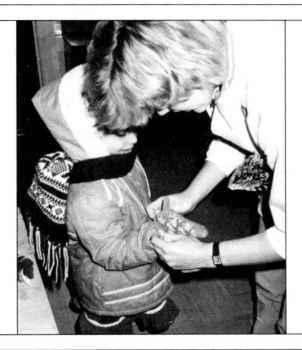

Have you ever

- Wished that you knew how to help a child feel better about herself?

- Wanted to know what to say when a 4-year-old says to a Mexican youngster, "You can't play—you're dirty!"

- Racked your brain for what you could do besides offering cross-gender activities to reduce sex stereotyping in children?

If you have, the material in this chapter will help you.

A Meditation for Children

I am a member of the world family . . .
I am related to those who stand next to me
. . . by the air we breathe
. . . by the light we share
. . . the hope we have for a better world.
I have a responsibility
. . . to give
. . . to receive
. . . to be open, tolerant, free.
I have inherited this world from those who have lived here
*   before . . .*
I occupy space and time for a few short years . . .
I hold this world in trust for those who will follow.
My life — with others — can fashion this world toward
. . . peace, rather than strife
. . . hope, rather than despair
. . . freedom, rather than slavery.
I, with those about me, can make the Brotherhood of Man a
*   living thing.*
I pledge my willing spirit to this thought.
We will do this together!

THE UNITED NATIONS (1981)

So far we have been talking about social competence in terms of the interpersonal social skills that parents and preschool teachers can help little children develop. This chapter considers some additional aspects of social development that, though more subtle, are equally important. These have to do with how children develop a sense of who they are and of their place in the world.

HOW DO CHILDREN DEVELOP A SENSE OF SELF?

In the beginning, it is thought that infants experience a sort of global oneness with their mothers and that an early task of infancy is to achieve a sense of separateness and a realization that the mother, as she comes and goes, continues to exist even when she is not within the baby's sight. As the infant gradually achieves this concept of mother separateness and continuing permanence, she also begins to sense herself as a separate, individual being. Piaget (1954) has called this sense of the separate other *the concept of object permanence,* and he regards it as being a fundamental prerequisite in the formation of later intellectual processes.

After infancy, children add to the sense of who they are by gaining identity from the people around them and becoming like them. This is the way children learn what constitutes basically acceptable ways for them to be and behave in their society. Freud postulated that this process of identification initially resulted from the child being dependent on her mother and wanting to incorporate her strength into herself. He maintained that the child gains security by acting as the mother acts, switching (if a boy) at about age 4 to identify with his father instead. Identification, then, as Freud sees it, is a complicated kind of substitution whereby a child comes to think, feel, and behave as though the characteristics of another person were her own. In a sense, she becomes as the other person is.

Proponents of behaviorism, on the other hand, subscribe to a different explanation of how children achieve a sense of identity and become like the people around them. Their approach, as exemplified in the work of B. F. Skinner (1954, 1974), favors the idea that, once the genetic endowment has been set, the individual's behavior is determined by external events. Put very simply, pure behaviorists maintain that behavior

is repeated only if it has been rewarded in some manner. Parents and other members of the larger society reward behavior they approve of, causing children to repeat it and gain a sense of how they should behave.

Albert Bandura (1977) makes use of this theory of behaviorism but also notes that some behavior is internalized by children even when external reinforcement for repeating it is not evident. He theorizes that children learn to be like other adults in their society by observing them and imitating what they do, as well as by having their behavior reinforced. Apparently

Name tags can confer a sense of identity while fostering the growth of literacy skills.

RESEARCH STUDY
How Might Culture Affect the Way People Teach?

Research Question   Lubeck asked the questions, "How is culture transmitted in the classroom?" "Do the teaching styles of Black and White preschool teachers differ from each other, and if they do, what are those differences and why do they exist?"

Research Method   Over the period of 1 year, Lubeck studied two half-day preschool classrooms. One was a middle-class group of 24 White children, ages 2 to 4½ years, taught by White middle-class teachers presenting a traditional preschool program. The other was a working class group of 21 Black children, aged 4 years, taught by Black working class teachers at a Head Start center. The rooms were similar in the amounts of equipment and space provided for the children.

Lubeck gathered her information by observing the White preschool and by observing and ultimately participating as a volunteer teacher for the entire school year at the Head Start center. This participation gradually earned her the trust and acceptance of the Head Start staff. In both situations she took extensive, daily field notes. (This is termed the *ethnographic approach* to doing research.) Teachers at the Head Start center were given the notes to read and agreed that her observations were correct.

Results   Lubeck's study covered the teachers' use of time, space, activities, and teacher/child relations, but due to limitations of space, only her conclusions about teacher/child relations will be included here.

She found that the Black and White teachers did indeed teach differently and did teach different values to the children. This happened despite the overall Head Start policies of encouraging free play and individualized attention—basic educational values similar to the values of the White preschool.

The middle-class White teachers, who came from nuclear families themselves, concentrated on children during the day and did not have very much contact with the other teachers, whereas the Black Head Start teachers, who came from extended families, were often involved in activities that were separate from what the children were doing. There was a sense of kinship among the Black teachers that was not as apparent among the White teachers.

The White teachers stressed freedom of choice, permitted divergent answers, and encouraged children to be independent, whereas the Black teachers emphasized the value of group solidarity and conformity rather than individual choice. Granting choices was feared as presenting opportunities for the children to get out of control. At the Head Start center the importance of giving convergent, right answers was stressed and the children were taught to obey authority unquestioningly.

In keeping with this sense of collective values, the language taught by the Black teachers was generalized, also. For example, toys would be referred to as "toys" rather than speaking of the little, red truck or the puzzle with the two roosters on it as was done in the middle-class school.

The White teachers typically influenced behavior by reasoning, suggesting, using indirect instruction and, when needed, firm, direct instruction. Lubeck comments that they appeared to believe that given time, reason would prevail. The Black teachers typically told the children exactly what to do and had a strong air of authority as they issued such directives.

Implications   When reading research, it is always important to remember its limitations. This study, intensive though it was, deals with only two classrooms of children. Therefore, it is inappropriate to conclude that every group of children in every other setting is taught using the same styles. On the other hand, it could also be the case that such differences may exist in many classrooms. If so, all teachers, whether they be Black or White, can benefit from thinking about the insights the study provides.

One thing Lubeck documents is that it is not easy to change cultural values. Teachers are likely to reflect their own cultural values and styles as they teach children despite what the philosophical system encourages. Witness the split between Head Start philosophy and what actually took place in that classroom.

It is easy for teachers who subscribe to the philosophy of the middle-class preschool to deplore the values taught by the Black teachers, but the truth is that these values have obvious worth as survival skills for Black children. The strong kinship patterns, the importance of conforming, following orders, and relying on the group for support have genuine short-term adaptive value for people growing up in a world where the most dominant group continues to be prejudiced against them. (Of course, there is also the possibility that teaching children to conform and take orders may not turn out to be to their ultimate benefit over the longer course of their lives.)

Rather than merely deploring these findings or planning how things should change, perhaps, after careful consideration, readers of this research will be willing to move beyond that point of view. Perhaps they may even begin to grasp what Lubeck said was her most profound learning from her study:

> I have had to reconstruct the history of the people with whom I worked, people who shared my community but not my ways, people who reared children in ways different from my own. My reactions to our differences have changed over time: early horror that I could see only stereotypes in what was being done 'wrong,' later conviction that, if they could only be shown a (my) 'better' way, they would change, and later still appreciation for a way of life that had possibilities different from my own—and dawning realization of my own—and my own culture's—limitations.

Note. From *Sandbox Society: Early Education in Black and White America* by S. Lubeck, 1985, Philadelphia: The Falmer Press.

this kind of imitative learning takes place simply because children want to be like their parents, and this is a gratification itself.

Whether one subscribes to the Freudian, Skinnerian, or Banduran point of view, it is worth noting that all of them emphasize that adults are powerful influences in establishing the child's identity. Both Freud and Bandura stress that nurturing, attractive adults are the ones most likely to be imitated, and considerable additional research supports this contention (Baumrind, 1971, 1972; Coopersmith, 1967; Harter, 1983). The implications of these findings for us as parents and teachers, who are all strong power figures in children's lives, is that if we want children to identify with us so that they want to "do as we do," we should be as warm and nurturing as possible, as well as being good examples.

One more factor worth mentioning is not directly discussed in these theories but also helps children develop a sense of self and of how to behave in their society. It is worth pointing out to teachers because adults frequently use it; that factor is direct instruction. Teachers and parents often tell children directly what are the acceptable and unacceptable ways to behave. How often adults say in essence, "We just don't do that. We never hurt animals," or "It isn't right to bite people!" or "Our family always . . .," or "Our family never . . . ." (Although I do recall a neighbor remonstrating with his 4-year-old, saying, "Clark! We never spit on sidewalks!" to which his swaggering 4-year-old replied, "Well, Dad, boys do!" We must admit such admonishments don't always work!)

To sum up socialization theory, after infancy children appear to gain their basic sense of who they are and what their place is in the world partly through the process of identifying with admired others and behaving as much like them as possible, and partly through conforming to the expectations of others to obtain their support and approval. Both these factors contribute to children's ideas of what it means to be a boy or a girl, what it means to be a member of a particular ethnic group, and even as early as 3 or 4 years of age, what they can look forward to becoming when they grow up. (Witness this chilling statement from a 4-year-old who was asked what he would be if he were a girl: "A girl?" he asked. "A girl? Oh, if I were a girl I'd have to grow up to be nothing!" [Leifer & Lesser, 1976, p. 18]).

But teachers and parents must realize that, in addition to these basic processes of socialization, many other factors contribute to children's developing sense of self as they become aware of the world outside their homes. These include many elements over which teachers and parents may have little control. Current usage speaks of such influences as being part of the *ecology of childhood* (Brim, Boocock, Hoffman, Bronfenbrenner, & Edelman, 1975; Mcloughlin & Gullo, 1985; West, 1987). Bansavage quotes Brim as defining this ecology as "the natural setting of developing children—the types of families, the types of communities, the friendship groups, the characteristics of their schools, contact with the adult world and similar environmental factors" (1978, p. 119). This focus is useful, not only because it helps pinpoint influences, but also because it reminds us that we must not underestimate the significance of slums, television, the neighborhood children, family size, an urban or rural setting, persistent high levels of noise, overcrowding, climate, population density, and so forth on the development of the children and their sense of who they are.

On the other hand, we must not underestimate the positive effect home and school can have on the way young children see themselves (Werner, 1984). As you read the description of Lubeck's research on the differing teaching styles of one group of Black and White preschool teachers, consider the effects the differing styles might have on the children in those classrooms.

ENHANCE THE CHILD'S FEELINGS OF SELF-ESTEEM

If we define the sense of self as being the child's gradually developing idea of who she is, we can say that self-esteem is present when she feels this self to be a valuable, worthwhile person. Many teachers think of self-esteem as being something they bestow on children by praising them or making them feel important, and it is true that merited praise and recognition are valuable ways of building self-esteem, since in the beginning these positive feelings come from outside the child. Over a period of time, however, we do not want children to remain dependent on a constant barrage of "you're wonderfuls" in order to feel good about themselves and who they are. Instead, we want to provide them with sources of positive self-esteem that come from within themselves whenever possible.

Build Self-Esteem by Providing the Child With Skills so That She Feels Competent

The child who is well coordinated and able to balance her way along a narrow wall or hang by her knees has a pleasant feeling of "I'm good—I can do it," as does the youngster who can pull up his pants himself or carry in the beans without spilling them. Acquisition of these skills requires that the teacher provide sufficient time and plentiful opportunities for practice and that he keep the level of challenge difficult enough to make things interesting, but not so hard that it scares children off from trying. If he also provides chances to carry out meaningful work and to help other people, as discussed in Chapter 11, the teacher will enhance the children's feelings of mastery and satisfaction even further. The goal in all these areas is to provide opportunities for children to feel successful so that they know deep inside that they are capable, adequate people.

Encourage Self-Esteem by Helping Children Do Things for Themselves

To paraphrase a better known statement, children should be encouraged to do things "of themselves, by themselves, and for themselves" to increase their autonomy and gain a positive sense of self. This is really another facet of competence. Allowing this independence to

develop can be especially difficult for teachers of such young children, since they must balance the children's needs for dependence and independence with their own need to keep the daily routines operating at a reasonable pace. It is not easy to tread the narrow path between lending a loving hand when it is needed so that children know we care and waiting quietly by when it is better for them to help themselves. Actually, waiting can be one of the hardest parts and most important skills in teaching. Even though teachers theoretically agree that the ultimate gains make waiting worthwhile, it may still be necessary for them to firmly remember this as they stand poised by the door while a group of threes fumble endlessly with their sweater buttons.

Encourage Self-Esteem by Providing Opportunities for Meaningful Work

Another way of enhancing children's sense of self-worth is to encourage them to be helpful by doing small jobs around the center. Young children love to participate in cleanup when it entails using water, just as they enjoy doing other "grown-up" jobs as long as these are reasonably within their abilities and are not too boring or long drawn out.

Unfortunately, adults often either underestimate children's abilities or pawn off the jobs that nobody really likes to do, such as putting all the blocks away. The kinds of jobs I have in mind are often one-time, short ones where the results are readily apparent. These might include washing the dishes after a cooking activity, sawing through a branch the wind has torn from the play yard tree and discarding it, or loading the wagon with hollow blocks to take outside. Or perhaps the birdhouse needs a spring cleaning, or leaves need raking in the fall, or the garden needs watering.

Many of these activities are so routine that adults do them just in order to get them over with, forgetting how much the children would love to participate. But such opportunities for participation should be seized on with joy by the teacher because they contribute to the welfare of

Shoveling snow like Mommy or Daddy does help children feel grown-up and empowered.

the group, and also because they can do so much to enhance children's sense of being competent, worthwhile people.

Being Creative Offers Satisfying Avenues for Building Self-Esteem

Early childhood teachers are generally quite strong in providing creative opportunities for children, although they do not always think of these as being esteem builders. Yet expressing ideas and feelings that come from within through the use of self-expressive materials can be a powerful source for enhancing self-esteem. Because creative activities are such esteem builders, it is particularly valuable to preserve the children's confidence that they are creative people so that this attitude and the resulting sense of personal worth can be retained in later life. What a pity it is that so many people, as they mature, come to feel apologetic and uncreative and close themselves off from one of the safest and potentially most rewarding avenues to self-satisfaction and self-esteem. Helping people re-

tain the freedom to be creative probably is best accomplished by teaching children that the most important aspect of creating something is to be satisfied with pleasing themselves rather than other people. We will learn more about how to do this in Chapter 13.

STRENGTHEN THE CHILD'S POSITIVE BODY IMAGE

The whole subject of body image as it relates to people's sense of self is a fascinating one, and, even as adults, some of us are still plagued with body images that adversely affect our behavior. For example, some of us still secretly picture ourselves as being the skinny or fat or poor-complexioned adolescent we were several years ago rather than the more attractive person we are now, and we continue to feel insecure because of this negative image.

Developing Body Awareness

The degree of awareness of the body and what it can do varies a good deal with different children. It is necessary with some Head Start youngsters, for instance, to begin by teaching them to point to their eyes and ears and hair before going on to the fun of identifying eyebrows, cheeks, and ankles. Children also enjoy naming things inside their bodies, such as bones and blood. (We even had one youngster who wanted to know where his gallbladder was.)

In addition to developing body awareness by learning the names of various parts, we also want children to appreciate what the body can do and to gain skill in its control. Movement education is probably the best way of accomplishing this. It makes a child aware of her body's position in space and its relation to other people and objects, as well as encouraging her to devise creative ways of moving around in that space. Moreover, physical prowess is much admired by other children and becomes even more important in elementary school, where proficiency in games is a basic key to popularity. Chapter 8, which deals with the development of physical competence, provides many suggestions for helping children gain confidence and competence in controlling physical movement.

Developing a Positive Body Image

Finally, the whole delicate matter of what children think of their bodies is an interesting one to consider. At such an early age, this is not often a conscious matter, although there is evidence that preschool children are already aware of the color of their and other people's skins. Nevertheless, even young children are affected by how attractive they feel they are and by the influence their physical appearance has on the way people respond to them.

I recall a little 3-year-old in one of my own groups—a sturdy, red-headed, freckle-faced boy with the build of a wrestler, but the personality of a retiring rabbit. I often saw fathers give him a playful poke as they passed by or jab his stomach or make playful sparring motions in his direction. Although initially dismayed, over a period of 2 years this youngster became increasingly aggressive—at least partially because of all these cues and expectations from men. His physique just seemed to elicit such responses.

Or how about the exquisite little girl with naturally curly hair, or the child whose nose is always runny, or the frail little boy with dark circles under his eyes? Nobody would dare poke him in the stomach, even though he might be yearning for this kind of masculine attention. I am not certain what teachers can actually do about these effects except try to see through the physical appearance of the youngster to the personality inside and encourage other people to do that, too.

It is not only physical characteristics that influence people's responses to children. Body postures influence responses and tell teachers a lot about how the child feels about herself (Szasz, 1978). The child who shrinks behind her mother's skirts on the first day reveals more of her

feelings than she possibly could with words. Often increased emotional and physical well-being is reflected in the easier, more open stance of children as the year progresses. Teachers respond continually to these physical signals, sometimes termed *body language*, just as children respond to theirs. Since these postures reveal so much about children (and adults), it would be wise for teachers to make a deliberate effort to take time to look closely at what the children's body language is telling them. They could learn much about how they feel about their world and about themselves if only they took time to notice.

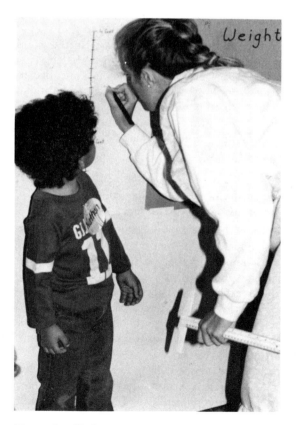

Measuring Nathan helps him develop a sense of self.

CULTIVATE POSITIVE FEELINGS IN CHILDREN ABOUT SEXUAL IDENTITIES AND ETHNIC AND RACIAL HERITAGES

The argument about how much of gender-linked (Tavris & Wade, 1984) and race-linked behavior (Hunt & Kirk, 1971; Jensen, 1969; Mercer, 1972; Yando, Seitz, & Zigler, 1979) is inherited and how much is the result of cultural influences continues, but few would dispute the value of reducing prejudice in both these areas and of widening opportunities for all people so that their true potential can be realized more completely. Suggestions concerning nonsexist and multicultural education are woven throughout this book (for example, bilingual education is discussed in Chapter 14), but they are such an important aspect of helping children gain a sense of who they are and of their place in the world that they warrant special discussion here. Many principles of presenting curriculum intended to widen horizons and reduce negative attitudes apply to both nonsexist and multicultural education. The curriculum suggestions in Table 12–1 are intended to draw some of these parallels to your attention.

Be on the Lookout for Opportunities to Confront Bias of All Sorts

Although this chapter confines itself to discussing nonsexist and multicultural education, we must remember that many other kinds of prejudice also exist. Some people are prejudiced against old people (witness the dearth of elderly people on television), while others assume that people with handicaps are helpless, or that early childhood teachers are "just babysitters."

Pacific Oaks, a college in Pasadena, California, has been a leader in advocating that even children as young as 2 and 3 years old should be presented with an anti-bias curriculum that actively takes a stand against all these forms of prejudice (Derman-Sparks, 1987; Derman-Sparks & the A. B. C. Task Force, 1989).[1]

To make this both real and relevant the anti-bias curriculum links such teaching to the children's lives, and approaches the subject three different ways. To begin with, children are encouraged to explore physical differences and similarities. For example, Derman-Sparks (1987) suggests that 3-year-olds might be encouraged to note the differences in skin colors among children in their group, matching those colors with paint or crayons; hear and talk over a related story such as *Colors Around Me* (Church, 1971); take color photos of children and staff; and make a poster of the differing colors of their skins.

As opportunities arise, other situations that have a potential for confronting bias can be included. Children can try out a child's crutches, for example, and then list all the things they do that do not depend on running around.

The second approach advocated in the anti-bias curriculum is to explore cultural variations and integrate material into the curriculum based on the cultural backgrounds of the children in the group. This might include cooking favorite family foods, sharing accounts of trips back to Mexico to visit relatives, or comparing hair styles. Books that reflect stereotyped ethnic or sex roles can be read and then discussed—the teacher may ask children if it is true that only men can be police officers or only women can take care of children.

Finally, the anti-bias curriculum of Pacific Oaks suggests that children learn to take direct action that challenges stereotypes and discriminatory behavior. For example, one group wrote a letter to a bandage manufacturer protesting the use of the term "flesh colored" to describe their product, and another group scrubbed offensive graffiti from a playground wall. Direct action of

---

[1]Please note that this description barely scratches the surface of the anti-bias curriculum. For further information refer to Derman-Sparks et al. (1989).

this kind empowers children and teaches them they can take an active role in protesting unfair or biased behavior.

Foster Positive Attitudes Toward Racial and Cultural Backgrounds

All too often it appears that teachers think of multicultural education only in terms of using integrated pictures in their rooms or making certain that the books they are reading to the children are not racially biased or that tortilla making is included as a multicultural experience. No one denies that this approach has value, and some suggestions for incorporating such ideas into the curriculum are included in Table 12–1.

What is disturbing is that some teachers fail to understand that the real purpose of offering multicultural materials should be *to foster positive attitudes in children about their own and others' racial and cultural backgrounds.* The purpose then of inviting a Mexican mother to help the children make tortillas is not just to teach them that tortillas are made of a special kind of cornmeal called *masa harina* or that Mexican people eat tortillas and that tortillas taste good. The purpose is to provide a real, involving experience that is so much fun for the children that they attach pleasant feelings to being Mexican and eating Mexican food. *In other words, making tortillas is merely the medium through which the message of positive respect for someone's culture is conveyed.*

Attitudes Are Caught, Not Taught. Since it is attitudes that matter most and children can sense teachers' feelings so keenly, teachers must search their own hearts and monitor their behavior to make certain that they are controlling the expression of their prejudices as much as possible. Of course, everyone prefers to believe they do not possess any prejudices, but it is more probable than not that we all do possess feelings of prejudice in some area (Leacock, 1982; Minuchin & Shapiro, 1983). For example, studies reveal that teachers pay less attention to

Mexican-American high school students than they do to Anglo ones (U. S. Commission on Civil Rights, 1973), and the effects of segregation on the self-esteem of Blacks is extensively documented (St. John, 1975).

Although it may not be possible to overcome deep-seated feelings of prejudice entirely, it is still valuable to know they exist inside oneself. Once bias is recognized and "owned," it can also be controlled. Every time a prejudiced remark is suppressed, a tiny blow for fairness has been struck.

For those who wish to go further and weed such uncomfortable feelings from their hearts, one fairly effective way of overcoming prejudice is to learn more about people of other groups by taking courses on their culture and by getting to know them personally. Attempting to learn their language reduces the feeling of distance. Some encounter groups also work toward the goal of increasing racial understanding.

Help Children Understand that All People Are Similar in Some Ways and Different in Others

Help Children Learn that Everyone Has Some Things in Common. Young children need to learn that people of every ethnic background have some human needs and characteristics in common: everyone needs shelter and rest and food, everyone's knees hurt when they get skinned, everyone bleeds when cut, and everyone's blood is the same color. Children can begin to gain an appreciation of these truths from such simple activities as leafing through a scrapbook of pictures showing children of various cultures all sleeping, but sleeping in all sorts of beds, ranging from hammocks to trundle beds.

Be aware that, although matters have improved somewhat in regard to multiethnic materials, many manufacturers still seem to interpret multiethnic to mean Black, and it remains nearly impossible, for example, to find educational materials that picture people with accurate His-

TABLE 12–1
Creating equal learning opportunities

Nonsexist possibilities	Multicultural possibilities
Human relations	

Human relations

Employ teachers of both sexes who participate equally in the majority of activities, that is, the male teachers don't always supervise carpentry and female teachers don't always present cooking. Everyone pitches in to teach everything, clean up, take children to the toilet, and so forth.

Know the preschool families well, and be on the lookout for members who have transcended the gender barrier in various occupations (women police officers, male nurses) and ask them to visit and acquaint children with what they do.

Be sensitive to men who have custody of their children. Offer assistence when they want it, but don't treat them as curiosities or objects of pity or condescension.

Arrange realistic visiting times at school when parents who work outside the home and siblings are free to attend—a Saturday morning play session, for example.

Encourage children of both sexes to have access to the full range of their feelings (see Chapter 10).

Visitors and field trips: It's worth mentioning once again that a point should be made of providing contacts with members of both sexes participating in a variety of occupations.

Many children have no idea what their parents do when they go to the office. Take a few youngsters to visit so they can find out what both mothers and fathers do who work outside the home.

Employ *teachers* from a variety of ethnic backgrounds. Make certain minority people are not relegated to only aide positions, but are placed in positions of authority also. Children are shrewd assessors of such power rankings.

Know the preschool families well. Encourage them to share interesting customs and traditions with the children at school as they do with their children at home. This might have to do with favorite ethnic foods, holidays, trips, and so on.

Make certain that all families are genuinely welcome. Help people meet each other, pick up each other for pot lucks, and plan together for workshops.

Remember that older family members are viewed somewhat as a culture apart in our society by some people. Make a point of including them and valuing their ideas and services.

Visitors and field trips: Be on the lookout for people from many ethnic groups in a variety of occupations—particularly occupations thought of as professional or skilled ones. Be casual about this, but make sure children have a chance to become acquainted with such people.

Take a small group and visit the homes of different families from time to time. This can emphasize both the things families have in common and special attributes, too.

Take the children to interesting places with a special ethnic flavor—the Greek delicatessen, the Chinese market, the Japanese kite shop.

Room climate and environment

Use pictures that show both boys and girls doing active things—beware of sweet little toilet paper type ads showing girls with kittens. Include pictures of boys in caring roles and pictures showing boys expressing feelings. Include pictures of fathers with children, mothers working outside the home, and so forth.

Use pictures that include children of all ethnic groups doing things the children in your school also do. (Incidentally, NAEYC offers a nice selection of multi-ethnic posters for sale using illustrations from *Young Children* covers.) Collect and use pictures of children in integrated groups doing things together.

TABLE 12–1 (*continued*)

Nonsexist possibilities	Multicultural possibilities
Follow policy of "open toileting" (boys and girls using same bathroom together) to reduce clandestine sexual interests.	Accumulate series of pictures showing how people of various cultures meet a universal need in a variety of ways—children taking baths in different ways, for example, or families eating together.
	Make certain pictures of older people in active roles are included. Beware of using only the grandparent stereotype.
	Whenever possible, use furnishings and equipment at the school that come from a variety of countries—perhaps a Mexican child's chair in housekeeping or a bedspread from India with deer and elephants on it. Speak of these appreciatively to the children.
Manipulative materials, such as lotto games, puzzles, and block accessories, should be scrutinized to make certain they include men and women in a wide range of occupations: Make certain an equal number of boys and girls are pictured.	Manipulative materials, such as puzzles and block accessories, should include people from differing ethnic groups.
Offer boy and girl dolls and boy and girl dress up clothes, and encourage both sexes to use all the equipment.	Dolls of various ethnic groups should be consistently available. Take a good look at these—are they true to ethnic type or just white dolls with different colored paint on their faces? Many manufacturers are guilty of this sort of racial insult.
	Include clothing typical of various cultures. Point out which culture they represent. Children's clothes are particularly appropriate.
Activities	
In general, encourage children of both sexes to try everything—involve girls in science and boys in washing up, for example. Encourage both sexes to engage in vigorous outdoor play, self-expressive activities, and blocks.	If the school operates on a bilingual base, consider alternating days of each language rather than only translating back and forth.
Occasionally keep a checklist to see if one area of the school is used more consistently by one sex than the other. Analyze why this is true, and attempt to correct it.	Foster children doing things together. When opportunities present themselves, pair ethnically different children together. Encourage intergroup mixing—sometimes, particularly when two languages are in use, children speaking the same language group together. Although this tendency is understandable, it is desirable to encourage children of all backgrounds to communicate as best they can while playing together. They manage surprisingly well.
Story time: Examine books with care. Train yourself to spot books that present boys as heroes and girls as passive admirers. Check bibliographies listed in References for suggestions of nonsexist books available for purchase. Check Ap-	Story time: Examine books carefully for racial ster-

TABLE 12–1 *(continued)*

Nonsexist possibilities	Multicultural possibilities
pendix E for guidelines on assessing books for sexist content. Music and dance: It may be necessary to call *dance* something else if boys have already learned to be wary of that "girl stuff." Widen the kind of material presented in dance so that it appeals to both sexes (see Chapter 8). Make certain to use male and female singers, ranging from Pete Seeger to Marlo Thomas. Also listen to what the lyrics are saying. Some of them are surprisingly sexist. Cooking: Although books on nonsexist education keep stressing that boys should participate in cooking, I've never seen a school in which this kind of participation was a problem. If it *is* a problem, boys should be deliberately drawn to participate. Blocks and other three-dimensional construction activities: For reasons described later in the section entitled "Foster Positive Attitudes Toward Gender Roles," it is particularly valuable to encourage girls to use blocks more frequently than they may have done in the past.	eotypes and overly quaint presentations of unfamiliar cultures, and also make certain that a balanced collection of books is purchased representing as many different kinds of children and adults as possible. Include ethnic folk tales. Check bibliographies in References for suggestions of resources and also check Appendix E for assessment guidelines. Offer an occasional folk dance, keeping it simple and bearing in mind it takes considerable repetition for the children to learn it. Beware of perpetuating such stereotypes of ethnic dancing as putting feathers in the children's hair and dancing around doing war whoops. Don't shun the music used in the children's homes. Popular music is very much a part of many families' culture. There are many excellent folk music records available from all sorts of cultures and suitable to use with young children. Ella Jenkins, for instance, has made a rich contribution to this area. Some resources for these are included in the References. Cooking: This is a wonderful way to learn to value other cultures as we discussed in Chapter 7. Make certain ethnic food is not presented as peculiar or unappetizing. Remember cooking can include going to speciality markets, cooking with culturally correct utensils, and eating in culturally appropriate style, such as using china spoons to eat egg noodle soup.

panic, Japanese, or Native American features. Even many of the "Black" materials are just White faces painted a different color (Wilson, 1981). Multiethnic books also require careful evaluation and selection.

Learning will be even more meaningful if the preschool group is a racially integrated one, since opportunities to teach about common needs and likenesses abound when children are together.

Teach That Different Cultures Are Unique. Sometimes teachers who feel quite comfortable when teaching about similarities are confused about whether to teach children that people are not completely alike. They seem to fear that mentioning cultural diversity, sometimes termed *teaching cultural pluralism*, encourages the formation of prejudice or that it somehow "isn't nice" to talk about such things. Perhaps these teachers hope that if they avoid mentioning differences, the children will not notice them—but this is not true.

Considerable research reports that children as young as age 3 are aware of the skin color of Blacks and Mexican-Americans (Derman-Sparks, Higa, & Sparks, 1980; Katz, P. A., 1982). Beuf (1977) states that this is also true for preschool Native American youngsters of the Southwestern and Plains tribes. Moreover, as children become older, awareness of ethnic group differences increases (Hess, 1970).

Since it is evident then that children *do* become aware of racial differences between people during their preschool years, it is only reasonable to conclude that teachers should be prepared to deal with questions about such differences in a positive way so that children learn to view diversity as a valuable part of being human.

Here is an example of how one teacher helped a youngster appreciate this truth as it relates to ethnic diversity[2]:

You're Black All Over?
My Lab Experiences With Isabella

Reba Gordon

My experience in the lab was an interesting and a memorable one. I was brought very close to a 5-year-old girl named Isabella. From our relationship, the impression I received is that she had never been in any contact with Blacks at all in her life.

My first contact with her was in the locker room. Isabella and Lynn were fingerpainting, and they had put it all over their faces. Afterwards I helped them wash up. Isabella then said, "You're a Black, you have Black hands."

I replied, "Yes," and that was the end of it. She didn't make any further comments for a while.

One day I sat down at the puzzle table with her and watched her complete a puzzle. She asked, "Were you born Black?"

"Yes, and my mother and father are Black, too."

She seemed shocked that I had parents, "You have a mother and father?"

"Yes, I also have a son, too, Isabella."

"Is your baby Black, too?"

"Yes."

Another day I wore my wig, and she was the only child that really noticed my hair was different.

"Why is your hair curly?"

"I'm wearing a different hairstyle today."

A week later I wore a semi-Afro hairstyle, and she said,

"Why did you wear your hair like that?"

"I like it this way."

"I don't like it."

Every week or so I would change my hairstyle, and every single time she always noticed the change. She might say, "Your hair looks different," or "How come you changed your hair?"

During all this time I had been telling Mrs. Warner about this situation, and she later had a conference with Isabella's parents on their daughter's new discovery. After the talk Mrs. Warner informed me that Isabella's mother had bought her a Black doll and said she was going to buy some books with Black people in them.

A few weeks later, Isabella and some other girls were in the locker room switching clothes, and I had come out of the bathroom buttoning up my pants. My blouse was up enough that she could see my stomach. Isabella went on to say,

"You have on nylons."

"No, I don't. See, I'm wearing knee socks," as I pulled up my pants leg so she could see. All the other girls just sat and listened.

"Oh, you're Black all over!"

"Yes, I am." I was totally shocked by her statement. I took it for granted that she knew I was Black all over. From here on in it was definite to me that she knew absolutely nothing about Blacks. She did not seem to correlate the Black doll to human Black people, which means children need concrete evidence at times.

When we left the locker room, she asked me to help her zip up the jump suit she was wearing. She watched me intensely as I zipped it up. Out of the blue she said, "Some are Black, huh?"

---

[2]The child's name has been changed to protect her privacy. My thanks to the author, Reba Gordon, and to Helen Ross and Mary Warner of San Diego State University for sharing this material from their classes with me.

I didn't want to put any ideas in her head so I asked, "Some of what are Black?"

"Some skins are Black."

"Yes, they are, and some are White."

This statement showed me that Isabella's parents had been talking to her about Black people at home.

Many times when the class was outside on the playground, she would run past me and hit me on the arm and say, "Hi, Black."

And I would reply, "Hi, White." This did not affect her one bit.

Toward the end of the semester the class was being split up into four reading groups, and the children were assigned to different teachers every day. While they were assigning them she yelled out, "I wanta go with the Black."

During this same week my neighbor had cornrowed my son's and my hair. I came to school the next day and many of the children made many comments.

"Why did you wear your hair like that?"

"What happened to your hair?"

"I don't like it that way."

"How did it get like that?"

And Isabella, to my surprise, said in a cool and calm way, "That's how Blacks wear their hair, huh?"

"Sometimes," I answered.

The next day I brought my son to the lab, and again the children noticed his hair was just like mine. Mrs. Warner asked Isabella if she had seen my son.

She replied, "Oh yeah, the Black down there." She didn't really come around him much, but came over to the block area and said,

"Your baby is Black, too," and left.

One more thing she said that I almost forgot was on a day I was head teacher and I was pinning on children's name tags. She hung around the table for a long while talking to me, at the same time keeping her face real close to my face whenever she got the chance. With a puzzled look on her face, she stuck out her lips and without sticking them back in their normal position she asked me, "Why do your lips stick out like this?"

Not really knowing how to answer her question, I said, "That is the way some Black people's lips are made."

Thinking about what she had asked me, I asked her why did her lips stick in. She answered, she didn't know why. She hung around a little bit more, examining my face, and then left to get involved in an activity.

At a picnic I wore my wig again and she ran past me and said,

"You got curly hair," and kept on running past.

One thing that sticks in my mind about the whole thing is that there was not any trace of viciousness in any of Isabella's comments. She never felt I was inferior compared to herself, which I felt was excellent, because many times I have come in contact with many White children, outside the lab, that are either frightened to death of Blacks or have some negative comments to make, which they probably picked up from their family or the street. I honestly believe she was very fond of me, and I too was very fond of her.

Isabella's mother talked to me one day and expressed she was embarrassed about the whole situation. I told her not to be, for Isabella had never tried to hurt my feelings. She went on to tell me that she had never been in contact with Blacks until she was in college, at the age of 20. She later went to teach at an all Black elementary school.

"I was so amazed by these Black children that I went around patting all their heads. And they are so rhythmic. But all in all I feel that you have been a great help to our daughter."

When she said that the children were "so rhythmic," I thought I would die. She sounded so typical of this day and age.

Since this situation has happened here and I know it has happened elsewhere, I hope it will help the present educator and future educators to see the importance of having multiethnic teachers and multiethnic education, for these types of children need to be exposed to people and cultures outside their own, along with this preschool experience. It is sad to see these same children go into adulthood and get jobs where they have to deal with society on the whole and not have any insight into any other race of people than themselves. I cannot see how they can represent all the people when they know nothing of all the people.

In conclusion, it was a good experience for me and I hope it was for Isabella also. I wish her all the luck in her future experiences and hope she keeps her beautiful curiosity and accepts all the new information as openly as she received my differences.

As this example demonstrates so clearly, the closer to home we can bring cultural diversity and richness to the actual lives of the children in our schools, the better will be our chances of substituting understanding and appreciation in place of prejudice. We do this in part by teaching each child that her own family and culture are worthwhile and in part by helping her enjoy the contributions of other families and cultures.

For instance, it can be interesting during holidays such as Thanksgiving to talk about the different ways families celebrate them. Do they have friends in or go to their grandparents? Do they have mince or pumpkin pie? Is there a special way their family celebrates birthdays? How do some Indian families feel about celebrating this day? Are there special holidays, such as Hannukah or Ramadan, that the family observes and would be willing to tell the other children about? Might some of the children be invited to a home for a Japanese bath, or might a Hopi youngster be encouraged to bring some of her Kachina dolls and tell the children about the characters they represent? Perhaps grandparents would come and tell stories to the children about what it was like when they were little ("You mean you didn't never even have television?"). All these kinds of opportunities have the potential for convincing a child that her own cultural background is interesting and admirable, and they also help the other children see her as being special and having special things to share with the group.

Use Comparison to Demonstrate the Positive Aspects of Cultural Pluralism. At the institute we have added comparison activities to such cultural sharings. These activities are intended to show the children that there is more than one way of reaching a common goal and that both ways are equally satisfactory. They always provide opportunities for real involvement and for positive comparisons to be made, too.

Some of the comparisons concocted by our student teachers have been quite simple; others have been elaborate, but all have been designed to encourage young children to compare their culture with another culture, see the advantages of each, and enjoy them both. These activities have included comparing[3]:

1. Black hair care with Anglo hair care
2. Cooking methods and eating styles of the West with those of Japan
3. Children's undergarments from the West with those from China
4. The open market of Jamaica with the supermarket of the United States
5. White bread (made into "French" toast) with Indian fry bread

The children loved participating in these experiences, and the adults have benefited, too. This is because our own horizons have widened as we have learned about the customs of other groups so that we could present them in an authentic way to the children.

Foster Positive Attitudes Toward Gender Roles

We all know there are physiological differences between the sexes that make each sex unique, and it is necessary to help children understand genital characteristics and cherish their inherent sexuality, as discussed in Chapter 9. The ability to feel good about his or her sexual role as it relates to procreation and childbearing should be a fundamental element in every child's sense of self.

Nonsexist Education. In addition to valuing the sexual aspects of the self, teachers should attempt to widen the horizon of both boys and girls so that they are no longer constrained and limited in their ideas about what activities are appropriate for children of either sex. This is what nonsexist education is all about. It teaches that people have many abilities, as well as needs, in common, no matter what their sex. Girls and women are encouraged to do things formerly

---

[3]Ideas kindness of the 1983 Fundamentals of Instruction Class, Institute of Child Development, University of Oklahoma.

the sole prerogative of boys and men, and vice versa.

At its best, nonsexist education opens new avenues for both boys and girls and helps them be complete, whole people. For example, girls are encouraged to see themselves as possessing a variety of potentials in addition to being wives and mothers, and boys are urged to remain sensitive to their caring and emotionally expressive side, a side that, in the past, our culture has frequently taught them to repress. As Honig (1983) says, "Caregivers need to celebrate competence in both males and females in *whatever* form competence appears" (p. 68).

What Can the Children's Center Do to Foster the Full Potential of Girls and Boys? Many sexist attitudes are conveyed to children by their

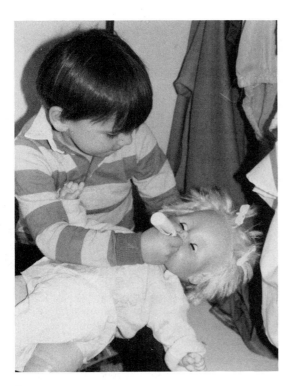

Boys should be encouraged to remain sensitive to their caring, nurturing side.

environments, as well as by other people's attitudes and behavior, and children's centers can make a positive contribution by being aware of this (Weinraub & Brown, 1983). Although our schools are generally quite open to both sexes in offering such activities as outdoor play or sewing, there is still a long way to go in building sensitivity to the content of books, which continue to show a preponderance of boys as heroes taking an active role in stories and girls taking more passive ones (Saario, Jacklin, & Tittle, 1973; Vukelich, McCarty, & Nanis, 1976; Yu, 1976).

Inspection of many equipment catalogs also supports the claim that the majority of toys and teaching materials related to occupations continue to be sexist. For example, those stand-up cut-out models of people frequently used in the block corner teach all too well the lesson that girls are nurses, teachers, and mothers and that boys are doctors, police officers, and motorcycle riders.

Moreover, teachers (often unintentionally) foster such attitudes, too. For many years I have observed the apprehension with which some of my young women students approach the carpentry table. Although it is true that such an activity requires careful supervision, there is little reason for it to arouse the degree of concern and even distaste I have seen reflected on their faces. They often protest that the children will hurt themselves with the saws or hammers, but I believe the real reason for their concern is that they know very little about the use of woodworking tools. In short, they are the victims of their previous sexist education. Instruction about the use of tools combined with a firm model of positive attitudes by the head teachers has helped overcome this concern, but it has also been necessary time and again to entice the adult students, as well as the girls and boys, to use carpentry materials. Otherwise, they may help perpetuate this particular kind of instrumental incompetence in the next generation. (Chapter 13 provides information on effective ways to present carpentry to all the children in the group.)

Suggestions From Research That May Enhance Nonsexist Teaching. Research also provides suggestions for ways teachers can reduce sexist practices in addition to simply encouraging cross-gender activities. A study by Honig and Wittmer (1982) documents that toddler boys more frequently used negative ways to elicit responses from teachers than the girls did. The caregivers, in turn, responded to this behavior from boys proportionately more often. Thus the boys' less desirable behavior was reinforced by the caregivers' attention in such circumstances — and so perpetuated itself. There is much value in recommending that caregivers make more of a point of responding to the positive behavior of little boys if they wish to increase this instead.

Another study reveals that parents of both sexes interrupt little girls when they are speaking more frequently than they interrupt their boys (Grief, 1983). When this happens, it seems probable that the message to little girls is that what they have to say matters less than what boys have to say. Could this behavior hold true for teachers, also? Do we interrupt girls more frequently? We may not know for certain, but if we want girls to feel their ideas have equivalent value, it is surely something we should be aware of as we talk with children.

Still another study (Serbin, O'Leary, Kent, & Toncik, 1973) reveals that preschool teachers tend to provide boys with more help when they ask for it and also to give them more information than they do the little girls in the group. Again, this tendency requires monitoring of behavior to make certain that teachers are explaining things as carefully to girls as boys and offering them just as much encouragement in solving problems when they request it.

Finally, a series of studies by Serbin (1980) indicates that there are some three-dimensional materials, such as blocks, that are generally preferred by boys. It is believed that using these materials contributes to the ability to solve the kinds of cognitive problems that require spatial visualization. (Visual-spatial ability is the ability to picture in the mind's eye how to rotate an object or mentally transform its shape. Remem-

ber those items on intelligence tests that ask you to predict how many blocks there are in an irregular stack or whether a hand seen from an unusual angle is the right or left one?) As Serbin points out, these visual-spatial skills are the ones most needed by people who become pilots, engineers, physicists, and architects—all fields in which few women currently excel. The question is, if girls used these materials more often, would their visual-spatial skills increase? And would new fields of endeavor be open to women as a result? Although we do not know the answers to these questions, we can reasonably assume that it would be worthwhile to encourage girls to play with blocks more often. Perhaps this early experience would help equalize their chances; certainly it could do no harm.

HELPING CHILDREN LEARN ABOUT THEIR PLACE IN THE WORLD BY MEETING OTHER PEOPLE

Besides learning about their place in the world in relation to developing self-esteem, in relation to their cultural and ethnic background, and in relation to their gender role, children also learn about the world around them and their potential place in it by meeting people and finding out what they do. In children's centers this can be accomplished by having visitors come in and by going on field trips. If these experiences are presented well, children can really benefit; if done poorly, both children and grown-ups can have a miserable time.

In both learning situations it is important to remember to plan events so the children are as involved as possible and so they are not overwhelmed by adults talking too long and telling them things that do not interest them. I will never forget the firefighter who insisted on telling us the gallons per minute his truck could pump, the diameter of the nozzles, and the length of the fire hoses, when we could have been trying on coats and helmets, sitting in the engine's seat, and watching the light go around. For such visits to be meaningful for the children, teachers must remember that many adults do not have the slightest idea about how to teach little children and that *they need to be coached beforehand to make the experience interesting for everyone.*

Having Visitors at School

Parents are wonderful resources for helping children learn about the world, so be on the lookout for ones who have skills or jobs that would appeal to the children. Some schools even inquire about these on their enrollment forms. Skills do not have to be extraordinary. The parent who has a camper and will let the children go through it or have a snack there or who will take time to let the children inspect a motorcycle adds real interest for the children and confers a certain glory on his or her own child,

too. Some parents can play guitars, others may be able to demonstrate a potter's wheel, or they know of someone who plays the flute. One of the mothers at our center was majoring in cosmetology and offered free haircuts occasionally. The children were enchanted—they loved watching, as well as having their own turn. Brothers and sisters can sometimes make special contributions, too. We recently had a 12-year-old bring in a garter snake and demonstrate what it could do.

Visitors offer a splendid way of widening children's occupational horizons—particularly if the teacher searches out women engaged in traditionally male vocations, such as telephone lines "man" or physician. Visitors also provide good opportunities for cross-age grouping experiences. Families are so mobile these days that

The firefighter is explaining to Todd that he shouldn't be frightened if there's a fire and he sees someone wearing a mask like this—he's just come to help him.

children are often deprived of contact with more mature adults, and some older people enjoy coming and reading to the children or sharing themselves in other ways in accordance with their talents and interests. Babies are also welcomed by children, who find their visits fascinating.

Still another value to having certain kinds of visitors come is that the experience helps children deal with their fears and apprehensions. Such people as police officers and ambulance attendants are often best seen at school rather than on a field trip, because the children are more secure on their home ground.

There are a few things the teacher should go over with the visitor in advance. Explain that the children are very young and cannot be expected to sit still for lengthy explanations, and suggest that the visitor give only a *short* talk or simply come in and sit down and let the children gather around in small groups as their interest moves them. Ask them to bring something interesting for the children to look at or try out. The doctor, for example, might bring her stethoscope and "ear light." The police officer might let the children look over his police car (children are half appreciative and half dismayed by the siren) and be prepared to answer questions about where he has left his gun and what he does with it. The ambulance attendants might give the children rides on their stretcher.

Taking Field Trips

There are many places young children can go on field trips, but the best have some qualities in common that are worth mentioning. These desirable destinations for field trips provide children with the opportunities to move around fairly freely, to make some noise, and to participate in an activity rather than just observe something. Most excursions cannot meet all three of these criteria, but a few that do include wading in a brook, going to the park, beach, or lake, visiting a farm to help milk a cow or goat, and walking to the market to buy ingredients for a recipe.

Although it is beneficial for children in all schools to go on such trips, it is particularly important that full-day centers provide such excursions regularly. It is not natural or good for children to stay cooped up in one building and yard 5 days a week, 10 hours a day. They must be taken places and have contact with many experiences and people. If staffing is short, every effort should be made to find volunteers who can come along and assist the teachers. Weekends at home with parents often cannot provide enough richness and variety for day-care youngsters, unless the school helps, too.

Some examples of trips our center children have enjoyed include:

- Walking to the library for a story hour
- Going to the Greek delicatessen to buy pickles
- Going to the pumpkin patch to get pumpkins before Halloween
- Taking a school pet to the veterinarian
- Collecting wood (with permission) at a nearby construction site
- Going to the nursery to buy little plants for Mother's Day
- Riding all the trikes around the block
- Attending a Cinco de Mayo celebration
- Visiting the cobbler's shop to see how shoes get fixed and buying polish to use on their own shoes back at school
- Visiting the teacher's house and having a snack there
- Visiting the college biology lab to see the skeleton
- Going to the post office to mail their valentines and visiting one of the parents who works there
- Walking to the office to pick up the mail
- Visiting the kindergarten they will attend in the fall
- Going to the wading pool in a nearby park
- Visiting a father at his pizza restaurant and making pizzas

Conducting a successful field trip requires careful planning. There are many matter-of-fact things to remember about this:

1. Keep excursion groups small but go frequently. Children have a better time in a small group, participate more, and are easier to control.
2. Notify parents in advance and obtain permission slips if necessary.

3. Leave a list at school of everyone who has gone on the trip.

4. *Visit first yourself* and, if necessary, obtain permission, check on appropriate times for the visit (find out, for example, when the park is sprinkled), and coach the adults about what will be expected of them.

5. Take two adults along if possible.

6. If going by car:
   a. Make certain the driver has adequate insurance.
   b. Talk rules over first. *Insist* that children remain seated and use seat belts at all times.
   c. If there is any misbehavior, pull over to the side and wait. If it continues, do not hesitate to return to school. This ensures better cooperation next time.

7. Whether you are going by car or not, it is only fair to tell the children how they will be expected to behave before starting out. Perhaps they will have to sit in the waiting room at the vet's for a little while, or say "thank you" to the butcher who takes them through his icebox. Telling them in advance helps avoid embarrassing them by having to correct or prompt them in public.

8. Encourage children to use the toilet before departure.

9. Keep a record to make sure that certain tractable children are not going on many trips while other less cooperative ones are always staying at school.

10. Stick carefully to your promised time of return. Tired parents hate standing around waiting for children at the end of the day.

11. Be prepared to take advantage of unanticipated, fortuitous happenings as they turn up. Seeing a fire fighter test a hydrant may be of much more interest to the children than what you originally had in mind to do.

12. Remember that field trips need not be elaborate—repeated trips to the house that is being built next door and taking a look under the street when the manhole cover is removed are both fascinating experiences for preschoolers.

13. *Always remember to send a thank-you note afterward.* This is excellent public relations, and the recipients enjoy them so much—especially if they include a few choice comments made by the children. It helps the children learn good social manners, too, if they dictate what the teacher should say.

Field trips widen children's horizons but also require careful advance arrangements to be successful.

When the trip is over, use it as a base for continued learning. It is good practice for children to recall what they did, and talking it over will provide them with new vocabulary to describe the experience and exercise their memory, too. They will do some evaluating if asked what they liked best or what they disliked or if anything scared them. Some trips lend themselves well to dramatic play afterward, also, and this can be encouraged if the teacher has a few props available and encourages the children to develop others on a spontaneous basis as they are needed.

If possible, it is a fine idea to take pictures during the trip. These can be used in many ways to remind the children of what happened. For example, some teachers bind these into storytelling books or use them as flannel board stories. They can also be turned into a temporal ordering game that encourages users to arrange events in the order in which they occurred.

The following account written by a Head Start staff member is a good example of a successful trip that incorporates many of the recommendations listed above. As you read it, try to identify all the positive social things the children were learning.

A Day in the Carrot Fields

A lot of our kids' fathers work harvesting carrots up around here at this time of year, and we thought it would be good for them to see what their dads do. The kids don't always know this, because there is just one car in the family and he goes off to work in it lots of times before they get up. So we checked with the foreman, and he said we could come if we stayed away from the machine that does the digging.

We loaded the kids in the Head Start busses (borrowing one from the other school) and started out. The only trouble was we couldn't find the field right off and spent about half an hour driving around and looking, but we finally saw the harvester, and the kids all cheered.

Oh yes—I forgot to say we had talked about staying out of the way of the machine before we left—they were good about that—I think they were afraid of it. We walked down the rows and watched the men harvesting the carrots and the machine working, and two of the children saw their fathers. Along the way, Ramiro found a big caterpillar, which was nice after the way he's been so mean lately. We put it in the glove compartment so we could bring it back with us.

The soil was real rich and soft and sandy where the machine had dug, and it left a lot of carrots behind, just lying there—what a waste—so all the children could take as many as they liked. They filled their arms with as much as they wanted, and then we got back in the bus and so to school.

The carrots were real dirty, so we got out our laundry tubs and vegetable brushes and let the kids wash them off in there and ate carrots for a snack.

Mrs. Sanchez (the cook) served them on orange paper plates we had left from Halloween with cheese slices and oranges. Maybe it tasted funny together, but it got the idea of orange across all right.

It worked out well at group time too because one group read *The Carrot Seed* (Krauss & Johnson, 1971) and the other group listened to the record about it. Next week we'll look at the snapshots we took and think about it again. I'm going to make them do like you said, and tell me which picture comes first.

When it was time to go, each kid had a big bag of carrots to take home. They were real fresh, and the children loved having so much of something. Their mothers were pleased, too. All in all, I'd say it was a good trip. The only thing I'd change is, next time we won't drive around so long looking for that field!

SUMMARY

The children's sense of who they are and of their place in the world has important ramifications for building their sense of social competence. Children gain their basic sense of who they are by identifying with the people around them whom they admire and want to be like. As they enter child care outside the home, the models teachers provide may socialize children into different ways of coping with their worlds. Teachers can influence children's feeling of self-esteem, their ideas of what constitutes appropriate sex roles for themselves, and what it means to belong to a particular ethnic and cultural group.

Teachers as well as families can help children build inner sources of self-esteem by (1) providing them with skills so that they feel competent, (2) including opportunities for them to do meaningful work, (3) helping them do things for themselves, and (4) encouraging them to be creative. A positive body image also contributes to children's sense of identity and can be developed in various ways.

In teaching about sexual and ethnic identity, the most important learning for children to internalize is a positive attitude toward members of the opposite sex and toward their own sex and toward their own and other's racial and cultural backgrounds. In addition, children need to learn that people of both sexes and various ethnic and cultural backgrounds are both alike and different from each other. There are many ways to make this teaching both positive and real for pre-schoolers as the work done by Pacific Oaks College demonstrates.

Children also learn about their place in the world by coming in contact with interesting people, and these encounters should be a carefully planned part of the curriculum. When they are well done, visits and field trips become rich sources of pleasurable learning for the children and for the adults who participate.

SELF-CHECK QUESTIONS FOR REVIEW

Content-Related Questions

1. Briefly summarize three theories describing how identity is achieved.
2. Give an example of a way to increase self-esteem that comes from outside the child. Now list several other strategies teachers can use that will help generate self-esteem from within the child.
3. Cite an example illustrating how body image might affect an individual's sense of self.
4. What does the anti-bias curriculum developed by Pacific Oaks College advocate?
5. If the purpose of multicultural curriculum is not to teach facts about various cultures, what *is* the real purpose or intention?
6. In addition to teaching children that all people are similar in some ways, what is the second concept about people that should be taught?
7. What is the fundamental concept on which nonsexist education should be based?
8. Describe some of the research findings about ways teachers can reduce sexist practices in addition to encouraging cross-gender activities.
9. There is something important teachers should do before a visitor talks to the children to prepare that person for the encounter, whether this is at the center or on a field trip. What is it?
10. This chapter includes many suggestions of ways to help field trips be as successful as possible. Pretend

you are helping an inexperienced teacher plan for his first trip. What suggestions would you give him to smooth the children's way?

Integrative Questions

1. Consult Table 12–1 where many parallels are drawn between nonsexist and multicultural education. Select a number of parallels and identify the common bond that links each pair together.
2. Review Lubeck's research in *Sandbox Society*. What strengths are present in the curriculum presented at the Head Start center that are lacking in the middle-class white school? How might these deficiencies be remedied?
3. Explain why being able to wait patiently is one of the most important skills in teaching.
4. There are a Navaho child and a Hopi child in your center, as well as a number of Anglos, and you have invited the Indian mothers to come and make Navaho fry bread and Hopi blue cornbread with the children. Explain what you want the children and their families to gain from this learning opportunity.

QUESTIONS AND ACTIVITIES

1. Every family has standards by which they expect their members to abide. Are you aware of some of the ones in your own family? Think of some examples of things your family "never" does or "always" does and share them with the class. Some examples might be "Everyone in our family always goes to college," or "It just isn't a home to my mother without a cat in it," or "My dad makes the money, but my mother always pays the bills."
2. List several new skills you have seen children in your school learn this week that increased their feelings of competence.
3. Have your ideas changed in recent years about what constitutes appropriate ways for men and women to behave? Are there still some activities you think it is only all right for one sex to do, such as asking for a date?
4. *Problem:* You are now the director of a children's center, and a father comes to school somewhat concerned about your nonsexist approach to early childhood education. He is quite frankly worried,

as are many people, that letting his son dress up in skirts may encourage him to become a homosexual. How would you reply to this concern? Might he be right?

5. Do you think it was all right for the little red-headed boy described in this chapter to be "roughed up" by the men? What might be the pros and cons of letting this kind of treatment continue?

6. Some students view themselves as having no cultural or ethnic heritage. They just say they are American. To demonstrate that you are more sophisticated than this, develop a project to do with the children that is based on some aspect of your own family's cultural or ethnic background.

7. *Problem:* As the children are assembling for group time, one of the little girls says distastefully, "I don't want to sit by Angelina—her skin's dirty!" (Angelina is brown because she is Puerto Rican, not because she is dirty.) How would you handle this incident? Be sure to think of practical, immediate and long-term approaches.

8. What was the best field trip you every took children on? Share with the class what made it so successful and how you would ensure that it would be as worthwhile when you do it the next time.

9. What other age-appropriate activities besides those suggested in the material from Pacific Oaks can you think of that would enable children to take direct action against bias?

REFERENCES FOR FURTHER READING

Developing a Sense of Identity

Damon, W. (1983). *Social and personality development: Infancy through adolescence.* New York: W. W. Norton & Co. This is a good, solid, wide-ranging discussion of social development. It includes a balanced discussion of theories of identification.

Developing Self-Esteem

Beme, P. H., & Savary, L. M. (1985). *Building self-esteem in children.* New York: Continuum. This book is filled with sound, clearly written advice. Highly recommended.

Briggs, D. C. (1970). *Your child's self-esteem: The key to his life.* This "oldy but goody" is written primarily with parents in mind but is also helpful reading for teachers. Available in paperback.

Developing Race Awareness

Derman-Sparks, L., Higa, C. T., & Sparks, B. (1980). Children, race, and racism: How race awareness develops. *Interracial Books for Children Bulletin, 11*(3, 4), 3–9. This is a practical discussion, divided according to children's ages of how such awareness develops and what teachers can do to facilitate positive attitudes.

Katz, P. A. (1982). Development of children's racial awareness and intergroup attitudes. In L. G. Katz (Ed.), *Current topics in early childhood education* (Vol. 4). Norwood, N. J.: Ablex Publishing Corp. Katz traces the development of race awareness through eight stages. She presents evidence that verbal expression of racial differences begins around age 4, but that children do exhibit awareness of differences by age 3.

Overviews of Multicultural Education

Banks, J. A. (1988). *Multiethnic education: Theory and practice* (2nd ed.). Boston: Allyn & Bacon. Banks, a distinguished authority in this area, concludes this analysis of multicultural education by listing 23 guidelines curriculum should follow to be truly multiethnic.

Derman-Sparks, L., & the A.B.C. Task Force. (1989). *Anti-bias curriculum: Tools for empowering young children.* Washington, D. C.: National Association for the Education of Young Children. *Anti-Bias Curriculum* explains in practical terms how that approach can be integrated into the early childhood curriculum. Highly recommended.

Edwards, C. P., & Ramsey, P. G. (1986). *Promoting social and moral development in young children: Creative approaches for the classroom.* New York: Teachers College Press. The authors present interesting suggestions for activities that can be used to broaden young children's understanding of the social world, including knowledge of gender roles and multicultural awareness. Excellent bibliographies of children's books accompany each chapter. An unusual and refreshing book.

Neugebauer, B. (Ed.). (1987). *Alike and different: Exploring our humanity with young children.* Redmond, Wash.: Exchange Press. *Alike and Different* covers usual and unusual aspects of living with differentness. Topics range from the "foreign" children to giftedness and children with handicaps. Outstanding bibliography of children's books. Highly recommended for the beginning student.

Sources of Information on Ethnic and Cultural Characteristics

Hale, J. E. (1986). *Black children: Their roots, culture, and learning style* (2nd ed.). Baltimore: Johns Hopkins University Press. A gold mine of information about the similarities and differences that exist between middle-class White and Black cultures is included in the book. Highly recommended.

Powell, G. J. (Ed.). (1983). *The psychosocial development of minority group children.* New York: Brunner/Mazel. This book offers a wealth of information about many kinds of children and how to teach them effectively. Highly recommended.

Saracho, O. N. & Spodek, B. (Eds.). (1983). *Understanding the multicultural experience in early childhood education.* Washington, D. C.: National Association for the Education of Young Children. The authors provide cultural information about Native Americans, Asians, Hispanics, and Blacks. They discuss problems related to teaching, but deal with curriculum only in passing.

Texas Department of Human Services. (1985). *Culture and children.* Austin: The Department. This a first-rate resource. It includes an overview of cultural characteristics of many groups and then provides examples of concrete ways to include ethnic experiences from those cultures in early childhood classrooms.

Wardle, F. (1987). Are you sensitive to interracial children's identity needs? *Young Children, 42*(2), 53–59. Wardle provides a wealth of practical recommendations and resources on this rarely treated subject. Highly recommended.

Multicultural Activity Books

There is a real need and place for publications of this sort, but I reiterate that *providing the kinds of environmental embellishments and activities suggested by these books should constitute only the beginning of true multicultural education.*

Cole, A., Haas, C., Heller, E., & Weinberger, B. (1978). *Children are children are children: An activity approach to exploring Brazil, France, Iran, Japan, Nigeria, and the U.S.S.R.* Boston: Little, Brown & Co. Although the title largely explains the contents, it should be added that each section contains recipes, games, holidays, suggestions for activities (some of which could be done by preschoolers), general information on the country, a few common words, and a map.

McNeill, E., Schmidt, V., & Allen, J. (1981). *Cultural awareness for young children: Asian, Black, cowboy, Eskimo, Mexican, and Native American cultures.* Mt. Rainier, Md.: Gryphon House. *Cultural Awareness* is distinguished by a good list of books, magazines, and films. It divides the children's activities into family living, foods, creative activities, nature-science, language development, and special events.

Bibliographies

Please note bibliographies cited in previous references.

Jenkins, E. C., & Austin, M. C. (1987). *Literature for children about Asians and Asian Americans: Analysis and annotated bibliography with additional readings for adults.* Westport, Conn.: Greenwood Press. Title is self-explanatory.

Klein, B. (1985). *Reading into racism: Bias in children's literature and learning materials.* London: Routledge & Kegan Paul. A thoughtful book that documents the current situation, carefully considers such problems as censorship, and mentions other methods of dealing with racist literature.

Schon, I. (1988). Hispanic books. *Young Children, 43*(4), 81–85. This reference includes references for adults plus a list of books for young children written in Spanish.

Information on Sex and Gender Roles

Greenberg, S. (1985). Educational equity in early education environments. In S. S. Klein (Ed.), *Handbook for achieving sex equity through education.* Baltimore: Johns Hopkins University Press. Greenberg summarizes research that identifies ways early childhood teachers perpetuate sex-role differences and then proposes ways to change each teaching. Highly recommended.

Tavris, C., & Wade, C. (1984). *The longest war: Sex differences in perspective.* New York: Harcourt Brace Jovanovich. The authors present an easy-to-read discussion of research about sex-role differences.

Resource Books for Producing Nonsexist Curriculum

Jenkins. J. K., & Macdonald, P. (1979). *Growing up equal: Activities and resources for parents and teachers of young children.* Englewood Cliffs, N.J.: Prentice-Hall. This book suggests a number of activities that could encourage children to try out nonsexist activities. It also includes facts about sex-role development that are intended to shoot down old sexist myths of various sorts.

Northwest Regional Educational Laboratory Center for Sex Equity. (1983). *Guide to nonsexist teaching activities (K–12).* Phoenix: Oryx Press. This is a terrific reference that covers films, textbooks, literature by women, and bibliographies.

Pogrebin, L. C. (1980). *Growing up free: Raising your child in the '80s.* New York: McGraw-Hill Book Co. A lengthy, well-written guide useful for teachers and parents in search of ideas about how to implement nonsexist attitudes in their families and themselves. Not exactly an activity book.

Shapiro, J., Kramer, S., & Hunerberg, C. (1981). *Equal their chances: Children's activities for non-sexist learning.* Englewood Cliffs, N. J.: Prentice-Hall. Written with elementary school teachers in mind, *Equal Their Chances* takes the curriculum of the school topic by topic and provides numerous examples of how nonsexist information could and should be incorporated into those studies. Enough of the ideas could be translated to the preprimary level that the book is worth examining.

Sprung, B. (1975). *Non-sexist education for young children: A practical guide.* New York: Citation Press. This paperback contains a wealth of practical ideas for conducting a nonsexist nursery school or center using five curriculum topics as examples. It remains the best reference in the field.

Field Trips

Courson, D. (1988). Field trips: New avenues for learning. *Dimensions, 16*(2), 15–18. Courson offers many practical suggestions about managing field trips and includes suggestions of trips that are suitable for a variety of ages.

Redleaf, R. (1983). *Open the door: Let's explore: Neighborhood field trips for young children.* Toys 'n Things Press (Mt. Rainier, Md.: Gryphon House, distributor). This is a thorough, delightful book that discusses what to do before and after each trip and includes thought (speculation) questions for the children. It also offers relevant songs, poetry, and children's books for each trip. Highly recommended.

For the Advanced Student

Allport, G. W. (1979). *The nature of prejudice, 25th anniversary edition.* Reading, Mass.: Addison-Wesley Publishing Co. This is a classic in the field of race relations that provides a valuable foundation for understanding the nature of prejudice.

Beuf, A. H. (1977). *Red children in white America.* Philadelphia: University of Pennsylvania Press. I include this book particularly because it contains the first study done on racial attitudes with Native American children from the tribes of the Southwest and Plains.

Halpern, D. F. (1986). *Sex differences in cognitive abilities.* Hillsdale, N. J.: Lawrence Erlbaum Associates. Halpern presents a thorough research-based review of gender-related differences, including a thoughtful discussion of possible reasons for such differences.

Harter, S. (1983). Developmental perspectives on the self-system. In P. H. Mussen (Ed.), *Handbook of child psychology* (4th ed.). E. M. Hetherington (Ed.), Vol IV: *Socialization, personality, and social development.* New York: John Wiley & Sons. This is a comprehensive review of the development of the self, including factors affecting self-esteem.

Huston, A. C. (1983). Sex-typing. In P. H. Mussen (Ed.)., *Handbook for child psychology.* E. M. Hetherington (Ed.), Vol. IV: *Socialization, personality, and social development.* New York: John Wiley & Sons. Huston's article is a thorough, valuable summary of what is known about how sex typing takes place.

Kitano, H. L., & Daniels, R. (1988). *Asian Americans; Emerging minorities.* Englewood Cliffs, N. J.: Prentice-Hall. Here in one place at last is a concise book relating the history of each Asian group as it has immigrated to the United States. Does not discuss cultural characteristics.

Low, V. (1982). *The unimpressible race: A century of educational struggle by the Chinese in San Francisco.* San Francisco: East/West Publishing Co. This book provides an example of how institutional racism can limit the development of young children and a heartening example of how parents can overcome such racism.

Maccoby, E. E., & Jacklin, C. N. (1987). Gender segregation in childhood. In H. W. Reese (Ed.), *Advances in child development and behavior.* New York: Academic Press. A well-written summary of research documenting that even children as young as 3 and 4 prefer to play with children of the same sex the majority of the time.

Philips, S. U. (1983). *The invisible culture: Communication in classroom and community on the Warm Springs Indian reservation.* New York: Longman. Philips describes her findings on how the behavior of this Oregon tribe compared to that of their Anglo peers. A rare and interesting analysis of school behavior.

Journals and Newsletters of Interest

The Black Child Advocate. 1463 Rhode Island Ave., N. W., Washington, D. C. 20005. This is the quarterly newsletter of the National Black Child Development Institute. It focuses primarily on current legislation that could affect the lives of all children, but Black children in particular.

Interracial Books for Children Bulletin. Published by the Council on Interracial Books for Children, 1841 Broadway, New York, New York 10023. Each issue focuses on a particular topic, which might be multicultural children or rethinking U.S. history. It also contains film and book reviews that mince no words. An invaluable resource.

Multicultural Leader. Educational Materials and Services Center. 144 Railroad Avenue, Suite 107, Edmonds, Washington 98020. This is a new, quarterly publication of great promise that covers research, journal articles, and books.

Nurturing News: A Forum for Male Early Childhood Educators. 187 Caselli Avenue, San Francisco, California 94114. Title is self-explanatory.

13 Freeing Children to Be Creative

Have you ever

- Dried up completely on ideas for creative activities?
- Needed to save money on art materials but didn't know how?
- Wished you could explain more clearly why coloring books are not creative?

If you have, the material in this chapter will help you.

> *Of all the qualities we seek to nurture in children as they grow, use of the imagination must be one of the most important. Indeed, our imaginings grow more important with every passing year as our technology develops and becomes even more amazing. We must remember that every machine first has to be imagined by someone.*
>
> JOHN COE (1987)

Creativity, as practiced by young children, is a dynamic, changing, fluid experience that derives its greatest satisfaction from the process, not the product. It is, in the best sense of the word, a state of "becoming." It is also an intensely personal process, since the wellspring of creativity lies within the child. For this reason, it contains the potential for both self-enhancement and self-despair. Because its manifestations are easily withered by disapproval, adults must be particularly careful to nourish rather than discourage creative self-expression in children, lest their criticism or domination blight its growth.

WHAT IS CREATIVITY?

Definitions of creativity vary widely according to the aspect being defined (Davis, 1983). For our purposes, the one proposed by J. A. Smith (1966) is most useful because it does not include the process of critical evaluation that is more appropriate to apply when working with older children and adults. He defines creativity as being the process of "sinking down taps into our past experiences and putting these selected experiences together into new patterns, new ideas or new products" (p. 43).

In preschool children, this putting together of new ideas and products based on past experience is expressed primarily through the use of self-expressive materials, through imaginative pretend play, and through creative thought. This chapter focuses on the first two of these creative media. Creativity in thought is discussed in the section on the cognitive self.

IMPLICATIONS OF SPLIT BRAIN RESEARCH FOR THE CREATIVE SELF

Before proceeding to the "how tos" of creativity, let us take a minute to acquaint ourselves with an interesting, rather new concept having to do with "split brain" research. The idea that underlies this work is a helpful one to understand when discussing the intuitive, creative side of human personality.

In recent years a number of psychologists have been investigating the differing capabilities of the left and right hemispheres of the brain (Ornstein, 1977, 1978; Restak, 1988; Sperry, Gazzaniga, & Bogen, 1969). Through a variety of experiments, ranging from the study of subjects who have undergone various types of brain surgery to studies using electroencephalograms, these researchers have established that the left hemisphere (in right-handed people) controls what we might describe as the rational, verbal, analytical kinds of mental processes, and the right hemisphere controls the nonverbal, spatial, intuitive ones.

To grasp this differentiation of function, some people have found it helpful to think of the brain as being like Siamese twins, who must go everywhere together, and who experience an intense mutuality of existence (Edwards, 1978). One of these twins (the left hemisphere) can talk, and talks all the time, makes decisions, is easily bored, dislikes ambiguity, and relishes solving problems in a rational, sequential reasoning way. The other hemisphere (the right one) has only a limited capacity for communicating directly with the outside world through exclamations, grimaces, and gestures, but it possesses the tremendously valuable capability of perceiving things, not as a series of separate parts, but as entities—wholes. This hemisphere's mode of thinking is intuitive and insightful rather than rational, and it is this part of us that is most active when we are involved in nonverbal creative activities. As Ornstein (1978) puts it, "The ability to create something no human being has ever imagined can never be reduced to a place on a machine scored pencil-and-paper exam. Artistic and musical abilities cannot be reduced to what can be expressed in words" (p. 76). It appears likely that different people, as they mature, develop different styles of learning that use one or the other of these hemispheres to a greater degree.

Teachers may find this concept helpful when considering how to maintain children's freedom to be intuitive and creative. If they want to give the second half of that Siamese twin combination a chance, they do not want to restrict schooling and learning to only the verbal, sequential, left hemisphere activities that currently dominate curriculum for older children. Instead, if teachers want to preserve children's wholeness, they should make certain that they offer that often underrated second twin many opportunities to express itself and to use its powers. The self-expressive, nonverbal activities and imaginative play situations discussed in this chapter suggest many ways of accomplishing this.

SOME GENERAL PRINCIPLES FOR FOSTERING CREATIVITY

There are some quite specific approaches that apply to the presentation of particular kinds of self-expressive materials, but there are also some more general principles that apply to all of them. These will be discussed first.

Create a Climate That Encourages Children to Feel Creative

A climate that encourages creativity is composed of a number of things; keeping anxiety low is certainly basic to it. When children feel they are living in a predictable environment where they know what is expected of them and the teacher is a reasonable person, they feel secure and so have more energy to devote to the pleasures of creativity.

Added to this is the general attitude of the teacher that could be summed up as "Let's try it!" or "Why not?" This attitude is expressed as an openness to suggestions from the children and a willingness to venture with them as they explore various creative mediums. It tells them that it is all right to try out something new and experiment with the possibilities of the materials being offered.

Teachers who wish to generate a creative climate must also be prepared to live with a certain amount of messiness. When children are caught up in the fever of creating things, their behavior is often somewhat helter-skelter, and it can really interfere with the creative process to insist that self-expressive or play materials be maintained in near perfect order at all times. (Note also that comments on cleaning up are sprinkled liberally through this chapter to balance this behavior.)

Finally, a general air of approval of what the children are doing does much to set the creative atmosphere for the group. This should be more a feeling of enjoying the experience *with* the children rather than singling out specific products for praise (Amabile, 1983). I still recall with pleasure a young three who turned to me after fingerpainting, sighed blissfully, and confided, "You know—this experience was udderly de-wightful!" Surely this is the climate we should aim for when building competence in the children's creative selves.

Remember That Process Is More Important Than Product

One reason it is better to emphasize the process is that young children are not skillful users of materials. Much of their creative effort is expended in the manipulative experience of trying

RESEARCH STUDY
What Is The Relationship Between Choice and Creativity?

Research Question   Does providing choices of materials motivate children to be more creative than giving them little or no choice does?

Research Method   Fourteen boys and fourteen girls between the ages of 2 and 6 who were attending a day-care center participated in the study. The teachers ranked each child in relation to creativity, interest in art, and level of independence. Then the children were randomly assigned to the choice or no-choice groups. (The purpose of the ranking was to determine whether there was an initial difference in creative ability between the choice and no-choice groups. No significant difference in ability was found.)

During a collage experience, children in the choice group were allowed to select any materials they wished from 5 out of 10 boxes. They were then asked by the experimenter to make a design of their choosing. The experimenter selected materials for the children in the no-choice group. (Each no-choice child was provided with a group of five collage boxes previously selected by a child in the "choice" group. Thus the pairs of choice/no-choice children were matched in terms of the materials used to make the collages.)

Then eight artists rated all the collages on a scale according to their being more or less creative.

Results   When the scores for the collages were analyzed statistically, the collages of the children who were encouraged to make their own choices were rated as significantly more creative than those of the children who had no opportunity for choosing their materials.

Implications for Teaching   This research supports the idea that allowing children to make choices from an array of creative materials rather than just telling them they must use particular materials can be an effective way of increasing the probability that they will express themselves more creatively.

Note. From "Children's Artistic Creativity: Effects of Choice in Task Materials" by T. M. Amabile and J. Gitomer, 1984, *Personality and Social Psychology Bulletin, 10*(2), pp. 209–215.

these out and becoming acquainted with them (Schirrmacher, 1988). Moreover, little children are more interested in doing than producing, and rarely, if at all, betray a planned intention when they take up their paintbrushes or select collage materials. This sort of advance planning belongs to older children on the verge of kindergarten. The other very important reason it is sound to emphasize process is that this reduces the temptation to provide models for children to copy. Copies are not originals, and it is originality that is the hallmark of creativity.

Remember That Encouraging Choices Fosters Creativity in Children

In order for an experience to be creative for children, it must be generated from within them, not be an experience "laid on" from outside. For this reason it is important to encourage children to make choices about the materials and activities for themselves. For example, rather than setting out three colors at the easel, why not suggest that each child choose which of four or five colors he wants to use, or select the nails he prefers, or accessories he requires in the block corner.

The research study presented in this chapter illustrates the effect that providing choices can have on motivating creative behavior in children.

Offer Support When Needed, but Interfere as Little as Possible

Children are entitled to assistance with creative materials when they need it, just as they are entitled to help with their shoelaces or having their meat cut up. If materials are too difficult to manage, the end result is frustration, not creative satisfaction. But there is a difference between suggesting that a child bear down on a brace and bit and telling him where to drill the hole. Teachers should offer technical help when necessary but not usurp the children's right to make their own creative decisions.

Teachers can also offer support by providing enough time for children to have thoroughly satisfying experiences. It takes a while for them to become deeply involved in play or get deeply

Ideas need not be elaborate to be creative.

into fingerpainting, and if the scheduled time for such activities is too short, the children are deprived of the leisurely richness they require to lose themselves in it entirely.

Still another important kind of support to offer is the provision of sufficient quantities of materials, as well as plenty of opportunity to use them. Children should be allowed to paint as many pictures or make as many collages as their fancy dictates rather than "just making one so Mary can have a turn, too."

Fortunately, many materials that are appropriate for self-expressive activities and for dramatic play are available free for the asking, and their reuse has the added virtue of helping children appreciate the value of recycling. All it takes is an imaginative eye, the courage to ask for them, and the energy to collect them regularly.

Provide Enough Variety in Creative Activities

Providing variety is important because different activities appeal to different children. Variety can be obtained in many ways. Sometimes simply moving an activity from one place to another will attract different children. Little boys, for example, who may shun dramatic house play activities indoors often participate more readily if the equipment is moved outside, or young threes may use the large hollow blocks more freely if they are placed around a corner of the building where the older children are less likely to intrude on them.

It is also valuable to make a point of varying the activities themselves, not only by varying such basic materials as dough and paint recipes, but also by offering different levels of difficulty that suit different levels of maturation and skill. Table 13–1 lists activities suitable for various ages of preschool children.

Make the Activity as Creative as Possible

Finally, when curriculum is developed that is intended to foster the creative aspect of the child's self, it is helpful for teachers to be quite clear in their own minds about just how creative

the contemplated activity is likely to be. Table 13–2 provides some examples of materials that offer varying degrees of freedom of self-expression.

Those activities with the greatest potential for creative self-expression are characterized by requiring the least amount of control and instruction by the teacher. Examples of these are included in Column I in Table 13–2. They are most open to being used in a dynamic, fluid, "becoming" sort of way. Variations of these activities concentrate on varying the material rather than varying what is made from it. The materials might be thought of as being generally less refined or sophisticated than the ones in Column II, since they do not require much skill for the children to have a satisfying experience using them. There is also more opportunity for direct involvement of the children with the materials, and there is more room left for them to express their intentions and feelings (their own, personal, creative selves), because they are not caught up in how to use the materials to such a marked degree. Because they are so satisfying, these materials can be offered over and over again, *and they should constitute the mainstays of the creative, self-expressive curriculum in the preschool.*

Column II also offers some valuable activities for preschoolers—typically the older ones in the school. However, these kinds of activities might be characterized as being more craftlike than creative. They generally require more skill on the part of the children and more instruction (at least initially) by the teacher. They tend to have more of a definite focus and direction, even though the teacher may meticulously avoid providing an actual model. There is considerable latitude allowed for individual ideas to be expressed (for example, children might be left free to arrange their flowers in the May baskets any way they wish or to stamp the Christmas paper in any pattern that appeals to them), but they do restrict freedom of expression more than the Column I materials do. To be successful, these materials usually require repeated presentation so

TABLE 13–1
Developmentally appropriate self-expressive activities

Two-year-olds	Three-year-olds	Four-year-olds
Easel painting		
Twos like to experience using brushes, paint, and paper. First offer primary colors. Twos sometimes use only one color and often like to cover the entire sheet with a rich-looking mass of color. Experimentation with materials is an important facet.	Threes often experience some of the same things as twos, except that they may have an idea of what they intend to paint or may name it afterward when it looks like something. Threes appreciate some variation, such as different-sized brushes.	Older fours often have definite ideas of what to paint. They also like to use different types of brushes, textures of papers, shapes of paper, and a selection of many colors and they enjoy mixing their own paints.
Fingerpainting		
Twos work mostly with starch and paint on paper. They smear and spread paint, enjoying large muscle movements. They sometimes watch a long time before beginning.	Threes can be encouraged to appreciate the possibility of making designs with their fingertips, palms, and so forth.	Fours enjoy variations in fingerpainting, as well as appreciating the possibility of making designs. Thick starch, negative prints from painting done on tables, or interesting scents such as vanilla or peppermint flavoring may be added to create variety.
Sponge painting		
Twos tend to use sponge painting in the same way as fingerpainting. They squeeze paint out of the sponge and smear it on the paper—they do not grasp concept of printing with a sponge.	Some threes will smear paint just as the twos do, but others will take time to make a sponge print.	Fours may take a conscious, active interest in the design they are creating. They deliberately experiment with using the sponge in different ways, such as dabbing lightly and pressing down hard.

My thanks to Clevonease Johnson, head teacher, Santa Barbara City College Children's Center (1979).

that the children can practice and gain skills in their manipulation; yet they are frequently offered as "one-shot" deals. They are valuable because they provide opportunities for purposefulness and challenges to skill that children appreciate. They also increase the variety of experience often needed desperately in full-day centers.

Column III presents activities at the restricted end of the creative continuum. The advantages of offering these kinds of activities are that they teach children to follow directions, to conform, and to learn something the teacher has decided is valuable for them to learn (such as being able to discriminate between what furniture belongs in a living room and what belongs in a kitchen or how to coil clay to make a bowl like the teacher's).

I would be the first to agree it is necessary for children to learn how to follow directions. However, this kind of activity is all too often passed off as being creative by teachers who do not grasp the difference between *creating* something and *making* something. Such an activity may be creative for teachers who invent the instructional idea, but it offers children almost no latitude for expressing their own responses, ideas, and feelings and hence should not be thought of as providing opportunities to develop their creative selves.

A Note About Expense

Throughout this book, suggestions are included about ways to save money while presenting a first-rate curriculum for the children. Nowhere is it more important to know how to stretch money than in the area of self-expressive activities, since children can use up materials faster than the blink of an eye when they are involved in creative endeavors. For this reason, teachers need to develop their scrounging instincts. Table 13–3 lists a number of sources for free materials, and additional economy measures are also included with many of the discussions on materials in the rest of this chapter. Following these suggestions will help keep expenses down, while providing the children with the plentiful amount of materials they require.

RECOMMENDATIONS FOR USING SELF-EXPRESSIVE MATERIALS TO FOSTER CREATIVITY

Easel Painting

One of the classic materials in almost all nursery schools and children's centers is the easel with its offering of tempera paint. Children of all ages enjoy this activity, and there are numerous ways to provide enough variety to sustain interest throughout the year.

Presentation of the Material. Needed equipment includes mixed paint, small containers for paint that fit the easel tray as nearly as possible, brushes, paper, a bucket, sponges and towels for washing hands, aprons, and a felt tip pen for labeling the paintings.

Sometimes teachers like to start with only the three primary colors (red, blue, and yellow) in the fall and then add others in the second month or so. Large newsprint paper is best so that the children have plenty of scope to paint, and soft, floppy camel hair brushes allow the children to swoop about the paper most freely. The stiff, flat kind of brush makes it harder to produce wavy lines. Although mixing paint in large quantities saves teacher's time, the children enjoy making it so much, and this is so educational for them to do that mixing a fresh batch each day with one or two children helping stir is generally better. A surprising amount of tempera is needed in relation to the quantity of water to make rich, bright, creamy paint; thus it is best to dump the tempera into a pint container first and then add water bit by bit. Instead of water, some teachers prefer using liquid starch because it thickens the paint mixture. However, it does increase the expense. It is helpful to add a dash of detergent, since this makes cleaning up easier.

A word of caution: some blue paints smell like rotten eggs if mixed in advance, so it is best to mix blue fresh each day. The use of a small electric hand mixer expedites paint mixing but is best used by the teacher before the children arrive.

Fruit juice cans make good paint containers, but only small amounts of paint should be poured in them at a time because many children put the same brush in different containers, which gradually turns all the colors dark gray. It is often necessary to cut off the wooden tips of the brushes because the tall handles get in the way of painting, they make it easier to tip the cans over, and they are hard for little children to handle. It is also helpful to stuff the empty end of the easel holder with newspaper to keep the cans from falling over. I do not favor the use of those lunch-size milk cartons for paint holders, unless

TABLE 13–2
Creative potential of self-expressive activities

I: Greatest potential	II: Medium potential	III: Very limited potential
Easel painting (and its variations)		
Using materials as the child wishes, provided he follows simple rules for positive social behavior, such as not painting his neighbor's picture or dripping paint on the floor. (Experience is varied by using several shades of same color, different-sized brushes, painting to music, and so on.*)	Painting in ways that allow less control by child, such as string painting, blowing paint around with straws, dropping food coloring on damp paper towels. Painting an object the child has made. Opportunities for genuine self-expression are sharply reduced because child cannot control the medium.	Painting or coloring in coloring books. Copying something the teacher has made, such as a sun, stick figure, or house.
Fingerpainting (and its variations)		
Fingerpainting as it is usually presented. (Experience is varied by presenting different textures of paint, a variety of colors, and so on.)	Foot painting, because it requires sitting down and needs careful control to avoid slipping. Taking "negative" prints from tabletop fingerpaintings.	I can't think of an example. One teacher commented that teachers are usually so busy helping the children "set up" that they haven't got time to think up more managing strategies.
Drawing		
Drawing with simple materials such as chalk, crayons, soft pencils, crayon "relief," chalk with starch, or felt pens.	Child encouraged to illustrate an experience, such as a previous field trip.	Drawing around stencils of animals, circles, triangles, and so forth. Using coloring books or mimeographed worksheets, keeping carefully within the lines.
Dough play		
Manipulating dough as child wishes and as an emotional release. (Variety is provided by many different kinds of doughs, colors, and so on.)	Selecting whatever cookie cutters he wishes to make Christmas ornaments, decorating them as he desires with red and green felt pens.	Making an ashtray according to a model provided by the teacher. Following a recipe for making biscuit dough.

*For more variations, refer to discussions of individual materials later in this chapter.

TABLE 13–2 *(continued)*

I: Greatest potential	II: Medium potential	III: Very limited potential
Collage making		
Child chooses from assortment of materials. (Teacher encourages child to consider qualities of design by asking what he thinks would look good together. Infinite variety is available in this medium through use of different materials and collage bases.)	Collage making centered on a theme—seaweed, shells, and sand after a visit to the beach; cotton balls, colored crushed egg shells, and Easter grass on lavender paper at Easter.	Cutting out pictures at the teacher's behest of all the chairs the child can find in a magazine and pasting them in a scrapbook. Gluing pre-cut eyes, nose, and mouth on a precut pumpkin head.
Dancing		
Dancing freely as the music suggests or feelings dictate.	Participating in movement education activities—"How many ways can you? . . ."	Folk dancing.
Puppet play		
Using puppets just to "fool around with" and to express feelings.	Making up a story together and using puppets to present it after considerable practice.	Presenting a puppet play of a well-known story, such as "The Three Bears."
Woodworking		
Using different kinds of wood, nails, and so forth. (Technical advice is provided when necessary, but children are left free to use materials as they wish, provided that safety is observed.)	Making an airplane or boat at the teacher's suggestion with no model provided, and materials chosen by child. (Advanced tools are provided that require considerable teacher instruction and supervision for successful use. As skill is gained, this activity probably moves over to Column I.)	Nailing together a precut birdhouse or shoeshine kit.
Unit block play		
Playing with blocks that are available and well sorted and with accessories that are brought out at child's request or with several different kinds of accessories that are available on nearby shelves for self-selection.	Playing with rubber zoo animals that are deliberately set out after trip to children's zoo to provide focus for play.	Teacher setting up cages made of blocks with animals inside them after a trip to the zoo and encouraging children to do likewise.

TABLE 13–3
Money stretchers: Sources of free or almost free materials for self-expressive activities

Materials	Sources
Empty ribbon rolls for wood gluing	Gift wrapping section of department stores
Wood shavings for collage	Scrap piles at building sites or cabinet shops
Scrap suede and leather pieces for collage	Leather stores
Boxes, large styrofoam pieces, and all sorts of things for construction	Trash bins of department and discount stores
Computer paper for coloring if the school uses crayons	Some computer places have reams of printouts used on one side — worthless paper (to them)
Empty fabric boards for large bases for group collages	Textile stores
Natural materials — bark, cones, seeds, leaves, dry flowers	Back yards — particularly in the fall — and hiking trails
Driftwood for collage	Beaches after a storm
Plastic and wood scraps for collage and woodworking	Plastic plants for trimmings, cuttings, and tubing; cabinetmakers
Five-gallon ice cream cartons for storage and for collaged wastebaskets as gifts	Ice cream stores
Rug scraps cut up to make wonderful textures for collage	Trash bins of carpet stores
Packing materials, including styrofoam, spongy materials, and excelsior for texture in collage and sheets of cardboard for collage bases	Electronic supply houses, china shops, and so on
Rolls from paper towels and toilet paper for glued constructions	Ask families to save
Coated, colored bits of wire as accessories for wood construction and for collage	Call public relations department of telephone company
Wood scraps for woodworking and gluing	Construction sites, cabinet shops, frame shops
Packing materials and large pieces of styrofoam for sawing	Hospitals, television stores, and electronic supply houses
Ends of newsprint rolls for easel paper and murals	Newspaper offices; there may be a slight charge for these

the tops are cut off so that the children can see the color of the paint more easily. These containers also encourage some teachers to seal the spout and save the paint, which is generally of a questionable color, for the next day — a poor economy measure in my opinion.

It will expedite matters if several pieces of paper are clipped to the easel at once. Many teachers prefer to write the child's name on the back of the paper to avoid the problem of having him paint over it. If a developmental file is kept at school for each child, dating a few paintings and saving them delights parents at conference time because it enables them to see how the child's skills have developed during the year.

TABLE 13–3 *(continued)*

Materials	Sources
Wallpaper sample books for collage bases and as sources of interesting textures and colors for collages, stamping, and so on	Paint and wallpaper stores
Naugahide and fabric samples; textures are quite different from ordinary material	Upholsterers
Free "art" paper—usually small, various colors, and textures	Print shops
Mat board for mounting poetry, use as collage bases; comes in lovely colors	Frame shops—cutouts from picture mats
Greeting cards and used gift wrapping for collage	Ask families to save
Molded cardboard packing from apples, peaches, and pears, cut up to make interesting shapes for collage—smells heavenly	Ask markets on days fruit is unpacked
Styrofoam meat trays for sewing and for collage bases	Supermarkets and ask families to wash and save
Aluminum pie pans and TV dinner plates for glue	Ask families to save
Plastic bottles for water play (wash thoroughly before using)	Beauty salons and homes
Egg shells, dried, crushed, and dyed, for collage—especially at Eastertime	Ask families to save
Boxes, cotton, and packing materials for collage (do not use medicine bottles)	Pharmacies
Plastic tubing and containers for water play and boxes	Hospitals have portions of disposable, one-use items that were *not* used in patient care and would be discarded otherwise; nurses are wonderful sources
Corks for collage and science experiments	Restaurants
Shingle scraps for collage bases	Houses under construction

Cleanup. Children often enjoy helping clean up this activity. They can spend considerable time squeezing the colored, soapy water through sponges, wiping off easels and aprons, and so forth.

Economy Measures. Putting a small amount of paint in a can at a time is one way to avoid waste. Ordering paint in quantity once a year is another way to make money go as far as possible, and if schools combine their orders, sometimes an even lower cost per can is offered. Children should be taught some practical techniques for handling paint to avoid waste, such as wiping the brush on the edge of the can and returning paintbrushes to the same color paint each time.

Easel painting should be a
mainstay of the creative curriculum.

(There is a difference, however, between teaching children enabling techniques like these and limiting their ideas by suggesting what they should paint.)

Some Suggested Variations of Easel Painting

- Use a number of shades of one color.
- Use colored paper—colored newsprint comes in pastel shades, or the backs of faded construction paper can be used.
- Use the same color of paint with same color of paper.
- Use black and white paint (fun at Halloween).
- Use colors that are traditionally associated with the particular holiday season.
- Use various sizes of brushes, or both flat and floppy ones, with the same colors of paint.
- Paint objects the children have made in carpentry or paint dried clay objects.

- Paint large refrigerator-type boxes.
- Work on a long piece of paper together to produce murals.
- Paint the fence with water and large brushes.
- Draw firmly on paper with crayons and paint over it to produce "crayon resist" art.
- Paint with undiluted food coloring (this is expensive but lovely).
- Use all pastel colors (start with white and add color a bit at a time when mixing).
- Use cake watercolors (teach children to wash brush before changing colors).
- Cut paper into various shapes—leave a hole in the middle or cut it like a pumpkin, a heart, a Christmas tree, and so forth.
- Set up a table with many colors of paint and encourage the children to select the colors they prefer.
- Paint to music.

Fingerpainting

Jean Stangl (1975) summarizes the value of fingerpainting very well:

> One cannot measure the satisfaction finger painting brings to the child who is tense, timid, autistic, shy, fearful, aggressive or hyperactive. It allows the child to get involved. It requires no help or skill, there is no fear of competition and the student is always successful. (How can the lesson fail?) Finger painting enables the individual to explore, to experiment, to be imaginative and creative, to be expressive and to get rid of many frustrations. It provides an opportunity for growth in self-confidence by allowing the student complete control over the paint. (pp. 4–5)

Fingerpainting seems to produce feelings of joy and peace more than any other activity. Thus teachers should offer it frequently, even though cleanup is somewhat time consuming.

Methods of Presentation. The quickest, simplest way to make fingerpaint is to combine liquid starch with dry tempera. This may be done by pouring a generous dollop of starch onto the paper and then sprinkling it with dry tempera. Alternatively, some teachers like to stir the dry pigment into an entire container of starch base.

However, I prefer to put spoonfuls of various plain bases onto the paper and then shake on whatever colors the children desire. No matter how the paint is originally prepared, teachers need to be ready to add more ingredients as the children work. The results to strive for are rich, brilliant color and sufficient paint to fill the paper completely if the child so wishes. Table 13–4 provides a number of pretested fingerpaint recipes.

Needed materials include *waterproof* aprons (old shirts are not satisfactory because they allow paint to soak through onto the children's clothing), large sheets of glazed fingerpaint paper, starch or some other medium to carry the color, pigment (either tempera or food color), and buckets of soapy water, sponges, and towels for cleanup.

Helping Children Who Feel Uncomfortable Enjoy the Experience. Although reluctant children should not be pressured unduly to participate in fingerpainting, those who are uneasy about getting their hands "dirty" can often be induced to try soap painting. This is a variation of fingerpainting using Ivory Snow whipped with a rotary beater until light and fluffy. It is best presented as tabletop painting rather than paper painting because it cracks and flakes as it dries, and parents do not welcome getting this all over their cars on the way home from school.

Children who are wary of becoming involved in such a messy activity also need plenty of opportunity just to stand and look, plus the assurance that they can wash the paint right off whenever they want to. For these youngsters, teachers should avoid using permanent colors, such as purple or orange. Occasionally, a very shy child, who seems torn between wanting and not wanting to participate, is willing to begin by placing his hand on top of the teacher's as she paints. However, most children find this expressive medium irresistible—and teachers need only to make sure that the children are clad in waterproof aprons before they plunge in.

Economy Measures. There are a few noteworthy ways to save money on materials for fingerpainting. Since fingerpainting paper is expensive, teachers may wish to substitute butcher paper, which also has a special finish (but does soak through faster than fingerpainting paper does). Because it comes in rolls, butcher paper has the added advantage of being any size the teachers wish to cut. (It is also available in a number of beautiful, bright colors if the budget is liberal.) Painting directly on a plastic tabletop or large tray makes paint go further, requires less restriction of the children than painting on paper does, and can be very satisfying for children to clean up with lots of soapy sponges and warm water. In addition, it is much less expensive for teachers to make their own paint than to buy it ready made. To prevent waste, they should shake on the tempera themselves rather than allowing the children to do this, though the children should be allowed to select the colors that they prefer. On the other hand, teachers should *not* economize by using small sizes of paper and insufficient quantities of base and tempera. The purpose of fingerpainting is to encourage deep, sensual, expressive pleasure in rich, bright, large, free painting. *Skimpy, restricted dryness of the paint should be avoided at all costs.*

Additional Drawing Materials: Chalk, Crayons, Felt Pens, and Pencils

Teachers should not overlook the potential of chalk, crayons, pencils, and felt pens, which are two-dimensional materials requiring fine muscle activity, although these do require practice for successful use. All of them have the advantage of being easy to get out and and clean up, and at the end of a long day this is important. Unfortunately, in a few schools they are the only expressive medium readily available to little children, and this is certainly undesirable.

Sometimes teachers have unrealistic expectations about the drawing and writing abilities of young children. Table 13–5 provides a helpful

TABLE 13–4
Tested fingerpaint recipes*

Method	Comments
Standard fingerpaint†	
Pour enough liquid starch on glazed paper to cover it, and shake on 1 to 2 tablespoons dry tempera to make a rich bright color. It may be necessary to add more starch or color as the children fingerpaint. Add more than one color in separate corners so children can enjoy blending them.	This is the quickest and easiest way to prepare fingerpaint. It dries dull and does not flake off. Liquid starch is somewhat costly. Try out the brand before buying a lot of it—a few off brands curdle and are not satisfactory.
Cornstarch fingerpaint	
Dissolve ½ cup cornstarch in 1 cup cold water. Pour mixture into 3 cups boiling water (it thickens suddenly). Stir constantly until shiny and translucent. Allow to cool and use as fingerpaint base, adding whatever color the children desire, or put in jars and stir in tempera or food coloring.	This is the least expensive form of fingerpaint base to make and is very satisfactory. It feels slick, spreads well, and is not sticky. If it is colored with food coloring, it should be stored in the refrigerator. *It can only be kept 1 or 2 days* before caking occurs and is best used the day it is made. This paint has an attractive "clear" but not shiny look when dry provided it is used when fresh. It also works well when mixed with tempera.
This cornstarch recipe does not store particularly well. Recipes that *do* keep several days without caking are given below.	
Easy-to-store fingerpaint no. 1	
Combine 2 cups water and ½ cup cornstarch, and boil until thick, stirring constantly. Add 1 cup Ivory Snow and coloring (if desired), cool, and use.	The addition of soap makes the base appear slightly curdled; material feels creamy when spread. Paintings, when dry, are dull and rich looking. Can be kept several weeks without refrigeration. Soap makes the cleanup easy.

*Thanks to Cené Marquis, head teacher, Institute of Child Development, for retesting these recipes (1984).
†Ready made, premixed fingerpaint is also available for purchase but is generally too expensive to use as frequently as the children need it.

list of what children at different ages can produce in the way of shapes and forms.

Are Ditto Sheets Creative? Sometimes teachers succumb to the use of mimeographed materials, which one of my friends terms, quite aptly,

"dictated art." Even though children are often permitted to use whatever colors they wish, such experiences are almost bound to stress staying within the lines, coloring in only one direction to "make it pretty," and using preselected subject matter. The result is a lesson in conformity, not

TABLE 13–4 *(continued)*

Method	Comments
Easy-to-store fingerpaint no. 2	
Dissolve 1 cup cornstarch in 1½ cups cold water. Soak 2 envelopes plain unflavored gelatin in an additional ½ cup water. Add cornstarch mixture quickly to 4 cups hot water. Cook over medium heat, stirring constantly, until mixture is thick and glossy. Blend in gelatin and 1 cup detergent until dissolved. Store in refrigerator. This makes a whiter base than the other recipes do.	This recipe seems like a lot of trouble, but if you need one that keeps, this is it! It cleans up easily because of so much detergent in it.
Thicker fingerpaint (modified Rhoda Kellogg recipe)	
Combine 2 cups flour with 2 teaspoons salt; beat in 3 cups cold water with rotary egg beater. Add 2 cups hot water, and boil until mixture looks shiny. (Start it on low heat to prevent lumping.) Stir in 2 tablespoons glycerine. (The glycerine prevents this heavy mixture from being too sticky to spread and use easily.)	Use of dry laundry starch makes a thicker paint, but since it is often hard to find, try this recipe instead. If food coloring is used with this (and it takes a lot to make it bright), it eventually dries shiny. Tempera is also satisfactory. This is thick and takes a long time to dry, but looks rich.
Soap fingerpainting	
Ivory Snow works well. Simply add water gradually while beating with a rotary egg beater until mixture is light and fluffy. Children enjoy making this, as well as using it.	This mixture often appeals to children who resist getting their hands in "dirty" paint. It is best to use it directly on a plastic tabletop. Scrape it up and reuse it as different children want a turn. If it is used on paper, it flakes off as it dries and is very messy. It is lovely when tinted in pastel tones with food coloring. It cleans up more easily if vinegar is added to the cleanup water. Dispose of soap mixture by flushing it down the toilet or putting it in the garbage (it clogs sinks). Material turns slimy if kept.
Shaving cream	
This can be used by several children if squirted on a plastic tray.	Shaving cream feels and smells nice, though it is expensive. When dry, it is dull and flakes off easily.

in exploring one's own ideas and feelings and putting these down on paper (Heberholz & Hanson, 1985).

I have heard beleaguered teachers say desperately that they hate using dittos but that the parents expect it. My guess is that parents expect dittoed worksheets because that is what they recall from their own early schooling experiences. I have found that once teachers explain the educational value of self-expression and originality, and also what constitutes developmentally appropriate activities for preschool

TABLE 13–5
Drawing and writing movements

Age (in years, months)	Behavior
0.1 to 1	Accidental and imitative scribbling.
1 to 1.6	Refinement of scribbles, vertical and horizontal lines, multiple line drawing, scribbling over visual stimuli.
2 to 3	Multiple loop drawing, spiral, crude circles. Simple diagrams evolve from scribblings by the end of the second year.
3	Figure reproduction limited to visually presented figures, circles, and crosses.
4	Laboriously reproduces squares, may attempt triangles but with little success.
4.6 to 5	Forms appear in combinations of two or more. Crude pictures appear (house, human form, sun). Can draw fair squares, crude rectangles, and good circles, but has difficulty with triangles and diamonds.
6 to 7	Ability to draw geometric figures matures. By 7 can draw good circles, squares, rectangles, triangles and fair diamonds.

Note. From *Perceptual-Motor Efficiency in Children: The Measurement and Improvement of Movement Attributes* (p. 85) by B. J. Cratty and M. M. Martin, 1969, Philadelphia: Lea & Febiger.

children, families no longer desire the mimeographed materials.

Chalk. Chalk is inexpensive and comes in pretty colors. Its most typical use is with blackboards, but little children do not seem to use it very effectively there. They do better if allowed to mark on the sidewalk with it—perhaps because the rougher texture of the cement more easily pulls the color off the stick, and the children seem more able to tell what they are doing as they squat down and draw. It is, of course, necessary to explain to them that they may "write" with chalk only on special places.

Chalk is also available in larger squares in a range of marvelous colors (be sure not to purchase oil pastels, which are beautiful but will not wash away). These can be used with rough paper and a liquid starch base for an interesting variation halfway between fingerpainting and drawing. Buttermilk is also recommended by many teachers as being a good liquid base to use with this medium on rough paper. Liquid tends to seal the chalk, so teachers must rub it occasionally on a piece of old sandpaper to break this seal so the color will continue to come off readily.

Crayons and Nonpermanent, Nontoxic Felt Tip Pens. Crayons are much more economical than pens (and who has not felt the thrill of pleasure over a new box of these), yet pens do come in beautiful clear colors. Compared with paint, they have the additional advantage of staying bright and unsullied until the children use them up.

Most schools set out crayons or pens jumbled together in a basket, but Thelma Harms recommends that they be kept assembled in separate boxes so that each user has an individual set. This cuts down on arguments and means that all the colors are available as the children require them. The use of thick crayons is general practice in preschools because they do not break as easily as thin ones do and, theoretically, because they are easier for children to hold. It is my opinion, however, that thinner crayons are probably easier to hold and manipulate. Perhaps preschools should offer both varieties, or try both out and decide for themselves.

Pencils. These require careful supervision. Children must not be allowed to run around with them, for they are somewhat dangerous. Previously our center did not offer them at all, until it became apparent that some of our children had almost no experience with them at home. Since they are widely used in kindergarten, it was evident that the children needed practice with them, so we have added them to the curriculum. For maximum success, teachers should purchase pencils with rich, soft "lead" cores and instruct children on the rules about where these can and cannot be used.

Printing and Stamping

Printing and stamping have some value in helping children develop a sense of design and understand cause-and-effect relationships, but the materials of these activities do not allow as much latitude for creative self-expression as other forms of self-expressive materials do. Nevertheless, information is presented here because so many questions are asked about how to use them effectively.

There are several kinds of stamps that are simple enough for little children to use, although any printing that involves paint is likely to change into fingerpainting as it smears—an indication of what the children would probably prefer to do. Commercially made rubber stamps work well with ink pads of various colors. Cookie cutters dipped in shallow paint trays print without distortion and can be used to stamp paper for various holiday events. Bits of sponges cut into different shapes can also be used effectively to create stamped designs. Clothespins make nice handles for these when clipped to one end of the sponge. Potato stamps can also be dipped in shallow paint and used for printing. These seem to work best if the design is incised rather than cut out. The best potato stamps I have seen were carved like pumpkins, with the features dug deeply into the round potato surface.

For those teachers who are feeling brave, here are some instructions for a more elaborate printing technique.[1]

Steps for Printing

Step I: Squeeze some Speedball ink on the pane of glass (about as much as the amount of toothpaste you would use to brush your teeth, or an inch-long ribbon). Roll it with a brayer in several directions until it sounds sticky. This means the ink is thoroughly distributed and will print well.

Step II: Take your leaf, flower, or grass and place it on the inked glass. Cover with a piece of scrap paper and press it into the ink.

Step III: Lift the leaf and place it on the paper you wish to print. Cover the leaf with a sheet of clean paper. Follow the outline of the leaf through the paper with your fingers, pressing on the stem and veins and following them out to the edges. Lift the top paper and the leaf and examine print.

Aids: If your print is too dark and you cannot see the veins and outline, it means you had too much ink on the glass. Try printing it again. If the print is too faint and the veins and outlines do not show up, the leaf was not inked thoroughly.

If this technique is too advanced, Speedball ink can also be rolled out on the glass and children can place their hands on the inked surface and then make handprints on scraps of mat board acquired from frame shops. These make striking, personalized gifts on holidays. The ink can be wiped off their hands with vegetable oil.

Dough and Clay

As is true with fingerpainting, play with dough or clay offers direct contact with the material and provides particularly rich opportunities for the expression and relief of feelings as children push, squeeze, and pound. These materials are three-dimensional in effect, and clay, in particular, provides opportunities for "clean" smearing, which many children enjoy.

Suggestions for Making Dough. Children should participate in making dough whenever possible (the only exception being cooking the cornstarch mixtures, which become stiff so suddenly that they really require the teacher's strong arm and careful use of very hot materials). If allowed to help make the dough, children learn about measuring, blending, and cause and effect and

---

[1] From FOXTAILS, FERNS AND FISH SCALES by Ada Graham, Four Winds Press. Copyright © 1976 by Ada Graham. Reprinted by permission of JCA Literary Agency, Inc.

Cookie cutters provide a pleasant variation to dough play but should not be allowed to replace the satisfaction of pounding and squishing this expressive material.

also have the opportunity to work together to help the school.

The doughs that require no cooking are best mixed two batches at a time in separate deep dishpans. Using deep ones keeps the flour within bounds, and making two batches at a time relieves congestion and provides better participatory opportunities. Tempera powder is the most effective coloring agent to add because it makes such intense shades of dough; adding it to the flour *before* pouring in the liquid works best. Dough can be kept in the refrigerator and reused several times. Removing it at the beginning of the day allows it to come to room temperature before being offered to the children—otherwise it can be dishearteningly stiff and unappealing. The addition of flour or cornstarch on the second day is usually necessary to reduce stickiness.

Variations. All the dough recipes in Table 13–6 have been carefully tested and are suitable for various purposes, as the comments explain. In preschool centers where process, not product, is emphasized, the dough and clay are generally used again and again rather than the objects made by the children being allowed to dry and sent home. For special occasions, however, it is nice to allow the pieces to harden and then to paint or color them. Two recipes are included in Table 13–6 that serve this purpose particularly well (Ornamental Clay and Baker's Dough).

Presenting Dough. Once made, dough is easy to get out and simple to supervise. Usually all the children have to remember is to keep it on the table and out of their mouths. It is a pleasant material to bring out toward the end of the morning or in late afternoon when children and teachers are tired and cleanup needs to be quick and easy.

For dough to be truly satisfying, children need an abundance of it rather than meager little handfuls, and they should be encouraged to use it in a manipulative, expressive way rather than in a product-oriented manner. For this reason, the usual practice of offering it with cookie cutters should be varied by offering it alone or only with rolling pins.

Cleanup. The cooked cornstarch recipes are the only ones that are particularly difficult to clean up because they leave a hard, dry film on the pan during cooking. However, an hour or two of soaking in cold water converts this to a jellylike material that is easily scrubbed off with a plastic pot scrubbing pad. If pans are soaked during nap time, the children will be quite interested in the qualities of this gelatinous material when they get up.

Other Molding and Modeling Materials

Potter's Clay. Potter's clay may be purchased at any art supply store in moist form. This is much easier to deal with than starting with dry powder. It is available in two colors—gray and terra cotta (terra cotta looks pretty but seems harder to clean up). Clay requires careful storage in a watertight, airtight container to retain its malleable qualities. When children are through with it, form it into large balls, press a thumb into it, and then fill that hole with water and replace in container.

Clay that is too soft for easy handling can be kneaded on a plaster "bat" board to remove excess moisture.

If oilcloth table covers are used, they can simply be hung up to dry, shaken well, and put away until next time. Formica-covered boards (sink cut-outs left over from new counter tops) also make nice large surfaces to use with dough or clay.

Snow, Sand, and Mud. Remember that snow, sand, and mud also have molding properties and that children enjoy forming shapes from these materials. In particular, do not overlook the real pleasure little children take in making large snowmen, shoveling and hauling snow, and so forth. (See also the discussion of mud and sand on pp. 180–81.)

Self-Expressive Materials Requiring Glue—Collage and Assemblage and Wood and Box Gluing

Collage and assemblage (three-dimensional collage) offer the best available mediums in the center for helping children think about such qualities of design as the way colors, textures, and forms look when arranged together. For this reason, *collage should not be considered primarily a paper-on-paper experience.* Instead, it is best thought of as being a three-dimensional expressive experience that provides opportunities for children to become acquainted with innumerable materials and build their appreciation of and sensitivity to color, substance, and design.

Presentation. Collages and assemblages require a firm base of some sort for their construction. This can be anything from construction paper to large pieces of tree bark, scraps of wood shingles, meat trays, discarded mat board from frame shops, or bolt boards from fabric stores. The base should be large enough to allow plenty of space for the arrangement of materials; therefore, such picayune things as cottage cheese lids are unsuitable.

The only substance that really sticks well enough that it can be used to glue all kinds of collage is white glue. Though not cheap in any size, it is least expensive when bought in gallon jugs. It cleans up readily with hot water until it dries. After that, it is very difficult to remove, so be sure to clean up carefully when the collage experience is finished—and this includes wiping the neck of the glue bottle.

Children should be taught that glue is not paint (the use of brushes and its thick appearance

TABLE 13–6
Tested play dough recipes*†

Ingredients and method	Comments
Basic play dough I‡	
3 cups flour, ¼ cup salt, 6 tablespoons oil, enough dry tempera to color it, and about ¾ to 1 cup water. Encourage children to measure amounts of salt and flour and mix them together with the dry tempera. Add tempera *before* adding water. If using food coloring, mix a 3 ounce bottle with water before combining with salt and flour. Combine oil with ¾ cup water and add to dry ingredients. Mix with fingers, adding as much water as necessary to make a workable but not sticky dough.	Many basic recipes do not include oil, but using it makes dough softer and more pliable. It also makes it slightly greasy, and this helps protect skin from the effects of the salt. Dry tempera gives the brightest colors, but food coloring may be used instead if desired. Advantages of this recipe are that it can be totally made by the children, since it requires no cooking and it is made from ingredients usually on hand that are inexpensive. This dough stores in the refrigerator fairly well. It gets sticky, but this can bo corrected by adding more flour. This is a good, standard, all-purpose, reusable dough. Others, listed below, are for special purposes and are nice to use for variety.
Basic play dough II§	
Combine 3 cups *self-rising* flour, 1 cup salt, 5 tablespoons alum (purchase at drug store) and 1 tablespoon dry tempera. Boil 1¾ cups water, add ⅓ cup oil to it, and pour over flour mixture, stirring rapidly. Use.	This dough is lighter and more plastic than the first one—feels lovely. It thickens as boiling water is poured in and cools rapidly so that children can finish mixing. It keeps exceptionally well in the refrigerator, oil does not settle out and it does not become sticky; a paragon among doughs! Beautiful to use at Christmas, if colored with white tempera.
Basic play dough III‖	
Stir together 2 cups flour, 2 tablespoons cream of tartar, and ½ cup salt. Combine 2 cups water with 2 tablespoons oil, food coloring, and oil of cloves (if desired for scent). Combine wet and dry ingredients, stir, and cook over medium heat until it forms a ball.	This dough has an excellent texture and keeps well in the refrigerator.
Cooked play dough¶	
Blend 1 cup flour, ½ cup cornstarch, and 1 cup water together to make a batter in top of double boiler. Boil 3 cups of water and 1 cup of salt to-	This is a resilient, springy dough, somewhat firm but not stiff, similar to commercial play dough in texture. Quantity is liberal for three or four children. Cooking must be done by adult because it gets very stiff quite suddenly and requires

*Thanks to Cené Marquis, head teacher, Institute of Child Development, for retesting these recipes (1984).
†Remember, flours vary. Adjustments, therefore, are sometimes necessary as dough is made. If too sticky, add more dry ingredients. If too dry, add more liquid.
‡From Santa Barbara City College Children's Center.
§Kindness of Sharon Brownette, California Preschool Program, Santa Barbara, California.
‖Kindness of Angie Dixon, parent of Dru Dixon, Institute of Child Development, 1984.
¶Kindness of Barbara Berton, Happyland Preschool, Costa Mesa, California.

TABLE 13–6 *(continued)*

Ingredients and method	Comments

gether and pour it into cornstarch-flour mixture. Cook in double boiler until dough looks shiny and translucent, stirring firmly and constantly. Allow to cool enough so children can handle mixture, then stir in coloring. Gradually work in 3 to 4 more pounds (12 to 16 cups) of flour until of good handling consistency.

firm control of hot, slippery double boiler. This is a nice recipe because children can see and make the batter first and witness the dramatic change. It keeps well in refrigerator, but does become firmer when chilled.

Cornstarch dough#

Mix thoroughly 1 cup salt, ½ cup cornstarch, and ¾ cup water to which food coloring has been added, and cook in a double boiler until thick and translucent. This happens suddenly, and it is very difficult to stir but worth it. Allow to cool to lukewarm on an aluminum pie plate.

This is one of the prettiest doughs I know. It sparkles while moist and resembles gumdrops! It has little grains of salt throughout so it feels mildly grainy but not unpleasant. For "gumdrop" effect, food coloring, *not* tempera, must be used. Quantity is sufficient for one child. It dries to a dull finish and does not break easily. Stirring *must* be done by an adult. It will keep overnight.

Ornamental clay**

Mix 1 cup cornstarch, 2 cups baking soda, and 1¼ cups water. Cook together until thickened, either in double boiler or over direct heat—*stir constantly*. When it is cool enough, turn it out and let children knead dough and make it into whatever they wish. If used for ornaments, make hole for hanging ornament while it is still moist.

This is a brilliant white dough that does well if dried overnight in an oven with pilot light on. It is quite strong when dry. If dried in air, it doesn't seem to be quite as strong. It has a kind of crisp though malleable texture when handled. Ideally it should be used same day it's made—preferably while still warm. If it is saved for next day, it can still be used, does not get sticky, but does become somewhat drier, crumbly, and a little stiff. It can be rolled very thin and cut with cookie cutters. Makes enough for one child or perhaps two, depending on what they do with it. When dry, it has a slight sparkle and is snowy white. It can be drawn on easily with felt tip pens and is very lightweight if used for tree ornaments.

Baker's dough††

Mix 4 cups flour, 1 cup salt, and 1 to 1½ cups water as needed to make dough nice to handle. Knead and handle as desired. Bake at 350° F for 50 to 60 minutes. Material will brown slightly, but baking at lower temperatures is not as successful.

This recipe makes enough for two or three children and keeps well in refrigerator. When baked, it becomes very light and very strong. It can be painted or drawn on with felt tip pens to add color and requires no cooking, except for final baking if preservation is desired.

#Modified from *A Curriculum for Child Care Centers* by C. Seefeldt, 1973, Columbus, Ohio: Merrill Publishing Co.
**Reprinted by permission of Doreen J. Croft (1976). *Recipes for busy little hands.* Palo Alto, Calif.: Author.
††From *A Curriculum for Child Care Centers* by C. Seefeldt, 1973, Columbus, Ohio: Merrill Publishing Co.

encourage this notion) and that it should be used with care. It can be set out in flat, untippable TV dinner trays or in little, flat pans. Some schools use squeeze bottles, but these have to be watched closely and cleaned very carefully so they do not clog. Children should brush the glue onto the place where they want something to stick, but not all over the paper. An alternative to brushing is dipping the object to be glued lightly into a shallow pan of glue and placing it on the paper, but this tends to get fingers stickier and stickier!

Collage materials should be placed on a separate choosing table and sorted into shallow containers, such as baskets, so that children can readily appraise the kinds of things that are available and consider how they will look when arranged together. Teachers can foster this awareness, particularly with older threes and fours, by asking them what they think would make an interesting contrast, what colors would be attractive together, and so forth. Children also should be encouraged to modify the materials to suit their needs. Perhaps they want to cut off just a snippet of styrofoam to use, or scrunch up a twist of tissue paper rather than leaving it flat, or bend a piece of wire to just the right shape.

Some Suggested Variations for Collage. The range of materials for collage is almost endless, and teachers should devote careful thought to selection of the materials presented together so that variety, contrast, and harmony are all present. The following are some possibilities for materials:

- All shades and colors of yarns, strings, ribbons, pipe cleaners, and colored wire
- All varieties of paper—corrugated, tissue, dull rough cardboard, old blotters, gilt papers from greeting cards, print shop papers, can labels, used gift wrapping papers, and so on
- Buttons of all sizes and colors
- Bottle caps and corks
- All forms of styrofoam packing (the white makes a nice contrast to other materials) and torn foam egg cartons

- Rock salt sprinkled on as the collage is completed for a snowy effect (can be colored by shaking it in a bottle with a little food color)
- All kinds of natural materials are exquisite—small pine cones, seeds, berries, leaves, twigs, bits of bone, bits of bark, small lustrous pebbles, feathers (though these can be difficult for small, gluey fingers), shells, pods, starfish, and so on
- Small tiles (require a strong collage base)
- Leather scraps and trimmings
- Spongy materials
- Wood chips and interesting wood shavings
- Netting and other see-through materials, such as cellophane, and old theatrical gelatins
- Beads from broken strings (colored beads make handsome accents)
- Cloth and wallpaper for adding patterns and textures—particularly fleeces, burlaps, velvets, and cloth and paper with interesting patterns
- Scraps and trimmings (such as rickrack), lace, and embroidery ends
- Colored glue with tempera for an interesting accent

The following are additional variations closely related to collage:

- Offer wood gluing—using styrofoam meat trays or roofing shingles to provide firm support. Painting or shellacking these later is a real pleasure and extends the experience for fours who can endure waiting for their constructions to dry.
- Small boxes (hearing aid boxes and film boxes, for example), combined with other bits and pieces of things, provide satisfying, quick methods of "assemblage"
- Arrange flat materials such as bits of tissue paper between layers of waxed paper and iron. The melted wax intensifies the colors. The result can be taped to a window and can be quite beautiful.
- Use felt pieces of a flannel board for a more temporary kind of collage. Many children like to do this, and it fosters an interest in design.

Woodworking

Some schools shun presenting carpentry, perhaps because some teachers have had little experience with woodworking tools and therefore think they are dangerous, but the activity is so satisfying for children that teachers should learn to use tools with care and competence so they can help children be successful, too. Women teachers who use tools in a confident, competent way provide good behavioral models for the children to emulate—models that may be particularly important for little girls who, in the past, have all too frequently been instrumentally incompetent in the area of woodworking.

Tools can be frustrating and tempers can mount as a result, so it is important to provide continual, attentive supervision for safety's sake. Teachers should be aware of children who are finding the activity too frustrating and offer help and encouragement in time to prevent explosions. As with the other self-expressive activities, it is possible to help children learn techniques in working with wood without restricting what they are creating with it.

Basic Tools. The most basic woodworking tools are hammers and saws. The hammers should be good, solid ones—*not* tack hammers. The saws should be crosscut ones so that they can cut with or across the grain of the wood, and they should be as short as possible. A well-made vise in which to place wood securely while sawing is invaluable. Preferably, there should be two of these, one at each end of the table. (C-clamps can be also used for this purpose and are less expensive, or a board can be nailed to the table while the child saws it, but this leaves the troublesome chore of removing the nails afterward.)

As the year progresses, additional tools should be added from time to time. A brace and bit are desirable (much better than "egg beater" drills, which are almost hopeless for little children to use); the brace and bit can be taken apart by the children, and different-sized bits can be inserted for variety. Rough and fine rasps and a light plane are also worthwhile. (Stanley Surform rasps are particularly good because they can be held with two hands and are very safe.) At our center, we have never had much luck using screws or screwdrivers, however. A general and important principle to remember is that, whatever tools are selected, they must be of good quality and really work. *Never* give children miserable little toy replicas; they are too unsatisfying to use.

Very young children enjoy sawing up the large pieces of styrofoam that come as packing for electronic equipment. Hammering into such material or into plasterboard is also quick and easy and does not require more force than twos and threes can muster. Older children need plentiful amounts of soft wood to work with. This is commonly available as scrap at construction sites and at some lumber mills. Cabinet shops are also good sources of wood; however, many of their scraps are hardwood and are more suitable for gluing than carpentry because they are too tough for children to saw through. Plywood is too tough and hard to be satisfying for children to manipulate. An old tree stump is great fun for children to pound countless nails into.

Some Suggested Variations for Woodworking

- Remember to vary the tools the children use as their skill (and self-control) increases.
- Purchase a variety of nails by the pound, not by the little box, from a hardware store. Children love an assortment of these. They can be set out in small foil pie plates to keep them from getting mixed up. Some schools nail these pie plates to a long board to prevent spilling.
- Offer various kinds of trims to go with woodworking, such as wire, thick colorful yarn, and wooden spools (with nails long enough to go through the spool).
- Offer round things for wheels, such as bottle caps, buttons, or the lids of 35mm film containers.
- Provide dowels of various sizes that will fit the holes made by the different sizes of bits.
- As previously mentioned, children like to paint what they have made, but this must be done another day or supervised by a second person because *it is vital to stay right beside the carpentry table at all times.*

Creative, Self-Expressive Dancing

Dancing offers another kind of self-expressive opportunity that is of great value in the lives of children. A full discussion of how to present a successful, free dance experience is included in Chapter 8.

FOSTERING PRETEND PLAY

No matter what else is discussed in relation to the various selves of the child, discussions of play keep cropping up in almost every chapter. This is because play is the great medium through which children learn and understand their world. In this chapter, once again, it is essential to talk about play to explain how it contributes to the development of the creative self. (The reader also may wish to review Chapter 2 at this point.)

Benefits of Imaginative, Pretend Play

Creative, dramatic play provides limitless opportunities for children to imagine and pretend themselves into roles ranging from parents to babies to ogres to bears. Within a matter of minutes, their imaginations can transform a simple object such as a piece of wood into a little car, a baby bottle, a gun, or a bit of roof. Thus, imagination enables children to become in play what they cannot be in real life, and doing this exercises their intellects, since there is an obvious mental operation involved in substituting symbols for reality (Piaget, 1962, 1976b; Segal & Adcock, 1981). Such play allows children to be masterful. It permits them to experiment with tentative solutions to problems, and it provides unparalleled opportunities for them to use their own ideas.

Sylva, Bruner, and Genova (1976) list some additional characteristics of play that are worth noting here because they apply particularly well to a discussion of the creative aspects of play. As they phrase it, "The essence of play is the

Play is the great medium through which children understand their world.

dominance of means over ends" (p. 244)—a statement that certainly sounds familiar and comfortable to process-not-product devotees. Other characteristics of play cited by them include a lessening of the risk of failure and an increased "freedom to notice seemingly irrelevant detail" because people involved in play are less preoccupied with specific, focused tasks and so are more open to the world around them. Finally, the authors point out that play is voluntary and self-initiated, that is, it comes from within the person. These qualities of freedom and self-initiation are what teachers wish to favor in creative play situations. The problem for beginning teachers is how to translate these high-sounding purposes into actual, down-to-earth practice. Fortunately, providing for such play need not be expensive, as Table 13–7 illustrates.

Some Practical Ways to Encourage Imaginative, Creative Play

The following are important factors in encouraging the creative, imaginative aspect of play:

1. Providing a background of actual experiences that may suggest possibilities for the children to pretend, such as a trip to a doctor's office
2. Providing plentiful equipment of the right kind (unstructured materials lend themselves to imaginative play most readily)
3. Allowing children to use this equipment in creative, possibly unconventional, but harmless ways to meet the needs of their play
4. Providing accessories to enhance play when children request them or to suggest a possible theme for play
5. Providing unusual rearrangements and juxtapositions of equipment to stimulate and extend play (combining the unit and hollow blocks, for example)
6. Keeping the play area appealing and the materials accessible
7. Most important of all, supporting but not dominating the children's play by offering whatever assistance is necessary to continue or enrich it

Since I have already used the housekeeping corner as an example of how a play area can foster social development and provide emotional relief (Chapter 11, Table 11–12), the following discussions will use hollow and unit blocks to illustrate how the practical principles for supporting creative play listed above can be put into practice in the preschool.

Unit Blocks. Unit blocks are those small hardwood blocks so dear to the hearts of children and so filled with potential for creative play. Designed by Caroline Pratt more than half a century ago, they remain one of the most enduring mediums for early childhood education. They are valuable because they suit the developmental needs and capabilities of a wide range of children, and they lend themselves to achieving large, spacious effects rather quickly. In imaginative play, unit blocks have another special quality that they share with models of animals and dolls. To use them for pretend purposes, children must project their imaginations even more than they do when involved directly in housekeeping play, because blocks are less structured.

Hardwood blocks are expensive but well worth the investment, and a children's center should add more every year, if at all possible, until they have a plentiful supply and a variety of shapes available (Reifel, 1984). The various-sized blocks should always be multiples of each other to facilitate comprehension of mathematical concepts of equality and to make building with them more satisfactory. If new blocks are waxed with heavy duty paste wax upon arrival, they will stay much cleaner and more appealing over the years.

A temporary set can be made from softwood with an electric saw, but unit blocks undergo such harsh use that these softwood substitutes are not permanently satisfactory because they splinter and their corners get knocked off. In a real financial pinch, teachers can use flat-topped milk cartons for blocks rather than offer no blocks at all.

Presentation. *Unit blocks should always be stored, same size together, long side in view, on shelves —not in tubs or bins.* If they are dumped in bins, children cannot find just the size they want when

TABLE 13–7
Sources of free or almost free materials for imaginative, dramatic play

Materials	Sources
Large appliance boxes for houses, markets, trains, or whatever; also nice for group painting projects	Appliance stores—kitchen, radio, and TV stores
Discarded furniture, cut down and repainted, for pretend play corner—high chairs, small beds, and so forth	Attics, rummage sales, thrift stores
Sandbox and housekeeping equipment	Rummage sales, thrift stores; ask families to donate extras
Telephones for promoting social interaction in play	Often on loan from public relations office of telephone company
Props for play, such as used envelopes, aged typewriters, pieces of hose, rope, discarded backpacks, hats of all descriptions	Families, paint stores, fast food places, workers, thrift stores, garage sales
Used gift wrappings—fun to use to play birthday party	Ask families to save
Dress-up clothes; provide a good assortment of clothes for both sexes; add multiethnic touches if possible; cut garments down to reasonable size so children can move freely in them	Ask families to save; garage sales, thrift shops
Large outdoor blocks	Milk companies sometimes donate old cases; computer packers and shippers sometimes donate foam, packing blocks

they need it; they also have no opportunity to perceive the relationships between the different sizes.

If children are taught to build slightly away from the shelves, fighting and stress will be reduced as other youngsters try to reach in for blocks also. The construction area needs to be shielded from traffic to discourage children from delivering a kick at some treasured structure as they pass by, and it should be as large as possible and capable of being extended when necessary. A carpeted space is nice to use for this activity because it is warmer to kneel on while working and also quieter for play. The carpet has to be very flat and tight so that the blocks stand up easily.

According to Harriet Johnson (Provenzo & Brett, 1983), who wrote a classic pamphlet on

block play, this kind of play progresses through a series of stages, beginning with simply carrying blocks around and progressing to stacking, simple bridging, and then to building enclosures with them. Following that, children begin to add decorative touches and also to use the structures for imaginative play. Ultimately they attempt to replicate actual buildings with which they are familiar (this stage is rarely seen at the preschool level).

I have visited many schools where I have seen unit blocks just sitting on shelves, and not generally used by the children. Sometimes teachers even complain to me that the children have no interest in them. I suspect two reasons for this: the teachers have made such a chore of picking them up that the children have learned to avoid the area, or the children are unfamiliar with the joys of blocks, since many homes do not offer them, and the teachers do not know how to get such play started.

Getting Play Started. It often does require attention from the teacher to draw children into block play. One way of doing this is to use the "nest-egg" approach—perhaps setting out a few of the cars on the beginning of a road made of blocks or stacking up some of the blocks in an inviting way before the children arrive. This is not intended to provide a model for the children to copy but to attract them and prompt the beginning of their play.

The teacher who quietly pulls up a chair and sits near the block corner while keeping an eye on the room in general will also draw children to that area and can encourage the play with an occasional supportive comment or question. Drawing diagrams occasionally of their constructions (using carbon paper so that one copy can be kept as a developmental record and the other sent home) also stimulates such play. One school

I know of even takes Polaroid shots of the children's work from time to time.

Tabletop blocks of various descriptions cultivate the use of smaller muscles, facilitate eye-hand development, and foster creative play, particularly if they are combined with little, plastic figures of animals and people. Lego toys, log-type blocks, and similar toys appeal to fours and fives, and Bristle Blocks can be used even with twos and threes because the pieces fasten together in such an easy, satisfactory way. Once again, it is important to have a large enough supply of these so that children can really build something with them and not run out of what they require.

Cleanup. The block area is much more appealing if blocks are not allowed to accumulate in a jumbled mess, so it makes sense that the children be encouraged to pick them up before leaving the area. Yet if this rule is enforced too rigidly or if the teacher refuses to help with the task, it certainly does discourage play. It seems better to

Older fours may reproduce a familiar structure in their block play. Soroosh has just constructed a model of the University of Oklahoma stadium.

strive for a general effect of tidiness without being disagreeable about it—thanking the children who do help and pitching in oneself to provide a good example. Children do not mind picking up so much if they can make a game of delivering the blocks to the shelves on trucks or shoving them over, train style, and they do experience satisfaction in getting them all marshalled neatly back in place.

Some Suggested Variations for Unit Block Play

- Widen the variety of shapes of blocks as the year progresses—include cylinders, pillars, and ramps, gothic arches, switches, and triangular blocks.
- Add cubical counting blocks; the touches of color these provide are exquisite.
- Use a dollhouse and furniture and dolls to go with it.
- Offer little cars and trucks.
- Provide a small wood train and tracks (a wonderful accessory for such play).
- Include additional transportation toys, such as boats and airplanes.
- Include wooden or rubber animals.
- Combine unit blocks with blocks of other kinds; they work well with both larger and smaller ones.
- Suggest that children incorporate tables into their block structures, particularly when combining them with smaller blocks.
- Offer the long boards as accessories.
- Move the block cases to other areas in the room; this often stimulates play by children who have not been attracted to them before.
- Remember that there is a tremendous variety of blocks (Provenzo & Brett, 1983), ranging from Bristle Blocks to Legoes; all have their place in the playful, learning activities children enjoy.

Large Hollow Blocks and Boards. There is simply nothing that matches the value of boards and large hollow blocks for fostering creativity in play. Their manipulation requires children to involve both their minds and bodies together in a total way as they lug them about and hoist them into position. Their very nature and size suggest construction of structures large enough to play in when completed. Play periods should be long enough that there is time for this activity, as well as for actual building.

Hollow blocks are expensive and do require protection, either by using them on carpeting inside or on grass or some other resilient material when outdoors. (One center, for example, uses artificial grass laid over cement as a cushioning surface to keep the blocks from breaking when they fall.) If used outdoors, they also require sanding and painting once a year with quick-drying lacquer, such as Deft, to preserve them.

Presentation. Once again, the nest-egg approach can prove useful as a starting point for large block play. The "egg" can be as simple as arranging four boards leaning against a few blocks to suggest a ramp or setting up a ladder to bridge two walls.

Providing accessories, such as ropes, lengths of hose, ladders and telephones, dolls, or housekeeping furniture, will also suggest possibilities and attract children. If the blocks are used in conjunction with other outdoor equipment, such as a boat, trikes, or a climbing gym, or are used around the sandbox to make a house, play in those areas will increase rapidly.

The teacher should be attentive to what is going on and be willing to serve as helper and supplier of needs rather than as dominator and controller of ideas. It facilitates play if such objects as sawhorses, hats, telephones, and old bedspreads are stored nearby so they can be produced at a moment's notice. To tell a child, "I can't get it right now—you'll have to wait until tomorrow," is unsatisfactory, since it is likely that the play will have moved on to something else by then.

Hollow blocks and boards should be used both indoors and out, since they generate different kinds of play when moved around. A nice, inexpensive large block that is satisfactory for use indoors where it is dry is the kind made of corrugated cardboard. Children can help assemble these and glue them closed, and a goodly supply can be obtained for a reasonable sum of money. Some computer firms also ship their products wedged between large blocks of spongy plastic (about 2 feet × 1½ feet × 1 foot). These make very light, surprisingly tough blocks.

Boards. Boards are one of the most useful and underrated pieces of equipment in a children's center. They should be made of ⅝- or ¾-inch all-weather plywood and cleated on the ends so that they hook safely over the edge of blocks and **A**-frames. They should be cut to fit other playground equipment when this exists. For example, it increases their usefulness if they hook across the bars of climbing gyms so that the children can use them to build floors within the gym for "tree houses."

Recently I have seen children use our set of boards in the following ways in their creative play: as an extension of the slide; as roofs for block structures; as decking on the row boat; as a network of roads on an elevated roadway; as a table in the sandbox; as part of an intricate, child-constructed obstacle course; as a ramp for climbing up to the **A**-frames; as a corral to keep bad horses out; and as a cage to keep bad lions in.

Boards are indispensable, and their usefulness is increased even more when sawhorses, barrels, tires, and large boxes are provided along with them. An adequate supply consists of 25 to 30 boards, of whatever two lengths adapt best to existing equipment. All it takes is one bake sale to raise enough money to purchase the wood and a handful of adults to cut, make, and finish them. The children's delight should be ample repayment for this effort.

Storage and Cleanup. Blocks and boards are cumbersome to move, although children are often of considerable help in doing this, particularly if they use a wagon. There are large, low carts made for this purpose, and if these materials must be stored far from the play area where they are used, such a cart can be a worthwhile investment. It is ideal to have the storage closet near a large, level area appropriate for large block play; it is also best to store the boards in racks, tray style, along one side of the storage wall rather than behind the blocks, so they will be used more freely. For added convenience, ladders can be hung on the wall also and sawhorses and **A**-frames stacked nearby.

SUMMARY

Young children express their originality and creativity primarily through the use of self-expressive materials, imaginative play, and creative thought. This chapter discusses methods of fostering creativity by means of expressive materials and imaginative play.

Some general principles of teaching that foster creative self-expression include (1) maintaining a climate that encourages children to feel creative, (2) remembering that process is more important than product, (3) encouraging children to make choices, (4) interfering as little as possible with the children's creative activities, but offering support and encouragement when necessary, (5) providing enough variety to the activities and keeping them developmentally appropriate, and (6) making certain that the activities are genuinely creative.

More specific recommendations related to the presentation of particular materials are presented for easel painting, fingerpainting, various drawing materials, printing and stamping, dough and clay, collage and assemblage, and woodworking. The chapter concludes with a discussion of the value of play as an imaginative, creative activity. It uses hollow and unit blocks to illustrate how to provide play opportunities that will enable children to make the best use of their creative powers.

SELF-CHECK QUESTIONS FOR REVIEW

Content-Related Questions
1. How is creativity usually expressed by young children?
2. Describe some of the functions of the right hemisphere of the brain, and explain why these are valuable.

3. The text lists six general principles that underlie successful presentation of most creative activities. Name what these are and explain why each is important.

4. What did Amabile and Gitomer find out in their research study on providing choices to children?

5. Select one of the self-expressive activities listed in Table 13–1 and describe how you would expect children of various ages to respond to it.

6. Imagine you are preparing to present easel painting or fingerpainting to the children in your group. How can you set it up most efficiently? What are some variations you could use to add variety to the experience? Answer the same questions for dough, collage, and woodworking.

7. Review the benefits of imaginative, pretend play for children and use block play to illustrate some practical ways to encourage such play.

Integrative Questions

1. The text points out there is a difference between suggesting that a child bear down on a brace and bit and telling her where to drill the hole. Please explain just what the difference is.

2. Refer to Table 13–2. What are the basic differences between Column I, II, and III activities? Which column provides the greatest opportunities for children to be creative? Why is this true?

3. What is the difference between *creating* something and *making* something? Explain how carpentry could be presented to fit either of these verbs.

4. Can you find examples of the principles for fostering creative play actually illustrated in the discussion on creative block play? Are all the principles there, or are some of them left out?

QUESTIONS AND ACTIVITIES

1. Do you think of yourself as being a person who uses the left or the right side of the brain more frequently? How do you know?

2. It is hard to really appreciate the individual merits of the dough recipes unless they are actually available for inspection and experimentation. As a class project, have volunteers make them up and bring them to class to try out.

3. As a class, brainstorm a list of "creative" activities appropriate for young children and then go back

and decide whether they belong in Column I, II, or III of Table 13–2.

4. Suppose a bad fairy has waved her wand and ruled that you could only select three basic types of creative self-expressive activities to use for a whole year in your preschool. Which three would you select and why?

5. Suppose that same bad fairy has waved her wand again and now you are allowed to *purchase* only paint and glue (no paper even!) for your creative curriculum. How limiting is this? What self-expressive activities would you actually be able to offer under these circumstances? How might you go about acquiring the necessary free materials to make them possible? Be specific.

6. Every community has its own special resources for free self-expressive materials. Gather these tidbits of information from members of the class and compile a resource list of these for everyone to use.

7. Copy some of the children's block constructions and ask the class to identify which developmental stage the construction represents.

REFERENCES FOR FURTHER READING

Overviews

Belliston, L., & Belliston, M. (1982). *How to raise a more creative child.* Allen, Texas: Argus Communications. This is a good book about what to do and *not* to do to foster creative self-expression.

Brittain, W. L. (1979). *Creativity, art and the young child.* New York: Macmillan Publishing Co. This excellent book discusses research findings on the creative use of art materials by preschool children and then makes recommendations based on these findings for presenting those materials in the early childhood classroom. Highly recommended.

Schirrmacher, R. (1988). *Art and creative development for young children.* Albany, N. Y.: Delmar Publishers. Schirrmacher's comprehensive approach deals with theory as well as practice.

Striker, S. (1986). *Please touch: How to stimulate your child's creative development.* New York: Simon & Schuster. Though written for parents, *Please Touch* is useful for beginning teachers, too, because of its clear discussions about, defense of, and practical suggestions for fostering various creative activities. Highly recommended.

Left and Right Sides of the Brain

Brooks, R. L., & Obrzut, J. E. (1981). Brain lateralizations: Implications for infant stimulation and development. *Young Children, 36*(3), 9–16. An interesting article that presents a discussion of left and right sides of the brain theory and then suggests what parents and teacher can do to promote adequate development for both hemispheres.

Information on Safe Art Materials

Peltz, P. A., & Rossol, M. S. (1984). *Children's art supplies can be toxic.* New York: Center for Occupational Hazards. An unusual and useful pamphlet that identifies various dangerous substances. It also includes a lengthy list of safety-approved art materials with their trade names. Available from the Center, 5 Beekman St., New York, New York 10038.

Money Savers

Sunderlin, S., & Gray, N. (Eds.). (1967). *Bits & Pieces: Imaginative uses for children's learning.* Wheaton, Md.: Association for Childhood Education International. This is such a good pamphlet that it is still in print. Many suggestions for scroungers and packrats are included here.

Collections of Creative Activity Suggestions

Newcomers to the field of early childhood education should bear in mind that, when looking for resource books of creative activities, it is strictly buyer beware. Many so-called creative books are really collections of highly structured craft ideas that leave little or nothing to the child's imagination. The books included here are happy exceptions to this problem.

Bos, B. (1982). *Please don't move the muffin tins: A hands-off guide to art for the young child.* Roseville, Calif.: Turn the Page Press. Nicely illustrated, this book has many practical suggestions and draws a clear distinction between crafts and art.

Chenfield, M. B. (1983). *Creative activities for young children.* New York: Harcourt Brace Jovanovich. In this very good book, Chenfield divides activities according to topics such as bodies or people we meet. She suggests creative activities, including art, movement, and discussion activities related to the topic. Excellent bibliographies for children and adults complete each chapter.

Cherry, C. (1972). *Creative art for the developing child: A teachers's handbook for early childhood education.* Belmont, Calif.: Fearon Publishers. Cherry's books are always filled with practical suggestions and this one on art is no exception.

Kane, J. A. (1985). *Art through nature: An integrated approach to art and nature study with young children.* Holmes Beach, Fl.: LP Learning Program. Kane presents new ideas for using natural materials in art projects. A few of these are "craft type" experiences but the majority are quite open.

Lasky, L., & Mukerji, R. (1980). *Art: Basic for young children.* Washington, D.C.: National Association for the Education of Young Children. This is one of the better books because it discusses the values of art activities as well as provides many suggestions and variations for them.

Painting

Smith, N. R. (1983). *Experience and art: Teaching children to paint.* New York: Teachers College Press. The title of this book is misleading since Smith's intention is not so much teaching as enabling children of various ages to use paints with satisfaction.

Fingerpainting

Stangl, J. (1986). *Magic mixtures: Creative fun for little ones preschool–grade 3.* Belmont, Calif.: David S. Lake Publishers. Recipes range from fingerpaints to many kinds of molding materials.

Clay

Hagen, J., Lewis, H., & Smilansky, S. (1988). *Clay in the classroom: Helping children develop cognitive and affective skills for learning.* New York: Peter Lang. The authors describe a research project that used three methods of instruction about modeling clay. The chapter "Clay in Your Classroom" is a gold mine of information on the practical aspects of presenting clay to young children.

Langstaff, N., & Sproul, A. (1979). *Exploring with clay.* Wheaton, Md.: Association for Childhood Education International. The joy of clay is presented in pictures accompanied by the children's own words. Technical information for the teacher is also included.

Woodworking

Skeen, P., Garner, A. P., & Cartwright, S. (1984). *Woodworking for young children.* Washington, D.C.: National Association for the Education of Young Children. At last, a truly practical book about woodworking for teachers and young children. This book deals with everything from how to tell soft and hard woods apart to describing how tools should be used and nails straightened. Highly recommended.

Creativity in Play

Hendrick, J. (1988). *The whole child: Developmental education for the early years* (4th ed.). Columbus, Ohio: Merrill Publishing Co. Chapters 13 and 14 discuss fostering creativity by means of self-expressive materials and fostering creativity in play. These chapters contain additional information on theory and research it is not possible to include in *Total Learning.*

Blocks

Cartwright, S. (1988). Play can be the building blocks of learning. *Young Children, 43*(5), 44–47. This article analyzes the learnings available from blocks in terms of all the selves and includes recommendations for the successful presentation of this material.

Hirsch, E. S. (Ed.). (1984). *The block book.* Washington, D.C.: National Association for the Education of Young Children. This is the most comprehensive discussion of block play presently available.

Provenzo, E. F., Jr., and Brett, A. (1983). *The complete block book.* Syracuse, N.Y.: Syracuse University Press. Lavishly illustrated, *The Complete Block Book* covers the history, as well as the potential uses, of blocks in the curriculum. Moreover, it reprints Harriet Johnson's famous pamphlet, *The Art of Block Building.*

Reifel, S. (1984). Block construction: Children's developmental landmarks in representation of space. *Young Children, 40*(1), 61–67. Reifel presents a well-documented discussion of the developmental changes in block construction as children develop more sophisticated concepts of space.

Methods of Evaluating the Creative Environment

Harms, T., & Clifford, R. M. (1980). *Early childhood environment rating scale.* New York: Teachers College Press. Although it is not exactly a book, I want to call the reader's attention to this scale because it offers a valuable way to assess the presence of creative activities in early childhood settings.

For the Advanced Student

Albert, R. S. (Ed.). (1983). *Genius and eminence: The social psychology of creativity and exceptional achievement.* Elms-ford, N.Y.: Pergamon Press. A fascinating collection of articles on genius and creativity (not always the same thing). A good book to browse through.

Amabile, T. M. (1983). *The social psychology of creativity.* New York: Springer-Verlag. This is a rare book in which the author substantiates her premises with research.

Corballis, M. C., & Beale, I. L. (1983). *The ambivalent mind: The neurophysiology of left and right.* Chicago: Nelson-Hall Publishers. This is a readable, interesting discussion of laterality (left and right sidedness) and its possible effect on human development. A chapter on hemispherical specialization is included.

Gardner, H. (1980). *Artful scribbles: The significance of children's drawings.* New York: Basic Books. Gardner carefully considers the relationship between drawing, development, and the other "evolving capacities" of the child. A readable, interesting, provocative book profusely illustrated.

Gowan, J. C., Khatena, J., & Torrance, E. P. (1981). *Creativity: Its educational implications* (2nd ed.). Dubuque, Iowa: Kendall/Hunt Publishing Company. What a pleasure it is to have this important book revised and in print once again. It covers a great many topics related to creativity, including what parents and educators can do to facilitate its development.

Rubin, J. A. (1984). *Child art therapy: Understanding and helping children grow through art* (2nd ed.). New York: Van Nostrand Reinhold Co. The material focuses mainly on older children. Interesting reading.

Wohl, A., & Kaufman, B. (1983). *Silent screams and hidden cries: An interpretation of artwork by children from violent homes.* New York: Brunner/Mazel. A valuable but depressing introduction to the subject of art therapy as it relates to abused children.

14 Developing Verbal Competence

Have you ever

- Worked in a multiethnic classroom and wondered whether you should make all the children speak English all the time?
- Worried what to do about a 3-year-old who hardly ever says a word?
- Wished that you could get the children to sing more?

If you have, the material in this chapter will help you.

There is no better play material in the world than words. They surround us, go with us through our work-a-day tasks, their sound is always in our ears, their rhythms on our tongue. Why do we leave it to special occasions and to special people to use these common things as precious play material? Because we are grownups and have closed our ears and our eyes that we may not be distracted from our plodding ways! But when we turn to the children, to hearing and seeing children, to whom all the world is as play material, who think and feel through play, can we not then drop our adult utilitarian speech and listen and watch for the patterns of words and ideas? Can we not speak in rhythm, in pleasing sounds, even in song for the mere sensuous delight it gives us and them even though it adds nothing to the content of our remarks? If we can, I feel sure children will not lose their native use of words: What's more, I think those of six and seven and eight who have lost it in part—and their stories show they have,—will win back their spontaneous joy in the play of words.

LUCY SPRAGUE MITCHELL (1948)

The last chapter discussed helping children develop their right hemisphere, nonverbal capacities. Now it is time to give the other side of the brain its due and discuss how to help children learn and use language. The ability to do this is a vital one, since using language and expressing rational, cognitive thought go hand in hand (Sugarman, 1983).

HOW DO CHILDREN LEARN TO TALK?

Arguments continue over how children actually acquire the ability to use language, and no definitive answer has been settled on yet (Rebok, 1987). However, it is valuable for teachers to be acquainted with the current state of theories of language acquisition, since this field of study is very active at present and the conclusions about how language is learned have important implications for teaching.

What is known so far is that the development of language is a gradual process that proceeds in predictable order and that parents and teachers (as representatives and conveyers of culture) can be powerful influences in fostering the acquisition of vocabulary and the growth of fluency as they help children acquire concepts and attach words to those concepts (Clark, 1983).

One school of thought favors the importance of imitation and reinforcement as the most probable acquisition device (Bandura, 1977; Skinner, 1957, 1974), but many people feel that these theorists have difficulty explaining how children can produce novel, previously unheard utterances by means of these processes. Another group postulates that children develop a language in accordance with a basic, universal linguistic structure inherent in all people that is gradually acted on by different cultures to produce diverse languages (Chomsky, 1987; McNeill, 1970). According to this linguistic theory, novel utterances are the result of applying abstracted, linguistic rules rather than merely imitating what has been heard. Still another theory is that children simply derive abstract rules of language structure as they use it and hear it spoken around them (Maratsos, 1983). Such formulations of rules are not deliberate and consciously determined. It is impossible to picture little children saying to themselves, "If I want to tell my mother I see more than one cat, I must add an *s* at the end of *cat.*" As Herriot puts it, "They use the rule though they cannot describe it" (1987, p. 427).

Since anyone who has worked with little children can cite numerous examples of their acquiring language through imitation and equally numerous examples of spontaneous, novel speech, it seems probable that several factors operate together in language learning and that teachers should take them all into account (Genishi, 1987). If imitation and reinforcement play a part in language acquisition, it behooves teachers to provide good examples for children to imitate and to make the process of using language to communicate satisfying for them. Such gratifications need not be elaborate. Paying attention to what children are saying, for instance, is a very effective way of encouraging them to continue speaking. If teachers also believe that children use experience with language to somehow arrive at linguistic rules for speaking, they will want to expose them to hearing a great deal of language. They then should encourage the children to use it in expressive, spontaneous ways as often as possible.

Teachers also need to have in mind a developmental timetable of when various language skills appear. Table 14–1 provides a list of readily observable behaviors that can help teachers and parents identify children who are lagging too far behind or who are exceptionally advanced. These youngsters can then be offered the special help and opportunities they require.

BLACK ENGLISH AND BILINGUALISM IN THE CHILDREN'S CENTER

Since many youngsters come to preschool programs speaking only the language of their homes, which may differ from what is spoken at school,

it is important for teachers to be well informed about Black English and bilingualism.

Black English

Because the structure of Black English differs from that of Standard English, in the past some teachers have assumed that it was an inferior form of Standard English (Hill, C.A., 1977). However, Black English has been analyzed and shown to possess a sophisticated grammatical structure different from, but not necessarily inferior to, that of Standard English (Labov, 1970; Roy, 1987).

Such research has helped teachers understand that this lect has a definite place in the culture of Black people and that it is not "baby talk." Actually, anyone who has been privileged to be included in the conversations, vivid insults, and other verbal games that go on between older Black children or adults really cannot fail to acknowledge the quickness of verbal wit and humor displayed at these times. Unfortunately, most White teachers do not have this kind of contact with the children they teach, nor is this kind of verbal gamesmanship evident in children of preschool age. The reader can gain at least a partial idea of this humor by watching some of the television programs featuring casts of Black actors. These occasionally provide mild examples of this sort of wit in their exchanges of friendly insults.

Teachers must also be aware of the negative effect that disapproval of something so personal as the child's means of expressing herself could have on her self-image. Because Black English is not an inferior form of Standard English, and because it is important to sustain the child's self-esteem, many authorities now suggest that teachers not deplore or attempt to suppress this form of speech (Daniel, 1981).

Perhaps the most effective way for White, middle-class teachers to regard Black English is to think of it as being another language instead of a lower-class lect. To function successfully in our world today, Black children need to acquire

TABLE 14–1
Milestones in the development of language ability in young children

Average age	Question	Average behavior
3 to 6 months	What does he do when you talk to him?	He awakens or quiets to the sound of his mother's voice.
	Does he react to your voice even when he cannot see you?	He typically turns eyes and head in the direction of the source of sound.
7 to 10 months	When he can't *see* what is happening, what does he do when he hears familiar footsteps . . . the dog barking . . . the telephone ringing . . . candy paper rattling . . . someone's voice . . . his own name?	He turns his head and shoulders toward familiar sounds, even when he cannot see what is happening. Such sounds do not have to be loud to cause him to respond.
11 to 15 months	Can he point to or find familiar objects or people when he is asked to? **Example:** "Where is Jimmy?" "Find the ball."	He shows his understanding of some words by appropriate behavior; for example, he points to or looks at familiar objects or people, on request.
	Does he respond differently to different sounds?	He jabbers in response to a human voice, is apt to cry when there is thunder, or may frown when he is scolded.
	Does he enjoy listening to some sounds and imitating them?	Imitation indicates that he can hear the sounds and match them with his own sound production.
1½ years	Can he point to parts of his body when you ask him to? **Example:** "Show me your eyes." "Show me your nose."	Some children begin to identify parts of the body. He should be able to show his nose or eyes.
	How many understandable words does he use—words you are sure *really* mean something?	He should be using a few single words. They are not complete or pronounced perfectly but are clearly meaningful.
2 years	Can he follow simple verbal commands when you are careful not to give him any help, such as looking at the object or pointing in the right direction? **Example:** "Johnny, get your hat and give it to Daddy." "Debby, bring me your ball."	He should be able to follow a few simple commands without visual clues.
	Does he enjoy being read to? Does he point out pictures of familiar objects in a book when asked to? **Example:** "Show me the baby." "Where's the rabbit?"	Most 2-year-olds enjoy being "read to" and shown simple pictures in a book or magazine, and will point out pictures when you ask them to.

Note. From *Learning to Talk: Speech, Hearing and Language Problems in the Pre-School Child* by the National Institute of Neurological Diseases and Stroke, 1969, Washington, D.C.: U.S. Department of Health, Education, and Welfare.

TABLE 14-1 (continued)

Average age	Question	Average behavior
	Does he use the names of familiar people and things such as *Mommy, milk, ball,* and *hat?*	He should be using a variety of everyday words heard in his home and neighborhood.
	What does he call himself?	He refers to himself by name.
	Is he beginning to show interest in the sound of radio or TV commercials?	Many 2-year-olds do show such interest, by word or action.
	Is he putting a few words together to make little "sentences"? **Example:** "Go bye-bye car." "Milk all gone."	These "sentences" are not usually complete or grammatically correct.
2½ years	Does he know a few rhymes or songs? Does he enjoy hearing them?	Many children can say or sing short rhymes or songs and enjoy listening to records or to mother singing.
	What does he do when the ice cream man's bell rings, out of his sight, or when a car door or house door closes at a time when someone in the family usually comes home?	If a child has good hearing, and these are events that bring him pleasure, he usually reacts to the sound by running to look or telling someone what he hears.
3 years	Can he show that he understands the meaning of some words besides the names of things? **Example:** "Make the car go." "Give me your ball." "Put the block in your pocket." "Find the big doll."	He should be able to understand and use some simple verbs, pronouns, prepositions, and adjectives, such as *go, me, in,* and *big.*
	Can he find you when you call him from another room?	He should be able to locate the source of a sound.
	Does he sometimes use complete sentences?	He should be using complete sentences some of the time.
4 years	Can he tell about events that have happened recently?	He should be able to give a connected account of some recent experiences.
	Can he carry out two directions, one after the other? **Example:** "Bobby, find Susie and tell her dinner's ready."	He should be able to carry out a sequence of two simple directions.
5 years	Do neighbors and others outside the family understand most of what he says?	His speech should be intelligible, although some sounds may still be mispronounced.
	Can he carry on a conversation with other children or familiar grown-ups?	Most children of this age can carry on a conversation if the vocabulary is within their experience.
	Does he begin a sentence with "I" instead of "me"; "he" instead of "him"?	He should use some pronouns correctly.
	Is his grammar almost as good as his parents'?	Most of the time, it should match the patterns of grammar used by the adults of his family and neighborhood.

proficiency in both Black and Standard English, because, as they mature, they will need to shift gears back and forth between them depending on whom they are talking to. As is true in other bilingual situations, teachers must realize that for Black children to acquire Standard English as their second language, it is not necessary for them to abandon their first one (Pflaum, 1986; Smitherman, 1981).

Bilingualism

The subject of bilingualism and bilingual education is simply too vast to be discussed in detail in a general education text of this kind. We must content ourselves here with pointing out the value of accepting that the child's dominant language is an important part of herself, just as it is vital to honor the other aspects of her cultural heritage.

At the preschool level, this is usually accomplished by employing teaching staff who are bilingual. In earlier years, the skills of such staff were most often used for interpretation rather than for preservation of the children's native tongue. It frequently happened that, as the children gained facility in English, the school dropped the use of the other language.

Now in some areas of the country there is more of an attempt to operate truly bilingual classrooms, in which a genuine effort is made to teach and sustain both languages and to perpetuate other cultural values, too. This kind of bilingual education is often termed a *maintenance bilingual model* (Ruiz, 1987). Harrington (1978) describes this succinctly:

> *Maintenance* models, if they are truly bilingual, are in fact trying to get at both cultural pluralism and structural pluralism. That is, they are trying to foster cultural and linguistic pluralism at the same time that they are providing students with the skills necessary to get resources within the larger society. Realistically . . . true maintenance programs are relatively rare. (p. 3)

Even though such programs may still be relatively rare in public schools, this need not be the case for children's centers, which have much greater opportunities for autonomy. If teachers so choose, they can make a point of combining the multiethnic educational model and environment discussed in Chapter 12 with a balanced bilingual program, thereby providing good quality language maintenance programs for the children they serve (Cazden, 1984).

The Child Who Is Not Fluent in Any Language

The foregoing discussion assumes that children who are not speaking Standard English do speak some other language or lect fluently. However, there are some youngsters who arrive at the center who are not verbal at all. Teachers must be on the lookout for such youngsters and not make the mistake of assuming, for example, that they must be fluent in their "home" language just because they do not speak in English. This is not always the case. It is particularly valuable to check about such nonverbal behavior with the children's families. This will help determine whether they do not talk at school but *do* talk at home, or whether they say very little in either circumstance.

Children who are generally nonverbal at home and at school need special attention and stimulation to develop their verbal and mental capacities. When these are provided, they often make very dramatic progress at school (Dumtschin, 1988). However, if they are still not talking after 2 to 3 months of regular attendance, it is vital to seek the help of specialists, since there is often a significant reason for the delay.

Perhaps the child is hard of hearing or is developmentally delayed in some way. Referrals should be made to the child's pediatrician, an otolaryngologist (a physician specializing in diseases of the ear, nose, and throat), or a speech pathologist. If retardation is suspected, referral should be made to a child psychologist for testing. Once the reason for the delay in speech has been determined, a plan for remediation should be developed, and the teacher should make certain the specialist keeps him informed about what he should be doing to help carry the plan out. The sooner these conditions are identified, the sooner they can be treated. *Teachers must never wait an entire year with a nonverbal 3- or 4-year-old in the hope that she will suddenly blossom forth and begin talking.* All too often this fails to happen.

GOOD TEACHING HABITS THAT FOSTER CHILDREN'S USE OF LANGUAGE

Chapter 10 on emotional health has already discussed how important it is for the teacher to "hear" the children's feelings and, by describing these to them, let them know that he understands what is going on inside them. This kind of interested concern is also a fundamental way of encouraging children to talk, since the teacher who truly listens draws forth conversation from children as a magnet attracts iron.

Of course, if teachers have packed the day too full so that everyone must be pushed from one activity to the next or if there is not enough teaching staff, the leisure that good conversational opportunities require is hard to come by. But even in centers where these circumstances prevail, teachers can encourage children to chat with them, if they realize how valuable such opportunities are for encouraging verbal fluency.

The research study by McCartney (1984) included in this chapter provides evidence of just how important it can be for teachers to involve themselves in quality talk with the children in their care.

Learn to Conduct a Conversation, Not an Interrogation

Teachers frequently see themselves as being primarily information givers and getters: that is, they are forever telling children important facts or asking them questions so the children will prove they already know the facts or are thinking about them—but good conversation rarely dwells on such matters.

Witness the following variations on the same topic and then ask yourself which of the two you would prefer to take part in if you were the child. Also, ask yourself what the child *learned* from each of the two encounters and which one fostered the greater fluency and development of thought.

Example 1

Child: Guess what, Teacher, I got new shoes!

Teacher: No kidding! My, my! They're real pretty!

Child: They got chuckles!

Teacher: Chuckles?

Child: Yeah, *you* know! *Chuckles!* Here on the side. (points to buckles)

Teacher: (light dawning) Oh, you mean *buckles!* That word sounds like buck—buck-buck-buck-buck-buck-a-luck *buckles!*

Child: (amused) Buck-buck-buck-buck-buck-a-luck buckles!

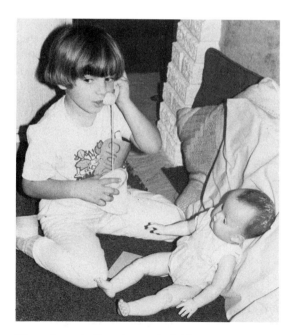

There is no better play material in the world than words.

RESEARCH STUDY
How Does the Day-Care Environment Affect Children's Language Development?

Research Question   McCartney asked the question, "Does the quality of the day-care environment affect children's language development?"

Research Method   Fifty-six children were randomly selected from seven day-care centers in Bermuda. All the children had attended the centers for more than half a year and were at least 3 years of age.

The investigators assessed the quality of the centers on a number of scales. The quality was found to vary widely. Next they observed and classified the verbal behavior of the children and their caregivers, and, finally, they evaluated the children's intellectual and language development on a series of measures.

Results   Analyses revealed that the quality of the day-care environment had a very significant effect upon language development. Children who were enrolled in the better-quality centers scored consistently higher on all the measures of intellectual and language ability than did the children who were enrolled in the poorer-quality centers.

More specifically, the *amount of verbal interaction* taking place between caregivers and children was identified as being a good predictor of how high the children would score on the tests. The more talking that took place between the caregivers and children, the higher the scores were for the children. The high-scoring children also initiated more conversations with staff.

The *kind* of verbal interaction was important, too. Observations revealed that the caregivers of higher-scoring children used fewer controlling comments and provided more information-giving comments. They also requested more information when talking with the children. In turn, the children talked more with the staff.

Teacher: That's right—buckles. (pause) Are they hard to get through that hole? (meaning the straps)

Child: Yeah, but I don't mind. I just worm 'em through!

Teacher: Yeah, just wiggle the edge that way—into the side place!

Child: *I* can do it! Into the side place! (pause) They make marks on my socks!

Teacher: Oh, yeah, I see. Does it hurt?

Child: Nope. My foot's sweaty, that's all—makes the red come off.

Teacher: You take those shoes off at night, you'll still have little red feet on!

Child: (thinks this over, laughs) Well, yeah—little

pink feet! Just like wearing shoes to bed! (laughs) My Momma sure won't like that, no way! (runs off to play)

Example 2

Child: Guess what, Teacher, I got new shoes!

Teacher: Yes, I see you did. They're pretty, Tania. What color do you think they are?

Child: (pause) Red.

Teacher: And what else is special about them?

Child: (shakes head) I don't know.

Teacher: Oh, yes, now—think a minute. What's that on the side of your red shoe? Right there? (she points to the buckle)

Child: It makes red marks.

This kind of thought-provoking exchange took place more frequently during group times than during free play.

The amount of talking the children did with each other was also assessed, and analysis showed that talking between children did not influence how well the children did on the measures of verbal and intellectual ability.

Implications This study provides clear evidence that just letting children talk with each other does not provide enough stimulation for them to develop sufficient language and intellectual skills. It emphasizes how important it is for adults to make plenty of time to talk with the children and encourage them to respond. It is these opportunities for interchange that foster the growth of language skills and related intellectual ability. Indeed, it may ultimately turn out that the provision of such opportunities is the hallmark of the successful developmental program.

The fact that in this study these opportunities occurred mainly during group instruction times should give the reader pause for thought. Does that finding imply that group instruction is more effective? Or could it mean that the caregivers in the study were simply not taking advantage of the free-play time to do more than control and guide the children?

Although McCartney's study cannot provide the answer to this question, it does draw attention to the possibility that teachers should take better advantage of one-to-one opportunities to create quality talk during free play. Certainly such open time *can* present wonderful opportunities for teachers to build language skills with the children—opportunities to question, listen, explain, and discuss all the interesting things that come up as children play. Capitalizing on these possibilities should help teachers enjoy the children as they also help them increase their language skills.

Note. From "Effect of Quality of Day Care Environment on Children's Language Development" by K. McCartney, 1984, *Developmental Psychology, 20*(2), pp. 244–260.

Teacher: That isn't what I mean! What's *this* called? (she points to the buckle again)

Child: Don't know.

Teacher: It's called a *buckle. Buckle*—can you say that?

Child: Fix it for me!

Teacher: "What's the magic word?"

Child: (pause) Please.

Teacher: Please what?

Child: Please fix that.

Teacher: (persistently but not unpleasantly) What's that called? I just told you.

Child: (says nothing)

Teacher: (patiently) Buckle—remember? That's a buckle!

Child: Buckle!

Teacher fixes the shoe while child stands silently, then runs off.

I hope the reader concludes from these examples that there is a place for fun in talking with children and that it is not always necessary to use high-pressure techniques to obtain valuable educational results. Note also how in example 1 the ideas build on each other and the talk flows freely and increases in quantity. These are the most important goals to work toward when building language skills in young children. They are certainly more important then driving and driving to add one new word, *buckle*, to the child's vocabulary.

Learn How to Ask Questions That Invite Children to Respond

Questions should relate to topics that children are interested in and that they know something about—preferably, even more than the teacher does. For example, "Where did you get that wonderful hat?" or "How come you like this book so much?" or "I saw you helping your Momma in the market yesterday. Were you telling her what to get?" all invite replies that will tell the teacher something he does not already know, and they cast the child in the role of the authority.

If these invitations to chat are coupled with nonjudgmental replies to what the children say, they will encourage talk even further. For example, consider the effect of the two kinds of teacher responses in the following dialogues:

Example 3

Teacher: (playfully picking up the child and hugging her) I saw you helping your Momma in the market yesterday. Were you telling her what to get?

Child: Yeah! I told her to get pickles, and ice cream, and sugar buns!

Teacher: Why did you do that? You know that isn't good for you! You ought to tell her to get cereal and vegetables and the things that we talked about at lunch that are good for you to eat! They'll make you grow up strong like your brother!

Child: (says nothing—just wiggles to get down)

Example 4

Teacher: (playfully picking up the child and hugging her) I saw you helping your Momma in the market yesterday. Were you telling her what to get?

Child: Yeah, I told her to get pickles, and ice cream, and sugar buns!

Teacher: I guess you were really hungry!

Child: I sure was—and those little crackers, and chicken, and corn . . . .

Teacher: That's what makes you grow—good stuff like that. (meaning chicken and corn)

Child: And shoe polish!

Teacher: Shoe polish! (playfully) I don't want to eat that!

Child: (grinning and with great emphasis) And *shoe polish!* We had shoe polish frosting for dessert!

Teacher: (laughs) Yum, yum. It must have looked like chocolate!

Child: Yeah, chocolate shoe polish frosting. (laughs) Dyn-o-mite!

Teacher: Well, it's *real* chocolate pudding for lunch today. Want to set out the napkins?

Child: Sure! (wiggles to get down)

Learn to Use an Attractive Speaking Voice

When teachers are under stress, their voices sometimes rise in pitch or take on a hard, nasal quality that is unpleasant to listen to and that creates tension in the children, too. Other teachers may have monotonous voices and thereby fail to attract or hold the children's attention.

The best remedy for these problems is for teachers to tape record themselves regularly during group or lunchtime and actually listen to what they are saying and how they sound while saying it. This is because it is impossible to correct a voice quality problem until they are aware of it. The next step is catching themselves in the act and consciously modulating the tone of voice to a more pleasant level. One way teachers can keep track of voice quality is to put five pennies in a pocket at the beginning of the day and transfer one to another pocket every time they hear their voices rising too far. It only takes a few days to keep all the pennies in the beginning pocket.

PRESENTING MATERIALS AND RESOURCES

As we have seen, the basic tool for developing language in children is the way teachers use their time with them to generate satisfying episodes of dialogue. Preschool also abounds with additional opportunities for emphasizing more specific language activities, and the remainder of this chapter discusses principles related to their presentation. Group time, which is discussed in Chapter 15, also provides many opportunities for building language skills.

Language Without Experience and Experience Without Language Is Almost Meaningless to Children

The work of Eve Clark (1983) on how children learn to attach meaning to words reminds us of the importance of tying experience to language. She points out that children originally establish word meanings on the basis of salient perceptual features of objects: shape, movement, size, sound, taste, and texture—all sensory experiences. The moral for early childhood teachers (even though they are dealing with children slightly older than the ones in Clark's studies) is that they must be careful to offer language activities related to those tangible, concrete things children know about because of their direct sensory experience with them.

It makes no sense to read a poem about snow to California children, many of whom have no idea of what it is, unless teachers also liken it to hail and include such experiences as taking them to visit an ice skating rink, showing them pictures of snow, and talking about how it feels when they put their hands in the refrigerator. Even then, these children do not really have the meanings associated with snow that youngsters in wintry climates do. Just because children can mouth a word does not mean they necessarily grasp the concept.

Auditory Discrimination Activities

Auditory discrimination is simply a fancy term for teaching children to pay attention to sounds and encouraging them to become discriminating so they can tell when the sounds are alike and when they are different. Being able to distinguish between sounds is an important skill because it

can help sensitize children who do not speak clearly to differences in the way words are pronounced. It is also a helpful prereading skill to foster because it helps them tell words apart.

Unfortunately, many schools seem unaware of the value of sharpening children's ears. Perhaps they feel this skill can only be taught through a lot of drill work, but this is untrue. There are many activities that can be used to build auditory discrimination skills and are just plain fun. Actually, anything that encourages children to listen closely to sounds and to signal in some way that they distinguish between them comes under this heading. The following are some suggestions[1]:

- Let the children pull pictures of animals or toy animals out of a "secret box." Next, make various animal sounds. When each child hears "her" animal, she jumps up and shows it to the other children. This activity can be made somewhat more challenging by using a tape recording instead of making the sounds yourself. This helps emphasize the aspect of sound more strongly.
- Tape record various common household sounds—a car starting, a toilet flushing, food frying, door shutting, an electric mixer, and so forth—and ask children to guess what they are hearing.
- Make up paired sets of sound cannisters (such as 35 mm film cases) with different contents, and see if the children can pair the ones together that sound just alike. (Experience proves that it is important to seal the tops of these so that children use their ears, not their eyes or fingers, to determine the source of the sound.)
- Fill a set of sturdy glass jars with different amounts of water, and encourage the children to strike them gently with a spoon and arrange them from lowest to highest tone. (This activity is appropriate for older fours and requires careful supervision because of the glass containers.)

---

[1]Two sources for additional activities and strategies are *Communicative Disorders: Prevention and Early Intervention* (2nd ed.) by C. E. Weiss and H. S. Lillywhite, 1981, St. Louis: The C. V. Mosby Co.; and *Speech Correction: An Introduction to Speech Pathology and Audiology* by C. Van Riper and L. Emerick, 1984, Englewood Cliffs, N.J.: Prentice-Hall.

- Divide a few children into two groups. While one group hides behind a sheet or screen, have one of them say something out loud and ask the other group to guess who is talking. Asking them to say a nursery rhyme will help overcome their self-consciousness about what to say.
- Let the children think up ways to make sounds using their bodies (such as stamping or clapping or yawning), and ask the other children to shut their eyes and guess what they are doing.

More Difficult Discrimination Activities:

- Have a small group of objects or even pictures and ask children to pick out the one that begins with "buh" or "a-a-a." A more advanced form of this activity is to ask them to look for something in the room that starts with a particular sound and point it out or ask the children to point out something that starts with the same sound as "baby" or "Mama."
- Have children listen to a series of words that are the same or almost alike, such as dog, log, fog, dog, dog. Every time they hear the same word they can take a marble from the pot. See how soon the children can empty the pot.

Songs and Records

Music should be part of the life of the school throughout the day and definitely not relegated just to group time. The use of a simple, familiar song can ease transitions between activities and deepen pleasure in activities themselves. Such a simple thing as singing the words, "Swing, swing, swingy, swing" to the tune of "Row, Row, Row Your Boat" can enchant a 2½-year-old, for example. Singing can pass the time while waiting for lunch or bind a group of parents and children together at a party. It can introduce the children to their cultural heritage, whether it be early American folk songs or ones from Africa or Germany or Japan (McLaughlin & Wood, 1973). It is the perfect medium for opening group time, since children can join in as they arrive without feeling they are interrupting or that they have been left out.

Choosing a Good Song. A good song for little children is one that is simple, short, and

Singing together is another easygoing way to encourage the development of language skills.

repetitive. It should have a range of only a few notes. If it can be personalized by inserting the children's names, so much the better. Careful thought should be devoted to the quality of the song, also. There is no need to settle for trivial material when we have people like Marcia Berman and Patty Zeitlin (1982)[2] and Alec Wilder (1965) writing contemporary music for children.

Traditional music should be included also. Many children today no longer hear nursery rhymes unless they are presented at school, yet many of these are set to tunes that have stood the test of time and are already familiar. "Twinkle, Twinkle Little Star," "Jack and Jill," and "Mary Had a Little Lamb" come instantly to mind.

American folk songs, although less familiar to some of us, offer another rich resource for singing with children. These are often written in a minor key—a useful quality, since it extends the children's "ear" for melody. Some folk songs are surprisingly funny and frank, also qualities that both children and adults appreciate (Landek, 1950; Seeger, 1948).

Remember too that many children hear music all day long in their own homes where radios or television sets are continually turned on. Although one might not want to use all such material, there certainly are many popular songs that will fit in; and since popular music is so much a part of the life of the children's homes, it makes sense to include it.

Finally, singing simple songs from many cultures offers an excellent way of fostering positive feelings toward other peoples. A child can glow with importance when the teacher mentions that a particular song comes from Puerto Rico—the same place his own family

comes from. The records of Ella Jenkins[3] are prime examples of how various cultures can be presented to young children in a pleasureful, participatory way, but it is desirable to explore even further than that. There are many records available today from such sources as Folkways Records or Bowmar[4] that are authentic and appropriate to use with children. Adding musical instruments that come from the same culture as the song is a delightful touch. These need be neither elaborate nor expensive. Hunter and Judson, for example, have written a helpful book entitled *Simple Folk Instruments to Make and Play* (1977), which is a good resource for making such equipment.

Here are five excellent books containing appropriate music for young children:

Bayless, K. M., & Ramsey, M. E. (1987). *Music: A way of life for the young child* (3rd ed.). Columbus, Ohio: Merrill Publishing Co.

Birkenshaw, L. (1982). *Music for fun; Music for learning* (3rd ed.). Toronto: Holt, Rinehart & Winston of Canada.

Jenkins, E. (1966). *The Ella Jenkins song book for children.* New York: Oak Publications.

Landek, B. (1950). *Songs to grow on: A collection of American folk songs for children.* New York: William Sloane Associates.

Seeger, R. C. (1948). *American folk songs for children.* Garden City, N.Y.: Doubleday & Co.

Zeitlin, P. (1982). *A song is a rainbow: Music, movement and rhythm instruments in the nursery school and kindergarten.* Glenview, Ill.: Scott, Foresman & Co.

Bayless and Ramsey, as well as Birkenshaw, go far beyond presenting songs per se. Their books are also rich resources of information on presenting all forms of music to young children—and these have the added advantage of providing *very*

---

[2]Two good examples of the Berman/Zeitlin work are "Spin, Spider, Spin" (AR 551) and "Rainy Day Dances, Rainy Day Songs" (AR 570). Both are available from Educational Activities, Freeport, New York 11520.

[3]Two good examples of her style are "Rhythms of Childhood with Ella Jenkins" (SC 7653) and "You'll Sing a Song and I'll Sing a Song" (SC 7664). Both are available from Scholastic Records, 906 Sylvan Ave., Englewood Cliffs, New Jersey 07632.

[4]Folkways Records, 43 W. 61st St., New York, New York 10023; Bowmar, 4563 Colorado Blvd., Los Angeles, California 90039.

simple arrangements scored for piano and Auto-harp. The Seeger and Landek books, which are still in print, are authentic resources for folk songs.

Teaching a Song to Children. Be prepared to repeat a song several times on several days for the children to learn it well enough to enjoy singing it freely. This is one of the primary reasons for choosing simple, repetitive songs of good quality. However, the children will be able to join in right away if there is a short chorus in which first the leader and then the group sing the same refrain.

Sing slowly, and teach only one verse at a time. It will contribute to the pleasure if the song is accompanied by an instrument, such a guitar or an Autoharp, but this is not essential. Indeed, unless done with care, using something like a piano can be more trouble then it is worth if it means the teacher must turn his back on the children while playing it. The advantage of using an Autoharp is that children can be invited to strum it in time to the singing, since all one must do to control the note is press down firmly on the correct key. (Incidentally, *anyone* can easily learn to play an Autoharp. Bayless and Ramsey provide helpful instructions for doing this in Appendix C of *Music: A Way of Life for the Young Child.*)

Remember, too, that one of the nicest things about singing with children is the freedom it gives the teacher to improvise and adapt a song to the circumstances of the day. Clare Cherry's book (1971) on movement is full of examples of how topical words can be set to tunes everyone knows.

Poetry and Finger Plays

Like singing, poetry should not be reserved just for group time, although it should always be part of that experience (Andrews, 1988). Teachers who take the trouble to commit some short poems to memory and who can quote these as the occasion arises can indeed make literature an integral, pleasureful part of the children's lives. I grew up in a school system that required us to learn a certain amount of poetry by heart, and that habit and those poems have never left me. Because of my own experience, I freely recommend the value of memorizing poetry to the reader. It can be a source of real delight for the children.

For teachers who do not wish to memorize verse, a poetry file is recommended as the quickest and best way to obtain access to poetry as it is needed. Relying on books as a resource really does not work out well. It is too hard to find just the right poem at the right time. Also, I have yet to find a completely satisfactory anthology of verse for preschool children, although if I were restricted to only one, I would choose Arbuthnot and Root's *Time for Poetry* (1968) because the majority of the poems are short and in excellent taste, and they are arranged by topic headings.

Our staff types out or photocopies appropriate, good quality poetry as they come across it and mounts it on mat board obtained as "leavings" from picture frame shops. This preserves the poem on a durable, hard-to-lose background and also makes it easy to file by topic so it can be immediately located when needed. Then when we need something on rain, or worms, or going to sleep, or shadows, we can put our hands right on it.

We have found the poetry of Dorothy Aldis, Marchette Chute, Aileen Fisher, Myra Cohn Livingston, Walter de la Mare, Miriam Clark Potter, Christina Rosetti, and Robert Louis Stevenson particularly appropriate—and of course Mother Goose should not be forgotten.[5] Many fine editions of her rhymes are available. My favorite is the one edited by Eulalie Osgood Grover (1971) based on Frederick Richardson's

---

[5]For an excellent bibliography of poetry books for very young children see *Handbook for Story Tellers* (pp. 147–149) by C. F. Bauer, 1977, Chicago: American Library Association. A bibliography of Mother Goose books also is included in that same volume on p. 150.

original edition, which as been reprinted by Hubbard Press.

No matter how complete the file, there will inevitably be times when no poem can be found that exactly suits a particular occasion. When this happens, try writing one yourself. The children will appreciate its timeliness. Its appropriateness for the occasion more than makes up for any potential lack of literary merit.

Finger Plays. Although the poetic quality of finger plays often leaves much to be desired, their ability to instantly involve children makes them a valuable addition to the language development arsenal. It is the old story of doing while saying—linking language and action—that helps children learn and enjoy this activity.

Finger plays are excellent ways to begin a group time, since they are so attractive to children. They also can provide relief in the middle of a group time by offering a change of pace and recentering their attention. Finger plays make good "time fillers" when the schedule goes awry and the children have to wait a little for something to happen. If the same one is presented repeatedly, they also enjoy saying it along with the teacher as they go through the actions. The actions themselves need not be limited just to fingers. Many successful "finger plays" actually involve larger muscles, such as getting up and sitting down. They can either be sung or recited.[6]

Books and Stories

Reading Stories. Teachers often think of reading stories to children as being primarily a receptive language situation where the children are expected to sit quietly and "receive" the story, but it should be both a receptive and expressive language opportunity. If stories are presented with this goal in mind, teachers no longer have to struggle to keep the children quiet. Instead, they can welcome the children's comments and questions and invite discussion about what may happen next in the story.

Teachers should read with expression and enthusiasm and should be familiar with the text so that they do not stumble over words. They should take time to enjoy what is happening with the children and to allow them to add their own comments. Bev Bos (1983) describes this process well:

> Slowly I started letting the children discuss many pages of the book as I read. I would stop. We would examine a picture, asking questions about what they could see. Often they would see details I hadn't. If I would ask them what they thought would happen next, they could frequently come up with wonderfully creative ideas. As this process continued, I began to see marvelous results. I started to see the children themselves emerging—attempting *their* language, attempting to communicate with me—and at the same time I could see that they were discovering that they were capable of complicated and delightful communication.
>
> I have often been asked in my workshops how we can allow time for such interruptions—such a slow pace—when there's so much to do. My answer is that if the interruption doesn't happen, it is very likely that learning isn't happening. We need to translate *interruption* as the child's entering the process. If we genuinely believe that language development is at the heart of the learning process, then we must allow time. Not only allowing for it, but planning for interruptions is our whole purpose. (p.7)

Of course, a balance is needed between encouraging children's comments and maintaining the momentum of the plot. Sometimes saying something such as "Just one more comment and then we'd better find out whether the Circus Baby could really sit on that chair" or "Well—let's go on now and see what's on the

---

[6]Two good sources of finger plays are *Move over, Mother Goose: Finger Plays, Action, Action Verses, and Funny Rhymes* by R. I. Dowell, 1987, Mt. Rainier, Md: Gryphon House; and *Do Your Ears Hang Low: Fifty More Musical Fingerplays* by T. Glazer, 1980, Garden City, N.Y.: Doubleday & Co.

You can do it!

next page" will usually lead the children back to the book without hurting anyone's feelings.

Good books for young children generally have brief texts, beautiful pictures, and subject matter that is interesting to children and presented in good taste.[7] Excellent books also have that extra note of originality combined with quality writing and a good story that enshrines them in the hearts of children forever. Some outstanding examples are *The Circus Baby* (Petersham & Petersham), 1950, *It's Just Me, Emily* (Hines, 1987), *Curious George* (Rey, 1941), *Bedtime for Frances* (Hoban, 1960), *The Snowy Day* (Keats, 1962), *Ask Mr. Bear* (Flack, 1932), *The Girl Who Loved Wild Horses* (Goble, 1978), *The Doorbell Rang* (Hutchins, 1986), *Madeleine* (Bemelmans, 1939), *Amigo* (Schweitzer, 1963), *The Goat in The Rug* (Blood & Link, 1976), *Where Does My Cat Sleep?* (Simon, 1982), and *Mary Betty Lizzie McNutt's Birthday* (Bond, 1983).

Books should be readily available throughout the day and should be varied from time to time—new ones brought out and more familiar

---

[7]In addition to the multiethnic resource lists previously cited, two additional bibliographies of books for young children may be found in *Helping Young Children Learn* (4th ed.) by E. G. Pitcher, S. G. Feinberg, and D. Alexander, 1984, Columbus, Ohio: Merrill Publishing Co.; and in *Guiding Your Child to a More Creative Life* by F. Maynard, 1973, Garden City, N.Y.: Doubleday & Co. An annual list of *Notable Children's Books* may be obtained from The Children's Service Division of the American Library Association, 50 E. Huron St., Chicago, Illinois 60611.

friends put away. Variety is as close as the nearest public library.

Particularly in full-day centers, it is important to provide a cozy oasis where children can withdraw and leaf through their favorites without interruption. Opening a book to an especially beautiful or interesting picture and placing it in a holder by the bookshelf often entices children to that area. Preschoolers should be taught to handle books with care. *Never* permit them to leave books lying on the floor for children to walk on or otherwise abuse.

Reading stories is a good example of an activity in which volunteers can excel with only a moderate amount of instruction from the staff. Encourage them to settle down in a comfortable place with several well-chosen books. This provides wonderful opportunities for one-to-one and one-to-two contacts that both children and volunteers find meaningful and satisfying.

Encouraging Children to Tell Stories. We have already spoken of the value telling stories can have for children in terms of expressing their feelings and clarifying their ideas (Chapter 10). Providing them with opportunities for doing this also develops language fluency.

To avoid long, rambling accounts at group time, which usually produce uncontrollable restlessness in the other children, it is best to pick times during the day when child storytelling can be done on a one-to-one basis between staff and youngster. Children particularly enjoy dictating stories in their own special books that the teacher has made by stapling a few sheets of paper together. As they approach kindergarten age, they may even enjoy adding illustrations to emphasize what they mean.

There are various ways of starting things off with the child. The teacher can simply ask her what she wants to tell about today, or inquire if she wants to have him write down how her puppy learned to stop barking, or even begin a story himself for the child to continue, perhaps

using those magical words, "Once upon a time . . . ."

Another way to encourage children to tell stories is to use pictures from the picture file. Younger children tend to use such single pictures more as opportunities to simply tell what is happening in the picture itself than as a starting point for a more extended story (Hough, Nurss, & Wood, 1987). Older children can go beyond that limited approach. Many times a picture of two little girls on a climbing gym or a lonely-looking boy holding a puppy can spark a long tale that uses the illustration as a take-off point, particularly if the teacher encourages such story telling by asking occasional questions or making comments such as "Then what do you think happened?" or "After she caught the fish, what did she do next?"

Books—A never-ending source of true delight!

Suggestions for Telling Stories. Like the children, teachers can also learn to tell stories with a little practice.[8] This often has a liberating, creative effect, since it allows them to tailor the tale exactly to the requirements of the youthful audience. Telling stories also offers the opportunity to include the children themselves as characters. It can recapitulate something the children themselves have done, or it can be based on one of the teachers' experiences that they think the children will enjoy. Stories can be based on books, as well as on personal experience, and this is a particularly useful technique to employ when the illustrations are delightful but the text too difficult for the children to comprehend. Learning to "edit" as they go along is also a useful strategy for teachers to cultivate when material is sexist or conveys an undesirable racist slant. (Guidelines on identifying sexist and racist materials are found in Appendix E.).

If you are insecure about storytelling, remember that children's librarians are often excellent storytellers and can frequently be prevailed on to present story hours for visiting preschoolers. Furthermore, many of them are also happy to impart their skills to other teachers if invited to participate in training workshops for this purpose.

Discussion and Conversation

Some examples of possible discussion openers include asking children to offer suggestions ("Visiting day is coming up. What activities do you think we should set up for your brothers and sisters to do? What would they enjoy?"), to consider alternatives ("It's such a beautiful day:

do you think we should have water play after snack, or would you prefer to walk to the park?" "Would you rather have Officer Thompson visit us at school or go the police station and meet him there?"), to make plans in advance ("You know, Cynthia is bringing her puppies to visit again tomorrow. Let's put our heads together and make a plan to keep them from being handled too much"), and to solve social problems ("We've been having so many fights over that trike with the license plate on it. I want to know what you children think we should do about it?").

Note that most of these gambits also require follow-up questions that encourage children to give the reasons for their opinions. Once all the possibilities, opinions, and reasons have been aired, it is best to reach a democratic group consensus—working out compromises where possible and, in the end, following the democratic principle of doing what the majority thinks best.

These decision-making opportunities should only be offered when the choices are real and are truly appropriate for children to evaluate. For example, it would *not* be appropriate to ask the children to decide what to do about a youngster who is wetting his pants or to expect them to made a decision on whether school fees should be raised, but it would be within their ability to ask them to suggest a number of ways Halloween might be celebrated or how they would help their friend Cindy feel better because her puppy died.

An alternative to taking the risk of abiding by a group decision, if you feel the children are too immature to reach an adequate one, is to tell them you want some ideas and suggestions that will help *you* arrive at a fair or good decision.

---

[8]Two good books about the art of storytelling are *Handbook for Story Tellers* by C. F. Bauer, 1977, Chicago: American Library Association; and *Just Enough to Make a Story: A Sourcebook for Storytelling* by N. Schimmel, 1978, Berkeley, Calif.: Sisters' Choice Press.

Link Language to the Printed Page

Parents often think of reading as being the first and fundamental building block of school success, and in a way, they are right. The ability to read and to grasp the meaning of what is read *is* basic to school success.

What they may fail to realize is that reading is actually just one link in a long developmental chain of broader literacy skills the child must forge from infancy onward, and that the concept of literacy extends far beyond the conventional idea of being able to read (Fields & Lee, 1987; Schickedanz, 1986).

Learning to substitute symbols for reality, for example, is a major step toward reading, and every time a child looks at a picture and talks about what it represents or pretends that something is something else, that is part of becoming literate, just as understanding how to hold a book right side up is also part of that process. Indeed, all of the skills described earlier in this

Note the way this storage helps children link real objects to their symbolic representations.

chapter—singing, telling stories, doing finger plays, and chatting with the teacher—are all important aspects of acquiring the language skills that underlie the later ability to read.

In addition to these more broadly based approaches to fostering the development of language and, ultimately, reading skills, there are many more specific ways to draw children's attention to the value of the printed word. Reading aloud to them is the most significant and satisfying way to convince children that print is important (Teale, 1984). Additional strategies can be as simple as pointing out the convenience of labelling a child's picture, so "we'll know I should give it to you when it's time to go home" or as complex as writing down a story the group dictates describing where the rabbit hid when he got out. Or perhaps the teacher can say, "Just a minute—I have to read the directions so I'll know how to put it together," or "Here, let's write a note to your mother telling her you went down the slide for the first time." Or the teacher might set out a picture recipe for the children to follow as they make individual fruit milk shakes.

It is also important to provide children with opportunities to use writing materials themselves as they move from scribbles, to pictures, and gradually incorporate the additional symbolic forms of letters and numbers in their work. Felt tip pens, crayons, old typewriters, and possibly computers can be used to good advantage in this regard (Von Sommers, 1984). Inclusion of writing materials during play is still another way to draw attention to the value of the printed page. Perhaps when the children are playing "McDonald's," order forms and play money can be included or letters can be addressed and mailed for Valentine's Day. All of these activities help children understand that there is a useful relationship between the printed word and what happens in life (Wolf et al., 1988).

Pflaum has provided a helpful checklist documenting some literacy skills that are appropriate for 3- to 5-year-olds to acquire (See table 14–2).

TABLE 14-2
Checklist for observing beginning literacy

Type	Independent level	Level with adult help
	Ages 3-4	
Storybook		
Interest	Has one or two very favorite books and poems. Knows them well, so recognizes when they are "misread"	Can become interested in new stories; asks questions
Story understanding	Can relate sequence of events	Can tell about a story in its absence
Story seeking	Is happy to participate in story-time	Is eager to help an adult find books
Notions about reading		
Print and picture	Can point to where story is contained	Can verbalize difference in what picture and print show
Purpose for reading	When asked, can find newspaper, book, etc.	Talks about the kind of reading done in various media
Parts of stories	Can answer question about sequence	Talks about parts of story explicity
Notion of word	Picks out word in title	Can identify where words begin and end
Writing		
Practice	"Writes" when asked (scribbles)	Is eager to show "writing" to an appreciative adult
Words	For example, has notion that big people ought to have big names	Talks about ideas regarding print
Letter	Learns letters of own name	Learns letters of name and asks for more
	Ages 4-5	
Storybook		
Familiarity	Knows several storybooks by name	Has specific things to say about several books
	Knows passages of at least one book	Knows several book segments by heart
Routine	Experiences a school and a home reading routine	Can be explicit about routines for reading
Preference	May have preference for one type of book	Is beginning to like certain types of storybooks
Purposes	Is quite specific about various reasons for reading	Can identify several purposes for reading

TABLE 14–2 *(continued)*

Type	Independent level	Level with adult help
Notions about books and print		
Books	Knows which way to hold a book, where beginning and end, pages, title, etc. are	Can describe how to handle a book for reading, and uses terms well
Reading terms	Points correctly to page, sentence, word, and letter; says sound	Uses terms correctly; page, sentence, word, letter, and sound
Notions about reading		
Print	Has no confusion about where a story comes from	
Stability	Knows that a story is always the same because of the print	Can explain why print tells the story
Words	Is familiar with terms and words and can point to printed words	Can identify oral and written forms and tries to describe the difference
Printed words	Has observed and spoken of the way words are printed with the same letters	Knows that words are written with the same letters and sequence each time
Sequence	Participates in talk about oral and written sequences in writing	Can identify how oral and written sound/symbol sequences occur
Letters		
Letters	Knows several letters in different settings	Can name many letters in different settings
Notion about alphabetic principle	Puzzles about word size and consistency of use for sounds	Begins to talk about stability of letters in different words to represent sounds
Writing		
Name	Writes name (possibly uses magnetic letters, but pencil use is preferred)	Asks for help to write other names
Practice	"Writes" when asked. Makes signs and labels	"Writing" may take on spontaneous spelling. Has a variety of writing purposes

Note. From *The Development of Language and Literacy in Young Children* (3rd ed.) (pp. 138–139) by S. W. Pflaum, 1986, Columbus, Ohio: Merrill Publishing Co. Reprinted by permission.

SUMMARY

One of the most important skills children acquire in the years before primary school is the ability to use language effectively. For this reason, teachers need to do all they can to facilitate such growth. Strategies include encouraging children to put their ideas into words as frequently as possible, maintaining the children's *home* languages in the school, and being aware of developmental timetables so that children who require special help can obtain it promptly. Conducting conversations rather than interrogations and asking questions that tend to prolong conversations are additional ways of facilitating the growth of language.

Specific curriculum activities to promote such growth include the use of auditory discrimination games, songs and records, poetry and finger plays, and books and stories.

It is also vital to link language to the printed page to help children forge still another link in the chain of literacy skills. Ways of weaving these activities into an attractive group time are suggested in Chapter 15.

SELF-CHECK QUESTIONS FOR REVIEW

1. List some average, "milestone" language behaviors typical for 2-, 3-, and 4-year-old children. Why is it important for teachers to know what these "milestones" are?
2. What are the three different theories explaining how children acquire language? Is there anything teachers can do, according to these theories, to help children acquire language?
3. Should teachers look down on children who speak Black English or require bilingual children to speak only English while they are at school?
4. Explain what teachers should do about the child who is not fluent in any language.
5. Think of a situation in which a teacher is talking with a child and practice including comments that would draw the child into more extended chatting.
6. Name three skills teachers should develop that will

foster the development of children's language skills.
7. Describe some ways children modify their speech when speaking to younger children. Do adults do this, too?
8. This chapter provides many suggestions for presenting language activities in seven areas. What are these areas? Be sure to include some specific recommendations for making each area more effective with children.
9. Does "literacy" mean that someone knows how to read? Be sure you can explain your answer and supply examples of skills young children must acquire before actually learning to read from the printed page.

Integrative Questions

1. Suppose that two 4-year-olds are investigating the Let's Find Out Table. They are using ice cubes— putting them in tubs of warm and cold water to see which temperature water makes the ice melt faster. They are also sucking on the ice cubes from time to time. Give several examples of controlling comments the teacher might make. Then cite some additional information that the teacher could give or ask instead. According to McCartney, which kinds of comments would be more likely to enhance the children's language skills? Why do you think that this is true?
2. Heather and Allison are talking with you about Christmas and making grandiose plans about their presents. Then Allison says, "And if my little brother gets *anything*—even *one* thing—I'm gonna take it away and flush it down the toilet!" Give an example of a reply that would be moralistic and would probably put an end to further conversation. Then give two examples of replies that would extend the conversation further.
3. Pick out a song you think would be appropriate to teach young children. Then explain why you selected it, basing your explanation on the criteria recommended in the book for selecting children's songs.

QUESTIONS AND ACTIVITIES

1. *Problem:* You are teaching in a Head Start center, and you have a 4-year-old Mexican girl in the group who only replies in single English words

when asked a question. What factors and possibilities would you want to consider before deciding how to deal with this behavior?

2. There are many interesting questions that arise when bilingual education is discussed. For example, the following question has been a "hot" topic in recent years: Do you think that staff members who are able to speak two languages (both of which are needed in the particular children's center where they teach) should receive additional compensation because they possess this special skill? Why or why not?

3. Imagine that some 4-year-olds you know have begun a conversation with you with the following statements: "Teacher, Teacher, Mindy had puppies last night." (Mindy is a cat!) "Guess what, Teacher, it's raining, and I got my head all wet!" "My Mother says I don't have to go outside today!" Now make up two conversational scripts for each of the children's statements — one script that you feel would deaden the conversation and one that would encourage children to continue it.

4. Is it possible to ask children too many questions? What might be some alternative ways of keeping conversation going instead of always asking questions?

5. Go to the corner drugstore or variety store and look over the inexpensive books offered there for children. Select and purchase a desirable and undesirable one and bring them to class. Be ready to explain their weak and strong points.

6. Listen to the children as they play house. Can you detect any differences in the way they speak when addressing "babies" in the family? Now listen to yourself when you speak to infants. Do you do the same thing? Why or why not might this "switch" be desirable?

REFERENCES FOR FURTHER READING

Overviews

Lindfors, J. W. (1987). *Children's language and learning* (2nd ed.). Englewood Cliffs, New Jersey: Prentice-Hall. This is an excellent, readable presentation of an important subject. Highly recommended.

Bilingual and Multilectical Information

Dyson, A. H., & Genishi, C. (1984). Nonstandard dialects in day care. *Dimensions, 13*(1), 6–9. This valuable article reviews problems associated with the use of dialects in preschools and concludes that using language with meaning is more important than correct form at that level.

Interracial Books for Children: Bulletin. (1986). Bilingual education and equity. *The Bulletin, 17*(3 & 4). Reading this issue is the quickest way to acquire information about the status and political problems of bilingual education in the United States.

Pflaum, S. W. (1986). *The development of language and literacy in young children* (3rd ed.). Columbus, Ohio: Merrill Publishing Co. Pflaum's chapter on "Variations in Language and Literacy Development" provides a good overview of Black English and other language variations.

Practical Suggestions for Generating Conversation With Children

Bos, B. (1983). *Before the basics: Creating conversations with children.* Roseville, Calif.: Turn the Page Press. This book is an utter delight! It is mostly about generating happy, wholesome relationships with children through the medium of music, conversation, and movement. A good bibliography of children's books is included.

Dumtschin, J. U. (1988). Recognize language development and delay in early childhood. *Young Children, 43*(3), 16–24. Dumtschin offers guidelines for determining developmental language delay and suggests practical ways teachers can help remediate such delayed speech through the appropirate use of conversation.

Weiss, C. E., & Lillywhite, H. S. (1981). *Communicative disorders: Prevention and early intervention* (2nd ed.). St. Louis: C. V. Mosby Co. The chapter entitled "101 Ways to Help Children Learn to Talk" contains exactly that—101 helpful, basic ideas about how to increase fluency in children. Highly recommended.

Songs and Music

Note also the list of music books featured on p. 291.

Andress, B. (1980). *Music experiences in early childhood.* New York: Holt, Rinehart & Winston. Andress provides a wide-ranging book that features simple arrangements of music, brief instructions on playing various instruments, and many ideas for activities. The book is particularly strong on suggestions for making interesting equipment.

Bayless, K. M., & Ramsey, M. E. (1987). *Music: A way of life for the young child* (3rd ed.). Columbus, Ohio: Merrill Publishing Co. This may be the most satisfactory single resource on music for preprimary teachers to own since it combines a sensible, thorough text with simple arrangements scored for piano and Autoharp and lists of records for dancing and singing.

Harrop, B., Blakely, P., & Gadsby, D. (1981). *Apusskido.* London: A & C Black. This is a collection of funny, cheerful songs divided according to topic. Highly recommended.

Poetry

Andrews, J. H. (1988). Poetry: Tool of the classroom magician. *Young Children, 43*(4), 17–24. Practical and inspiring ways to integrate poetry into the life of the school are presented.

Arbuthnot, M. H., & Root, S. L., Jr. (1968). *Time for poetry* (3rd ed.). Glenview, Ill.: Scott, Foresman & Co. This book is a treasure. It is filled with poetry arranged by topic and also contains a valuable chapter on sharing poetry with children.

Prelutsky, C. (Ed.). (1986). *Read aloud rhymes for the very young.* New York: Alfred A. Knopf. Delightfully illustrated, these poems *are* simple. They are also arranged somewhat according to subject.

Resources of Children's Books and Reading Aloud Materials

Binkley, M. R. (1988). *Becoming a nation of readers: What parents can do.* Washington, D.C.: United States Department of Education. (Available from the Consumer Information Center, Pueblo, Colorado 81009). This inexpensive pamphlet summarizes practical advice for parents on how to help their children love to read.

Child Study Children's Book Committee. (1988). *Children's books of the year.* (Available from Bank Street College, 610 W. 112th St., New York, New York 10025). The Committee annually provides an annotated, trustworthy source of excellent books. It lists the best choices of the year selected from several thousand possibilities.

Engle, R. (1980). Understanding the handicapped through literature. *Young Children, 35*(3), 27–32. Engle discusses the value of these books and provides a list of suggested choices.

Glazer, J. I. (1986). *Literature for young children* (2nd ed.). Columbus, Ohio: Merrill Publishing Co. This book works particularly well for students using *Total Learning* because most of it is divided into chapters dealing with literature and the social self, the intellectual self, and so forth.

Jalongo, M. R. (1988). *Young children and picture books: Literature from infancy to six.* Washington, D.C.: National Association for the Education of Young Children. The joy of really good picture books is captured here. Jalongo explains how to select quality books and how to present them so effectively that children will fall in love with them and with reading, too. Highly recommended.

Pellowski, A. (1984). *The story vine: A source book of unusual and easy-to-tell stories from around the world.* New York: Macmillan Publishing Co. Pellowski offers examples of stories told with string, with pictures drawn as the teacher goes along, with finger plays, and much more.

Schon, I. (1986). *Basic collection of children's books in Spanish.* Metuchen, N.J.: Scarecrow Press. Title is self-explanatory.

Shelton, H., Montgomery, P., & Hatcher, B. (1989). *Bibliography of books for children, 1989 edition.* Wheaton, Md.: Association for Childhood Education International. In this updated version of a favorite reference, ACEI includes annotated lists of fiction, picture books, nonfiction, and reference books. The inclusion of magazines and newspapers for children makes this an unusual and welcome resource.

Trelease, J. (1982). *The read-aloud handbook.* New York: Penguin Books. A sensible, easy-to-read paperback that is filled with good advice for parents and teachers on how to enjoy books with children. It features an annotated bibliography of outstanding read-alouds for children from toddler age to grade 6.

Development of Literacy Skills

Fields, M. V., & Lee, D. (1987). *Let's begin reading right: A developmental approach to beginning literacy.* Columbus, Ohio: Merrill Publishing Co. This sensible book traces the numerous ways children are involved with reading at the preschool level. It goes on to cover reading in elementary school. Highly recommended.

Schickedanz, J. A. (1986). *More than the ABCs: The early stages of reading and writing.* Washington, D.C.: National Association for the Education of Young Children. Schickedanz traces reading from the infant's first encounter with books through storybooks and the beginning of writing. She offers many developmentally appropriate suggestions for fostering literacy in young children.

For the Advanced Student

Allen, H. B., & Linn, M. D. (Eds.). (1986). *Dialect and language variation.* New York: Academic Press. This book reviews research related to dialects and language variation and includes information on Mexican-American and American Indian English as well as Black English.

Escobedo, T. H. (Ed.). (1983). *Early childhood bilingual education: A Hispanic perspective.* New York: Teachers College Press. The articles in this book present research to substantiate their practical recommendations for instructing the bilingual child who speaks Spanish and English.

Genishi, C. (1987). Acquiring oral language and communicative competence. In C. Seefeldt (Ed.), *The early childhood curriculum: A review of current research.* New York: Teachers College Press. This is a brief, useful review of current research.

Genishi, C. (1988). Children's language: Learning words from experience. *Young Children, 44*(1), 16–23. In this well-documented research review, Genishi makes a valuable point about the relationship of language to plentiful experience.

Kontos, S. (1986). What preschool children know about reading, and how they learn it. *Young Children, 42*(1),

58–66. This helpful review of research includes implications for teaching.

Labov, W. (1980). The logic of nonstandard English. In F. Williams (Ed.), *Language and poverty*. Chicago: Markham Publishing Co. In this classic work, Labov provides a spirited analysis and defense of the strengths and values of the language used by children from urban ghetto areas.

Opie, I., & Opie, P. (1980). *A nursery companion*. Oxford, England: Oxford University Press. The Opies have spent their lives studying children and their games and chants, and they have contributed some classic material to the literature in that area. This particular book is a collection of old-time alphabet picture books from the 1800s.

Additional Resources of Particular Interest

The Children's Book Council, 67 Irving Place, New York, New York 10003. This wonderful nonprofit organization sponsors Children's Book Week and is an excellent source of posters and pamphlets. A one-time fee entitles you to issues of the informative "Calendar" forever, as well as announcements of pamphlets and posters. Highly recommended.

15 Putting It All Together for a Good Group Time

Have you ever

- Wanted to offer more than songs and stories in group time but did not know what else to include?
- Worried about how to control restless children while you were reading to them?
- Needed help in planning language experiences for two different age groups?

If you have, the material in this chapter will help you.

Responding to children's spontaneous impulses to speak at the story table seems preferable to suppressing speech at one time and trying to draw it out at another. Remarks in the middle of a story may add to its significance for everyone, and if a discussion then developed, that would be the time to give language expression preference.

ELINOR FITCH GRIFFIN (1982)

Language-enhancing experiences should be present throughout the day, as we have seen in Chapter 14. In addition to this continual interweaving of language with activity, a discussion of group time is included here because group time presents the opportunity par excellence for putting all the language and cognitive activities together in an integrated way, while also nourishing the child's social self.

We should bear in mind that the fundamental purpose of group time is to generate an occasion when everyone enjoys being together. It should be a happy time, not one marred by constant reprimands and unpleasantness.

Well-presented group times provide opportunities for learning to do many things. Children are expected to focus their attention, to listen while others speak, to participate in discussions, to control wiggly impulses, and to keep themselves from being distracted by rambunctious neighbors. This is a great deal to expect from such young human beings. Fortunately, there are many things that teachers can do to help children meet these expectations and promote harmony as well.

STRUCTURING THE GROUP FOR SUCCESS

Keep the Groups as Small and Stable as Possible

The larger the group, the less personal attention each child receives, the fewer opportunities he has to participate, and the more waiting he must do. If this were stated as an equation, it would look like this:

$$\text{Less personal attention} + \text{More waiting} =$$
$$\text{Reduced learning} + \text{Increased discipline} + \text{Control problems}$$

Some teachers try to solve this by having a second adult do "police duty" on the fringes of the group, but it is more effective to have the second person conduct an additional group, instead.

If the same children are divided into the same groups each day, it is easier to continue interests from time to time as these build. Keeping the group population stable also fosters a sense of belonging among the children.

Choose a Time and Place That Minimize Tension and Distractions

Just before lunch is about the most stressful point of the day to offer group time. It is much better to choose a time when the children are rested and not hungry. For example, many teachers begin the day with this experience.

Stress can also be reduced by locating groups as far away from each other as possible. Try to shield each group from the others by placing a low barrier between them, such as a screen or bookcase.

Choose a place that offers few distractions. If you sit in front of a shelf of toys, for example, children's eyes are bound to wander to delights on the shelves behind you. It is also wise to seat the children far enough away from any equipment so that it is out of their reach. An ideal site is a cozy corner with rugs and a feeling of softness about it.

Plan Carefully and Be Flexible

An important part of promoting harmonious learning at group time is being relaxed yourself. Nothing fosters this as much as careful planning and advance preparation. Always assemble the ingredients of the group time curriculum beforehand, and have them in reach but as much out of the sight of the children as possible. Be sure to read books and poetry all the way through in advance to make certain that they are what you really want and to familiarize yourself thoroughly with the material.

Peace of mind is increased if more materials are selected than there will be time to use (two cognitive activities, for example, or several books), since it is almost impossible to know, in the beginning, what will be effective in group time and what will not. There is no sin in simply setting a book aside that the children do not enjoy and going on to something else.

Readiness to extend or contract an activity, to change the order of presentation, and to improvise spontaneously as needed are the hallmarks of the truly master teacher.

Start Group Time as Soon as Children Begin to Gather

Do not expect the children to sit quietly and wait until the last straggler appears. Simply waiting encourages youngsters to think of all kinds of things to do! It is far better to begin group immediately with a song or finger plays. These activities are so attractive that laggards will want to hurry over. Moreover, these particular activities are easy for children to join in as they arrive.

Present Difficult or New Experiences Early

Decide in advance what activity is likely to require the most concentration or effort by the children. Perhaps this is the cognitive game or learning a new song. Present this early when the children are still fresh and attentive.

Change the Pace and Include Variety

Group time should generally be "up beat"; do not allow anything to drag on too long. Since it is so taxing for young children to sit still for extended periods, some kind of exercise and movement should be provided as part of this experience. Typically this takes the form of finger plays and body movement ideas. It also might involve a relaxation exercise in which the children practice stretching out and letting go.

Encourage Discussion Among the Children

It seems that new teachers in particular fear being interrupted by the children during the group experience, so they read breathlessly through a book, brushing the children's interested comments aside as distractions. This is probably because they dread losing control, but allowing the children to respond to questions and volunteer information increases their interest in what is happening. It also encourages them to put their ideas into words and to share experiences with the group.

Kindergarten teachers often plan for this deliberately by including a sharing time when every child contributes something. At the preschool level, doing this usually causes the other children to fidget and lose interest because it takes too long. For this reason, it seems best to allow time for children to interject spontaneous remarks and comments as group progresses. Often such remarks can be developed into a valuable discussion that involves many of the children. When it is time to return to the story, all the teacher has to do is say, for example, "Well, that certainly was interesting hearing about how Anselmo caught that fish. Now let's go back to Curious George and see if he caught one, too."

Draw the Group to a Close Before It Falls Apart

It is always better to stop a little too soon than to go on and on until the children end up frantic to get away. Quit while you are ahead; then everyone will want to come back next time.

What to Do When a Child Continues to Distract the Group

Even when all these strategies are practiced faithfully, all teachers encounter children from time to time who are unable to conform to reasonable standards of behavior during group. The first thing to consider under such circumstances is whether the child is physically *able* to conform. Does he see well? How is his hearing? Consider also whether he might be developmentally younger than the other children so that the material presented is inappropriate for his interests.

When such problems create group time difficulties, special plans have to be made that will enable the child to participate. Perhaps he needs to sit closer to the teacher to see or hear, or perhaps he can be dismissed early from the group or be read to by himself. Sometimes a number of such youngsters can be gathered into a separate group by another staff member so that the material is more appropriate to their age and interests.

Many children, however, do not seem to suffer from any of these problems, but they continue to be disruptive. The solution to this depends a lot on the philosophy of the particular teacher. Some teachers believe it is acceptable for children who do not want to be part of group time to play by themselves, as long as they are quiet and do not disturb the group. It is often, but not always, the case that such youngsters gradually return and join with the others as they become aware of the fun going on in the group.

Other teachers feel that this time of being together is so important that all children should attend. They have the restless one sit beside them, separating him from particular friends who may be drawn into misbehavior and then giving him a special role in the group. Perhaps he can turn the pages during story reading or hold the flannel board while others put on special items. Firm expectations of desirable behavior have to be projected to such a child as well.

If all else fails, it is occasionally necessary to have another adult remove the obstreperous one from the group. That person should explain to the child that he has lost the privilege of staying and may only return when he has made up his mind to be more cooperative. (This essentially is an application of the six learning steps described in Chapter 11.)

Finally, Enjoy the Children

There is no substitute for your interest and enthusiasm. Be well enough prepared that you do not have to worry about how group time will go. Forget about the little, irritating things that do not really matter, and concentrate on relaxing and letting the children know you like them and that you are excited about what you are going to do together. This will make group time a pleasure for everyone.

PLANNING THE CURRICULUM FOR SUCCESS

What Should a Good Group Time Include?

The basic educational goals of a good group time should be the development of receptive and expressive language, the enhancement of thinking processes, and the provision of a positive social experience for the children.

At first, planning a comprehensive group time may seem overwhelming because there are so many things to take into account. However, these basically boil down to just two considerations: the variety of content to include and the reason for including each item.

Contents of a Good Group Time. To provide variety of content in group time, each of the following ingredients should be included at least once during the week—and the more of them that can be used every day, the better.

RESEARCH STUDY
Do Plans and Practice Match?

Research Question   McAfee asked the question, "How do teachers think about, plan, and conduct group time activities?"

Research Method   In this exploratory study, 35 teachers teaching children from ages 2½ through kindergarten were interviewed, and five classrooms from that group were selected for intense observation. The programs all met the standards for good quality, with adequate or better than adequate adult/child ratios. About half of the teachers had a degree in early childhood education, child development, or a related area.

Teachers were asked to list types of activities commonly used during group times and to also include the most frequent difficulties they encountered while leading group times. Then during group time each classroom was observed for 48 1-minute time samples, and the results were recorded.

Results   The teachers listed 14 types of activities commonly used during group time. These were books/stories, music, songs, movement, finger plays, discussion, sharing/show-and-tell, lessons and demonstrations, traditional opening activities, planning and review, dramatizations, games, films, poetry and "other" (such as relaxation and news time).

However, when the analysis of the observations was completed, it turned out that the only activities usually included were books (33% of the time), music (10% of the time), sharing/show-and-tell (23% of the time), and traditional opening activities such as calendar and taking roll (13% of the time). The kinds of activities did not vary according to the children's ages. Advance planning in order to realize long-term educational goals was not typical.

When listing management difficulties the teachers said that some children's disruptive behaviors and the need to balance individual needs with group needs were the hardest things to cope with. The teachers reported that 75% of the time the reasons for these problems were beyond their control; they ascribed the

1. Practice in auditory discrimination
2. Songs
3. Poetry
4. Stories (not necessarily a book)
5. Finger plays and action activities
6. Discussions
7. Practice in a cognitive activity (discussed in Chapters 16 and 17)
8. Something that is multiethnic or nonsexist

Unfortunately, as the research by McAfee (1985) reveals, all too often this kind of variety is not provided during group time. This is a

shame because a well-planned group experience offers opportunities for a multitude of language, social, emotional, and cognitive learning experiences that are unsurpassed during the center day.

Basic Curriculum-Planning Principles. The following are fundamental principles to remember when planning a curriculum for group time:

- It is fun and helps tie learning together if you include one or two activities in group time that are related to the focus of interest for the week.

difficulties to developmental levels, emotional or behavioral problems, home background, or classroom conditions such as too many children.

Implications for Teaching If this sample, which was admittedly exploratory, is typical of what happens in most preschool and kindergarten classrooms, the news is not good. Teachers who rely on the same repetitive routines of calendar, weather, books, and songs are depriving themselves and the children of wonderful opportunities to expand their worlds. Moreover, using some of these strategies with children as young as 2 or 3 years of age is inappropriate. No wonder the children were restless and inattentive and that control situations proliferated.

It is clear from the original list that the teachers knew of many activities that should be included in group times, and it is just as clear from the observations that they did not include them. We must ask ourselves why those teachers did such a mediocre job when they knew and would probably have liked to do better. Most likely, the poor quality was due to a number of factors such as fatigue, pressure to keep moving from one thing to the next during the day, and apathy.

Providing educationally worthwhile group times takes self-discipline and energy combined with the sincere convictions that group time presents invaluable opportunities to promote thinking and reasoning skills, as well as developing language and social expertise. It requires self-discipline to sit down and plan such experiences in advance, energy to carry the plans out once they have been made, and sufficient conviction that group time is valuable to make careful planning a consistent part of the program. To ensure the success of group time, sustained effort is required not just once in a while, but daily.

Finally, teachers need to see themselves as being more in control of the situation than did the teachers in the sample. For example, rather than blaming the children for misbehaving because they are immature, it makes better sense to adjust what the teacher is doing and to suit the activities being offered to the age of the children rather than making impossible demands on them to behave better.

Note. From "Circle Time: Getting Past 'Two Little Pumpkins' " by O. D. McAfee, 1985, *Young Children, 40*(6), pp. 24–29.

- *Always* be sensitive to the importance of including multicultural and nonsexist materials—and *always* check the materials you are using for possible bias before presentation.
- Keep the materials appropriate for the age with which you are working. (Note how the same subject matter, holidays, is handled differently for twos and fours in Table 15–1 and 15–2 and how the subject of rabbits is presented for young threes and older fours in Tables 15–3 and 15–4.)
- Group times are precious—do not waste them. Be certain there is a valid reason for including every item you have selected.

- One selection can serve several purposes. For example, *Staying Home Alone on a Rainy Day* by Chiharo Iwasaki (1968) would fulfill the requirement for something that is multiethnic, could be used for auditory training if the teacher had the children make loud and soft rain sounds with their fingers, and could serve as a takeoff point for discussing loneliness as well.
- Good group times require not only careful planning and advance preparation but also the freedom to deviate from the plan when something special comes up.
- Practice may not make perfect, but doing group

times over and over really helps. Seize every opportunity you can to practice this valuable skill.

Examples of 1-Day Plans for Group Time

The large-group planning and analysis sheets (Tables 15–1 and 15–2) are included here because it is easier for the beginning teacher to plan 1 day at a time. These groups were planned for 2- and 4-year-olds. Of course, the 4-year-olds were able to pay attention longer, and that group occupied about 25 minutes for group time. The focus for the week was on winter holidays. Note the slightly differing categories for the younger and older groups.

Planning for Young 3-Year-Olds

A group of threes (or twos) does best with short and simple stories, large picture books, and considerable repetition of material. This group also appreciates beginning with a familiar activity each time—perhaps "Head, Shoulders, Knees, and Toes" or "Where Is Thumbkin?" Group times should be kept fairly short for such young children and should use active participation whenever possible. Remember, there should

be a sound reason for including every piece of material (Table 15–3).

In Table 15–4 the focus of interest for this group of young threes is on dogs (carried over from the previous week) and rabbits, and materials were selected accordingly. A nonsexist component is not included because the material is about evenly divided between male and female animal stories or the animal's sex is not discernible.

Planning for Older 4-Year-Olds

Older fours can sit for fairly long periods of time, especially when they are interested in the material. They enjoy some repetition, but also relish diversity. They are thirsty for information per se and can deal with experience on a more verbal level. For example, they can grasp the idea that different languages can have different words for the same thing, and they enjoy learning some of these words. They are also partial to "nonsense" rhymes. Fours are able to talk about their feelings and can deal with simple social discussions of such things as the pleasures and perils of giving and receiving gifts. They are also interested in

Young threes need lots of active involvement during group time.

TABLE 15–1
Plan and analysis sheet for large-group presentation for 2-year-olds

Date: <u>December 19, 1988</u>

Category	Name of material	Reason for inclusion	Evaluation	Suggestions when repeated
Finger plays	I Am a Top Jack-in-the-box	Actually these are whole body poems. Children can use "I Am a Top" to pretend to be a top and dreidel—large-muscle activity. Draw children into group.	Children enjoyed being dreidels.	Turn slowly so children do not get dizzy (and teachers don't either!)
Auditory discrimination activity	Shaking jingle bells	Shaking bells slowly and loudly while singing softly and loudly. Children learn to control making loud and soft sounds.	Twos have difficulty shaking bells softly and singing softly although they did try.	Remember that twos will have trouble being soft—don't set sights too high.
Relaxation activity	After being dreidels, the children fall gently down and rest.	Children need to learn how to relax and it's easier to do a relaxing activity after a busy activity.	It worked; children rested a few minutes.	Next time emphasize resting more.
Large-muscle activity	Being dreidels Jack-in-the-Box poem	Spin a real dreidel. While singing the song, pretend to be a dreidel. Going from concrete to semi-abstract by pretending to be a dreidel. Fun poem involves jumping which twos like to do!	Children enjoyed the activity. There was some transfer of concepts.	Spin slow so children and teachers do not get dizzy.
Songs	"Rudolph" "Jingle Bells" "Dreidel"	Familiar songs. Jewish holiday song children enjoy.	Children enjoy it.	Will sing again.
Story	Christmas Tree Book "O Tannenbaum"	The children decorated the Christmas tree earlier in the day. The story is about a family buying a tree and decorating it.	I shortened the story by being selective with pictures I showed; this did help retain children's attention.	I will again have a tree ready to decorate before the children are dismissed from group.
What was multicultural	Menorah and dreidels	Major part of Jewish holiday Hanukkah which is this week. (Jacob is Jewish.)	Jacob told us some of what he got for Hanukkah, so I'd say this activity was well worth the time.	Next time I'll light the Menorah and count the candles with the children.

Note. My thanks to Cheryl Gaskins, student teacher, The Institute of Child Development, University of Oklahoma, 1988.

TABLE 15–2
Plan and analysis sheet for large-group presentation for 4-year-olds

Date: December 19, 1988

Category	Name of material	Reason for inclusion	Evaluation	Suggestions when repeated
Poetry	"Four Little Bells"	It is a finger play about bells that I thought would draw children actively into the group. It is easily learned and has a sequence to it.	The children learned it quickly, and since they were using their own hands, it kept their attention focused.	I'd like to have either real bells or flannel shapes of bells—another visual concrete aid to go to the abstract, pretending to have bells.
Auditory discrimination	Using real jingle bells to sing	Letting children experience the control they have over objects and voice. Children can sing song loud and jingle loud, sing soft and jingle soft. Also learning loud and soft.	Children easily manipulated the bells, requesting to sing soft after loud and loud after soft.	I would have bells with a wide range of rings, and use those as a game. When hidden which bell is being rung?
Mental ability activity	Flannelboard Story "Santa"	The story was repetitive. The children could easily join in, providing they remembered the order of the story. Pretending to be inside a present allows children to use their personal space. Children need more experiences in which body is confined then released, tense then relaxed. (Memory and Temporal Ordering)	Children easily remembered the sequence and clearly enjoyed helping tell the story. They requested to do it again. Wish I had planned more movements inside the box (i.e., If you were a ball how would you move if someone shook the box? Or if you were a doll what sound might you make?).	I would definitely have the children do the wind sound again. It kept their listening skills tuned in and added to the story.
Discussion subject	No material	Briefly asked about what changes have been happening around their homes, on their	I need to have some pictures to lead the children into the discussion more.	I would use the picture of a child frowning with Santa and talk with the children about

312

		...streets, at the mall so children would have opportunity to share in group.		how they are feeling during holiday season. Perhaps I would even add a play acting scene with a child and mother discussing shopping and staying at the babysitter's, or why children can't touch the Christmas decorations.
Songs	"Jingle Bells" "Rudolph" "Oh Tannenbaum" "We Wish You A Merry Christmas" and also sing "Happy Hanukkah" and "Dreidel"	Familiar songs for the children. Learn a new holiday song to sing for Winter Party. Jewish Hanukkah Songs to sing at Winter Party.	All songs were sung heartily, and the children really enjoyed them.	I would use again next time. They were simple songs, easy to learn.
Story	"Santa" Flannel board	An enjoyable story in which children could participate.	Definitely a story the children participated in.	Will use again.
What was multicultural	Menorah	Hanukkah is a holiday happening this week in Jewish families. I provided this activity so that children will realize that not everyone has Christmas in their homes but that Hanukkah is a holiday that Jewish children enjoy.	In trying to emphasize that not all families have Christmas and trying to do so in a positive way or by not emphasizing the difference, I almost forgot to tell the children Hanukkah is a Jewish holiday. Hannah and Moses were delighted to discuss their family customs.	After explaining that each candle is for one day of Hanukkah, except for the one candle that is for lighting the others, I will ask "How many days are included in Hanukkah?"

Note. My thanks to Cheryl Gaskins, student teacher, The Institute of Child Development, University of Oklahoma, 1988.

TABLE 15–3
Analysis of reasons for selection of literary materials to use with young threes (listed in the order of the days as they appear in Table 15–4)*

Resource†	Reasons for selection
Books	
Angus and the Cat Written and illustrated by Marjorie Flack (1931)	Beloved classic; continues dog focus from last week
Creatures Small and Furry Written by D. J. Crump (1983)	Use only rabbit pages. Good picture of how rabbits live underground
What Whiskers Did Written and illustrated by Ruth Carroll (1965)	A storytelling book that features a rabbit, uses no words, and requires children to tell story
The Wild Rabbit Oxford Scientific Films, photographs by George Bernard (1980)	Charming, accurate photographs of rabbits and how they live; simple text; has several pages of useful information for the teacher as an introduction
Where's the Bunny? Written and illustrated by Ruth Carroll (1950)	Another very simple book that requires children to hunt for hidden bunny (bunny is easy to find); also has dog, which continues dog focus
Whistle for Willie Written and illustrated by Ezra Jack Keats (1964)	Features a small Black child and his dog, and deals with a universal experience. Provides multiethnic experience; ties in with focus of previous week.
What's Your Name? Written and illustrated by Zhenya Gay (1955)	Lists characteristics of familiar animals and asks children to guess their identity—a good review of what children have learned this week about rabbits
Animals on the Farm Feodor Rojankovsky (1982)	Simple, handsome pictures; presents concept of farm animals per se
Goodnight, Moon Written by Margaret Wise Brown, illustrated by Clement Hurd (1947)	A classic beloved by young children; story focuses on rabbit going to sleep; helpful to relax children; children must search carefully for little mouse that is hiding in the room (mouse is hard to find)
The Snuggle Bunny Written by N. Jewell, illustrated by March Chalmers (1972)	About rabbits and also about loneliness, caring, and older people

---

*All the books for young threes and older fours have been selected with the criterion of age appropiateness in mind. They have also been selected because of their outstanding illustrations and good literary quality. The full names of authors and illustrators are given whenever possible because teachers should get to know these creative people as familiar, treasured friends of children.

†See material on pp. 322–327 for actual poems, songs, and finger plays.

TABLE 15–3 *(continued)*

Resource†	Reasons for selection
Poetry and finger plays	
"Listening" Miriam Clark Potter (1955)	For fun; short enough for children to learn; talks about mother-child relationship; flannel board provides variety and helps children remember as they say the poem
"My Rabbit"	Appropriate subject matter
A *Tale of Tales* Written by Elizabeth MacPherson, illustrated by Garth Williams (1962)	Charming illustrations; presents simple concept combined with poetry and has rabbit in it; might add song "Why Rabbits Have Bright Shiny Noses," if children can sit still that long
Songs	
"Head, Shoulders, Knees, and Toes"	Opening activity for the children
"Bye, Baby Bunting" and "Where Oh Where Has My Little Dog Gone?"	Rabbit and dog themes; familiar childhood songs
"Hop Se Hi"	Fits rabbit theme and provides the relief of large-muscle exercise for children
"Bingo"	Scottish-American folk song about dogs—repeat from previous week

the concept of growing up, and they are developing strong ideas about appropriate sex roles. The materials in Table 15–5 have been selected with these characteristics in mind.

In Table 15–6 the focus of interest for this group is rabbits and doing things for other people —in this case, making and receiving gifts. The tonsillectomy material is included to meet the need of a particular child and alleviate the anxiety of the group about what might happen to him.

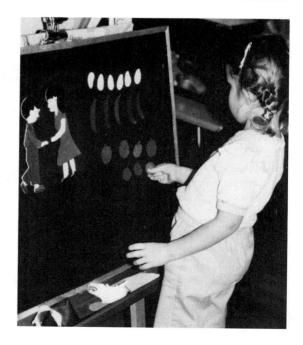

Flannel board stories also help children focus their attention, particularly when they participate by adding items as the story progresses.

TABLE 15–4
A weekly plan for group time with young threes (main topics are rabbits and dogs)

Monday	Tuesday	Wednesday
Stories to read and tell		
Angus and the Cat Flack (1931) *Farm Animals* Andrews (1968)	*What Whiskers Did* Carroll (1965) *The Wild Rabbit* Oxford Scientific Films (1980) or *Creatures Small and Furry* Crump (1983)	*Where's the Bunny?* Carroll (1950) *Whistle for Willie* Keats (1964)
Poetry and finger plays		
"Listening" Potter (flannel board)	"A Tale of Tales" MacPherson (1962) "Listening" (repeated)	"My Rabbit" (finger play)
Auditory training		
	Children pull animal pictures out of "secret box," then give them to teacher when they hear her make animal's sounds	Use tape recordings of familiar household sounds—children identify them
Songs		
"Head, Shoulders, Knees, and Toes" "Bingo Was His Name-O" (goes with Angus story) "Hop Se Hi" (action song)	"Bye Baby Bunting" (stand up and rock baby) "Hop Se Hi" (song and movement, repeated) "Where Oh Where Has My Little Dog Gone?"	"Head, Shoulders, Knees, and Toes" (repeated) "Hop Se Hi" (repeated) "Where Oh Where Has My Little Dog Gone?" (repeated)
Discussion and cognitive games		
Matching game: simple lotto game matching rabbit pictures cut from gift paper mounted on stiff cards to a second identical set	*What Whiskers Did* *Whiskers* has no words; have children tell story	Children hunt for hidden bunny in Carroll's book, *Where's the Bunny?*
Multiethnic component		
Pass around dolls brought back from Mexico by one of the children's families "Bingo," a Scottish-American folk song		*Whistle for Willie,* features a Black youngster

Thursday	Friday
What's Your Name? Gay (1955) *Animals on the Farm* Rojankovsky (1982) *Goodnight, Moon* Brown (1947)	*The Snuggle Bunny* Jewell (1972) *What's Your Name?* Gay (1955) (repeated)
"My Rabbit" (finger play, repeated)	"Listening" (flannel board, repeated)
With *Animals on the Farm*, teacher makes two animals noises for each picture and children decide which is the correct one	Play recordings of very familiar household sounds—children identify them (repeated)
"Head, Shoulders, Knees, and Toes" (repeated) "Bingo Was His Name-O" (repeated) "Bye Baby Bunting" (repeated)	"Hop Se Hi" (repeated) "Bye Baby Bunting" (repeated) "Bingo Was His Name-O" (repeated)
Guess animals in Gay's book, *What's Your Name?* Hunt for mouse in "Goodnight, Moon"	Use pictures of children of various cultures eating with their families, and ask children how they are alike, and so forth Guess animals in Gay's book, *What's Your Name?* (repeated)
"Bingo," a Scottish-American folk song	Pictures of families of different cultures eating together

TABLE 15–5

Analysis of reasons for selection of literary materials to use with older fours (listed in the order of the days as they appear in Table 15–6)

Resource*	Reasons for selection
Books	
A Story, A Story Written and illustrated by Gail Haley (1970)	African "Ananse" folk tale; Caldecott winner; good story with multicultural value
The Tale of Peter Rabbit Written and illustrated by Beatrix Potter (1903)	Timeless classic; rabbit focus
Marshmallow Written and illustrated by Clare Turlay Newberry (1942)	Story about a domesticated rabbit living "loose" in a home
Animals Every Child Should Know Written by Dena Humphreys, illustrated by Rudolf Freund (1951)	Handsome illustrations—all wild animals; contains many facts about wild rabbits that fours like to know; good contrast for discussion with *Marshmallow* story; continues theme of Coatsworth poem nicely from previous day
A Letter to Amy Written and illustrated by Ezra Jack Keats (1968)	A story with Black children as the central characters; universal theme of boys and girls getting along together and a birthday party that carries out the gift theme
Annie and the Old One Written by Miska Miles, illustrated by Peter Parnall (1971)	Navajo girl's relationship with an older person, her grandmother, shows caring for others, accepting death as part of the life cycle; a rather long book but worthwhile
The Nicest Gift Written and illustrated by Leo Politi (1973)	About Christmas in the barrio of Los Angeles; portrays life as many of the children in our center know it; interpolates familiar Spanish words and Mexican customs; out-of-season topic, but included because of gift theme and ethnic character
The Hare and the Tortoise Written by Aesop, illustrated by Paul Galdone (1962)	Rabbit theme; part of children's cultural heritage; uses unusual vocabulary in a "simple" text ("put forth," "so a course was fixed," "contempt," and so on); also used to balance very long book, *Annie and the Old One*
Curious George Goes to the Hospital Written and illustrated by H.A. and Margaret Rey (1966)	Included because one of the children is anticipating a tonsillectomy
Staying Home Alone on a Rainy Day Written and illustrated by Chiharo Iwasaki (1968)	Exquisite illustrations by a Japanese artist; talks about growing up, fear, and loneliness, a universal experience all children undergo sooner or later

*See material on pp. 322–327 for actual poems, songs, and finger plays.

TABLE 15–5 *(continued)*

Resource	Reasons for selection
Rosa-Too-Little Written and illustrated by Sue Felt (1950)	About a small girl working hard to achieve a goal (writing her name to get a library card); Hispanic background and feminist theme
A Hospital Story: An Open Book for Parents and Children Together Written by Sarah Stein, photographs by D. Piney (1974)	One of a series that includes other books on handicapped children, death, and so forth; contains text and pictures for children and also comments written for adult reading the story; selected because of impending tonsillectomy
No Roses for Harry Written by Gene Zion, illustrated by M.B. Graham (1958)	An amusing book, used here partly to balance *A Hospital Story* and partly to provide an opening for a discussion of the social problem of what to do when someone bestows an unwanted gift on you
Mr. Rabbit and the Lovely Present Written by Charlotte Zolotow, illustrated by Maurice Sendak (1962)	Accent in this story is about genuine caring for another person and about selecting a truly thoughtful gift; reviews colors; shows male (rabbit) in caring role
Poetry and finger plays	
"The Rabbits' Song Outside the Tavern" Elizabeth Coatsworth	A rather long, difficult poem; asks children to think about pros and cons of being wild and tame; beautiful language and images
"Once There Was a Bunny" traditional	Finger play—for fun
"The Rabbit" Elizabeth Madox Roberts	Captures a momentary encounter between child and rabbit; good poetry that carries out rabbit theme
"Listening" Miriam Clark Potter	For fun—easy for children to memorize
Songs	
"Little Peter Rabbit Had a Fly upon His Ear" "Pedro El Conejito Con La Mosca En Su Nariz" (same song, translated)	A funny song that also uses motions—use of English and Spanish desirable; gradually eliminating words as song is repeated causes children to concentrate on what they're doing.
"Hop Se Hi"	Large-muscle movement song; carries out rabbit focus; provides relief from sitting still
"Why Rabbits Have Bright Shiny Noses"	Finger play—for fun

TABLE 15-6
A weekly plan for group time with older fours (main topics are rabbits, gifts, caring for others, and tonsillectomy)

Monday	Tuesday	Wednesday
Books and stories to read and tell		
A Story, a Story Haley (1970) The Tale of Peter Rabbit Potter (1903)	Marshmallow Newberry (1942) Letter to Amy Keats (1968) Animals Every Child Should Know Humphreys (1951)	Annie and the Old One Miles (1971) The Nicest Gift Politi (1972) The Hare and the Tortoise Aesop (1962)
Poetry and finger plays		
"The Rabbits' Song Outside the Tavern" Coatsworth "Once There Was a Bunny" (finger play)	"The Rabbit" Roberts "Listening" Potter	"Once There Was a Bunny" (finger play, repeated)
Auditory training		
Teacher puts different objects in box while holding it behind her back and then lets one child shake box; others guess what's inside by identifying sound	Child goes behind low screen with teacher, selects object for sound box, and shakes it for other children to identify	Each child has box, shakes and listens to sound, and matches it to teacher's box when they sound the same (develops auditory memory)
Songs		
"Little Peter Rabbit Had a Fly upon His Ear" sung in English and Spanish	"Hop Se Hi" (song with movement)	"Why Rabbits Have Bright Shiny Noses" (song with finger play)
Discussion and cognitive activities		
Classification activity: Which objects would be best presents for baby, parent, dog, child, rabbit? Have five children wear appropriate hats or animal ears; others draw out pictures of gifts from bag and give to correct person or animal	Cause and effect: Discuss gift giving; also discuss where we'll move the rabbit cage now that it's warm outside; ask children to compare tame Marshmallow with the wild rabbit in Humphrey's book	Matching sound boxes: Show a few "storytelling" pictures, and ask children what is happening in them; discuss gift giving

Thursday	Friday
Curious George Goes to the Hospital Rey (1966) *Staying Home Alone on a Rainy Day* Iwasaki (1968) *Rosa-Too-Little* Felt (1950)	*No Roses for Harry* Zion (1958) *A Hospital Story* Stein (1974) *Mr. Rabbit and the Lovely Present* Zolotow (1962) (use flannel board with colors of felt to go with colors in story)
"Listening" Potter (flannel board, repeated) "The Rabbit" Roberts (repeated)	"The Rabbits' Song Outside the Tavern" (repeated)
Name all the children, using the "Carolyn, Bombarolyn" nonsense rhyme	Repeat the "Carolyn, Bombarolyn" rhyme
"Little Peter Rabbit" in Spanish and English (repeated) "Hop Se Hi" with movement (repeated)	"Why Rabbits Have Bright Shiny Noses" (repeated) "Little Peter Rabbit" in Spanish and English (repeated) "Hop Se Hi" (repeated)
Have you ever been in the hospital? What was it like?	Temporal ordering: Measure rabbit and compare it with previous measurements; discuss gift giving—unwanted gift (*Harry*) and thoughtfulness (*Mr. Rabbit and the Lovely Present*)

TABLE 15–6 (continued)

Monday	Tuesday	Wednesday
Multiethnic component		
A Story, a Story (Black) "Little Peter Rabbit" in Spanish (Mexican-American) Talk about rabbits' viewpoint of people and animals inside tavern	*Letter to Amy* (Black)	*The Nicest Gift* (Mexican-American) *Annie and the Old One* (Navajo) *Hare and the Tortoise* (folklore)
Nonsexist component		
Classification game deliberately nonsexist	*Letter to Amy* stresses boys and girls getting along together	*Annie* has girl as heroine and presents women in strong roles *Nicest Gift* has boy expressing feelings

Examples of Poetry, Finger Plays, and Songs for Group Time

Poetry

LISTENING[1]

Miriam Clark Potter

This is Mrs. Rabbit's house
   Up the stairs perhaps,
Hear the little bunnikins
   Taking sniffy naps.

Sniffy naps, small sniffy naps,
   With their eyes shut tight.
Mrs. Rabbit's listening,
   To hear if they're all right.

THE RABBIT[2]

Elizabeth Madox Roberts

When they said the time to hide was mine,
I hid back under a thick grapevine.

And while I was still for the time to pass,
A little gray thing came out of the grass.

He hopped his way through the melon bed
And sat down close by a cabbage head.

He sat down close where I could see.
And his big still eyes looked hard at me.

His big eyes bursting out of the rim.
And I looked back very hard at him.

---

[1]Adapted from "Mrs. Bunny's House" from *Sleepy Kitten* by Miriam Clark Potter. Copyright 1938 by E. P. Dutton, renewed 1966 by Miriam Clark Potter. Reprinted by permission of E. P. Dutton, a division of New American Library.

[2]From UNDER THE TREE by Elizabeth Madox Roberts. Copyright 1930, renewed © 1958 by the Viking Press, Inc. Reprinted by permission of Viking Penguin Inc.

	Thursday	Friday

Thursday

Staying Home Alone (point out lovely pictures are by a Japanese artist)
Rosa-Too-Little (Mexican-American)

Friday

Rosa-Too-Little has girl working against odds to achieve and assert herself
Curious George has a boy monkey feeling uncertain in hospital

Mr. Rabbit and the Lovely Present has both male (rabbit) and female (girl) being thoughtful and caring
Hospital Story has a girl feeling uncertain

NONSENSE NAMING RHYME[3]

Eula Mullins

This naming rhyme comes from the childhood of one of our center teachers and is much relished by 4-year-olds, who appreciate the silliness of it. In essence, the last one, two, or three syllables of the child's name are added to "bomb . . ." "see . . ." and "gof. . . ." For example:

Carolyn bombarolyn, seearolyn, gofarolyn!
Tee-legged, tie-legged, bow-legged Carolyn!
   or
Betty, bombetty, seaetty, gofetty!
Tee-legged, tie-legged, bow-legged Betty!
   or
Peter, bombeter, seacreter, gofeter!
Tee-legged, tie-legged, bow-legged Peter!

---

[3]Kindness of Eula Mullins, mother of Head Teacher Carolyn Mullins Mathews, Santa Barbara City College Children's Center.

THE RABBITS' SONG OUTSIDE THE TAVERN[4]

Elizabeth Coatsworth

We, who play under the pines,
We, who dance in the snow
That shines blue in the light of the moon,
Sometimes halt as, we go—
Stand with our ears erect,
Our noses testing the air,
To gaze at the golden world
Behind the windows there.

Suns they have in a cave,
Stars, each on a tall white stem,
And the thought of a fox or an owl
Seems never to trouble them.
They laugh and eat and are warm.
Their food is ready at hand,

---

[4]Reprinted with permission of Macmillan Publishing Co., Inc. from *Away Goes Sally* by E. Coatsworth. Copyright 1934 by Macmillan Publishing Co., Inc., renewed 1962 by Elizabeth Coatsworth Beston.

323

While hungry out in the cold
We little rabbits stand.

But they never dance as we dance!
They haven't the speed nor the grace.
We scorn both the dog and the cat
Who lie by their fireplace,
We scorn them licking their paws,
Their eyes on an upraised spoon—
We who dance hungry and wild
Under a winter's moon.

Finger Plays

MY RABBIT

(Traditional)

My rabbit has two big ears
  (hold up first two fingers to make ears)
And a funny little nose
  (join together all five fingers to make a pointy "nose")
He likes to nibble carrots
  (make nibbling motions with fingers)
And he hops wherever he goes.
  (make hopping movements with entire hand)

ONCE THERE WAS A BUNNY

(Traditional)

Once there was a bunny
  (make ears with first two fingers of left hand)
And a green, green cabbage head.
  (make a cabbage head with right fist)
"I think I'll have some breakfast," the little bunny
  said.
  (move bunny toward the cabbage)
So he nibbled and he nibbled,
  (move fingers on left, "bunny," hand)

Then he turned around to say,
"I think this is the time I should be hopping on
  my way!"
  (make left, "bunny," hand hop away)

Songs and Musical Finger Plays

*LITTLE PETER RABBIT HAD A FLY
UPON HIS EAR*

(sing with gestures if desired)
(sung to the tune of "Battle Hymn of the Republic")

Little Peter Rabbit had a fly upon his ear,
Little Peter Rabbit had a fly upon his ear,
Little Peter Rabbit had a fly upon his ear,
And he flicked it and it flew away!

(repeat, leaving off "ear," next verse; next
  verse leave out "fly" and "ear" and so forth)

Pedro el conejito con la mosca en su nariz,
Pedro el conejito con la mosca en su nariz,
Pedro el conejito con la mosca en su nariz,
La espanta y se asusta.

WHY RABBITS HAVE BRIGHT SHINY NOSES

Author unknown
(sung to tune of "My Bonnie Lies over the Ocean")

All rabbits have bright shiny noses
I'm telling you now as a friend,
The reason they have shiny noses—
Their powder puff's on the wrong end.

CHORUS
Wrong end, wrong end, wrong end,
  wrong end, wrong end, wrong end.
Wrong end, wrong end, wrong end,
  wrong end, wrong end, wrong end.

HOP SE HI

Words and music by K. BAYLESS

With a hop se hi and a hop se ho, With a

hop se hi and a ho, ho, ho, With a hop and a "bop" and a-

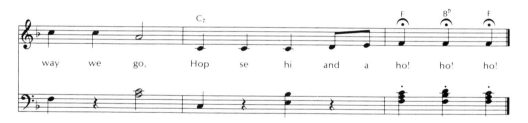

way we go, Hop se hi and a ho! ho! ho!

From *Music: A Way of Life for the Young Child* (3rd ed.) by K. M. Bayless and M. E. Ramsey, 1987, Columbus, OH: Merrill Publishing Co.

BINGO

Scottish song

Arranged by K. BAYLESS

There was a farm-er who had a dog, And Bin-go was his

name - O. B - I - N-G-O, B - I - N-G-O,

B - I - N-G-O, And Bin-go was his name - O

Suggestions

Sing the song through as written. Then repeat it and clap or tap instead of singing the letter ''B'' in ''B-I-N-G-O.'' On the next repetition substitute clapping the letters ''B'' and ''I,'' etc. (This song is excellent for helping develop concentration.)

From *Music: A Way of Life for the Young Child* (3rd ed.) by K. M. Bayless and M. E. Ramsey, 1987, Columbus, OH: Merrill Publishing Co.

HEAD, SHOULDERS, KNEES, AND TOES

From *Music: A Way of Life for the Young Child* (3rd ed.) by K. M. Bayless and M. E. Ramsey, 1987, Columbus, OH: Merrill Publishing Co.

SUMMARY

A well-presented group time provides opportunities for children and staff to come together in a pleasant, harmonious way, if the time is carefully structured so that it is easy for the children to function together. Some elements of structure that facilitate this include keeping groups small and stable, choosing a time for presentation when the children are rested and comfortable, planning carefully while retaining flexibility, beginning group as soon as children gather, keeping the pace "up beat," including sufficient variety, and drawing the group to a close before it falls apart.

In addition to songs and stories, group time curriculum should include opportunities for children to participate in discussions, to practice cognitive skills, and to develop their ability to tell various sounds apart. Since these times are so precious, teachers should think carefully about what materials they wish to include and always have a genuine reason for adding every one.

SELF-CHECK QUESTIONS FOR REVIEW

Content-Related Questions

1. List several different kinds of things children have the opportunity to learn during group time.
2. There are some fundamental principles to bear in mind when presenting group times that will help make them more successful. What are these principles?
3. List the eight ingredients that should be included as often as possible during a week of group times. Do most teachers include them when presenting group time? Why or why not is this the case? Why should they be included?
4. What are some important points to remember when planning a group time for young 3-year-olds? How would planning for a group of old fours differ from the plan for the younger children?

Integrative Questions

1. If you were the director of a center and realized that the teachers under your supervision were just relying on calendar, stories, and songs for group time, how would you go about changing their behavior? Would just telling them they should do

better be enough? If not, what kinds of practical help and motivation could you offer?

2. How do you expect the behavior of 2-year-olds and 4-year-olds to differ from each other during group time? Based on these differences, explain how you would adjust your group time plans to take those differences into account.

QUESTIONS AND ACTIVITIES

1. Students usually know more resources for group time activities than they realize they do. How many resources do *you* know? For practice, have the class choose a focus of interest for group time and then brainstorm in the group for sources of songs, poems, stories, auditory discrimination activities, and so forth that would fit that focus.

2. *Problem:* You have a little girl in your group who constantly interrupts what you are saying in group time. You believe children should participate in that experience, but this is too much! How would you solve this problem?

3. *Problem:* You want to present some group times that focus on water play, but you cannot find even one poem or finger play on that topic. Take 20 minutes and write one to share with the class.

4. *Problem:* You are now a director of a full-day center, and an inexperienced teacher comes to you and says she just cannot keep the children quiet during group time. What practical suggestions and help would you share with her that could make everyone's life easier during that period of the day?

5. Since the research shows that so many teachers present only a few activities during group time, is it possible that they are right and that the recommendations for including additional activities are too elaborate and should be ignored?

REFERENCES FOR FURTHER READING

It was surprising to find, as I sought out books dealing with the subject of group time, that there was very little available on this subject, except for discussions of how to share books with children. For this reason, the reader is asked to refer to the special topics listed in the references in the previous and following chapters, as well as to the resources given below.

Overviews

Beaty, J. J. (1988). *Skills for preschool teachers* (3rd ed.). Columbus, Ohio: Merrill Publishing Co. Beaty offers a useful discussion of ways to get children's attention and ways to extend the book experience in the chapter "Preschool Book Experience."

McAfee, O. D. (1985). Circle time: Getting past "Two Little Pumpkins." *Young Children* 40(6), 24–29. In addition to presenting the research discussed in this chapter, McAfee includes many practical suggestions for conducting more successful group times than the ones she observed in the study. Highly recommended.

Oken-Wright, P. (1988). Show-and-tell grows up. *Young Children* 43(2), 52–58. The author explains how to use discussion and evaluation with older fours and fives to increase their participation in group time.

Material on Telling Stories

In addition to the Bauer (1977) and Schimmel (1978) references listed on p. 296, the following references are helpful.

Anderson, P. S. (1963). *Story telling with the flannel board: Book 1.* Minneapolis: T. S. Dennison & Co. This book contains both stories and poems and many patterns for flannel board use.

MacDonald, M. R. (Ed.). (1982). *Storytellers' sourcebook: A subject, title and motif index to folklore collections for children.* Detroit: Gale Research Co. Title is self-explanatory.

Magee, M. S., & Sutton-Smith, B. (1983). The art of story telling: How do children learn it? *Young Children, 38*(4), 4–12. As the authors recount a study describing the way one little girl's storytelling ability developed, they interweave suggestions about how this skill can be encouraged in all children.

16 Helping Children Learn to Think for Themselves

Increasing Cognitive Competence

Have you ever

- Wanted to know how to ask the children better questions?
- Felt nervous about setting up a science table?
- Thought that teaching facts was not enough but didn't know how else to get the children to think?

If you have, the material in this chapter will help you.

I want to launch a nationwide anti-smug campaign. I am meeting more and more children who already know everything!

"We already studied colors!"

"We had the human body in second grade!"

"We did nutrition last year!" (I told them about the scientist Dr. McClintock who has been studying kernels of corn on the cob for 60 years and she hasn't finished corn yet.)

I asked a group of kids if they had been following Halley's comet. They answered, "We finished the Solar System."

I'm worried about the shrinking of minds, the closing of doors and windows, the shriveling of curiosity and wonder.

As I believe, so I teach. Educators and parents, join the anti-smug campaign! Down with convergent thinking, closed absolute right-and-wrong answers! Up with divergent thinking, open-ended exploring, brainstorming, wonder-full discussions and questions!

MIMI B. CHENFIELD (1987)

One of the most interesting aspects of teaching young children lies in the area of mental development, because young children usually come to school filled with curiosity, wonder, and the wish to learn. This eagerness makes cognitive education a delight for both teachers and children, *if the teachers have a clear idea of the children's capabilities and how to develop these further in an appropriate way.*

To accomplish this most effectively, teachers must take time to clarify their own educational values and decide for themselves what the real purpose of educating the children's cognitive selves should be. Should mental development consist only of learning a large array of facts, recognizing the alphabet, and parroting memorized replies to questions? Or should such education foster the ability to think and reason, to generate new ideas, to relish learning about a fascinating world, and to feel confident and enthusiastic when approaching new intellectual challenges?

While acknowledging the value of factual knowledge, the majority of teachers would want to include opportunities for thinking and reasoning in the curriculum, too. They want to nourish that spark of intellectual curiosity, develop that ability to think, and sustain that interest in the world and all it contains, as well as furnish the children with facts and information. This chapter offers some suggestions about what teachers can do to provide a balanced curriculum for mental development that includes both facts and thinking so that the curriculum is truly comprehensive.

BASIC WAYS TO HELP CHILDREN ENJOY COGNITIVE LEARNING

Keep Cognitive Learning Appropriate to the Children's Age and Abilities

One of the best ways to foster enthusiasm in any area of learning is to provide children with learning activities that are within their ability to master. This statement is generally accepted as an educational truism; yet it is a strange phenomenon that preschool teachers, who would never feel apologetic about not teaching baseball or needlepoint to preschoolers, still sometimes feel defensive about their refusal to push children ahead in the area of mental development. Yet the reasons for not attempting such acceleration are basically the same in all areas of instruction. Teachers do not force children beyond their depth in any curriculum area (whether it be physical, social, or intellectual), because doing this breeds discouragement, saps motivation, reduces opportunities for learning what the children should be learning at that particular age, and results in tension and unhappiness (Elkind, 1981b; Gallagher & Coché, 1987). (For a developmental chart that includes cognitive skills, see Appendix A.)

On the other hand, activities that are developmentally appropriate intrigue children and lead them to further interests (Bredekamp, 1987). Some good indications of interest are whether children are attracted to the activity when it is presented, whether they persist in

working on it, and whether they show progress in learning to master the task. In short, activities should be difficult enough to invite interest, but not so difficult that they produce despair.

Keep Cognitive Learning a Part of Real Life

This book frequently extols the virtue of basing learning on concrete, actual involvement with the physical manipulation of materials—a position that is well supported in the literature (Kamii, 1985; Piaget, 1983). Besides actual involvement, there is a second aspect that should be emphasized when discussing cognitive learning. Intellectual learning should not only be based on the physical manipulation of materials, but should also be integrated into the everyday, real life of the center whenever possible. This is best achieved by selecting the focus of interest for developing thinking skills from among the

There is no substitute for curiosity and enthusiasm in learning.

children's current concerns. Such curriculum is often termed *emergent* or *responsive* curriculum because the curriculum emerges from the children's interests and responds to it.

Perhaps this week the children are interested in the subject of camping because some of the families have just returned from vacation trips, or they are interested in weather because school has been closed after a tremendous storm. Perhaps a youngster has brought a grasshopper to school, and this sparks their interest in insects. As we will see in this chapter and the next, any of these topics can be used to provide practice in a wide variety of mental abilities, and all will assuredly be relevant and interesting to the children because they come from the youngsters themselves.

Keep Feelings a Part of the Experience

Remember, too, that part of reality is having feelings. Feeling and knowing properly belong together. Even when the accent is on practicing an intellectual skill, whenever human beings are involved, feelings are there, also. Indeed, unless the emotional life of the child is reasonably calm and she has been able to achieve some degree of peaceful social coexistence with the other children, it is unlikely that she will be free to focus much of her energy on the more difficult task of intellectual learning. Therefore, teachers should be prepared to recognize feelings as they arise and not try to brush them aside "because we're playing lotto now." Teachers should also appreciate the opportunities for special emotional or social learning that some subjects afford and deliberately include these as part of that curriculum area. *Learning should take place for many selves on many levels at the same time.* Specific examples of ways all the selves can be included in the cognitive curriculum are provided in Chapter 17.

Model Joy and Interest in Learning Yourself

The verve and interest in a subject that teachers feel themselves is one of the most valuable ways to encourage children's enthusiasm for cognitive learning. If teachers are excited about whatever topic is used as a basis for developing mental ability, the children will sense this and become infected with the same enthusiasm.

Indeed, much of the creative satisfaction that comes from teaching arises from the fun of presenting a subject to the children in a fresh and interesting way. The feeling of "I can hardly wait to see how the children will respond" is one of the things that makes teaching continually fulfilling.

HELP CHILDREN FIGURE OUT ANSWERS FOR THEMSELVES

When Asking Questions, Keep the Pace Reasonably Slow

A teacher can ask the best, most interesting and age-appropriate questions in the world and still experience discouragement if he fails to allow enough time for the children to reply before rushing on to the next question or, worse yet, answering it himself.

Rushing ahead of the children's ability to think is more typical of teachers than we would like to believe. As the research by Rowe illustrates so clearly, there are tremendous benefits for the children when teachers discard this pressured approach and substitute a more extended period of wait-time between questions.

Encourage Children to Ask Questions Themselves

John Coe puts it well when he says, "The best school, after all, for the world of childhood is not the school where children know the most answers, but the school where children ask the most questions" (1987, p. 70).

There are several practical things teachers can do to encourage question-asking behavior in their classrooms. Staying open and listening for questions is a fundamental part of such encouragement. Sometimes, particularly when the question is not clear, the teacher might ask the child to repeat or rephrase it, which helps both child and teacher understand what is being asked. Finally, as Rowe's research reminds us, waiting and resisting the impulse to provide the answer oneself can stimulate the child to answer and ask more questions on her own.

These responses are highly desirable because every time a child figures out an answer for herself, she has gained independence and confidence and a good feeling about herself because she has been able to rely on herself instead of on someone else. Of course, sometimes there is just no way for a child to learn something unless she is told—names of things or certain facts fall into this category. But there are many other times when, *if the teacher asks the right question,* the child can have a pleasureful "aha!" experience as she discovers or thinks through an idea on her own. These learning experiences are to be cherished, since they contribute much to the child's sense of happiness and feeling of intellectual competence.

Use Children's Questions to Help Them Learn

Answering a child's information-seeking questions requires two skills. First, it requires asking the right kind of question in reply to the child's query. This is often spoken of as "answering a question with a question," but there is more to it than that. The question the teacher asks in return ideally focuses the child's attention on something she can figure out from what she is involved with at that time, rather than asking the child to respond with factual information. Second, after the teacher asks the question, he should wait while the child thinks through and formulates her reply. Witness the differences in the following dialogues.

Example 1

The children, who have returned from a visit to the veterinarian, have found the doctor's kit all set up for them in the housekeeping corner. The teacher begins to unpack it.

Erin: (to the teacher) What are you doing with those things?

Teacher: I'm getting out the stethoscopes. They help us hear noises in our bodies. Doesn't your doctor ever listen to your chest with one of these?

Erin: He listens to my heart. Where *is* my heart?

Teacher: In your chest. (he points) Right there! Here, Erin, listen! (he puts the stethoscope on the child's chest)

Erin: (whining) I can't hear it. What does it sound like?

Teacher: Listen to mine. Don't you hear it go thump-thump?

Erin: Oh, yeah, now I do. It *does* go thump!

Teacher: Now listen to yours. What does *it* do?

Erin: It goes thump, too.

The above situation does not seem limiting to the child, until you contrast it with the following one.

Example 2

On the way back from a trip to the veterinarian, Hank and Maggie decide they want to play hospital when they return to school; so upon arrival, they hurry to get out the medical kits.

Maggie: (to the teacher) What's in that box?

Teacher: This one? Want to look? (hands the box to Maggie)

Maggie: Oh, it's that thing my doctor uses. It's a—what's it called?

Teacher: Anybody know? (total silence) It's called a stethoscope. (pause) Does it tickle when your doctor uses it?

Maggie: Yes, and it's cold, too. What good is it anyway?

Hank: He listens to your heart. I've heard it—it goes kuh-thump. There, I'll show you. (they listen to each other's hearts and to the teacher's, too)

Teacher: But how come the dog doctor had one?

Maggie: Do dogs have hearts?

Teacher: (pause) Well, *you* know a dog. (the children's center is frequently visited by a forbearing springer spaniel named Lady)

Hank: Lady! Let's get Lady! (the children proceed to the director's office where, providentially, Lady is stretched out, snoring)

RESEARCH STUDY
How Long Is Long Enough?

Research Question Rowe wanted to find out why a variety of science programs used in elementary school were not as effective in fostering inquiry skills as their developers had hoped.

Before beginning the study reported here, she had already analyzed hundreds of tapes of teachers talking with children in elementary school while they were teaching science units. She found out that differences in the inquiry abilities of the children were not due to lack of materials or science knowledge, group size, types of science curricula, age of children, or regionalism because she had controlled all these variables. The one thing almost all of the programs had in common was that the pace of instruction was very fast. When she measured the amount of time teachers waited for children to reply after asking a question she discovered the wait-time was only *1 second!* It was so short she couldn't use a stopwatch to time it but had to use special mechanical equipment instead.

Rowe began to wonder if this short wait-time could be the reason why the children were not responding well and developing their inquiry skills satisfactorily. To find out the answer, she posed the following research question: What would happen if teachers waited a little longer for the children to reply after asking a question? What if they didn't interrupt so quickly? Would that affect the quality of the children's replies?

Research Method Twelve classroom teachers working with children of various ages participated, using the same science lessons grouped into differing sequences. During the year of the experiment, the classes were recorded with audio and video tape, and the teachers were trained to provide more wait-time—allowing at least 3 seconds instead of the typical 1 second for replies.

Teacher: Now, don't surprise her. Speak to her first.

Maggie: Hi, there, Lady, old girl. (Lady looks up and wags her tail) (to Hank) Where's her heart?

Hank: (authoritatively, pointing to Lady's hindquarters) Down there!

Teacher: Is it?

Maggie: (putting stethoscope on Lady's rear) I don't hear nothing. She hasn't got one!

Teacher: Are you sure?

Hank: Let me listen! Nope, nothing there.

Teacher: Gee, *I* thought dogs had hearts. Where could it be?

Hank: On her back maybe.

Maggie: I want a turn. Let me do it. (she slides the stethoscope around Lady's chest) I hear it! I hear it!

Here it is! (Lady, gratified by the attention, licks her hand) Yuck, her mouth is sticky—yuck, yuck! I gotta wash.

Hank: But lemme hear her heart first. (Maggie runs off, but Hank continues to listen, ultimately distinguishing the sounds of the dog's breathing and stomach growling, also)

Note that this kind of teaching does not mean that the teacher never provides information or never makes a suggestion in the form of a guiding question (the teacher in Example 2 did both), but it does mean that he continually asks himself the question, "How can I help the children discover the answer for themselves?"

Research Results   When the post training tapes were analyzed and compared with prior tapes, the results showed that as the teachers allowed more time for the children to think, the length of the children's responses increased, the number of unsolicited but appropriate responses increased, failures to respond decreased, incidence of speculative responses increased, child-child debate increased, conclusions increased, the number of children's questions increased, and children rated by teachers as being "slower" gave more responses. The quality of the teachers' follow-up replies changed, too. Their replies were more flexible (i.e., their follow-up comments more frequently related to what the children had said), they asked better questions, and their expectations of the children previously rated as "slow" rose.

Implications for Teaching   Although this research deals with school-age children, it seems highly probable that teachers of preschool-age children also need to increase their wait-time between questions and answers. If anything, young children require even longer to formulate their replies because it takes more effort for them to put ideas into words.

A glance at the second hand of a watch illustrates how surprisingly brief 1 second actually is. Surely, once the matter is raised to a conscious level, it is relatively easy to remember to wait those few additional seconds—precious seconds that enable children to gather their thoughts together and put them into words. That brief pause can make the difference between allowing children to feel competent or undercutting their sense of ability.

Note. From "Wait-Time and Rewards as Instructional Variables, Their Influence on Language, Logic, and Fate Control: Part One—Wait-Time" by M. B. Rowe, 1974, *Journal of Research in Science Teaching, 11*(2), 81–94.

ASK CHILDREN TO THINK OF WAYS TO SOLVE PROBLEMS AND PROPOSE ALTERNATIVE POSSIBILITIES

In the discussion on encouraging conversation in Chapter 14, it was pointed out that conversation should be an interchange rather than a continual interrogation. In the preceding section of this chapter, it was recommended that, when teachers do ask questions, these should encourage children to investigate further and draw their own conclusions.

One final function of asking questions must be added. To encourage the generation of ideas, teachers should cultivate the ability to ask questions that cause children to think about how to solve problems or even to propose alternative solutions. Such questions are intended to encourage original solutions and so are called *creative thought questions.*

Creative thought questions are characterized by having more than one "right" (alternative) answer because a number of possible replies may be of equal worth. This sort of open-ended thinking has been christened *divergent thinking* by Guilford (1967, 1981). Guilford contrasts it with its opposite, *convergent thinking,* which could be defined as thinking in which only one correct answer is possible. When teachers are developing *convergent* thinking in children, they ask questions that require information in reply. Such questions as "How old are you?" "What's your name?" "Where's your coat?" and "What do we call this?" anticipate one correct, factual response. Note that much "discovery" learning, which fosters reasoning and process thinking, also produces convergent replies. For example, in the dialogue about finding Lady's heart, the children figured out the *facts* that a dog does have a heart and that it is located in its chest. However, if the children had been asked to figure out additional ways to hear Lady's heart, *then* it would have been an example of creative problem solving.

The following are examples of questions that stimulate *creative* problem solving and divergent thinking:

• How could we fix it?
• What else could we do?
• What do you think would happen if . . .?
• But what if that won't work. What else could we use?
• What could you use to make it?
• What do *you* think? What's your opinion?

Such creative thought questions invite a multitude of answers and possibilities.

Four-year-olds, in particular, relish thinking about funny problems—what if everybody had a tail like a monkey, or what if we lived under water the way fish do?—as well as solving more serious ones, such as how to keep the rabbit from getting too warm, or where to hang all the bulky coats now that winter is here, or how best to dry the dog after its bath.

Little children usually come up with one idea each, but if these single ideas are pooled in a group discussion, they can learn to appreciate that there is often more than one good way to solve a problem.

Reinforce the Production of Creative Ideas by Recognizing Their Value

Holman, Goetz, and Baer (1976) summarize considerable research that supports the importance of providing positive rewards for children

who are producing many different ideas, are engaging in other forms of original, creative behavior, or are doing both. It is all too easy for adults, who have had so much more experience, to unintentionally discourage creative thinking by evaluating the results too critically too soon, or by applying unreasonably high standards of accomplishment to what the children are doing, or by showing amusement at the unexpected novelty of a suggestion. Children are extraordinarily sensitive to these "put-downs" and quickly learn to hold their tongues and stop sharing their ideas when this occurs. Perhaps they may even stop thinking up alternative solutions to problems when subjected to such negative responses or, worse yet, to what they sense is subtle ridicule.

On the other hand, children will continue to be adventurous if teachers provide positive reinforcement by paying attention to their ideas, treating them with serious respect, and encouraging them to try their suggestions out whenever possible. Even an idea that does not turn out to be practical can have a beneficial result if it is used to teach the children that making an attempt is worthwhile and that failure just means it is time to propose another alternative.

Often, of course, the children's ideas are sound ones, and when this is the case and the group adopts the suggestion, the delight of the children is obvious. Their self-esteem, as well as their mental ability, has been enhanced.

HELP CHILDREN LEARN FACTS AND USE THOSE FACTS TO PRACTICE THINKING AND REASONING SKILLS

In addition to asking the right kinds of questions, waiting long enough for answers, and reinforcing the children's creative ideas, there is another aspect to planning cognitive curriculum that teachers need to understand thoroughly. There is a difference between teaching children facts and teaching them to use those facts to think and reason.

Unfortunately, many teachers never quite understand the difference between the two and, with the best of intentions, wind up concentrating mostly on teaching facts—sharing information with the children and then asking them to regurgitate it back.

There is no denying that facts are useful. However, they should form only the foundation upon which higher-order thinking skills should be constructed. For example, 4-year-olds may know the facts that holding ice under hot water makes it melt, that holding ice in their hands also makes it melt, and that ice melts faster in the sun than in the shade. These are all facts about ice. The teacher who goes one step further and asks, "How come all these things make ice melt?" is asking the children to put the facts together—to figure out an answer. What is it that warm little hands, sun, and hot water all have in common? Of course, they will not conclude that they all radiate energy, but they can deduce that the three agents have something in common—heat. By reaching this conclusion, they have participated in using facts to reason out an answer.

If the teacher continues with the subject, he could then ask the children to propose ways to make the ice melt faster. Perhaps they would suggest wrapping it in a blanket, using a hair dryer, or putting it in the oven. Then he might ask them to predict which of these ways is likely to produce the quickest result, help the children try those suggestions out, and encourage them, once again, to put their conclusions into words.

Table 16–1 provides a number of examples of fact and thought learning. Note how facts are used as the underpinning for thinking and reasoning skills.

SETTING UP A SCIENCE TABLE THAT ENCOURAGES THINKING

Ideally, opportunities to ask and answer thought-provoking questions, foster problem-solving skills, learn facts, and think and reason should be incorporated throughout the school environment. Many teachers also like to include a special interest area, sometimes called the "science table" or the "let's-find-out table," where children are particularly encouraged to explore something about their world in more detail. Such tables have the advantage of combining a number of different learning materials in one place and drawing them to the children's attention in a specific way.

Science Tables Can Introduce Children to the Scientific Method

The let's-find-out table provides many valuable opportunities for cause-and-effect learning to take place, because children can carry out simple experiments there. This introduces them to the concept of the scientific method, which involves (1) making observations, (2) thinking of possible reasons why things happen, (3) trying out these reasons or potential causes, (4) observing the results, and (5) then drawing conclusions.

With little children, such opportunities should be uncomplicated, straightforward ones. The experiments will be most successful if they provide chances to figure out the answers to such questions as "What made that happen?" "What would happen if . . .?" or "How could we find out if . . .?" These questions should be followed by, "Let's try it and see!"

The experiments can be as informal as seeing how a dog reacts when scratched in different places, or finding out how to make a kitten purr, or discovering what happens when red and yellow are mixed together. Perhaps it is a hot day, and the metal slide is hot, too. The teacher might ask the children, "How can we cool the slide?" If the children suggest pouring water down it, the teacher might ask, "How can we get the water there? What if the hose won't reach? Then what?" These opportunities for thinking and reasoning abound for the teacher who is on the lookout for them.

Remember that part of the learning experience should always include having the children

TABLE 16–1
A comparison of turtles and guinea pigs

Teaching facts	Teaching thinking and reasoning
Learning facts requires such mental abilities as paying attention, observing, remembering, and recalling (retrieving something from memory). Child has practice looking closely at turtle and guinea pigs and replies with facts when questioned by teacher or volunteers them because of interest.	Learning to reason requires mental reasoning abilities.* Child must understand a concept (such as matching or cause and effect), combine it with facts, apply it, and draw a conclusion—which, in turn, may produce a new fact. Child looks at tracks made by guinea pig and turtle, sees the tracks are different, and grasps that the cause of this difference is the tail mark left by the turtle as he moves along.
Factual learning focuses on learning facts and information. Turtles have hard shells. They have four legs and a tail. They can live on land or in the water (depending on the kind). They eat vegetables, fruit, insects, and bits of raw meat. They reproduce by laying eggs. They hiss. They are alive. Guinea pigs have fur. They have four legs and no tail. They live on land but can swim. They eat vegetables. They reproduce by giving live birth. They say "yeep." They are alive.	Thinking skills focus on using a learned fact to reason and figure out things. Matching: Are the two animals identical? Observation shows they are not the same, and application of that concept (same-different) shows they are not the same. Grouping: Do they belong to the same family? What do they have in common? They both have four legs. They are both alive. They both make noise when frightened. They eat many but not all the same things. How are they different? One has fur; the other has a shell. One lays eggs; the other gives live birth. Cause and effect: What makes something else happen? What made the turtle draw his head in?

*These mental abilities, along with some additional ones, are discussed in detail in Chapter 17.

put their conclusions into words. ("Well, what *did* make the kitten purr? Did the squirt bottle or the bucket of water work better? How come, do you think, the bucket was better?")

The following are examples of spontaneous situations in which the children could formulate reasons (hypotheses) for something happening:

- What makes the play dough so sticky? What could we add to make it drier?
- Can we turn Jell-O back to water? And then back to Jell-O again?
- How did you make that shadow? Can you make it go away?

The children may need to be helped along in their thinking by questions posed by the teacher

TABLE 16–1 (Continued)

Teaching facts	Teaching thinking and reasoning
	How come there is that line in the sand from the turtle track? How do we know it's a turtle track and not a guinea pig track? Does the guinea pig only "yeep" when frightened? What else makes her say "yeep"?
Benefits of factual learning are that it enables the child to know more about the world and provides a basis of information to be used with reasoning skills. Child recognizes turtles and guinea pigs and has a fund of information about their characteristics and care.	Benefits of learning to figure out answers are that the child uses her interest, combined with the facts, and, stimulated by the teacher's questions, practices some reasoning skills. Child uses subject of turtles and guinea pigs to practice the mental ability skills of matching, grouping, and determining cause and effect.
Typical teacher questions that encourage content learning are: What is it called? What do we do with it? What do you know about it? What do you remember that we have already learned? What did we say his name was? Does he have a tail? What is he eating? Who do you think is making that funny noise? What did we see the turtle eat yesterday?	Typical teacher questions that encourage reasoning skills are: How are these (legs, claws, ears, and so forth) different? What do you think made it happen? Why do you think these are just the same? Can you tell me any way the turtle and guinea pig are alike? What do you think made the guinea pig say "yeep"? Which would you rather have for a pet? Why did you choose that?

or by other children, but the test of a truly successful experiment is that the children can answer most of their own questions as a result of their experience with the materials.

Topics That Can Be Used Successfully for Let's-Find-Out Tables

The subject matter used for science tables is often some kind of natural history, but physical science subjects, such as pulleys, levers, and objects that sink and float, are also effective. Some topics used by our staff in the past are:

- A comparison of rabbits, gerbils, and guinea pigs
- What firefighters do, and how they put out fires safely
- How volcanoes work
- Growing seeds: what do plants need to grow?
- Various properties of water: how does it freeze, what mixes with it, can it run up hill?

Aaron concocted this hammer for himself when the teacher refrained from suggesting a solution.

- What sinks and what floats?
- An investigation of textures
- What do birds eat? (a wintertime project that included making pinecone bird feeders)
- What happens in the fall to plants and animals?
- Where do peanuts come from? (peanuts are a big crop in our state)
- How heavy is it? How do we measure weight?

Some Basic Principles to Apply When Setting Up a Let's-Find-Out Table

1. It is much more satisfactory for children to learn about something when they can learn from real experience and by doing. For example, the inclusion of live animals, such as turtles,[1] enhance both interest and learning.

2. For the sake of comparison and asking questions, it is generally helpful to provide a contrast of some kind—such as between guinea pigs and turtles as shown in Table 16–1 or between two species of turtle.

3. Provide activities the children can do with what is displayed. For turtles and guinea pigs this might include offering them food, analyzing which animal eats what, taking them out and holding them, and watching them move.

4. Unless you happen to know a lot about a particular subject already, it will be necessary to do at least a little reading about the topic.

5. Be prepared to offer some especially interesting tidbits of information, as well as basic facts, about what the children are studying. For example, did you know that the oldest known turtle lived 152 years? And did you know that in Peru, guinea pig is considered a delicacy? A nearby reference shelf of a few books is a real help.

6. Have in mind various questions you might ask the children to help them think up ways of finding out the answer.

7. Be as prepared as possible to let them try out their ideas and suggestions.

8. Do your best to combine beauty with learning: neat printing, beautifully illustrated books, pictures, and touches of color all do their part in making the let's-find-out area appealing. *National Geographic* publishes an outstanding series of natural history books suitable for little children. Librarians are also more than willing to help teachers locate appropriate support materials.

9. Remember to change such areas regularly. Rather than setting out everything about turtles at once, for instance, it would sustain interest more effectively to introduce the turtle one day with some getting-acquainted activities about what it eats and does, then add guinea pigs for comparison toward the middle of the week, and perhaps

---

[1] The health department has assured me that it is only the little, green turtles that sometimes spread the disease salmonella and that should not be used in child-care centers. Land turtles are all right because they are dry. They also suggested it is wise to wash hands after handling any animal.

This let's-find-out area provided the children with many different items to weigh and many ways to weigh them. The basket was used to hold stones so investigators could find out how many stones it took to equal their body weight.

add the large turtle shell after that for the children to try out being turtles themselves.

10. The let's-find-out area can also be tied nicely into the rest of the curriculum plan to extend learning further. For example, the children would enjoy moving like turtles and guinea pigs at dance time. Threes would appreciate hearing the story *Turtle Tale* (Asch, 1978), and fours would like *Molly's Woodland Garden* (Rockwell & Rockwell, 1971) or *Let's Get Turtles* (Selsam, 1965).

Examples of Experiments at the Turtle Table

Rather than just giving the children information, it is helpful to have in mind things they can find out for themselves as they participate at the science table. If the right question is asked (such as, "Are all turtles the same size?"), the children need only look at the assortment of shells, pictures, and animals to deduce the answer for themselves.

What is even more interesting (and fun) is to ask them a question and then follow up with, "How could you find out?" Remember, it is this kind of question that leads to simple experiments in which ideas are tried out and the answer is obtained. Of course, the experiments have to be supervised by the teacher to protect the animals from harm, and they need to be spread out throughout the weeks's time for the same reason. The following are some questions about turtles that could be answered by simple experimentation:

- Do turtles really move slowly when compared with guinea pigs? When compared with snails?
- What do they like to eat? What won't they eat?
- Do they act differently when they feel warm or cold?
- Are they afraid of guinea pigs?
- Do turtles talk?
- What frightens turtles?
- How do turtles protect themselves?

Questions for the Children to Think About to Develop Specific Mental Abilities

The let's-find-out table can also provide many opportunities to practice thinking skills, as noted

What do you suppose it would feel like to be a real turtle?

in the examples in Table 16–1. Some additional suggestions might include:

- *Matching:* Make a lotto game with pictures of turtles. (Turtles are easy to draw, and the drawings can be easily photocopied; stickers or duplicate sets of wildlife stamps also work well.)
- *Grouping:* This could be handled through discussion, comparing the qualities that animals have in common with the qualities of inanimate objects, or comparing turtles with animals that live only in water or that can fly.
- *Pairing common relations:* Looking up the visiting animal in a book and finding a picture of the turtle that goes with the live animal is a good example of one kind of common relations, relating two- or three-dimensional objects. It answers the question, "What picture goes with which turtle?"
- *Seriation:* Do big turtles eat only big things and small turtles only small things? Arrange several lettuce leaves in order from large to small and find out if the size of the leaf makes any difference to the turtle.
- *Temporal ordering:* A filmstrip on how turtles reproduce and grow would help the children understand that process as it occurs through time.

- *Cause-and-effect learning:* The figuring-out suggestions on p. 332 present fine opportunities for cause-and-effect learning. Such questions as "How do we know it's a turtle track and not a guinea pig track?" or "What makes the turtle draw his head in?" present fine opportunities for cause-and-effect learning.

SUMMARY

When curriculum is generated for the cognitive self, the most important goal to work toward is helping children feel confident, happy, and enthusiastic when engaged in mental activity. This can be accomplished by keeping the activities appropriate to the children's age and abilities, making cognitive learning a part of real life, allowing sufficient wait-time, and helping children feel competent by enabling them to figure out answers for themselves.

Teachers need to understand the difference between teaching facts and helping children learn to think and reason if they wish to offer a cognitive curriculum to the children that provides opportunities for comprehensive mental development. Children can also learn to express creativity in thought if teachers encourage them to propose alternative solutions to problems. This strategy works particularly well when teachers stress the desirability of considering more than one solution and when they emphasize that sometimes more than one "right" answer is possible. An example of how to set up a let's-find-out table illustrates how these goals can be accomplished.

SELF-CHECK QUESTIONS FOR REVIEW

Content Questions

1. Explain why children should not be pushed beyond their depth in any area of learning.
2. Define *emergent* and *responsive* curriculum.
3. What are three important things teachers can do that will help children enjoy cognitive learning?
4. This chapter suggests several strategies that will help children figure out answers for themselves. What are these strategies? Give an example illustrating how a teacher might use each one to further the children's learning.
5. What is the difference between fact and thought learning? Explain why each is a valuable part of the curriculum.

Integrative Questions

1. How would an emergent, responsive approach to developing curriculum differ from the way most curriculum is developed? Provide an example of an emergent possibility you have come across in recent weeks while working with children. Would you describe the curriculum in your current school as emergent or conventional?
2. In order to demonstrate that you understand the difference between teaching facts and teaching reasoning skills, select a topic of recent interest to the children and provide examples of both teaching approaches.
3. The children have been playing with beanbags, and one of the bags has got stuck in a tree beyond reach. Propose a dialogue between teacher and child that would discourage the child from think-

ing of a way to retrieve the beanbag. Now rewrite the dialogue demonstrating how the teacher might ask a series of questions that could help the child figure out ways to retrieve the beanbag.

QUESTIONS AND ACTIVITIES

1. In Examples 1 and 2 on pages 333–334, identify the teacher's statements that provided factual answers. Were some of these necessary? Is it any better for another child to tell a child a fact than for the teacher to do it? Consider the incorrect information Hank gave Maggie about the location of Lady's heart—do you think the teacher should have said anything about that?
2. Movement education offers many opportunities for creative, alternative solutions to problems—for example, "If you couldn't use your arms at all, is there another way you might catch a ball?" Take a few minutes with the class and produce some more questions related to movement education that would be fun to pose to the children about turtles.
3. Select a topic from a subject that has interested the children during the past week and have the adult class contribute suggestions on how it could be used for a let's-find-out table. Be sure to include a list of questions that would encourage the children to figure out answers and another list that would encourage them to do some additional thinking about the topic so that their reasoning skills are employed.
4. *Problem:* One of the parents has volunteered to bring three harmless snakes to your school room to demonstrate them to the children. You are genuinely afraid of such animals—they fill you with a deep revulsion. Under these circumstances do you think it would be desirable to accept the offer of the visit? What might be the pros and cons of having the snakes visit?
5. Try some brainstorming yourself. What else might a potato masher be used for? A rubber tire? A piece of cloth? A box of matches, contents included? Try to go beyond ordinary uses—have fun—take risks! (And if this exercise is especially difficult for you, analyze what has made it so hard and *not* fun. What are ways you can use these insights when teaching children in order to foster a more positive response from them?)

6. Do you think that waiting longer for preschool children to respond to questions might improve the quality of their replies? Propose an experiment that could help you find out if this is true.

REFERENCES FOR FURTHER READING

Overviews — Helping Young Children Have Ideas and Solve Problems

Forman, G. E., & Hill, F. (1980). *Constructive play: Applying Piaget in the preschool.* Monterey, Calif.: Brooks/Cole Publishing Co. *Constructive Play* is filled with fascinating examples of ways to present problems to young children that should arouse their curiosity and stimulate their questions.

Goffin, S. G., & Tull, C. (1984). Ideas! Creating possibilities for problem solving. *Dimensions, 12*(2), 15–19. This is a good article explaining strategies for problem solving that are appropriate for each age.

Paley, V. (1981). *Wally's stories.* Cambridge, Mass.: Harvard University Press. This *delightful* book illustrates how Paley encouraged her kindergartners to propose creative, imaginary solutions to problems posed in stories and discussion.

Creating the Right Atmosphere for Thinking

Smith, R. F. (1987). Theoretical framework for preschool science experiences. *Young Children, 42*(2), 34–40. Smith proposes practical guidelines for determining whether scientific topics are developmentally appropriate to use with 3- and 5-year olds.

How to Ask Questions That Help Children Think

Campbell, K. C., & Arnold, F. D. (1988). Stimulating thinking and communicating skills. *Dimensions, 16*(2), 11–13. The article features a developmentally based series of question types, moving from "what is . . .?" to "what else . . .?" to "what if . . .?"

Carin, R. B., & Sund, A. (1978). *Creative questioning and sensitive listening techniques: A self-concept approach* (2nd ed.). Columbus, Ohio: Merrill Publishing Co. Though really written for teachers of older children, this book is useful for preprimary teachers, too, because it covers so many different aspects of asking questions and *waiting* for answers. Highly recommended.

Sigel, I. E., & Saunders, R. (1979). An inquiry into inquiry: Question asking as an instructional model. In L. G. Katz (Ed.), *Current topics in early childhood education* (Vol. II). Norwood, N.J.: Ablex Publishing Co. This wonderful chapter presents a list (with examples) of all sorts of questions teachers ask or *should* ask. Highly recommended.

Resources for Developing Let's-Find-Out Experiences

Ayers, J. B. & Ayers, M. N. (1984). Popcorn, Piaget and science for preschoolers. *Dimensions, 12*(2), 4–6. The Ayers use popcorn to illustrate how even such a simple and popular item can be used to teach basic scientific skills linked to the preoperational stage of development.

Embery, J. (1983). *Joan Embery's collection of amazing animal facts.* New York: Dell Publishing Co. This paperback is full of the odd little tidbits of information about animals that children find fascinating.

Harlan, J. D. (1988). *Science experiences for the early childhood years* (4th ed.). Columbus, Ohio: Merrill Publishing Co. I recommend this book as being a particularly rich source of additional curriculum-related ideas, including music, finger plays, lists of children's books, creative ideas, and even some examples of "thinking games."

Lima, C. W. (1982). *A to zoo: Subject access to children's picture books.* New York: R. R. Bowker Co. Have you ever hunted desperately for a picture book to fit a particular subject? If so, this is the answer to your prayers. It indexes everything from turtles to robots by subject, author, title, and illustrator. Available in most libraries.

Neuman, D. B. (1978). *Experiences in science for young children.* Albany, N.Y.: Delmar Publishers. This very good book talks about teaching strategies and approaches, as well as things to do. All the science activities have been tried out with preschool children, and a chart is included that indicates which ones are appropriate for which age.

Rights, M. (1981). *Beastly neighbors: All about wild things in the city, or why earwigs make good mothers.* Boston: Little, Brown & Co. A delightful book whose subtitle does a good job of describing its contents. It includes a timely chapter on recycling.

Rockwell, R. E., Sherwood, E. A., & Williams, R. A. (1983). *Hug a tree and other things to do outdoors with young children.* Mt. Rainier, Md: Gryphon House. I highly recommend this book as a resource for activities, labeled according to age and as a resource for additional resources.

Sprung, B., Forschl, M., & Campbell, P. B. (1985). *What will happen if . . . .: Young children and the scientific method.* New York: Educational Equity Concepts (Gryphon House, distributor). The authors single out a few topics and illustrate how they might be used to teach the scientific method. Outstanding because of the nonsexist, age-appropriate emphasis. Highly recommended.

Williams, R. A., Rockwell, R. E., & Sherwood, E. A. (1987). *Mudpies to magnets: A preschool science curriculum.* Mt. Rainier, Md: Gryphon House. Another first-rate book that suggests many investigatory science experiences that are arranged according to topic and age. Highly recommended.

Woodard, C., & Davitt, R. (1987). *Physical science in early childhood.* Springfield, Ill.: Charles C Thomas, Publisher. This book is replete with *appropriate* examples of exploratory activities that illustrate basic principles of physics. It includes suggestions for extending the experiences and for simplifying them for very young children. Highly recommended.

For the Advanced Student

Deci, E. L., & Ryan, R. M. (1982). Curiosity and self-directed learning: The role of motivation in education. In L. G. Katz (Ed.), *Current topics in early childhood education* (Vol. 4). Norwood, N.J.: Ablex Publishing Corp. Deci and Ryan are primarily concerned with the role of intrinsic motivation, and they hypothesize that children who are intrinsically motivated because of interest, rather than extrinsically motivated because of external rewards, will be more curious, self-motivated learners.

Gall, M. (1984). Synthesis of research on teacher questioning. *Educational Leadership, 42*(3), 40–47. Gall provides a good review of this important subject.

Gallagher, J. M., & Sigel, I. E. (Eds.). 1987. *Early Childhood Research Quarterly, 2*(3). The entire issue is devoted to the dangers of forcing children into inappropriate curriculum.

Lay-Dopyera, M., & Dopyera, J. E. (1987). Strategies for teaching. In C. Seefeldt (Ed.), *The early childhood curriculum: A review of current research.* New York: Teachers College Press. This chapter contains a helpful section on question asking.

17 Building for Future Academic Competence

Developing Specific Mental Abilities

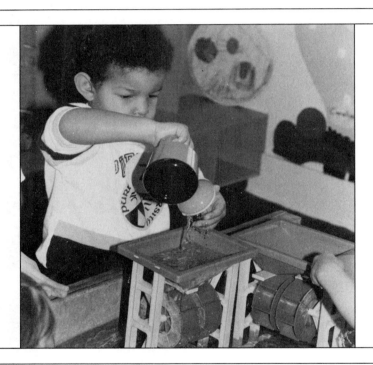

Have you ever

- Heard people refer to Piaget but did not really understand why his theories are so valuable?
- Wondered how to go about developing mental abilities in the children without pushing them beyond their depth?
- Wished that you knew more about presenting "pre-academic" skills so the children would find them fun?

If you have, the material in this chapter will help you.

The point is that you always pay a price for what you do in life. Certainly children can be accelerated in particular skills if they are worked long and hard enough. But the price may be too steep in regard to what the child missed or the emotional problems that ensue in the process. Moreover, there is no clear-cut evidence that early acceleration in any particular academic skill has long-lived benefits. . . . In general, a child who elaborates the skills he does have such as the ability to order materials according to size, on a wide range of different materials (blocks, sticks, dolls, dogs, and so on), is likely to be better prepared for future learning than a child who has learned a great deal in a short time but who has not really had the opportunity to assimilate and practice what he has learned.

DAVID ELKIND (1981a)

In addition to helping children sustain a zest for intellectual learning and develop creativity in thought, teachers should also foster some more specific mental abilities in young children, since practice in these skills favors the development of more advanced thinking and reasoning skills as the children mature.

CONTRIBUTIONS OF JEAN PIAGET

To understand more about such mental abilities, it is first necessary to review the most basic conclusions of Jean Piaget, because his work has made such a significant contribution to what is known about the development of cognitive structures in childhood. (Piaget and his associates are prolific writers, and their publications are too numerous to list here in their entirety. For a convenient collection of the most important Piagetian publications, the reader may wish to refer to a copy of *The Essential Piaget* by Gruber and Vonèche, 1977.)

Piaget has long maintained that children's mental growth is the result of dynamic *interaction* between children and their environments and that the activity of play and actual, involving experience are vital ingredients in fostering mental development. He also maintains that the thought processes of children differ from those of adults and that these processes pass through a series of development stages as the child matures. He has demonstrated the truth of this contention quite convincingly in several areas, the most familiar being his demonstrations of preschoolers' inability to master the principle of conservation (the fact that the total amount or quantity of material remains unchanged even though the shape or number of parts may be altered). Young children will maintain stoutly, for instance, that the amount of water in a tall, thin beaker is greater than an identical amount of water in a squat jar, even though they may have just witnessed that the quantities were originally the same. As Charles (1974) puts it, preschool-age children lack "the ability to consider, at the same time, the whole and various arrangements of its parts" (p. 14). In our culture, it is not until about age 7 that children grasp the principle of "reversibility" and can, in their mind's eye, return a substance to its original state while viewing it in its altered state. This is, of course, only one of numerous examples Piaget and other scholars of the Genevan school have investigated over the past 50 years that demonstrate the perception-bound quality of thinking characteristic of preschool-age children. For children of this age, seeing is, quite literally, believing.

347

RESEARCH STUDY
A Piagetian Experiment: Conservation of a Discontinuous Quantity

Research Question   After Piaget conducted his pouring experiment with liquids and found out that children of preschool age were unable to master the principle of conservation, he asked these questions—What if pieces of solid material were used in place of liquids? Would the children reason differently about whether *that* material stayed the same even if put into different-sized containers?

Research Method   To determine the answer, Piaget substituted red and green beads in place of liquid, and proceeded as follows. While the child watched, he poured the red beads into one container and then filled up an identical container to the same level with green beads. Next, as the child watched, he transferred the red and green beads into containers of differing sizes. During the experiment he asked the child questions phrased in the following manner.

[Subject is a child aged 5 years, 10 months.]* "What are these?" *Little green and red beads.* "Is there the same amount in the two glasses?" *Yes.* "Why?" *Because there's the same height of green and red.* "If we put the beads in there, what would happen?" [The investigator points to a tall, thin glass.] *They would be higher.* "Would there be the same amount?" *No.* "Where would there be more?" [Child points to tall, narrow container.] *There.* [The investigator pours the red beads into the container.] "Do you really think there are more beads there than here?" *Yes.* "Why?" *Because it's narrow and they go higher.* "If I poured them all out [pretends to pour the red beads on one side and the green on the other], would they be the same or not?" *More red ones.* "Why?"

Piaget's research is very different in style from the other research studies cited in this book. For this reason an actual excerpt of his approach is included in this chapter. In order to study children's thinking he used a combination of interview and observation to develop and then confirm his theories.

He has been criticized because it is not possible to repeat a Piagetian experiment exactly (Centre for Educational Research and Innovation, 1977). This is because his data often lack precise ages and numbers and are not statistically analyzed. Moreover, rather than using control groups and carefully presenting exactly the same situation to every child, he thought it was more valuable to conduct open-ended discussions with children on a one-to-one basis so every interview was somewhat different since he followed the child's lead as he formulated his questions.

Despite these criticisms, Piaget's clever investigations have blazed new trails in the study of children's development, particularly in the realm of cognition, and teachers as well as children owe him a debt of gratitude for the remarkable insights he contributed.

Stages of Mental Development

Piaget has divided mental development roughly into four stages as shown in Table 17–1, and although the age of onset and discreteness of these stages varies somewhat from culture to culture, the order in which the stages occur appears to be fairly regular (Cohen, 1983).

Because that one is narrow. "And if I make a necklace with the red beads and one with the green beads, will they be the same, or not?" *The red one will be longer.* "Why?" *Because there'll be more in there.* [The investigator pours the red beads back into the original container.] "And now?" *They're the same height again.* "Why?" *Because you've poured them into that one.* "So are there more red ones or green ones?" *The same.* (Piaget, 1952, page 26)

The experiment is repeated once more, with identical responses from the 5-year-old, demonstrating that the child judges quantity based on the appearance of the quantity in the container, not on the inherent amount of material.

On the other hand, when this experiment is carried out with older children (ranging in age from 6 to 9 years), they are no longer beguiled by the shape of the container. They are able to "conserve" the idea of quantity, and understand that the actual amount of beads has not changed despite the fact that the taller cylinder makes it look like there are now more of them. Therefore, they answer correctly that the number of red and green beads remains the same, no matter how the shape of the container changes.

Implications for Teaching   Nothing demonstrates more clearly than Piaget's numerous investigations that children really do reason differently from adults and that their mental abilities develop sequentially as the child matures. When teachers understand this fact, it becomes apparent how important it is to suit learning to the correct developmental level. Otherwise instruction becomes a waste of time for the teacher and a source of frustration for the children in her care.

Note: From *The Child's Conservation of Number* by J. Piaget, 1952, New York: Humanities Press.
*Piaget's queries are in quotation marks. The child's replies are italicized.

Argument continues over whether it is possible (or desirable) to accelerate children and move them from one stage to the next by means of various teaching techniques (Bruner, Olver, & Greenfield, 1966; Elkind, 1981b; Henderson & Bergan, 1976). However, it appears that the main value for the teacher of knowing about such stages and the characteristics of children who are in them lies in understanding how children see the world and in suiting learning opportunities to what they are able to grasp at each stage.

All children benefit from such learning opportunities, but it is particularly important to offer them to children who come from families of the poor (Almy, Chittenden, & Miller, 1966; Golden, Bridger, & Martare, 1974; Sigel &

Cocking, 1977), since these kinds of activities may not be part of the culture of their homes. Special attention should also be paid to other children whose life experiences may have been restricted because of such things as extensive hospitalization or overexposure to television.

Conditions That Favor Optimum Development

According to Piaget, development is influenced by physical maturation, experience, interaction with other people (socialization), and equilibration. This information has important implications for teachers and parents, since adults can influence all these elements, at least to a degree, thereby helping ensure the most favorable climate for the child's growth.

TABLE 17–1
Summary of the Piaget model

Basic stages	Behavior commonly associated with the stage
Sensorimotor stage **(0 to 2 years)** Understanding the present and real	Composed of six substages that move from reflex to intentional activity involving cause-and-effect behavior Involves direct interactions with the environment
Preoperational stage **(2 to 7 years)** Symbolic representation of the present and real Preparation for understanding concrete operations	Child uses signifiers: mental images, imitation, symbolic play, drawing, language Understands verbal communication Believes what he sees—is "locked into" the perceptual world Sees things from his own point of view and only one way at a time ("centering") Thinking is *not* reversible Busy laying foundations for understanding concrete operations stage, which involves grasping concepts of conservation, transitivity, classification, seriation, and reversibility
Concrete operational stage **(7 to 11 years)** Organization of concrete operations	Has probably acquired the following concepts: conservation, reversibility, transitivity, seriation, and classification; that is, now believes that length, mass, weight, and number remain constant; understands relational terms such as "larger than" and "smaller than"; is able to arrange items in order from greatest amount to least amount; can group things, taking more than one quality into account at the same time
Formal operational stage **(11 to 15 years)** Hypothesis making Testing the possible	Age of abstract thinking Able to consider alternative possibilities and solutions Can consider "fanciful," hypothetical possibilities as a basis for theoretical problem solving Sees the world not only as it *is*, but as it *could* be

For instance, although physical maturation depends primarily on built-in timetables, the role of good nutrition, adequate health procedures, and ample physical activity should not be ignored. The Romans summed this up to perfection when they spoke of the importance of *mens sana in corpore sano*—a sound mind in a sound body.

The significance of experience—in particular concrete, tangible experience—has been stressed throughout this book as being a fundamental, essential component of teaching young children, yet it must be mentioned once again in this discussion of mental growth, lest the reader be tempted to suddenly abandon the real world for the solely verbal-visual one.

The third enhancer of growth, social interactions, requires a bit more comment. Although teachers of young children are usually well aware of the kind of *social* benefits children gain through interaction with other children, they tend to be less familiar with Piaget's idea that discussion and argument (in the sense of debate) among children is an important avenue of mental growth. It is very helpful for children to discuss reasons and thinking problems among themselves, as well as directly with teachers. This encountering of experience together, combined with putting their ideas about it into words and engaging in back-and-forth comparison of their thoughts, is a productive mode of learning that teachers should make greater use of as a teaching method.

Finally, the process of equilibration, or bringing ideas into balance with reality; is valuable to understand. Piaget maintains that there are two ways children deal with information; they either assimilate it or accommodate to it, and both of these processes contribute to equilibration. Quite simply, when children *assimilate* information, they add new facts to what they know already; if they *accommodate* to information, they change what they know to fit the new experience.

Mental activity usually involves a combination of these two processes working together. For example, years ago I had a child in my day-care group who found his little dog lying dead in the gutter one day, run over by a car. Weeks later, his mother reported that he was insisting on walking along the edge of the curb every time they went somewhere, and this almost fanatical preoccupation was driving her crazy! In approved counseling style, I asked her how long he had been doing this and what else had happened or changed in his life at about the same time. At first she maintained that nothing much had changed, but upon thinking it over, she commented that he had begun doing that about the same time his grandfather had died. It turned out that the reason he had been so insistent on walking along the curb was that he was looking for his beloved Grandpa. Once his mother realized this, she explained to him that dead people are not generally found in gutters and that Grandpa had been buried in the cemetery, which

they then visited. This anecdote illustrates that this little boy had formerly *assimilated* his Grandfather's dying (that is, he interpreted it in the light of what he knew of death). The additional information required him to *accommodate* to it by changing his prior knowledge to include new experience. The new situation required new learning and a rebalancing of what he already knew about the world with what he had just learned.

Much learning involves this process of rebalancing, and teachers tend to accept this fact routinely. What they may be insensitive to, however, is that sometimes accommodating to new information also requires considerable tact by teachers so that the child can save face while he literally is changing his mind.

WHICH MENTAL ABILITIES ARE PARTICULARLY IMPORTANT?

Readers will no doubt realize that they already provide some practice in the mental abilities discussed in this chapter. However, experience has taught me that such practice often appears to be inadvertent or a by-product of activities whose primary purpose seems to be providing children with factual information rather than providing practice in reasoning skills. This is unfortunate because it emphasizes the wrong end of the learning continuum.

As we saw in the last chapter, teachers do not have to opt for either teaching facts or providing opportunities for developing mental abilities. Almost any subject or focus of interest that appeals to the children can be used for both these purposes as Tables 17–2 and 17–3 demonstrate. *What does matter is that teachers attain a better, clearer idea of what some of the mental abilities are and of how to deliberately include them in curriculum plans to make certain that the children have opportunities to practice them, as well as to acquire factual information.*

Piaget (1983) has identified various mental abilities that form the foundation for later

TABLE 17-2
Links between mental abilities and later school-related skills

Ability	Value
Matching: Can identify which things are the same and which things are different *Basic question:* Can you find the pair that is exactly the same?	The ability to discriminate is crucial to development of other mental abilities. An important aspect of gaining literacy: discriminate between letters (such as "m" and "w"). Promotes understanding of equality. Encourages skill in figure and ground perception (separating a significant figure from the background).
Grouping: Can identify common property that forms a group or class *Basic question:* Can you show me the things that belong to the same family?	Fosters mathematical understanding; set theory and equivalency. Children must discriminate, reason, analyze, and select in order to formulate groups. Regrouping encourages flexibility of thought. Depending on manner of presentation, may foster divergent thinking—more than one way to group items. Requires use of accommodation and assimilation. Classification is a basic aspect of life sciences: allows people to organize knowledge.
Common relations: Can identify common property or relationship between a *nonidentical pair* *Basic question:* Which thing goes most closely with what other thing?	Fosters mathematical understanding: one-to-one correspondence. Fosters diversity of understanding concepts: many kinds of pairs (opposites, cause-effect, congruent). Can teach use of analogies and riddles.
Cause and effect: Can determine what makes something else happen: a special case of common relations *Basic question:* What makes something else happen?	Basis for scientific investigations. Conveys sense of order of world. Conveys sense of individual's ability to be effective: act on his world and produce results, make things happen. Encourages use of prediction and generation of hypotheses. Introduces child to elementary understanding of the scientific method.
Seriation: Can identify what comes next in a graduated series *Basic question:* What comes next?	Fosters mathematical understanding. Relationship between quantities: counting (enumeration) with understanding, one-to-one correspondence, equivalency, estimation. If teacher presents series going from left to right, fosters basic reading skill.
Temporal ordering: Can identify logical order of events occurring in time *Basic question:* What comes next?	Fosters mathematical understanding. Conveys a sense of order and a sense of time and its effect. Relationship between things: cause-and-effect and other relationships. Prediction. Requires memory: what happened first, then what happened?
Conservation: Can understand that a substance can return to its prior state and that quantity is not affected by mere changes in appearance *Basic question:* Are they still the same quantity?	Idea of constancy (reversibility) is fundamental as a foundation for logical reasoning, basic for scientific understanding; it is also the basis for mathematical calculations involving length, volume, area, and so forth.

Note. From *The Whole Child: Developmental Education for the Early Years* (4th ed.) by J. Hendrick, 1988, Columbus, Ohio: Merrill Publishing Co.

TABLE 17–3

Suggestions for mental development activities using typical preschool activities as the focus of interest

Activity	Reasoning skills	Factual learning possibilities
Cooking with older fours (making whole wheat muffins)		
Eating muffins after they are baked	Generate *emotional gratifications* Satisfaction in eating Pride in accomplishment Increased self-esteem	"I like to eat" New foods taste good sometimes Cooking is fun New vocabulary "crumbs," "steam," "temperature," etc.
Sharing muffins with other children for snack	Generate *social learning* Doing something for self and others to enjoy Working together for a common goal	"I have to cooperate to get things done" It's fun to do something for someone else
Cleaning up the cooking activity	Opportunity for meaningful work	"I know what it's like to be my mother or father cooking in the kitchen"
Answering questions and solving problems while making muffins	Foster *creative thinking* What shall we do so Charlie can have a muffin? He's allergic to raisins. We only have two muffin tins. What else can we use to bake the muffins in?	"I may be little, but I can solve hard problems"
Day before: take label from flour sack and egg carton to market and match labels to shelf products	Provide practice in *matching* (Basic question: "Are these the same or different?")	Products have labels that tell us what they are; might learn informally that an item begins with a specific letter (flour begins with *f*, for example) There's more than one kind of flour or eggs in the market. They don't all have identical labels
Weighing flour: use a balance scale to measure identical quantities, such as two cups of flour	Provide practice in matching by weight	One way to "prove" that things are identical is to weigh them
As tools are being used, talk about what goes with what (flour with sifter, spoon with batter, egg with shell); repeat at group time in riddle form	Provide practice in *pairing common relations* (Basic question: "Which two things go most closely together?")	Different tools have different purposes; some tools work best with some foods and processes, others with others
After visiting the market, provide equipment for playing store. Where should different foods be placed? What belongs where?	Provide practice in *grouping* (Basic question: "Which things belong to the same group or family?")	Food products have different qualities and are stored in the market accordingly—vegetables together, baking products together, and so on

TABLE 17–3 *(continued)*

Activity	Reasoning skills	Factual learning possibilities
Allow children to taste ingredients and compare them for sweetness. Are raisins or honey sweeter? How about salt? Flour? Baking powder? Vanilla? How would you arrange them from sweet to not sweet?	Provide practice in *ordering: seriation* (Basic question: "What comes next?") "What is sweetest?"	Foods have varying degrees of sweetness
Read recipe out loud, and let children arrange ingredients in the order they will be mixed together	Provide practice in *temporal ordering* (Basic question: "What happens next?")	In recipes, sometimes it really matters what comes first, second, and third
How do grapes turn into raisins? (Try drying grapes in food dryer.) Can we turn them back into grapes? What made the muffins rise? (Experiment with leaving some ingredients out; putting some in oven, leaving others out of oven.)	Provide practice in determining *cause and effect* (Basic question: "What makes that happen?")	Drying grapes turns them into raisins. You can't turn a raisin back into a grape Heat and baking powder make muffins rise

Unit blocks with 3- and 4-year-olds

Activity	Reasoning skills	Factual learning possibilities
Use blocks as vehicles for dramatic play Child might build a structure with a specific purpose in mind or one that satisfies an emotional need such as a corral to sit in.	Generate *emotional gratifications*, such as relief of anxiety, or expression of feeling	"If I build a corral and sit inside it, it makes me feel safe and protected" "Now that I've knocked down that hospital and pretended to kill those doctors inside it, I feel better!"
Use blocks in the company of other children	Generate *social learning* Blocks offer innumerable opportunities for social interaction and learning—how to enter a group, the limits of acceptable behavior, and respect for others' accomplishments	"If I bring them a truck, they will allow me to join in" "The rule says, 'I can only knock down the things I've built myself' "
Unstructured quality of blocks favors use of creative imagination; a block can be anything the child wishes; play is imaginative and various	Foster *creative thinking* "All the cylinders are in use. What can we use in place of them?" "How could you make that?"	There are endless possibilities for building with blocks "I don't have to worry if there are not enough blocks to go around. I can always use something else as a substitute"

TABLE 17–3 *(continued)*

Activity	Reasoning skills	actual learning possibilities
Unit blocks with 3- and 4-year-olds—cont'd		
Putting away all the same kind of *identical* blocks together Young children tend to use only one size for one purpose and to select only identical ones for that purpose	Provide practice in *matching* (Basic question: "Are these the same or different?")	There are many blocks that are exactly the same because they're made out of wood and are the same size If blocks of the same size are stored together, it's much easier to find the needed block when building with them
Block construction that requires stacking to build towers or walls of the same height using blocks of various unit multiples	Provide practice in *pairing common relations* (Basic question: "Which two things go most closely together?")	Various "number" facts, such as two unit blocks are equivalent to one double unit and two triangle blocks are equivalent to one unit block
Teacher might store all curved blocks in one case and all straight-sided ones in another; ask children to guess why some are in one case, some in the other one	Provide practice in *grouping* (Basic question: "Which things belong in the same group or family?")	Some blocks that look different have common properties
Older children might be helped to understand twoness, threeness, and so on by counting pairs or triplets of blocks of various dimensions (three unit blocks are the same number of blocks as three triangle blocks)—the common property is twoness or threeness		Particular number groups (or sets) always contain the same total amount, that is "three" is "three" whether three triangles, three pillars, or three unit blocks
Child might construct flight of stairs or tiers of a building using blocks	Provide practice in *ordering: seriation* (Basic question: "What comes next?")	Unit blocks increase in size in a predictable, orderly way
Teacher might make a series of drawings as a block construction progresses or take Polaroid pictures, then ask children to arrange the pictures later in order construction occurred	Provide practice in *temporal ordering* (Basic question: "What happens next?")	Block construction has a beginning, middle, and end
Many principles of construction can be learned that basically have to do with what makes blocks stay up or fall down Many opportunities for trial-and-error, cause-and-effect learning related to balance	Provide practice in determining *cause and effect* (Basic question: "What makes that happen?")	Facts about the force of gravity: if you want something to stay up, it's important to balance the blocks; if it's heavier on one side than on the other, it will tip over

concrete operational thought in older children. In our culture, these are children aged approximately 7 years and older. Constance Kamii (1972), who has had an important role in implementing Piagetian principles in early childhood classrooms, lists these primary concrete operational abilities as including classification, seriation, structuring of time and space, social knowledge, and representation.

Ways of gaining social knowledge and using such symbols as language and imaginative play to represent reality have already been discussed in previous chapters, so we will concentrate here on how to develop the beginning skills that underlie classification, seriation, and structuring time and space.

Lest we become too parochial, I want to point out that readers should also look beyond Piaget and realize there are other taxonomies and theories that identify many additional kinds of mental abilities. Guilford's Structure of Intellect, for instance, identifies 120 different ones (Guilford, 1967, 1979). I have found that particular outline of value when describing how people think, because its arrangement is so comprehensive and logical. However, it is too extensive to consider using in its entirety at the preschool level. Also, many of the abilities described therein are undeveloped at that early age.

To develop curriculum for very young children, it is necessary to select skills that appear to be particularly significant for later mental development. They must also be ones that are developmentally appropriate, that is, ones that are not beyond the ability of the children to achieve. For this reason, the reader will find the activities recommended for developing the various cognitive abilities to be simple ones. These have all been used successfully, not only in our own children's center and institute, but also in many other preschool settings, such as Head Start, so we know that young children enjoy them and are able to perform them satisfactorily. To make doubly certain that we are not tied to just one theory of cognitive structure, all the abilities selected (with the exception of simple

matching) were chosen because they have reasonably similar counterparts in both the Piagetian and Guilfordian theories. (For a more complete discussion of parallel skills in Piaget and Guilford, see Hendrick [1973, 1988]).

These skills include matching, pairing common relations, grouping, graduated ordering (seriation), temporal ordering, and determining simple cause-and-effect relationships.

Relationship Between the Mental Abilities and Later School Success

The mental abilities selected for discussion have great value in themselves because they encourage children to use their mental powers without asking them to do things that are beyond their grasp to achieve. These abilities are also valuable because they can help lay a foundation for later success in developing reading, mathematical, and scientific skills. Table 17–2 illustrates some of the links that exist between these abilities and later competence at a higher academic level.

GENERAL PRINCIPLES FOR WORKING ON SPECIFIC MENTAL ABILITIES

Make a Plan (But Be Prepared to Seize the "Teachable Moment")

To make certain that all the important mental abilities are covered on a regular basis, it is absolutely necessary to make a plan for each week, lest some of them be forgotten or overlooked. This need not be an elaborate outline (Tables 17–3 and 17–4), but it *is* necessary to think activities through in order to ensure their inclusion.

Admittedly, this can be difficult for the beginning teacher to do. One must realize that the only effective way of becoming more familiar with cognitive curriculum possibilities is to make a special effort and work hard for a few months at learning to identify and develop appropriate

TABLE 17–4
Suggestions for mental development activities using a theme based on the interests of the children

Activity	Reasoning skills	Factual learning possibilities
Growing and eating vegetables with 3- and 4-year olds		
Gardening and growing things to eat Working in dirt	Generate *emotional health* Gardening enables them to experience the satisfaction of eating what they have grown Feelings of competence from caring for garden and actually producing a worthwhile result Involvement with dirt, mud, and water offers emotional relief	"Achieving something makes me feel good" "Mucking about in dirt is pleasurable"
Any child who wishes to can work in the garden	Generate *social learning*—nonsexist emphasis Everyone participates in gardening and growing vegetables Gardening provides opportunity for meaningful work	Gardening is both men's and women's work Working can be fun
Ask questions Propose problems	Foster *creative thinking* "What if roots grew up instead of down?" "How can we make something that will just sprinkle the seeds very lightly?"	Roots usually grow down Punching holes in a can lets water run through
Weed the garden, leaving only lettuce and radish seedlings	Provide practice in *matching* (Basic question: "Are these the same or different?")	Every plant has its own distinctive characteristics: radishes look like radishes, lettuce like lettuce, dandelions like dandelions
Offer cooked foods at lunch and ask children to choose raw vegetable each came from: potato/mashed potato; spinach/cooked spinach; tomatoes/tomato sauce; peas in	Provide practice in *pairing common relations* (Basic question: "Which two things go most closely together?")	Cooking really changes some things, but they're still called by the same name and are still related to each other

My thanks to Janelle Colleran and Cathy Dunlap for many of the suggestions contained in this table (1979).

activities. After that, it becomes easier and easier to blend mental ability activities into the rest of the center day and to make use of spontaneous opportunities as they arise, also.

Keep It Fun

In Chapter 16 we spoke of the importance of helping children feel confident and happy in the cognitive realm by providing them with men-

TABLE 17–4 *(continued)*

Activity	Reasoning skills	Factual learning possibilities
pod/cooked peas. Or pair can labels with what's inside the can		
At group time or snack time have many samples of food (real or pictures), and ask children to decide if they come from plants or animals	Provide practice in *grouping* (Basic question: "Which things belong in the same group or family?")	Vegetables and meats come from very different sources Fruits are sweet, vegetables aren't
Growing and eating vegetables with 3- and 4-year-olds—cont'd		
Are they fruits or vegetables? How do they know?		
In the garden, ask children to water first the smallest, then find the medium, and then water the largest plants	Provide practice in *seriation* (Basic question: "What comes next?")	Learn vocabulary describing size and the concept of size
Put together a sequential pumpkin puzzle showing its life cycle, or dance through the life cycle of plants at dance time. Ask children how could they be a seed? Roots?	Provide practice in *temporal ordering* (Basic question: "What comes next? What happens next?")	Vegetables go through an orderly, predictable life cycle: first a seed, then sprouts, and so forth
Tell "Jack and the Bean Stalk," encouraging children to tell what comes next in the story		
Start bean seeds in pots, some in dark with and without water, some in light with and without water	Provide practice in determining *cause and effect* (Basic question: "What makes that happen?")	Plants need light, water, and warmth to grow
Observe tender plants after a hard frost. What happened to them? What made it happen? (Try putting lettuce in the freezer section of refrigerator)		
What if we didn't weed the garden? (leave a section and find out)		

tal challenges that are appropriate for their developmental level, by relating cognitive learning to real life, and by enabling children to figure out answers for themselves. All these contribute to the basic pleasure and rewards related to intellectual learning. In addition to these fundamental principles, teachers should apply a few others when working with specific skills to increase the pleasure of that experience for the children.

Integrate practice in mental skills into regular activities and play situations whenever possible. As the following examples illustrate, many ordinary daily activities at school provide opportunities for practice in various thinking skills. Using them for that purpose helps integrate such learning into the lives of children and keep it pleasureful at the same time.

Realize that just doing those activities will not provide sufficient learning. *It is necessary to talk about what the children are doing, too, so that they are aware of what they are doing while they are doing it.* Otherwise such learning is likely to remain on the intuitive level longer than need be.

For example, while putting the blocks away, you might use terms that young 3-year-olds understand and speak of putting away all the big "daddy" blocks first, the medium "mommy" ones next, and the little "baby" blocks last to encourage the concept of graduated ordering (seriation). Or you might discuss with the children what it was that made the egg become hard when they boiled it to emphasize cause-and-effect learning.

Integrate Cognitive Learning into the Regular Curriculum

Table 17–3 shows how activities, such as block play and cooking, that are part of the everyday curriculum can be used to enrich the emotional, social, and, particularly, the cognitive selves of the children if a little extra time and thought is devoted to their presentation.

In these tables the learning possibilities have been divided into learning facts and practicing reasoning skills to demonstrate once again the differences between them. Table 17–4 illustrates how teachers might use a subject (or theme) for the same purpose. It is my impression that teachers tend to use themes or specific topics more frequently for building cognitive skills, so the example in Table 17–4 may seem a bit more familiar to the reader. Using themes or topics offers the additional advantage of directly re-

flecting the children's current interests. Basing learning on what the children want to know is a wonderful way to increase their pleasure in learning.

Make as Many Materials as You Can Yourself

Although much cognitive learning need not rely on tabletop or small-group activities for its implementation, sometimes table materials, such as lotto boards or puzzles, can be very effective learning accessories. When they are used, try to make as many of them yourself as possible.

There are several reasons for advocating this. First, such materials are usually much less expensive to make (if you do not include the teacher's time in the calculation), and making them provides creative satisfaction for the teacher, as well as pleasure for the children. Second, the materials can be designed to fit a particular topic. (Just try to find a classification game that deals with camping, for instance, or with going to the hospital.) Finally, teacher-made materials are usually more attractive than commercial ones. I am always impressed by the color and spirit of the ones my own students concoct, and the children find them irresistible. Teachers seem to have a better idea of what will actually appeal to little children than most manufacturers do.

When making such materials, remember that durability is important. Glue pictures to a sturdy cardboard backing. Rubber cement works best as the adhesive, and matboard is both colorful and strong. Take time to spray the results with clear acrylic spray or cover them with clear contact paper to keep the materials permanently fresh and attractive.

It is easy to make inexpensive materials by drawing pictures or by using rubber stamps or paper stickers. Gift wrapping paper is a fine, frequently overlooked resource that is especially useful when making materials with a holiday theme. Catalogs, which are often arranged by category, are particularly good sources for sets of grouping pictures. Inexpensive "picture dictionaries" are still another source of colorful, attractive illustrations. Once made, the items

Pairing the dinosaurs with their pictures provides a good opportunity for practicing common relations.

can either be stored in neat boxes with a picture on the top so that children can tell what is inside or popped into ziplock bags where the contents are readily visible.

Provide Plentiful Opportunities for Practice

Repeated practice is necessary to learn any skill, and mental skills or abilities are no exception to this rule. Not only should opportunities for practice be repeated, using the same materials, but practice in the same skill should be provided over a long span of time, using different topics or themes and offering a range of levels of difficulty so that the children may progress as they become more proficient.

To Keep Activities Appropriate, Understand How to Make Them Very Simple and Also More Difficult

Very young children and ones who are just beginning to work on developing skills need to start with very simple activities, but they become quickly bored by these as their expertise increases. For this reason, each discussion of specific abilities offers suggestions for designing practice opportunities that range from easy to difficult.

Basic ways to increase the challenge or difficulty of these skills include:

• Increase the number of items the child has to work with at one time, such as providing two lotto boards to scan instead of one.

- Require that memory be used as part of the process—turning cards over so that the children have to remember which one is where is enjoyed by many 4-year-olds.
- Shift to a different sensory modality, such as moving to activities that require feeling instead of seeing or matching by tasting alone.
- Increase the amount of detail that has to be analyzed while figuring out the answer.
- Asking children to give verbal reasons for their decision will certainly make the activity more challenging, and such answers may be within the ability of many 4-year-olds. However, an extensive explanation will probably be beyond the ability of most of them.

CURRICULUM SUGGESTIONS FOR DEVELOPING SPECIFIC MENTAL ABILITIES

Matching

To understand matching, children must be able to understand the concepts *same* and *different*. Teachers need to understand this, too. Same should mean "just the same" or identical. If one item is a two-dimensional picture of a dog, for example, the item it matches must be the same two-dimensional picture, not a three-dimensional little model of a dog.

The questions and directions that go with this activity should be, "Is this just the same?" or "Find me the one that is just the same," or "Show me the one that is different, or not the same."

Matching is the easiest of the mental skills described here for children to acquire. For that reason, matching activities are particularly appropriate to use with older twos and young threes, although older preschoolers also enjoy these activities. When developing specific mental abilities, it is desirable to begin with teaching this concept of same versus different, because children must be able to perform this basic discrimination task before they can learn the more difficult discriminations required for successfully accomplishing relational, grouping, and

ordering skills. Moreover, the ability to perceive sameness and differentness is a vital element in learning to read, since children must be able to perceive such subtle differences as the one between *d* and *b* or *m* and *w* to tell the difference between *dog, bog, God,* and *gob* or *mood, wood,* and *doom.*

Matching Activities That Children Enjoy

- Throw beanbags with pictures pinned on them into boxes with matching pictures.
- Put stickers on hands and have the children hunt for a matching child to sit with at lunch.
- Use "mirror" dancing in which one child imitates the actions of another as closely as possible.
- Put identical objects mixed in with other objects in a feel box or bag and have the child identify the identical pair by feel.
- Put one item in the bag or box and put three choices where the child can see them. The child matches the item in the box or bag with one of the three choices.
- Duplicate handclap patterns.
- Match sets of identical pairs of sound shakers.
- Match tastes or smells.
- Cut up varieties of apples and ask children if they can match the pieces by taste. (This is really hard!)
- Match paired pieces of various white vegetables, such as radishes, turnips, jicama, sunchokes, and potatoes.

Suggestions for Making the Task More Challenging. The difficulty level for matching activities can be increased by adding more detail to the pictures or making the differences less conspicuous. Using other sensory modalities adds challenge, too. For example, even children as young as 3 enjoy using their hands to search out the differences between two or possibly three objects in a feel bag, with the goal of identifying the one in the bag that is just the same as the one the teacher is holding.

Paired Common Relations

It is easiest to grasp the difference between common relations and matching skills if one realizes that, although relations always involve pairs of items (as matching does), these are *never identical* pairs. Instead, they are pairs because they have some common element or bond between them that associates them. Perhaps they are opposites, such as up and down or hot and cold; or perhaps they are items that usually go together as do shoes and socks, pots and lids, cords and sockets, hats and heads, and flowers and vases. (Some of these relationships are the very simplest examples of what Piaget terms "one-to-one correspondence.") The basic question the children must be able to answer to succeed in these activities is "What belongs most closely or goes most closely together?"

Children really enjoy paired associate activities. Learning to see the relationships between things underlies the ability to appreciate riddles at a later age. It also prepares the way for the mental leap necessary to grasp analogies, such as "Hat is to head as lid is to . . .?" or "Belt is to waist as ring is to . . .?" or "Two is to four as three is to . . .?" Such analogies are thought to be excellent tests of genuine reasoning and thinking abilities. (Witness the fact that the Miller Analogies Test is one the most frequently used criteria for admission to graduate school.)

Common Relation Activities That Children Enjoy

- Children love to pore through a box of mixed items and put pairs together, such as salt and pepper shakers, leash and toy dog, nuts and bolts, and shoe and sock.
- Develop a game that involves putting picture and object together, such as ball with pictured ball and comb with pictured comb. (This provides valuable symbolization practice.)
- Use pictures of things that go together, such as animals and their homes or mothers and babies.
- Use flannel board sets of pairs, such as raincoat with hat or swimsuit and cap.
- Put nonsense pairs together and ask children to identify what is wrong with the pair.
- Have children hold a particular item at group time, then wait suspensefully until you or another youngster draws its pair from a box or from behind their backs, at which point they can shout its name out loud.
- Give children a particular picture of an animal and, as you produce a picture of its correct food, have them get up and "feed" their animal its dinner.

Grouping

Grouping involves being able to identify what a number of items, either pictures or objects, have in common. Thus, basically, the children's task is to "Show me which things belong together," or (the opposite task) "Show me what does not belong to this group or family."

Note that grouping differs from common relations because grouping always involves just what the word says: dealing with a group rather than a pair. At least three or four items possessing a common property are needed for the children to successfully determine what the group has in common. Grouping differs from matching because in grouping none of the items are identical; matching items are always exactly the same.

Grouping is a beginning form of the more sophisticated hierarchical classification identified by Piaget (1983) as being the intellectual prerogative of children who have attained the concrete operational stage of development. The concept of grouping is valuable to understand because the ability to perceive common properties not only underlies all the classification systems of science, but also contributes to understanding set theory in mathematics. However, its greatest value is that grouping requires reasoning and thinking even at the preschool level, although children of that age may not always be able to put the reasons for their placing items into particular groups into words. (Piaget speaks of such grouping activity as being on the intuitive level—an apt description of how the children proceed. They appear to determine the reasons for the grouping as they do it, rather than determining the common property in advance. This accounts for the fact that the basis for forming the group often shifts as the activity progresses.)

There are many opportunities during the day for such grouping activities. If children are asked to sort all the foods they think should go into vegetable soup onto one tray and the ones for fruit salad onto another, that is a grouping activity. Or if they fish all the goldfish out of the aquarium and leave in the others, that too is grouping. If they take a field trip to the dog show and return with the concept that there is a large category "dog" composed of many subclasses, such as poodles, spaniels, and terriers, once again they are exposed to the idea of grouping according to common properties. In all these situations, the basic question the children must answer is, "Which things belong to the same group or family?"

Be Careful to Talk About the Result. Simply doing the activity, however, is not enough. The teacher should clarify what the children have intuitively perceived by asking questions about why things do or do not belong to the same group. For example, she might ask why German shepherds are different from poodles, or inquire if poodles and shepherds are cats—and if not, why not. She also might ask why cats are cats and dogs are dogs. The children will be able to give only very simple answers, such as "Dogs bark and cats meow," or "Dogs eat dog food, and cats eat cat food," or "Dogs are bigger than cats." Any of these answers should be accepted by the teacher without a lot of hairsplitting, because they are the result of the children identifying some attribute or quality generally possessed in common by one group and not possessed by the other one.

One of the most frequently used strategies for providing practice in classification or grouping is for adults to identify the group first and then ask the children to add things that belong to this category or to remove items that do not belong. For example, teachers frequently direct children to "Find all the things with fur on them" or to "Give me all the red beads." Unfortunately, this kind of teaching requires almost no thinking on the children's part. They only have to know what *red* means or what *fur* is and pick out all the items that possess this quality.

The way to elicit more thinking from children is to ask them to identify the common quality themselves and to sort items or pictures according to that property. For example, children love to sort buttons of all descriptions, and the opportunities buttons offer for composing groups according to differing properties is large indeed.

Younger children will most likely sort them according to color or size or shape, but older ones may sort according to whether the buttons are plastic, metal, or shell or according to how many holes they possess. It is often obvious to the teacher what the basis of the grouping is, and if the children are too young to put it into words themselves, she can clarify what they have done by saying, "It looks to me as if you are putting all the red ones here and all the blue ones there. Is that your idea?"

Slightly older children also enjoy the challenge of guessing what should be added to an already existing group. The teacher might set out pictures of furniture on the flannel board without telling the children the common property (namely, furniture) and then ask the children to select the item from an additional group of pictures that belongs to that same group.

Grouping Activities That Children Enjoy
- Use the dollhouse and ask children what furniture belongs in which room.
- Supply a large number of wildlife stamps, mounted on cardboard, and ask the children to sort which animals belong together.
- Acquire a large number of buttons, each one different, and encourage the children to sort the buttons into whatever categories appeal to them (egg cartons make good sorting trays).
- Dismiss the children according to whether they are wearing a particular color. To make it more difficult, dismiss according to stripes, plaids, and so forth.
- Provide a grocery store and have the children set it up by sorting empty boxes and cans onto the shelves as "they go together."
- Let them pin up, in one place (such as on a bulletin board), the things they saw at the dog show and, in another place, the things they did not see there.
- Provide them with flannel board groups, such as vegetables and other foods, and ask them to remove what does not belong.
- At dance time, ask the children what can they do with their arms that they cannot do with their feet.
- There are also many commercially made classification games that can be used to provide practice in this concept.

Suggestions for Making the Task More Challenging. The easiest grouping activities are ones in which the common property or attribute is very obvious, such as color or shape. The less obvious the property, the more difficult is the category; thickness, for instance, is an attribute much less commonly identified by little children than color (Hendrick, 1973). Asking the children to name the category also increases the degree of difficulty; so does asking them to regroup the materials another way or to group them according to several properties at the same time.

Ordering

There are two systems of arranging things according to some form of order or regularity that are valuable to include in cognitive curriculum for preschool children. One is arranging items according to some form of *graduated order* (termed *seriation* by Piaget), and the other is arranging them according to the order in which they occur in time *(temporal ordering)*. In both cases, the basic question the children must answer to perform these thinking tasks successfully is, "What comes next?"

Seriation. Seriation, or arranging items according to a graduated order, is most frequently thought of in terms of gradations of size. Montessori cylinders are good examples of a regular change of dimension, and any kind of nested equipment can be used to teach the same concept. Measuring cups, measuring spoons, nested blocks, or those little wooden dolls or eggs that fit inside each other are all examples of seriated ordering. Nuts and bolts come in a wonderful array of sizes, too, and children enjoy arranging these in order and also performing the one-to-one correspondence involved in screwing the right-sized nut onto the correct bolt.

To teach the concept in a broader sense, it is also possible to teach gradations of color (ranging from palest pink to deep red, for example), taste (sweet to sour), or sound (loud to soft).

Cuisinaire rods and unit blocks whose sizes are all based on multiples of one basic unit measurement can also be used to teach seriation, if they

Nesting these Russian dolls presents an attractive invitation to practice seriation.

are stacked in regular order beside each other for comparison. These are particularly valuable because they help children grasp the idea that 2 is composed of two 1s, 3 of three 1s or of one 2 and one 1, and so forth. This results in a much more meaningful concept of enumeration than merely learning to parrot "1, 2, 3 . . . ."

Seriation Activities That Children Enjoy

- Make a slot box with slots for different-sized and shaped objects—a small circle, a larger square, a still larger rectangle, and so forth.
- Gather as many nested objects from around the house or school as possible (sets of spoons and cups, for example), and offer them during house play or at the water table. Talk about how one fits inside another.
- When putting things away, hang them up in graduated order—for example, in the house play area hang up all the cooking spoons in order from small to large.

- Offer varying shades of the same color paint at the easel, from light to dark.
- Offer a feeling game in which various grades of sandpaper, mounted on cardboard, are put in the bag, then the children try to draw out the smoothest first, the the next smoothest, and so forth.
- Ask the children to line up according to size and record the order. Repeat during the year to see if there is any change in the relationship.
- Throw beanbags or balls into larger and gradually smaller rings drawn on the cement.
- Build a family of snowmen according to size.
- Fill plastic eggs with differing amounts of beans or pebbles. *Seal tightly.* Have children arrange these in an egg carton according to the volume of sound they make when shaken. Have older children do this activity with their eyes shut.

Suggestions for Making the Task More Challenging. The easiest kind of what-comes-next seriation problem is asking youngsters to continue a trend by showing you what comes at the end of an established row or what comes at its beginning. The problem becomes much more difficult for them to solve as the number of choices is increased or if all the items are presented jumbled together. More difficult still is having them fill in the spaces left unfilled in a series.

Temporal Ordering. Temporal ordering is the logical order of events as they occur through time. Sometimes a change in size, as well as an advance in time occur, if it involves the life cycle. For example, as babies mature, they also become larger, as do young plants and animals. When not dealing with the life cycle, temporal ordering is exemplified in such things as following a recipe (the cake cannot go in the oven until the ingredients have been measured, mixed together, and put in a pan), sliding down a slide (you have to climb up before sliding down), or taking a bath (you have to get wet before you get dry). Remember that children should be encouraged to work from left to right when developing these sequences to help them acquire the left-to-right habit necessary in our culture for learning to read.

Temporal Ordering Activities That Children Enjoy

- Take pictures of a field trip the children went on, have each child draw one picture out of a hat, then ask them to arrange themselves with pictures in hand in a line according to what happened when.
- Be on the lookout for comic strip stories that can be mounted and used for temporal ordering sequence practice. ("Peanuts" is a good source for these.)
- Encourage children to tell stories that involve events happening in order—"The Three Little Pigs," for example, or "The Three Bears." (The latter teaches both graduated and temporal ordering.)
- Plan with the children in advance what the steps in a process will be and illustrate it as they tell you what these are—carving a pumpkin is easily drawn on a blackboard, for instance.
- Make a time line, such as showing how the baby rat changes as it grows.
- For church-related schools, advent calendars can be fun. Nonreligious calendars can also be made to help children anticipate how many days are left until some important event takes place (but do not start too soon.)
- Use some of the commercially made sequence puzzles; these are quite good and show such sequences as getting dressed and making a snowman.
- Make illustrated recipe cards so children may prepare a snack by following these in order.

Suggestions for Making the Task More Challenging. Temporal ordering depends partly on a knowledge of circumstances and partly on reasoning and common sense. Difficulty can be increased by adding more stages in the sequence and by asking children to interject events into the middle of the sequence. Older fours particularly enjoy being asked to arrange events backward (and for this reason they relish Ruth Krauss's book *The Backward Day* [1950]). They can also be challenged by out-of-order, "silly" questions, such as "What would happen if we ate the birthday cake and then the children came to the party?" or "What would happen if we frosted the cookies before we put them in the oven?"

It stimulates the use of memory and makes the task harder if the children are asked to recall exactly which step in a process they actually did first. The older children in school also enjoy simple, illustrated sequences that they can "read" by looking at the pictures as they follow a recipe. Such a chart for making soup, for example, might show pictures of meat cut up in pieces, a frying pan, 4 cups of tomato juice, and a number of vegetables and their needed quantities. Experienced older fours love the independence of "reading" such recipes entirely by themselves, assembling the ingredients, and following the illustrated steps with little or no additional guidance from the teacher.

Cause-and-Effect Relationships

Children begin to understand the relationship between cause and effect in infancy when they first determine that shaking their crib makes a little, attached bell jingle, for example. But as

Many principles of construction related to balance and equality provide Carly with experience in cause and effect.

Piaget points out, the distinction of which event is the cause and which is the effect remains confusing for many years. For this reason, when providing cause-and-effect learning experiences for preschoolers, keep them uncomplicated and quite obvious—obvious in the sense that the cause and the results can be readily observed.

Cause-and-effect learning is often thought of as being part of the world of science, and many illustrations of such scientific cause-and-effect relationships are included in the discussion of developing the let's-find-out table in Chapter 16. However, many additional, simple cause-and-effect relationships occur everywhere and should be discussed with children.

Here are some examples of common ones that can be used to help children realize that a particular action brings about a particular result: squeezing whipped soap through a pastry decorator, blowing a whistle, turning on a flashlight, using a garlic press, blowing soap bubbles, squeezing an oil can, using wind-up toys (such as little paddleboat bath toys), grinding nuts in a grinder, shooting a squirt gun, using a flashlight to make shadows come and go, weighing objects on a balancing scale, pushing a swing, turning a kaleidoscope, or blowing on a pinwheel.

Children use such items every day but probably remain unaware of cause-and-effect relationships unless the teacher queries them about the relationships. The questions should be very simple ones, such as, "What makes the picture change in the kaleidoscope?" or "What makes the garlic come out?" The teacher should not expect highly technical explanations about energy and force in reply, nor should she attempt to provide these. However, the children are perfectly capable of answering that the picture changes because they are turning the cylinder or that the garlic is coming out because they are squeezing the handle.

In cause-and-effect learning situations, the basic question to ask the children is "What do you think made it happen?" and the basic question for the teacher to ask herself is "How can I help the children figure out the answer?"

SUMMARY

During the past half century, Jean Piaget has made a tremendous contribution to our understanding of how young children think. He has maintained that children's understanding of the world and the way they think about it varies at different ages, that the development of thought results from dynamic interaction between children and their environments, that play is an important means of learning, and that movement from one state to the next depends on maturation, experience, socialization, and equilibration.

Among the skills identified by Piaget as being significant are those related to classification and seriation, and this chapter emphasizes how to provide cognitive learning opportunities for preschool children that contribute to their later understanding of these more sophisticated concepts, as well as to their success in school.

These learning experiences should include work on the skills of matching, pairing common relations, grouping, graduated and temporal ordering, and understanding simple cause-and-effect relationships. To make such learning a positive experience for teachers and children, it is necessary to formulate a curriculum plan, make certain the activities are fun for the children, provide plentiful opportunities for practice, and offer both simple and more taxing activities to sustain the children's interest and continue their growth. The chapter discusses each skill in detail and also includes many examples and suggestions for activities that meet those criteria.

SELF-CHECK QUESTIONS FOR REVIEW

Content Questions

1. Name two ingredients Piaget feels are vital components in fostering mental development.
2. List each of the basic stages of cognitive development according to Piaget, and give examples of behavior that are commonly associated with each stage.

3. Explain what teachers can do to facilitate the conditions Piaget says are necessary for optimum development to take place. These include physical maturation, experience, interaction with other people, and equilibration.
4. What is the difference between *assimilation* and *accommodation?*
5. The six mental abilities discussed in detail in the chapter include *matching, pairing common relations, grouping, seriated ordering, temporal ordering* and *cause and effect.* Define each of these abilities; explain how each of them is linked to later school-related skills.
6. Describe an activity you could use with the children that would provide practice in each of the six mental abilities discussed in detail in the chapter. Explain how you would make each one very easy for younger children and more challenging for older ones.

Integrative Questions

1. Explain how the experiment described on pages 348–349 supports Piaget's sequential theory of cognitive development.
2. What is the difference between grouping, matching, and paired common relations. How can one tell these particular mental abilities apart from each other?
3. Select an area such as housekeeping or outdoor play and propose activities that could take place there which would provide practice in each of the six mental abilities discussed in detail in Chapter 17.
4. How could you use the material from this chapter to defend your curriculum when worried parents come to you and ask, "Why aren't the children learning the alphabet and how to count so they will be ready for school?"

QUESTIONS AND ACTIVITIES

1. *Problem:* At one of the parent meetings, some of the parents say that they love the school but are worried because they have heard that the kindergarten teacher at their neighborhood school expects every child to be able to count to 20 and read his name and address as he enters kindergarten. How would you reply to this concern?

2. Select a holiday that is coming up and discuss with the class some ways that the mental abilities outlined in this chapter could be practiced using the holiday as the focus of interest.

3. Bring a commercially produced or teacher-made cognitive learning activity to class and explain how you might vary the presentation of the basic materials to make it simple enough for young threes or difficult enough for older fours to enjoy.

4. Appoint a committee to watch *Sesame Street* for two or three programs. Are there opportunities provided to learn thinking skills, as well as the alphabet and rote counting? What do you think of television as a learning medium for such skills?

5. You have just purchased some attractive wrapping papers that have lots of little valentine and birthday pictures. Explain how you might use these papers to construct a matching game and a grouping game. What would be different about the way the two games are designed?

REFERENCES FOR FURTHER READING

Development of the Brain

Brierley, J. (1987). *Give me a child until he is seven.* New York: The Falmer Press. In this very good book, Brierley explains what is known about principles of brain physiology and development. The author includes discussions about the educational implications of this information for teachers of young children. Highly recommended.

Healey, J. M. (1987). *Your child's growing mind. A parent's guide to learning from birth to adolescence.* Garden City, N.Y.: Doubleday & Co. This sensible book discusses everything from how the brain develops to lateralization and learning to read.

Explanations of Piagetian Thought

Bybee, R. W., & Sund, R. B. (1982). *Piaget for educators* (2nd ed.). Columbus, Ohio: Merrill Publishing Co. A detailed explanation of Piaget's theory is offered here. The explanations are clear, and the book includes a brief biography.

Wadsworth, B. J. (1984). *Piaget's theory of cognitive and affective development* (3rd ed.). New York: Longman. Wadsworth presents a straightforward explanation of the high points of Piagetian theory sprinkled liberally with quotations from Piaget's work that help convey the flavor and substance of this thinking.

Activities that Facilitate Use of Specific Mental Abilities

Baratta-Lorton, M. (1972). *Workjobs: Activity-centered learning for early childhood education.* Reading, Mass.: Addison-Wesley Publishing Co. Photographs accompany every suggested activity, showing how a wide variety of cognitive materials can be made and used by the teacher.

Cratty, B. J. (1973). *Intelligence in action: Physical activities for enhancing intellectual abilities.* Englewood Cliffs, N.J.: Prentice-Hall. This book is still worth seeking out because it reminds us that cognitive learning can and should be implemented by the use of large-muscle skills.

Richardson, L. I., Goodman, K. L., Hartman, N. N., & LePique, H. C. (1980). *A mathematics activity curriculum for early childhood and special education.* New York: Macmillan Publishing Co. This book is crammed with ideas for teaching such concepts as grouping and seriation.

Saunders, R., & Bingham-Newman, A. M. (1984). *Piagetian perspectives for preschools: A thinking book for teachers.* Englewood Cliffs, N.J.: Prentice-Hall. This book offers many excellent ways to implement Piagetian principles throughout the classroom. *Highly recommended.*

Sparling, J., & Lewis, I. (1984). *Learning games for threes and fours.* New York: Walker & Company. The authors break learning games into activities appropriate for four stages of development. These cover many mental abilities and sound like genuine fun. Developmental checklists are also included. Highly recommended.

For the Advanced Student

DeVries, R., & Kohlberg, L. (1987). *Programs of early education: The constructivist view.* New York: Longman. The authors discuss Piagetian theory and present three programs that implement it in somewhat differing ways. Also includes a comparison of Piagetian and Montessorian education.

Gardner, H. (1986). Notes on cognitive development: Recent trends, new directions. In S. L. Friedman, K. A. Livingston, & R. W. Peterson (Eds.). *The brain, cognition, and education.* New York: Academic Press. Gardner presents an interesting, readable review of past, present, and future trends in the study of cognitive development.

Gregory, R. L. (Ed.). (1987). *The Oxford companion to the mind.* Oxford, England: Oxford University Press. This book is an encyclopedia offering concise discussions of everything ranging from invertebrate learning to memory skills.

Gruber, H. E., & Vonêche, J. J. (Eds.). (1977). *The essential Piaget.* London, England: Routledge & Kegan Paul. This is an anthology of the more important contributions of Piaget. It is convenient to have these all in one place;

selections are preceded by brief introductory explanations.

Kamii, C. (1985). *Young children reinvent arithmetic: Implications of Piaget's theory*. New York: Teachers College Press. Although most of this book is devoted to first grade and beyond, Kamii also includes a clear discussion of general Piagetian principles as they apply to the development of mathematical concepts.

Piaget, J. (1983). Piaget's theory. In P. H. Mussen (Ed.), *Handbook of child psychology* (4th ed.). W. Kessen (Ed.), Vol. I: *History, theory, and methods*. New York: John Wiley & Sons. This is, of course, a classic explanation by the master himself.

Shulman, V. L., Restaino-Baumann, L. C. R., & Butler, L. (Eds.). (1985). *The future of Piagetian theory: The neo-Piagetians*. New York: Plenum Press. Title is self-explanatory.

Thomas, R. M. (1985). *Comparing theories of child development*. (2nd ed.). Belmont, Calif.: Wadsworth Publishing Co. This invaluable book discusses a range of theories, including that of Piaget. Highly recommended for its clarity and comprehensiveness.

18 Making Special Celebrations Part of the Life of the School

Have you ever

- Wondered how to help children enjoy holidays without having them become overtired and cranky?
- Needed ideas for holiday activities that enhance the children's creative selves?
- Wanted to know how to run a trouble-free potluck dinner for the families in your school?

If you have, the material in this chapter will help you.

Children and parents like "art" to hang up for the holidays. Holidays are important in our culture; we make a production of Halloween, Thanksgiving, Mother's Day, Father's Day. Holiday art can be a trap for both children and teachers. The trap, as I see it, is that teachers, in wanting to send home holiday art, get "craft" ideas, which are usually much too difficult for the young children to execute successfully. To solve the problem of difficulty, the teacher then makes a model for the child to look at—the ditto of a turkey, for example, that children must cut and color and paste exactly like the model the teacher has presented.

BEV BOS (1982)

The celebration of days having special significance for children offers great opportunities to enrich the social, emotional, and creative aspects of the early childhood curriculum, and the end result of such celebrations can be wonderful—or absolutely terrible—depending on how much foresight and common sense the staff brings to these celebrations.

The holidays most widely observed in the United States have been singled out for discussion here, but I hope that staff will add other celebrations as well that are appropriate to the ethnic and cultural backgrounds of the children in their particular schools. The following suggestions are offered in the interest of keeping these occasions the cheerful, caring experiences teachers and families prefer.

KEEP HOLIDAYS SATISFYING AND MEANINGFUL FOR CHILDREN AND FAMILIES

Decide Which Values You Want Children to Learn from the Holiday, Then Plan Curriculum Accordingly

Unfortunately, just about all major holidays in the United States have developed an aura of commercialism that can pervert their true value and purpose if we do not resist this influence.[1] Think, for example, of the stress on candy that is associated with everything from Halloween to Mother's Day, Easter, and even chocolate cherries for Washington's Birthday. Or consider the emphasis on gluttony at Thanksgiving or the deluge of toy advertisements before Christmas.

Surely these are not aspects of holidays we want to emphasize with children, when so many other more wholesome values abound. At Thanksgiving it is just as easy to dwell on the plenitude of the earth and our gratitude for its bounty by sharing a snack of fruits and vegetables from each family as it is to lead discussions about how much you plan to eat on "Turkey Day." Or the school may share by sending each family a little pot of cranberry-orange relish for the Thanksgiving table. Either of these experiences

---

[1]To provide the widest possible application for this chapter, I have deliberately avoided discussion of religious teachings associated with church and temple holidays. In my opinion, religiously oriented schools are indeed fortunate that they can include such aspects of holidays in their curriculum, because such inclusions do much to retain the basic meaning in holidays so often neglected in secular schools.

is more genuine and meaningful for 3- and 4-year-olds than discussing the Pilgrims, and both reach the heart of the Thanksgiving experience.

While speaking of the values we want children to learn, we should also ask ourselves if we really want children to conclude that holidays are times when adults become irritable and there is increased stress between people. All too often poor planning and too much stimulation produce this result. *It is important to understand that excitement is not the same thing as enjoyment* (Katz, 1975). Allowing plenty of time for unhurried, simple holiday pleasures and at the same time not beginning so early that the children are kept in a dither of anticipation are important keys to keeping all these occasions pleasureful. A week of preparation is about the longest period of time that children can endure without going to pieces.

Stress during that week can be held to a minimum by reasonably observing routines, by deliberately including tension-reducing activities such as water play and vigorous outdoor exercise, and by not stuffing the day full of too many unusual activities.

How to Teach These Values

Once again, I want to emphasize the truth that children learn best through participation and firsthand experience. We all know this, yet holidays can lead us into thinking we have done a good job of teaching when actually we are depending on words and concepts that may have little or no real meaning for the youngsters. For this reason, preschool teachers must make special efforts not only to consciously choose the values they wish to teach but also to ask themselves how they can turn these experiences into more than words. Certainly they can tell simple stories to children about Martin Luther King, Jr., and what a great man he was, but real valuing of Black people is more likely to result from the children's daily encounter with their own firm but kind Black teachers.

Help Parents Think Their Values Through

During the early years, parents of young children are often in the process of establishing family philosophies and traditions that they will follow all their lives. Teachers can contribute to this process by helping families think their values all the way through. For example, it could be worthwhile to plan a parent meeting before Christmas to discuss various ways to make the holiday truly meaningful and satisfying for everyone. Perhaps the group would want to spend an evening discussing ways little children can do something positive to help the family enjoy the holiday season. Ideas could be shared about simple gifts young children can make, ways they can participate successfully in trimming the tree with homemade decorations, or simple, thoughtful things they could do for someone they care about.

Families may also want to talk over their expectations of their children's behavior at that time. Perhaps they are unintentionally burdening the children with the expectation of overresponse; the expression "being overjoyed" has real meaning in this context. Perhaps they want to learn how to deal with their children's unrealistic expectations of being given everything in the world. Then, too, the matter of what are safe and appropriate toys can be touched on, or suggestions for holding fatigue to a minimum can be presented.

Sharing family traditions is still another way everyone's lives can be enriched, as these shared bits of fun spark ideas for possibilities in young families who may be just beginning to build traditions into their family lives. And, of course, there is no better way to widen people's cross-cultural horizons than to exchange descriptions of family customs for the holidays.

Another valuable discussion topic could be the problem of depression during the holidays. Single parents appear to be particularly prone to this condition, but depression seems to strike almost everyone sometime, and many adults confess to feelings of hollowness or sadness from time to time during this season. Since everyone else may appear to them to be joyful, a real sense of hurt and isolation can accompany this feeling. One parent expressed this feeling to me this way: "There must be something wrong with me to feel this way. I feel like all I'm doing, doing, doing, is for others, and nobody really cares about doing anything for me!" A tactfully led discussion with a group of sympathetic people can offer the comfort of sharing these feelings. It could also encourage people to take an active part in planning for their own happiness by getting out and doing something they really want to do, rather than just feeling low. This sort of response ultimately increases the pleasure of both children and adults as holidays approach (Dyer, 1986).

PLAN HOLIDAY CURRICULUM WITH VARIOUS SELVES IN MIND

The Social and Emotional Selves

The opportunity for sharing joyful experiences together that holidays provide makes them particularly promising subjects for the development of the social and emotional selves. Because such events inevitably include the receiving of gifts, attention, and care, they can enhance the children's feelings of being wanted and recognized. Less obvious but of equal importance is the opportunity these occasions provide for children to do satisfying things for others, whether making valentines or helping arrange the room for a pot-luck dinner. Older fours also derive benefit from planning together for such events. ("How can we fix it so that the younger children can find eggs, too?" or "What could we do to celebrate our director's birthday?") Such experiences provide simple but valuable opportunities for children to be generous, helpful, and kind. These opportunities are sometimes overlooked by teachers who assume that preschool children are too little or not skillful enough to do something for someone else. The research study included in this chapter provides interesting evidence that children as young as 3½ can learn to be helpful and kind if the proper atmosphere and teaching methods are employed.

Then, too, the celebration of holidays from various cultures is one of the traditional social activities advocated in multicultural education as a means of teaching cross-cultural values (Goodwin & Pollen, 1980; McNeill, Schmidt, & Allen, 1981; Warren & McKinnon, 1988). However, just as teaching about famous people is difficult to make truly meaningful to preschool children, so can be the celebration of Chinese New Year or Cinco de Mayo. The most effective way to go about observing such holidays is to concentrate on the ones that are relevant to the families in your particular group. For example, because our center is blessed with several Mexican-American children and many Mexican-American student teachers, we are able to celebrate Cinco de Mayo with authentic verve.

Parents of various cultural backgrounds are often gracious about suggesting traditional ways for children to participate; some are willing to come to school and help with a special dish or tell stories of how they celebrated a particular holiday when they were little; they may even invite a group of children to visit their home. However, a thoughtful teacher should also bear in mind that holiday time means that the families observing them are already especially busy, so adjusting the date of the school celebration may make it easier for the family to participate.

In the emotional realm, holidays not only furnish special opportunities to experience love and caring but can also help children learn to deal with fear. Many children are afraid of Santa Claus or the Easter Rabbit; and Halloween, in particular, has its component of scariness, as well as pleasure, for young children. Advance preparation at group time, such as passing some of the more bizarre rubber masks around for inspection, may prevent a crisis of terror for an unprepared 3-year-old.

RESEARCH STUDY
Do Children Do as We Say or Do as We Do?

Research Question "What are the most effective ways to teach kindness and altruism to young children?"

Research Method The sample consisted of 104 children aged 3½ to 5 who came from White, middle-class backgrounds. They were divided into two groups. During the hours of the experiment one group was taught by a nurturant teacher. (The nurturant teacher offered help, was sympathetic and protective, praised frequently, and paid attention to the children.) The other group was taught by a non-nurturant teacher. (The non-nurturant teacher acted reserved, responded matter-of-factly to children's approaches, tended to ignore requests for attention, and disregarded or critically evaluated the children's achievements. She acted aloof and did not involve herself in the children's play. The investigators state that "precautions were taken so that children would not experience undue anxiety.")

The nurturant and non-nurturant groups were then subdivided into four groups. Group A1 had a nurturant teacher; Group A2 had a non-nurturant teacher; Group B1 had a nurturant teacher; Group B2 had a non-nurturant teacher.

Groups A1 (nurturant) and A2 (non-nurturant) were taught about being kind and helpful, using little models of animals and people. For example, one setup had a monkey who could not reach his banana. Both nurturant and non-nurturant teachers of Groups A1 and A2 modeled helping behavior by giving the monkey his banana and then letting the children repeat that action.

The children in the nurturant Group B1 and non-nurturant Group B2 used the same little models and situations to learn about kindliness, but they also participated in discussions of pictured incidents and witnessed example of real-life situations in which the teachers acted kindly toward someone else. For instance, in one of the real-life situations, their teachers comforted another adult who bumped her head.

Following conclusion of the lessons, the children were tested for their ability to demonstrate kindly, helping behavior using models, pictures, and real-life situations. Groups B1 and B2 were retested in real-life situations 2 weeks later.

Results Analysis of the first set of posttest results revealed no difference between the behavior of the children who had been in the nurturant environments and those in non-nurturant environments. Apparently, the way the teachers acted toward the children did not affect the way the children behaved.

What *was* different about the groups was that the A1 and A2 children who had only worked with the little models did not transfer their learning about kindliness to either pictures or real-life situations.

On the other hand, the children in Groups B1 and B2 who had been taught with the little models, pictures, and real-life examples *did* show positive changes in their responses to both model situations and pictures, but not to real-life situations.

But the investigators did not stop at that point. They conducted a retest of Group B1 and Group B2 children 2 weeks later. That retest produced quite different and interesting results. At this time the children were presented with real-life situations that were conducted in a more natural, homelike setting. For example, they were provided with what appeared to be spontaneous opportunities to retrieve a baby's toys for him without being asked to, or to pick up spools from a spilled workbasket.

That retest revealed significantly different results between the behavior of the children in Group B1 who had been with a nurturant teacher, and the behavior of the children in Group B2 who had been with the non-nurturant teacher.

When presented with the opportunity to be kind and helpful, 84% of the children who had worked with the nurturant teacher responded by retrieving the baby's toys or the spools without being asked, whereas only 43% of the children who had worked with the non-nurturant teacher did so.*

The investigators concluded that, when tested under more natural circumstances, it was evident that the modeling of helpfulness by the nurturant teacher had taken root and produced a behavioral as well as a symbolic change in the children's responses.

Implications for Teaching   This research provides evidence that it is possible to teach children even as young as 3½ to 5 years of age to reach out and do something kind and helpful for someone else if the correct methods of instruction are employed.

It also supports the idea that teaching the concept of kindliness on only a symbolic level by using models, pictures, and discussion is not sufficient if we want children to go beyond paying lip service to that ideal.

If we want young children to translate what they are told into action and become kind and helpful, we must provide them with real-life examples of that behavior. Moreover, if we want them to act spontaneously in a helpful and kindly way, then we need to combine that instruction with behaving in a kindly, nurturant way toward them ourselves. It is this nurturant approach that encourages them most effectively to do as we do, rather than merely doing as we say.

Note. From Learning Concern for Others by M. R. Yarrow, P. N. Scott, and C. Z. Waxler, *Developmental Psychology, 8* (2), pp. 240–260.

*Responses were significant at the .001 level.

In addition, children need the opportunity to talk over important occasions afterward or play them through to clarify how they really felt about it. Once again, Halloween offers a particularly good example because of the thrill of going out in the dark to strange houses, the presence of mysterious visitors, and so forth.

The Creative Self

Frequently the social-emotional satisfaction of doing things for other people can be combined with doing something that satisfies the creative aspect of the child's self, too. Usually this involves making something for someone she cares about. The pitfall here is that sometimes such gifts violate another principle to which early childhood teachers are usually devoted. This is the principle that children should be encouraged to be creative and self-expressive. Unfortunately, all too often as Mother's and Father's Day or Valentine's Day approaches, mass production of identical gifts becomes the case. Most teachers are bothered by this contradiction of values and yet allow themselves to be trapped into such sweatshop activities time after time in the name of pleasing parents and including all the children.

One way to avoid this situation is to offer two or three different items for children to make and allow them to choose not only what appeals to them the most but also whatever they think the recipient may like the best. Uniquely self-expressive items such as fingerpainting can be given a holiday flavor if traditional color schemes are used. For example, red fingerpainting on white paper framed by green construction paper is very Christmasy. Or shaking gold or silver glitter on anything it will stick to can turn almost any object into a festive yuletide gift.

Anything the children can decorate themselves in their own way leaves at least some room for creativity. Iron-on crayons are a god-send for dishtowels or pot holders, although these objects do have the drawback of requiring the teacher to hem the edges. Permanent felt tip markers are excellent to use for this purpose, too, and their colors are particularly bright and clear. The use of collage for Valentine's Day is well known, and this technique can also be used to decorate simple frames for snapshots of each child for Mother's and Father's Day.

A good test of just how creative and child oriented the project is is how much the teacher has to do to complete it herself or how much teacher supervision and direction it requires. The more teacher participation, the less creative it is likely to be for the children. Remember that children also enjoy wrapping such gifts, and there are many ways to create attractive wrapping papers that allow individuality of expression.

The Cognitive Self

Although holiday curriculum's major strength lies in the areas of the social, emotional, and creative selves, as with any focus of interest, holidays can and should be enriched with appropriate books, music, poetry, and flannel board stories. These contribute to language development, aesthetic appreciation, and the acquisition of factual knowledge.

Particular mental ability activities with a holiday flavor can easily be developed by using holiday stickers or pictures cut from wrapping paper. These lend themselves very well to the construction of matching and grouping games, and children love them. Since the events of many celebrations occur in a prescribed order, they are also excellent resources for practice in sequential reasoning: birthday parties, for example, often begin when the birthday child opens his presents, then games are played, and finally refreshments are served, with the party culminating in the arrival of the birthday cake.

The ability to recall the past can be stimulated by asking children to dictate stories such as "What I did on my birthday" or "What happened at the potluck dinner." Waiting a week or two and then reminiscing also helps children begin to develop a sense of time passing and exercise their capacity to remember. And, of course, holidays can be used as stepping-stones to new interests for the children—the living Christmas tree can be planted outside, the Easter animals raised to maturity, and (my favorite!) the Halloween pumpkin allowed to rot and dug back into the garden.

SUREFIRE HINTS FOR OBSERVING SPECIAL DAYS[2]

Birthdays

Primary Values. Honor the birthday child and mark her progress toward maturity (growing up is an idea dear to the hearts of most children).

Things to Avoid. Undue emphasis on the number of presents expected and received, and who is and is not going to be invited to the birthday party; overlooking a child's birthday at school (this can really hurt feelings, so it is wise to keep a calendar of these events); neglecting to celebrate the birthdays of children whose birthdays fall in the summer.

Activities. An activity that allows the child to assess her personal growth, such as measuring her or making a book about what she did when she was younger, is satisfying.

It helps to keep a special box that has a variety of birthday things all assembled, such as a birthday puzzle, some stories and poems about birthdays, and cognitive games using that theme. If these are kept all in one place, it makes life much easier for the teacher, and the children look forward to getting down the "birthday box" with great pleasure.

Singling the child out by making her a special crown to wear is usually much enjoyed; parents can be encouraged to provide a special snack—ideally one with good nutritional value that is not as costly as an elaborately decorated birthday cake, which the child is likely to have at home, anyway.

Our staff also have a special tradition of celebrating their own birthdays with the children by bringing a special snack to share with everyone. The children are often surprised to discover that everyone gets older—even teachers!

Appropriate Books

Bond, F. (1983). *Mary Betty Lizzie McNutt's Birthday*. New York: Thomas Y. Crowell. This is a little bitty book about a little bitty pig's birthday—delightful. (2 years and older)

Hertz, O. (1981). *Tobias has a birthday*. Minneapolis: Carolrhoda Books. One of a series, this is a simple story of how a child in Greenland celebrates his birthday.

Keats, E.J. (1968). *A letter to Amy*. New York: Harper & Row, Publishers. This is a story about a young boy who invites a little girl to his birthday party—a multiethnic book with a universal theme. (3 to 5 years)

Shiman, S. (1976). *A special birthday*. New York: McGraw-Hill Book Co. Here is a beautifully illustrated book without words. Children will enjoy following the ribbon to various gifts. (2½ to 5 years)

Uchida, Y. (1975). *The birthday visitor*. New York: Charles Scribner's Sons. This story focuses on a Japanese-American family; in an unusual approach, it deals with both death and life. (4 to 6 years)

Halloween

Primary Values. More than any other holiday except birthdays, Halloween remains a children's day with all the fun of dressing up and carving pumpkins. If well handled, it can also help children learn to cope with half-way delicious fears.

---

[2]The following material is included to illustrate how the suggestions in the previous discussion might be implemented in a children's center. Note that the emphasis here is on social, emotional, and creative growth; general methods of developing appropriate cognitive material are described in Chapter 17. These suggestions should not be taken as gospel but only as possibilities that will stimulate teachers to develop similar experiences particularly suited to the children in their groups.

Things to Avoid. Prolonged glutting on candy and overstimulation; wearing costumes to school.

Activities. Allow the children to draw the features on the jack-o'-lantern, but an adult should do the cutting. (Knives coated with pumpkin pulp are dangerously slippery.) The children can scrape out all the seeds, though. (One of our children commented, "Gee, teacher, it feels just like wet cobwebs inside!") They can also light the candle if long, hearth-type matches are provided.

Eat snack by pumpkin light; serve an orange and black snack (perhaps oranges and raisins and toasted pumpkin seeds, or orange-colored pancakes with raisin faces). Use an additional pumpkin to make cookies or pumpkin cake.

If the center is fortunate enough to have access to a pumpkin field, as is often true in warm climates, be sure to bring back a vine with flowers and green fruit still attached, or grow and harvest your own (this can be difficult to do if older children intrude on the playground from time to time). Keep one jack-o'-lantern and

Simple games based on holiday themes add to the fun.

place it in a shallow pan and allow it to deteriorate. The mold is beautiful if examined with a magnifying glass, and digging the remains back into the soil helps children understand how the life cycle produces more life.

Some schools have a tradition of a Halloween parade. I prefer to leave this to the grammar school crowd; however, if the staff wants to do this, remember to keep the parade short, do not make the children wait too long to participate in it, make certain every child has a costume (this usually requires extra adults around to help dress the children), and do not rely on paper costumes, which are too delicate for little children to wear successfully.

It is also a good idea to send a safety reminder home to parents about Halloween precautions. Parents should be encouraged to go with children for tricks or treats, rather than sending them along with an older child. Remind them, too, about the dangers of candles combined with flimsy costumes and the unfortunate possibility that candy may be contaminated with pins, razor blades, or poison. Light reflecting tape stuck on costumes will increase the children's visibility and safety.

After Halloween Is Over. Provide Halloween paraphernalia for imaginative play so that children can play through their feelings about this event. Plan a very easygoing day afterward if Halloween comes on a school evening.

Appropriate Books

Kroll, S. (1984). *The biggest pumpkin ever.* New York: Scholastic. There is a wholesome moral included here about the joys of working cooperatively together.

Lystad, M. (1973). *Halloween parade.* New York: G. P. Putnam's Sons. This book is nice to use because the story centers around being creative in making homemade costumes. (4 to 6 years)

Miller, E. (1972). *Mousekin's golden house.* Englewood Cliffs, N.J.: Prentice-Hall. The first, and in my opinion, the best of the Mousekin books focuses on what happens to a little mouse and the jack-o'-lantern in which he makes his home during the winter. (3 to 5 years)

Schweninger, A. (1984). *Halloween surprises.* New York: Viking Kestrel Books. The charming illustrations depict the joys of Halloween with almost no language.

Sendak, M. (1963). *Where the wild things are.* New York: Harper & Row, Publishers. A 4-year-old triumphs over a variety of horrifying monsters. (4 to 6 years)

Thanksgiving

Primary Values. The pleasure of families gathering together and sharing food together as a social experience; appreciating and being grateful for the earth's plenty.

Things to Avoid. Overemphasis on how much everyone expects to eat—an obsession only with turkeys (there are other valuable things to talk about besides these ungainly birds); reliance mainly on the discussion of Pilgrims and Indians to make the day meaningful; encouraging racial stereotypes of all Indians wearing paint on their faces and feathers in their hair.

Activities. Make something at school to send home with the youngster to share on Thanksgiving Day, such as cranberry-orange relish, pumpkin bread, or a holiday decoration.

Children can be encouraged to bring an assortment of fruits and vegetables from home, which they can handle and talk about and then prepare together to share as a wonderfully varied Thanksgiving snack, or they can be taken to a large market to buy one of every kind of fruit and vegetable they find there for the same purpose.

Afterward. Ask the children to talk about the family and guests who came to share the holiday or tell where their family went to be with others. Children also enjoy picking out a variety of flannel board family members (including pets of course) who attended; a few older children may wish to attempt to describe how these people are related to each other ("She's my Mother and she's my Grandmother's daughter"), but this is usually too difficult for preschoolers.

Appropriate Books

Child, L. M. (1974). *Over the river and through the woods.* New York: Coward, McCann & Geoghegan. Beautiful illustrations of an idealized 1890 family's trip to Grandmother's house accompany the familiar words of this poem-song. (4 years and older)

Gibbons, G. (1983). *Thanksgiving Day.* New York: Holiday House. Gibbons tells the Pilgrim story in simple language and ties it to current traditions.

Janice. (1967). *Little Bear's Thanksgiving.* New York: Lathrop, Lee & Shepard Co. This simple tale tells how Little Bear struggles to stay awake until Thanksgiving arrives.

Spinelli, E. (1982). *Thanksgiving at the Tappleton's.* Reading, Mass. Addison-Wesley Publishing Co. The plot focuses on how a family comes to realize that it is being together, not eating special things, that makes Thanksgiving a special time.

Christmas

Primary Values. Doing thoughtful and loving things for others; participating in various craft activities[3]; sharing in family customs and festivities; this is a particularly good time to share customs of other families, also. Remember that not everyone celebrates Christmas; be sensitive to the needs of children who do not and discuss this with their parents, asking for their suggestions and point of view (Gelb, 1987). For example, many Jewish families will graciously contribute to the richness of the holiday season by sharing their Hanukkah traditions with the children if they are invited to do this. This will help everyone understand that Hanukkah is not the Jewish equivalent to Christmas.

Afterward. Reminisce about the joys of this holiday, encouraging children to discuss a variety of satisfactions rather than just enumerating everything they received as gifts. If weather permits, plant a living Christmas tree outdoors.

---

[3]See, particularly, the recipes for the basic dough and ornamental clay on pp. 266–267.

Appropriate Books

Briggs, R. (1973). *Father Christmas*. New York: Coward, McCann & Geoghegan. Children will pore for hours over the odd little illustrations in *Father Christmas*; a truly one-of-a-kind book that should not be missed. (3 to 6 years)

Budbill, D. (1974). *Christmas tree farm*. New York: Macmillan Publishing Co. Nicely illustrated, *Christmas Tree Farm* is particularly enjoyed by fours, whose interest in facts is satisfied by this description of where Christmas trees come from.

Ets, M. H., & Labastida, A. (1959). *Nine days to Christmas*. New York: Viking Press. Beautifully illustrated, this book deals with Christmas in Mexico. The text is somewhat lengthy. (4 to 6 years)

Kent, J. (1969). *The Christmas piñata*. New York: Parents Magazine Press. Here is a delightful little book that describes a Christmas celebration in Mexico. (3 to 5 years)

Moore, C. C. (1961). *The night before Christmas*. New York: Grosset & Dunlap. The exquisite illustrations by Gyo Fujikawa make this a particularly attractive presentation of this old classic. (2 years and older)

Spier, P. (1983). *Christmas!* New York: Doubleday & Co. In a wordless, attractively illustrated book Spier includes pictures having to do with preparations for, celebrations of, and the day after Christmas. Could be used with any age, with some judicious shortening for younger children.

Stock, C. (1984). *Sampson, the Christmas cat*. New York: G. P. Putnam's Sons. Sampson is a cat who has some funny adventures on Christmas day as he adopts a family.

Willson, R. B. (1983). *Merry Christmas: Children at Christmastime around the world*. New York: Philomel Books. The text is way too grown up for preschoolers, but information could be paraphrased. The book has exquisite illustrations of Christmas celebrations in many cultures.

Valentine's Day

Primary Values. The pleasure of telling someone else you like them and the pleasure of being liked; receiving letters (a rare, intense pleasure for many little children).

Things to Avoid. The popularity contest often inherent in having a Valentine's box at school—many early childhood teachers put up a tactful notice ahead of time explaining why this is not done at their school and how the holiday will be celebrated instead; precocious comments on "boyfriends" and "girlfriends" are also inappropriate.

Activities. Valentine's Day calls out for pretty collage materials—white lace, red hearts, and so forth. Although costs of mailing can be prohibitive if the school must bear it alone, it *is* possible to ask each family to provide a stamp and then encourage the children to make a valentine that they can mail at the post office to their families.

It can be fun to carry out the holiday theme by having an all red and pink day, including easel paints, play dough, snack, and even lunch.

Children do love dramatic play involving sending and receiving mail. It can be worth the investment to have lots of cheap or recycled envelopes in the housekeeping corner that they can use for making and mailing valentines.

Appropriate Books

Schweninger, A. (1976). *The hunt for Rabbit's galosh*. New York: Doubleday & Co. Various animals help Rabbit hunt for his galosh so he can mail a valentine to his mother. (3 to 5 years)

Easter

Primary Values. This is an excellent time to teach about the beauty of the renewal of life by celebrating such springtime rites as planting seeds and enjoying baby animals.

Things to Avoid. Stressing the omnipresent candy; letting children mix all the egg dye into one bowl of dull gray; labeling each egg and trying to make sure each child gets that particular egg to take home!

Activities. It can be difficult to control the experience if everyone is allowed to crowd around and slosh eggs in the dye at the same time. The best way I have seen this presented was by a teacher at the Oaks Parent/Child Workshop who brought a tray to each snack table with enough eggs for two apiece and cups of various colored dyes from which the children could choose. When the eggs were bright enough, they were spooned out and put in cartons to dry.

If an egg hunt is planned, it is necessary to hide eggs in different areas for different age children. Otherwise the fours find all the "easy" ones immediately and the threes have an unsatisfying time of it. At our center, we separate age groups and also explain in advance that each child may find two dyed eggs to keep and as many foil wrapped jelly beans (yes, I know they are made of sugar!) as they can locate. This works out all right for everyone but the 2-year-olds, who seem to think that anything wrapped in foil must be litter.

Wheat or corn may be planted in eggshell halves and sent home when sprouted; the shells are biodegradable and only need to be crushed a little when the plants are set out in the garden.

If planned in advance, the school rabbit will produce babies at this time, which has the added advantage of increasing the likelihood of their later adoption.

Appropriate Books

See also group time recommendations about bunny rabbit materials in Chapter 15.

Balian, L. (1974). *Humbug rabbit.* Nashville: Abingdon. (Still in print). This is an amusing story about baby rabbits and Easter eggs.

Milhous, K. (1950). *The egg tree.* New York: John Scribner's Sons. This story describes an Easter egg hunt and the old custom of using the eggs to decorate a tree. (4 to 6 years)

Tresselt, A. (1967). *The world in the candy egg.* New York: Lothrop, Lee & Shepard Co. Many animals look into this old-fashioned candy egg and see what they love best. (4 to 5 years)

Mother's and Father's Days

Primary Values. Can contribute to an understanding and valuing of family relationships— and an opportunity to reciprocate parental affection by doing something for that parent. In our center, where so many of the parents are single, we have found that such days take on a very special meaning to parents, as well as to chil-dren, and a special sensitivity is required because of this.

Things to Avoid. Insensitively assuming that all the children have both parents readily available. By that time of the year, teachers usually know who in the child's life might serve as a surrogate parent if the natural parent is not in evidence. They can then propose that the youngster make a present for that person instead. Also to be avoided are presents that are more teacher than child made.

Activities. There are a variety of small gifts that can be simply made by a child for the parent. Among these are cards made from paintings the youngster has done with a dictated message inside about "What my Mother does . . . " or "I like my Father because . . . . " Or the card may describe in the child's words some special, kindly thing she intends to do for the parent on that special day.

Handprints made in plaster of paris are another longtime favorite. The plaster can be tinted any color the child prefers by adding tempera to the dry plaster, but the whole process has to be done very speedily, and it is wise to realize that some prints will have to be done more than once to obtain a clear one. Children also enjoy potting up small, quick-blooming plants, such as dwarf marigolds, for gifts.

Some of the best presents we ever made for parents of either sex were the soap balls described by Lewis (1975). Mix 2 teaspoons of hot water with liquid food color and scent if desired (such as lemon or clove). Add colored liquid to ½ cup soap flakes and mold and squeeze until it can be rolled into small balls. Or the material can be rolled out thick and cut with cookie cutters, or formed around colored heavy cotton yarn for a bath ball. To go with the soap, we made bath salts composed of baking soda colored with several drops of food coloring and worked together with fingers or a spoon. These salts are nice to put in small baby food jars and give with the soap.

Appropriate Books

Just about any good book on family life will do here, depending on the children's favorites.

Holiday Books

A few additional books about holidays and seasons that may be of interest follow:

Coleridge, S. (1986). *January brings the snow*. New York: Dial Books. This old rhyme is beautifully illustrated by Jenni Oliver. It takes the reader through the year month by month.

Friedrich, P., & Friedrich, O. (1957). *The Easter bunny that overslept*. New York: Lothrop, Lee & Shepard Co. This presents a review of major holidays throughout the year as the bunny attempts unsuccessfully to participate in each one of them with his Easter eggs. (4 to 5 years)

Parsons, V. (1975). *Ring for liberty*. New York: Golden Press. This attractively illustrated book tells the story of the signing of the Declaration of Independence as told through the eyes of a little boy. Although the children's grasp of this subject is necessarily limited, I would attempt to use this book with older fours to help them understand that the Fourth of July is more than just fireworks.

Rockwell, A. (1985). *First comes spring*. New York: Thomas Y. Crowell. Rockwell provides numerous charming pictures of what people do and wear at various seasons of the year.

Zolotow, C. (1957). *Over and over*. New York: Harper & Row, Publishers. Beautifully illustrated, this book also uses a simple story line to trace the progression of holidays throughout the year, including birthdays. (4 to 6 years)

Celebrating Holidays with Families by Having a Children's Program

Some schools like to make an occasion of holidays by having the children present a program for the parents to enjoy. If this can be a very simple occasion that involves a brief period of preparation, it can add to the pleasure of the holiday. However, if the program becomes so elaborate that it requires months of practice, it not only places stress on everyone but may go stale long before the actual presentation takes place.

One approach our staff has found that works well is to teach the children a few songs or finger plays related to the particular holiday. When the adults have assembled, the children sit down together with their families and sing these for the parents. We also include copies of the words for the visitors to use and ask them to join in with us on the second time around. Following this, we provide a simple, festive snack for everyone. Such an event is enough of a "program" and is not too stressful for the young participants to enjoy. If costumes are thought to be necessary, hats are enough for the children to wear. These can be made at school so that parents are spared the problem and expense of producing elaborate costumes.

Suggestions for Managing a Successful Family Picnic or Potluck[4]

Signing Up. To make adequate potluck plans, it is necessary to have an attractive poster available for signing up; otherwise, one can end up with all desserts and no hot dishes. These posters can also mitigate one of the real problems at potlucks: occasionally the food runs out before the people do. This situation can be alleviated by specifying clearly on the sign-up sheet how many people each dish should be expected to serve (for example, "It should be a casserole for 6 or 8" or "Please bring enough for two families"). If there are going to be many children attending, it may be necessary to ask people to sign up for two items so there will be enough to go around. If families in the school are on slim budgets, it is wise to plan such dinners early in the month so that more people will feel able to participate. It is also helpful to be very definite on the sign-up sheet about details, such as "Bring your own

---

[4]Detailed suggestions for potlucks are included here because I have never been able to find such suggestions elsewhere. Yet potluck dinners remain one of the most successful ways to draw families together, and the more planning and care that goes into them, the more delightful the outcome is likely to be for everyone.

table service," and to specify the exact time the meal will be served.

A poster will help catch people's attention, but it may also be necessary for teachers to invite individuals specifically. People are often shyly reluctant to participate in such events—particularly at the beginning of the year when they do not know other families or that the potlucks are fun. Of course, the more responsibility that is spread around, the more likely people are to come. For example, asking families to provide transportation for other families means that both will show up and that they will have become acquainted before arrival. This is especially helpful for single parents, who may otherwise dread being one of a kind. (You might consider asking the single parent to do the picking up to avoid the connotation of being a "charity case.")

Choosing the Place. Some staffs never consider having any gathering away from the school site; however, we have found that there are real advantages to planning a potluck or picnic at a park when weather permits. Quite frankly, this is because there is a subtle difference in the attitude of the families when we move off school premises. When parties are held at the school, parents assume the teachers are in charge of the children and leave this responsibility, as well as more of the setting up and cleaning up, to the staff. As a result, the staff spends most of the next day recovering. When the gathering is "off campus," parents assume more of the responsibility. Besides this, if a park is selected, there is the advantage that some of the play equipment is larger and more appropriate for older children, and for family potlucks this is a real boon. On the other hand, having the event at school does

Family potlucks are a fine way to make celebrations part of the life of the school.

present the different advantage of giving parents and older children an opportunity to see what the school itself is like.

Some Recommendations on Serving Food. There are always a handful of people who forget to bring either dishes, cups, silverware, or serving spoons, so it is a good idea to have some extras on hand to avoid embarrassing them. Serving will go faster if tables are arranged so that people can go down both sides at the same time. We have found it wise to bring out a few hot dishes and salads later so that people at the end of the line have fresh foods from which to choose.

Beverages can be offered most economically if hot water is heated in large coffee urns and instant coffee and tea provided to mix individually as desired. We always serve lemonade for the children (and for anyone else who wishes it), because red colored juices stain if spilled and milk has to be refrigerated. If it has been a hot day, almost everyone will prefer juice, and quantities should be adjusted accordingly.

Plan the Purpose of the Potluck Carefully. There are two kinds of potluck dinners: those with and those without children. The purpose of having such events vary accordingly, although the basic purpose should always be to help people get to know each other and feel comfortable with the staff. Eating together helps people become acquainted. Thoughtful introductions by the staff can provide parents with some common ground for conversation; for example, the teacher may say, "Maggie, I want you and your husband to meet the Smiths. Your Dorothy and their Emily have a mutual interest in our rabbit."

Picnics may not require any special focus other than having some simple equipment such as Frisbees available, but indoor evening potlucks do. If they are dinners with the children attending, it is helpful to have something for the children to do before dinner because this is when the adults are preoccupied with setting things up and the children are likely to be tired and hungry. Our staff has solved this problem by

showing a couple of children's movies or video tapes while the crowd is gathering. There are many Weston Woods films of high caliber that fulfill this need admirably; many public libraries make these available at no cost. After dinner, because the children are so young, activities should be simple, if offered at all. Perhaps the evening can draw to a close with each group singing a few of their best loved songs for the parents.

We have also found that the parents appreciate having an occasional evening potluck when the children are left at home. After a quick cleanup, it is especially easy to move on to an evening program because people are already "warmed up" to participate.

GET INTO THE SPIRIT OF THE HOLIDAY YOURSELF!

Finally, I can do no better when discussing holidays than to close this chapter with the following suggestions that appeared in an advertisement for Bullock's Wilshire, a West Coast department store:

102 Gifts for Any Season,
to Give With All Your Heart

1. Smile. 2. Provide a shoulder to lean on. 3. Pat someone on the back. 4. Say "thank you." 5. Give an unexpected kiss. 6. Or a warm hug. 7. Say "Gosh you look good!" 8. Rub a tired back. 9. Apply a cold compress. 10. Whistle when you're feeling down. 11. Keep the 55 MPH speed limit. 12. Say "good morning" even if it isn't. 13. Mail a letter to an old friend. 14. Place a surprise phone call. 15. Wash the dishes when it's her turn. 16. Empty the trash when it's his turn. 17. Ignore a rude remark. 18. Help a friend move her piano. 19. Or clean his garage. 20. Or paint his house. 21. Make the coffee at the office. 22. Save the want-ads for a job hunter. 23. Write a nice letter to the editor. 24. Take Grandma to lunch. 25. Don't discuss the election with your mother-in-law. 26. Don't discuss the Superbowl with your father-in-law. 27. Send a "thinking of you" card. 28. Wave at a meter maid. 29. Just use one parking space. 30. Pay your doctor bill. 31. Give your used clothes to a

needy person. 32. Pass on some good news. 33. Send a complimentary letter about a great product. 34. Buy the wine she likes. 35. Buy the cheese he likes. 36. Say something nice, instead. 37. Consider a different point of view. 38. Loan a favorite book. 39. Return a friend's favorite book. 40. Let him win at golf. 41. Let her win at tennis. 42. Play catch with a little boy. 43. Or a little girl. 44. Take a box of homemade cookies to work. 45. Visit an elderly shut-in. 46. Forgive an old grudge. 47. Talk to a lonely child. 48. Laugh at an old joke. 49. Laugh at a boring joke. 50. Tell him he's wonderful. 51. Tell her she's beautiful. 52. Take the kids to the park. 53. Or the zoo. 54. Or the show. 55. Serve breakfast in bed. 56. Make the music soft and the lights low. 57. Clean the house for Mom. 58. Share a dream. 59. Jog with her. 60. Walk with him. 61. Adopt a stray cat. 62. Or a lost dog. 63. Keep a confidence. 64. Try to understand a teenager. 65. Try to understand an adult. 66. Squeeze the toothpaste tube from the bottom. 67. Relay an overheard compliment. 68. Let someone ahead of you in line. 69. Say "You're doing a good job." 70. Send a friendly note to a computer. 71. Tell your optometrist he has pretty eyes. 72. Laugh when the joke's on you. 73. Say you were wrong. 74. Say someone else was right. 75. Say "please." 76. Say "yes." 77. Help someone change a tire. 78. Be quiet in the library. 79. Type a term paper for a friend. 80. Explain, patiently. 81. Tell the truth. 82. Encourage a sad person. 83. Take a problem upon yourself. 84. Spread a little joy around. 85. Remain calm. 86. Leave your mailman a little gift. 87. And your milkman. 88. Change someone's typewriter ribbon. 89. Cut the grass. 90. Tell a bedtime story to a little one. 91. Do a kind deed, anonymously. 92. Share your umbrella. 93. And your vitamin Cs. 94. Talk to a friend's plant. 95. Mail someone a poem. 96. Leave a funny card under a windshield wiper. 97. Tape a love note to the refrigerator. 98. Be quiet while he watches the game. 99. Be quiet while she watches the movie. 100. Give a flower you picked yourself. 101. Point out a beautiful sunset. 102. Say "I love you," often.

SUMMARY

The celebration of special events at the children's center can make a rich contribution to the developing selves of the child, but such celebra-

tions are of particular value to the social, emotional, and creative selves.

Many holidays present excellent opportunities to do things for other family members that are kind and thoughtful, and such actions should be encouraged. However, the most effective way to instill the impulse to be kind in the hearts of children is for the teacher to set an example of kindly nurturance toward the youngsters in his care.

Successful curricular usage of these festive occasions is ensured if the staff thinks carefully about what they want the children to gain from the experience and how they intend to communicate these values. Many specific examples of how this can be accomplished for a variety of holidays ranging from Halloween to Father's Day are included.

SELF-CHECK QUESTIONS FOR REVIEW

Content-Related Questions

1. List several ways teachers can increase children's pleasure in celebrating holidays without increasing their level of stress to an intolerable degree.
2. Suggest some topics centering on holidays that could provide a focus for a parent meeting. Explain why each topic might be particularly valuable to present.
3. Suggest some holiday activities that would benefit the social and emotional selves of the children. Now suggest some activities that would benefit the creative and cognitive selves.
4. In the research study about learning concern for others, why was it important for Yarrow, Scott, and Waxler to conduct the second retest?
5. Select a holiday and give some examples of social values associated with that holiday that you feel are undesirable. Then identify additional social values you feel should be emphasized.

Integrative Questions

1. Select a holiday and, using it as your focus, outline activities you plan to include. Be sure to include a list of positive values you intend to teach, an analysis of any "creative" activities according to whether they should be classified as Column I, II, or III activities (see Table 13-2), and suggestions

for relieving stress for adults and children as the holiday approaches.

2. Reread the Yarrow, Scott, and Waxler research. *If the investigators had stopped their research at the end of the first posttest, what conclusions might they have drawn from the experiment?*

QUESTIONS AND ACTIVITIES

1. Do you think that Santa Claus and the Easter Rabbit should be included as part of the curriculum for holidays? How about ghosts and witches? How do you plan to handle these subjects in your own school?

2. Are there special traditions observed by your own family for some particular holiday? For the pleasure of it, share these with the class.

3. Describe five Christmas craft projects that would be more *teacher* than child produced.

4. Review Column I, II, and III activities described in Table 13–2, and decide in which column the holiday activities used at your school belong.

5. Take a look at the population of children where you teach. What cultural resources are available among these families on which you might draw to increase multicultural awareness and appreciation by the children as holidays approach?

REFERENCES FOR FURTHER READING

Presentation of Holidays

Bos, B. (1982). *Don't move the muffin tins: A hands-off guide to art for the young child.* Roseville, Calif.: Turn the Page Press. Bos's book has been already recommended in the chapter on self-expressive materials but merits mention here because of a sensible chapter on creative holiday activities.

Dyer, W. W. (1986). *Happy holidays! How to enjoy the Christmas and Hanukkah season to the fullest.* New York: William Morrow and Co. Dyer has filled this brief book with positive, practical suggestions for enjoying the holiday season.

Gelb, S. A. (1987). Christmas programming in schools: Unintended consequences. *Childhood Education, 64* (1), 9–13. The author outlines undesirable aspects of such celebrations and concludes with positive remedies.

Activity Suggestions for Preschool Children

Goodwin, M. T., & Pollen, G. (1980). *Creative food experiences for children* (rev. ed.). (Available from Center for Science in the Public Interest, 1501 16th St., N.W., Washington, D.C. 20036-1499.) Although not restricted to holiday recipes, this book does have a special section on appropriate holiday foods combined with an accent on sound nutrition.

Higgins, S. O. (1984). *The pumpkin book. Full of Halloween history, poems, songs, art projects, games and recipes.* Shasta, Calif.: Pumpkin Press. This is a useful resource—art projects are mostly Column III (see Table 13–2) suggestions.

Warren, J., & McKinnon, E. (1988). *Small world celebrations: Around-the-world holidays to celebrate with young children.* Everett, Wash.: Warren Publishing House. The authors provide a multicultural resource of holidays, ranging from a Vietnamese mid-autumn festival to an American Indian intertribal ceremony. Stories, songs, crafts, and activities are included for each culture.

Wilmes, L., & Wilmes, D. (1982). *The circle time book.* Dundee, Ill.: A Building Blocks Publication. This book covers a wide variety of holidays, including those from many cultures. It provides suggestions for language games, creative activities, poetry, books, and recipes.

19 Including Families in the Life of the School

Have you ever

- Wanted to get to know the parents in your center better but felt uncertain about how to achieve this?
- Fretted over how to produce an interesting parent meeting?
- Gotten angry when a parent asked you a critical question?

If you have, the material in this chapter will help you.

Glooskap and the Baby

Now it came to pass when Glooskap had conquered all his ene-mies, even the Kewahqu', who were giants and sorcerers, and the M'teoulin, who were magicians, and the Pamola, who is the evil spirit of the night air, and all manner of ghosts, witches, devils, cannibals, and goblins, that he thought upon what he had done, and wondered if his work was at an end.

And he said this to a certain woman. But she replied, "Not so fast, Master, for there yet remains one whom no one has ever conquered or got the better of in any way, and who will remain unconquered to the end of time."

"And who is he?" inquired Glooskap.

"It is the mighty Wasis," she replied, "and there he sits; and I warn you that if you meddle with him you will be sorry."

Now Wasis was a baby. And he sat on the floor sucking a piece of maple sugar, greatly contented and troubling no one.

As Glooskap had never married or had a child, he knew little of the way of managing children. But he was quite certain, as such people are, that he knew all about it. So he turned to the baby with a bewitching smile and bade him come to him.

The baby smiled again, but did not budge. And the Master spoke sweetly and made his voice like that of the summer bird, but it was of no avail, for Wasis sat still and sucked his maple-sugar.

Then the Master frowned and spoke terribly, and ordered Wasis to come crawling to him immediately. The baby burst out crying and yelling, but did not move for all that.

Then, since he could do but one thing more, the Master turned to magic. He used his most awful spells, and sang the songs which raise the dead and scare the devils. The Wasis sat and looked on admiringly, and seemed to find it very interesting, but all the same he never moved an inch.

So Glooskap gave up in despair, and Wasis, sitting on the floor in the sunshine, went "Goo! Goo!" and crowed.

And to this day when you see a baby well contented, going "Goo! Goo!" and crowing, and no one can tell why, you will know it is because he remembers the time when he overcame the Master who had conquered all the world. For of all the beings that have ever been since the beginning, the baby is alone the only invincible one. [1]

PENOBSCOTT INDIAN LEGEND
PETER ANASTAS (1973)

---

[1]From Anastas, P., GLOOSKAP'S CHILDREN. Boston: Beacon Press, 1973, pp. 14–15. Copyright © 1973 by Peter Anastas. Reprinted by permission of Beacon Press.

Numerous studies remind us once again of the vital role parents play in the lives of young children (Anthony & Pollock, 1985; Hinde & Stevenson-Hinde, 1988; Maccoby, 1980; Quinton & Rutter, 1988). For this reason, suggestions have been included throughout *Total Learning* about ways to encourage a sense of closeness between families and those of us who care for their children outside the home.

Because the subject is so important, this entire final chapter is also devoted to discussing ways of building bonds between home and school so that children will feel their world is a consistent whole rather than split into the unrelated halves termed *home* and *school*.

There are many ways of enriching this bond, and strategies must necessarily vary to suit individual school situations. But there are three basic home-school strands that all schools should strengthen, whether they are parent-child cooperatives or full-day centers. These are weaving strands of human relationships that let parents know we care about them and their children, strands that offer help to families to strengthen family life, and strands that accept help from families so that the lives of the children at the center are enriched.

LETTING PARENTS KNOW WE CARE ABOUT THEM AND THEIR CHILDREN

Building a Climate of Trust

There is no substitute for the gradual establishment of trust that can be built between teacher and parent when it is based on easygoing, consistent daily contact between them. It takes time and personal contact to make friends. To accomplish this, the teacher should make deliberate plans to be available while children are arriving to personally welcome each youngster and have a friendly word with the parent, too.

Strange as it may seem at first thought, the very beginning of the day is *not* the time for the teacher to be preoccupied with the children. If parents are truly part of the life of the school, this transition should be thought of as being the part of the daily curriculum intentionally devoted to "family time." This is the part of the day when the teacher takes a genuine interest in the small details of each family's life. Needless to say, it takes a good memory to remember to ask about the anticipated kittens or how the grandparent's visit is coming along, but doing this helps build the friendliness that fosters trust. It also makes it more likely that the parent will have opportunities to share helpful information about the child. Maybe Mary Lou has just gotten a new pair of shoes, or Aaron has lost a tooth. Perhaps the parent is worried because a youngster has been having nightmares, or the child is very tired because he stayed up late to meet his father's plane the night before. These tidbits can contribute a lot to the teacher's understanding of the child's behavior, as well as build bridges of deepened understanding between the home and center.

Building trust also means that the teacher refrains from talking about a family's affairs with other people. This requires good judgment, since sometimes families are in a position to help each other if they know that such help is needed. However, it is always wise to check with the family in difficulty first before violating their privacy. Good judgment is particularly necessary when discussing "problem children." Certainly the parent who is concerned because her child has a big bite mark on his shoulder has a right to know the general steps the school is taking to prevent that happening again, but if trust is to be maintained with everyone, privacy must be preserved at the same time. The teacher should particularly avoid "running down" the members of one family to members of another, since they are likely to assume that she will do the same thing about them behind their back. As one of my students put it, "Bad mouthin' makes bad feelin's."

First impressions can have a crucial effect on establishing a climate of trust and caring, also, and this is one of many reasons that the careful preparation for separating parent and child advocated in Chapter 10 is so important. The teacher who takes time to explain the reasons for gradual rather than sudden separation and who helps the parent through this experience with a mixture of assured kindness and sympathetic concern demonstrates to the family right at the start of the relationship that she can be trusted because she has the child's best interests at heart.

Keeping Parents Informed

A somewhat more impersonal but still useful way of emphasizing that the school cares about families, as well as the children, is by providing information to parents about what the children are doing in school. Many schools use a bulletin board by the sign-in sheet for this purpose, but some parents never seem to read this—and they certainly will not continue to check it unless the material is eye catching and frequently changed. When kept current and relevant, bulletin boards have real, practical value. For example, it is constantly necessary to make certain that parents understand that early childhood education is purposeful, and a weekly curriculum chart posted on the bulletin board will emphasize that teachers are not baby-sitters.

Many centers also make use of a monthly newsletter, and these are excellent public relations vehicles. One month a newsletter might concentrate on the cognitive skills the school is developing, and another could focus on ways the school fosters emotional health. In addition, it might include a calendar of events, recipes from the potluck dinner, general news about what the children will be doing during the coming month, or requests for "freebies" for the school. If bilingual families are part of the school, it is important to include material in both languages to make them feel welcome and let them know what is happening. Otherwise the language barrier may persist and perpetuate a feeling of being outside and apart from the school.

OFFERING HELP TO FAMILIES TO STRENGTHEN FAMILY LIFE

Suggestions for Conferences With Parents

Private conferences with families are one of the most satisfactory ways of providing help on a personal basis, but they do have the unfortunate tendency to make both teacher and parents nervous. Realizing that this nervousness is typical and acknowledging this to the parents can help overcome such feelings. The daily informal chats recommended earlier help, too, but it really takes more than one conference to get past this hurdle.

Conferences are primarily useful because they provide private, uninterrupted opportunities for conversation, and there is no chance that the child might overhear himself being discussed. They are appropriate places to review the youngster's progress and to produce the checklists and observations that document that development (Bjorklund & Burger, 1987). If begun early in the year when the teacher is just becoming acquainted with the child, conferences can help establish a condition of mutual respect between teacher and family. This is because the parents can be cast in the role of knowing more about the child than the teacher can possibly know at this point.

Inevitably, conferences are also used to discuss problems, and if that is the case, it is sensible for the teacher to avoid giving the impression that she is taking the parents to task for their child's foibles. Each child has his own temperament from the time of birth, and it is not always within the parents' ability to change some of these characteristics. The child is a powerful agent in creating his own behavior (Maccoby & Martin, 1983). That is why this chapter opens with the Glooskap legend; it is intended to remind adults to retain their sense of proportion and remain aware of that personal, individual power that comes from within each person.

More productive than indulging in the shaming-blaming syndrome (which is likely to elicit a similar retaliatory attack on the teacher

Conference time should be an opportunity for sharing information and discussing alternative solutions.

by the parent) is using conference time for the mutual purpose of sharing information and discussing alternative solutions (Gelfer & Perkins, 1987).

In general, the teacher who has a listening ear and a quiet tongue will find the most positive changes taking place for the children and the families, should these be needed. Parents often know deep inside what would be a good solution; the well-done conference can provide parents with the chance to talk the situation through, weigh alternatives, and decide for themselves what action to take. Only in this way are changes really brought about. Listening more than talking does not mean that the teacher should not contribute suggestions and ideas drawn from professional experience and training—she should. It does mean that the right to make the decisions rests with the parents.

Meetings About Parenting

Many parents also benefit from opportunities to learn more about children in a general way, and, for this reason, parenting meetings are an additional helpful service offered by many preschools. A few cooperative schools meet every week for discussion, thereby providing splendid opportunities to develop an informed population of parents who form close bonds with the other families, as well as with the school. Parents in most schools do not meet that frequently, so special attention must be paid to keeping a thread of relationships and continuity stretching from one meeting to the next (Powell, 1986).

Finding Appropriate Topics. A good opening topic for the year might be a discussion of the curriculum and philosophy of the school, replete with visual aids. It often works well to ask parents at that meeting what they would like to discuss at the next one and to build continuing meetings from their input. Some additional topics that are usually of interest to parents include building inner controls in children, the father's influence in children's development, coping with jealousy in youngsters, nonsexist education, how to teach sharing, helping children through crisis situations, being a single parent, characteristics of good toys, and fostering mental ability in young children.

We have found that using an informative movie or video tape as a basis for discussion is particularly helpful early in the year, because it gives a group who may not be acquainted with each other something in common to talk about. Such media can be rented from various university media centers and are well worth the rental fees. Write to the ones at the universities nearest to your school and request a film catalog.

Presenting the Topic. Many teachers feel very anxious about leading such meetings and so, time after time, fall back on guest speakers. Although such visitors can bring special expertise and information with them, they have no way of knowing the people in the group and the particular significance of questions they may ask. The presence of visitors also reduces the chance for parents and teachers to talk together about a topic of general, mutual interest.

For these reasons, it is more desirable for teachers to pluck up their courage and lead the meetings themselves. They must remember that these do not have to be, and really *should not* be, presented as lectures anyway. People learn much more from a combination of discussion and information giving than they do from just sitting and listening.

The secret of leading successful discussions is identifying the important points for people to learn before beginning, making certain that these points are covered during the discussions, developing a good selection of thinking questions in advance to pose to the group, and having the patience and courage to wait for the

replies—particularly at the beginning of the discussion when people are feeling shy. It is really the same strategy recommended in Chapter 16, in which the generation of creative thinking skills was discussed in relation to young children.

Role playing, breaking into small groups to discuss special points, and participating in panel discussions are additional, effective ways to produce interesting parent nights.

Including Time for Socializing to Take Place. Although education is often the ostensible reason for holding parent meetings, there is another important value that should not be overlooked. Meetings can also provide valuable social opportunities for parents. These are especially nice for young homemakers, who may not get out much and are feeling isolated and lonely. The chance to be with other people who have similar problems and concerns can furnish real emotional support for such people, as well as simply providing fun for them. Therefore, part of every meeting should allow time for human friendliness. Refreshments offered beforehand or at mid-break give people something to do with their hands so they feel less self-conscious and furnish chances for them to become acquainted, too.

Sometimes it can be worthwhile to dispense with the program altogether and have a potluck dinner instead. There is no better way to build a comfortable, relaxed bond between home and school than by eating together. It is easy to run a successful potluck if attention is paid to the kinds of details discussed in Chapter 18.

ACCEPTING HELP FROM FAMILIES THAT WILL ENRICH THE LIVES OF THE CHILDREN AT THE CENTER

Perhaps the words *accepting help* in this heading may seem peculiar at first glance, but they were chosen deliberately because sometimes teachers do not find it comfortable to accept such assistance.

Accepting and Using Criticism

It can be difficult to regard critical comments and questions as a form of help, but it is important to pay attention to parents when they express such concerns and to benefit from what they have to say. Sometimes, if teachers listen instead of rushing in with a lot of defensive remarks, it can lead to changes in procedures or policies that are better for the children, as well as more satisfactory for parents. Teachers should remember that if one parent complains, it possibly means that others are also dissatisfied but are too intimidated to speak up. For example, we recently had a parent complain after her little boy arrived home for the third time in 2 weeks wearing someone else's sneakers. (At least one other family must have been unhappy.) She had a well-taken point, which we ultimately solved by color-coding 11 identical pairs of dark blue sneakers with dabs of tape so that children could match them up themselves.

Sometimes parents criticize policies because they do not understand what is going on. A father may be uneasy when he finds his little boy trucked out in a dainty petticoat. Another parent may wonder (as many do) when the children are "really going to learn something." It is best to view such critical-sounding queries as presenting opportunities for explaining the educational purposes behind what is going on at school. Parents are entitled to such information. *If, by chance, teachers find themselves unable to produce sound reasons for the inclusion of particular activities, it should indicate to them that they should think further about whether something else might be more profitably substituted for them in the future.*

Of course, it is not always possible for family and school values to coincide (Kontos, 1984). The staff of our center believes that parents' wishes should be honored whenever possible,

and so we are willing to cut naps short when a parent tells us her 4-year-old won't go to bed until 10 if we don't, or to help children follow religious dietary rules, or to change an occasional youngster into school clothes before letting him play in the mud.

On the other hand, we would not be willing to allow a child to roam around the room during lunch, eating as he goes, nor would we ever spank a child who has messed her pants, no matter what the parent advised. When this kind of conflict occurs between home and school values and, for one reason or another, neither side feels it can compromise, we just say clearly to the child, "Well, there are home rules, and that's what you do at home, and there are school rules, and this is what the rule says you do here." In other words, when necessary, we are frank about the fact that different places have different rules; this is not too difficult for children to understand. We feel that teaching them this is better than undercutting parents by secretly defying their standards or implying to the children that the school is totally right and their homes are totally wrong.

It is interesting to note there has been some research in the area of teacher/parent values that questions whether teacher disapproval of parenting skills affects the way the teachers act toward the children of those parents. The research study by Kontos and Wells provides reassuring evidence that teachers do not hold grudges against the children because of such differences.

Drawing on Parents as Resources

Examples have been cited throughout this book of ways parents can serve as resources for enriching the children's lives, so I will only briefly recapitulate them here. It is remarkable the kinds of contacts parents have within a community and the amount of help they can offer once they are aware of what is needed. Remember to be precise about the need and to furnish examples if possible, so that people really understand what you are looking for.

RESEARCH STUDY
Can Teachers Separate Their Attitudes Towards Parents and Children?

Research Question The investigators wanted to find out if teachers act differently toward children according to whether the teachers thought the children's parents had good parenting abilities or poor parenting abilities. Does a negative attitude toward parents carry over to the children?

Research Method In an earlier, related study, Kontos and Wells asked directors of several centers to identify parents whose parenting skills they held in low or high esteem. Upon completion of the first investigation, the investigators turned next to observing the behavior of the teachers toward the children of those parents. The sample consisted of 17 children whose parents demonstrated high parenting skills, and 10 children whose parents demonstrated low parenting skills. Their ages ranged from 20 to 73 months, and the average age of both groups of children was not significantly different.

Each child's behavior was observed 3 times for 5 minutes each time. The observer did not know whether the child's family was included in the high or low skills group. The children were observed for task involvement, the way they used materials, cooperation, verbal behavior, and consideration of others.

The teachers' behavior was also observed and recorded. They were checked for such behaviors as being absent or present with the child, participating with the child, and for the quality of their verbal responses to the youngster.

Results When the observations of the children's behavior was analyzed statistically, the behavior of both groups of children was very similar—the children

---

In addition to unearthing sources of free materials, parents often know of special animals, or they are acquainted with people who would be of interest to the children, or they may know of a fascinating place to visit, such as the back room of a bakery or a goat farm, and will help make the arrangements. Then, too, families themselves are so varied and have so many talents, it would be a pity to overlook them. Remember that family members include grandparents and brothers and sisters, as well as parents, and these people often have special talents and free time they enjoy sharing with the children. In the past few weeks our center has had a flute player, the

owner of a large, interesting snake, and members of a Boy Scout troop all spend time with the children, while their young relatives basked in the reflected glory.

Parents as Volunteers

Not all parents like working directly in the preschool (after all, a perfectly valid reason for sending children to school is so mothers can have time to themselves, and many other parents work all day), so it makes sense to emphasize to families that volunteering can take many different forms. Producing the resources we discussed

with the parents in low parenting skills group rated slightly more likely to be considerate in relation to using materials and taking turns and they engaged in somewhat more recitation/task talk than did those children with parents who possessed high parenting skills.

When the behavior of the teachers was analyzed, once again their behavior toward both groups of children was more similar than it was different. In almost all aspects, teachers did not favor one group of children more than they did the other. Where differences *did* show up, they were differences that favored the children who belonged to the low parenting skills group. Teachers were present more of the time where low-group children were and also engaged in more social talk with them.

Implications for Teaching It is good to know that at least the teachers in question did not carry over their disapproval of parental child-rearing skills into dislike or avoidance of the children. If anything, they may have compensated for that dislike by paying extra attention to them. Or perhaps the child rearing judged less appropriate by professional teachers produced behavior in children that required more teacher attention to correct! Whatever the reason for the added attention, it is reassuring to know that teachers, at least in this study, are able to separate their feelings about children from their feelings for the parents and are able to behave in generous and unbiased ways toward the children in their care.

Note. From "Attitudes of Caregivers and the Day Care Experiences of Families" by S. Kontos and W. Wells, 1986, *Early Childhood Research Quarterly, 1,* pp. 47–67.

earlier is an example of such a variation. Serving on a parent advisory board, working on a potluck, or participating in a cleanup and paint-up day are other valuable contributions preferred by some parents.

Participating in the Classroom. When parents *do* want to participate directly with the children, there are several basic things to do to make them feel truly accepted and welcome. Always bear in mind that the primary purpose of having the volunteer at school is to provide a situation that both volunteer and children will enjoy and not just to comply with a mandated parent involvement component. This means that whatever activity is selected, it has to be something that does not entail a lot of potential discipline problems, it should not be demeaning (cleaning the animal cages, for example), and it should not be something that demands an expertise the visitor does not have (such as being in charge of an entire group time). It *should* capitalize on the interests and strengths of the volunteer, and if you make a consistent point of becoming acquainted with the families, you can usually develop a pretty good idea of what these abilities are.

HELPING FAMILIES IN NONTRADITIONAL SETTINGS

The number of families who fit the stereotyped picture of Father going out to work while Mother stays home and bakes cookies for the children as they return from school lies far from present-day reality for many people. (Please refer also to Chapter 10 for a discussion of handling crises and to Chapter 12 for information on families from various cultural and ethnic backgrounds.)

Some information to bear in mind about the real situation of families in the United States at this time includes:

- More than half (50.8%) of mothers with children under age 1 worked outside the home in 1987.[*]
- By 1995, it is estimated that two-thirds of all preschool children will have mothers working outside the home.[†]
- One in every four children is born in and spends some portion of his early years in poverty.[‡]
- The Census Bureau projects that almost half of all children born in 1979 will live, at some point, with only one parent.[‡]
- Between 1981 and 1986 preschool enrollment rose by 25% and the trend upward is expected to continue.[§]
- It is estimated that in the next decade the number of children younger than 6 needing care will rise by 50%.[§]

If we really pay attention to these facts, it means we must also rethink the kinds of services we offer to parents, because their needs are changing and will continue to change in the coming decade. For this reason, some specific suggestions are offered below about ways to assist these families while their children are at the center or preschool.

Some Suggestions for Helping Families in Which Both Parents Work Outside the Home

- Adapt center hours as much as possible to meet parents' needs in a realistic way.
- Plan events so that working parents can attend. Perhaps a Saturday visiting day could be included; night meetings are also helpful.
- Set aside an evening or early morning for parent conferences. If conference times are planned for late afternoon, be sure to provide a bite to eat also to reduce fatigue.
- Develop a list of people who are willing to care for children who are ill, and make this available to parents. (A handful of schools make provision for sick child care on their own premises. Some hospitals also provide daily sick child care opportunities at reasonable cost.
- Be careful to keep the emergency call list for each child up to date so that permission is on file when parents have someone else pick up the child from school.
- Reassure parents that good parenting is a matter of spending "quality time" with their children and does not depend on the total amount of time—and help them define what "quality time" means.
- Keep informed on tax information so that you can furnish correct information on child-care deductions to parents who ask about it.
- Make it clear that you respect whatever kind of work the parents do. If possible, arrange for a group of children to visit the work places. Encourage parents to come and explain their jobs to children at the school.

Evening programs of special interest might include:

- Spending quality time with my child—what does this mean?
- Balancing work and family life
- Finding time for myself
- Where can I turn when I must work, and my child is ill?

[*]New York Times (1988).
[†]Children's Defense Fund (1988).
[‡]Newberger, Melnicoe, and Newberger (1986).
[§]Bureau of the Census (1986).

Some Suggestions for Helping Families Headed by a Single Parent

Speaking as a single parent myself, I want to point out that there is still a stigma attached to being divorced. Therefore, try to overcome whatever critical feelings you may have about the pros and cons of divorce. Problems related to that situation are complex enough for the parents without having to deal with your prejudice, too. The following are some suggestions:

- Avoid using such terms as *broken home* and *fatherless children*. A more acceptable term could be *single parent family*, because being a family does not necessarily depend on having a mother and father present in the home.
- Avoid taking sides with one parent or the other; it is likely that neither is all right or all wrong.
- Remember that single parent families are very likely to have low incomes. Newly divorced families may experience special problems in this regard and will benefit from referral to appropriate social agencies.
- Many single parents are lonely; they find themselves gradually excluded from contact with couples and at a loss to know how to handle holidays without a former spouse. Suggestions and information can be very welcome if tactfully presented.
- Notices about community activities such as meetings of Parents Without Partners or We Care (for those whose spouse has died) should be routinely posted.
- Make it a point to introduce single parents to each other. They could be encouraged to develop a support group of their own within the school.
- Avoid deploring the fact the parents are divorced. Instead be on the lookout for the strengths demonstrated by the single parents and comment on these in an encouraging way.
- Be sure to send notices offering parent conferences to both parents. Occasionally both will attend the same meeting, but frequently the parents prefer to come separately, and so conferences will require more of your time.
- Be *sure* you are aware of the custody provisions for the child. Know who is permitted to take the child from the school. Although this is often a friendly arrangement between divorced parents, sometimes it is not, and the school is legally responsible for the child's safety while on those premises.
- For an interesting discussion of ethics related to difficult divorce/child-care situations, see Feeney (1988).

Programs of interest to single parents might include:

- Opportunities for meeting single parents of the opposite sex
- What should we tell the children?
- The strengths of single parents
- Legal rights of women
- When fathers have custody—how to make a go of it
- Dealing with children who are feeling emotional pain—how can parents help?

Some Suggestions for Helping Blended Families

The 40% rate of second-marriage divorce indicates that there is often considerable stress when parents remarry and blend families together. Centers can at least avoid contributing to such stress by doing some of the following:

- Understand that children going through the blending process may be confused or upset. They have to deal with emotional feelings related to loyalty, jealousy, anger about possible rejection, confusion over authority, and so forth (and so do all the parents).
- Joining a blended family often means a child's birth order shifts dramatically. For example, a former "only" child might become a middle child with both older and younger siblings.
- Be aware that stepparents often are not legally entitled to grant permission for medical treatment. Clarify this with the families *before* an emergency happens.
- Offer the children the opportunity to make something for both stepparents and natural parents at holiday times.
- Remember to include the stepparents in school functions—they are often ignored, and it should be their choice and the child's whether or not they will actually attend.

- Avoid the temptation to pass judgment on which reconstituted side of the family is doing the better job with the child in your care.

Programs of special interest to blended families might include:

- Living with other people's children
- Sharing children between two families
- Joint custody—how can we make it work?
- When the chips are down—who disciplines whom?
- Dealing with stepparent stereotypes
- Coping with jealousy

Some Suggestions for Helping Families Who Have Very Low Incomes

- Be matter of fact—not condescending or pitying.
- Be especially careful not to offend parents. Families on food stamps may not appreciate artwork made from macaroni or chocolate pudding fingerpainting. Nor do they feel comfortable with pictures of children who have heaps of presents about them at Christmas.
- Process agency papers, such as applications for child-care vouchers, as quickly as you can. Families' reimbursement or income may depend on your efficient paperwork.
- Be particularly aware of community resources: when

and where food stamps are available and what the hours are for the county health clinic.

- Deliberately build acquaintance with various social agencies yourself. A friendly call from you will often help a parent use the system more effectively.
- Provide a clothing exchange for outgrown but not wornout children's clothing.
- Offer a food coupon exchange in which people can leave or take whatever coupons they wish.
- Acquaint yourself with the AFDC (Aid to Families with Dependent Children) regulations. There may be portions of those regulations that parents do not know about that could benefit their children if used.

Programs of interest to families who are poor might include:

- A speaker from the social welfare office, explaining rights and obligations
- Speakers from unfamiliar agencies, such as those that sponsor special Christmas stores for low-income families
- Very practical discussions on child rearing (Although it is always important to be practical, these families are particularly likely to dislike theoretical, head-in-the clouds, professorial-type meetings.)
- What to do about specific community problems, such as how to get vicious dogs off the street.

It works best to get volunteers together ahead of time to talk over basic school ground rules and ask them what they would like to do. A list of possibilities can help stimulate ideas. These might include reading to the children, cooking something with them, bringing a baby to share, or coming along as the additional adult needed on a field trip. If the volunteers can choose what they prefer doing, they will be more at ease than if such activities are simply assigned to them.

When the volunteer comes to school, it is important to pay attention to him, so he feels truly welcome. The book by Miller and Wilmshurst, *Parents and Volunteers in the Classroom* (1975), is packed with useful suggestions about

how to do this even when the teachers are very busy.

Teachers sometimes fail to appreciate that being a volunteer is stressful. To feel competent, volunteers need specific instructions about what to do, and they also deserve to be thanked sincerely upon departure. Probably the best advice to give teachers working with volunteers is that they should ask themselves from time to time how *they* would feel if they were the volunteers and what they would say the staff could do that would make them want to return for another day. Then, of course, those teachers should accept their own advice and proceed accordingly.

Visiting grandparents add special delight to the day.

SUMMARY

Parents are a tremendously significant part of the child's life, and children's centers should make every effort to weave bonds between home and school that make the fabric of that life complete and whole. A basic strand in this process is letting parents know that teachers care about them and about their children. This can be accomplished by establishing a condition of trust between home and school through consistent, daily contact, handling separations with caring concern, and keeping parents posted on school activities by means of bulletin boards and newsletters.

An additional way of drawing families and teachers together is by offering help to families to strengthen family life. This should include adjusting the center's services to families who do not fit the traditional middle-class stereotypes of family life. Conducting individual conferences is one way of providing such help, and sponsoring meetings on parenting concerns is another. Potluck suppers and visiting days also offer

excellent opportunities for staff and families to become better acquainted so that more interchange can take place.

Accepting help from families is just as important as offering help. This is not always easy, particularly when the help comes in the form of critical comments and questions, but even these can benefit the school and the parent-teacher relationship if handled with maturity. Two other less threatening ways parents can offer the school help are by providing resources of various kinds and by participating directly in the school with staff and children. Such participation requires special preparation and planning by staff so that the volunteers and children gain feelings of competence and happiness as a result of that experience.

SELF-CHECK QUESTIONS FOR REVIEW

Content-Related Questions

1. Why should teachers not be preoccupied with children at the beginning of the center day?

2. List some practical things teachers can do to help establish a feeling of trust between themselves and parents.

3. Do you agree with the statement that children's misbehavior is usually the result of the way the child is handled at home? Be sure you can give reasons for your position.

4. Describe some important points to remember when planning a parent education meeting.

5. What does the author suggest teachers should do when home and school policies cannot agree?

6. Select an example of a nontraditional family, and provide some suggestions about how the school could help the family function effectively.

7. Regulations require that 40% of the parents in your center participate in the center in some fashion. Create a checklist of various ways parents might participate. Be sure to include such items as sharing resources from home and serving on the parent board.

Integrative Questions

1. Just suppose that a teacher did *not* want to have much contact with parents! Suggest some ways she could arrange her program so that it would be difficult for parents to have informal chats with her. How do your suggestions compare with the behavior of some teachers you recall from your days in elementary school?

2. You are now the teacher in a Head Start center, and you want to keep the parents informed about what is happening in your classroom. *If you could not use a newsletter to do this,* what other practical means of communication could you use to relay news to the families?

3. If the Kontos and Wells study had revealed that teachers were less helpful and friendly to children when they disapproved of their families' parenting skills, what would you suggest as a remedy? Would simply telling teachers they should "behave better" be enough?

QUESTIONS AND ACTIVITIES

1. Do you think all teachers should be required to have parents participate in their rooms? What might be some of the drawbacks to such a requirement?

2. *Problem:* One of your friends who is in her first year of teaching calls you and is feeling very depressed. She has gone to some lengths to plan a special parenting meeting and only half the parents actually showed up that night. What would be your response to her depression?

3. The next time your college class is shown a movie, take a few minutes and develop questions based on it that would encourage good discussion in a parenting group.

4. *Problem:* You are now a teacher in a full-day center, and a parent who lives near another one of the center's families takes you aside and tells you a lengthy story about the mischief the other child leads her son into at home. (They are no angels at school either!) She asks you not to allow the boys to play together at school anymore and threatens to withdraw her child if this is not enforced. As a teacher, how do you think you should handle this kind of request? What if her son, in your opinion, is actually the ringleader?

5. Think of a policy parents might legitimately complain about at a children's center or at the school where you are teaching. Now try role playing various responses to such complaints. These responses could include attacking back, refusing to listen, reflecting parent feelings, and explaining the reasons for the school policy.

REFERENCES FOR FURTHER READING

Overviews

Berger, E. H. (1987). *Parents as partners in education: The school and home working together* (2nd ed.). Columbus, Ohio: Merrill Publishing Co. Berger discusses parent involvement in both school- and home-based programs and has some sensible advice to offer on home-school relations.

Gestwicki, C. (1987). *Home, school, and community relations: A guide to working with parents.* Albany, N.Y.: Delmar Publishers. Here is a clearly written, practical book that provides real-life examples of responses by teachers and parents.

Joffe, C. E. (1977). *Friendly intruders: Childcare professionals and family life.* Berkeley, Calif.: University of California Press. This book offers valuable insights into the differing and similar needs and preferences of Black and White parents.

Taylor, K. W. (1981). *Parents and children learn together* (3rd ed.). New York: Teachers College Press. This classic discussion of teacher-parent interactions remains one of the best in the field. The material is presented in the framework of a cooperative nursery school.

Talking with Parents

Galinsky, E. (1988). Parents and teacher-caregivers: Sources of tension, sources of support. *Young Children, 43*(3), 4–15. Galinsky identifies many sources of stress experienced by parents and child-care staff, and then offers some practical suggestions for reducing stress between them.

Gelfer, J. I., & Perkins, P. G. (1987). Effective communication with parents: A process for parent/teacher conferences. *Childhood Education, 64*(1), 19–22. A series of checklists makes this article easy to use as a reference for planning quality conferences.

Hendrick, J. (1988). *The whole child: Developmental education for the early years* (4th ed.). Columbus, Ohio: Merrill Publishing Co. The chapters "What Parents Need" and "Tender Topics: Helping Children Master Emotional Crises" contain considerable information and recommendations about effective counseling with parents.

Rotter, J. C., Robinson, E. H., & Fey, M. A. (1987). *Parent-teacher conferencing* (2nd ed.). Washington, D.C.: National Education Association. This pamphlet includes many examples of sample questions, tips related to conferencing, and sensible advice. Highly recommended.

Information About Families in Nontraditional Settings

Dietl, L. K., & Neff, M. J. (1983). *Single parent families: Choice or chance?* New York: Teachers College Press. This is an unusual book that actively involves the reader by intertwining information and fictitious cases with opportunities to think answers through.

Quisenberry, J. D. (Ed.) (1982). *Changing family lifestyles: Their effect on children.* Washington, D.C.: Association for Childhood Education International. This pamphlet outlines how life-styles are changing and suggests many ways teachers can help families living with such changes.

Sue, D. W. (1981). *Counseling the culturally different: Theory and practice.* New York: John Wiley & Sons. Although this book goes more deeply into counseling than most teachers prefer; it is recommended because it provides a good deal of information about working with Blacks, Hispanics, Asians, and American Indian peoples.

Parent Education

Auerbach, A. B. (1968). *Parents learn through discussion: Principles and practices of parent group education.* New York: John Wiley & Sons. Auerbach includes many examples of how discussion groups function and offers practical suggestions for leading them. A very helpful book.

Berger (1987, already cited under "Overviews") offers a particularly good chapter on parent education.

Involving Parents in the Classroom

Frede, E. (1984). *Getting involved: Workshops for parents.* Ypsilanti, Mich.: High/Scope Press. Each chapter begins with a brief discussion of an important topic such as play and then offers a selection of activities parents could do as a group to deepen their understanding of the topic.

Honig, A. (1979). *Parent involvement in early childhood education.* Washington, D.C.: National Association for the Education of Young Children. In particular, the chapter "Why Parent Involving Is Sometimes a Hard Job" should be read with attention because of its frank discussion of possible pitfalls.

Tizard, B., Mortimore, J., & Burchell, B. (1983). *Involving parents in nursery and infant schools: A source book for teachers.* Ypsilanti, Mich.: High/Scope Press. An English book based on a research project, *Involving Parents* offers many practical suggestions about different ways to include parents in the life of the school. Delightful reading.

For the Advanced Student

Becher, R. M. (1986). Parent involvement: A review of research and principles of successful practice. In L. G. Katz (Ed.), *Current topics in early childhood education, Vol. VI.* Norwood, N.J.: Ablex Publishing Co. Becher provides a research-based overview of ways parents can be involved with schools.

Bronstein, P., & Cowan, C. P. (Eds.). (1988). *Fatherhood today: Men's changing role in the family.* New York: John Wiley & Sons. This book uses extensive research citations as bases for discussing everything from gay fatherhood to Chicano and Black fathers to fathers with toddlers.

Children's Defense Fund. (1988). *A children's defense budget, FY 1989.* Washington, D.C.: The Fund. CDF produces this annual compilation of information about the status of America's children and the probable impact of the federal budget on their well-being. A gold mine of facts is contained in this invaluable reference.

Maccoby, E. E., & Martin, J. A. (1983). Socialization in the context of the family: Parent-child interaction. In P. H. Mussen (Ed.), *Handbook of Child Psychology* (4th ed.). E. M. Hetherington (Ed.), *Volume IV: Socialization, personality, and social development.* New York: John Wiley & Sons. This is an extensive review of research that explores how parents and children influence each other as development takes place.

Other Resources of Special Interest

Child Care Information Exchange, P. O. Box 2890, Redmond, Washington 98073. CCIE invariably contains a wealth of useful information on child-care practice and management. It is listed here because it often includes practical information on working with parents.

Appendixes

A

Chart of Normal Development: Infancy to Six Years of Age*

The chart of normal development on the next pages presents children's achievements from infancy to six years of age in five areas:

- Motor skills (gross and fine motor)
- Cognitive skills
- Self-help skills
- Social skills
- Communication skills (understanding and speaking language)

In each skill area, the age at which each milestone is reached *on the average* is also presented. This information is useful if you have a child in your class who you suspect is seriously delayed in one or more skill areas.

However, it is important to remember that these milestones are only average. From the moment of birth, each child is a distinct individual and develops in his or her unique manner. No two children have ever reached all the same developmental milestones at the exact same ages. The examples that follow show what we mean.

By nine months of age Gi Lin had spent much of her time scooting around on her hands and tummy, making no effort to crawl. After about a week of pulling herself up on chairs and table legs, she let go and started to walk on her own. Gi Lin skipped the crawling stage entirely and scarcely said more than a few sounds until she was 15 months old. But she walked with ease and skill by 9½ months.

Marcus learned to crawl on all fours very early, and continued crawling until he was nearly 18 months old, when he started to walk. However, he said single words and used two-word phrases meaningfully before his first birthday. A talking, crawling baby is quite a sight!

Molly worried her parents by saying scarcely a word, although she managed to make her needs known with sounds and gestures. Shortly after her second birthday, Molly suddenly began talking in two- to four-word phrases and sentences. She was never again a quiet child.

All three children were healthy and normal. By the time they were 3 years old, there were no major differences among them in walking and talking. They had simply developed in their own ways and at their own rates. Some children seem to concentrate on one thing at a time—learning to crawl, to walk, or to talk. Other children develop across areas at a more even rate.

As you read the chart of normal development, remember that children don't read child development books. They don't know they're supposed to be able to point out Daddy when they are a year old, or copy a circle in their third year. And even if they could read these baby books, they probably wouldn't follow them! Age-related developmental milestones are obtained by averaging out what many children do at various ages. No child is "average" in all areas. Each child is a unique person.

One final word of caution. As children grow, their abilities are shaped by the opportunities they have for learning. For example, although many five-year-olds can repeat songs and rhymes, the child who has not heard songs and rhymes many times cannot be expected to repeat them. All areas of development and learning are influenced by the child's experiences as well as by the abilities they are born with.

*Note. From *Mainstreaming Preschoolers: Children with Health Impairments* by A. Healy, P. McAreavey, C. S. VonHippel, and S. H. Jones, 1978, Washington D.C.: U.S. Department of Health, Education, and Welfare, Office of Human Development Services, Administration for Children, Youth and Families, Head Start Bureau.

Chart of normal development

	0–12 months	12–24 months	24–36 months	36–48 months	48–60 months	60–72 months
MOTOR SKILLS						
Gross motor skills	Sits without support Crawls Pulls self to standing and stands unaided Walks with aid Rolls a ball in imitation of adult	Walks alone Walks backward Picks up toys from floor without falling Pulls toy, pushes toy Seats self in child's chair Walks up and down stairs (hand-held) Moves to music	Runs forward well Jumps in place, two feet together Stands on one foot, with aid Walks on tiptoe Kicks ball forward	Runs around obstacles Walks on a line Balances on one foot for 5 to 10 seconds Hops on one foot Pushes, pulls, steers wheeled toys Rides (that is, steers and pedals) tricycle Uses slide without assistance Jumps over 15 cm (6") high object, landing on both feet together Throws ball overhand Catches ball bounced to him or her	Walks backward toe-heel Jumps forward 10 times, without falling Walks up and down stairs alone, alternating feet Turns somersault	Runs lightly on toes Walks on balance beam Can cover 2 meters (6'6") hopping Skips on alternate feet Jumps rope Skates
Fine motor skills	Reaches, grasps, puts objects in mouth Picks things up with thumb and one finger (pincer grasp)	Builds tower of three small blocks Puts four rings on stick Places five pegs in pegboard	Strings four large beads Turns pages singly Snips with scissors Holds crayon with thumb and fingers, not fist	Builds tower of nine small blocks Drives nails and pegs Copies circle Imitates cross	Cuts on line continuously Copies cross Copies square Prints a few capital letters	Cuts out simple shapes Copies triangle Traces diamond Copies first name Prints numerals 1 to 5

Transfers object from one hand to other hand	Turns pages two or three at a time Scribbles	Uses one hand consistently in most activities	Manipulates clay materials (for example, rolls, balls, snakes, cookies)	Colors within lines Has adult grasp of pencil	Demonstrates preacademic skills
Drops and picks up toy	Turns knobs Throws small ball Paints with whole arm movement, shifts hands, makes strokes	Imitates circular, vertical, horizontal strokes Paints with some wrist action. Makes dots, lines, circular strokes Rolls, pounds, squeezes, and pulls clay		Has handedness well established (that is, child is left- or right-handed) Pastes and glues appropriately	

COMMUNICATION SKILLS
Understanding language

Responds to speech by looking at speaker	Responds correctly when asked *where* (when question is accompanied by gesture)	Points to pictures of common objects when they are named	Begins to understand sentences involving time concepts (for example, *We are going to the zoo tomorrow*)	Follows three unrelated commands in proper order	
Responds differently to aspects of speaker's voice (for example, friendly or unfriendly, male or female)	Understands prepositions *on*, *in*, and *under*	Can identify objects when told their use	Understands size comparatives such as *big* and *bigger*	Understands comparatives like *pretty*, *prettier*, and *prettiest*	
Turns to source of sound	Follows request to bring familiar object from another room	Understands question forms *what* and *where*	Understands relationships expressed by *if . . . then* or *because* sentences	Listens to long stories but often misinterprets the facts	
Responds with gesture to *hi*, *bye-bye*, and *up* when these words are accompanied by appropriate gesture	Understands simple phrases with key words (for example: *Open the door. Get the ball.*)	Understands negatives *no*, *not*, *can't* and *don't* Enjoys listening to simple storybooks and requests them again	Carries out a series of two to four related directions	Incorporates verbal directions into play activities Understands sequencing of events when told them (for example, *First we have to go to*	

Chart of normal development *(continued)*

0–12 months	12–24 months	24–36 months	36–48 months	48–60 months	60–72 months
Stops ongoing action when told *no* (when negative is accompanied by appropriate gesture and tone)	Follows a series of two simple but related directions		Understands when told, *Let's pretend*	the store, then we can make the cake and tomorrow we will eat it)	There are few obvious differences between child's grammar and adult's grammar
Spoken Language					Still needs to learn such things as subject-verb agreement, and some irregular past tense verbs
Makes crying and noncrying sounds	Says first meaningful word	Joins vocabulary words together in two-word phrases	Talks in sentences of three or more words, which take the form agent-action-object (*I see the ball*) or agent-action-location (*Daddy sit on chair*)	Asks *when*, *how*, and *why* questions	Can take appropriate turns in a conversation
Repeats some vowel and consonant sounds (babbles) when alone or when spoken to	Uses single words plus a gesture to ask for objects	Gives first and last name	Tells about past experiences	Uses models like *can*, *will*, *shall*, *should*, and *might*	Gives and receives information
Interacts with others by vocalizing after adult	Says successive single words to describe an event	Asks *what* and *where* questions	Uses "s" on nouns to indicate plurals	Joins sentences together (for example, *I like chocolate chip cookies and milk*)	Communicates well with family, friends, or strangers
Communicates meaning through intonation	Refers to self by name	Makes negative statements (for example, *Can't open it*)	Uses "ed" on verbs to indicate past tense	Talks about causality by using *because* and *so*	
Attempts to imitate sounds	Uses *my* or *mine* to indicte possession	Shows frustration at not being understood	Refers to self using pronouns *I* or *me*	Tells the content of a story but may confuse facts	
	Has vocabulary of about 50 words for important people, common objects, and the existence, nonexistence and recurrence of objects and events (for example, *more* and *all gone*)		Repeats at least one nursery rhyme and can sing a song		
			Speech is understandable to strangers, but has still some sound errors		

COGNITIVE SKILLS

Follows moving objects with eyes
Recognizes differences among people.
Responds to strangers by crying or staring
Responds to and imitates facial expressions of others

Responds to very simple directions (for example, raises arms when someone says, *Come,* and turns head when asked *Where is Daddy?*)
Imitates gestures and actions (for example, shakes head no, plays peek-a-boo, waves bye-bye)
Puts small objects in and out of container with intention

Imitates actions and words of adults
Responds to words or commands with appropriate action (for example: *Stop that. Get down*)
Is able to match two similar objects

Looks at storybook pictures with an adult, naming or pointing to familiar objects on request (for example: *What is that? Point to the baby*)
Recognizes difference between *you* and *me*
Has very limited attention span
Accomplishes primary learning through own exploration

Responds to simple directions (for example: *Give me the ball and the block. Get your shoes and socks*)
Selects and looks at picture books, names pictured objects, and identifies several objects within one picture

Matches and uses associated objects meaningfully (for example, given cup, saucer, and bead, puts cup and saucer together)
Stacks rings on peg in order of size
Recognizes self in mirror, saying *baby,* or own name
Can talk briefly about what he or she is doing
Imitates adult actions (for example, housekeeping play)

Recognizes and matches six colors
Intentionally stacks blocks or rings in order of size
Draws somewhat recognizable picture that is meaningful to child, if not to adult. Names and briefly explains picture

Asks questions for information (*why* and *how* questions requiring simple answers)
Knows own age
Knows own last name
Has short attention span
Learns through observing and imitating adults, and by adult instruction and explanation. Is very easily distracted
Has increased understanding of concepts of the

Plays with words (creates own rhyming words; says or makes up words having similar sounds)
Points to and names four to six colors
Matches pictures of familiar objects (for example, shoe, sock, foot; apple, orange, banana)

Draws a person with two to six recognizable parts, such as head, arms, legs.
Can name or match drawn parts to own body
Draws, names, and describes recognizable picture
Rote counts to 5, imitating adults
Knows own street and town
Has more extended attention span.
Learns through observing and listening to adults as well as

Retells story from picture book with reasonable accuracy
Names some letters and numerals
Rote counts to 10
Sorts objects by single characteristics (for example, by color, shape, or size if the difference is obvious)

Is beginning to use accurately time concepts of *tomorrow* and *yesterday*
Uses classroom tools (such as scissors and paints) meaningfully and purposefully
Begins to relate clock time to daily schedule
Attention span increases noticeably. Learns through adult instruction. When interested, can ignore distrac-

Chart of normal development (continued)

0–12 months	12–24 months	24–36 months	36–48 months	48–60 months	60–72 months
COGNITIVE SKILLS (continued)					
		Has limited attention span. Learning is through exploration and adult direction (as in reading of picture stories) Is beginning to understand functional concepts of familiar objects (for example, that a spoon is used for eating) and part/whole concepts (for example, parts of the body)	functions and groupings of objects (for example, can put doll house furniture in correct rooms), and part/whole (for example, can identify pictures of hand and foot as parts of body) Begins to be aware of past and present (for example: *Yesterday we went to the park. Today we go to the library*)	through exploration. Is easily distracted Has increased understanding of concepts of function, time, part/whole relationships. Function or use of objects may be stated in addition to names of objects Time concepts are expanding. The child can talk about yesterday or last week (a long time ago), about today, and about what will happen tomorrow	tions. Concepts of function increase as well as understanding of why things happen. Time concepts are expanding into an understanding of the future in terms of major events (for example, *Christmas will come after two weekends*)
SELF-HELP SKILLS					
Feeds self cracker Holds cup with two hands. Drinks with assistance Holds out arms and legs while being dressed	Uses spoons, spilling little Drinks from cup, one hand, unassisted Chews food Removes shoes, socks, pants, sweater	Uses spoon, little spilling Gets drink from fountain or faucet unassisted Opens door by turning handle Takes off coat	Pours well from small pitcher Spreads soft butter with knife Buttons and unbuttons large buttons Washes hands unassisted	Cuts easy foods with a knife (for example, hamburger patty, tomato slice) Laces shoes	Dresses self completely Ties bow Brushes teeth unassisted Crosses street safely

SELF HELP SKILLS (*continued*)

Unzips large zipper	Puts on coat with assistance	Blows nose when reminded			
Indicates toilet needs	Washes and dries hands with assistance				

SOCIAL SKILLS

Smiles spontaneously	Recognizes self in mirror or picture	Plays near other children	Joins in play with other children. Begin to interact	Plays and interacts with other children	Chooses own friends(s)
Responds differently to strangers than to familiar people	Refers to self by name	Watches other children, joins briefly in their play	Shares toys. Takes turns with assistance	Dramatic play is closer to reality, with attention paid to detail, time, and space	Plays simple table games
Pays attention to own name	Plays by self, initiates own play	Defends own possessions	Begins dramatic play, acting out whole scenes (for example, traveling, playing house, pretending to be animals)	Plays dress-up	Plays competitive games
Responds to *no*	Imitates adult behaviors in play	Begins to play house		Shows interest in exploring sex differences	Engages with other children in co-operative play involving group decisions, role assignments, fair play
Copies simple actions of others	Helps put things away	Symbolically uses objects, self in play			
		Participates in simple group activity (for example, sings, claps, dances)			
		Knows gender identity			

B

A Suggested Method for Preparing Summarizing Reports for Official Boards and Funding Agencies

With increasing frequency, teachers and directors of day care centers are required to present annual summaries of the children's progress to justify continuation of funding. Many staff members are uncertain about how to present such information effectively even though they have faithfully kept track of the children's growth during the year. For this reason, the following information is included.

One useful method of summarizing such data that is relatively easy for all teachers, even those untrained in statistics, to employ is the simple numerical summary of checklist material. In this method, answers are tallied for the various categories on the checklists, and the totals are converted to percents to simplify drawing comparisons.

COMPUTING A NUMERICAL SUMMARY FOR A CHECKLIST

Only checklists of children who have remained throughout all three testing periods should be used. If there are more than 10 children in each age group, it may be worthwhile to sort the children into the smaller groups and compute the percent for separate ages. This separation will demonstrate change between categories more clearly.

- **Step 1** Tally (count up) answers for each category on a master sheet. For example, tally all the answers in the "not able to observe" category for the Self-Confidence Pretest; next, tally answers for the "hardly ever" category, and so forth.

- **Step 2** Add the number of tallies in each column.
- **Step 3** Add the totals of the four columns for the Pretest together to obtain the total number of answers given in all the columns. (This same total is used in the Midtest and Posttest calculations.)
- **Step 4** Find the percent of replies for each column by dividing the number of answers in each column by the total number of answers for all the Pretest columns.
- **Step 5** Repeat this process to calculate the percent replies for the Midtest and Posttest.

Once the percents have been calculated, they may be used to draw a variety of comparisons among the results of the test periods. Thus if the chart shown on the next page were used in a fiscal report, it could be pointed out that although only 38% of the children were rated as usually appearing to be self-confident in September, by May the percent had increased to 62. Or the analysis might be phrased, "The percent of 4-year-old children who rated high on measures of self-confidence almost doubled in the period from September to May."

Although the teacher will no doubt wish to attribute such a favorable change to the educational program, it must be emphasized that this method draws no comparisons between that group and a control group not undergoing instruction. Thus, it documents change but does not provide evidence that the change could not be due to other influences, such as maturation. To be on safer scientific ground, the teacher will need to use a control group and more sophisticated statistical methods to obtain such evidence.

USING STATISTICAL METHODS FOR THE ANALYSIS OF DATA

It is important to know that methods that are vastly superior to the scheme proposed above exist for the statistical analysis of data. In particular, such techniques as t-tests and the analysis of variance are helpful. These methods are superior because they may be used to determine whether there is a significant differ-ence between pretest, midtest, and posttest results or between the test results of the school population and those of a control group.

Although these techniques usually lie beyond the expertise of the center teachers, they should realize that such techniques have been developed and are of real value in assessing data. Occasionally, a statistician can be prevailed on to carry out such calculations should they be needed.

Computation of Percent Representation in Various Categories of a Checklist

Self-confidence	Pretest				Midtest				Posttest			
	Not able to observe	Hardly ever	About half the time	Usually	Not able to observe	Hardly ever	About half the time	Usually	Not able to observe	Hardly ever	About half the time	Usually
Able to hold her own when challenged (confident, not unduly intimidated)	1	2	7	5	0	2	7	6	0	1	6	8
Likes to try new things	2	2	6	5	0	0	8	7	0	0	6	9
Takes criticism and reprimands in stride (not overwhelmed or crushed)	0	4	4	7	0	3	3	9	0	2	2	11
Able to adjust to change in routines or people in the center	0	1	8	6	0	1	7	7	0	0	6	9
Number of tallies in each column	3	9	25	23	0	6	25	29	0	3	20	37
Column answer divided by total of all columns	.05	.15	.42	.38	0	.10	.42	.48	0	.05	.33	.62
Percent of replies in each category	5%	15%	42%	38%	0%	10%	42%	48%	0%	5%	33%	62%

Number of participating children = 15
Total answers for pretest = 60

$$\text{Percent} = \frac{\text{Number of answers in column}}{\text{Total number of answers in pretest, midtest, or posttest}}$$

C

Communicable Disease Chart for Schools*

Incubation and symptoms	Methods of spread
Chicken pox (varicella) *Incubation:* 2-3 weeks, usually 13-17 days. *Symptoms:* skin rash often consisting of small blisters which leave a scab. Eruption comes in crops. There may be pimples, blisters, and scabs all present at the same time.	Direct contact, droplet, or airborne spread of secretions of respiratory tract of an infected person or indirectly with articles freshly soiled with discharges from such persons.
Common cold *Incubation:* 12-72 hours, usually 24 hours. *Symptoms:* irritated throat, watery discharge from nose and eyes, sneezing, chilliness and general body discomfort.	Direct contact with an infected person or indirectly by contact with articles freshly soiled by discharges of nose and throat of the infected person.
Flu (influenza) *Incubation:* 1-3 days. *Symptoms:* abrupt onset of fever, chills, headache, and sore muscles. Runny nose, sore throat, and cough are common.	Direct contact with an infected person or indirectly by contact with articles soiled by discharges of nose and throat of the infected person. Possibly airborne in crowded areas.
German measles (rubella) (three-day measles) *Incubation:* 14-21 days, usually 16-18 days. *Symptoms:* skin rash and mild fever. Glands at back of head, behind ear, and along back of neck are often enlarged. Some infections may occur without evident rash.	Direct contact with an infected person or indirectly by contact with articles freshly soiled by discharges of nose and throat of the infected person.
Hepatitis A (infectious) *Incubation:* 10-50 days; average 25-30 days. *Symptoms:* usually abrupt onset with loss of appetite, fever, abdominal discomfort, nausea and fatigue. Jaundice may follow in a few days.	Person to person contact, presumably in the majority of cases by fecal contamination. May be spread by ingestion of fecally contaminated water and food.

Note. References: American Academy of Pediatrics; Report of the Committee on Infectious Diseases (18th ed.), 1977, Evanston, Ill.; Control of Communicable Diseases in Man (12th ed.) by Abram S. Berenson (Ed.), 1975, Washington, D.C.; American Public Health Association.

*Courtesy the Ohio Department of Health, Bureau of Preventive Medicine, Columbus, Ohio.

Period of communicability: communicable at least 5 days before blisters appear and until all scabs are crusted.

Control: exclude from school until all scabs are crusted.

Children with certain chronic diseases, like leukemia, are at extreme high risk for complications.

Period of communicability: 24 hours before onset of symptoms until 5 days after onset. (However, period may vary.)

Control: exclude from school until symptoms are gone.

Period of communicability: probably shortly before onset of symptoms and at least 3 days after onset of symptoms.

Control: exclude from school until symptoms are gone.

Routine immunization is not recommended for children.

Period of communicability: most highly communicable from 7 days before and at least 4 days after the onset of rash.

Control: exclude from school for a least 4 days after the onset of symptoms.

Immunization of all children entering school is required by law. The disease, while mild in children, is very serious for unborn babies if it is contracted by a pregnant woman.

Period of communicability: most highly communicable during the last half of the incubation period and continuing for approximately 1 week after jaundice.

Control: exclude from school until at least 7 days after onset of jaundice. Student should be under physician's care.

Consult the local health department for help in controlling the disease within the school. Adequate sanitation facilities are necessary in reducing the spread of this disease. An adequate supply of soap and paper towels is essential. Students should wash their hands after each toilet use and before meals. Observe cafeteria personnel for symptoms of the disease and give particular attention to handwashing practices of all food handlers. Gamma globulin is usually *not* recommended for classroom contacts.

Incubation and symptoms	Methods of spread

Hepatitis B (serum)
Incubation: 45-160 days, average 60-90 days.
Symptoms: usually inapparent onset with loss of appetite, vague abdominal discomfort, nausea, vomiting; often progresses to jaundice. Fever may be absent.

Chiefly through blood or blood products by inoculation or ingestion of blood from an infected person. Contaminated needles and syringes are important vehicles of spread. Also may be spread through contamination of wounds or lacerations.

Impetigo
Incubation: 2-5 days, occasionally longer.
Symptoms: blisterlike lesions which later develop into crusted pus-like sores which are irregular in outline.

Direct contact with draining sores.

Head lice (pediculosis)
Incubation: the eggs of lice may hatch in 1 week and sexual maturity is reached in approximately 2 weeks.
Symptoms: irritation and itching of scalp or body; presence of small light gray insects or their eggs (nits) which are attached to the base of hairs.

Direct contact with an infested person and indirectly by contact with the *personal* belongings, especially clothing and headgear.

Measles (rubeola)
Incubation: 8-13 days; usually 10 days.
Symptoms: acute highly communicable disease with fever, runny eyes and nose, cough, and followed by a dark red elevated rash that occurs in patches.

Direct contact with secretions of nose, throat and urine of infected persons; indirectly airborne and by articles freshly soiled with secretions of nose and throat.

Meningitis (bacterial)
Incubation: 1-7 days.
Symptoms: acute disease with sudden onset of fever, intense headache. Behavioral changes may occur including irritability or sluggishness.

Direct contact with secretions of nose and throat of infected persons or carriers.

Meningitis (aseptic-viral)
Incubation: varies with causative agent.
Symptoms: acute disease with sudden onset of fever, intense headache, nausea, forceful vomiting, and stiff neck. Behavioral changes may occur including irritability and sluggishness.

Varies with causative agent.

Mononucleosis
Incubation: 2-8 weeks.
Symptoms: fever, sore throat, swollen lymph glands.

Direct contact with saliva of infected person.

Mumps
Incubation: 12-26 days, commonly 18 days.
Symptoms: usually fever followed by painful swelling under the jaw or in front of the ear.

Direct contact with saliva of infected person, or indirectly by contact with articles freshly soiled with discharges of such persons.

Period of communicability: most highly communicable during latter part of incubation period and during acute illness.

Control: exclude from school until symptoms are gone. Students should be under a physician's care.

Notify your local health department.

Period of communicability: from onset of symptoms until sores are healed.

Control: exclude from school until adequately treated and sores are no longer draining.

Early detection and adequate treatment are important in preventing spread. Infected individual should use separate towels and wash cloths. All persons with lesions should avoid contact with newborn babies.

Period of communicability: while lice remain alive on the infested person or in his clothing and until eggs (nits) have been destroyed.

Control: exclude from school until disinfection is accomplished.

The local health department should be notified of any occurrence of lice. When a student is found with head lice, all family members should be inspected and those infected should be treated.

Period of communicability: from onset of symptoms until a few days after rash appears.

Control: exclude from school until at least 4 days after the rash appears.

Immunization of all children entering school is required by law. Notify the local health department if a case occurs in the school. One of the most readily transmitted communicable diseases.

Period of communicability: no longer than 24 hours after initiation of antibiotic therapy.

Control: exclude from school until adequately treated. Student must be under a physician's care.

Notify the local health department if a case occurs in the school. Antibiotic therapy may be necessary for intimate contacts. Classroom contacts are usually *not* candidates for antibiotic therapy.

Period of communicability: varies with causative agent.

Control: exclude from school during fever period. Student must be under a physician's care.

It is important to determine whether meningitis is aseptic or bacterial since the symptoms are essentially the same. Aseptic meningitis is a much less serious disease.

Need not be excluded from school under ordinary circumstances.

Not highly communicable.

Period of communicability: 48 hours before onset of swelling and up to 9 days after swelling occurs.

Control: exclude from school for at least 9 days after swelling occurs.

Immunization against mumps is available. The disease may have serious complications to adults.

Incubation and symptoms	Methods of spread

Ringworm (scalp, skin, and feet)

Incubation: Unknown.

Symptoms:

Scalp: scaly patches of temporary baldness. Infected hairs are brittle and break easily.

Skin: flat, inflamed ringlike sores that may itch or burn.

Feet: scaling or cracking of the skin, especially between the toes, or blisters containing a thin watery fluid.

Directly by contact with infected persons or animals or indirectly by contact with articles and surfaces contaminated by such infected persons or animals.

Scabies (itch)

Incubation: first infestation in 4-6 weeks; reinfestation symptoms may occur in a few days.

Symptoms: small raised areas of skin containing fluid or tiny burrows under the skin resembling a line which appear frequently on finger webs, under side of wrists, elbows, armpits, thighs, and belt line. Itching is intense, especially at night.

Direct contact with sores and, to a limited extent, from undergarments or bedding freshly contaminated by infected persons.

Scarlet fever and strep throat (streptococcal)

Incubation: 1-3 days, but may be longer.

Symptoms:

Strep throat: fever, sore and red throat, pus spots on the back of the throat, tender and swollen glands of the neck.

Scarlet fever: all symptoms that occur with strep throat as well as strawberry tongue and rash of the skin and inside of mouth. High fever, nausea, and vomiting may occur.

Direct or intimate contact with infected person or carrier, rarely by indirect contact through transfer of objects or hands. Casual contact rarely leads to infection. Explosive outbreaks of strep throat may follow drinking of contaminated milk or eating contaminated food.

Venereal diseases (gonorrhea, syphilis, herpes simplex)

Incubation:

Gonorrhea: 3-9 days.

Syphilis: 10-90 days.

Herpes simplex II: up to 2 weeks.

Symptoms:

Gonorrhea: early symptoms in the male are a thick yellow discharge from the sex organs appearing 3-9 days after exposure, and a painful burning sensation during urination. The same symptoms may also appear in the female, but often are so mild that they are unnoticed.

Gonorrhea: direct personal contact—usually through sexual intercourse.

Minimum control measures	Other information
Period of communicability: as long as sores are present. *Control:* exclusion from school is necessary for ringworm of the scalp and skin until treatment has begun.	Preventive measures are largely hygienic. All household contacts, pets, and farm animals should be examined and treated if infected. Scalp ringworm is seldom, if ever found in adults.
Period of communicability: until student and household contacts have been adequately treated (usually requires one treatment). *Control:* exclude from school until student and household contacts have been treated adequately. (Single infection in a family is uncommon.)	Disinfection of the general environment is not necessary. After treatment of student and family *no* waiting period for reentry is necessary.
Period of communicability: with adequate treatment, communicability is eliminated within 24 hours. *Control:* exclude from school until 24 hours after treatment is started.	Early diagnosis and medical treatment are essential in the care of the student and in the prevention of serious complications.
Period of communicability: *Gonorrhea:* communicable until treated (up to 8 months).	The control of the venereal diseases is the responsibility of the physician and the health department. Information must be held in the utmost confidence in order to successfully control these diseases.

Incubation and symptoms	Methods of spread
Symptoms: Syphilis: may include a sore which develops at the site the organism enters the body; a rash, unexplained and prolonged sore throat, fever and headache. *Herpes simplex II:* very painful sores or blisters on or around the sex organs.	*Syphilis:* direct personal contact—usually through sexual intercourse. *Herpes simplex II:* direct personal contact—usually through sexual intercourse.

Whooping cough (pertussis)

Incubation: 7-21 days, usually 10 days.
Symptoms: begins with cough which is worse at night. Symptoms may at first be very mild. Characteristic "whooping" develops in about 2 weeks and spells of coughing sometimes end with vomiting.

Direct contact with discharges of an infected person, or indirectly by contact with articles freshly soiled by discharges of infected persons.

Tuberculosis

Very few students have been found to be infected with tuberculosis.
Skin testing policies for tuberculosis testing in students are determined by local health departments.

Animal bites

1. The community should be made aware of the potential dangers of animal bites.
2. Preventive vaccination of owned dogs and control of all stray dogs should be encouraged.
3. All biting animals should be confined for a 10-day observation period.
4. All unprovoked attacks by wildlife should be considered as potential exposures to rabies.
5. All animal bites should be reported to the local health department so that an investigation of the case may be made.

Minimum control measures	Other information

Period of communicability:
   Syphilis: as long as early symptoms are present (up to 3 years).

Herpes simplex II: most contagious when blisters are moist; however, may remain communicable for several weeks.

Control: herpes, gonorrhea, and syphilis—there is no reason for restricting attendance except in the specific recommendation of the health department or family physician.

Pelvic inflammatory disease (PID) is a serious complication of gonorrhea and requires medical treatment.

Period of communicability: from 7 days after exposure to 3 weeks after onset of "whooping" in untreated children, or 5-7 days after treatment is started.

Immunization is required by law for entrance into school.

If an animal bite occurs:
1. Confine biting animal if possible.
2. Try to obtain as complete a description as possible if the animal escapes.
3. Give first-aid immediately by copious flushing of wound with water or soap or detergent with water.
4. Refer for medical treatment by or under direction of physician.
5. Report all animal bites to the local health department serving the area where the bite occurred.
6. Work with animal control officials to keep dogs off school grounds as much as possible.

In health instruction classes:
1. Teach the proper conduct toward animals to avoid being bitten.
2. Emphasize the dangers in handling stray dogs, cats, and wild animals.
3. Stress the necessity of students reporting bites of all animals, especially bats.
4. Encourage immunization of pets.

D Sample Daily Food Plans for One Meal and Snack*

Pattern	I	II	III	IV
Snack†	Orange juice Whole wheat bread Butter	Apple wedge Cheese	Milk Banana	Hard cooked egg Tomato juice
Lunch or supper††	Ground beef patty Peas Carrot strips Enriched roll Butter or margarine Milk	Roast turkey Broccoli Mashed potatoes Whole wheat bread Butter or margarine Milk	Fish sticks Scalloped potatoes Stewed tomatoes Whole wheat bread Butter or margarine Milk	Blackeyed peas with ham Mustard greens Purple plums Corn bread Butter or margarine Milk

*Note. From *Nutrition: Better Eating for a Head Start* by U.S. Department of Health, Education and Welfare, 1976, Washington D.C.: Author.

†Include one or more of the following: Milk, fruit, vegetable, juice or protein-rich food; may include a bread or cereal product in addition.

††Protein-rich food, vegetable and/or fruit (at least two kinds), bread, enriched or whole grain, butter or margarine as needed, milk.

Pattern	V	VI	VII	VIII
Snack	Celery stuffed with liver sausage Apple juice	Milk Peanut butter on cracker	Apple juice Cheese toast	Milk Raisins and peanuts
Lunch or supper	Scrambled eggs Spinach Fried apples Biscuit Butter Milk	Oven-fried drumsticks Corn on the cob Sliced tomato/green pepper rings Whole wheat bread Butter or margarine Milk	Meat loaf Green beans Baked potato Carrot strips Enriched bread Butter or margarine Milk	Tuna sandwich on whole wheat bread Tomato juice Raw cabbage (small pieces) Apricots Milk

Pattern	IX	X	XI	XII
Snack	Grapefruit juice Finger-size pieces of leftover meat	Raw carrots, celery, green pepper with cottage cheese dip	Tomato juice Flour tortilla with melted cheese	Fresh fruit in season (Strawberries, melons, tangerines, etc.)
Lunch or supper	Pinto beans with melted cheese Chili peppers, chopped tomato, onion, lettuce Flour tortilla Milk	Meat balls in tomato sauce over spaghetti Zucchini Peaches French bread heated with butter or margarine Milk	Liver fingers Sweet potato Apple, banana, and orange salad Fry bread Milk	Swiss steak cubes Cauliflower Cooked carrots Whole wheat roll Butter or margarine Milk

E

Ten Quick Ways to Analyze Children's Books for Racism and Sexism*

Both in school and out, young children are exposed to racist and sexist attitudes. These attitudes—expressed over and over in books and in other media—gradually distort their perceptions until stereotypes and myths about minorities and women are accepted as reality. It is difficult for a librarian or teacher to convince children to question society's attitudes. But if a child can be shown how to detect racism and sexism in a book, the child can proceed to transfer the perception to wider areas. The following ten guidelines are offered as a starting point in evaluating children's books from this perspective.

1. CHECK THE ILLUSTRATIONS

Look for stereotypes. A stereotype is an oversimplified generalization about a particular group, race, or sex, which usually carries derogatory implications. Some infamous (overt) stereotypes of Blacks are the happy-go-lucky watermelon-eating Sambo and the fat, eye-rolling "mammy"; of Chicanos, the sombrero-wearing peon or fiesta-loving, macho bandito; of Asian Americans, the inscrutable, slant-eyed "Oriental"; of Native Americans, the naked savage or "primitive" craftsman and his squaw; of Puerto Ricans,

the switchblade-toting teenage gang member; of women, the completely domesticated mother, the demure, doll-loving little girl, or the wicked stepmother. While you may not always find stereotypes in the blatant forms described, look for variations which in any way demean or ridicule because of their race or sex.

Look for tokenism. If there are non-White characters in the illustrations, do they look just like Whites except for being tinted or colored in? Do all minority faces look stereotypically alike, or are they depicted as genuine individuals with distinctive features?

Who's doing what? Do the illustrations depict minorities in subservient and passive roles or in leadership and action roles? Are males the active "doers" and females the inactive observers?

2. CHECK THE STORY LINE

The Civil Rights Movement has led publishers to weed out many insulting passages, particularly from stories with Black themes, but the attitudes still find expression in less obvious ways. The following checklist suggests some of the subtle (covert) forms of bias to watch for.

Standard for success. Does it take "White" behavior standards for a minority person to "get ahead"? Is "making it" in the dominant White society projected as the only ideal? To gain acceptance and approval, do non-White persons have to exhibit extraordinary qualities—excel in sports, get A's, etc.? In friendships between White and non-White children, is it the non-White who does most of the understanding and forgiving?

*Reprinted with permission from the *Bullletin* of the Council on Interracial Books for Children, Inc., 1841 Broadway, New York, NY 10023. The Council also publishes the *Bulletin* (eight issues a year), which reviews new children's books for the human and antihuman messages they convey.

Resolution of problems. How are problems presented, conceived, and resolved in the story? Are minority people considered to be "the problem"? Are the oppressions faced by minorities and women represented as causally related to an unjust society? Are the reasons for poverty and oppression explained, or are they accepted as inevitable? Does the story line encourage passive acceptance or active resistance? Is a particular problem that is faced by a minority person resolved through the benevolent intervention of a White person?

Role of women. Are the achievements of girls and women based on their own initiative and intelligence, or are they due to their good looks or to their relationship with boys? Are sex roles incidental or critical to characterization and plot? Could the same story be told if the sex roles were reversed?

3. LOOK AT THE LIFESTYLES

Are minority persons and their setting depicted in such a way that they contrast unfavorably with the unstated norm of White middle-class suburbia? If the minority group in question is depicted as "different," are negative value judgments implied? Are minorities depicted exclusively in ghettos, barrios, or migrant camps? If the illustrations and text attempt to depict another culture, do they go beyond oversimplifications and offer genuine insights into another lifestyle? Look for inaccuracy and inappropriateness in the depiction of other cultures. Watch for instances of the "quaint-natives-in-costume" syndrome (most noticeable in areas like costume and custom, but extending to behavior and personality traits as well).

4. WEIGH THE RELATIONSHIPS BETWEEN PEOPLE

Do the Whites in the story possess the power, take the leadership, and make the important decisions? Do non-Whites and females function in essentially supporting roles?

How are family relationships depicted? In Black families, is the mother always dominant? In Hispanic families, are there always lots and lots of children? If the family is separated, are societal conditions—unemployment, poverty—cited among the reasons for the separation?

5. NOTE THE HEROES AND HEROINES

For many years, books showed only "safe" minority heroes and heroines—those who avoided serious conflict with the White establishment of their time. Minority groups today are insisting on the right to define their own heroes and heroines based on their own concepts and struggles for justice.

When minority heroes and heroines do appear, are they admired for the same qualities that have made White heroes and heroines famous or because what they have done has benefitted White people? Ask this question: Whose interest is a particular figure really serving?

6. CONSIDER THE EFFECTS ON A CHILD'S SELF-IMAGE

Are norms established that limit the child's aspirations and self-concepts? What effect can it have on Black children to be continuously bombarded with images of the color white as the ultimate in beauty, cleanliness, virtue, and the color black as evil, dirty, menacing, etc.? Does the book counteract or reinforce this positive association with the color white and negative association with black?

What happens to a girl's self-image when she reads that boys perform all of the brave and important deeds? What about a girl's self-esteem if she is not "fair" of skin and slim of body?

In a particular story, is there one or more persons with whom a minority child can readily identify to a positive and constructive end?

7. CONSIDER THE AUTHOR'S OR ILLUSTRATOR'S BACKGROUND

Analyze the biographical material on the jacket flap or the back of the book. If a story deals with a minority theme, what qualifies the author or illustrator to deal with the subject? If the author and illustrator are not members of the minority being written about, is there anything in their background that would specifically recommend them as the creators of this book?

Similarly, a book that deals with the feelings and insights of women should be more carefully examined if it is written by a man—unless the book's avowed purpose is to present a strictly male perspective.

8. CHECK OUT THE AUTHOR'S PERSPECTIVE

No author can be wholly objective. All authors write out of a cultural as well as a personal context. Children's books in the past have traditionally come from authors who are White and who are members of the middle class, with one result being that a single ethnocentric perspective has dominated American children's literature. With the book in question, look carefully to determine whether the direction of the author's perspective substantially weakens or strengthens the value of his/her written book. Are omissions and distortions central to the overall character or "message" of the book?

9. WATCH FOR LOADED WORDS

A word is loaded when it has insulting overtones. Examples of loaded adjectives (usually racist) are savage, primitive, conniving, lazy, superstitious, treacherous, wily, crafty, inscrutable, docile, and backward.

Look for sexist language and adjectives that exclude or ridicule women. Look for use of the male pronoun to refer to both males and females. While the generic use of the word "man" was accepted in the past, its use today is outmoded. The following examples show how sexist language can be avoided: ancestors instead of forefathers; chairperson instead of chairman; community instead of brotherhood; firefighters instead of firemen; manufactured instead of manmade; the human family instead of the family of man.

10. LOOK AT THE COPYRIGHT DATE

Books on minority themes—usually hastily conceived—suddenly began appearing in the mid-1960s. There followed a growing number of "minority experience" books to meet the new market demand, but most of these were still written by White authors, edited by White editors, and published by White publishers. They therefore reflected a White point of view. Only very recently in the late 1960s and early 1970s has the children's book world begun to even remotely reflect the realities of a multiracial society. And it has just begun to reflect feminists' concerns.

The copyright dates, therefore, can be a clue as to how likely the book is to be overtly racist or sexist, although a recent copyright date, of course, is no guarantee of a book's relevance or sensitivity. The copyright date only means the year the book was published. It usually takes a minimum of one year—and often much more than that—from the time a manuscript is submitted to the publisher to the time it is actually printed and put on the market. This time lag meant very little in the past, but in a time of rapid change and changing consciousness, when children's book publishing is attempting to be "relevant," it is becoming increasingly significant.

F   Suggested Equipment for Block Building*

Set of blocks for a group of 15 to 20 children (Numbers in parentheses refer to drawing on page 430)

	3 years	4 years	5 years
Half units (1)	48	48	60
Units (2)	108	192	220
Double units (3)	96	140	190
Quadruple units (4)	48	48	72
Pillars (5)	24	48	72
Small cylinders (6)	20	32	40
Large cylinders (7)	20	24	32
Circular curves (8)	12	16	20
Elliptical curves (9)	8	16	20
Pairs of triangles—small (10)	8	16	18
Pairs of triangles—large (11)	4	8	12
Floor boards—11″ (12)	12	30	60
Roof boards—22″ (not illustrated)	0	12	20
Ramps (13)	12	32	40
Half pillars (not illustrated)	0	12	16
Y switches (14)	2	2	4
Right angle switches (15), and/or X switches (not illustrated)	0	4	8

*Note. From Jessie Stanton, Alma Weisberg, and the faculty of the Bank Street School for Children, *Play equipment for the nursery.* Bank Street College of Education, New York. © 1962, Bank Street College of Education. Used by permission.

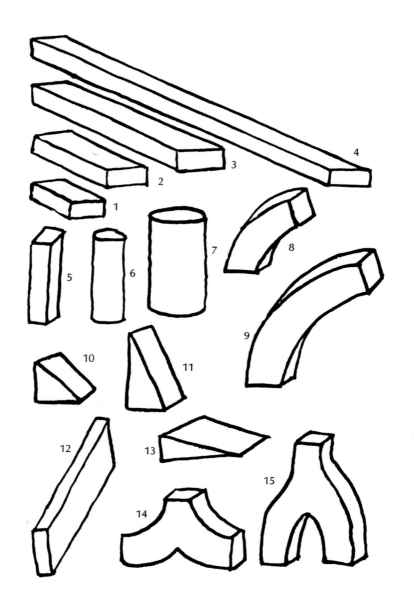

G Educational Organizations, Newsletters, and Journals Associated with Early Childhood

EDUCATIONAL ORGANIZATIONS

AAHPER
American Alliance for Health, Physical Education, and Recreation
1900 Association Dr.
Reston, VA 22091

ACEI
Association for Childhood Education International
11141 Georgia Ave., Suite 200
Wheaton, MD 20902

ACT
Action for Children's Television
46 Austin St.
Newtonville, MA 02160

ACYF
Administration for Children Youth and Families
P.O. Box 1182
Washington, DC 20013

American Montessori Society
175 Fifth Ave.
New York, NY 10010

CEC
Council for Exceptional Children
1920 Association Dr.
Reston, VA 22091

Children's Defense Fund
122 C St., N.W.
Washington, DC 20001

CWLA
Child Welfare League of America, Inc.
440 First St., N.W., Suite 316
Washington, DC 20001

DCCDCA
Day Care and Child Development Council of America
1401 K St., N.W.
Washington, DC 20005

ERIC/ECE
Educational Resources Information Center on Early Childhood Education
805 W. Pennsylvania Ave.
Urbana, IL 61801

NAEYC
National Association for the Education of Young Children
1834 Connecticut Ave., N.W.
Washington, DC 20009-5786
(1-800-424-8777)

National Committee for the Prevention of Child Abuse
332 S. Michigan Ave., Suite 950
Chicago, IL 60604-4357

SACUS
Southern Association for Children Under Six
P.O. Box 5403
Brady Station
Little Rock, AR 72215

NEWSLETTERS

The Black Child Advocate
Black Child Development Institute
1463 Rhode Island Ave., N.W.
Washington, DC 20005

Child Health Alert
P.O. Box 338
Newton Highlands, MA 02161

ERIC/ECE Newsletter
805 W. Pennsylvania Ave.
Urbana, IL 61801

Multicultural Leader
Educational Materials and Services Center
144 Railroad Ave., Suite 107
Edmonds, WA 98020

Nurturing News: A Forum for Male Early Childhood Educators
187 Caselli Ave.
San Francisco, CA 94114

Report on Preschool Education
Capitol Publications, Inc.
2430 Pennsylvania Ave., N.W., Suite G-12
Washington, DC 20037

JOURNALS

American Journal of Orthopsychiatry
American Orthopsychiatric Association
49 Sheridan Ave.
Albany, NY 10010

Child Care Information Exchange
P.O. Box 2890
Redmond, WA 98073-2890

Child Development
Society for Research in Child Development
University of Chicago Press
5801 Ellis Ave.
Chicago, IL 60637

Childhood Education
ACEI
11141 Georgia Ave., Suite 200
Wheaton, MD 20902

Children Today
Office of Human Development Services
Superintendent of Documents
U.S. Government Printing Office
Washington, DC 20402

Day Care and Early Education
Human Sciences Press
72 Fifth Ave.
New York, NY 10011

Developmental Psychology
American Psychological Association
1200 17th St., N.W.
Washington, DC 20036

Dimensions
Southern Association for Children Under Six
P.O. Box 5403, Brady Station
Little Rock, AR 72215

Early Childhood Research Quarterly
National Association for the Education of Young Children
Ablex Publishing Company
355 Chestnut Street
Norwood, NJ 07648

Exceptional Children
Council for Exceptional Children
1920 Association Dr.
Reston, VA 22091

Harvard Educational Review
Longfellow Hall
13 Appian Way
Cambridge, MA 02138

Interracial Books for Children Bulletin
1841 Broadway
New York, NY 10023

Journal of Children in Contemporary Society
Haworth Press
28 E. 22nd St.
New York, NY 10010

Journal of Research in Childhood Education
Association for Childhood Education International
11141 Georgia Ave., Suite 200
Wheaton, MD 20902

Nutrition Action
Center for Science in the Public Interest
1501 16th St.
Washington, DC 20036-1499

Pediatric Mental Health
P.O. Box 1880
Santa Monica, CA 90406

Young Children
NAEYC
1834 Connecticut Ave., N.W.
Washington, DC 20009-5786

References

Abbot, S. (1972). *Old dog*. New York: Coward, McCann, Geohegan.

Adcock, D., & Segal, M. (1983). *Making friends: Ways of encouraging social development in young children*. Englewood Cliffs, N.J.: Prentice-Hall.

Aesop. (1962). *The hare and the tortoise*. New York: McGraw-Hill Book Co.

Albert, R. S. (Ed.). (1983). *Genius and eminence: The social psychology of creativity and exceptional achievement*. Oxford: Pergamon Press.

Allen, H. B., & Linn, M. D. (Eds.). (1986). *Dialect and language variation*. New York: Academic Press.

Allen, Lady of Hurtwood. (1968). *Planning for play*. Cambridge, Mass.: MIT Press.

Allport, G. W. (1979). *The nature of prejudice, 25th anniversary edition*. Reading, Mass.: Addison-Wesley Publishing Co.

Almy, M., Chittenden, E., & Miller, P. (1966). *Young children's thinking*. New York: Teachers College Press.

Almy, M., & Genishi, C. (1970). *Ways of studying children: An observation manual for early childhood teachers* (2nd ed.). New York: Teachers College Press.

Amabile, T. M. (1983). *The social psychology of creativity*. New York: Springer-Verlag.

Amabile, T. M., & Gitomer, J. (1984). Children's artistic creativity: Effects of choice in task materials. *Personality and Social Psychology Bulletin, 10*(2), 209–215.

American Academy of Pediatrics. (1986). *Report of the Committee on Infectious Diseases*. Elk Grove Village, Ill.: The Academy.

Ames, L. B., & Chase, J. A. (1980). *Don't push your preschooler* (rev. ed.). New York: Harper & Row, Publishers.

Anastas, P. (1973). *Glooskap's children*. Boston: Beacon Press.

Anderson, P. S. (1963). *Storytelling with the flannel board: Book 1*. Minneapolis, Minnesota: T. S. Dennison & Co.

Andress, B. (1980). *Music experiences in early childhood*. New York: Holt, Rinehart & Winston.

Andrews, J. H. (1988). Poetry: Tool of the classroom magician. *Young Children, 43*(4), 17–24.

Andry, A. C., & Schepp, S. (1968). *How babies are made*. New York: Time-Life.

Anthony, E. J., & Cohler, B. J. (Eds.). (1987). *The invulnerable child*. New York: The Guilford Press.

Anthony, E. J., & Pollock, G. H. (1985). *Parental influences in health and disease*. Boston: Little, Brown & Co.

Arbuthnot, M. H., & Root, S. L., Jr. (1968). *Time for poetry* (3rd ed.). Glenview, Ill.: Scott, Foresman and Co.

Arlow, J. A., & Kadis, A. (1976). Fingerpainting in the psychotherapies of children. In D. Schaefer (Ed.), *The therapeutic use of children's play*. New York: Jason Aronson.

Arnheim, D. D., & Pestolesi, R. A. (1978). *Elementary physical education: A developmental approach*. St. Louis: C. V. Mosby Co.

Arnheim, D. D., & Sinclair, W. A. (1979). *The clumsy child: A program of motor therapy* (2nd ed.). St. Louis: C. V. Mosby Company.

Aronson, S. S. (1987). Health update: AIDS and child care programs. *Child Care Information Exchange, 58*, 35–39.

Asch, F. (1978). *Turtle tale*. New York: Dial Press.

Axline, V. (1964). *Dibs: In search of self*. Boston: Houghton Mifflin Co.

Axline, V. (1969). *Play therapy* (rev. ed.). New York: Ballantine Books.

Axtmann, A., & Bluhm, C. (1986). In D. P. Worf (Ed.), *Connecting: Friendship in the lives of young children and their teachers*. Redmond, Wash.: Exchange Press.

Ayers, J. B., & Ayers, M. N. (1984). Popcorn Piaget and science for preschoolers. *Dimensions, 12*(2), 4–6.

Baird, J. C., & Lutkus, A. D. (Eds.). (1982). *Mind child architecture*. Hanover, N.H.: University Press of New England.

Balaban, N. (1985). *Starting school: From separation to independence*. New York: Teachers College Press.

Balian, L. (1974). *Humbug rabbit*. Nashville: Abingdon Press.

Bandura, A. (1973). *Aggression: A social learning analysis*. Englewood Cliffs, N.J.: Prentice-Hall.

Bandura, A. (1977). *Social learning theory*. Englewood Cliffs, N.J.: Prentice-Hall.

*For the addresses of organizations given here, refer to Appendix G.

Banks, J. A. (1988). *Multiethnic education: Theory and practice* (2nd ed.). Boston: Allyn & Bacon.

Bansavage, J. C. (1978). Ecology of child development. *Children in Contemporary Society, 11*(4), 119–121.

Barbour, N., Webster, T. D., and Drosdeck, S. (1987). A resource for the language arts. *Young Children, 42*(2), 20–25.

Barker, R. G., Dembo, T., & Lewin, K. (1976). Frustration and regression. In J. S. Bruner, A. Jolly, & K. Sylva (Eds.), *Play—Its role in development and evolution*. New York: Basic Books.

Barrata-Lorton, M. (1972). *Workjobs: Activity-centered learning for early childhood education*. Reading, Mass.: Addison-Wesley Publishing Co.

Barrett, D. C. (1987). Undernutrition and child behaviour: What behaviours should we measure and how should we measure them? In J. Dobbing (Ed.), *Early nutrition and later achievement*. London: Academic Press.

Bauer, C. F. (1977). *Handbook for story tellers*. Chicago: American Library Association.

Baumrind, D. (1971). Current patterns in parental authority. *Developmental Psychology Monographs, 1*, 1–103.

Baumrind, D. (1972). The development of instrumental competence: Focus on girls. Minneapolis: *Minnesota Symposium in Child Development*.

Baxter, K. M. (1978). *Come and get it: A natural foods cookbook for children*. Ann Arbor, Mich.: Children First Press.

Bayless, K. M., & Ramsey, M. E. (1982). *Music: A way of life for the young child* (2nd ed.). St. Louis: C. V. Mosby Co.

Bayless, K. M., & Ramsey, M. E. (1987). *Music: A way of life for the young child* (3rd ed.). Columbus, Ohio: Merrill Publishing Co.

Beaty, J. J. (1988). *Skills for preschool teachers* (3rd ed.). Columbus, Ohio: Merrill Publishing Co.

Beaty, J. J. (1989). *Observing development of the young child* (2nd ed.). Columbus, Ohio: Merrill Publishing Co.

Becher, R. M. (1986). Parent involvement: A review of research and principles of successful practice. In L. G. Katz (Ed.), *Topics in early childhood education* (Vol. VI). Norwood, N.J.: Ablex Publishing Co.

Beckwith, J. (1980). *Make your backyard more interesting than TV*. New York: McGraw-Hill Book Co.

Bellack, A. S., Hersen, M., & Kazdin, A. E. (Eds.). (1982). *International handbook of behavior modification and therapy*. New York: Plenum Publishing Corp.

Belliston, L., & Belliston, M. (1982). *How to raise a more creative cihld*. Allen, Tex.: Argus Communications.

Beme, P. H., & Savary, L. M. (1985). *Building self-esteem in children*. New York: Continuum.

Bemelmans, L. (1939). *Madeline*. New York: Simon & Schuster.

Benham, N., Miller, T., & Kontos, S. (1988). Pinpointing staff training needs in child care centers. *Young Children, 43*(4), 9–16.

Bentzen, W. R. (1985). *Seeing young children: A guide to observing and recording behavior*. Albany, N.Y.: Delmar Publishers.

Bereiter, C., & Engelmann, S. (1966). *Teaching disadvantaged children in the preschool*. Englewood Cliffs, N.J.: Prentice-Hall.

Bergen, D. (1988). *Play as a medium for learning and development: A handbook of theory and practice*. Portsmouth, N.H.: Heinemann.

Berger, E. H. (1987). *Parents as partners in education: The school and home working together* (2nd ed.). Columbus, Ohio: Merrill Publishing Co.

Bernstein, A. (1978). *The flight of the stork*. New York: Delacourte Press.

Bernstein, J., & Gullo, S. (1976). *When people die*. New York: E. P. Dutton.

Berrueta-Clement, J. T., Schweinhart, L. J., Barnett, W. S., Epstein, A. S., & Weikart, D. P. (1984). *Changed lives; The effects of the Perry Preschool Program on youths through age 19*. Ypsilanti, Mich.: High/Scope Educational Research Foundation.

Beuf, A. H. (1977). *Red children in white America*. Philadelphia: University of Pennsylvania Press.

Biber, B. (1984). *Early education and psychological development*. New Haven: Yale University Press.

Binkley, M. R. (1988). *Becoming a nation of readers: What parents can do*. Washington, D.C.: United States Department of Education.

Birch, H. G. (1980). Malnutrition, learning, and intelligence. In S. I. Harrison & J. F. McDermott (Eds.), *New directions in childhood psychopathology. Volume I: Developmental considerations*. New York: International Universities Press.

Birch, H. G., & Gussow, J. D. (1970). *Disadvantaged children: Health, nutrition & school failure*. New York: Harcourt Brace Jovanovich.

Birch, L. L. (1980a). Effect of peer models' food choices and eating behavior on preschoolers' food preferences. *Child Development, 51*, 489–496.

Birch, L. L. (1980b). Experiential determinants of children's food preferences. In L. G. Katz (Ed.), *Current topics in early childhood education* (Vol. 3). Norwood, N.J.: Ablex Publishing Corp.

Bjorklund, G., & Burger, C. (1987). Making conferences work for parents, teachers and children. *Young Children, 42*(2), 26–31.

Blank, M. (1982). Moving beyond the difference. In L. Feagans & D. C. Farron (Eds.), *The language of children reared in poverty*. New York: Academic Press.

Blatchford, P., Battle, S., & Mays, J. (1982). *The first transition: Home to pre-school: A report on the "Transition from Home to Pre-School" project*. Windsor, Berkshire, England: NFER-Nelson Publishing Co.

Blood, C. L., & Link, M. (1976). *The goat in the rug*. New York: Parent's Magazine Press.

Bloom, B. S. (1964). *Stability and change in human characteristics.* New York: John Wiley & Sons.

Bloom, B. S., Engelhart, M. D., Furst, E. J., Hill, W. H., & Krathwohl, D. R. (1956). *Taxonomy of educational objectives.* New York: David McKay Co.

Boehm, A. E., & Weinberg, R. A. (1987). *The classroom observer: Developing observation skills in early childhood settings* (2nd ed.). New York: Teachers College Press.

Boguslawski, D. B. (1975). *Guide for establishing and operating day care centers for young children.* New York: Child Welfare League of America.

Bond, F. (1983). *Mary Betty Lizzie McNutt's birthday.* New York: Thomas Y. Crowell.

Bos, B. (1982). *Please don't move the muffin tins: A hands-off guide to art for the young child.* Roseville, Calif.: Turn the Page Press.

Bos, B. (1983). *Before the basics: Creating conversations with children.* Roseville, Calif.: Turn the Page Press.

Bowlby, J. (1969). *Attachment and loss: Vol. 1: Attachment.* New York: Basic Books.

Bowlby, J. (1973). *Attachment and loss: Vol. 2: Separation.* New York: Basic Books.

Brazelton, T. B. (1984). *To listen to a child: Understanding the normal problems of growing up.* Reading, Mass.: Addison-Wesley Publishing Co.

Bredekamp, S. (Ed.). (1987). *Developmentally appropriate practice in early childhood programs serving children from birth through age 8* (expanded edition). Washington, D.C.: National Association for the Education of Young Children.

Brehm, M., & Tindell, N. T. (1983). *Movement with a purpose: Perceptual motor lesson plans for young children.* West Nyack, N.Y.: Parker Publishing Co.

Brenner, B. (1973). *Bodies.* New York: Dutton.

Bretherton, I. (Ed.). (1984). *Symbolic play: The development of social understanding.* New York: Academic Press.

Brewster, L., & Jacobson, M. F. (1978). *The changing American diet.* Washington, D.C.: Center for Science in the Public Interest.

Briggs, D. C. (1970). *Your child's self esteem: The key to his life.* Garden City, N.Y.: Doubleday & Co.

Briggs, R. (1973). *Father Christmas.* New York: Coward, McCann & Geoghegan.

Brim, O., Boocock, S., Hoffman, L., Bronfenbrenner, U., & Edelman, M. (1975). *Ecology of child development.* Philadelphia: American Philosophical Society.

Brittain, G. (1979). *Creativity, art and the young child.* New York: Macmillan Publishing Co.

Brody, J. (1981). *Jane Brody's nutrition book.* New York: W. W. Norton & Co.

Bronson, W. J. (1974). Competence and the growth of personality. In K. Connolly & J. S. Brunner (Eds.), *The growth of competence.* London: Academic Press.

Bronstein, P., & Cowan, C. P. (Eds.). (1988). *Fatherhood today: Men's changing role in the family.* New York: John Wiley & Sons.

Brooks, R. L., & Obrzut, J. E. (1981). Brain lateralization: Implications for infant stimulation and development. *Young Children, 36*(3), 9–16.

Brown, J. F. (Ed.). (1982). *Curriculum planning for young children.* Washington, D.C.: National Association for the Education of Young Children.

Brown, M. W. (1947). *Goodnight moon.* New York: Harper & Row, Publishers.

Brown, M. W. (1965). *The dead bird.* New York: Young Scott Books.

Bruner, J. S. (1978). Learning the mother tongue. *Human Nature, 1*(9), 42–49.

Bruner, J. S., Olver, R., & Greenfield, P. (1966). *Studies in cognitive growth.* New York: John Wiley & Sons.

Budbill, D. (1974). *Christmas tree farm.* New York: Macmillan Publishing Co.

Bureau of the Census. (1986). *School enrollment—Social and economic characteristics of students: October 1986.* (Series P-20, No. 429). Washington, D.C.: Superintendent of Documents.

Buros, O. K. (1965). *The 6th mental measurements yearbook.* Highland Park, N.J.: Gryphon Press.

Buscaglia, L. (1984). *Loving each other: The challenge of human relationships.* New York: Holt, Rinehart & Winston.

Butler, A. L., Gotts, E. F., & Quisenberry, N. L. (1978). *Play as development.* Columbus, Ohio: Merrill Publishing Co.

Bybee, R. W., & Sund, R. B. (1982). *Piaget for educators* (2nd ed.). (1982). Columbus, Ohio: Merrill Publishing Co.

Calderone, M. S., & Ramey, J. W. (1982). *Talking with your child about sex: Questions and answers for children from birth to puberty.* New York: Ballantine Books.

Campbell, K. C., & Arnold, F. D. (1988). Stimulating thinking and communicating skills. *Dimensions, 16*(2), 11–13.

Campbell, S. D., & Dill, N. (1985). *The impact of changes in spatial density on children's behaviors in a day care setting.* Wheaton, Md.: Association for Childhood Education International.

Carin, R. B., & Sund, A. (1978). *Creative questioning and sensitive listening techniques: A self-concept approach* (2nd ed.). Columbus, Ohio: Merrill Publishing Co.

Carlsson-Paige, N., & Levin, D. E. (1987). *The war play dilemma: Balancing needs and values in the early childhood classroom.* New York: Teachers College Press.

Carr, R. (1980). *See and be: Yoga and creative movement for children.* Englewood Cliffs, N.J.: Prentice-Hall.

Carroll, R. (1950). *Where's the bunny?* New York: Henry Z. Walck.

Carroll, R. (1965). *What Whiskers did.* New York: Macmillan Publishing Company.

Carson, R. (1956). *The sense of wonder.* New York: Harper & Row, Publishers.

Cassidy, D. J., Myers, B. K., & Benion, P. E. (1987). Early childhood planning: A developmental perspective. *Childhood Education, 64*(1), 2–8.

Cazden, C. (1981). *Language in early childhood education.* Washington, D.C.: National Association for the Education of Young Children.

Cazden, C. (1984). *Effective instructional practices in bilingual education.* Washington, D.C.: National Institute of Education.

Centre for Educational Research Innovation. (1977). *Piagetian inventories: The experiments of Jean Piaget.* Paris, France: Organisation for Economic Co-operation and Development.

Charles, C. M. (1974). *Teacher's petit Piaget.* Belmont, Calif.: Fearon Publishers.

Chenfield, M. B. (1983). *Creative activities for young children.* New York: Harcourt Brace Jovanovich.

Chenfield, M. B. (1987). The first 30 years are the hardest: Notes from the Yellow Brick Road. *Young Children, 42*(3). 29–32 .

Cherry, C. (1971). *Creative movement for the developing child: A nursery school handbook for non-musicians* (rev. ed.). Belmont, Calif.: Fearon Publishers.

Cherry, C. (1972). *Creative art for the developing child: A teacher's handbook for early childhood education.* Belmont, Calif.: Fearon Publishers.

Cherry, C. (1976). *Creative play for the developing child: Early lifehood education through play.* Belmont, Calif.: Fearon Publishers.

Cherry, C. (1981). *Think of something quiet: A guide to achieving serenity in early childhood classrooms.* Belmont, Calif.: Pitman Learning.

Child, L. M. (1974). *Over the river and through the wood.* New York: Coward.

Child Study Children's Book Committee. (1988). *Children's books of the year.* New York: Bank Street College.

Children's Defense Fund. (1988). *A children's defense budget, FY 1989.* Washington, D.C.: The Fund.

Chomsky, N. (1987). Language: Chomsky's theory. In R. L. Gregory (Ed.), *The Oxford companion to the mind.* Oxford, England: Oxford University Press.

Church, V. (1971). *Colors around me.* Chicago: Afro-American Publishing Co.

Cicerelli, V. G., Evans, J. W., & Schiller, J. S. (1969). *The impact of Head Start on children's cognitive and affective development: Preliminary report.* Washington, D.C.: Office of Economic Opportunity.

Clark, E. (1983). Meanings and concepts. In P. H. Mussen (Ed.), *Handbook of child psychology* (4th ed.). J. H. Flavell & E. Markman (Eds.), *Volume III: Cognitive development.* New York: John Wiley & Sons.

Clemens, P. S. (1983). *The psychologist's test file.* Novato, Calif.: Academic Therapy Publications.

Coatsworth, E. (1934). The rabbit's song outside the tavern. In *Away goes Sally.* New York: Macmillan Publishing Co.

Coe, J. (1987). Children come first. *Childhood Education, 64*(2).

Cohen, D. (1983). *Piaget: Critique and reassessment.* New York: St. Martin's Press.

Cohen, M. D., & Hadley, S. (1986). *Selecting educational equipment for home and school.* Wheaton, Md.: Association for Childhood Education International.

Cole, A., Haas, C., Heller, E., & Weinberger, B. (1978). *Children are children are children: An activity approach to exploring Brazil, France, Iran, Japan, Nigeria, and the U.S.S.R.* Boston: Little, Brown & Co.

Coleridge, S. (1986). *January brings the snow.* New York: Dial Press.

Combs, A. W. (1972). *Educational accountability: Beyond behavioral objectives.* Alexandria, Va.: Association for Supervision and Curriculum Development.

Comer, D. (1987). *Developing safety skills with the young child: A common sense nonthreatening approach.* New York: Delmar Publishers.

Connolly, K., & Bruner, J. (Eds.). (1974). *The growth of competence.* London: Academic Press.

Cooper, T. T., & Ratner, M. (1980). *Many friends cooking: An international cookbook for girls and boys.* New York: Philomel Books.

Coopersmith, S. (1967). *The antecedants of self-esteem.* San Francisco, Calif.: W. H. Freeman & Co., Publishers.

Corballis, M. C., & Beale, I. L. (1983). *The ambivalent mind: The neuropsychology of left and right.* Chicago: Nelson-Hall.

Courson, D. (1988). Field trips: New avenues for learning. *Dimensions, 16*(2), 15–18.

Crase, D. R. (1986). Ideas! Helping young children deal with death. *Dimensions, 14*(3), 15–18.

Cratty, B. J. (1973). *Intelligence in action: Physical activities for enhancing intellectual abilities.* Englewood Cliffs, N.J.: Prentice-Hall.

Cratty, B. J. (1979). *Perceptual and motor development in infants and children.* Englewood Cliffs, N.J.: Prentice-Hall.

Cratty, B. J., & Martin, M. M. (1969). *Perceptual-motor efficiency in children: The measurement and improvement of movement attributes.* Philadelphia: Lea & Febiger.

Croft, D. (1967). *Recipes for busy little hands.* Palo Alto, Calif.: Author.

Croup, E. H. (1978). Feeding the special needs child. *Children in Contemporary Society, 12*(1), 7–9.

Crump, D. J. (1983). *Creatures small and furry.* Washington, D.C.: National Geographic Society.

Cryan, J. R. (1987). *The banning of corporal punishment in child care, school and other educative settings in the United States*. Wheaton, Md.: Association for Childhood Education International.

Cryan, J. R. (1988). Evaluation: Plague or promise? In J. S. McKee & K. M. Paciorek (Eds.), *Early childhood education 88/89*. Guilford, Conn.: Dushkin Publishing Group.

Curry, N. (Ed.). (1986). *The feeling child: Affective development reconsidered*. New York: The Haworth Press.

Curry, N. E., & Arnaud, S. H. (1982). Dramatic play as a diagnostic aid in the preschool. *Journal of Children in Contemporary Society, 14*(4), 37–46.

Curry, N. E., & Bergen, D. (1987). The relationship of play to emotional, social, and gender/sex role development. In D. Bergen (Ed.), *Play as a medium for learning and development: A handbook of theory and practice*. Portsmouth, N.H.: Heinemann.

Curtis, S. A. (1982). *The joy of movement in early childhood*. New York: Teachers College Press.

Curtis, S. A. (1987). New views on movement development and the implications for curriculum in early childhood. In C. Seefeldt (Ed.), *The early childhood curriculum: A review of current research*. New York: Teachers College Press.

Damon, W. (1983). *Social and personality development: Infancy through adolescence*. New York: W. W. Norton & Co.

Daniel, J. L. (1981). Black culture (English) in perspective. In G. Smitherman (Ed.), *Black English and the education of black children and youth: Proceedings of the National Invitational Symposium on the King decision*. Detroit: Center for Black Studies, Wayne State University.

Davis, G. A. (1983). *Creativity is forever*. Dubuque, Iowa: Kendall/Hunt Publishing Co.

Deacon, G. (1981). *Kid-tested menus with kitchen and luncheon techniques for day care centers*. North Wilkesboro, N.C.: Gold Crest.

Deci, E. L., & Ryan, R. M. (1982). Curiosity and self-directed learning: The role of motivation in education. In L. G. Katz (Ed.), *Current topics in early childhood education* (Vol. 4). Norwood, N.J.: Ablex Publishing Corp.

De Paola, T. (1973). *Nana upstairs and Nana downstairs*. New York: Putnam.

Derman-Sparks, L. (1987). "It isn't fair!" Anti-bias curriculum for young children. In B. Neugebauer (Ed.), *Alike and different: Exploring our humanity with young children*. Redmond, Wash.: Exchange Press.

Derman-Sparks, L., & the A.B.C. Task Force. (1989). *Anti-bias curriculum: Tools for empowering young children*. Washington, D.C.: National Association for the Education of Young Children.

Derman-Sparks, L., Higa, C. T., & Sparks, B. (1980). Children, race, and racism: How race awareness develops. *Council for Interracial Books for Children Bulletin, 11*(3/4), 3–9.

DeVries, R., & Kohlberg, L. (1987). *Programs of early education: The constructivist view*. New York: Longman.

Dickerson, M. (1977). *Developing the outdoor learning center*. Little Rock, Arkansas: Southern Association for Children Under Six.

Dietl, L. K., & Neff, M. J. (1983). *Single parent families: Choice or chance?* New York: Teachers College Press.

Dobbing, J. (Ed.). (1987). *Early nutrition and later achievement*. London: Academic Press.

Dougherty, D. M., Sax, L. M., Cross, T., & Silverman, N. (1987). *Children's mental health: Problems and services: A report by the Office of Technology Assessment*. Durnham, N.C.: Duke University Press.

Dowell, R. I. (1987). *Move over Mother Goose: Finger plays action verses and funny rhymes*. Mount Rainier, Md.: Gryphon House.

Duke, K. (1983). *The guinea pig ABC*. New York: E. P. Dutton.

Dumtschin, J. U. (1988). Recognize language development and delay in early childhood. *Young Children, 43*(3), 16–24.

Dyer, W. W. (1986). *Happy holidays! How to enjoy the Christmas and Hanukkah season to the fullest*. New York: William Morrow and Co.

Dyson, A. H., & Genishi, C. (1984). Nonstandard dialects in day care. *Dimensions, 13*(1), 6–9.

Early Childhood Research Quarterly. (1987). Vol. 2(3).

Ebel, R. L. (1970). Behavioral objectives: A close look. *Phi Delta Kappan*, November, pp. 171–173.

Education Week. (1988a, January 13). Proportion of infants immunized is declining, CDF study finds. *Education Week*, p. 8.

Education Week. (1988b, May 18). Recent outbreaks of mumps linked to immunization delays. *Education Week*, p. 3.

Edwards, B. (1978, November). *Left and right brain research*. Paper delivered at the Montessori Conference, Santa Barbara, Calif.

Edwards, C. P., & Ramsey, P. G. (1986). *Promoting social and moral development in young children: Creative approaches for the classroom*. New York: Teachers College Press.

Eisenberg, N. (Ed.). (1982). *The development of prosocial behavior*. New York: Academic Press.

Eisner, E. (1969). Instructional expressive educational objectives: Their formulation and use in curriculum. In W. J. Popham, E. W. Eisner, H. J Sullivan, & L. L. Tyler (Eds.), *Instructional objectives*. Chicago: Rand McNally, American Educational Research Association.

Eisner, E. (1985). *The art of educational evaluation: A personal view*. London: The Falmer Press.

Eliason, C. F., & Jenkins, L. T. (1986). *A practical guide to early childhood curriculum* (3rd ed.). Columbus, Ohio: Merrill Publishing Co.

Elkind, D. (1981a). *Children and adolescents*. New York: Oxford University Press.

Elkind, D. (1981b). *The hurried child: Growing up too fast, too soon*. Reading, Mass.: Addison-Wesley Publishing Co.

Elkind, D. (1983). The nature and function of play. In H. N. Schefler (Ed.), *Resources for early childhood: An annotated bibliography and guide for educators, librarians, health care professionals and parents*. New York: Garland Publishing.

Embery, J. (1983). *Joan Embery's collection of amazing animal facts*. New York: Dell Publishing Co.

Endres, J. B., & Rockwell, R. E. (1985). *Food, nutrition, and the young child* (2nd ed.). Columbus, Ohio: Merrill Publishing Co.

Engle, R. (1980). Understanding the handicapped through literature. *Young Children, 35*(3) 27–32.

Erikson, E. H. (1963). *Childhood and society* (2nd ed.). New York: W. W. Norton & Co.

Erikson, E. H. (1971). A healthy personality for every child. In R. H. Anderson & H. G. Shane (Eds.), *As the twig is bent: Readings in early childhood education*. New York: Houghton Mifflin Co.

Erikson, E. H. (1982). *The life cycle completed: A review*. New York: W. W. Norton & Co.

Escobedo, T. H. (Ed.). (1983). *Early childhood bilingual education: A Hispanic perspective*. New York: Teachers College Press.

Espenschade, A. S., & Eckert, H. M. (1967). *Motor behavior in early childhood: Motor development*. Columbus, Ohio: Merrill Publishing Co.

Ets, M. H., & Labastida, A. (1959). *Nine days to Christmas*. New York: Viking Press.

Eyre, L., & Eyre, R. (1980). *Teaching children joy*. New York: Ballantine Books.

Fassler, J. (1971). *My Grandpa died today*. New York: Behavioral Publications.

Feeney, S. (1988). Ethics case studies: The divorced parents. *Young Children, 43*(3), 48–51.

Fein, G., & Rivkin, M. (Eds.). (1986). *The young child at play: Reviews of research* (Vol. 4). Washington, D.C.: National Association for the Education of Young Children.

Feitelson, D., & Ross, G. (1973). The neglected factor: play. *Human Development, 16*, 202–223.

Feldman, W. W., & Nash, S. C. (1986). Antecedants of early parenting. In A. Fogel & G. F. Melson (Eds.), *Origins of nurturance: Developmental, biological and cultural perspectives of caregiving*. Hillsdale, N.J.: Lawrence Erlbaum Associates, Publishers.

Felt, S. (1950). *Rosa-too-little*. Garden City, N.Y.: Doubleday & Co.

Feree, M. J., & Groppe, C. C. (1975). In F. Cook, C. Groppe, & M. Feree, *Balanced food values and sense* (Pamphlet #2220, pp. 6–7). Berkeley, Calif.: University of California, Division of Agricultural Science.

Ferreira, N. (1982). *Learning through cooking: A cooking program for children two to ten*. Palo Alto, Calif.: R&E Associates.

Fields, M. V., & Lee, D. (1987). *Let's begin reading right: A developmental approach to beginning literacy*. Columbus, Ohio: Merrill Publishing Co.

Flack, M. (1931). *Angus and the cat*. Garden City, N.Y.: Doubleday & Co.

Flack, M. (1932). *Ask Mr. Bear*. New York: Macmillan Publishing Co.

Flemming, B. M., Hamilton, D. S., & Hicks, J. D. (1977). *Resources for creative teaching in early childhood education*. New York: Harcourt Brace Jovanovich.

Forman, G. E., & Hill, F. (1980). *Constructive play: Applying Piaget in the preschool*. Monterey, Calif.: Brooks/Cole Publishing Co.

Fowler, W. (Ed.). (1986). Early experience and the development of competence. In W. Damon (Ed.), *New directions for child development*. San Francisco: Jossey-Bass, Publishers.

Frank, L. (1968). *Play is valid*. Wheaton, Md.: Association for Childhood Education International.

Frankenburg, W. K., Emde, R. N., & Sullivan, J. W. (Eds.). (1985). *Early identification of children at risk: An international perspective*. New York: Plenum Press.

Franklin, M. B., & Biber, B. (1977). Psychological perspectives and early childhood education: Some relations between theory and practice. In L. G. Katz (Ed.), *Current topics in early childhood education*, (Vol. 1). Norwood, N.J.: Ablex Publishing Co.

Frede, E. (1984). *Getting involved: Workshops for parents*. Ypsilanti, Mich.: High/Scope Press.

Friedrich, P., & Friedrich, O. (1957). *The Easter bunny that overslept*. New York: Lothrop, Lee & Shepard Co.

Frost, J. L., & Klein, B. L. (1979). *Children's play and playgrounds*. Boston: Allyn & Bacon.

Frost, J. L., & Sunderlin, S. (Eds.). (1985). *When children play: Proceedings of the International Conference on Play and Play Environments*. Wheaton, Md.: Association for Childhood Education International.

Frost, J. L., & Wortham, S. C. (1988). The evolution of American playgrounds. *Young Children, 43*(5), 19–28.

Fuchs, N. R. (1976). Play therapy at home. In C. Schaefer (Ed.), *The therapeutic use of children's play*. New York: Jason Aronson.

Furman, E. (1974). *A child's parent dies: Studies in childhood bereavement*. New Haven, Conn.: Yale University Press.

Furman, E. (1984). Children's patterns in mourning the death of a loved one. In H. Wass & C. A. Corr (Eds.), *Childhood and death*. Washington, D.C.: Hemisphere Publishing Corp.

Furman, E. (Ed.). (1986). *What nursery school teachers ask us about: Psychoanalytic consultations in preschools*. Madison, Conn.: International Universities Press.

Galinsky, E. (1988). Parents and teacher-caregivers: Sources of tension, sources of support. *Young Children, 43*(3), 4–15.

Gall, M. (1984). Synthesis of research on teacher questioning. *Educational Leadership, 42*(3), 40–47.

Gallagher, J. M., & Coché, J. (1987). Hothousing: The clinical and educational concerns over pressuring young children. *Early Childhood Research Quarterly, 2*(3), 203–210.

Gallahue, D. L. (1982). *Developmental movement experiences for children.* New York: John Wiley & Sons.

Garber, J., & Seligman, M. E. P. (Eds.). (1980). *Human helplessness: Theory and applications.* New York: Academic Press.

Gardner, H. (1980). *Artful scribbles: The significance of children's drawings.* Chicago: Nelson-Hall Publications.

Gardner, H. (1986). Notes on cognitive development: Recent trends, new directions. In S. L. Friedman, K. A. Klivington, & R. W. Peterson (Eds.), *The brain, cognition, and education.* New York: Academic Press.

Gärling, T., & Valsiner, J. (1985). *Children within environments: Toward a psychology of accident prevention.* New York: Plenum Publishing.

Garvey, C. (1983). Some properties of social play. In M. Donaldson, R. Grieve, & C. Pratt (Eds.), *Early childhood development and education: Readings in psychology.* New York: Guilford Press.

Gassier, J. (1984). *A guide to the psycho-motor development of the child.* London: Churchill Livingstone.

Gay, Z. (1955). *What's your name?* New York: Viking Press.

Gearhart, B. R. (1985). *Learning disabilities: Educational strategies* (4th ed.). St. Louis: C. V. Mosby Co.

Gelb, S. A. (1987). Christmas programming in schools: Unintended consequences. *Childhood Education, 64*(1), 9–13.

Gelfer, J. I., & Perkins, P. G. (1987). Effective communication with parents: A process for parent/teacher conferences. *Childhood Education, 64*(1), 19–22.

Genishi, G. (1987). Acquiring oral language and communicative competence. In C. Seefeldt (Ed.), *The early childhood curriculum: A review of current research.* New York: Teachers College Press.

Genishi, C. (1988). Children's language: Learning words from experience. *Young Children, 44*(1), 16–23.

Gesell, A., Halverson, H. M., Thompson, H., Ilg, F., Costner, R., Ames, L. B., & Amatruda, C. S. (1940). *The first five years of life: A guide to the study of the preschool child.* New York: Harper & Row, Publishers.

Gesell Institute. (1987). The Gesell Institute responds. *Young Children, 42*(2), 7–8.

Gestwicki, C. (1987). *Home, school, and community relations: A guide to working with parents.* Albany, N.Y.: Delmar Publishers.

Gibbons, G. (1983). *Thanksgiving day.* New York: Holiday House.

Ginott, H. G. (1965). *Between parent and child: New solutions to old problems.* New York: Macmillan Publishing Co.

Ginott, H. G. (1972). *Teacher and child.* New York: Macmillan Publishing Co.

Ginsberg, S. (1984). *Parenting programs. A paper from the Resource Center in Early Childhood: Reconsidering the essentials: A collection of papers.* New York: Bank Street College.

Glazer, J. I. (1986). *Literature for young children* (2nd ed.). Columbus, Ohio: Merrill Publishing Co.

Glazer, T. (1980). *Do your ears hang low? Fifty more musical fingerplays.* Garden City, N.Y.: Doubleday & Co.

Gnepp, J. (1982). Psychological preparation for children going into the hospital. In J. Klayman & S. Moore (Eds.), *Reviews of research for practitioners and parents* (No. 2). Minneapolis: Center for Early Education, University of Minnesota.

Goble, P. (1978). *The girl who loved wild horses.* Scarsdale, N.Y.: Bradbury Press.

Goffin, S. G. (1987). Cooperative behaviors: They need our support. *Young Children, 42*(2), 75–81.

Goffin, S. G., & Tull, C. (1984). Ideas! Creating possibilities for problem solving. *Dimensions, 12*(2), 15–19.

Gold, D. L. (1987, December 2). "Readiness" goal seen producing harmful policies. *Education Week,* pp. 1 & 6.

Golden, M., Bridger, W. H., & Martare, A. (1974). Social class differences in the ability of young children to use verbal information to facilitate learning. *American Journal of Orthopsychiatry, 44*(1), 86–91.

Goodwin, M. T., & Pollen, G. (1980). *Creative food experiences for children* (rev. ed.). Washington, D.C.: Center for Science in the Public Interest.

Goodwin, W. L., & Driscoll, L. A. (1980). *Handbook for measurement and evaluation in early childhood education.* San Francisco: Jossey-Bass Publishers.

Gordon, S. (1979). *Girls are girls and boys are boys: So what's the difference?* Fayetteville, N.Y.: Ed-U Press.

Gordon, S., & Gordon, J. (1974). *Did the sun shine before you were born?* Fayetteville, N.Y.: Ed-U Press.

Gordon, S., & Gordon, J. (1986). *Raising a child conservatively in a sexually permissive world* (rev. ed.). Fayetteville, N.Y.: Ed-U Press.

Gordon, T. (1976). *P. E. T. in action: Inside P. E. T. families, new problems, insights and solutions in Parent Effectiveness Training.* New York: Peter H. Wyden Publisher.

Gorlitz, D., & Wohlwill, J. F. (Eds.). (1988). *Curiosity, imagination and play: On the development of spontaneous cognitive and motivational processes.* Hillsdale, N.J.: Lawrence Erlbaum Associates, Publishers.

Gottfried, A. W., & Brown, C. C. (Eds.). (1986). *Play interactions: The contribution of play materials and parental involvement to children's development.* Lexington, Mass.: D. C. Heath and Co.

Gowan, J. C., Khatena, J., & Torrance, E. P. (1981). *Creativity: Its educational implications.* Dubuque, Iowa: Kendall/Hunt Publishing Co.

Graham, A. (1976). *Foxtails, ferns and fish scales: A handbook of art and nature projects.* New York: Four Winds Press.

Grantham-McGregor, S. (1987). Field studies in early nutrition and later achievement. In J. Dobbing (Ed.), *Early nutrition and later achievement.* London: Academic Press.

Greater Minneapolis Day Care Association. (1983). *Sick child care: A problem for working parents and employers.* Minneapolis: The Association, 1006 West Lake Street, Minneapolis, Minnesota 55408.

Greenberg, S. (1985). Educational equity in early education environments. In S. S. Klein (Ed.), *Handbook for achieving sex equity through education.* Baltimore, Md.: Johns Hopkins University Press.

Greenman, J. (1988). *Caring spaces, learning places: Children's environments that work.* Redmond, Wash.: The Exchange Press.

Gregory, R. W. (Ed.). (1987). *The Oxford companion to the mind.* New York: Oxford University Press.

Grief, E. B. (1983). Sex differences in parent-child conversations: Who interrupts who? Paper presented at the Biennial Meeting of the Society for Research in Child Development, San Francisco, March 1979 as quoted in Honig, A. S. (1983). Sex role socialization in early childhood. *Young Children, 38*(6), 57–69.

Griffin, E. F. (1982). *Island of childhood: Education in the special world of nursery school.* New York: Teachers College Press.

Grover, E. O. (Ed.). (Originally by F. Richardson). (1971). *Mother Goose: The classic Volland edition.* Long Beach, Calif.: Hubbard Press.

Gruber, H. E., & Vonèche, J. J. (Eds.). (1977). *The essential Piaget.* London: Routledge & Kegan Paul.

Guerney, L. F. (1984). Play therapy in counseling settings. In T. D. Yawkey & A. D. Pellegrini (Eds.), *Child's play: Developmental and applied.* Hillsdale, N.J.: Lawrence Earlbaum Associates.

Guilford, J. P. (1967). *The nature of human intelligence.* New York: McGraw-Hill Book Co.

Guilford, J. P. (1979). *Cognitive psychology with a frame of reference.* San Diego: EdITS, Publishers.

Guilford, J. P. (1981). Developmental characteristics: Factors that aid and hinder creativity. In J. C. Gowan, J. Khatena, & E. P. Torrance (Eds.), *Creativity: Its educational implications* (2nd ed.). Dubuque, Iowa: Kendall/Hunt Publishing Co.

Gustafson, B. E., et al. (1954). The Vipeholm Dental Caries Study: The effect of different levels of carbohydrate intake on dental caries in 436 individuals observed for five years. *Acta Odontol Scandanavia, 11,* 232.

Hagen, J., Lewis, H., & Smilansky, S. (1988). *Clay in the classroom: Helping children develop cognitive and affective skills for learning.* New York: Peter Lang.

Hale, J. E. (1986). *Black children: Their roots, culture, and learning style* (2nd ed.). Baltimore, Md.: Johns Hopkins University Press.

Haley, G. W. (1970). *A story, a story.* New York: Atheneum.

Halpern, D. F. (1986). *Sex differences in cognitive abilities.* Hillsdale, N.J.: Lawrence Erlbaum Associates.

Halpern, R. (1987). Major social and demographic trends affecting young families: Implications for early childhood care and education. *Young Children, 42*(6), 34–40.

Harms, T. (1972). Evaluating settings for learning. In K. R. Baker (Ed.), *Ideas that work with young children.* Washington, D.C.: National Association for the Education of Young Children.

Harms, T., & Clifford, R. M. (1980). *Early childhood environment rating scale.* New York: Teachers College Press.

Harrington, C. (1978). Bilingual education, social stratification and cultural pluralism. *Equal Opportunity Review,* ERIC Clearinghouse on Urban Education, Teachers College, Columbia University.

Harrop, B., Blakely, P., & Gadsby, D. (1981). *Apusskido.* London, England: A&C Black.

Harter, S. (1983). Developmental perspectives on the self-system. In P. H. Mussen (Ed.), *Handbook of child psychology* (4th ed.). E. M. Hetherington (Ed.), *Volume IV: Socialization, personality, and social development.* New York: John Wiley & Sons.

Harter, S. (1985). Competence as a dimension of self-evaluation: Toward a comprehensive model of self-worth. In R. L. Leahy (Ed.), *The development of the self.* New York: Academic Press.

Hartley, R. E., Frank, L. K., & Goldenson, R. M. (1952). *Understanding children's play.* New York: Columbia University Press.

Hartup, W. W. (1983). Peer relations. In P. H. Mussen (Ed.), *Handbook of child psychology.* E. M. Hetherington (Ed.), *Volume IV: Socialization, personality, and social development.* New York: John Wiley & Sons.

Hayes, D. S. (1978). Cognitive bases for liking and disliking among preschool children. *Child Development, 49,* 906–909.

Henderson, R. W., & Bergan, J. R. (1976). *The cultural context of childhood.* Columbus, Ohio: Merrill Publishing Co.

Hendrick, J. (1973). *The cognitive development of the economically disadvantaged Mexican-American and Anglo-American four-year-old: Teaching the concepts of grouping, ordering, perceiving common connections and matching by means of semantic and figural materials.* Unpublished doctoral dissertation, University of California at Santa Barbara.

Hendrick, J. (1988). *The whole child: Developmental education for the early years* (4th ed.). Columbus, Ohio: Merrill Publishing Co.

Henninger, M. L. (1985). Preschool children's play behaviors in an indoor and outdoor environment. In J. L. Frost & S. Sunderlin (Eds.), *When children play.* Wheaton, Md.: Association for Childhood Education International.

Herberholz, B., & Hanson, L. (1985). *Early childhood art* (3rd ed.). Dubuque, Iowa: William C. Brown, Publisher.

Herriot, P. (1987). Language development in children. In R. L. Gregory (Ed.), *The Oxford companion to the mind.* Oxford, England: Oxford University Press.

Hertz, O. (1981). *Tobias has a birthday.* Minneapolis: Carolrhoda Books.

Hess, R. D. (1970). Social class and ethnic influences upon socialization. In P. H. Mussen (Ed.), *Carmichael's manual of child psychology* (3rd ed., Vol. 2). New York: John Wiley & Sons.

Hetherington, E. M. (Ed.). (1983). *Volume IV: Socialization, personality and social development.* In P. H. Mussen (Ed.), *Handbook of child psychology.* New York: John Wiley & Sons.

Hewes, J. J. (1974). *Build your own playground: A sourcebook of play sculptures, designs, and concepts from the work of Jay Beckwith.* Boston: Houghton Mifflin Co.

Higgins, S. O. (1984). *The pumpkin book: Full of Halloween history, poems, songs, art projects, games and recipes.* Shasta, Calif.: Pumpkin Press.

Hildebrand, V. (1984). *Management of child development centers.* New York: Macmillan Publishing Co.

Hildebrand, V. (1986). *Introduction to early childhood education* (4th ed.). New York: Macmillan Publishing Co.

Hill, C. A. (1977). A review of the language deficit position: Some sociolinguistic and psycholinguistic perspectives. *IRCD Bulletin, 12*(4), 1–13.

Hill, D. M. (1977). *Mud, sand, and water.* Washington, D.C.: National Association for the Education of Young Children.

Hills, T. W. (1987). Children in the fast lane: Implications for early childhood policy and practice. *Early Childhood Research Quarterly, 23,* 265–273.

Hinde, R. S., & Stevenson-Hinde, J. (Eds.). (1988). *Relationships within families: Mutual influences.* Oxford, England: Clarendon Press.

Hines, A. G. (1987). *It's just me, Emily.* New York: Ticknor and Fields.

Hirsch, E. S. (Ed.). (1984). *The block book* (rev. ed.). Washington, D.C.: National Association for the Education of Young Children.

Hoban, R. (1960). *Bedtime for Frances.* New York: Harper & Row, Publishers.

Hoban, R. (1964). *Bread and jam for Frances.* New York: Harper & Row, Publishers.

Hoepfner, R., Stern, C. & Nummedal, S. G. (1971). *CSE-ECRC preschool/kindergarten test evaluations.* Los Angeles: School Evaluation Project, Center for the Study of Evaluation and the Early Childhood Research Center, UCLA Graduate School of Education.

Hoffman, M. L. (1970). Moral development. In P. H. Mussen (Ed.), *Carmichael's manual of child psychology* (3rd ed., vol. 2). New York: John Wiley & Sons.

Hohmann, M., Banet, B., & Weikart, D. P. (1970). *Young children in action: A manual for preschool educators.* Ypsilanti, Mich.: High/Scope Educational Research Foundation.

Holman, J., Goetz, E. M., & Baer, D. M. (1976). The training of creativity as an operant and an examination of its generalization characteristics. In B. C. Etzel, J. M. LeBlanc, & D. M. Baer (Eds.), *New developments in behavioral research: Theory, method, and application.* Hillsdale, N.J.: Lawrence Erlbaum Associates.

Honig, A. (1979). *Parent involvement in early childhood education.* Washington, D.C.: National Association for the Education of Young Children.

Honig, A. S. (1983). Sex role socialization in early childhood. *Young Children, 38*(6), 57–70.

Honig, A. S. (1985a). Compliance, control, and discipline. *Young Children, 40*(2), 50–58.

Honig, A. S. (1985b). Compliance, control, and discipline. *Young children, 40*(3), 49–51.

Honig, A. S., & Wittmer, D. S. (1982). Teachers and low-income toddlers in metropolitan day care. *Early Child Development and Care, 10*(1), 95–112.

Hough, R. A., Nurss, J. R., & Wood, D. (1987). Making opportunities for elaborated language in early childhood classrooms. *Young Children, 43*(1), 6–12.

Humphrey, J. D. (Ed.). (1984). *Stress in childhood.* New York: AMS Press.

Humphreys, D. (1951). *Animals every child should know.* New York: Grosset & Dunlap Publishers.

Hunt, J. McV. (1986, June). The effects of variation in quality and type of early child care on development. In W. Fowler (Ed.), Early experience and the development of competence. *New Directions in Child Development, 32.*

Hunt, J. McV., & Kirk, G. E. (1971). Social aspects of intelligence: Evidence and issues. In R. Cancro (Ed.), *Intelligence and environmental influences.* New York: Grune & Stratton.

Hunter, I., & Judson, M. (1977). *Simple folk instruments to make and play.* New York: Simon & Schuster.

Huston, A. C. (1983). Sex-typing. In P. H. Mussen (Ed.), *Handbook of child psychology.* E. M. Hetherington (Ed.), *Volume IV: Socialization, personality, and social development.* New York: John Wiley & Sons.

Hutchings, J. J. (1988). Pediatric AIDS: An overview. *Children Today, 17*(3), 4–7.

Hutchins, P. (1986). *The doorbell rang.* New York; Greenwillow Books.

Hymes, J. L. (1981). *Teaching the child under six* (3rd ed.). Columbus, Ohio: Merrill Publishing Co.

Hyson, M. C., Whitehead, L. C., & Prudhoe, C. M. (1988). Influences on attitudes toward physical affection between adults and children. *Early Childhood Research Quarterly 3*(1), 55–75.

Interracial Books for Children: Bulletin. (1986). Bilingual education and equity. *The Bulletin, 17*(3 & 4).

Isaacs, S. (1986). *Who's in control? A parent's guide to discipline.* New York: Putnam Publishing Group.

Iwasaki, C. (1968). *Staying home alone on a rainy day.* New York: McGraw-Hill Book Co.

Jacobson, E. (1976). *You must relax* (5th ed.). New York: McGraw-Hill Book Co.

Jalongo, M. R. (1983). Using crisis-oriented books with young children. *Young Children, 38*(50), 29–36.

Jalongo, M. R. (1987). Do security blankets belong in preschool? *Young Children, 42*(3), 3–8.

James, J. C., & Granovetter, R. F. (1987). *Water works: A new book of water play activities for children ages 1 to 6.* Lewisville, N.C.: Kaplan Press.

Janice. (1967). *Little bear's Thanksgiving.* New York: Lothrop, Lee & Shepard.

Javernick, E. (1988). Johnny's not jumping: Can we help obese children? *Young Children, 43*(2), 18–23.

Jenkins, E. (1966). *The Ella Jenkins song book for children.* New York: Oak Publications.

Jenkins, E. C., & Austin, M. C. (1987). *Literature for children about Asians and Asian Americans: Analysis and annotated bibliography with additional readings for adults.* Westport, Conn.: Greenwood Press.

Jenkins, J. K., & Macdonald, R. (1979). *Growing up equal: Activities and resources for parents and teachers of young children.* Englewood Cliffs, N.J.: Prentice-Hall.

Jensen, A. R. (1969). How much can we boost I.Q. and scholastic achievement? *Harvard Educational Review, 39*(1).

Jervis, K. (1987). *Separation strategies for helping two to four year olds.* Los Angeles: Reiss Davis Clinic.

Jewell, N. (1972). *The snuggle bunny.* New York: Harper & Row, Publishers.

Joffe, C. E. (1977). *Friendly intruders: Childcare professionals and family life.* Berkeley, Calif.: University of California Press.

Johnson, H. W. (1979). *Preschool test descriptions: Test matrix and correlated test descriptors.* Springfield, Ill.: Charles C Thomas, Publisher.

Johnson, J. E., Christie, J. F., & Yawkey, T. D. (1987). *Play and early childhood development.* Glenview, Ill.: Scott, Foresman and Co.

Johnson, J. E., & Ershler, J. (1982). Curricular effects on the play of preschoolers. In D. J. Pepler & K. H. Rubin (Eds.), *The play of children: Current theory and research.* Basel, Switzerland: S. Karger.

Joiner, L. M. (1977). *A technical analysis of the variation in screening instruments and programs in New York State.* New York: City University of New York. (New York Center for Advanced Study in Education. ED 154 596)

Jones, D. P. H., & McGraw, J. M. (1987). Reliable and fictitious accounts of sexual abuse to children. *Journal of Interpersonal Violence, 2*(1), 27–45.

Jones, E. (1977). *Dimensions of teaching-learning environments: Handbook for teachers.* Pasadena, Calif.: Pacific Oaks.

Jones, E., & Prescott, E. (1978). *Dimensions of teaching learning environments. II: Focus on day care.* Pasadena, Calif.: Pacific Oaks.

Kamii, C. (1972). A sketch of the Piaget-derived preschool curriculum developed by the Ypsilanti Early Education Program. In S. J. Braun & E. P. Edwards (Eds.), *History and theory of early childhood education.* Worthington, Ohio: Charles A. Jones Publishing Co.

Kamii, C. (1985). *Young children reinvent arithmetic: Implications of Piaget's theory.* New York: Teachers College Press.

Kane, D. N. (1985). *Environmental hazards to young children.* Phoenix: Oryx Press.

Kane, J. A. (1985). *Art through nature: An integrated approach to art and nature study with young children.* Holmes Beach, Fla.: LP Learning Program.

Kantrowitz, M. (1973). *When Violet died.* New York: Parent's Magazine Press.

Katz, L. (1975). *The second collection of papers for teachers.* Urbana, Ill.: College of Education, University of Illinois.

Katz, L. G. (1977, October). What is basic for young children? *Childhood Education,* p. 18.

Katz, P. A. (1982). Development of children's racial awareness and intergroup attitudes. In L. G. Katz (Ed.), *Current topics in early childhood education* (Vol. 4). Norwood, N.J.: Ablex Publishing Corp.

Keats, E. J. (1962). *The snowy day.* New York: Viking Press.

Keats, E. J. (1964). *Whistle for Willie.* New York: Viking Press.

Keats, E. J. (1968). *A letter to Amy.* New York: Harper & Row, Publishers.

Kelly, F. J. (1981). Guiding groups of parents of young children. *Young Children, 37*(1), 28–32.

Kelly, N. T., & Kelly, B. J. (1985). *Physical education for pre-school and primary grades.* Springfield, Ill.: Charles C Thomas.

Kendrick, A. S., Kaufmann, R., & Messenger, K. P. (Eds.). (1988). *Healthy young children: A manual for programs.* Washington, D.C.: National Association for the Education of Young Children.

Kent, J. (1969). *The Christmas piñata.* New York: Parents Magazine Press.

Kessler, J. W. (1966). *Psychopathology of childhood.* Englewood Cliffs, N.J.: Prentice-Hall.

Kinsey, A. C., Pomeroy, W. B., & Martin, C. E. (1948). *Sexual behavior in the human male.* Philadelphia: W. B. Saunders.

Kinsey, A. C., Pomeroy, W. B., Martin, C. E., & Gebhard, P. H. (1953). *Sexual behavior in the human female.* Philadelphia: W. B. Saunders.

Kitano, H. H. L., & Daniels, R. (1988). *Asian Americans: Emerging minorities.* Englewood Cliffs, N.J.: Prentice-Hall.

Klein, G. (1985). *Reading into racism: Bias in children's literature and learning materials.* London: Routledge & Kegan Paul.

Kliman, A. S. (1978). *Crisis: Psychological first aid for recovery and growth.* New York: Holt, Rinehart & Winston.

Knight, F. D. (1962). *The Ebony cookbook: A date with a dish.* Chicago: Johnson Publishing Co.

Knowles, D., & Reeves, N. (1983). *But won't Granny need her socks? Dealing effectively with children's concerns about death and dying.* Dubuque, Iowa: Kendall/Hunt Publishing Co.

Koblinsky, S. A. (1983). *Sexuality education for parents of young children: A facilitator training manual.* Fayetteville, N.Y.: Ed-U Press.

Koblinsky, S. A., Atkinson, J., & Davis, S. (1980). Sex education with young children. *Young Children, 36*(1), 21–31.

Koblinsky, S. A., & Behana, N. (1984). Child sexual abuse: The educator's role in prevention, detection, and intervention. *Young Children, 39*(6), 3–15.

Kohlberg, L. (1978). Revision in the theory and practice of moral development. In W. Damon (Ed.), *New directions for child development: Moral development* (Vol. 2). San Francisco: Jossey-Bass, Publishers.

Kohlberg, L. (1985). *Essays on moral development: Vol. II. The psychology of moral development, the nature and validity of moral stages.* San Francisco: Harper & Row.

Kontos, S. (1984). Congruence of parenting and early childhood staff perceptions of parenting. *Parenting Studies, 1*(1), 5–10.

Kontos, S. (1986). What preschool children know about reading, and how they learn it. *Young Children, 42*(1), 58–66.

Kontos, S., & Wells, W. (1986). Attitudes of caregivers and the day care experiences of families. *Early Childhood Research Quarterly, 1*(1), 47–67.

Koocher, G. P. (1973). Childhood, death and cognitive development. *Developmental Psychology, 9*(3), 369–375.

Kornhaber, A. (1983). Grandparents are coming of age in America. *Children Today, 12*(4), 31.

Krauss, R. (1950). *The backward day.* New York: Harper & Row, Publishers.

Krauss, R. & Johnson, C. (1971). *The carrot seed.* New York: Scholastic Books.

Kritchevsky, S., Prescott, E., & Walling, L. (1969). *Planning environments for young children: Physical space.* Washington, D.C.: National Association for the Education of Young Children.

Kroll, S. (1984). *The biggest pumpkin ever.* New York: Scholastic Books.

Kübler-Ross, E. (1969). *On death and dying: What the dying have to teach doctors, nurses, clergy and their own families.* New York: Macmillan Publishing Co.

Labov, W. (1970). The logic of nonstandard English. In F. Williams (Ed.), *Language and poverty.* Chicago: Markham Publishing Co.

Lally, J. R., & Honig, A. S. (1977). The family development research program. In M. Day & R. Parker (Eds.),

The preschool in action (2nd ed.). New York: Allyn & Bacon.

Landek, B. (1950). *Songs to grow on: A collection of American folksongs for children.* New York: William Sloane Associates.

Langstaff, N., & Sproul, A. (1979) *Exploring with clay.* Wheaton, Md.: Association for Childhood Education International.

Lasky, L., & Mukerji, R. (1980). *Art: Basic for young children.* Washington, D.C.: National Association for the Education of Young Children.

Lay-Dopyera, M., & Dopyera, J. E. (1987). Strategies for teaching. In C. Seefeldt (Ed.), *The early childhood curriculum: A review of current research.* New York: Teachers College Press.

Lazar, I., Darlington, R., Murray, H., Royce, J., & Snipper, A. (1982). Lasting effects of early education: A report from the Consortium for Longitudinal Studies. *Monographs of the Society for Research in Child Development 47*(2–3, No. 195).

Leacock, E. (1982). The influence of teacher attitudes on children's classroom performance: Case studies. In D. M. Borman (Ed.), *The social life of children in a changing society.* Hillsdale, N.J.: Lawrence Erlbaum Associates.

Lee, B. N., & Merrill, M. D. (1972). *Writing complete affective objectives: A short course.* Belmont, Calif.: Wadsworth Publishing Co.

Leeper, S. H., Witherspoon, R. L., & Day, B. (1984). *Good schools for young children* (5th ed.). New York: Macmillan Publishing Co.

Leifer, A. D., & Lesser, G. S. (1976). *The development of career awareness in young children.* NIE papers on education and work: Number one. Washington, D.C.: United States Department of Health, Education, and Welfare, National Institute of Education.

Lemley, V., & Lemley, J. (1975). *Zucchini cookbook.* Escondido, Calif.: Wilderness House.

LeShan, E. J. (1971). *The conspiracy against childhood.* New York: Atheneum Publishers.

Lewis, A. G. (1975). *Lotions, soaps and scents.* Minneapolis: Lerner Publications.

Lichtenstein, R., & Ireton, H. (1984). *Preschool screening: Identifying young children with developmental and educational problems.* New York: Grune & Stratton.

Lima, C. W. (1982). *A to zoo: Subject access to children's picture books.* New York: R. R. Bowker Co.

Lindberg, L. (no date). *Facility design for early childhood programs: An NAEYC resource guide.* Washington, D.C.: National Association for the Education of Young Children.

Lindfors, J. W. (1987). *Children's language and learning* (2nd ed.). Englewood Cliffs, N.J.: Prentice-Hall.

Lonetto, R. (1980). *Children's conceptions of death.* New York: Springer Publishing Co.

Lovell, G., & Harms, T. (1985). How can playgrounds be improved: A rating scale. *Young Children, 40*(3), 3–8.

Low, V. (1982). *The unimpressible race: A century of education struggle by the Chinese in San Francisco.* San Francisco: East/West Publishing Co.

Lubeck, S. (1984). Kinship and classrooms: An ethnographic perspective on education as cultural transmission. *Sociology of Education, 57*(October), 219–232.

Lubeck, S. (1985). *Sandbox society: Early education in black and white America.* Philadelphia: The Falmer Press.

Lystad, M. (1973). *Hallowe'en parade.* New York: George Putnam's Sons.

Maccoby, E. E. (1980). *Social development: Psychological growth and the parent-child relationship.* New York: Harcourt Brace Jovanovich.

Maccoby, E. E., & Jacklin, C. N. (1987). Gender segregation in childhood. In H. W. Reese (Ed.), *Advances in child development and behavior* (Vol. 20). New York: Academic Press.

Maccoby, E. E., & Martin, J. A. (1983). Socialization in the context of the family: Parent-child interaction. In P. H. Mussen (Ed.), *Handbook of child psychology.* M. B. Hetherington (Ed.), *Vol. IV: Socialization, personality, and social development.* New York: John Wiley & Sons.

MacDonald, M. R. (Ed.). (1982). *Storytellers' sourcebook: A subject, title and motif index to folklore collections for children.* Detroit: Gale Research Co.

MacFarlane, K., Waterman, J., Conerly, S., Damon, L., Durfee, M., & Long, S. (1986). *Sexual abuse of young children: Evaluation and treatment.* New York: The Guilford Press.

Macpherson, E. H. (1962). *A tale of tails.* New York: Golden Press.

Magee, M. S., & Sutton-Smith, B. (1983). The art of storytelling: How do children learn it? *Young Children, 38*(4), 4–12.

Maratsos, M. (1983). Some current issues in the study of the acquisition of grammar. In P. H. Mussen (Ed.), *Handbook of child psychology.* J. H. Flavell and E. M. Markman (Eds.), *Volume III: Cognitive development.* New York: John Wiley & Sons.

Marion, M. (1987). *Guidance of young children* (2nd ed.). Columbus, Ohio: Merrill Publishing Co.

Marston, L. (1984). *Playground equipment: Do-it-yourself, indestructible, practically free.* Jefferson, N.C.: McFarland and Co.

Martorella, P. H. (1975). Selected early childhood affective learning programs: An analysis of theories, structure and consistency. *Young Children, 30*(4), 289–301.

Maxim, G. (1989). *The very young* (3rd ed.). Columbus, Ohio: Merrill Publishing Co.

May, R. (1977). *The meaning of anxiety* (rev. ed.). New York: W. W. Norton & Co.

Mayle, P. (1973). *Where did I come from?* Secaucus, N.J.: Lyle Stuart.

McAfee, O. (1981). Planning the preschool program. In M. Kaplan-Sanoff & R. Yablans-Magid (Eds.), *Exploring early childhood: Readings in theory and practice.* New York: Macmillan Publishing Co.

McAfee, O. D. (1985). Circle time: Getting past "Two Little Pumpkins." *Young Children, 40*(6), 24–29.

McCartney, K. (1984). Effect of quality of day care environment on children's language development. *Developmental Psychology, 20*(2), 244–260.

McClenahan, P., & Jaqua, I. (1976). *Cool cooking for kids: Recipes and nutrition for preschoolers.* Belmont, Calif.: Fearon Pitman Publishers.

McClosky, R. (1948). *Blueberries for Sal.* New York: Viking Press.

McGinnis, K., & Oehlberg, B. (1988). *Starting out right: Nurturing young children as peacemakers.* Oak Park, Ill.: Meyer, Stone, and Co.

McKee, J. S. (Ed.). (1986). *Play: Working partner of growth.* Wheaton, Md.: Association for Childhood Education International.

McLaughlin, E., & Wood, L. (1973). *Sing a song of people.* Glendale, Calif.: Bowmar.

Mcloughlin, C. S., & Gullo, D. F. (1985). *Young children in context: Impact of self, family and society on development.* Springfield, Ill.: Charles C Thomas.

McNeill, D. (1970). The development of language. In P. H. Mussen (Ed.), *Carmichael's manual of child psychology* (3rd ed., Vol. 1). New York: John Wiley & Sons.

McNeill, E., Schmidt, V., & Allen, J. (1981). *Cultural awareness for young children: Asian, Black, cowboy, Eskimo, Mexican, and Native American cultures.* Mt. Rainier, Md.: Gryphon House.

Meisels, S. J. (1985). *Developmental screening in early childhood: A guide* (rev. ed.). Washington, D.C.: National Association for the Education of Young Children.

Meisels, S. J. (1987). Uses and abuses of developmental screening and school readiness testing. *Young Children, 42*(2), 4–6, 68–73.

Merahn, S., Shelov, S., & McCracken, G. H. (1988). Special report: AIDS: What teachers, directors and parents want to know. *Pre-K Today, 2*(6), A1–A7.

Mercer, J. R. (1972). I.Q. the lethal label. *Psychology Today, 6*(4), 44–97.

Michigan Department of Education. (1984). *Superintendent's Study Group on Early Childhood Education.* Lansing, Mich.: The Department.

Miles, M. (1971). *Annie and the old one.* Boston: Little, Brown & Co.

Milhous, K. (1950). *The egg tree.* New York: John Scribner's Sons.

Miller, B. L., & Wilmshurst, A. L. (1975). *Parents and volunteers in the classroom: A handbook for teachers.* San Francisco: R&E Associates.

Miller, C. S. (1984). Building self-control: Discipline for young children. *Young Children, 40*(1), 15–19.

Miller, E. (1972). *Mousekin's golden house.* Englewood Cliffs, N.J.: Prentice-Hall.

Miller, J.B., & Miller, K. M. (1979). Informed purchasing can stretch short dollars. *Young Children, 34*(6), 15–20.

Miller, K. (1989). *The outside play and learning book: Activities for young children.* Mount Rainier, Md.: Gryphon House.

Minuchin, P. P., & Shapiro, E. K. (1983). The school as a context for social development. In P. H. Mussen (Ed.), *Handbook of child psychology.* E. M. Hetherington (Ed.), *Vol. IV: Socialization, personality, and social development.* New York: John Wiley & Sons.

Mitchell, G. (1982). *A very practical guide to discipline with young children.* Marshfield, Mass.: Telshare Publishing.

Mitchell, J. (Ed.). (1985). *The 9th mental measurements yearbook.* Lincoln, Nebr.: University of Nebraska Press.

Mitchell, L. S. (1921). *Here and now story book.* New York: E. P. Dutton.

Monighan-Nourot, P., Scales, B., Van Hoorn, J. V., & Almy, M. (1987). *Looking at children's play: A bridge between theory and practice.* New York: Teachers College Press.

Moore, C. C. (1961). *The night before Christmas.* New York: Grosset & Dunlap.

Moore, N. R. (Ed.). (1983). *Free and inexpensive learning materials* (21st ed.). Nashville: George Peabody College for Teachers. (Distributed by Incentive Publications.)

Moore, S. G. (1982). Prosocial behavior in the early years: Parent and peer influences. In B. Spodek (Ed.), *Handbook of research in early childhood education.* New York: The Free Press.

Morningstar, M. (1986). *Growing with dance: Developing through creative dance from ages two to six.* Point Roberts, Wash.: Windborne Publications.

Morrison, G. (1988). *Early childhood education today* (4th ed.). Columbus, Ohio: Merrill Publishing Co.

Moustakas, C. (1959). *Psychotherapy with children.* New York: Ballantine Books.

Moustakas, C. E. (1966). *The authentic teacher: Sensitivity and awareness in the classroom.* Cambridge, Mass.: Howard A. Doyle.

Murphy, L. B. (1962). *The widening world of childhood.* New York: Basic Books.

Murphy, L. B. (1987). Further reflections on resilience. In E. J. Anthony & B. J. Cohler (Eds.), *The invulnerable child.* New York: The Guilford Press.

Murphy, L. B., & Moriarty, A. E. (1976). *Vulnerability, coping and growth from infancy to adolescence.* New Haven, Conn.: Yale University Press.

National Association for the Education of Young Children. (1984). *Accreditation criteria & procedures of the National Academy of Early Childhood Programs.* Washington, D.C.: The Association.

National Association for the Education of Young Children. (1987). *Child care center diseases and sick child care* (rev. ed.). Washington, D.C.: The Association.

National Association for the Education of Young Children. (1988). NAEYC position statement on standardized testing of young children 3 through 8 years of age. *Young Children, 43*(3), 42–47.

National Commission on Excellence in Education. (1983). *A nation at risk: The imperative for education reforms.* Washington, D.C.: United States Department of Education.

National Institute of Neurological Diseases and Stroke. (1967). *Learning to talk: Speech, hearing and language problems in the pre-school child.* Washington, D.C.: United States Department of Health, Education and Welfare.

Nelson, E. (1987). Learned helplessness and children's achievement. In S. Moore & K. Kolb (Eds.), *Reviews of research for practitioners and parents.* Minneapolis: Center for Early Education and Development, University of Minnesota.

Nelson, M., & Clark, K. (Eds.). (1986). *The educator's guide to preventing child sexual abuse.* Santa Cruz, Calif.: Network Publications.

Neugebauer, B. (Ed.). (1987). *Alike and different: Exploring our humanity with young children.* Redmond, Wash.: Exchange Press.

Neuman, D. B. (1978). *Experiences in science for young children.* Albany, N.Y.: Delmar Publishers.

Newberger, C., Melnicoe, L., & Newberger, E. (1986). The American family in crisis: Implications for children. *Current Problems in Pediatrics, 16*(12), 671–737.

Newberry, C. T. (1942). *Marshmallow.* New York: Harper & Row, Publishers.

New York Times. (1988, June 19). Working mothers. *The Times*, p. 33.

Nilsson, L. (1975). *How was I born?* New York: Delacourt Press.

Northwest Regional Education Laboratory Center for Sex Equity. *Guide to nonsexist teaching activities* (K–12). Phoenix: Oryx Press.

Noyes, D. (1987). Indoor pollutants: Environmental hazards to young children. *Young Children, 42*(6), 57–65.

Numeroff, L. J. (1985). *If you give a mouse a cookie.* New York: Harper & Row, Publishers.

Oakley, M. (1984). The year we had Aaron. In J. L. Thomas (Ed.), *Death and dying in the classroom: Readings for reference.* Phoenix: Oryx Press.

Oken-Wright, P. (1988). Show-and-tell grows up. *Young Children, 43*(2), 52–58.

Oklahoma City-County Health Department. (1988). *Important information about Haemophilus Influenzae Type B (HIB) The b-capsa I vaccine (Haemophilus b Polysaccharide Vaccine).* Oklahoma City: The Health Department.

Opie, I., & Opie, P. (1969). *Children's games in street and playground.* Oxford, England: Clarendon Press.

Opie, I., & Opie P. (1980). *A nursery companion.* Oxford, England: Oxford University Press.

Orlick, T. (1982). *The second cooperative sports & games book.* New York: Pantheon Books.

Ornstein, R. (1977). *The psychology of consciousness* (2nd ed.). New York: Harcourt Brace Jovanovich.

Ornstein, R. (1978). The split and whole brain. *Human Nature, 1*(5), 76–83.

Oxford Scientific Films. (1980). *The wild rabbit.* New York: G. P. Putnam's Sons.

Paley, V. (1981). *Wally's stories.* Cambridge, Mass.: Harvard University Press.

Pangrazi, R. P., & Dauer, V. P. (1981). *Movement in early childhood and primary education.* Minneapolis: Burgess Publishing Co.

Pardeck, J. A., & Pardeck, J. T. (1986). *Books for early childhood: A developmental perspective.* New York: Greenwood Press.

Parke, R. D., & Slaby, R. G. (1983). The development of aggression. In P. H. Mussen (Ed.), *Handbook of child psychology* (4th ed.). E. M. Hetherington (Ed.), *Vol. IV: Socialization, personality, and social development.* New York: John Wiley & Sons.

Parkinson, K. (1986). *The enormous turnip.* Niles, Ill.: Albert Whitman and Co.

Parsons, V. (1975). *Ring for liberty.* New York: Golden Press.

Parten, M. (1932). Social participation among preschool children. *Journal of Abnormal Psychology, 27,* 243–269.

Patterson, G. R. (1986). Maternal rejection: Determinant or product for deviant child behavior? In W. W. Hartup & Z. Rubin (Eds.), *Relationships and development.* Hillsdale, N.J.: Lawrence Erlbaum Associates.

Patterson, G. R., Littman, R. A., & Bricker, W. (1967). Assertive behavior in children: A step toward a theory of aggression. *Monographs of the Society for Research in Child Development, 32*(5, No. 113).

Paulston, C. B. (Ed.). (1987). *International handbook of bilingualism and bilingual education.* New York: Greenwood Press.

Pellowski, A. (1984). *The story vine: A source book of unusual and easy-to-tell stories from around the world.* New York: Macmillan Publishing Co.

Peltz, P. S., & Rossol, M. S. (1984). *Children's art supplies can be toxic.* New York: Center for Occupational Hazards.

Pepler, D. J. (1982). Play and divergent thinking. In D. J. Pepler & K. H. Rubin (Eds.), *The play of children: Current theory and research.* Basel, Switzerland: S. Karger.

Pepler, D. J., & Ross, H. S. (1981). The effects of play on convergent and divergent problem solving. *Child Development, 52,* 1202–1210.

Petersham, M., and Petersham, M. (1950). *The circus baby.* New York: Macmillan Publishing Co.

Pflaum, S. W. (1986). *The development of language and literacy in young children.* (3rd ed.). Columbus, Ohio: Merrill Publishing Co.

Pfluger, L. W., & Zola, J. M. (1972). A room planned by children. In K. R. Baker (Ed.), *Ideas that work with young children.* Washington, D.C.: National Association for the Education of Young Children.

Philips, S. U. (1983). *The invisible culture: Communication in classroom and community on the Warm Springs Indian Reservation.* New York: Longman.

Phyfe-Perkins, E., & Shoemaker, J. (1986). Indoor play environments: Research and design implications. In G. Fein & M. Rivkin (Eds.), *The young child at play: Reviews of research* (Vol. 4). Washington, D.C.: National Association for the Education of Young Children.

Piaget, J. (1952). *The child's conception of number.* New York: Humanities Press.

Piaget, J. (1954). *The construction of reality in the child.* New York: Basic Books.

Piaget, J. (1962). *Play, dreams and imitation in childhood.* New York: W. W. Norton & Co.

Piaget, J. (1976a). Piaget's theory. In P. B. Neubauer (Ed.), *The process of child development.* New York: Jason Aronson.

Piaget, J. (1976b). Symbolic play. In J. S. Bruner, A. Jolly, & K. Sylva (Eds.), *Play—Its role in development and evolution.* New York: Basic Books.

Piaget, J. (1976c). *To understand is to invent.* New York: Penguin Books.

Piaget, J. (1983). Piaget's theory. In P. H. Mussen (Ed.), *Handbook of child psychology.* W. Kessen (Ed.), *Volume I: History, theory and methods.* New York: John Wiley & Sons.

Piaget, J., & Inhelder, B. (1969). *The psychology of the child.* New York: Basic Books.

Pipes, P. L. (1985). *Nutrition in infancy and childhood.* St. Louis: C. V. Mosby Co.

Pitcher, E. B., Feinberg, S. G., & Alexander, D. (1989). *Helping young children learn* (5th ed.). Columbus, Ohio: Merrill Publishing Co.

Pogrebin, L. C. (1980). *Growing up free: Raising your child in the 80s.* New York: McGraw Hill Book Co.

Politi, L. (1973). *The nicest gift.* New York: Charles Scribner's Sons.

Popovich, D. (1981). *Effective educational and behavioral programming for severely and profoundly handicapped students: A manual for teachers and aides.* Baltimore: Paul H. Brookes Publishing Co.

Potter, B. (1903). *The tale of Peter rabbit.* New York: Franklin Warne.

Potter, M. C. (1955). Sleepy kitten. *The golden book of little verses.* New York: Simon & Schuster.

Powell, D. R. (1986). Research in review: Parent education and support programs. *Young Children, 41*(3), 47–53.

Powell, G. J. (1983). *The psychosocial development of minority group children.* New York: Brunner/Mazel.

Prelutsky, C. (Ed.). (1986). *Read aloud rhymes for the very young.* New York: Alfred A. Knopf.

Prescott, E. (1984). The physical setting in day care. In J. T. Greenman & R. W. Fuqua (Eds.), *Making day care better: Training, evaluation, and the process of change.* New York: Teachers College Press.

Prescott, E., Jones, E., & Kritchevsky, S. (1972). *Environmental inventory*. Pasadena, Calif.: Pacific Oaks.

Provenzo, E. F., Jr., & Brett, A. (1983). *The complete block book*. Syracuse, N.Y.: Syracuse University Press.

Quinton, D., & Rutter, M. (1988). *Parenting breakdown: The making and breaking of inter-generational links*. Aldershot, England: Avebury.

Quinsenberry, J. D. (Ed.). (1982). *Changing family lifestyles: Their effect on children*. Washington, D.C.: Association for Childhood Education International.

Raper, J., & Aldridge, J. (1988). What every teacher should know about AIDS. *Childhood Education, 64*(3), 146–149.

Rasmussen, M. (1979). *Listen! The children speak*. Washington, D.C.: Organisation Mondiale pour l'Education Prescolaire, United States National Committee, Region III.

Rathbone, J. L. (1969). *Relaxation*. Philadelphia: Lea & Febiger.

Ramey, C. T., Holmberg, M. C., Sparling, J. J., & Collier, A. M. (1977). An introduction to the Carolina Abecedarian Project. In B. M. Caldwell & D. J. Stedman (Eds.), *Infant education for handicapped children*. New York: Walker.

Read, K., Gardner, P., & Mahler, B. C. (1987). *Early childhood programs: Human relationships and learning* (8th ed.). New York: Holt, Rinehart & Winston.

Rebok, G. W. (1987). *Life-span cognitive development*. New York: Holt, Rinehart & Winston.

Redleaf, R. (1983). *Open the door: Let's explore*. Mt. Rainier, Md.: Toys 'n Things Press (Gryphon House, distributor.)

Reifel, S. (1984). Block construction: Children's developmental landmarks in representation of space. *Young Children, 40*(1), 61–67.

Restak, R. M. (1988). *The mind*. New York: Bantam Books.

Rey, H. A. (1941). *Curious George*. Boston: Houghton Mifflin Co.

Rey, H. A., & Rey, M. (1966). *Curious George goes to the hospital*. Boston: Houghton Mifflin Company.

Reynolds, C. (Ed.) (1984). *Perspectives on bias in mental testing*. New York: Plenum Press.

Rholes, W. S., Blackwell, J., Jordan, C., & Walters, C. (1980). A developmental study of learned helplessness. *Developmental Psychology, 16*, 616–624.

Richardson, L. I., Goodman, K. L., Hartman, N. N., & LePique, H. C. (1980). *A mathematics activity curriculum for early childhood and special education*. New York: Macmillan Publishing Co.

Riggs, M. L. (1980). *Movement education for preschool children*. Reston, Va.: American Alliance for Health, Physical Education, Recreation and Dance.

Rights, M. (1981). *Beastly neighbors: All about wild things in the city, or why earwigs make good neighbors*. Boston: Little, Brown & Co.

Riley, S. S. (1984). *How to generate values in young children*. Washington, D.C.: National Association for the Education of Young Children.

Riley, S. S. (1989). Pilgrimage to Elmwood Cemetery. *Young Children, 44*(2), 33–36.

Roberts, E. M. (1950). The rabbit. *Under the tree*. New York: Viking Press.

Rockwell, A. (1985). *First comes spring*. New York: Thomas Y. Crowell.

Rockwell, A., & Rockwell, H. (1971). *Molly's woodland garden*. Garden City, N.Y.: Doubleday & Co.

Rockwell, R. E., Sherwood, E. A., & Williams, R. A. (1983). *Hug a tree and other things to do outdoors with young children*. Mt. Rainier, Md.: Gryphon House.

Rogers, C. S., & Sawyers, J. K. (1988). *Play in the lives of children*. Washington, D.C.: National Association for the Education of Young Children.

Rojankovsky, F. (1982). *The great big animal book*. New York: Golden Press.

Roopnarine, J. L., & Johnson, J. E. (Eds.). (1987). *Approaches to early childhood education*. Columbus, Ohio: Merrill Publishing Company.

Rotter, J. C., Robinson, E. H., & Fey, M. A. (1987). *Parent-Teacher conferencing* (2nd ed.). Washington, D.C.: National Education Association.

Rowe, M. B. (1974). Wait-time and reward—Part One—Wait-time. *Journal of Research on Science Teaching, 11*(81–94).

Roy, J. D. (1987). The linguistic and sociolinguistic position of Black English and the issue of bidialectalism in education. In P. Homel, M. Palij, & D. Aronson (Eds.), *Childhood bilingualism: Aspects of linguistic, cognitive and social development*. Hillsdale, N.J.: Lawrence Erlbaum Associates.

Rubin, J. A. (1984). *Child art therapy: Understanding and helping children grow through art* (2nd ed.). New York: Van Nostrand Reinhold Co.

Rubin, K. H. (1977a). The play behaviors of young children. *Young Children, 32*(6), 16–24.

Rubin, K. H. (1977b). The social and cognitive value of preschool toys and activities. *Canadian Journal of Behavioural Science, 9*, 382–385.

Rubin, K. H. (Ed.). (1980). *Children's play*. San Francisco: Jossey-Bass Publishers.

Rubin, K. H. (1982). Early play theories revisited: Contributions to contemporary research and theory. In D. J. Peplar (Ed.), *The play of children: Current theory and research*. Basel, Switzerland: S. Karger.

Rubin, K. H., Fein, G. G., & Vandenberg, B. (1983). Play. In P. H. Mussen (Ed.), *Handbook of child psychology*. E. M. Hetherington (Ed.), *Volume IV: Socialization, personality, and social development*. New York: John Wiley & Sons.

Rubin, K. H., and Howe, N. (1986). Social play and perspective taking. In G. Fein & M. Rivkin (Eds.), *The young child at play: Reviews of research* (Vol. 4). Washington, D.C.: National Association for the Education of Young Children.

Rubin, K. H., & Ross, H. S. (Eds.). (1982). *Peer relationships and social skills in childhood*. New York: Springer-Verlag.

Rubin, K. H., Watson, K. S., & Jambor, T. W. (1978). Free-play behaviors in preschool and kindergarten. *Child Development, 49,* 534–536.

Rubin, Z. (1980). *Children's friendships*. Cambridge, Mass.: Harvard University Press.

Rudman, M. K. (1984). *Children's literature: An issues approach* (2nd ed.). New York: Longman.

Ruiz, R. (1987). Bilingualism and bilingual education in the United States. In C. B. Paulston (Ed.), *International handbook of bilingualism and bilingual education*. New York: Greenwood Press.

Saario, T., Jacklin, C. N., & Tittle, C. K. (1973). Sex role stereotyping in the public schools. *Harvard Educational Review, 43*(3), 386–416.

Sachs, J., & Devin, J. (1988). Young children's use of age-appropriate speech styles in social interaction and role-playing. In M. B. Franklin & S. S. Barten (Eds.), *Child language: A reader*. Oxford, England: Oxford University Press.

Sacks, H., Schegloff, E. A., & Jefferson, G. (1978). A simplest systematics for the organization of turn taking for conversation. In J. Schenkein (Ed.), *Studies in the organization of conversational interaction*. New York: Academic Press.

Sahler, O. J. Z. (Ed.). (1978). *The child and death*. St. Louis: C. V. Mosby Co.

St. John, N. H. (1975). *School desegregation: Outcomes for children*. New York: John Wiley & Sons.

Saltz, E., & Brodie, J. (1982). Pretend-play training in childhood: A review and critique. In D. J. Pepler & K. H. Rubin (Eds.), *The play of children: Current theory and research*. Basel, Switzerland: S. Karger.

Samalin, N., & Jablow, M. M. (1987). *Loving your child is not enough*. New York: Viking Press.

Saracho, O. N., & Spodek, E. (Eds.). (1983). *Understanding the multicultural experience in early childhood education*. Washington, D.C.: National Association for the Education of Young Children.

Satir, V. (1975). *People making*. Palo Alto, Calif.: Science & Behavior Books.

Saunders, R., & Bingham-Newman, A. M. (1984). *Piagetian perspectives for preschools: A thinking book for teachers*. Englewood Cliffs, N.J.: Prentice-Hall.

Schaefer, C. E. (Ed.). (1976). *The therapeutic use of children's play*. New York: Jason Aronson.

Schaefer, C. E. (1984). *How to talk to children about really important things*. New York: Harper & Row, Publishers.

Schaefer, C. E., & Millman, H. L. (1981). *How to help children with common problems*. New York: Van Nostrand Reinhold Company.

Schaefer, C. E., & O'Conner, K. J. (1983). *Handbook of play therapy*. New York: John Wiley & Sons.

Schickedanz, J. A. (1986). *More than the ABCs: The early stages of reading and writing*. Washington, D.C.: National Association for the Education of Young Children.

Schimmel, N. (1978). *Just enough to make a story: A sourcebook for storytelling*. Berkeley, Calif.: Sisters' Choice Press.

Schirrmacher, R. (1988). *Art and creative development for young children*. Albany, N.Y.: Delmar Publishers.

Schon, I. (1986). *Basic collection of children's books in Spanish*. Metuchen, N.J.: Scarecrow Press.

Schon, I. (1988). Hispanic books for young children. *Young Children, 43*(4), 81–85.

Schowalter, J. E., Buschman, P. Patterson, P. R., Kutscher, A. H., Tallmer, M., & Stevenson, R. G. (1987). *Children and death: Perspectives from birth through adolescence*. New York: Praeger.

Schowalter, J. E., Patterson, P. R., Tallmer, M., Kutscher, A. H. Gullo,, S. V., & Peretz, D. (Eds.). (1983). *The child and death*. New York: Columbia University Press.

Schwartz, R., & Trabasso, T. (1984). Children's understanding of emotions. In J. Kagan & M. Zajonc (Eds.), *Emotions, cognition and behavior*. Cambridge: Cambridge University Press.

Schwartzman, H. B. (1978). *Transformations: The anthropology of children's play*. New York: Plenum Press.

Schweinhart, L. J., & Weikart, D. P. (1980). Young children grow up: The effects of the Perry Preschool Program on youths through age 15. *Monographs of the High/Scope Educational Research Foundation*. Ypsilanti, Mich.: High/Scope Press.

Schweinhart, L. J., Weikart, D. P., & Larner, M. B. (1986). Consequences of three preschool curriculum models through age 15. *Early Childhood Research Quarterly, 1*(1), 15–46.

Schweitzer, B. (1963). *Amigo*. New York: The Macmillan Company.

Schweninger, A. (1976). *The hunt for Rabbit's galosh*. Garden City, N.Y.: Doubleday & Co.

Schweninger, A. (1984). *Halloween surprises*. New York: Viking Kestrel.

Scott, D. K. (1985). Child safety seats — They work! *Young Children, 40*(4), 13–17.

Seefeldt, C., & Barbour, N. (1990). *Early childhood education: An introduction* (2nd ed.). Columbus, Ohio: Merrill Publishing Co.

Seefeldt, V. (Ed.). (1986). *Physical activity and well-being*. Reston, Va.: American Alliance for Health, Physical Education, Recreation and Dance.

Seeger, R. C. (1948). *American folksongs for children*. Garden City, N.Y.: Doubleday & Co.

Segal, M., & Adcock, D. (1981). *Just pretending: Ways to help children grow through imaginative play*. Englewood Cliffs, N.J.: Prentice-Hall.

Selman, R. L. (1971). Taking another's perspective: Role-taking development in early childhood. *Child Development, 42,* 1721–1734.

Selsam, M. (1965). *Let's get turtles.* New York: Harper & Row, Publishers.

Sendak, M. (1962a). *Chicken soup with rice.* New York: Harper & Row, Publishers.

Sendak, M. (1962b). *Where the wild things are.* New York: Harper & Row, Publishers.

Serbin, L. A. (1980, Fall). Play activities and the development of visual-spatial skills. *Equal Play,* pp. 6–9.

Serbin, L. A., O'Leary, K. D., Kent, R. N., & Toncik, E. J. (1973). A comparison of teacher response to preacademic and problem behavior of boys and girls. *Child Development, 22,* 796–804.

Sgroi, S. (Ed.). (1982). *Handbook of clinical intervention in child sexual abuse.* Lexington, Mass.: D. C. Heath & Co.

Shapiro, J., Karmer, S., & Hunerberg, C. (1981). *Equal their chances: Children's activities for non-sexist learning.* Englewood Cliffs, N.J.: Prentice-Hall.

Sharmat, M. (1980). *Gregory the terrible eater.* New York: Four Winds Press.

Shearer, D. E. (1987). The Portage Project: A home approach to the early education of young children with special needs. In J. L. Roopnarine & J. E. Johnson (Eds.), *Approaches to early childhood education.* Columbus, Ohio: Merrill Publishing Co.

Sheffield, M. (1972). *Where do babies come from?* New York: Alfred A. Knopf.

Shelton, H., Montgomery, P., & Hatcher, B. (1989). *Bibliography of books for children, 1989 edition.* Wheaton, Md.: Association for Childhood Education International.

Shiman, S. (1976). *A special birthday.* New York: McGraw-Hill Book Co.

Shulman, V. L., Restaino-Bauman, L. C. R., & Butler, L. (Eds.). (1985). *The future of Piagetian theory: The neo-Piagetians.* New York: Plenum Press.

Shure, M. B., & Spivak, G. (1978). *Problem-solving techniques in childrearing.* San Francisco: Jossey-Bass, Publishers.

Sigel, I. E., & Cocking, R. R. (1977). *Cognitive development from childhood to adolescence: A constructivist perspective.* New York: Holt, Rinehart & Winston.

Sigel, I. E., & Saunders, R. (1979). An inquiry into inquiry: Question asking as an instructional model. In L. G. Katz (Ed.), *Current topics in early childhood education, vol. II.* Norwood, N.J.: Ablex Publishing Co.

Simon, N. (1982). *Where does my cat sleep?* Niles, Ill.: Albert Whitman and Co.

Sinclair, C. B. (1973). *Movement of the young child: Ages two to six.* Columbus, Ohio: Merrill Publishing Co.

Skeen, P., Garner, A. P., & Cartwright, S. (1984). *Woodworking for young children.* Washington, D.C.: National Association for the Education of Young Children.

Skeen, P., & Hodson, D. (1987). AIDS: What adults should know about AIDS (and shouldn't discuss with very young children). *Young Children, 42*(4), 63–71.

Skinner, B. F. (1954). The science of learning and the art of teaching. *Harvard Educational Review, 24,* 86–97.

Skinner, B. F. (1957). *Verbal behavior.* New York: Appleton-Century-Crofts.

Skinner, B. F. (1974). *About behaviorism.* New York: Alfred A. Knopf.

Smilansky, S. (1968). *The effects of sociodramatic play on disadvantaged children.* New York: John Wiley & Sons.

Smilansky, S., Hagan, J., & Lewis, H. (1987). *Clay in the classroom: Helping children develop cognitive and affective skills for learning.* New York: Peter Lang Publishing.

Smith, J. A. (1966). *Setting conditions for creative teaching in the elementary school.* Boston: Allyn & Bacon.

Smith, M. S., & Bissell, J. S. (1970). Report analysis: The impact of Head Start. *Harvard Educational Review, 14,* 51–104.

Smith, N. R. (1983). *Experience and art: Teaching children to paint.* New York: Teachers College Press.

Smith, P. K., & Connolly, K. J. (1980). *The ecology of preschool behavior.* Cambridge, England: Cambridge University Press.

Smith, R. F. (1987). Theoretical framework for preschool science experiences. *Young Children, 42*(2), 34–40.

Smitherman, G. (1977). *Talkin' and testifyin': The language of Black America.* Boston: Houghton Mifflin Co.

Smitherman, G. (1981). Black English and the education of Black children and youth: Proceedings of the National Invitational Symposium on the King Decision. Detroit: Center for Black Studies, Wayne State University.

Snow, C. (1972). Mother's speech to children learning language. *Child Development, 43,* 549–565.

Snyder, M., Snyder, R., & Snyder, R., Jr. (1980). *The young child as person.* New York: Human Sciences Press.

Sparling, J., & Lewis, I. (1984). *Learning games for threes and fours.* New York: Walker & Co.

Sperry, R. W., Gazzaniga, M. S., & Bogen, J. E. (1969). Interhemispheric relationships: The neucortical commissures, syndromes of hemisphere disconnection. In P. K. Vinkin & G. W. Bryn (Eds.), *Handbook of clinical neurology* (Vol. 4). Amsterdam, Holland: North Holland Publishing Co.

Spier, P. (1983). *Christmas!* Garden City, N.Y.: Doubleday & Co.

Spinelli, E. (1982). *Thanksgiving at the Tappleton's.* Reading, Mass.: Addison-Wesley.

Sprung, B. (1975). *Non-sexist education for young children: A practical guide.* New York: Citation Press.

Sprung, B., Forschl, M., & Campbell, P. B. (1985). *What will happen if . . . .: Young children and the scientific method.* New York: Educational Equity Concepts (Gryphon House, Distributor).

Stangl, J. (1975). *Finger painting is fun.* Camarillo, Calif.: Educational Techniques.

Strangle, J. (1986). *Magic mixtures; Creative fun for little ones preschool–grade 3.* Belmont, Calif.: David S. Lake Publishers.

Stein, S. B. (1974a). *About dying: An open family book for parents and children together.* New York: Walker & Co.

Stein, S. B. (1974b). *A hospital story: An open book for parents and children together.* New York: Walker & Co.

Stein, S. B. (1974c). *Making babies.* New York: Walker & Co.

Stephens, K. (1988). The first national study of sexual abuse in child care: Findings and recommendations. *Child Care Information Exchange, 60,* 9–12.

Stevens, C. (1969). *The birth of Sunset's kittens.* New York: Young Scott Books.

Stiker, S. (1986). *Please touch: How to stimulate your child's creative development.* New York: Simon & Schuster.

Stinson, S. (1988). *Dance for young children: Finding the magic in movement.* Reston, Va.: American Alliance for Health, Physical Education, Recreation and Dance.

Stock, C. (1984). *Sampson, the Christmas cat.* New York: G. P. Putnam's Sons.

Suchman, J. R. (1961). Inquiry training: Building skills for autonomous discovery. *Merrill Palmer Quarterly, 7,* 147–169.

Sue, D. W. (1981). *Counseling the culturally different: Theory and practice.* New York: John Wiley & Sons.

Sugarman, S. (1983). *Children's early thought: Developments in classification.* Cambridge, England: Cambridge University Press.

Sullivan, H. S. (1940). *Conceptions of modern psychiatry: The first William Alanson White Memorial Lectures.* Washington, D.C.: The William Alanson White Psychiatric Foundation.

Sullivan, M. (1982). *Feeling strong, feeling free: Movement exploration for young children.* Washington, D.C.: National Association for the Education of Young Children.

Sunderlin, S., & Gray, N. (Eds.). (1967). *Bits and pieces: Imaginative uses for children's learning.* Wheaton, Md.: Association for Childhood Education International.

Sutton-Smith, B. (1987, December 9). Commentary: The domestication of early childhood play. *Education Week,* p. 28.

Sylva, K., Bruner, J. S., & Genova, P. (1976). The role of play in the problem-solving of children 3–5 years old. In J. S. Bruner, A. Jolly, & K. Sylva (Eds.), *Play—Its role in development and evolution.* New York: Basic Books.

Szasz, S. (1978). *The body language of children.* New York: W. W. Norton & Co.

Tavris, C., & Wade, C. (1984). *The longest war: Sex differences in perspective.* New York: Harcourt Brace Jovanovich.

Taylor, S. D. (1984). Teachers make curriculum decisions. *Dimensions, 12*(3), 21.

Taylor, K. W. (1981). *Parents and children learn together* (3rd ed.). New York: Teachers College Press.

Teale, W. H. (1984). Reading to young children: Its significance in literacy development. In H. Goelman, A. Oberg, & F. Smith (Eds.), *Awakening to literacy.* Exeter, N.H.: Heinemann.

Texas Department of Human Services. (1985). *Culture and children.* Austin, Tex.: The Department.

Tharlet, E. (1987). *The little cooks: Recipes from around the world for boys and girls.* New York: UNICEF.

Thomas, J. L. (Ed.). (1984). *Death and dying in the classroom: Readings for reference.* Phoenix: Oryx Press.

Thomas, R. M. (1985). *Comparing theories of child development* (2nd ed.). Belmont, Calif.: Wadsworth Publishing Co.

Tizard, B., Mortimore, J., & Burchell, B. (1983). *Involving parents in nursery and infant schools: A source book for teachers.* Ypsilanti, Mich.: High/Scope Press.

Tourse, P., & Gundersen, L. (1988). Adopting and fostering children with AIDS: Policies in progress. *Children Today, 17*(3), 15–19.

Trawick-Smith, J. (1988). "Let's say you're the baby, OK?" Play leadership and following behavior of young children. *Young Children, 43*(5), 51–59.

Trelease, J. (1982). *The read-aloud handbook.* New York: Penguin Books.

Tresselt, A. (1967). *The world in the candy egg.* New York: Lothrop, Lee & Shepherd Co.

Tresselt, A. (1972). *The dead tree.* New York: Parents Magazine Press.

Turiel, E. (1980). The development of social-conventional and moral concepts. In M. M. Windmiller, N. Lambert, & E. Turiel (Eds.), *Moral development and socialization.* Boston: Allyn & Bacon.

Tyler, R. W. (1950). *Basic principles of curriculum and instruction.* Chicago: University of Chicago Press.

Tyler, R. W. (1973, September). The father of behavioral objectives criticizes them: An interview. *Phi Delta Kappan, 55.*

Uchida, Y. (1975). *The birthday visitor.* New York: Charles Scribner's Sons.

United States Commission on Civil Rights. (1973). *Teachers and students: Differences in teacher interaction with Mexican American and Anglo students. Report V: Mexican American Study.* Washington, D.C.: The Commission.

United States Department of Agriculture. (1985). *Your money's worth in foods.* Washington, D.C.: Superintendent of Documents.

U.S. Department of Health, Education and Welfare. (1976). *Nutrition: Better eating for a head start.* Washington, D.C.: Author.

Vandenberg, B. (1986). Play theory. In G. Fein & M. Rivkin (Eds.), *The young child at play: Reviews of research* (Vol. 4). Washington, D.C.: National Association for the Education of Young Children.

Van Riper, C., & Emerick, L. (1984). *Speech correction: An introduction to speech pathology and audiology.* Englewood Cliffs, N.J.: Prentice-Hall.

Viorst, J. (1972). *The tenth good thing about Barney.* New York: Atheneum Press.

Von Sommers, P. (1984). *Drawing and cognition: Descriptive and experimental studies of graphic production processes.* Cambridge, England: Cambridge University Press.

Vukelich, C., McCarty, C., & Nanis, C. (1976). Sex bias in children's books. In M. D. Cohen (Ed.), *Growing free: Ways to help children overcome sex-role stereotypes.* Washington, D.C.: Association for Childhood Education International.

Wadsworth, B. J. (1984). *Piaget's theory of cognitive and affective development* (3rd ed.). New York: Longman.

Wardle, F. (1987). Are you sensitive to interracial children's needs? *Young Children, 42*(2), 53–59.

Warren, J., & McKinnon, E. (1988). *Small world celebrations: Around-the-world holidays to celebrate with young children.* Everett, Wash.: Warren Publishing House.

Warren, R. M. (1977). *Caring: Supporting children's growth.* Washington, D.C.: National Association for the Education of Young Children.

Wass, H., & Corr, C. A. (Eds.). (1984). *Helping children cope with death: Guidelines and resources* (2nd ed.). Washington, D.C.: Hemisphere Publishing Corp.

Weber, E. (1984). *Ideas influencing early childhood education: A theoretical analysis.* New York: Teachers College Press.

Weikart, P. (1987). *Round the circle: Key experiences in movement for children ages 3 to 5.* Ypsilanti, Mich.: The High/Scope Press.

Weikart, P. (1988). *Movement plus rhymes, songs, and singing games: Activities for children ages 3 to 7.* Ypsilanti, Mich.: High/Scope Press.

Weinraub, M., & Brown, L. M. (1983). The development of sex role stereotypes in children: Crushing realities. In V. Franks & E. Rothblum (Eds.), *The stereotyping of women: Its effect on mental health.* New York: Springer Publishing Co.

Weinstein, C., & David, T. (1987). *Spaces for children: The built environment and children's development.* New York: Plenum Press.

Weiss, C. E., & Lillywhite, H. S. (1981). *Communicative disorders: Prevention and early intervention* (2nd ed.). St. Louis: C. V. Mosby Co.

Wenning, J., & Wortis, S. (1984). *Made by human hands: A curriculum for teaching young children about work and working people.* Cambridge, Mass.: The Multicultural Project for Communication and Education.

Werner, E. E. (1984). Resilient children. *Young Children, 40*(1), 69–72.

Werner, E. E., & Smith, R. S. (1982). *Vulnerable but invincible.* New York: McGraw-Hill Book Co.

West, B. (1987). Children are caught—between home and school, culture and school. In B. Neugebauer (Ed.), *Alike and different: Exploring our humanity with young children.* Redmond, Wash.: Exchange Press.

Westland, C., & Knight, J. (1982). *Playing, living, and learning: A worldwide perspective on children's opportunities to play.* State College, Penn.: Venture Publishing.

White, B. L., & Watts, J. C. (1973). *Experience and environment: Major influences on the development of the young child* (Vol. I). Englewood Cliffs, N.J.: Prentice-Hall.

White, E. B. (1952). *Charlotte's web.* New York: Harper & Row, Publishers.

White, R. W. (1968). Motivation reconsidered: The concept of competence. In M. Almy (Ed.), *Early childhood play: Selected readings related to cognition and motivation.* New York: Simon & Schuster.

Whitener, C. B., & Keeling, M. H. (1984). *Nutrition education for young children: Strategies and activities.* Englewood Cliffs, N.J.: Prentice-Hall.

Wickstrom, R. L. (1983). *Fundamental motor patterns* (3rd ed.). Philadelphia: Lea & Febiger.

Wilder, A. (1965). *Lullabies and night songs.* New York: Harper and Row, Publishers.

Wildsmith, B. (1985). *Give a dog a bone.* New York: Pantheon Books.

Williams, R. Q., Rockwell, R. E., & Sherwood, E. A. (1987). *Mudpies to magnets: A preschool science curriculum.* Mt. Rainier, Md.: Gryphon House.

Williams, S. R. (1986). *Essentials of nutrition and diet therapy* (4th ed.). St. Louis: C. V. Mosby Co.

Willson, R. B. (1983). *Merry Christmas: Children at Christmastime around the world.* New York: Philomel Books.

Wilmes, L., & Wilmes, D. (1982). *The circle time book.* Dundee, Ill.: A Building Blocks Publication.

Wilson, G. (1981). The values conveyed in children's toys. *Council on Interracial Books for Children Bulletin 12*(6), 3–9.

Winters, R. (1985). *Choosing a child care center.* Tampa, Fla.: Child Abuse Digest.

Wishik, C. S. (1982). *Kids dish it up. . . . Sugar-free.* Port Angeles, Wash.: Peninsula Publishing.

Wohl, A., & Kaufman, B. (1983). *Silent screams and hidden cries: An interpretation of artwork by children from violent homes.* New York: Brunner/Mazel.

Wohlwill, J. F., & Van Vliet, W. (Eds.). (1985). *Habitats for children: The impacts of density.* Hillsdale, N.J.: Lawrence Earlbaum Associates.

Wolf, D., Davidson, L., Davis, M., Walters, J., Hodges, M., & Scripp, L. (1988). Beyond A, B, and C: A broader and deeper view of literacy. In A. D. Pellegrini (Ed.), *Psychological bases for early education.* New York: John Wiley & Sons.

Wolf, D. P. (Ed.). (1986). *Connecting: Friendship in the lives of young children and their teachers.* Redmond, Wash.: Exchange Press.

Wolf, J. M., & Kessler, A. L. (1987). *ERS Monograph: Entrance to kindergarten: When is the best age?* Arlington, Va.: Educational Research Service.

Wolfgang, C. H., & Glickman, D. C. (1986). *Solving discipline problems: Strategies for classroom teachers* (2nd ed.). Boston: Allyn & Bacon.

Wood, C., Powell, S., & Knight, R. C. (1984). Predicting school readiness. *Journal of Learning Disabilities, 17,* 8–11.

Yando, R., Seitz, V., & Zigler, E. (1979). *Intellectual and personality characteristics of children: Social-class and ethnic-group differences.* New York: John Wiley & Sons.

Yarrow, M. R., Scott, P., & Waxler, C. Z. (1973). Learning concern for others. *Developmental Psychology, 8,* 240–260.

Yawkey, T. C., & Pellegrini, A. D. (1984). *Child's play: Developmental and applied.* Hillsdale, N.J.: Lawrence Erlbaum Associates.

Yu, C. Y. (1976). How children's books distort the Asian American image. *Council on Interracial Books for Children Bulletin, 7*(2/3), 78–81.

Zeitlin, P. (1982). *A song is a rainbow: Music, movement and rhythm instruments in the nursery school and kindergarten.* Glenview, Ill.: Scott, Foresman and Co.

Zimiles, H. (1987). The Bank Street approach. In J. L. Roopnarine & J. E. Johnson (Eds.), *Approaches to early childhood education.* Columbus, Ohio: Merrill Publishing Co.

Zion, G. (1958). *No roses for Harry.* New York: Harper & Row, Publishers.

Zolotow, C. (1957). *Over and over.* New York: Harper & Row, Publishers.

Zolotow, C. (1962). *Mr. Rabbit and the lovely present.* New York: Harper & Row, Publishers.

Zolotow, C. (1963). *A tiger named Thomas.* New York: Lothrop, Lee & Shepard.

Zolotow, C. (1974). *My grandson Lew.* New York: Harper & Row, Publishers.

Author Index

Subject Index